Legal Writing for Legal Professionals

Terry S. Bingham
Cuyahoga Community College, Cleveland, Ohio

Susan L. Majka
Cuyahoga Community College, Cleveland, Ohio

PEARSON

Boston   Columbus   Hoboken   Indianapolis   New York   San Francisco
Amsterdam   Cape Town   Dubai   London   Madrid   Milan   Munich   Paris   Montreal   Toronto
Delhi   Mexico City   Sao Paulo   Sydney   Hong Kong   Seoul   Singapore   Taipei   Tokyo

Editorial Director: Andrew Gilfillan
Executive Editor: Gary Bauer
Editorial Assistant: Lynda Cramer
Director of Marketing: David Gesell
Marketing Manager: Thomas Hayward
Product Marketing Manager: Kaylee Carlson
Marketing Assistant: Les Roberts
Program Manager: Tara Horton
Project Manager Team Lead: Bryan Pirrmann
Project Manager: Patricia Gutierrez
Operations Specialist: Deidra Smith
Creative Director: Andrea Nix
Art Director: Diane Six
Manager, Product Strategy: Sara Eilert

Product Strategy Manager: Anne Rynearson
Team Lead, Media Development & Production: Rachel Collett
Media Project Manager: Maura Barclay
Cover Designer: Studio Montage
Cover Image: "Blind Lady Justice" Courtesy Shutterstock/wacpan
Full-Service Project Management: Chandrasekar Subramanian, SPi Global
Composition: SPi Global
Text Printer/Bindery: Edwards Brothers/ Malloy, Jackson Road
Cover Printer: Phoenix Color/ Hagerstown
Text Font: Goudy Oldstyle Std, 11/13

Credits and acknowledgments borrowed from other sources and reproduced, with permission, in this textbook appear on the appropriate page within the text.

Acknowledgements of third party content appear on page with the borrowed material, which constitutes an extension of this copyright page.

Unless otherwise indicated herein, any third-party trademarks that may appear in this work are the property of their respective owners and any references to third-party trademarks, logos or other trade dress are for demonstrative or descriptive purposes only. Such references are not intended to imply any sponsorship, endorsement, authorization, or promotion of Pearson's products by the owners of such marks, or any relationship between the owner and Pearson Education, Inc. or its affiliates, authors, licensees or distributors.

Many of the designations by manufacturers and sellers to distinguish their products are claimed as trademarks. Where those designations appear in this book, and the publisher was aware of a trademark claim, the designations have been printed in initial caps or all caps.

Library of Congress Cataloging-in-Publication Data

Bingham, Terry S., author. | Majka, Susan L., author.
Legal writing for legal professionals / Terry S. Bingham, Susan L. Majka.
Hoboken : Pearson Education, Inc, 2016.
LCCN 2015044455
ISBN 978-0-13-378617-0
LCSH: Legal composition. Law—United States—Language.
LCC KF250 .B48 2016 | DDC 808.06/634—dc23 LC record available at
http://lccn.loc.gov/2015044455
10 9 8 7 6 5 4 3 2 1

ISBN 10: 0-13-378617-X
ISBN 13: 978-0-13-378617-0

DEDICATIONS

Terry S. Bingham

This book is dedicated to my husband, Lynn, for his immeasurable love, patience, and support. To our children Jeffrey, Jordin, Brett, Whitney, Darren, and Kelsey, to Dr. Steve Perkins who taught me how to enjoy life, and to the women who taught by example: Dr. Lynn Callister, Shauna Stephenson, Nancy Bennett, and Dr. Qetler Jensrud.

Susan L. Majka

This book is dedicated to my late husband, John, and to the wonderful family he gave me: Ron, Laurie, Tim, Rhonda, Sam, Libby, and Kaia. It also is dedicated to my best friends, Nancy Mason Babb and Tina Wallace.

DEDICATIONS

CONTENTS

CHAPTER 8

CHAPTER 9

CHAPTER 10

ONLINE CHAPTERS

PREFACE TO LEGAL WRITING FOR LEGAL PROFESSIONALS

■ THE PURPOSE OF THE BOOK

We have taught and continue to teach the legal writing course for paralegals that we developed for an ABA-accredited paralegal program. As we developed materials for our classes over the years, we discovered increasingly effective methods for clarifying complex legal concepts and ideas for our students. After we had refined our materials to the point that the students were requesting extra copies and sharing them with other paralegal students in other class sections, we realized that what we had created could be helpful to students at other colleges and to other instructors. We therefore decided to write this textbook. We have class-tested the contents of this book over years of working with paralegal students, and the text is directly focused on the areas of educational weakness and the needs that these students have demonstrated. We focused on the careful curriculum development needed to teach students the organizational methods required for legal writing, the proper style and tone required in legal writing and the IRAC format that is so integral to legal writing. We created a fictional law office with attorneys and clients that are followed throughout the book. We have found that this approach of recreating the actual office setting and experiences captures and retains the students' interest. We incorporated real-life ethical dilemmas and clients both to prepare the students for the situations they will encounter in the workplace and to introduce them to the concept of the ethical challenges they will face. We are happy to report that this textbook has been very highly reviewed, and we hope this text fits the Instructors' needs and helps their students learn a sometimes complex subject.

■ ORGANIZATION OF THE BOOK

This text is divided into four discrete sections. The layout of the book provides a logical structure for Instructors to teach the course and for the students to learn; it starts the students with basic organization, proceeds on to the IRAC structure of legal writing, and then moves the students into writing the types of legal documents they will be writing during their careers.

Although the book is organized to guide the student through learning the writing process, it also is structured to allow Instructors to select only the sections needed for their specific class or program. Each of the individual sections can be used independently as a stand-alone text. The online section of the book, the Legal Writing Handbook, provides remedial material to which Instructors can refer students who need work in grammar and punctuation.

The **FIRST SECTION** shows the students how to organize and includes discussion regarding the organization of multiple facts onto paper in order to produce clearer and more coherent writing. This first step is essential for students who do not have experience with organizing multiple facts and complex ideas. Outlining provides students with a visual system of organization that is systematic and allows them to construct a logical and effective document. By organizing and outlining, the students learn which elements of their research take priority and most effectively support their argument.

The first section also introduces the students to formal letter writing, a task many have never undertaken. It explains to the students that effective letter writing is based on considering the identity of the recipient, and it provides specific examples of letters addressed to clients, the court, or opposing counsel. It also cautions the students about the common pitfalls that those new to the formal legal environment often encounter. This section includes additional warnings concerning avoiding the use of colloquial words and slang in their correspondence and legal documents, as well as avoiding reliance on computer provided spell and grammar check, another common pitfall for younger students.

Finally, the first section gives the students their initial exposure to the concept of plagiarism Students are so accustomed to finding information through Internet searches that they often do not understand that they cannot simply insert someone else's words or ideas into their own writings without acknowledging their sources. This text explains and clarifies what constitutes plagiarism through explanation and examples.

The **SECOND SECTION** is the heart of the book: it provides a clear explanation of the IRAC method of organizing legal documents. Because this method of organization is new to almost all paralegal students, we have provided copious examples of correctly and incorrectly written IRAC issues, rules analyses, and conclusions. We have devoted individual chapters to each of the four IRAC elements, and we fused the individual elements in the following chapter, IRAC as a whole. Then we conclude the IRAC section with a chapter addressing more the complex task of addressing multiples issues in the same document. This section also could be used for law students starting legal writing courses, and it would be an excellent reference for paralegals planning to continue on to law school.

In the ISSUE chapter, we explain how essential a carefully crafted issue is to the effectiveness of the rest of the document. We also provide examples of incorrectly and correctly drafted issues and we explain why the incorrect examples fail to meet requirements. The chapter begins by explaining the concept of the issue, and then challenges the students to identify or detect the issue in several fact patterns. The chapter moves on to require the students to revise three existing incorrect issues and then evaluate each of the incorrect and correct issue statements. Finally the student is ready to create a correct, succinct issue for any given fact pattern. Additionally, our examples of issues include both the traditional "whether" version and the more contemporary full sentence version.

The RULE chapter introduces the students to the way case law and statutes are written, and it demonstrates how to incorporate the law into their documents. It provides incorrect and correct examples along with explanation of why the incorrect examples are wrong. It illustrates the techniques for directly quoting the law, interweaving the law into text, and paraphrasing the law.

The ANALYSIS chapter is crucial for students who are learning to write legal documents or are planning to continue on to law school. In our experience, students have difficulty grasping the process of applying the law to the facts of their cases. Even more challenging for students is then organizing their analysis in a clear and logical manner. This chapter provides them with guidance and examples to help them understand how the analysis should be crafted. Again, we provide copious examples of incorrectly and correctly drafted analyses along with explanation concerning why the incorrect examples are wrong. In this chapter, therefore, students progress from understanding and writing analyses at a low level to comprehending and composing them at a very high level.

Finally, the CONCLUSION chapter focuses on the common problem new legal writers encounter, erroneously including analysis material in their conclusions. We have found this to be a very common difficulty for new legal writers, and this chapter helps them understand the purpose and correct form of the IRAC conclusion. As with all the chapters, we include incorrect and correct examples with explanations.

The IRAC section, therefore, helps the students learn to think and approach the material in a logical and systematic manner. It also emphasizes both the need and the techniques for learning to focus on the important facts in a case and incorporate the appropriate legal arguments.

The **THIRD SECTION** of the book teaches the students a commonly used format for legal documents as well as the content of basic legal documents, including complaints, answers, memoranda of law, motions to dismiss, and motion to compel. The text also provides examples of motions for summary judgment and briefs in opposition to motions for summary judgment. In this section, the students gain valuable practice in drafting authentic work product that they can transfer directly to the work place.

This section also addresses emails and the hazards of unprofessional emails. Because many younger students have been emailing all of their lives, they are not aware of the necessity of writing professionally, even in emails. This section discussing professionalism in emails continues the running thread of ethics that is integrated subtly throughout the story line in the textbook.

The third section of the book also includes a chapter on proofreading and editing. Too often students omit this essential step, and the quality of the assignments they turn in demonstrates their failure to take the important step of rereading and correcting their errors. The chapter provides specific examples of well-edited and unedited writings, many of which were adapted from our own students' papers. It also cautions the students to take care in documenting client interviews, so they do not repeat grammatical errors the clients may have made. These examples also help the students to realize that many of their clients will come from diverse backgrounds that they will need to accommodate.

The last chapter of the third section of the book highlights the pitfalls and errors legal writers often make. Many of these problems involve honesty, brevity, accuracy, and tone. The chapter demonstrates the effect of inadvertent errors on the reader, and it emphasizes the need to consult not only the Civil Rules of the jurisdiction, but also the Local Rules. The chapter also focuses on ethics and contains numerous examples of ethical dilemmas taken from real life situations the authors have encountered. The chapter, and indeed the entire text, not only provides examples of and cautions against the unauthorized practice of law, but it also includes numerous ethical situations that require the students to ponder the correct course of action in potentially compromising situations. Some of these situations are obvious, but others are subtle and demonstrate to the students how common ethical dilemmas are in the law.

Additionally, the last chapter revisits the passive voice and how it can weaken the effect of writing. All of the examples of badly written documents in this chapter were adapted from real-life motions attorneys had submitted to various courts.

The book provides many valuable tools for both the student and the Instructor. Among these tools are Learning Objectives, Chapter Outlines, and numerous examples contrasting incorrect and correct versions of the material being covered to aid with visual recognition. The text also contains copious scaffolded exercises, including exercises comparing A to B examples to engage the learner in the skill of analysis. The exercises in each chapter are designed to reinforce the material the student has just learned by progressing from a low level of learning to an advanced level of learning.

Additionally, the text contains other valuable learning tools like grids, a writing checklist, mnemonics for remembering key elements, tables, bullet-pointed chapter summaries, end of chapter assignments that incorporate all the material covered in each chapter to help students maintain newly acquired skills learned in that chapter. An especially innovative feature of this text is the introduction of formulas for IRAC: Fact + Rule = Analysis, which the authors have found be very effective in helping students understand and apply IRAC in their documents.

The **FOURTH SECTION** of this text is the **Online Legal Writing Handbook**, which is available at the open-access book website www.pearsonhighered.com/careersresources. As noted above, the Handbook addresses grammar and punctuation. We have found that many students have not learned these lessons in the course of their primary and secondary education, and we therefore often have to cover this material before we can get to the actual paralegal material. For those students returning to school for a career change, most find this review very helpful. Student evaluations from the courses we have taught consistently have mentioned this part of the course as being one of the most valuable sections to the students. Even if the Instructor does not need to use this section for the majority of students in any given class, the Instructor will find it useful for the student needing remedial education.

In our years of teaching paralegal students, we have found that students possess a wide variety of writing skills and deficits in writing knowledge. This Handbook contains sections specifically designed to address the various problem areas students need to correct in their writing. A student who has problems with verbs, for example, could be directed to that chapter for remedial help.

Alternatively, the Handbook could be used at the beginning of a quarter or semester to assess the students' writing abilities. However, this textbook also could be used in a two semester format, with the Handbook beginning the first semester, and the organization and IRAC chapters completing the courses.

■ PEDAGOGY

This text employs many traditional pedagogical features, including chapter outlines, examples, and a summary. Additionally, the text's curriculum design has the exercises scaffolded from a basic level to a very difficult level. This scaffolding progresses the students through the material and builds upon previously learned material. This allows students to gain confidence while their newfound skills become embedded and entrenched in their long-term memories. The text contains mnemonics to aid memory, grids to provide clarity, and numerous examples of incorrect and correct versions of the material to develop the analytical learning of the student. The examples also give the students a concrete understanding of often abstract concepts.

In addition, this text provides a unique approach; it is designed to immerse the paralegal students into the real-life experiences and tasks they will face in their professional careers. The text follows a story line; in a continuing attempt to expose students to the actual situations they will encounter in their careers, from intake until the case is resolved, we have designed this book with the gender-neutral fictional paralegal working for the same attorneys who represent the same clients with real-life legal situations throughout the litigation process.

An important feature of this text is the common thread of ethics found throughout the chapters. Another distinctive feature of this text is the Legal Writing Handbook section, which consists of basic and more advanced grammar and punctuation.

■ RESOURCES FOR STUDENTS

Online Legal Writing Handbook

This student resource that is designed to address common grammar, mechanics, and writing issues that students can access at any time during the course at the open-access book website www.pearsonhighered.com/careersresources. This Handbook contains sections specifically designed to address common writing issues. It contains clear and basic explanations of proper sentence structure, common punctuation problems, frequently encountered verb tense and agreement errors, and improper pronoun shifts. The Legal Writing Handbook also includes abundant exercises for students who need work in basic areas that may be outside the scope of a college course. Instructors can refer students who have problems with basic writing skills to the Handbook so they can strengthen their abilities without taking time away from the material of the class. Instructors will have the answers to these exercises along with additional explanation of the material for individual instruction, if desired.

■ RESOURCES FOR INSTRUCTORS

This text is designed to facilitate the Instructor's job. In every chapter, each concept that is discussed is followed by one or more exercises that both reinforce the material for the students and allow the Instructors to assess the students' comprehension and learning needs. These exercises allow the students to learn and understand more of the material outside the classroom, thus allowing Instructors more flexibility in deciding the content of their lectures. Each exercise has been carefully crafted to build on the information the student has learned earlier in the chapter or in earlier chapters. The Instructor's Manual provides answers for each of these exercises, along with an explanation of the approach taken in the chapter, lecture outlines for that chapter, and assessments that coordinate with the progression of the chapter.

Instructor's Manual.

The instructor's manual also includes content outlines for classroom discussion, teaching suggestions, and answers to selected end-of-chapter questions from the text. The Instructors' Manual additionally provides syllabi designed for varying length quarters and semesters that are designed for either single or two quarter or semester courses. Each syllabus also is divided into educational levels for introductory, intermediate, and advanced classes to accommodate varying levels of programs.

Another valuable feature found in the Instructors' Manual are the pre- and post-tests for each of the four sections. These tests give Instructors an overview of a new class's strengths and deficits, allowing the Instructors to focus lectures on the areas where the students have demonstrated needs. These tests also provide measurable data regarding the degree of the students' comprehension of the material after it has been covered. These pre- and post-tests easily could be adapted as quizzes or exams rather than used initially to assess the students' abilities and weaknesses. Alternatively, even after they were used for initial assessment, Instructors could use them for assignments or tests to ensure that the students absorbed and retained the material covered. Alternatively, many of the exercises and assignments in each chapter could be adapted as midterm and final exams. Instructors will be able to copy these exercises and assignments and have the added advantage to having the answers to them in their Instructors' Manual.

Resources for Improving Student Writing Skills.

Another valuable tool in the Instructors' Manual is the material relating to the online open-access Legal Writing Handbook, with not only answers to the exercises contained in the Legal Writing Manual, but also clear explanations of the concepts and lessons that are covered in the Manual. Just as with the hard copy text, the Instructors' Manual contains pre-and post-tests for the open-access online Legal Writing Handbook. These pre- and post-tests will be available only in the Instructors' Manual, and they provide all the advantages of that the tests provide for the other chapters.

PowerPoint Presentations.

Our presentations offer clear, straightforward outlines and notes to use for class lectures or study materials. Photos, illustrations, charts, and tables from the book are included in the presentations when applicable. With a total of 523 power points with interactive slides that promote in-class discussion and in-class exercises closely paired to the textbook, the power points for each chapter are extensive and comprehensive aids for Instructors' lectures.

To access supplementary materials online, instructors need to request an instructor access code. Go to **www.pearsonhighered.com/irc,** where you can register for an instructor access code. Within 48 hours after registering, you will receive a confirming email, including an instructor access code. Once you have received your code, go to the site and log on for full instructions on downloading the materials you wish to use.

eBooks.

This text is also available in multiple eBook formats. These are an exciting new choice for students looking to save money. As an alternative to purchasing the printed textbook, students can purchase an electronic version of the same content. With an eTextbook, students can search the text, make notes online, print out reading assignments that incorporate lecture notes, and bookmark important passages for later review. For more information, visit your favorite online eBook reseller or visit www.mypearsonstore.com.

ACKNOWLEDGMENTS

From both the authors:

We would like to thank our editor, Elisa Rogers, for her continuous input and sage advice, and our publisher, Gary Bauer, for his unflagging belief in and ongoing support of our book. We truly owe this book's existence to Gary and his determination to ensure that it proceeded to publication.

We also must give credit to the reviewers who provided numerous suggestions and valuable critiques. This book was greatly enhanced by their comments. These outstanding reviewers were Carol Brady, Milwaukee Area Technical College; Steve Dayton, Fullerton College; Lara O'Dell, Ivy Tech Community College; Sondi A. Lee, Camden County College; Beth R. Pless, Northeast Wisconsin Technical College; Paula J. Sinopoli-Bascom, Madisonville Community College; John A. Whitehead, Kilgore College; and Lindsay Willis, Central Piedmont Community College. We especially want to thank Lara O'Dell of Ivy Tech Community College, who reviewed the last five chapters, for the meticulous and detailed corrections she made. These were invaluable.

Finally, we want to thank Lisa O'Rear Lassen, the previous Director of Paralegal Studies at Cuyahoga Community College for arranging for us to work on this book with Pearson Publishing. Without Lisa, this book never would have been started. We also thank Mardy Chaplin, Director of Paralegal Studies at Cuyahoga Community College for his continued support, encouragement, and faith in our legal writing class and our ability.

From Terry S. Bingham

I would like to acknowledge Dr. Qetler Jensrud of Akron University for caring enough to teach with exactness, for maintaining patience with all my questions, and for insisting on excellence. Without her detailed and superb instruction, this book would lack the superior curriculum design, structure, and organization she taught me.

I would like to thank my students for refining my teaching skills and helping me to facilitate better learning.

Most of all, I want to thank my husband, Lynn, for his support, love, and patience, and my children, Jeffrey, Jordin, Brett, Whitney (who contributed art work), Darren, and Kelsey for their encouragement and belief in my talents and skills.

From Susan L. Majka

I want to thank the people who provided professional assistance with the writing of this book, first and foremost Sue Altmeyer, the law librarian at Cleveland-Marshall College of Law, who saved me countless hours in the research process. I also want to thank the following attorneys for their input, proofreading, and suggestions: the Honorable Diane M. Palos, Tina Wallace, Michael Geary, Maureen Brett, and Margaret Terry. I also want to thank my sister, Dr. M. Katherine Jung, for close proofreading of some of the chapters. Her feedback was very valuable.

This book would not have been possible without Sister Mary Dion Horrigan, SND, who taught me self-discipline and the art of studying. Everything I have accomplished in my careers I owe to her strict, yet caring, instruction. Sr. Dion refused to accept anything less than my best from me, and she instilled these standards in me.

I also would like to thank the many people who provided moral support and wise advice during the process of writing this book, including, but certainly not limited to, my aunt and uncle, Claire Marie and Jack Langkau, and my dear friends Tina Wallace, Nancy Mason-Babb, Jeff and Pam Peacock, Jim Gettys, Margaret Terry, and Felicia DiLappi.

ABOUT THE AUTHORS

Terry Bingham has a Bachelor of Science degree in Postsecondary Technical Education with a specialty in curriculum development and instructional training from University of Akron, where she was valedictorian of the College of Education graduating class. She holds a Paralegal Studies Post-degree Professional Certificate, ABA approved program, from Cuyahoga Community College in Cleveland, Ohio and has five years of experience as a paralegal. Mrs. Bingham co-developed a first run college level Introduction to Legal Writing course for paralegals for an ABA accredited paralegal program, incorporating her extensive educational background in curriculum development and her paralegal education and professional experience to construct the course.

This book is the culmination of many years of successfully shepherding willing learners through the course. Terry has 30 years' experience as an advanced piano instructor. In the course of her music teaching career, she also develops age- and ability-suitable lesson plans to achieve desired student skill level and modifies teaching method and resource selection to maximize student interest and participation. Terry is a member of the North Eastern Ohio American Society for Training and Development and the American Society for Training and Development, Cleveland Association of Paralegals, and National Association for Legal Professionals. For over three decades, Terry has been an active mentor, volunteering for children's and youth organizations. Mrs. Bingham has received multiple recognitions, including Boy Scouts of America, leadership awards, and she has cherished the satisfaction of seeing many of her wards (including all three of her sons) earn the Eagle Scout Rank. She and her husband enjoy traveling, their four children, and their many grandchildren.

Susan Majka has been an attorney in the state of Ohio since 1995, when she graduated magna cum laude from Cleveland-Marshall College of Law and won the award for Excellence in Legal Writing. She has worked in a medical malpractice firm and volunteered at the Legal Aid Society. Ms. Majka also worked as an attorney serving various judges in the Cleveland Municipal Housing Court, the Cuyahoga Common Pleas Court, and the Ohio Eight District Court of Appeals. She is currently an attorney for the Federal Government. While she was in law school, Ms. Majka worked as a nurse/paralegal/law clerk at a medical malpractice firm. Also while in law school, Ms. Majka worked in the operating room as a Registered Nurse, which had been her career from 1980 until 1995. Prior to her career in nursing, Ms. Majka had earned a Bachelor's Degree in English Literature and pursued graduate work in English literature at Auburn University in Auburn, Alabama, where she taught Freshman Composition. She also has taught at Malone College in the accelerated Bachelor's Degree program. Ms. Majka co-developed a course in legal writing for paralegals at Cuyahoga Community College with Mrs. Bingham, and she has taught the course for many years. Ms. Majka has also taught Civil Procedure, Introduction to Paralegal Studies, and Introduction to Nurse Paralegal Studies. Ms. Majka's volunteer activities include the Junior League of Cleveland, particularly the Scholarship Committee. She also has been a Long Term Care Ombudsman and a member of the Junior Committee for the Cleveland Orchestra.

■ REVIEWERS TO ACKNOWLEDGE:

Legal Writing for Legal Professionals

by

Carol Brady, Milwaukee Area Technical College

Steve Dayton, Fullerton College

Lara O'Dell, Ivy Tech Community College

Sondi A. Lee, Camden County College

Beth R. Pless, Northeast Wisconsin Technical College

Paula J. Sinopoli-Bascom, Madisonville Community College

John A. Whitehead, Kilgore College

Lindsay Willis, Central Piedmont Community College

LEARNING OBJECTIVES

1. Comprehend the process and purpose of outlining

2. Perform outlining

3. Analyze important versus unimportant facts for your outline

4. Construct an outline using the three step process

5. Separate facts for sequencing

6. Structure an outline with roman numerals, capital letters, and Arabic numbers format

7. Develop an outline incorporating the important facts, using sequencing, and applying parallel structure.

CHAPTER 1

Outlining

■ LEGAL OUTLINING

Every significant writing, especially a writing that will be submitted to the court, should be written in three stages: organizing, writing, and revising. Some teachers refer to these three stages as prewriting, writing, and post writing, and we will use these terms here. Prewriting consists of outlining, which includes gathering your data, then sorting, prioritizing, and organizing it. An outline is like the skeleton or blueprint of the written work. It gives the writer a map of the direction he or she plans to use to state or explain the content of the work. We use outlining to help us organize what we want to say in a logical order so that the reader can follow our thoughts, arguments, or story.

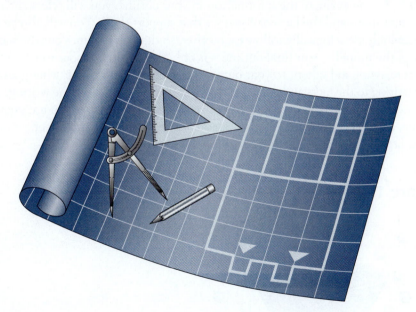

We outline so that what we have to say is in a logical order or a persuasive layout for the reader. The more complicated or involved the subject, the more important it is to outline before attempting to write the actual document. This prewriting process is essential for an effective document.

An outline is important, therefore, for all but the briefest of writings. Although sometimes we outline short simple works in our heads, we will be more effective writers if we organize longer or more complex works on paper.

By outlining a writing before we begin, we can prioritize what is important and place the ideas or facts that support each important point underneath. We can see the relationship between various ideas or facts in a way that may not have occurred to us without the outline. Sometimes patterns appear that were not evident without the outline.

An outline can begin very casually, just thoughts jotted on a piece of paper. After we have written down all the thoughts about the subject, we can look for patterns or subjects that should be grouped together. Once we formalize the outline, however, it is best to make it grammatically correct and parallel. That way, when we go to write the work from the outline, portions of the writing might be almost prewritten.

It is impossible to be an effective legal writer without correct grammar and punctuation. Grammatical and punctuation errors, at best, will distract the reader, and, in the worst case, will fail to convey the meaning the writer intended. Please refer to the *Legal Writing Handbook* for guidance on grammar and punctuation.

Thus, we use outlining to organize our thoughts in a logical, cohesive, and effective order so that when we begin to write, our thoughts will flow coherently and our writing will be persuasive and convincing. By creating a grammatically correct outline before starting to write, we can avoid including errors inadvertently.

■ CONTENT OF THE OUTLINE

Your first, rough outline will contain numerous facts and ideas that might or might not be important and/or helpful to your writing. One way to picture how your outline will organize your thoughts is to picture a funnel (Figure 1.1). The top of the funnel will contain all the facts and ideas you have written in your rough outline. As you evaluate the information in your outline, you will select the most important items and the facts or concepts that support them. You will also be able to see which ideas logically follow each other, so that what comes out the narrow neck of the funnel—your final outline—is only the portion of your rough outline that is relevant and salient to your purpose. It is important to limit what goes into your writing to the facts and concepts that will further the goal of the writing. This does not mean that you can omit things to the point that what you are saying is untrue, but it does allow you to organize your writing to minimize the effect of the cases, laws, facts, or ideas that hurt your purpose.

Figure 1.1 Outline funnel

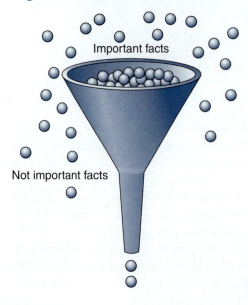

EXAMPLE ONE

After graduating from law school and passing the bar exam, Brad and Ana opened their law office in a storefront a few doors down from Cherelle's boutique on Main Street. One day early in their careers, Tommy Williams walked into the office with a concerned look. After Tommy requested a consultation, Brad welcomed him into his office. Tommy proceeded to recount a phone call he had received from his father on Sunday morning around 4 a.m. His father was using his one phone call after being arrested for drunk driving, resisting arrest, and assaulting a police officer. Tommy explained that he was embarrassed to have to reveal this to his former classmate, but he needed someone to represent his father in court the following day.

Brad assured Tommy that he was not responsible for his father's actions and promised to do his best to represent him. "Please don't repeat anything my father or I say to anyone. I am upset enough as it is," Tommy pleaded. Brad explained that legal ethics forbade him from revealing the confidences of a client and asked if Mr. Williams was still in jail. Tommy answered that he was, but Tommy wanted to get him legal representation before paying his bail. "He'd better not jump bail," Tommy said. "I'm using the money I've been saving for an engagement ring for Sheila." Grinning at this news, Brad then instructed his paralegal, Pat, to go to the police station to get a copy of the police report.

After bailing his father out of jail, Tommy brought his father to Brad's office. Mr. Williams admitted that Saturday evening he had "had a few beers" at the Dew Drop Inn, but he denied being drunk. "The bartender don't serve no one who had too much to drink," he stated. He said he left around 11 p.m. and drove around looking for a place to get something to eat. He did not know why the police pulled him over, and he told the policeman so. The officer was rude and abrupt, according to Mr. Williams, and ordered him out of his prized Trans Am. Mr. Williams said he thought the officer was jealous because his car was so nice. When Mr. Williams attempted to walk the straight line, he recounted, the officer actually tripped him and then arrested him for driving under the influence. "Him and me been fighting since we was in school. I think he pulled me over just 'cause he hates me," Mr. Williams said. Mr. Williams said the officer tripping him made him angry, and he began to argue with the officer. Mr. Williams said that after the officer pushed him toward the patrol car, he pushed back. The officer must have been standing on a soft shoulder, he continued, because he lost his footing and fell into the storm ditch, which happened to be full of muddy water. After Mr. Williams finished his story, Brad instructed him not to leave home until he was headed to the courthouse the next day. Tommy promised that he would make sure his father stayed home, and that they would meet at the courthouse in the morning.

Pat returned to the office with the police report. Brad read it and saw that it recorded Mr. Williams' blood alcohol as 0.2%, with .08% being legally intoxicated. The police report also stated that Mr. Williams had been unable to walk a straight line, that he had assaulted the police officer, and had pushed him into the storm ditch.

Brad asked Pat to outline the facts of the case for him as he researched the law in preparation for the court appearance the next day.

BAD EXAMPLE

   I. When Mr. Williams called Tommy

      A. Four in the morning

      B. Said he left the bar at 11 pm

      C. Reported being sober

   II. What make of car he was driving

      A. Wouldn't risk his Trans Am by driving it drunk

      B. Officer could have been jealous of the nice car

  III. Whether the officer was stronger than Mr. Williams and assaulted him

      A. The officer did not like Mr. Williams

      B. The officer tripped Mr. Williams

      C. The officer tripped and fell into the ditch

The main headings in this outline are incorrect because they give trivial facts a position of importance instead of focusing on the important legal issues. Also, the points listed underneath each of these main headings do not follow logically from the main heading. Even if the time at which Mr. Williams called Tommy were important, items B and C are irrelevant to that question. When Mr. Williams left the bar has no bearing on when he called Tommy. Whether he said he was sober also has no bearing on the timing of his phone call. In summary, none of the main headings is of any legal significance. The make of car he was driving does not affect the question of whether he was drunk or assaulted the officer. When he called Tommy also makes no difference to these issues. Finally, it does not matter whether the officer or Mr. Williams was stronger. Even when a 100 pound weakling hits an officer built like a body builder, the result is an assault on an officer.

GOOD EXAMPLE

   I. Whether Mr. Williams was intoxicated

      A. Mr. Williams' statement

      B. Blood alcohol level per police breathalyzer test

      C. Possible witnesses from Saturday evening

   II. Whether Mr. Williams failed the roadside test

      A. Mr. Williams' statement that the officer tripped him

      B. The police report's version

      C. Any possible witnesses

  III. Whether Mr. Williams intentionally assaulted the officer

      A. Mr. Williams' statement

      B. The police report's version

      C. Any possible bystanders/witnesses

You may be wondering how the three main headings were chosen. We chose these because they focus on the three main legal issues the fact pattern presents. Mr. Williams was arrested for allegedly being intoxicated, failing the roadside test, and assaulting the officer. The points noted below each of the main headings break down the potential evidence that would address each of the legal issues.

EXAMPLE TWO

One day Cherelle stopped into Ana and Brad's law office. At first Ana thought she stopped to chat, but Ana quickly realized that Cherelle was upset. Ana led her into the office, gave her a cold drink, and asked her what was wrong.

"I cannot believe that this is the way she 'thanks' me for all I did for her," she muttered.

"Who?" asked Ana.

"That young woman I hired as a part time sales clerk. She had no job history, but she told me she was working her way through school toward a job in fashion retail. I thought I could help her learn the ropes and that I was helping her by giving her a job. Now she turns around and sues me! She says I discriminated against her because she's black. But I'm black! How could I have discriminated against her?"

Ana was quite surprised to see Cherelle this emotional. She was usually cool and calm regardless of the situation. She asked Cherelle what she could have done that the girl construed as discrimination.

"The clothing she was wearing to work was not appropriate for an upscale shop. Her clothing was too casual and some of it was worn or stained. I am trying to project a certain image, and her way of dressing did not convey the image I want.

"Well, I offered to sell her items from the shop at cost so that she could wear them to work. She became offended and said I was trying to make her dress like someone she wasn't. I tried to explain that to succeed in fashion, a person has to project a certain image. I told her I was trying to help her, but she quit and walked out. Two weeks later, I got this mailing from the court; it is titled a complaint, saying she is suing me for discrimination. What a little brat! I have never been a vengeful person, but I don't mind who hears about her behavior."

"Ok, let's look at this analytically. What is the date on the complaint?" Ana asked.

"The envelope is postmarked two days ago, but the complaint is dated two weeks ago," Cherelle replied.

"Who is her attorney?" Ana inquired. She looked at the complaint. The ink was smeared and the wording was confusing. She turned to the attorney's signature and said, "No wonder. This guy is such a bottom feeder. He never goes to trial; he tries to bully the other side into settling. I bet the court will throw this out before it even gets to trial."

"What are you talking about?" asked Cherelle. Ana explained that when one side could not produce enough evidence to support its case, opposing counsel could write a motion for summary judgment saying so. If the other side could not produce evidence, the judge would dismiss the case.

"But I still have to pay an attorney to do this for me! That is so unfair. I didn't do anything wrong," Cherelle protested.

"I know it isn't fair, but that is the system. Fortunately for you, you have a roommate who is an attorney," Ana answered.

Ana proceeded to review the court filing. The complaint, although it was poorly written, appeared to say that Cherelle had denigrated the girl's taste in clothing. It also said that, although Ana never overtly said so, she wanted a sophisticated, lighter skinned clerk, not someone with the girl's dark complexion. Ana chuckled, because Cherelle's skin was quite dark as well. Ana began to jot down her thoughts for her response to the complaint.

BAD EXAMPLE

  I. Cherelle was upset and wanted everyone to know what the girl did to her.
  A. The girl quit without notice.
  B. The girl dressed trashy to go to work.
  C. The girl made up stories about Cherelle.
 II. Cherelle did not want a more sophisticated, lighter-skinned clerk.
  A. Cherelle was as dark as the girl.
  B. Cherelle never said that anyway.
  C. The girl's attorney is a jerk.
  D. Cherelle even offered to let the girl buy clothes at cost.
III. It is unfair that Cherelle has to pay an attorney when she did nothing wrong.
  A. Cherelle should withhold the girl's last pay.
  B. Cherelle should tell everyone in town not to hire her.
  C. Cherelle should tell everyone the girl is a liar.

The incorrect outline not only focuses on facts that are not important, it makes up facts. Unfortunately, it is not uncommon for beginning paralegals to embellish a fact pattern to make it more persuasive. It is extremely important to include only the facts, even if they are weak, unhelpful, or unappealing. Once an attorney or paralegal loses credibility, the reputation for untruthfulness stays with him or her. The legal community in most cities is very close, and misbehavior gets discussed widely and frequently.

Another problem with this outline is the fact that the first main heading focuses on the defendant's emotions. Rarely are a party's emotions legally significant, and focusing on emotions often weakens the attorney's case.

GOOD EXAMPLE

  I. The girl alleged wrongs in the complaint.
  A. Cherelle insulted her taste in clothing.
  B. Cherelle implied she needed a sophisticated, lighter-skinned clerk.
 II. Facts that are in agreement.
  A. The girl worked for Cherelle.
  B. Cherelle spoke to the girl about her dress while working in the shop.
  C. The girl quit.
III. Facts that are in dispute.
  A. Cherelle's comments about the girl's clothes were insults.
  B. Cherelle wanted a different type of person as a clerk.
  C. Cherelle implied she wanted someone lighter-skinned.
  D. Cherelle implied she wanted someone more sophisticated.
IV. Allegations that are not legally actionable.
  A. An employer may criticize an employee's attire.
  B. An employer may require an employee to be sophisticated.
  C. An employer may dictate an employee's work attire.

V. Allegations that could be legally actionable.

    A. An employer may not discriminate against an employee because of race.

    B. An employer may not discriminate against an employee because of gender.

We chose the first main heading because it focuses on the things the girl, who is now called the Plaintiff, states Cherelle, who is now called the defendant, did that the girl claims were illegal. These claims are the heart of the legal action. The next two main headings separate the fact pattern into facts both parties agree are correct and the facts they do not agree are true. The final two main headings address whether the appellant, that is, the girl who quit, has alleged that Cherelle has done something illegal or not. Each of these main headings will be important in the lawsuit.

EXAMPLE THREE

Two days after his preliminary hearing, Mr. Williams, the client accused of driving under the influence and assaulting an officer, walked into Brad's office. He informed Brad that he had been carrying a refrigerator for a friend in the bed of his pick up truck when the truck hit a huge bump. The bump had caused the refrigerator to fall off the back of the truck onto a car following it.

"That guy what was tailgating me, he got what he had coming to him. I was driving real slow so the refrigerator wouldn't shift and this guy was trying to make me speed up. So I speeded up, and this is what happened. It's all his fault, but he did get hurt when the refrigerator went through his windshield."

Brad asked if the driver of the car had been taken to the hospital, and Mr. Williams said he didn't stick around to see if EMS actually took him.

"I figured I was in enough trouble with this drunk driving thing, so I hightailed it out of there. Me and my buddy put the refrigerator back on the truck and took it to his house. Darn thing still works, too!"

Brad asked Mr. Williams if he got the driver's license plate or the make of the car. Mr. Williams said he had not bothered, because he did not intend to be involved. He had just stopped by the office to let Brad know in case it ever became a problem.

"I presume the EMS or police got the license number and make of your truck, though," Brad said.

Mr. Williams said that they might have gotten the make and color of the truck, but because he had not put plates on it or registered it, they would not be able to trace it to him.

"I got it parked in my buddy's barn. He messed with the engine so that it would look like it ain't been run in years. He put a bunch of hay and dust all over it. No one would believe it was ever run.

"You ain't gonna tell the police about this, are you?" Mr. Williams asked with alarm.

"I am forbidden to tell anyone what you tell me, unless you tell it to them first," Brad replied. "The only time I can repeat something is if you tell me you are planning to hurt someone. Then I have a duty to warn."

Mr. Williams laughed, saying, "I already hurt him good, so I done enough. As far as I'm concerned, it's all over."

Brad advised Mr. Williams that he had violated several laws, some more serious than others. He told him he did not condone his actions, but he was his lawyer and would defend him in a court of law.

"Tommy done me right when he brought me to you," Mr. Williams said. "I like you."

"I won't do anything illegal or unethical," Brad warned. Mr. Williams laughed and said, "You don't got to. I do enough for both of us." He walked out of the office, still laughing.

Important facts

- Refrigerator was not safely secured in the truck bed.
- Mr. Williams caused an accident.
- The driver following was injured.
- The driver's car was damaged.
- Mr. Williams left the scene of an accident.
- Mr. Williams operated an unregistered vehicle, the truck.
- Mr. Williams aided and abetted tampering with evidence, the truck.
- Mr. Williams does not believe he is liable for the driver's injuries.
- Mr. Williams intends to hide the evidence and avoid admitting involvement.

BAD EXAMPLE

I. Chances Mr. Williams will get caught

 A. If his buddy snitches on him

 B. If someone at the scene recognized him

 C. If someone goes into his buddy's barn and sees the truck

II. Might happen if he got caught

 A. Probably jail because of the DUI being a prior

 B. The guy in the car maybe suing him

 C. The police maybe confiscating his truck

 D. His buddy getting in trouble for helping hide the truck

GOOD EXAMPLE

I. Potential criminal actions

 A. Leaving the scene of an accident

 B. Driving an unregistered vehicle

 C. Operating the vehicle unsafely, so that it lost its load

 D. Damaging another vehicle

 E. Tampering with evidence

II. Potential civil actions

 A. Injuring the driver whose car was hit by the refrigerator

 B. Damaging the car

Note the parallelism of each subheading. Each "A," "B," etc. begins with a verb ending in "-ing." Using parallel structure in your outlines will aid you in writing your final document. It provides a structure and logic that an outline that is not parallel lacks.

STEP ONE For many writers, outlining is a three step process. First, the writer accumulates all the information and summarizes it concisely. A first summary of the incident with Mr. Williams and the refrigerator might look like the following:

- Mr. Williams caused an accident when a refrigerator fell off the back of the unregistered truck he was driving.
- The refrigerator hit another vehicle and reportedly hurt the driver and damaged the vehicle.
- Mr. Williams and his companion placed the refrigerator back into the truck and left the scene.
- Mr. Williams and his companion hid the truck, attempted to make it look like it had not been run recently, and had no intention of reporting the incident to the authorities.

We have jotted down notes regarding the legally significant events concerning the incident with the refrigerator.

STEP TWO The second step narrows the focus by weighing the importance of each fact and analyzing which facts are important to the final document. Taking the incident with Mr. Williams and the refrigerator, we see this in the bullet-point list.
Important facts

- Refrigerator was not safely secured in the truck bed.
- Mr. Williams caused an accident.
- The driver following was injured.
- The driver's car was damaged.
- Mr. Williams left the scene of an accident.
- Mr. Williams operated an unregistered vehicle, the truck.
- Mr. Williams aided and abetted tampering with evidence, the truck.
- Mr. Williams does not believe he is liable for the driver's injuries.
- Mr. Williams intends to hide the evidence and avoid admitting involvement.

Here we have refined the notes we jotted down in step one and have broken them down into the individual legal issues.

STEP THREE In the third step, we take the important facts and organize them in a logical way. There is not necessarily only one way to organize a set of facts. Part of the organization depends on the goal of the writing. If the goal is to provide an objective summary of the facts, then the outline above would be appropriate. If, however, the goal is to minimize the seriousness and/or effect of Mr. Williams's actions, the outline would look very different.

    I. Liability

        A. Damage to car and injury to driver

            1. Driver failed to maintain assured clear distance.

            2. Driver was inattentive to potential hazards on the road.

        B. Proof of responsibility for the accident

            1. Driver cannot identify the truck's plates.

            2. Driver cannot identify owner or driver of the truck.

II. Damages

    A. Medical damages

        1. Driver may have had preexisting condition. (research)

        2. Driver may have experienced medical situation causing his inattention. (research through discovery)

    B. Vehicle damage

        1. Driver's car was old and had a low value for replacement.

        2. Driver's car may have had preexisting damage. (research)

III. Mr. Williams's actions

    A. Driving an unregistered vehicle

        1. Truck would not pass inspection/he could not afford repairs.

        2. He drove the truck on the road only this once.

    B. Leaving the scene of an accident

        1. Mr. Williams might not have been aware of the seriousness of this.

        2. Mr. Williams was afraid to get in trouble so soon after his DUI.

Although the major headings, "Liability," "Damages," and "Mr. Williams's actions" and the first subheadings, "Damage to car and injury to driver," etc. are not parallel with the second subheadings, "Driver failed to maintain assured clear distance," etc, the headings and first subheadings are parallel with each other, and the second subheadings are parallel with each other. The parallelism in your outlines does not need to be slavishly followed, but it should be helpful in guiding your writing. When writing a document from this outline, the headings will provide an organizational guide to direct us, and the second subheadings will provide us with prewritten sentences that we can adapt to the document. This way, we have saved time in our writing process and insured consistency in our draft.

EXERCISE

Using the prior three steps, that is, summarizing the important parts of the fact pattern, narrowing the focus, and organizing the important facts in a logical way, outline the following fact pattern using the funnel method.

FACT PATTERN

Sheila Kowalski made an appointment for a legal consult with Ana. At the meeting, Sheila explained that after apartment shopping for a long time, she had finally found an apartment she really loved. It had all the things she had wanted in her first apartment: a large, open kitchen, a view of the town square, a spacious closet, and close proximity to the hospital. She told Ana that any apartment she was considering had to be walking distance to the hospital, even though she would drive when her nursing shift was scheduled at night.

She showed Ana the ad she had answered when she first called about the apartment. The ad stated that it had a large, open kitchen, generous storage, and was newly remodeled. It was one block from the hospital where Sheila worked. After touring the apartment, Sheila signed the lease, specifying the precise apartment, stating its address and apartment number.

When she went to move in, however, the landlord told her that the particular apartment she had toured was no longer available. He pointed to a clause in the lease, which Sheila had not noticed when she signed it, saying that the landlord could substitute a similar apartment for the one the tenant had toured. She pointed to the language she had added specifying that the lease covered one specific apartment unit.

The landlord proceeded to show Sheila an apartment with a closed-off galley kitchen;

(continued)

only one small closet; an old, dirty carpet; and a view of the garbage dumpster. Additionally, the apartment the landlord showed Sheila was five blocks further from the hospital than the one she had toured. Sheila handed her copy of the lease contract to Ana and said that she hoped Ana could help her. She told Ana that the landlord had threatened to sue her for breach of contract when she refused to accept the substitute apartment.

EXERCISE

Read the fact pattern below and again use the three step funnel structured approach to outline it.

The next day, Sheila returned to Ana's office in tears. She handed Ana a Complaint that the landlord had filed against her. In Count One of the Complaint, he alleged breach of contract, stating that Sheila had refused to honor the lease agreement she had signed and that he was losing rental income by her breach of the lease contract.

In Count Two, the landlord alleged that Sheila had slandered him when she told her boyfriend Tommy about the incident, because Tommy had told everyone that the landlord had pulled a bait and switch on Sheila. He had discussed this with everyone who came into the scrap yard, everyone he saw at the diner where he had lunch, and everyone at the bar where he stopped after work.

Count Three of the landlord's complaint alleged that Sheila had further damaged the premises by kicking a hole in the door on the way out of the apartment. He further alleged that she had threatened to sue him for every piece of property he owned.

Sheila told Ana that she had not kicked anything; she had been wearing sandals that day, and she would have hurt her foot if she had kicked the door. She also told Ana that it was the landlord, and not she, who had threatened a lawsuit.

As she discussed the situation with Ana, Sheila became angry. They agreed that Sheila would file a counterclaim and try to force the landlord to either rescind the contract or rent Sheila an apartment that was comparable to the one she had toured, and to the description in the ad; he would have to provide an apartment with a large, open kitchen, one with spacious closets, one that was close to the hospital, and one that was newly remodeled.

EXERCISE

Read the following continuation of the fact pattern and use the three step structured funnel approach. Select the important facts and issues and outline them.

Ana has asked Sheila to write down everything she can remember about the tour of the apartment and her conversations with the landlord. By having Sheila do this, Ana will learn facts that did not come out in her interview with Sheila. Further, Sheila might remember something she had forgotten to mention in the interview. This method of acquiring information from a client can be useful, provided the paralegal or attorney is careful to identify the important information. Below is what Sheila has written.

"I had been saving up for an apartment since I graduated from nursing school. I knew exactly what I was looking for; I wanted a big kitchen, because I love to cook. I needed the apartment to be close to the hospital so I could walk to work on nice days that I was working day shift. I had looked at a lot of apartments, but I did not see anything I could afford that met my wish list. I also wanted a good view,

(continued)

because after work I like to sit by the window with my feet up while I sip a beverage. After a really hard day, I bring home a pizza and eat by the window, but usually I just I drink a cool beverage. A good view has always been very important to me. I remember my first dorm room looked at a parking lot, and it was a depressing view. Even though I wear a uniform for work, I wanted a big closet so I can finally buy all the nice clothes I now can afford. My closet in the dorm was so small it was hard to even fit my uniforms, much less anything else. When I saw the ad on March 14th, I got really excited and called the number right away for an appointment to see it. I knew the apartment would not last at that price. I got in to see it the very next day and signed the lease. The apartment looked out on the town square, with all the oak trees. It is so charming to watch the squirrels chasing each other up and down the oak trees. I loved the color of the granite in the kitchen; it was black with sparkly flecks. The cupboards were white, which made the kitchen look clean. The closet had two sets of hanging rods as well as a lot of shelf space. I probably should have had my father or my boyfriend look at it before I moved so quickly, but the landlord said he had another appointment to tour the apartment immediately after my appointment. I was afraid that I would lose the apartment. I wrote on the lease the exact address and apartment number, because the landlord said he had several apartments that were open, and I wanted to be sure I would get that exact apartment. Right after I signed the lease, I took my copy of it and showed it to my dad. He said it looked good to him, but he is not an attorney."

■ SEQUENCING

Sequencing is important when making an outline. Although the most obvious way to sequence a group of facts is by time, that is, consecutively, it is not the only way. An outline can be sequenced by the subject, by the laws or cases that apply, or by the consequences resulting from the facts.

Lack of sequencing results in confusion for the reader, and, more importantly, lack of effectiveness for the writer. A poorly sequenced outline can cause the writer to miss an important fact or issue.

> **EXAMPLE**
> - Sheila was all set to move into her new apartment.
> - She answered the ad she saw online.
> - The landlord threatened to sue her.
> - She had saved the ad that she responded to.
> - The apartment the landlord wanted her to move into was dirty.
> - It had a small kitchen.
> - She had toured a beautiful apartment.
> - The apartment had only one small closet.
> - It was five blocks from the hospital.

You can see how jumbled the facts are when they are related in this order. If we organize them consecutively, the story becomes clearer.

- Sheila answered an ad for an apartment.
- The ad said the apartment had a large open kitchen.
- The ad said the apartment had a spacious closet.

- She toured the apartment.
- It had a large open kitchen and spacious closet, and was close to the hospital.
- She signed the lease expecting to move into the apartment she saw.
- On the day she was to move, the landlord gave her a different apartment.
- The substitute apartment had a closed-off galley kitchen.
- The substitute apartment had only one small closet
- The substitute apartment had an old, dirty carpet.
- Sheila refused to accept the apartment.
- The landlord sued Sheila for breach of contract.
- Sheila countersued for breach of contract.

Now the facts make sense.

Another way of sequencing is organizing the consequences that resulted from the facts. Again, this will be somewhat consecutive, but it does not have to be as clearly consecutive as the previous example.

Looking at Sheila's situation again, we also can sequence and outline the facts by event and consequence, instead of by time.

When Sheila was working with Ana to write the counterclaim, she told Ana that she had spent $500 on movers. The cost was supposed to be $250, but because they had to move her things back to her parents' house after she refused the substitute apartment, her cost was double. Sheila had also arranged with another nurse to share the expenses on the apartment, so her potential roommate was also inconvenienced. Additionally, Sheila had organized a housewarming party, and she had bought the food, which had cost her $300. Because she was not able to have the party, she donated the food to the food bank. She also had spent money on invitations and a special outfit for the party. Because she wore a uniform at work, the outfit was not something she was likely to use.

Sheila had taken two vacation days to move and to organize her new apartment. Because she only had two weeks of vacation a year, she had lost 20% of her vacation time.

Sheila's mother had hired a contractor to redo Sheila's room after she moved out. Because she moved back, her mother had to cancel the contractor and lost her deposit.

Here, each consequence would be preceded by its corresponding fact.

Sheila hired movers; she paid $500 and did not get her new home.
Sheila took two vacation days; she did not get to use them as she had planned.
Sheila's roommate had counted on moving in; she is without a place to live.
Sheila prepared for a housewarming party; she lost the money spent on food, invitations, etc.
Sheila bought an outfit for the party; she now has no use for it.
Sheila's mother hired a contractor; she lost her deposit because Sheila had to move back into the room her mother had planned to renovate.

Note that sometimes you will include ideas or facts in your first jottings that you might decide not to include in your final outline, either because they are extraneous or because they will not be helpful. For example, the fact that Sheila bought an outfit for her party that had to be canceled, and that she is listing this as one of her damages, seems to contradict the fact that she wanted large closets so she could buy lots of clothes. We might not use that particular argument in our final document.

EXERCISE _____

Read the following scenario and determine what is important and also sequence by *time*.

Cherelle stopped at into Ana's office to chat. She told Ana that Ana would never believe what had happened that day; Cherelle had caught a shoplifter. Cherelle confronted her outside the store. She caught the girl walking out the door wearing an expensive scarf she had tried on. By a stroke of luck, a police car was driving by, and Cherelle flagged the officers down. The police asked both Cherelle and the girl what was going on. There were two officers, and each took one person aside and questioned her. The tag was hanging down the girl's back. The girl claimed that Cherelle was trying to steal her scarf. Cherelle told the officer she spoke with that the girl had taken the scarf without paying for it.

EXERCISE _____

Read the following scenario and determine what is important and also sequence by *consequence*.

Mr. Williams stood outside gazing at the charred timbers that a short time ago had been his home. He cursed himself for forgetting to make the house insurance payment. He shivered in the cold of the clear night. His son Tommy had warned him to stay home and to not drink any alcohol. Mr. Williams was his own man, he thought, but he could see it made sense to stay home with all the trouble he was in. It did not make sense to not drink, though. Tommy had tried to take all the alcohol out of Mr. Williams's home, which made Mr. Williams mad. What Tommy did not know, however, was that Mr. Williams always kept a bottle of bourbon in a secret cubicle he had fashioned years earlier, when Tommy's mother was still alive. Mr. Williams pondered how similar Tommy was to his mother. She had taken his alcohol away too. That was why he had made the secret cubicle.

Mr. Williams had poured himself a generous drink and lit a cigarette. He listened to the World Series on the radio, but he was not interested in either team. He woke up to find himself surrounded by flames and smoke. He managed to get out of the house, but within minutes it had burned to the ground. He wished he had thought to grab the bottle on his way out; he yearned for a drink.

EXERCISE _____

Read the following fact pattern and determine what is important using the funnel approach. Then sequence the facts in the way you consider most effective.

Tommy pulled his car quickly into his father's driveway. Stunned, he looked at the ruins of his childhood home. He spotted his father and gave him a hug. Realizing that his father was shivering, he took off his coat and wrapped it around his father. He also realized that his father smelled of cigarettes and alcohol.

Thoughts swirled through Tommy's brain; his father would never repay the bail money. He would never be able to propose to Sheila. His father would have to live with him until the insurance rebuilt the house. Sheila would break up with him, not wanting to be related to a person like his father. His life was ruined. His father had been drinking, even though Tommy thought he had removed all the alcohol. How had the fire started? Was anyone else inside? Maybe another person had brought the alcohol and that person had died in the fire.

Tommy asked his father what had happened. His father looked dazed, and Tommy realized his father was staggering: not from shock, but from inebriation.

The fire department arrived, and as they shot water on the embers, Tommy mentioned his suspicions that another person may have been in the house. One of the firemen began searching in the embers when the floor gave way, dropping him to the basement. The EMS

(continued)

had arrived with the fire truck, and as they carried the fireman on a stretcher to the ambulance, Tommy overheard the fireman speaking. He was telling the paramedics that he could not feel or move his legs, and that his back hurt terribly.

Tommy sank to the ground and put his head in his hands. His father berated him, pointing out that it was he, the father, who was now homeless and had lost all his possessions. Rather than punch his father, Tommy walked to his car and drove away.

■ INFORMAL AND FORMAL OUTLINING

There are two styles of outlining: informal and formal. The informal outline often is the earlier version of the formal outline, used when researching, interviewing a client, or putting down thoughts as they occur. Another use for informal outlining is for a writing that is simple or less important. Informal outlines may consist of phrases or clauses, but they are sufficient to record the thought or idea.

EXAMPLE OF INFORMAL OUTLINING

Ana wanted to tell her grandmother in her weekly letter about a number of events that had happened the previous week. She jotted them as follows on the back of an envelope as she waited for an appointment:

- Mr. William's house burned down
- Cherelle caught shoplifter
- Her sympathy for Tommy
- Wondering if Sheila would stay with Tommy

Ana knew that she could not tell her grandmother about Mr. Williams' DUI, Sheila's apartment disappointment, or the refrigerator falling off a truck and blinding the driver, because they all involved clients of her firm. Ana was ethically barred from discussing anything related to her clients' cases.

Formal outlining, unlike the outlining we have discussed so far, is essential for more complicated or sophisticated writings. Later in this textbook you will learn to write Memoranda of Law, briefs, and motions that will require a formal outline. Just as the name suggests, a formal outline follows a specific structure and each line of the outline is parallel.

Parallelism occurs when like elements are written in the same form. The abstract concept is difficult to understand, but an example makes the concept clear. We will discuss parallelism at greater length later in the chapter because it is important not only in outlining, but also in all writing.

Say Ana decided to formally outline her letter to her grandmother. She might write it as follows:

EXAMPLE OF FORMAL OUTLINING

I. Mr. Williams

   A. Mr. Williams received a DUI.

   B. Mr. Williams's house burned down.

   C. A fireman broke his back fighting the fire.

II. Tommy
    A. Tommy had to take his father in.
    B. Tommy could lose Sheila because of his father's actions.
III. Cherelle
    A. Cherelle caught a shoplifter.
    B. Cherelle was able to have the police arrest the shoplifter.
IV. Sheila
    A. Sheila took time off and hired a truck to move.
    B. The landlord tried to give Sheila a different, less nice apartment.
    C. Sheila refused the replacement apartment.
    D. Sheila's prospective roommate had nowhere to live.
    E. Sheila had to cancel her housewarming party.
V. Injured driver
    A. A driver was seriously injured when something smashed his windshield.
    B. The driver could not remember what had happened.
    C. The driver was blinded by something penetrating his eyes.
    D. The police had no leads on what caused the accident.
    E. The driver's car had paint from the object that hit it.
    F. The paint was not automotive paint.

Notice two things about this outline. First, each Roman numeral heading addresses one person. These are parallel; they are similar in subject and in form. Each is a person, and each is a noun. Second, notice that for every A there is a B. In other words, it would be incorrect to outline as follows:

I. Tommy is depressed.
    A. He had to take his father in.
II. Sheila's disappointment
    A. Could not move in when she wanted to

First, the elements of the outline are not parallel. Roman numeral "I" contains a full sentence; Tommy is depressed. Roman numeral "II," on the other hand, is a phrase. It contains the possessive of Sheila and the noun disappointment. These two elements are not parallel. Further, the subelements, the "A" for the Roman numerals, also are not parallel. The subelement under Tommy is again a full sentence. The subelement under Sheila's disappointment is a clause. More importantly, there is no "B" to correspond with the two "A"s. An outline cannot have an "A" without at least one more subheading, that is without at least a "B." See Table 1.1 for an explanation of Roman Numerals.

When the elements of an outline are not full sentences, they should begin with the same form of speech. If the first element is a noun, all the subsequent elements also should begin with nouns or pronouns. If the first part of the element is a verb, all the following elements should begin with verbs in the same form.

The second important thing to notice is the way a formal outline is structured. Most outlines using Roman numerals proceed from the capitalized form of the Roman numeral to a capital letter. If the topic in the capital letter has subheadings, Arabic numerals begin each subelement. If the Arabic numeral has subelements, lower case letters precede each subelement. If the lower case letters have subelements, then lower case Roman numeral precede them.

EXAMPLE

I. Sheila lost money as a result of the landlord's switch.

   A. She paid the movers.

      1. She paid them to move her things to the apartment.

      2. She paid them to move her things back to her parents' home.

   B. She planned a housewarming party.

      1. She bought a new outfit she could not use.

      2. She spent money on the party.

         a. She mailed invitations.

            i. She paid for invitations.

            ii. She paid postage to send them.

            iii. She bought cards to send to cancel the party.

         b. She spent money on food that she did not serve at the party.

II. Sheila's mother lost money, because she had to cancel the contractor.

Notice that the fact that Sheila's mother had to cancel the contractor is not a subelement under Roman numeral II. That is because there is no second element that would make a "B" for the "A."

One caveat: Federal statutes do not follow this form. Instead, after the Roman numerals, they use a lower case letter, then a number, then an upper case letter, then the lower case Roman numerals. See example of 7 USC § 136a - Registration of pesticides - in the box. In some versions of statutes, the text does not even contain a space between the sections, making them harder to navigate. In volumes that we own, we have found that highlighting all the capital Roman numerals in one color, then all the capital letters in another color, etc, makes the volume far easier to use.

Table 1.1 Roman Numerals

Roman Numerals
Roman numerals are not always taught in schools today, so below is an explanation and example of how they work. I = one II = two III = three So far, so good. Now it gets a little complicated.
The Roman numeral for five is the letter "V." Instead of the Roman numeral for four being "IIII," it is "IV." In a way, it is as though the "I" preceding the "V" is subtracted from the "V," making the number four. IV = four V = five
For the Roman numeral six, the "I" is placed after the "V," so it is added to the five. VI = six VII = seven VIII = eight
Just as a fourth "I" is not added to make the number four, the number nine does not add a fourth "I" to the right of the "V." Rather, it places the "I" before the Roman numeral for ten, which is "X." So the Roman numeral for nine is "IX." This is the same concept as used to make the Roman numeral for 4, IV, as shown above. IX = nine X = ten XI = eleven
Following this logic, the number nineteen is XIX. The number twenty is designated by two tens, "XX." The next nine numbers add the original nine after the "XX." So twenty-six would be "XXVI. This continues in format with different letters representing higher numbers. For example, the letter "L" represents 50. For more details, search the Internet for charts delineating Roman numerals.

EXAMPLE

7 USC § 136a - Registration of pesticides

(a) Requirement of registration

Except as provided by this subchapter, no person in any State may distribute or sell to any person any pesticide that is not registered under this subchapter. To the extent necessary to prevent unreasonable adverse effects on the environment, the Administrator may by regulation limit the distribution, sale, or use in any State of any pesticide that is not registered under this subchapter and that is not the subject of an experimental use permit under section 136c of this title or an emergency exemption under section 136p of this title.

(b) Exemptions

A pesticide which is not registered with the Administrator may be transferred if—

(1) the transfer is from one registered establishment to another registered establishment operated by the same producer solely for packaging at the second establishment or for use as a constituent part of another pesticide produced at the second establishment; or

(2) the transfer is pursuant to and in accordance with the requirements of an experimental use permit.

(c) Procedure for registration

(1) Statement required

(1) Each applicant for registration of a pesticide shall file with the Administrator a statement which includes—

(A) the name and address of the applicant and of any other person whose name will appear on the labeling;

(B) the name of the pesticide;

(C) a complete copy of the labeling of the pesticide, a statement of all claims to be made for it, and any directions for its use;

(D) the complete formula of the pesticide;

(E) a request that the pesticide be classified for general use or for restricted use, or for both; and

(F) except as otherwise provided in paragraph (2)(D), if requested by the Administrator, a full description of the tests made and the results thereof upon which the claims are based, or alternatively a citation to data that appear in the public literature or that previously had been submitted to the Administrator and that the Administrator may consider in accordance with the following provisions:

(i) With respect to pesticides containing active ingredients that are initially registered under this subchapter after September 30, 1978, data submitted to support the application for the original registration of the pesticide, or an application for an amendment adding any new use to the registration and that pertains solely to such new use, shall not, without the written permission of the original data submitter, be considered by the Administrator to support an application by another person during a period of ten years following the date the Administrator first registers the pesticide, except that such permission shall not be required in the case of defensive data.

(ii) The period of exclusive data use provided under clause (i) shall be extended 1 additional year for each 3 minor uses registered after August 3, 1996, and within 7 years of the commencement of the exclusive use period, up to a total of 3 additional years for all minor uses registered by the Administrator if the Administrator, in consultation with the Secretary of Agriculture, determines that, based on information provided by an applicant for registration or a registrant, that—

(I) there are insufficient efficacious alternative registered pesticides available for the use;

(II) the alternatives to the minor use pesticide pose greater risks to the environment or human health;

(III) the minor use pesticide plays or will play a significant part in managing pest resistance; or

(IV) the minor use pesticide plays or will play a significant part in an integrated pest management program.

The registration of a pesticide for a minor use on a crop grouping established by the Administrator shall be considered for purposes of this clause 1 minor use for each representative crop for which data are provided in the crop grouping. Any additional exclusive use period under this clause shall be modified as appropriate or terminated if the registrant voluntarily cancels the product or deletes from the registration the minor uses which formed the basis for the extension of the additional exclusive use period or if the Administrator determines that the registrant is not actually marketing the product for such minor uses.

■ FORMATTING OUTLINES

Formats are important to the organization of an outline both for the writer and the reader. If the writer can clearly, effectively, and logically create a well-written outline, the reader will be able to understand and follow the writer's logic and purpose. The writer will be able to draft a document that is organized and logical.

As mentioned earlier, note that you will never have only one heading. For every "I," you must have a "II." For every "A," you must have a "B." If you find that you have only one subheading, that item actually belongs in the heading above. Being able to write only one subheading means there is not enough material to divide the heading above it, and the material belongs above.

Two types of formats are the general (letter-number system) and the legal format (decimal system). The most common format within the legal field is the general format which uses the Roman numeral system, which was discussed above under sequencing.

General Format

Under the general format system of outlining, the Roman numerals are used to signify the major topics or points. Thus, the major topics, issues, or points would be headed I, II, III, etc. The supporting information would be headed first with a capital letter, A, B, C, etc. Information that supports the material in the A, B, C and following headings would be listed as Arabic numbers 1, 2, 3, etc. Material under the Arabic numerals is designated with lower case letters, a, b, c, etc. When the materials in the lower case letters requires further breakdown, lower case Roman numerals are used, i, ii, iii, etc. (Figure 1.2).

Traditionally, each subsection was indented, making the different sections easy to see. In more recent volumes of statutes, perhaps in an effort to save paper, all the headings and subheadings have been printed flush with the left margin. This makes the outline more difficult to use, but reduces the amount of paper used. See box with an Ohio State statute for an example.

Figure 1.2 Outline format

```
Outline Format Example:
  I. Main Point

      A. Subordinate Point
          1. Supporting data
          2. Supporting data

      B. Subordinate Point
          1. Supporting data
          2. Supporting data

  II. Main Point

      A. ....
```

EXAMPLE

4511.21 Speed limits - assured clear distance.

(A) No person shall operate a motor vehicle, trackless trolley, or street-car at a speed greater or less than is reasonable or proper, having due regard to the traffic, surface, and width of the street or highway and any other conditions, and no person shall drive any motor vehicle, trackless trolley, or streetcar in and upon any street or highway at a greater speed than will permit the person to bring it to a stop within the assured clear distance ahead.

(B) It is prima-facie lawful, in the absence of a lower limit declared or established pursuant to this section by the director of transportation or local authorities, for the operator of a motor vehicle, trackless trolley, or streetcar to operate the same at a speed not exceeding the following:

(1)

(a) Twenty miles per hour in school zones during school recess and while children are going to or leaving school during the opening or closing hours, and when twenty miles per hour school speed limit signs are erected; except that, on controlled-access highways and expressways, if the right-of-way line fence has been erected without pedestrian opening, the speed shall be governed by division (B)(4) of this section and on freeways, if the right-of-way line fence has been erected without pedestrian opening, the speed shall be governed by divisions (B)(9) and (10) of this section. The end of every school zone may be marked by a sign indicating the end of the zone. Nothing in this section or in the manual and specifications for a uniform system of traffic control devices shall be construed to require school zones to be indicated by signs equipped with flashing or other lights, or giving other special notice of the hours in which the school zone speed limit is in effect.

(b) As used in this section and in section 4511.212 of the Revised Code, "school" means any school chartered under section 3301.16 of the Revised Code and any nonchartered school that during the preceding year filed with the department of education in compliance with rule 3301-35-08 of the Ohio Administrative Code, a copy of the school's report for the parents of the school's pupils certifying that the school meets Ohio minimum standards for nonchartered, nontax-supported schools and presents evidence of this filing to the jurisdiction from which it is requesting the establishment of a school zone. "School" also includes a special elementary school that in writing requests the county engineer of the county in which the special elementary school is located to create a school zone at the location of that school. Upon receipt of such a written request, the county engineer shall create a school zone at that location by erecting the appropriate signs.

(c) As used in this section, "school zone" means that portion of a street or highway passing a school fronting upon the street or highway that is encompassed by projecting the school property lines to the fronting street or highway, and also includes that portion of a state highway. Upon request from local authorities for streets and highways under their jurisdiction and that portion of a state highway under the jurisdiction of the director of transportation or a request from a county engineer in the case of a school zone for a special elementary school, the director may extend the traditional school zone boundaries. The distances in divisions (B)(1)(c)(i), (ii), and (iii) of this section shall not exceed three hundred feet per approach per direction and are bounded by whichever of the following distances or combinations thereof the director approves as most appropriate:

(i) The distance encompassed by projecting the school building lines normal to the fronting highway and extending a distance of three hundred feet on each approach direction.

(ii) The distance encompassed by projecting the school property lines intersecting the fronting highway and extending a distance of three hundred feet on each approach direction;

(iii) The distance encompassed by the special marking of the pavement for a principal school pupil crosswalk plus a distance of three hundred feet on each approach direction of the highway.

> Nothing in this section shall be construed to invalidate the director's initial action on August 9, 1976, establishing all school zones at the traditional school zone boundaries defined by projecting school property lines, except when those boundaries are extended as provided in divisions (B)(1)(a) and (c) of this section.

The easier way to make your own outline is to indent each subheading as we did above and repeat below:

I. Sheila lost money as a result of the landlord's switch.
    A. She paid the movers.
        1. She paid them to move her things to the apartment.
        2. She paid them to move her things back to her parents' home.
    B. She planned a housewarming party.
        1. She bought a new outfit she could not use.
        2. She spent money on the party.
            a. She mailed invitations.
                i. She paid for invitations.
                ii. She paid postage to send them.
                iii. She bought cards to send to cancel the party.
II. Sheila's mother lost money, because she had to cancel the contractor.

See how much easier that format is to use.

Some legal books use a different form of outlining, using the section symbol and numbers. This form of outlining is found in Treatises of Law, American Jurisprudence (AmJur), and other legal writings. See the side bar with an example of this format.

Another outlining format you will encounter during your paralegal career is the legal format (decimal system). In this outlining format, the main points are preceded by the section symbol "§" followed by a number, a decimal point, and another number. This form of outlining is harder to follow, but probably easier to revise. A volume that is organized this way will refer the reader to a section number rather than the page number. The section numbers are usually located at the top of the page.

Table 1.2 Legal Format

LEGAL FORMAT
EXAMPLE
§ 1.1 Case #1 (Main Point)
§ 1.11 Dependent point
§ 1.12 Dependent point
§ 1.2 Case #1 (Main Point)
§ 1.21 Dependent point
§ 1.22 Dependent point
§ 2.1 Case #2 (Main Point)
§ 2.11 Dependent point
§ 2.12 Dependent point

■ PARALLELISM IN OUTLINING

Parallelism exists when like elements are written in the same form. The abstract concept is difficult to understand, but an example makes the concept clear.

> **EXAMPLE**
>
> Each of the women found the line of work they wanted; Sheila loved nursing, Cherelle liked sales, and Ana enjoyed law.
>
> Notice that the descriptions of the three women's jobs are written in the same form. Each is a simple independent clause written subject-action verb-object.

If this sentence were written poorly, without parallelism, it might sound like this:

Each of the women found the line of work they wanted; nursing had always been Sheila's goal, Cherelle liked sales, and the law, even though it was difficult, had always been Ana's interest.

This version is harder to follow and is not pleasing to the ear. It is not parallel.

Parallelism goes beyond independent clauses, however. Consider the following sentence.

EXAMPLE

When they were preparing to hire a paralegal, Brad and Ana sought a candidate with several important qualities: punctuality, thoroughness, honesty, and discretion.

This sentence would not be correct if it were written differently:

When they were preparing to hire a paralegal, Brad and Ana sought a candidate with several important qualities: able to be punctual, thoroughness, honest, and a discreet person.

Similarly, the elements of an outline must be parallel. The following segment of an outline is not parallel.

EXAMPLE

I. Tommy is depressed.
   A. He had to take his father in.
II. Sheila's is disappointment.
   A. Could not move in when she wanted to.

Roman numeral "I" contains a full sentence; Tommy is depressed. Roman numeral "II," on the other hand, is a phrase. It contains the possessive of Sheila and the noun disappointment. These two elements are not parallel. Further, the subelements, the "A" for the Roman numerals, also are not parallel. The subelement under Tommy is again a full sentence. The subelement under Sheila's disappointment is a clause.

When the elements of an outline are not full sentences, they should begin with the same form of speech. If the first element is a noun, all the subsequent elements also should begin with nouns. If the first part of the element is a verb, all the following elements should begin with verbs.

EXAMPLE ONE

I. Hiring a paralegal
   A. Advertising
   B. Interviewing
   C. Making an offer

II. Finding essential qualities in a paralegal
A. Being punctual
B. Being responsible
C. Being diplomatic
D. Being organized

All the elements in Example One are verbs with an "-ing" ending.

We could write the same outline and be parallel in another way.

EXAMPLE TWO

I. Paralegal employment
A. Advertisement
B. Interview
C. Offer
II. Paralegal's essential qualities
A. Punctuality
B. Responsibility
C. Diplomacy
D. Organizational skills.

EXERCISE

Read the following fact pattern. Outline only the important facts, using the structured funnel approach. Sequence the information using the general format of the main points and the subordinate numbers using parallelism.

Concepts to use are: 1. important vs. not important, 2. funnel, 3. then sequence, 4. outline in general format, 5. parallelism.

Brad and Ana, who in addition to being law partners were engaged to be married, were in Ana's kitchen eating supper and discussing the cases they had in their office. Ana mentioned that a new potential client had asked for a consult. As it turned out, the would-be client was the man who had been blinded when the refrigerator fell off the truck Mr. Williams was in. Ana knew that they could not accept the man as a client, because his legal interests were diametrically opposed to their existing client, Mr. Williams. They also knew that they were ethically forbidden to let the man know that Mr. Williams was their client, or that he had any connection to the refrigerator incident. Fortunately, they had been able to handle the situation in an ethical manner. This man's inquiry, however, made them realize that as their practice was growing, they had to be sure to avoid conflicts of interest in the clients they accepted. Their office of two attorneys was too small for a "Chinese wall," that is, a separation adequate to allow them to represent clients with conflicting interests. They decided then and there to outline all their existing clients and be sure there were no conflicts.

Ana remembered Sheila Kowalski and her problem with the apartment being switched. Brad mentioned that he had been talking to a man at the gym who complained about the same landlord and inquired about Brad representing him as a tenant against the same landlord. Brad had handed him his business card and now questioned whether he could represent both Sheila and this other tenant. Brad and Ana agreed that they could never represent the landlord, and they decided they would give thought and put research into representing another tenant against the same landlord.

(continued)

Then Brad mentioned Mr. Williams, whose multiple legal problems involved several parties. Clearly, they were barred from representing the driver of the car who had been injured by the falling refrigerator. But were they also barred from ever representing any police officers, because they had represented Mr. Williams in the DUI case?

Cherelle's case involving the former employee presented a simpler situation. That girl already had her own counsel, and to their knowledge, no one else was involved in the case.

Brad suddenly remembered that he had spoken to his third grade teacher, Mrs. Pritchett, who had asked if she could see him about a roofing problem. She was scheduled to come in to the office the next week. They realized they would have to check their client list to be sure they did not represent any building contractors or workers.

SUMMARY

- Outlining is an important step in writing effective documents.

- Outlining allows writers to organize their material logically.

- With outlining, writers cannot recognize what facts are important for their purpose and which to omit.

- Outlining also gives writers an overview of their material, allowing them to evaluate several different ways to organize their material and then select the most effective format.

ASSIGNMENTS

I. Answer the following questions:

1. A _____ is used to keep information organized.

2. What does the funnel help the writer decide?

3. Name three important concepts in outlining that were discussed in this chapter.

4. Grouping alike categories such as time, case, event, or similarity are examples of _____.

5. What are two types of outlines?

6. The format of an outline includes designated main points with Roman numerals. After the Roman numeral, the next subheading is designated with _____, and subheadings under that are designated with _____.

7. One subordinate point should not stand alone; what are several alternatives?

8. Making each element in an outline a subordinate clause beginning with a preposition is an example of _____.

II. Write only the important facts from the following incident.

On the day of his father's trial for driving under the influence of alcohol, resisting arrest, and assaulting a police officer, Tommy started the coffee and went to wake up his father. He turned on the light in the room where his father was staying since Mr. Williams' house had burned down. When he went to shake his father's shoulder, he realized that the bed was empty except for the pillows placed under the covers.

Tommy sighed. He then phoned Brad at his home and told him that his father, the defendant in the trial that day, was missing. Brad's heart sank, both because he dreaded facing the judge that morning without his client, but mostly because he felt bad for Tommy. He told Tommy he would stop by to pick him up in a little while.

When they arrived at the courthouse, each man glanced around, hoping futilely that Mr. Williams would appear. Tommy said he would be glad to see his father, even if he were drunk. Brad nodded, and they slowly entered the courthouse.

When Mr. Williams's case was called, Brad had to inform the Judge that his client had disappeared from his son's house during the night, and that his location was unknown. Although he expected a reprimand from the judge, instead the judge called Brad to the bench. Tommy saw Brad's face break into a huge smile. Brad glanced at Tommy and gave him a signal that all was ok.

Just then, the deputy brought Mr. Williams into the courtroom. He was dressed in a jail uniform, and he had a large cut on his cheek, as well as two black eyes. For a moment, Tommy wished he had punched his father himself. Quickly, though, his feelings changed to relief.

Brad requested a brief recess to allow him to discuss this new turn of events with his client, but the judge refused. The judge then told Brad that because Mr. Williams had appeared on time for his trial, Tommy would get the bail money back. The judge also informed Brad that Mr. Williams's bail was revoked, because he had violated its terms by drinking and being arrested for drunk and disorderly, assault, and disturbing the peace.

III. Read the following fact pattern and the two outlines of it. Compare the outlines and decide which is better. Explain in detail why you did not choose the other outline.

Brad realized that Mr. Williams would not make a very good impression on a jury with black eyes and cuts on his face. It would be difficult, Brad realized, to convince a jury that Mr. Williams had not assaulted the police officer when it was clear he had been in a fight the night before. Brad was also concerned about what had happened to result in Mr. Williams being in custody again. He also knew that with bail revoked, he did not have to worry about Mr. Williams missing any further court dates.

Brad asked the judge if he could approach the bench. The judge waved him up, and Brad requested a continuance of the trial. He told the judge that he needed to investigate the previous night's incident so he could be fully prepared to defend his client. The judge agreed that continuing the trial was prudent and granted a one month continuance. The judge then reminded

Mr. Williams that he would be returning to jail until the trial.

When Brad and Mr. Williams got to a room where Brad could talk with him confidentially, Mr. Williams began to yell. Why, he asked, did Brad continue the trial? Now he would have to spend an entire month in jail, had Brad thought of that? Brad outlined his reasoning to Mr. Williams, who calmed down.

FIRST OUTLINE FOR EXERCISE ONE

I.   Advantages of continuing the trial
  A. Mr. Williams' appearance would improve
    1. Black eyes would not convince the jury he was not violent
  B. Brad would have time to investigate most recent charges.
    1. Why Mr. Williams was in jail
    2. could the trials be combined?
  C. Tommy could get his bail money back
    1. Tommy could propose to Sheila
    2. Tommy not worry where father was

II. Disadvantages of continuing the trial
  A. Mr. Williams spends a month in jail.
  B. Mr. Williams might go through alcohol withdrawal.
    1. Tommy would not smuggle liquor into jail.

SECOND OUTLINE FOR EXERCISE TWO

I.   Mr. Williams would gain from having the trial postponed.
  A. He would be easier to defend in a month.
    1. His facial injuries would heal.
      a. The jury would not assume he was a fighter.
      b. His appearance would be more appealing.
    2. Gossip about the most recent arrest would reduce.
  B. Brad would have time to investigate the recent arrest.
    1. He could find out if Mr. Williams had another DUI.
    2. He could prepare a comprehensive defense.

II. Mr. Williams would lose a month of his life in jail with the trial postponed.

LEARNING OBJECTIVES

1. Identify the difference between the barbell and arrowhead paragraph patterns

2. Reproduce the barbell and arrowhead paragraph patterns

3. Eliminate poorly written and choppy writing

4. Compose well organized paragraphs

5. Apply unity and coherence to written paragraphs

6. Sequence well written paragraphs by using transitional words

Paragraphs and Functions

CHAPTER 2

■ PARAGRAPHS

We discussed prewriting in the outlining chapter. Composing your document, which will consist of paragraphs, is stage two of the outlining process writing.

A paragraph is a group of sentences discussing, describing, or explaining a cohesive idea or concept. An effective paragraph is well organized and self contained. It should not contain extraneous thoughts or ideas. It should have a clear beginning and end, with the middle of the paragraph fleshing out the basic concepts addressed in the beginning and summarized at the end.

Functions

Paragraphs are necessary in writing for many reasons. First, they provide a ready-made method for placing different ideas or aspects of a writing into discreet segments. Second, they give the reader a built-in breathing point. An effective writer considers the reader's attention span and crafts the length of the paragraphs to account for it. If a paragraph is too long, the writer risks losing the reader's attention part way through. By breaking a writing into manageable portions, the writer encourages the reader to continue.

Paralegals use outlines and compose paragraphs in the workplace every day when they draft documents like memoranda of law, letters to clients, and motions. This organization makes the paralegal's work product useful for the attorney. Organization, especially in written communications and documents, is an essential trait for a paralegal.

Remember, your writing should be "invisible," so that what you are saying, and not how you are saying it, is what the reader sees. If paragraphs are overly long or are too short, the reader's attention can be distracted from the point of the writing by the style of the writing. Therefore, most concepts should be presented in "bite-sized" portions.

By writing an outline before actually beginning to write, a paralegal has organized his or her thoughts into a form that is conducive to creating effective paragraphs. The paralegal's main point and supporting points are already grouped together in order of importance in the outline. Thus, the paralegal can control and manage the information being provided to the reader. Now the writer only has to construct effective sentences into a coherent paragraph. The paragraph is already organized.

Barbell Pattern

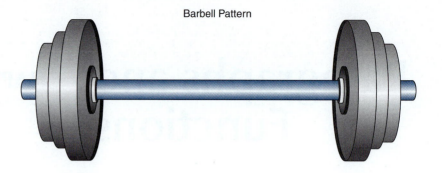

Patterns

Writers use one or more of several patterns of paragraph organization. Varying your paragraph structure will provide interest to the readers and prevent your writing from sounding monotonous. Also, as we learned in the outlining chapter, the way you organize your material allows you to emphasize what is important and downplay areas and facts that you have to mention but prefer to minimize.

Barbell Paragraph Pattern

The three sections, a beginning, a middle, and an end, are in the barbell pattern. By picturing a barbell, the writer can see that the weight of the paragraph will be found in the first and the last sentences of the paragraph. The first sentence of the paragraph will be the topic sentence, the sentence that tells the reader what the paragraph will discuss. It provides the focus and often a persuasive description of the subject of the paragraph.

Similarly, the last sentence of the paragraph will summarize what the writer has said in the paragraph. It will also try to persuade or inform, and it will incorporate the material found in the middle of the paragraph to support the conclusion. The last sentence of the paragraph is the writer's chance to solidify the point or argument set forth in the paragraph.

The middle of the barbell, where the person grasps it, contains the substance: the essence of the argument or specific facts that support the beginning and ending sentences. Just as the ends of the barbell provide the weight that builds muscle, while the middle provides the essential bond between the two weights, so the middle section of the paragraph provides the substance and facts that bond the topic sentence and the concluding sentence together. Without the middle of the paragraph, the writer has only bald assertions without support. Although the beginning and ending sentences are the "stars of the show," without the substance in the middle, they are very weak indeed.

EXAMPLE

Brad worked hard to represent his clients zealously while remaining ethical. Sometimes this was far more difficult than it sounded. When Mr. Williams informed Brad that he was responsible for the accident that blinded the driver whose car was hit by the refrigerator, Brad had to remember his ethical duty concerning the confidences of a client. This was especially hard when the broadcasters on the evening news repeated the police department's pleas to viewers to come forward with information concerning the accident. It was even more difficult, though, when Mr. Williams gloated about getting away without getting caught. Nonetheless, Brad clearly understood the ethical rules and never told even his law partner, Ana, what Mr. Williams had told him.

Brad warned Pat, the paralegal, that this duty of confidentiality extended to the paralegal, and applied equally.

The beginning, or topic, sentence is "Brad worked hard to represent his clients zealously while remaining ethical."

The ending, or concluding, sentence is "Nonetheless, Brad clearly understood the ethical rules and never told even his law partner, Ana, what Mr. Williams had told him."

The middle portion of the paragraph provides the substance to support the assertion contained in the first sentence. The concluding sentence repeats the concept contained in the first sentence, but it adds the substance found in the middle of the paragraph to emphasize the point put forth in the first sentence.

EXAMPLE

Brad was prepared for Mr. Williams's hearing. He had filed a motion challenging the accuracy of the breathalyzer reading by ascertaining when it had last been calibrated. He also had his paralegal, Pat, research the animosity and long-standing feud Mr. Williams had claimed existed between him and the arresting officer. His strongest piece of evidence, however, was the eye witness Pat found who had used his phone to visually record Mr. Williams's arrest. Brad had entered the visual recording into evidence, but, to his surprise, the prosecutor had not bothered to review it. Brad knew that although he might not win on the accuracy of the breathalyzer argument, he would prevail on the resisting arrest and assaulting an officer charges.

The beginning sentence appears to be quite simple: "Brad was prepared for Mr. Williams's hearing."

The ending sentence, on the other hand, incorporates the information in the middle of the paragraph and clearly and succinctly summarizes it while repeating and supporting the information in the first sentence.

EXERCISE _____

Identify and label the topic sentence (T), the middle section, which may have more than one sentence (M), and the concluding sentence (C). Draw a vertical line between the transitions.

The prosecutor's opening statement was quite forceful. He told the jury that the evidence would show that Mr. Williams was dangerously drunk on the evening in question. Not only was he drunk, the prosecutor continued, but he was violent and aggressive. The prosecutor told the jury that Mr. Williams had attacked the officer, not once, but twice. First, he said, Mr. Williams pulled the officer down after falling during the roadside sobriety test. More egregious, the prosecutor went on to say, was the fact that Mr. Williams had shoved the officer into the filthy, vermin infested storm ditch. The prosecutor pointed out that Mr. Williams was actually lucky that the officer had not sustained serious injury or infection from being forcefully shoved into the ditch. The prosecutor had presented his version of the facts in a very effective manner.

EXERCISE

Identify and label the topic sentence (T), the middle section, which will have more than one sentence (M), and the concluding sentence (C). Draw a vertical line between the transitions.

The prosecutor had the jury's rapt attention. Each juror visually followed his every move. They hung on his every word, and they reacted emotionally and even physically to parts of his opening statement. One woman audibly gasped when the prosecutor described Mr. Williams pushing the officer into the ditch. Another woman shuddered when the prosecutor mentioned the officer falling in with vermin. Some of the men's faces hardened when they heard the prosecutor's description of Mr. Williams' aggression and excessive drunkenness. Many sat with their arms folded against their chests, like an angry parent scrutinizing a wayward child. All the jurors were clearly impressed and even swayed by the prosecutor's dramatic rendition of the events of the evening of Mr. Williams' arrest. The prosecutor successfully impressed the jury with his opening statement.

EXERCISE

Select from the two paragraphs which paragraph follows the barbell pattern.

1. Mr. Williams began to sweat, listening to the prosecutor. Maybe the jury will believe what that lying attorney is saying, he thought. I could spend a lot of time in jail. The thought of being without his one pleasure in life, alcohol, made him tremble. Brad placed his hand on Mr. Williams's arm to calm him. He whispered in Mr. William's ear, "Don't let the jury see you shake. It makes you look guilty."

2. Brad's opening statement helped to calm Mr. Williams. Brad told the jury that although some of what the prosecutor had told them had a basis in truth, much of his opening statement was fabricated. For example, Brad pointed out, although it was true that the officer had fallen twice during the course of the arrest, the evidence would prove that neither fall was Mr. Williams's fault. Additionally, Brad noted, the evidence would demonstrate that the officer had a long-standing grudge against Mr. Williams and had intentionally altered the results of the breathalyzer test to make the results of the test read higher than they really were. In short, Brad concluded, the only facts he and the prosecutor agreed on were that the officer pulled Mr. Williams over, both men fell during the roadside sobriety test, and the officer landed in the ditch. After hearing Brad's opening statement, Mr. Williams's breathing slowed to normal and his hands stopped shaking.

If the sentences are out of order, you can see how confusing the paragraph is. The following example will clarify this concept.

EXAMPLE OF A POORLY ORGANIZED PARAGRAPH

The officer then described how Mr. Williams fell out of the car when he tried to stand. The arresting officer made a compelling case on his own behalf. The officer's testimony repeated the arrest report almost word for word. The prosecutor put on his case first, beginning with his star witness, the arresting officer. He described Mr. Williams's erratic control of his Trans Am weaving dangerously into the oncoming lane, the difficulty Mr. Williams had had in pulling over without driving into the ditch, and the strong smell of alcohol that blasted out of the window when Mr. Williams opened it.

However, if the paragraph follows an organized sequence then the information is much easier for the reader to understand.

EXAMPLE OF A WELL ORANIZED PARAGRAPH

The prosecutor put on his case first, beginning with his star witness, the arresting officer. The officer's testimony repeated the arrest report almost word for word. He described Mr. Williams's erratic control of the Trans Am, weaving dangerously into the oncoming lane, the difficulty Mr. Williams had had in pulling over without driving into the ditch, and the strong smell of alcohol that blasted out of the window when Mr. Williams opened it. The officer then described how Mr. Williams fell out of the car when he tried to stand. The arresting officer made a compelling case on his own behalf.

EXERCISE

The following three sections from the barbell pattern, topic sentence, supporting information, and conclusion, are out-of-order. The middle of the paragraph often consists of several sentences. Place them in order #1 (topic), #2 (middle), #3 (conclusion).

_____ First he presented evidence from his eye-witness, and then he showed the jury the actual recording of the entire encounter.

_____ Clearly, Brad's presentation of evidence was a resounding success.

_____ He approached his case methodically, chipping away at the credibility of the officer.

_____ Brad had quite a challenge when his turn to present evidence came.

_____ When the jury saw that Mr. Williams had not been weaving while driving, had been tripped when he got out of his car, and had passed the roadside sobriety test, they were not surprised to see that the officer actually had tried to push Mr. Williams into the ditch.

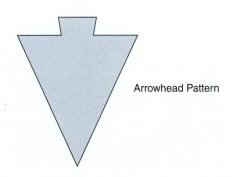

Arrowhead Pattern

Arrowhead Pattern

The arrowhead pattern is used many times in the legal field. The beginning sentence is broad, and each subsequent sentence continues to narrow to a point called the conclusion. This method is more difficult to use, but it can be very effective. It leads the readers through the facts to a surprising conclusion that nonetheless is inevitable based on the facts. This method is not uncommon in speeches meant to persuade a group.

EXAMPLE

After the debacle with her prospective apartment, Sheila felt discouraged and depressed. She also felt awful that her mother had had to cancel her redecorating plans because of Sheila's apartment problem. She struggled to think of a way to show her mother how much she appreciated her sacrifice, but she needed something that would also lift her own spirits. Suddenly she remembered how much her mother had enjoyed the chicken and dumplings Sheila had made when her mother was sick. Sheila made the chicken and dumplings again, and both she and her mother felt better.

EXAMPLE

In her motion for summary judgment, which is a document that can allow the judge to decide the case without a trial(which we will cover later), Ana wrote the following:

> Cherelle Jackson opened a boutique on Main Street a year and half ago. At first she ran the store alone, but as she became more successful, she hired a young woman to help with sales. As a member of a minority, Cherelle wanted to help another minority student with an interest in fashion. She therefore hired the plaintiff in this lawsuit, who had expressed an interest in fashion and a need for tuition money to pursue her dream. Cherelle undertook guiding this young woman in the field of fashion. Despite Cherelle's offer of providing the boutique's clothing to the young woman at cost, and despite Cherelle's well-intended guidance on presenting a professional image, the young woman not only quit her job without notice, leaving Cherelle in a lurch, she also sued Cherelle for race discrimination. As the attached pictures from each of their identification cards demonstrate, however, both women are equally dark. The plaintiff cannot prove racial bias on the part of this defendant who is a member of the same minority group.

EXAMPLE

In his trial brief, Brad had used the arrowhead technique to persuade the Court:

> Mr. Williams's pride and joy is his Trans Am. He drives it only in the summer and only in good weather. He was driving this car on the evening in question, so he was cautious to avoid drinking too much. After two beers in the course of as many hours, he left the Dew Drop Inn and drove around the countryside, enjoying the warm evening. He was puzzled when the officer pulled him over, and he was angered when the officer pushed him to the ground as he tried to exit his car. He was further upset when the officer tripped him during the roadside sobriety test, and he protected himself when the officer tried to push him into the drainage ditch. The officer was the one who ended up in the ditch. Mr. Williams was not surprised by the events after he realized who the officer was; it was his lifelong nemesis, a man who wanted nothing more than to see Mr. Williams squirm and suffer. Mr. Williams knew that he would have trouble with this event.

EXERCISE

Identify only the broadest beginning point (B) and only the narrowest ending point (N) of the following paragraph using the letters B or N.

> The jury studied both attorneys closely. They also noticed the demeanors of the officer and Mr. Williams. During deliberation, the jury agreed that although Mr. Williams was far from a stellar citizen, the officer appeared to have been lying during his testimony. Mr. Williams was a more credible witness, and his counsel presented the more credible side in this case.

EXERCISE

Identify only the broadest beginning point (B) and only the narrowest ending point (N) of the following paragraph with the associated letters.

> The prosecution presented its case first, as always, because it had the burden of proof. After the prosecution rested, Brad called his first witness, a man who had been in school with both the officer and Mr. Williams. This witness described the irrational dislike the officer had always had for Mr. Williams. Brad then called his star witness, who, unfortunately, was not a person of high repute. Everyone on the jury knew this witness, and every single one of them wondered why Brad would use him. Then Brad introduced the phone visual recording this witness had taken of the entire incident, from the time Mr. Williams stopped his car until he was placed into the police cruiser. Stunned, the jury realized that the events had occurred exactly as Mr. Williams and the witness had stated.

EXERCISE

Sequence all of the facts from broadest to narrowest in the arrowhead pattern from the paragraph below.

> Even worse, some witnesses would provide testimony that was entirely different from what they had told him prior to trial. Brad had learned that he had to accept his witnesses as they were. He had learned that phrasing his questioning carefully and controlling the witness as much as possible was essential for providing his client with the best representation. Unfortunately, not all witnesses were pillars of society, and not all witnesses were as credible as he would wish.

As the above exercises have demonstrated, both the barbell pattern and the arrowhead pattern work well in legal writing. As a paralegal, your goal is to make the writing as clear and functional as it can be for the reader.

Unity

The writer's goal is a unified writing. Although the writing often will include varied topics or facets of the whole, the writer can achieve unity by keeping like information together and expanding it. A paragraph is unified if it stays on one topic and does not stray off point. A unified paragraph is also organized in a logical manner. Each component of the paragraph should serve the purpose by validating or supporting the purpose of the paragraph. The paragraphs should sequence in a logical order, by chronology, or cause and effect, or order of importance, etc.

BAD EXAMPLE

The jury was on the third day of deliberation. Deliberation started late in the afternoon on a Friday. One juror, however, was being troublesome. The second day of deliberation had been wasted with arguments over who would be the jury foreman. She had been daydreaming during some of the testimony and kept arguing that the rest of the jurors were inventing testimony. She had been planning her grocery list so she could shop on the way home. They finally selected an unexpected person to be the foreman. The foreman had to chastise the problem juror. Finally, they were able to address the issues in the case.

GOOD EXAMPLE

Deliberation started late in the afternoon on a Friday. The second day of deliberation had been wasted with arguments over who would be the jury foreman. They eventually selected an unexpected person to be the foreman. Finally, they were able to address the issues in the case. One juror, however, was being troublesome. She had been daydreaming during some of the testimony and kept arguing that the rest of the jurors were inventing testimony. The foreman had to chastise the problem juror.

Note that the correct example omits the sentence about the subject of the problem juror's daydreams. This sentence strays off the point of the paragraph. The remainder of the paragraph puts the events in the paragraph in chronological order.

Paragraphs should vary in length, both to address the amount of information needed for each topic as well as to prevent tedium for the reader. Obviously, the paragraph should not be any longer than necessary, because unnecessary repetition will bore the reader. Just as the length of the paragraphs should vary, so should the length of the sentences in the paragraph. A paragraph in which each sentence is the same length and the same structure becomes sing-song and is ineffective, unless this is done for rhetorical effect.

EXAMPLE OF CHOPPY WRITING

Brad's new paralegal, Pat, wrote the following draft summary of the police report:

Mr. Williams was pulled over at 2:34 a.m. Mr. Williams drove a Trans Am. The Trans Am was light blue. The officer ordered Mr. Williams out of the car. Mr. Williams fell as he got out of the car. The officer ordered him to walk a straight line. Mr. Williams fell again. Mr. Williams pushed the officer into the ditch.

This writing is tedious and dull, even though it contains the information from the police report. Brad worked with the paralegal and suggested the following changes:

EXAMPLE OF FLUID WRITING

At 2:34 a.m., the officer pulled over Mr. Williams, who was driving a light blue Trans Am. Mr. Williams fell when he tried to get out of his car. Then, when the officer ordered him to walk a straight line, Mr. Williams fell again. Finally, after having fallen twice, Mr. Williams pushed the officer into the ditch.

This paragraph contains the same information as the first one, but it flows more smoothly and does not bore the reader. Of course accuracy is primary, but good writing adds to the effectiveness of the piece.

EXAMPLE OF CHOPPY WRITING

Pat, the paralegal, was very motivated to do well, so the next writing submitted to Brad read as follows:

The witness stopped in the office. He gave me his phone with the video of Mr. Williams's arrest. I took the phone to the videographer's office. The videographer copied it onto a CD. I brought both the phone and the CD back to the office. Ana got an affidavit from the witness. The witness also is willing to testify at trial. I copied the CD onto the office network. You can view it anytime. It is saved as "Williams arrest video" in the H drive.

Although this paragraph might be slightly better than the first one, it is still very rote and dull. One reason the paragraph sounds stilted is that each sentence begins with a noun or pronoun, is followed by the verb, and completed by the direct object or subject complement. Additionally, the paragraph lacks any transitions. We will discuss transitions when we address coherence later in this chapter.

EXAMPLE OF FLUID WRITING

The witness stopped in the office in order to give me his phone with the video of Mr. Williams's arrest. I took the phone to the videographer's office, where he copied it onto a CD. I brought both the phone and the CD back to the office. Meanwhile, Ana got an affidavit from the witness, even though he is willing to testify at trial. I also copied the CD onto the office network where you can view it anytime. It is saved as "Williams arrest video" in the H drive.

You can see how much better this version sounds.

EXAMPLE OF CHOPPY WRITING

Although frustrated, Pat continued to try to improve the variety and length of the sentences. The first draft of an office memo read as follows:

Mr. Williams came to the office today. He was with his son Tommy. He wanted to pay you. Tommy had the checkbook. He wrote the check. I put it in the safe. Tommy wanted to thank you. Your help meant the world to him. He is sorry he beat you up on the playground in first grade. Mr. Williams wanted to thank you too. He said you are his lawyer for the rest of his life.

EXAMPLE OF FLUID WRITING

Pat reread the paragraph and realized that it could be improved by varying the sentence lengths and adding transitions, and wrote the following:

Mr. Williams and his son Tommy came to the office today to pay you. Actually, it was Tommy who had the checkbook and wrote the check. I put the check in the safe. Tommy said to be sure to thank you, since your help meant the world to him. He also apologized for beating you up on the playground in first grade. Mr. Williams also wanted to thank you. He said you are his lawyer for the rest of his life.

Brad smiled when he read this memo, not just because Tommy had apologized, and not just because he had gotten paid. He smiled because he saw the improvement in Pat's writing.

In the following examples, notice that the sentence that does not create unity is highlighted.

EXAMPLES

Pat left the following memos for Brad:

1. Tommy came in to see you. He is worried about his father again. His father got drunk and started to tell everyone at the Dew Drop Inn about the refrigerator, whatever that means. Tommy said you would understand. *Mr. Williams sure has a drinking problem.* Tommy wants you to call him as soon as you can.
2. A police officer came in today to ask if you would help him interview Mr. Williams. *The officer was sure easy on the eyes!* The officer left a phone number for you to call. He referenced a driver who was blinded in an accident.
3. Mr. Williams stopped by, and he was very upset. He said someone has been telling stories about him that could get him into a lot of trouble. *It seems to me that he does not need help getting into trouble.* Mr. Williams said he needs to talk to you right away.
4. The officer stopped by again. He implied that you will be in trouble if you do not cooperate with the police on this. *The officer is not so hot after all.* I left the number and the officer's name on your chair.
5. Ana called to tell you that Cherelle won her case. The clerk who quit and then sued her was reprimanded and ordered to pay Cherelle's court costs. *I love the clothes Cherelle sells.* Ana said she would tell you all about the trial at dinner.
6. The clerk who sued Cherelle came into the office today. She said that Ana had better watch her back, because she will get even. *Cherelle was right; the girl dresses like a tramp.* She did not stay long, but I did call the police to report the threat. They took a statement and have put the office and both your apartment and Ana's apartment under surveillance.

EXERCISE

In the following examples underline the sentence that does not create unity. These examples are more subtle.

Pat, the paralegal, wrote the following police statement concerning the incident in which Cherelle's former clerk had threatened Ana and Brad.

1. At 3:30 p.m. on Tuesday, a young woman entered the office reception area and asked to speak with Ana. I informed her that Ana was not available and offered to take a message. She gave me a message all right. She said to tell Ana to watch her back.

2. She also said that if she had to hurt Ana by hurting Brad, she would. I do not even know if she knows what Brad looks like. She said that she always gets even and that Ana cost her money. Because she has to pay court costs, she said, she cannot pay the tuition for next semester. She will make sure that whatever she does to Ana will cost Ana a lot more.

3. The young woman was approximately five feet four inches tall and weighed around 150 pounds. I can guess that weight because she was about my height and I am thinner, weighing 135. She had dark skin and short cropped hair. I did not see her get into a car when she left.

4. I believe she knows what car Ana drives, because she said something about a red Corolla. She even recited a license plate number, but I am not sure what Ana's plate number is. This girl seemed very mean and a little unhinged. I know she scared me. She also told me Ana's home address, which I know was correct.

5. Ana's law partner, Brad, will be coming in as soon as he can get here to provide more information. He is worried sick about Ana. He will be able to provide the make, model, and license number of his car, as well as his home address.

6. One more thing; this girl threatened to have Ana deported to Mexico. She said she had proof that Ana's birth certificate was a fake. She said she wanted to hurt Ana first. She made some comment about Ana not being so pretty when she was done with her. She is probably jealous because this girl is no beauty queen, and she is stupid too, because Ana is Puerto Rican.

Coherence

Writing that is coherent follows logically. It does not ramble. Its parts are connected in a rational manner. A coherent writing contains logical and well-reasoned information. It avoids the off-topic types of sentences referenced in the unity section earlier in this chapter.

Coherent writing is made even more logical by the use of transitions. Transitional words are those that make the connection between two ideas, phrases, clauses, and/or sentences. They often provide the reader with a clue about the text that follows the transition.

EXAMPLE

Ana was frightened of the girl who was threatening her. She went about her normal day.

Each sentence may state a true fact, but they do not seem to make sense together. By the addition of a transitional word, however, they are coherent:

EXAMPLE

Ana was frightened of the girl who was threatening her. Nonetheless, she went about her normal day.

Now the reader understands that although Ana is frightened, she refuses to be cowed.

Below in Table 2.1 is a grid with some transitional words or phrases that writers use to make their writing both more coherent and easier to read. While it is important not to overuse transitional words, when they are used properly, they greatly enhance the effectiveness of a writing.

Table 2.1 Transitional Words

Purpose	Transitional Words
Addition	Also And Besides Furthermore In addition In order to maintain Moreover Similarly
Cause and Effect	Accordingly After all And yet As a result As a consequence At the same time Because Consequently Even though For For that reason Hence However Nevertheless Otherwise Since So So that Still Therefore To do this Yet
Comparison	For the same reason In the same way Likewise Similarly

(continued)

Contrast	Alternatively
	But
	Despite
	However
	Instead
	On the other hand
	Unlike
Conclusion	Consequently
	Finally
	In summary
	In conclusion
	Thus
	To review
Emphasis	Certainly
	Clearly
	Indeed
	In fact
	Still
Examples	For example
	For instance
	To illustrate
	Specifically
	That is
Similarity	Again
	As well as
	And
	Besides
	For example
	Furthermore
	In the same way
	Once more
Sequence	Above
	After that
	Beside that
	Final
	Finally
	Former/Latter
	First, Second, Third, ...
	Next
	The later
Time	Afterwards
	Earlier
	Eventually
	Initially
	Later
	Meanwhile
	Shortly thereafter
	Simultaneously
	Since
	Subsequently

In the sentences below, by using a transitional word, we have enhanced the meaning of the sentence. Notice how using a variety of transitional words in the examples below makes the writing more interesting and effective. Transitions help avoid choppiness in writing.

In the following examples, the transitional words are italicized.

EXAMPLES

1. Brad stayed close to Ana and *also* monitored her phone calls and texts. Ana knew that the police were monitoring her; *therefore*, she was more worried about Brad's safety. Ana need not have worried about Brad, *however*, because the police were watching him as closely as they were watching her. The police were keeping a close watch on Ana and Brad; *similarly*, they were closely monitoring the young woman who had made the threats. The police were also keeping a close watch on Cherelle and the boutique: *in conclusion*, every player in this drama was being watched.

EXAMPLE

2. Ana jumped when she heard a knock at her apartment door. *After* looking through the peephole, *however*, she realized she was not under immediate threat. She opened the door and let Brad in; *still*, she peeked around him to see if he had been followed. He had, *in fact*, been followed, but by a plainclothes policewoman. *Even though* the police were in the hall outside her apartment, *nevertheless*, Ana still had trouble relaxing.

Notice the difference in the following two examples. Look for words which create unity and coherence. In the first example of choppy writing there are a few transitions but not enough.

EXAMPLE OF CHOPPY WRITING

3. Ana ate breakfast the next day. Ana used the remote to start her car. It did not explode. She cautiously got into it. She tried to back out of the parking space. Someone was standing behind her car. She was annoyed. She was gripped with fear. The person began to come around the car. When the rear of the car was clear, Ana gunned the engine and backed out. She realized that the person was not the woman threatening her. The person was a police officer. Her heart returned to its normal rhythm. She rolled down her window. She informed the officer that he had terrified her. She realized that he was on her side. She did not want to anger him. He apologized for frightening her. He appeared very sheepish. Ana caught movement out of the corner of her eye and ducked. A large rock struck the officer in the middle of his chest. He took off running after the woman who had thrown it. Ana called the police on her cell phone. She did not like to talk on the phone while she was driving. The dispatcher assured her that the officer had backup. The dispatcher told her to drive directly to her office. Another unmarked police car would be following her. Ana locked the office door after she entered.

Compare the above paragraph with the one that follows. Notice how the italicized transitional words clarify the sentence.

EXAMPLE OF FLUID WRITING

4. *After* eating breakfast the next day, Ana used the remote to start her car. Surprisingly, it did not explode, *so* she cautiously got in to it. *As* she was trying to back out of the parking space, unfortunately, someone was standing behind her car. *At first* she was annoyed; *then*

suddenly she was gripped with fear. The person began to come around the car, and *as soon as* the rear of the car was clear, Ana gunned the engine and backed out. She *then* realized that the person was not the woman threatening her, *but* instead was a police officer. *When* her heart returned to its normal rhythm, she rolled down her window. She informed the officer that he had terrified her. *Despite* this, she realized that he was on her side *and* did not want to anger him. He apologized for frightening her; in fact, he appeared very sheepish. Suddenly, Ana caught movement out of the corner of her eye and ducked. A large rock struck the officer in the middle of his chest, *and* he took off running after the woman who had thrown it.

Ana called the police on her cell phone, *even though* she did not like to talk on the phone while she was driving. The dispatcher assured her that the officer had backup. *Additionally*, the dispatcher told her to drive directly to her office, *because* another unmarked police car would be following her. *Despite* the presence of the officers, Ana locked the office door after she entered.

EXERCISE

Underline the transitional words or phrases in the following paragraph.

While Cherelle, Ana, and Brad ate dinner that evening in the apartment that Cherelle and Ana shared, Cherelle apologized to Ana and Brad. Surprised, they asked her why she needed to apologize. Slowly, she admitted that she felt guilty that her former clerk was stalking and threatening them. Immediately Brad put his arm around Cherelle's shoulder and reassured her. Unfortunately, he told her, attorneys sometimes endured threats from unbalanced litigants. In fact, he went on, it was not uncommon for a former client who was unhappy with the outcome of a case to harass or threaten an attorney. Nonetheless, he said, he was very happy with his work. Ana added, furthermore, she was glad that Cherelle was not in this alone. Cherelle was likewise in danger, because the woman owed her the court costs. Ana also reassured Cherelle that she was glad to have been able to help her, and regardless of the young woman's threats, she felt the woman would be caught soon, and subsequently be locked up so that they all could feel safe.

EXERCISE

Meanwhile
Then
After
Therefore
While

From the list provided, choose and insert the transitional words that are needed to create a smooth transition in the sequence of sentences in the following paragraph. A transitional word is not necessary at the beginning of each sentence. The transitional word is used to create writing that is smooth and connects the thoughts clearly and effectively. You might not need to use all the words listed.

Ana and Cherelle cleared the dinner dishes. Brad washed them and put them in the drainer. After the dishes were done, they decided to go out for ice cream. They realized that they might not be safe outside the apartment; they decided to bake cookies instead. Brad called the police department to find out whether there were any further developments in the case.

EXERCISE

Insert the transitional words that are needed to create a smooth transition in the following sequence of sentences. A transitional word is not necessary at the beginning of each sentence. The transitional word is used to create writing that is smooth and connects the thoughts clearly and effectively. Refer to the chart provided in this chapter for transitional words and phrases.

Ana was taking the cookies from the oven when she heard a loud explosion. Brad ran into the kitchen and pushed both women to the floor.

Another explosion went off. Cherelle began to shake uncontrollably, and passed out. Ana tended to Cherelle. Brad redialed the police. They heard shouting outside, but they were afraid to move. They had to move. They crawled to a room in the middle of the apartment, away from the windows. Brad's phone rang, and the police informed him that when they had surrounded the girl, she had turned her gun on herself. The girl was dead.

EXERCISE

Read the facts in the following outline. You will draft a paragraph or paragraphs describing these events. Looking at the grid, use at least 10 transitional words as you merge the facts to provide smooth transitions between ideas in order to create a unified and coherent, well-written paragraph.

   I. Brad informed Ana and Cherelle that they were safe.
      A. He put his arms around both of them.
      B. They cried with relief.
  II. They heard a knock at the door.
      A. They jumped.
      B. They realized they were safe.
      C. They realized the girl could not hurt them.
 III. They opened the door to the police officer.

  IV. The officer told them what had happened.
      A. He saw the girl with a gun approaching Ana's car.
         1. The girl shot the gas tank of Ana's car.
         2. Ana's car exploded.
      B. The girl approached Brad's car.
         1. The officer could not get close enough to the girl.
         2. The girl shot the gas tank of Brad's car.
         3. Brad's car exploded.
   V. Backup officers arrived.
      A. They shouted for the girl to drop the gun.
      B. The girl turned the gun on herself.
      C. The officers had not had time to stop the girl.

EXERCISE

Read the following paragraph. Notice that the italicized transitional words provide a negative slant. Using the list below the paragraph, rewrite it to give it a positive slant.

The morning paper contained a complete article about the incident; *unfortunately*, it was even the banner headline. Brad and Ana were in the office discussing the previous evening with Pat. Brad was aware of the publicity the article would bring to the law firm. *Nevertheless*, he knew that they could not avoid the attention it would draw. *Even though* they had not sought this notoriety, *still* they would deal with it. *Certainly*, it might increase the number of people who sought their help with legal issues. *Consequently*, they instructed Pat to prepare for an increase in phone calls and foot traffic.

In fact
Indeed
Clearly
However
For that reason
Therefore

A common error new writers make is poorly organizing their material. Believe it or not, legal writing instructors get papers similar to the exercise below fairly frequently.

EXERCISE

The following paragraph contains facts that are out of order. Reorganize them in a logical sequence in an outline. Be sure to prioritize the facts. Then construct well-written paragraphs from your outline. Be sure to use appropriate transitional words to improve the meaning and flow of your writing. After you have written the paragraph logically, evaluate what you have written and revise it to improve it.

Pat, the paralegal, interviewed a prospective client for Brad while Brad was in court. Because Pat took the notes quickly and typed them as they were written, the notes were not well organized. Take the following memo and reorganize it into a coherent set of paragraphs.

He also wonders if his buddy started telling people about it. I suspect he was slightly tipsy, but he wanted me to report the following information to you. He said that a woman he did not remember told him she knew about the refrigerator. He is afraid that $500 will not be enough to satisfy her. Mr. Williams came in today. She will keep hounding him for money every time she needs it. He does not remember telling anyone about the refrigerator incident and he is afraid if he did say something there will be others to come forward and blackmail him, too. She told him he had talked about it at the Dew Drop Inn, but for $500 she would keep it to herself. Since it was Mr. Williams's truck, his buddy would not be in as much trouble. Then he got frightened and said I could not tell anyone what he had said to me. I assured him that as your paralegal, I was as bound by client confidentiality as you were.

SUMMARY

- Writing logical, organized paragraphs is the best way for writers to convey the ideas they want to express.

- A paragraph should consist of unified ideas and concepts, and material that is not related should be addressed in its own paragraph.

- Using different paragraph patterns prevents writing from being dull and repetitive.

- Writers can emphasize their important points by using the appropriate paragraph pattern.

- Two paragraph patterns are the barbell and the arrowhead.

- Coherence is as important in paragraphs as unity.

- Transitions help writing to flow smoothly and to enhance facts, ideas, and concepts the writer is conveying.

- Transitions also provide context and add meaning to the paragraph.

- Providing variety for readers is important, and varying both sentence and paragraph length achieves this.

- Well written paragraphs contain logical writing that flows well and results in an effective, persuasive document.

ASSIGNMENTS

I. Below is a rambling, grammatically incorrect story that a potential client recounts to you. You need to organize it, first by outlining it, then by composing it into a memo for your attorney. Your memo must be grammatically correct and properly punctuated. Think carefully, and prioritize the important facts. Be sure to sequence the facts logically and write the memo coherently.

Potential client: "I sure hope you guys cin help me. I done heered that Smith & Garcia is the bestest law firm in the county. Lemme tell you what happened. I was driving home from work last week, Friday I think it were, no it were Thursday. Anyways, my gal done texted me, and I was most home. My old lady don't know that I got a girlfriend—just a little soming on the side, you know what I mean? Did you know they got a law says you can't text in the car? I ain't never seen that on the driving test. So anyhoo, I had to read the text and delete it afore I gotted home cuz my old lady'd kill me iffen she found out. Well, I weren't goin very fast cuz I know the cops got a speed trap on that stretch a road but doesn't some brat ride his bike right into the front a my car! Lucky my car didn't get messed up but the kid did. And that @#!% cop done seen the whole thing. My old lady bailed me out a jail, and good thing I deleted the text afore she got there!

Can youse guys help me out? I sure hate to lose my license over this. My gal lives perty far aways you know.

II. Below is a rambling, grammatically incorrect story that a potential client recounted to you. You need to organize it, first by outlining it, then by composing it into a memo for your attorney. Your memo must be grammatically correct and properly punctuated. Think carefully, and prioritize the important facts. Be sure to sequence the facts logically and write the memo coherently.

Potential client: "Hi, I hope that Smith & Garcia law firm can help me. I worked for the power company for about 5 years, but one day my safety belt busted. I was up at the top of a pole working on a line. You remember that song, "Wichita Lineman?" It was like that. So anyway, my belt broke and I fell 20 feet. I busted my back and a bunch of other stuff. Of course I had sick time then I used disability. But I was still hurting when the doctor said I could go back to work. And the doctor wouldn't give me no more pain pills. So I had to go to another doctor. He gave me pills and he was a great guy he didn't give me any trouble when I needed pills but now he got in trouble cause someone got mad at him and he lost his medical license. Anyway, I went back to work when the power company's doctor said I was cleared to go back even though I was still hurting. I didn't know that they would give me a drug test before I could go back on the poles. Well, I had been taking the medicine the other doctors had prescribed it was all legal. I got fired because I didn't pass the drug test but I think that was discrimination because I had an injury on the job but the worker's compensation people did not agree. I think the woman who was the person in charge of the hearing hates men because I heard her tell the woman whose case was before mine that she had a good case but she turned down three men including me so I want my job back and I want them to pay me what I would have made if they hadn't fired me and it is there fault that I got hurt because they issued me bad equipment. They had a responsibility to make sure their workers are safe and I am going to lose my house and my wife left me and I barely can pay for my prescriptions that I need because the pain just won't let up.

"Can you help me?"

III. Below is a rambling, grammatically incorrect story that a potential client recounted to you. You need to organize it, first by outlining it, then by composing it into a memo for your attorney. Think carefully, and prioritize the important facts. Be sure to sequence the facts logically and write the memo coherently.

In this scenario, you are a paralegal working for Brad and Ana. Ana approached you one day and handed you the following letter. She told you that it came in the mail and might present a valid legal case, but it was so badly written that she couldn't tell. She instructed you to try to decipher what the person who wrote the letter was saying and to summarize it for her. You need to organize it, first by outlining it, then by composing it into a memo for your attorney. Your memo must be grammatically correct and properly punctuated. Think carefully, and prioritize the important facts. Be sure to sequence the facts logically and write the memo coherently.

Dear law firm of Smith & Garcia,

I need your help. My sister is a crazy shrew and she is stealing my parent's blind. Our Mom is almost out of money because my sister won't give me her money to help with the cost of Mom's care who has some memory loss but she still remembers that I am her favorite daughter and she wishes I were her only daughter because I am a nice girl who loves her and stays with her and makes sure my bad sister doesn't get the family heirlooms like grandma's diamond ring and great grandpa's Civil War sword (it is Confederate but we support the United States now) because my evil sister Pam would take all that stuff and give it to her rotten daughter and grandkids. Just because I don't have any kids doesn't mean that she should get all the good stuff does it. You have to help me stop her mom is out of money and I know that mom and dad gave me a lot of money because they knew I needed it after my husbands business when bankrupt and Pam's husband makes lots of money he is a doctor and she could help me pay for moms care if she loved mom she says I forged the checks but I just helped dad write them because his hand was shaky before he died and the one I signed after he died was one he said he would write but he died first so I did it for him and made the date before he died even though he was in a coma because it was what he wanted he told me so. Pam is so evil she has told the Judge that I stole the money I didn't steal it dad gave it to me he wanted me to have it she should just curl up and die with all the lies she tells.

So now mom is in a nursing home because she is out of money and Pam says I have to pay back the money that dad wanted me to have because mom won't be able to get government help to pay for her nursing home because the money she says I owe is an asset of moms but it isn't because dad gave it to me before he ever knew mom would need it.

Can you help me?

IV. Below is a rambling, grammatically incorrect story that a potential client has recounted to you. You need to organize it, first by outlining it, then by composing it into a memo for your attorney. Your memo must be grammatically correct and properly punctuated. Think carefully, and prioritize the important facts. Be sure to sequence the facts logically and write the memo coherently.

Prospective client: You got to scuse me I get to America just one year ago. I try good English but hard for me. I try to tell you what happen best what I can. I buy house with money I bring with me from man who say is good house. I move in house not so good. I meet man at hall my people have for we from old country. I trust man he say is from my hometown back in old country. He say son of friend my father. I know name my father's friend so I believe man. I buy house people from my country proud to be honest. Man not honest. Roof leak, basement got crack, big problems with house. I say to man house he sell me no good house and he laugh at me. Now I mad. He say try and get him. He keep laughing he walks away. House he say is good neighborhood I got to pay money to mean kids so they no burn house up. House he say build good is leaking and walls crack. He say I illegal alien but I got green card from lottery. I know I legal. I think man not from my country but from enemy country so he trick me. I need lawyer help me make this man give me back money I pay for house. House no good. No can live there. Not safe. Wife say she go back to old country if I no move her some other house near her sister way out. No bus go by sisters house how I get to work?

I need lawyer help can you help me?

LEARNING OBJECTIVES

1. Organize the material for the prewriting step

2. Draft the original outline and document

3. Detect problems through upside-down writing

4. Critique the document by proofreading

5. Revise the document for a finished writing

Organization of Material | CHAPTER 3

■ STEPS TO WRITING

Every significant writing, especially a writing that will be submitted to the court, should be written in three stages: organizing, writing, and revising (Figure 3.1). Some teachers refer to these three stages as prewriting, writing, and post writing, and we will use these terms here. Each of these three writing stages is essential to drafting an effective document In the outlining chapter, we learned about organizing and how important it is to have a plan before starting to write a document. In the chapter explaining how to draft a paragraph from an outline, we learned about the actual act of putting words together to convey an idea, concept, or facts. Unfortunately, this is the point at which mediocre writers stop. Ineffective writers merely put their paragraphs together without evaluating the whole document for flow or effectiveness. But by stopping at the end of the second stage, you lose the chance to correct mistakes, clarify concepts that were not stated clearly enough, and remove extraneous material that can weaken your writing.

Prewriting and Organization of the Material

When new writers omit the prewriting step, they risk having a disorganized, incoherent document. Too often new writers believe that they do not need to outline and that they do not need to sort the facts and ideas they are discussing. Documents that were written without the writers engaging in this important stage, however, almost always are confusing and ineffective. Instead of presenting their material in a logical, effective manner, these writers submit muddled, jumbled ideas, and information.

Too often, as instructors we have received documents that were completely confusing because their writers failed to prewrite and organize the material. Until you have sorted out the important facts from the irrelevant ones, you cannot organize your material. Until you have organized your material effectively, you cannot present a persuasive argument or articulate document.

Thus, you first must determine what the goal of your document is, and what facts before you are pertinent to that goal. If your goal is to persuade the court that your client was harmed, for example, you need to separate the facts addressing the cause of your client's harm from the facts demonstrating the amount of harm your client incurred. Further, you need to separate the facts demonstrating the types of harm involved. Only then will you be able to draft a convincing document.

Figure 3.1 Three stages of writing

51

Writing the Rough Draft

All writers complete a rough draft; good writers know that this is only their initial draft. Even after you have outlined and organized your material, during the process of writing, you may discover that you have omitted something important, or that what appeared to be organized in your outline is less effective in writing. Once you begin writing, you may realize that the flow of your document needs to be revised.

In the chapter discussing how to write a paragraph from an outline, you learned different paragraph structures. You may find that you have several effective paragraphs, but you might not be able to make them flow articulately. In your rough draft, you will incorporate these various paragraphs into a coherent whole. You likely will find yourself rearranging sentences, clauses, phrases, and whole paragraphs while you are writing this rough draft. Even the authors of this book find themselves moving modifiers, clauses, and entire paragraphs during the writing of their rough drafts. Additionally, we sometimes have to discard something we have spent a lot of time on and start over with an entirely new approach. Although this is frustrating, an effective final document is what is important.

Furthermore, it is essential to reread as you move things around when you write, or you risk leaving parts of sentences or ideas behind when you have moved text to another section of the document. Once you are relatively satisfied with the document, you need to walk away from it, preferably overnight or for several hours. Then you can reread it with a fresh eye.

Post Writing and Proofreading for a Finished Document

This third stage of the writing process, post writing, involves proofreading and checking your document against a writing checklist for grammatical or punctuation errors, as well as re-outlining the actual written document to ensure that it is clear, well organized, and comprehensive. In reality, the third stage of this process, post writing, also involves writing, because you are revising and improving the writing of the first draft of the document.

In this all-important revision stage, you begin by proofreading your document for errors, organization, and clarity. When you are first starting out, you may even ask a better writer to review your work to point out errors or weaknesses that are not obvious to you as the writer.

Eventually, though, it is up to you, the writer, to learn to proofread to ensure that you have said what you meant to say in a way that your reader can understand. The writing checklist provided in this chapter will help you identify grammatical and punctuation errors when you review your draft. The upside-down outlining will reveal any sequencing errors, extraneous or inadvertently omitted material, or organizational problems.

For example, read the following two paragraphs. Each says the same thing, but one conveys the ideas effectively, and the other does not.

BAD EXAMPLE

Brad knew while he was in law school what he would do. Brad would accept only interesting cases. He would not represent a client he did not respect. He cannot take a criminal or bad person as a client. The other attorneys might think he had no ethics if he represented someone who was evil or a criminal. He did this when he opened his own practice. He waited for good people with interesting problems to come in to his office and ask for his help. No one came. The rent was due. The paralegal needed a paycheck. The electric bill was not paid. He realized he had to bite the bullet and take cases and clients that were distasteful.

It bothered him to represent bad people. He talked about it with Jeremy. Jeremy was home one weekend. Jeremy was doing a medical residency at a big hospital in the inner city. A lot of bad people came to that hospital for medical care. Jeremy told Brad about how different the people were that he treated than he knew before. Jeremy said one patient was a disgusting criminal. He hurt little children. He did not want to take care of this evil man. The senior fellow explained it to Jeremy. Even if Charles Manson came in the emergency room with a heart attack, they had an obligation to treat him. Charles Manson had headed a cult in the 1960s and he led them to a house and killed a lot of people in cold blood, including a pregnant woman, the actress Sharon Tate, who had starred in *Valley of the Dolls*. The senior fellow made him realize that he had an obligation to treat all patients.

Jeremy told Brad that it was the same with law. Brad did not have to take every client. He was not unethical if he did take bad people for clients. Brad could not be sure every client was a good person. Brad had to be a good lawyer and follow the rules of the justice system. Brad learned about the Rules of Professional Conduct and the Ethical Consideration.

Brad thought about the conversation with Jeremy a lot. Brad felt better about representing Mr. Williams. He was a good client. His son paid the bills. Brad could use that money to pay his staff. He could use that money to pay the rent. Ana agreed with him. He was a little sad that he could not practice law the way he thought he would.

The example above contains several problems that could have been avoided if the writer had outlined the material both before and after drafting it. First, it contains extraneous information that is not essential or helpful to the goal of the writing. For example, Brad's worrying about what other attorneys would think of him if he took a bad person as a client is not necessary to the purpose of the writing, which is to demonstrate the evolution of Brad's understanding of running a law office.

Additionally, the writing is redundant. It states that Brad "would not represent a client he did not respect. He cannot take a criminal or bad person as a client." The revised version of this paragraph below conveys the same idea more succinctly and eloquently.

Another important problem with the bad example is the failure to maintain consistency in verb tense. The verbs in the example shift from past to present and back, which is incorrect and distracting to the reader.

Also, the sentences and paragraphs lack transitions between them, causing the writing to be choppy. In the correct example, appropriate transitions help the writing to flow smoothly, and they add to the meaning of the writing.

If the writer had outlined this first draft, he or she could have seen the shift in verb tense, the lack of flow between ideas that transitions would have provided, and the extraneous and redundant material.

GOOD EXAMPLE

When he was in law school, Brad had believed he would be able to work only on cases that interested him, with clients he respected. Upon opening his own practice, however, he learned quickly that he had to pay the rent, the utilities, and his staff. He learned that he had to bite the bullet and accept cases and clients he found distasteful. Brad worried that he was compromising his principles and risking sliding down the "slippery slope" of ethical behavior by providing these people with legal representation.

One weekend when Jeremy was home for a visit during his medical residency, Brad and he discussed this situation. Jeremy clarified the situation in a way that had not occurred to Brad. Jeremy mentioned that one of his patients was a criminal who had hurt little children. Jeremy felt repulsed by this man and did not want to treat him. His senior fellow had taken him aside and told him that if the infamous mass murderer and cult leader Charles Manson came in the emergency room with a heart attack, the doctors would have a moral and ethical obligation to try to save his life, no matter what they thought of him and his actions. Jeremy then realized that the man had a right to health care.

Similarly, he told Brad, every accused person had a right to legal representation. Although he pointed out that Brad could refuse any case he did not want to take, he should not consider himself unethical by accepting cases that were repulsive. All Brad could do, Jeremy went on, was to do his best to ensure that the justice system worked as effectively as it could. Brad realized he knew how he could best do this. He would follow the guidelines written expressly for lawyers, the Ohio Rules of Professional Conduct, and pattern his actions after the Supreme Court of Ohio Professional Ideals for Ohio Lawyers and Judges.

After giving a lot of thought to their conversation, Brad felt much more comfortable representing Mr. Williams, who was, after all, one of their most regular clients. And as a practical matter, the checks Mr. Williams's son Tommy wrote always cleared. As long as Mr. Williams was in town, Brad knew he would be able to make payroll and pay the rent. His law partner and fiancée, Ana, agreed on this point. Nonetheless, he had to smile ruefully when he remembered his idealistic notions from his law school days.

In this version, the redundant and extraneous material is omitted, and the ideas are connected with appropriate transitions. The verb tenses are consistent, and the writing flows smoothly.

■ WRITING CHECKLIST

A writing checklist is an important tool for the post writing step of drafting a document. Some of the sections in the list that follows address material covered in previous chapters. For example, the section on coherence was covered in the chapter explaining how to write a paragraph from an outline. Other items on this checklist are addressed in the online *Legal Writing Handbook*. If you find you have problems in an area of grammar or punctuation, consult the *Handbook* for more in-depth guidance in these areas.

Although we have provided a checklist, it is prudent for writers to compile an individual checklist of the errors they commonly make so that they can use the list to search their drafts for their own problem areas.

In the post writing step, writers analyze their document for flow, clarity, accuracy, and grammatical correctness. The post writing step, also known as proofreading, can make the difference between an average or below average document and a good or excellent document.

However, learning to identify errors is difficult. Writers know in their own minds what they are trying to say and cannot always spot areas where they have not expressed their ideas clearly.

The checklist is designed to help writers identify the weaknesses and errors in their documents. The following exercises will demonstrate how to analyze documents using the checklist. By proof reading, i.e. post writing, writers can make their writing more effective and can correct any grammatical errors they may have missed.

Table 3.1 Writing Checklist

	Writing Checklist
	Coherence
1.	Prioritize
2.	Sequence
3.	Organize
4.	Outline
5.	Analyze
	Sentence Structure
6.	Sentence fragments
7.	Subordinate clauses as independent clauses
8.	Fused sentences
9.	Run on sentences
	Grammar
10.	Subject verb agreement
11.	Verb tense consistency
12.	Adverbs modifying verbs and adjectives
13.	Consistent pronoun person throughout document
14.	Correct pronoun number
	Punctuation
15.	Semicolons
16.	Colons
17.	Commas
18.	No contractions
19.	Possessives
20.	Punctuation inside quotation marks
21.	Long quotes blocked and single spaced
22.	Proper use of ellipses
	Fine-Tuning
23.	Eliminate unnecessary words—be succinct
24.	Vary sentence structure
25.	Vary sentence length
26.	Read for clarity of sentences
27.	Be specific
28.	Evaluate for flow
29.	All sentences in context
30.	Paragraph placement
31.	Provide transitional words
32.	Correct spelling

EXERCISE

Using the writing checklist, compare the good and bad examples provided in pages 52-54 of this chapter to determine what is wrong with the bad example. Identify ten errors contained in the bad example and explain in detail why they are errors and what you would do to fix them. Your answers must be written in full, well constructed sentences, and your combined explanations should be at least one page long.

EXERCISE

Using the writing checklist, identify the problems in the following paragraph. Mark each error or problem with the corresponding number from the writing checklist and explain how you would correct the problem. Your answers must be written in full, well constructed sentences, and your combined explanations should be at least one page long.

Jeremy thinks about his conversation with Brad. A lot of life involved compromise. He never would have thought about taking care of people which were different from the ones he had always knew. Although he should have realized. You can't go through life without dealing with different people. Some not bad, just different. I will be a good doctor I will treat all patients equally he swore. That was not as easy as it sounds, he had some patients he wanted to shake sense into them. She may be a lady of ill repute; but she was still a person, just like the rich patient. What made people decide to do what they do in life. He wondered. Then he remembered his own life. Where he had stupidly punched Tommy. Who only tried to help him. Some of his patients he did not like are far worse than Tommy he will think. Looking stupid to all his college classmates. Tommy a hero! No point in getting depressed. Jeremy, going back to research on a strange disease. Ironically, for a patient he did not like.

EXERCISE

Now that you have identified the problems and errors in the above paragraph, revise it and correct the errors you have found.

■ UPSIDE-DOWN OUTLINING

Writers usually outline before drafting a document, but one effective form of revision is outlining the document after you have written it. We call it "upside-down" or "backward" outlining, but whatever it is called, it is helpful in pointing out flaws in the draft.

It is common for writers to be so familiar with the subject matter they are addressing that they lose sight of what they have not said and not explained in the document. By outlining the actual document after it is written, writers can see exactly what points they glossed over or missed entirely. In the appellate courts, this problem arises in specialty areas of the law. Practitioners of probate or domestic law take for granted the basic elements of their field. But by failing to explain those basics in a paragraph or two, they leave the readers searching for the concepts they have omitted.

By outlining the draft of the document, writers will be able to see whether they have omitted anything, or worse, have failed to be logical and clear. Begin this process by writing the topic sentence of each paragraph or a summary of it, starting at the beginning. Then add the sub-points from each paragraph.

EXAMPLE

The paralegal, Pat, has interviewed a potential client. Read the account of the client interview first. Then read the written memorandum based on the client interview. Finally, notice the topic sentence taken from each paragraph. By reading only the topic sentence ideas, can you understand the contents of the interview?

The paralegal, Pat Peters, had the following interview with Sheila Kowalski, R.N.

SHEILA: I know that Brad and Ana are both busy; you said they are in court, but I think I need their help with a situation at work. I don't want to take this to my supervisor until I know I am doing the right thing and doing it legally. I don't know where to start.

Do you know what a drug cart is? It is the cart where the narcotics are locked up. Every shift, the charge nurse from the shift going off and the charge nurse from the shift coming on count the narcotics together and make sure they match the count from the previous shift change, subtracting the drugs that the nurses have signed out for specific patients. Occasionally, there are miscounts, but I have begun to notice that when one particular nurse has worked on a shift, there is almost always a miscount. I can't believe I am the only one who has noticed this, but no one else has said anything, and if there is one thing you can count on in a hospital, it's gossip.

And I am pretty sure that one time, after this particular nurse had signed out some morphine for a patient who was supposed to get half the dose in the prefilled syringe, I saw her come out of the restroom with the syringe in her hand. It was half full, and the medication is the color of water. She asked me to witness her wasting the extra—that's what we do with prefilled syringes if the patient doesn't get the full dose. We have to account for all of the narcotic, so one nurse witnesses another nurse shooting the extra into the trash. Then both nurses sign that they witnessed the excess drug being wasted.

I felt uncomfortable signing, because I suspected she had used the extra drug on herself then refilled the syringe with water. But I can't prove anything.

PAT: Did she show any effects from the drug that would make you suspect she had taken some of it?

SHEILA: It was the end of the shift, so I only saw her for the time it took to give report before she left the hospital. So I can't say that I have ever noticed her acting as though she were under the influence of a drug. That is what makes me hesitant to say anything to anyone. It was strange that she took the syringe into the rest room with her, but if she really needed to use the rest room badly, she couldn't leave the syringe unattended. So maybe that was why she did it. What bothers me is that she acted startled and shook up when she realized I had seen her come out with the syringe, and she didn't make any explanation, like most people would have. She acted very nervous until she left. I sure hope Ana or Brad can advise me on this.

EXAMPLE OF A MEMORANDUM

MEMORANDUM
To: Ana Garcia, Esq.
From: Pat Peters, paralegal
Re: Sheila Kowalski

Sheila Kowalski, a registered nurse at Parkhurst Hospital, wishes to consult with an attorney concerning the proper approach for dealing with possible narcotic abuse by a coworker. Ms. Kowalski suspects, but has no definitive proof, that another nurse who works in the same unit has been using narcotics from the narcotics cart.

Ms. Kowalski has noticed a pattern of miscounts at the end of shifts on which this nurse has worked. She believes the pattern is clear, but she is hesitant to say anything to a supervisor for fear of accusing an innocent person. No one else in the hospital appears to have commented on this pattern, which makes Ms. Kowalski reluctant to discuss it with anyone there.

Her suspicions were piqued recently when she saw this nurse leaving the rest room with a narcotics syringe. The nurses have a system for checking each other when a patient does not need the whole dose of a syringe that is already pre-filled. They witness each other shooting the drug into the trash, and then each signs that they were witnesses.

When the nurse realized that Ms. Kowalski saw her coming out of the rest room with the half-full syringe, she looked startled and shaken. She acted nervous for the rest of the shift, which was almost over. Ms. Kowalski witnessed this nurse wasting the contents of the syringe, but she suspects perhaps the nurse had substituted water for the medication.

Ms. Kowalski suspects that she does not have enough hard information to say anything to the supervisors about this nurse, and she is reluctant to risk damaging the nurse's reputation if her suspicions are wrong. She would like to discuss it with you at your earliest convenience.

The table below demonstrates the way to break down, that is, separate out, the portions of a document into an upside-down grid. This provides writers with a method for seeing whether their writing flows logically and clearly. Sometimes writers think their paragraphs are logical, because in their own minds the paragraphs make sense. Once the writers lay out the paragraphs in a grid or table like the one below, however, they can see that there are flaws and omissions in their writing.

Table 3.2 Upside-Down Grid

Upside-Down Grid	
Detailed Facts of Memorandum	**Abbreviated Facts of Upside-Down Outlining**
1. Sheila Kowalski, a registered nurse at Parkhurst Hospital, wishes to consult with an attorney concerning the proper approach for dealing with possible narcotic abuse by a coworker.	Concerned about possible narcotic abuse by a coworker, but not sure
2. Ms. Kowalski has noticed a pattern of miscounts at the end of shifts on which this nurse has worked.	Pattern of narcotic miscounts when this nurse is working
3. Her suspicions were piqued recently when she saw this nurse leaving the rest room with a narcotics syringe.	Nurse had narcotics syringe in rest room

(continued)

4. When the nurse realized that Ms. Kowalski saw her coming out of the rest room with the half-full syringe, she looked startled and shaken.	Nurse acted suspiciously when seen leaving rest room with syringe.
5. Ms. Kowalski suspects that she does not have enough hard information to say anything to the supervisors about this nurse, and she is reluctant to risk damaging the nurse's reputation if her suspicions are wrong.	Ms. Kowalski not sure whether to say anything with this scant information.

EXERCISE

Read the following document in which the paragraphs are out of order. Put them in the correct order. Create an upside-down grid for the corrected document. There is a preliminary grid below for starting. By organizing the topic sentences into a grid, you can see if they flow logically. The grid provides a succinct visual overview of the contents, which can be extremely helpful, particularly with a long or complex document. One of your authors recently drafted a memorandum on a complex area of law, and using this technique helped her to identify redundancies and see the way it needed to be reorganized.

Although professional writers use this technique, new writers need to use backward outlining even more to avoid falling back into ineffective old habits that lack organization.

Note that there may be more or fewer than six points for the grid.

Because their interests and skills covered several areas of law, Ana and Brad developed a successful and well respected legal practice within several years of graduation from law school. They knew when to obtain more experienced co-counsel on a case when the area of law was unfamiliar to them, and they learned as much as they could from every attorney they encountered, whether as opposing counsel, co-counsel, or through continuing education courses.

Not only did the criminal defendants like Brad, the courts also liked dealing with him in criminal matters; he always told the truth and never hid anything that he was obliged to disclose. He was straightforward and professional but was a good advocate for his client. He never shouted or dramatized in court. His soft spoken, respectful manner impressed the judges, and their positive feelings about Brad carried over to his clients.

From the start, Brad, to his surprise, enjoyed criminal law. When he was in law school, he thought criminal law would be the last area he would want to practice. But after representing several clients with criminal charges against them, he discovered that he had a knack for getting the courts to give them less severe sentences than they expected, which of course made them happy with Brad.

When they first started in practice after law school, Brad and Ana were a good team for their law office because they each preferred different areas of the law. Nonetheless, they both knew enough about the different areas of their practice that they could bounce ideas off one another.

After their first year in practice, despite their relative inexperience, Brad and Ana quickly gained the respect of the legal community for their integrity and professionalism. Whether Brad was trying a driving under the influence case or Ana was trying a motor vehicle accident case, opposing counsel and the courts were happy to see either of them on a case.

Brad had found his niche immediately, but Ana, on the other hand, took a while to discover that she preferred personal injury and medical malpractice cases. She found the medicine fascinating, and she enjoyed the fact that each case was different and interesting. She too was respected by the courts because she did not try cases that were not valid. She did not make unreasonable settlement demands, yet she always got the best result she could for her clients.

Upside-Down Grid	
Detailed Facts of Document	**Abbreviated Facts for Upside-Down Outlining**
1.	
2.	
3.	
4.	
5.	
6.	

EXERCISE

Read the document and draw your own upside-down outlining grid. Note that there may be more or fewer than six points for the grid. Remember, completing this step will reveal flaws in the flow and organization of your document so you can revise and improve your writing. If you fail to perform this step, you risk submitting poorly organized, illogical documents. This step is an effective way to avoid repeating old bad habits.

Ana learned a lot from her first medical malpractice case. The client, a well-dressed woman in her forties, had consulted Ana because she was unhappy with the results of the plastic surgery she had had done on her eyelids. Ana could see what she meant. One of her eyelids formed a peak in the middle, making it impossible for the woman to close her eye completely. Ana sympathized with the woman; not only were her eyes unsightly, but they also looked painful. Ana could not help but blink more frequently than normal when speaking to the woman, as though she were trying to blink for her.

Ana learned, however, that even the most credible, sympathetic clients were not always truthful. When she deposed the plastic surgeon, she learned that her client had disobeyed the physician's orders. The client had resumed wearing her contact lenses two days after the surgery. She had applied eye makeup before the stitches had been removed. And she had brushed against her eyelid with a large, multi-pronged ring within days of the surgery, snagging one of the sutures on the ring. The doctor testified that the client did not seek his help after this mishap until a week later, despite the fact that the snagged suture caused her eyelid to form a peak in the center.

Ana also learned that witnesses will lie during depositions. When opposing counsel deposed her client, the woman admitted that she had worn her contact lenses soon after surgery. She also admitted catching the suture on her ring. She testified, though, that she had called the doctor's office immediately after this happened, and he had refused to see her before her next scheduled appointment the following week.

Ana realized she would have to depose a witness she had not originally intended to use. She interviewed the doctor's office manager, who confirmed the testimony of Ana's client. The doctor was angry that his patient had been so careless. He was about to leave for a brief vacation, and he refused to miss his flight because of her carelessness and refusal to follow orders. What the office manager said that really took Ana by surprise, however, was that the office manager had given the client the name and phone number of the plastic surgeon who was covering for the doctor leaving on vacation.

Ana finally realized that not every case that looked like a winner was one. Her client confirmed that the office manager had encouraged her to contact the alternate doctor, but the client was so angry that her operating surgeon would leave town and leave her in such a lurch that she decided to wait and to sue him for his indifference to her plight.

Ana's first medical malpractice case taught her lessons she had not anticipated existed. She learned that every client and every defendant had some grain of truth in his or her testimony. She learned that the real truth, if it were ever revealed, existed somewhere in the middle of each party's point of view. And she learned to never answer the phone on the way to the airport for vacation.

EXERCISE

Read the paragraphs and draw your own upside-down outlining grid. Note that there may be more or fewer than six points for the grid. Remember, completing this step will reveal flaws in the flow and organization of your document so you can revise and improve your writing. If you fail to perform this step, you risk submitting poorly organized, illogical documents. This step is an effective way to avoid repeating old bad habits.

A tort consists of four elements: a duty, a breach of that duty, an injury resulting from the breach, and damages from the injury. An inexperienced paralegal might not realize that each of these elements is essential for an actionable tort.

Without a duty, there cannot be a tort. For example, anyone operating a car on a public road has a duty to everyone else to drive the car safely. Driving the car safely includes driving in a manner that does not put any other person or any other person's property at risk. Not every instance of operating a car entails a duty; if the person is operating the car on his own private property and there is no one and no one else's property around that he could put at risk, he does not have a duty to drive safely. Similarly, if a person is driving in a demolition derby, it is expected that he will be driving with the intention of damaging the other cars in the derby.

Even where there is a duty, for a tort to exist, there must be a breach of that duty. If the driver of the car were driving safely, he would not be breaching his duty, even if his passenger was injured when he was in a collision caused by an unsafe driver. The safe driver would not have breached his duty to drive safely. The unsafe driver, on the other hand, would have breached that duty.

In addition to a duty and a breach of that duty, for a valid tort, that breach of the duty must have caused an injury. If the unsafe driver drove through a red light, he breached his duty to drive safely. Unless he actually caused an accident or injured someone by running the red light, however, there is no tort, because there is no injury. If, on the other hand, the unsafe driver broadsided a car proceeding lawfully through the intersection when the unsafe driver ran the red light, there would be an injury, at least to the lawful driver's car, if not also to the lawful driver and his passengers.

A tort still cannot exist, even when the breach of a duty caused an injury, unless there are actual damages. This concept confuses those new to the law, because they use injury and damages interchangeably. Damages are the amount or form of compensation for the injury incurred by the breach. When the unsafe driver ran the red light and broadsided the other driver's car, the amount needed to repair the property damage to the car would constitute the damages. The injury was the actual dents, scratches, and broken parts on the car. The damages consist of the cost of repairing those damages to return the car to the condition it was in before the accident. If, however, the car that was struck was being towed to the junkyard and was not even useful for spare parts, then there would be no legal damages. Despite the dents and scratches the unsafe driver made on the car, because the dents and scratches did not affect the car's value, there would be no damages.

There is not an actionable tort without the four required elements: a duty, a breach of that duty, an injury, and damages resulting from the injury.

■ FINAL DOCUMENT WRITING

After you have assessed the flow and identified the flaws in your writing by upside-down outlining it, you can correct any logical and continuity errors in your next draft. At this point, you should walk away from the writing and focus your attention on something else, even if you merely get a drink of water or do some stretches. Preferably, however, you would spend at least a half an hour or overnight to get some distance from your writing. Then reread it with a fresh eye, and you will notice errors or weak spots in the draft. After you have corrected and improved these areas, you will have your final document.

SUMMARY

- By breaking down the task of writing a legal document, it becomes more manageable.

- Before you begin writing every document you should organize the material.

- Organizing the material consists of several steps.

- The first step in organizing is deciding the purpose of the document.

- The next step in organizing is determining what facts or ideas are important to include for achieving the purpose of the document.

- Once you have determined the important facts and ideas, you must determine the most logical order for presenting it.

- Only then are you ready to write your first draft, which will be rough.

- After writing your first draft, upside-down outline it to ensure it has flow and continuity.

- The next to last step you will take is to correct the errors that your upside-down outlining reveals.

- The extremely important final step is to step away, at least mentally, and return to your document and proofread it, correcting any flaws or errors you notice in this proofreading.

- For difficult, long, or challenging documents, you may have to repeat these steps.

- Using this process will allow you to approach the task of writing efficiently and effectively.

ASSIGNMENTS

I. Read the following scenario. Use the "pre-writing step" and organize and outline the material.

As he sat at his desk working, Brad felt that someone was watching him. He looked up and saw Mr. Williams, who was ashen. Startled, Brad asked him what was wrong. Speechless, Mr. Williams, his hand shaking, placed a sheet of paper on the desk in front of Brad. Without touching it, Brad read the crudely printed words. "I HEERDED YOU BRAGGING ON GITTING AWAY WITH THAT FRIDGE THING. LEAVE $500 UNDER THE BARREL BEHIND THE DEW DROP INN AN NO ONE WON'T EVER KNOW." Finally, Mr. Williams spoke. Hoarsely, he said, "Someone is blackmailing me."

Looking up at Mr. Williams, Brad told him that now that another person knew what had happened, it was only a matter of time until word got to the police. Brad reminded him that the police investigation was ongoing, and they were actively seeking the person or persons who were responsible.

The court would be less harsh, Brad went on, if Mr. Williams turned himself in rather than waiting for the police to find out what happened. Even turning himself in late would be better than continuing to hide, especially now that the circumstances of the incident were no longer a secret. The more time, police resources, and taxpayer money expended on the search for the culprit, the angrier the court would be.

By turning himself in, Brad continued, they also could report the blackmail to the police. With any luck, the blackmailer would be convicted, so Mr. Williams's being in trouble would not have been totally in vain.

II. Use the "writing" step and draft a one page document from the outline you composed for assignment I.

III. Use the "post writing" step to proofread and revise the draft document you wrote for Assignment II. Outline your draft, as demonstrated in the upside-down outlining section, to ensure it flows clearly and is well organized. Then use the writing checklist to review the document for grammatical or punctuation errors. Type your final version of the document, and turn it in along with a typed copy of the outline from Assignment I and the draft from Assignment II.

IV. Read the following scenario and use the 3 steps of writing to produce an excellent paper. Your assignment will have 5 separate papers. First, you will organize and outline the scenario. This outline is your first paper. Second, you will compose your first draft. This is your second paper. Third, you will create and complete a grid that upside-down outlines your first draft. This is your third paper. Fourth, rewrite the draft, correcting errors revealed by the upside-down outline. This is your fourth paper. Fifth, using the writing checklist, review your second draft for grammar and punctuation. Write your final draft with the necessary corrections. This is your fifth paper.

The nicest supervisor was on duty one evening. Sheila was troubled because she was working with the nurse whose narcotics counts were so often wrong. No one else seemed to have noticed this pattern; she could not understand why. It was not that she disliked the nurse. She just wanted to be sure the patients were cared for properly.

Once again at the end of the shift, the narcotics count was wrong. Sheila counted with a different nurse, not the one connected with the miscount pattern. Neither Sheila nor the nurse counting with her met each other's eyes when they discovered the miscount.

The nursing supervisor asked them to report any other incidents they thought were suspicious.

She asked them to go home and separately write down what they had seen. Further, they were to report any incidents that they found suspicious. The supervisor repeated that they were not to discuss this with anyone, including each other.

When they were talking with the supervisor, neither of them named the nurse they suspected of narcotics abuse. The supervisor did not ask them to name names out loud.

Because she was thinking about the narcotics count situation, Sheila discovered after she had changed into her street clothes in the locker room that only one other nurse was still there. The other nurse was the one she had done the narcotics count with.

Both the nurses left the nursing office focused on the gravity of the situation.

The nursing supervisor warned them not to discuss the situation with anyone. Both nurses wrote the name of the person they suspected was responsible for the narcotics miscounts on a piece of paper and folded it. The nursing supervisor did not open the papers while they were in the room.

Sheila said she never wanted to get anyone in trouble, and without proof she did not want to point to any one person as being responsible for the narcotic miscounts.

In the locker room, the other nurse who had done the narcotics count with Sheila asked her if she had noticed a pattern in the narcotics miscounts. They decided they had to discuss the situation with the nursing supervisor. Sheila told the other nurse in the locker room that two weeks earlier she had seen a nurse leaving the rest room with a partially filled morphine syringe. The fellow nurse's eyes widened, and she said she had seen the same thing the day before yesterday.

Once they were in the supervisor's office, the other nurse was too nervous to talk. But she did add that once she had seen the suspected nurse leaving the rest room with a half full morphine syringe and a spot of blood on the front of her uniform pants.

Sheila told the supervisor that both the nurses had seen a pattern in the problem with the narcotics counts. Each of the two nurses wrote the name of the person they suspected was responsible for the narcotics miscounts on a piece of paper and folded it. They handed the papers to the nursing supervisor.

The nurses both blurted out to the supervisor that they were there because of the narcotics count problem. The office had found that the staffing pattern matched a pattern of patients assigned to a certain nurse who complained of not getting relief from their pain medications. Without opening the folded pieces of paper, the supervisor thanked them for their concern. She told them that the nursing office had also noticed a pattern and that they had reviewed the patient charts for the effectiveness of the pain medications the patients had received shortly before the end of each shift. Sheila had not wanted to say anything until someone else mentioned it, in case she was the only one who suspected something. The two nurses were not even certain that they were thinking of the same person.

While Sheila and the nurse were talking in the locker room, they did not tell each other the name of the nurse who they suspected was the nurse guilty of narcotics abuse.

Sheila paged the supervisor, who agreed to meet them in the main nursing office for the hospital.

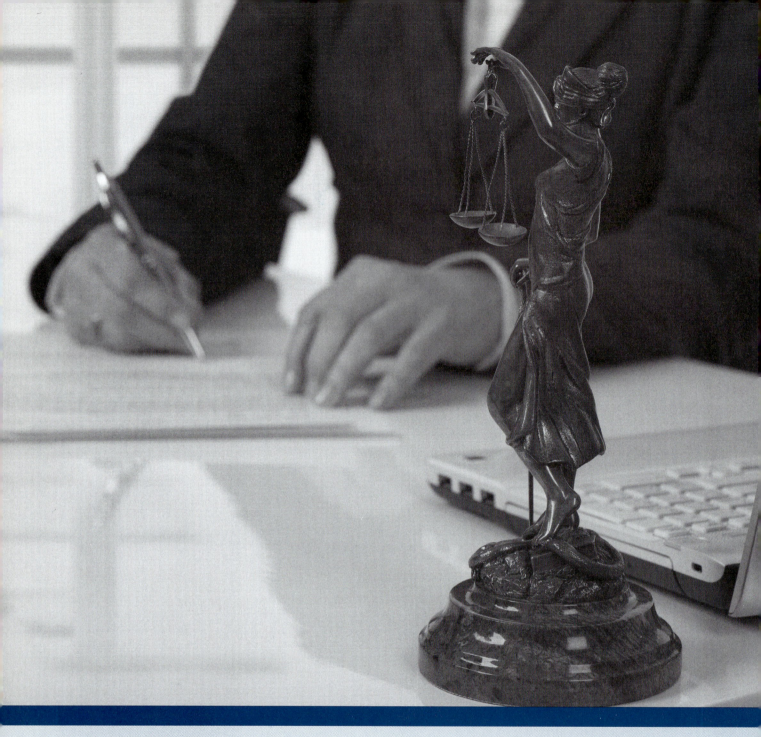

LEARNING OBJECTIVES

1. Identify the importance of legal correspondence in letter and electronic form

2. Evaluate the purpose for the correspondence

3. Assess the audience for the correspondence

4. Select effective and appropriate correspondence for your audience's characteristics

5. Write grammatically correct correspondence

6. Incorporate a professional tone in correspondence

Letters to Clients

CHAPTER 4

■ CORRESPONDENCE

Paralegals often send and receive correspondence during their careers. There are many situations in which the attorney will need to have information sent to clients, opposing counsel, or expert witnesses. Additionally, there are times when a paralegals needs to send correspondence in the course of their job. Paralegals may send letters to counsel for the other parties to confirm a scheduled deposition, or they may need to write a cover letter for discovery requests. The forms of correspondence paralegals use are letters and electronic communications, that is, emails.

Letters

Until the last few decades, letters were the only form of correspondence used in legal practice. Professional letters have specific requirements, including a heading informing the recipient of the identity and address of the sender, which usually is centered at the top of the page.

It is imperative to include the date of any correspondence. This is the only way you can prove when it was sent. Omitting the date on correspondence could cause your client to lose the case, in which case, you would lose your job.

The next element of a formal letter is a block with the name and address of the recipient. This is positioned flush with the left margin.

In legal correspondence, you will almost always have a "re" line, containing the topic or purpose of the letter. This is placed above the salutation.

The salutation must begin with "Dear." It is always best to use the recipient's last name after the "Dear." For example, even if you were writing to another paralegal you knew from school, you would write "Dear Ms. Doe," not "Dear Jane." Remember that everything you write in the course of your professional duties is a legal document and is subject to being introduced in court at some time, perhaps during a discovery dispute. It is important that it appears professional.

Next comes the body of the letter, which contains the actual text of your correspondence.

The closing courtesy is a brief phrase that is placed one line after your last line of text in the body. Examples of closing courtesies are "Sincerely," Sincerely yours," "Very truly yours," etc. There is always a comma after the closing courtesy, followed by four blank lines.

The fifth line after the closing courtesy is the signature line. The sender's name is typed under a blank line for the signature. If the attorney is signing a letter you drafted, his or her signature block might go under the typed name.

If the correspondence includes any enclosures, you will type enclosures on the left margin, and you might include the name of the enclosure. For example, you may write "Enclosure: Interrogatories."

If you are sending a copy of the correspondence to others in addition to the recipient, you would add on the left margin "cc" along with the names of the persons who are also receiving the correspondence.

Electronic Communications

In recent decades, correspondence has been altered radically by electronic communications. Most of you use various types of electronic communication in your personal lives, including email, Twitter, Instagram, Facebook, and Pinterest.

The tone and form of personal electronic communications, though, differ significantly from the electronic communications you will engage in during your professional paralegal career. First, your emails written for work must maintain a professional tone. If you have not been exposed to professional writing, you will need to work hard to recognize unprofessional tone and correct it.

In addition to tone, you will need to make sure that the grammar and punctuation in your electronic correspondence is correct. In your personal emails, you may write in sentence fragments, and you might not worry about verb tenses and subject-verb agreement. But in professional emails, writing a grammatically correct communication is extremely important. Unprofessionally written correspondence reflects poorly on you and your attorney. It also risks failing to provide the recipient with the correct information.

■ DETERMINE THE PURPOSE

Paralegals write letters for a number of reasons, and the paralegal must determine the purpose of the letter before starting to draft it. One of the most common letters a paralegal will draft is the client letter. Other documents are common to most civil litigation. These include deposition notices, notices of court dates, appointments, continuances, and discovery requests. Most of these will be sent with a cover letter. Paralegals also may draft letters to confirm deposition schedules with opposing counsel, to solicit or confirm the engagement of an expert witness, or to provide cover letters for settlement packages or discovery requests for the attorney to sign.

The greeting line for a legal correspondence should use a colon, rather than a comma. Your correspondence should include only the information necessary, and should not include information that may harm the case.

The types of correspondence and forms you will draft as a paralegal will depend on the area of law the attorney or firm you work for practices. If the firm specializes in family law, you might be sending clients a proposed shared parenting agreement, a proposed support agreement, or a proposed separation agreement, for example.

If the firm specializes in real estate, you might be sending requests to the auditor's office, letters to surveyors requesting a survey, or letters to a title company requesting a title search. You will deal with various types of deeds, eviction notices, and rent deposits.

If you work in a medical malpractice (commonly called "med mal") or personal injury (commonly called "P.I.") firm, in addition to the types of documents common to most areas of law, you will also work with medical authorizations, medical record releases, letters to expert witnesses, and for personal injury, requests for police reports and witness affidavits.

In criminal law, you might be drafting requests to change a plea, requests for police reports, witness affidavits, subpoenas to witnesses, motions for release of impounded property, or motions to suppress.

Some of the routine correspondence you draft will rely partially on form letters or partially pre-drafted documents, commonly referred to as "boilerplates." We will discuss boilerplates in more detail in a later chapter. The discussion of boilerplates in this chapter is limited to its use in correspondence. Boilerplate is a term used in the legal field that describes a partially pre-written document into which the writer inserts the specifics that fit his or her particular purposes. In strict legal terms, boilerplate has a more limited definition, but within the legal field, it often is used in this more general way. An everyday example of a boilerplate document is a rental application. In this contract, most of the language is already written on a lease. The specifics, including, but not limited to, the date of the agreement, the name of the person renting, the term of the lease, and payment terms are blank and are filled in to meet the needs of the specific rental agreement.

Similar to this, when a law firm writes the same sort of letter frequently, it may have a template or boilerplate version that the drafter completes as needed. When using a boilerplate document, it is important to be sure that it contains all the information needed and no information left over from another client. This is a surprisingly common error, and it makes the attorney and the firm look careless, which is never reassuring to a client, and never impresses the court or opposing counsel. After you have written the letter, you will proofread it to ensure that it satisfies the purpose for which you wrote it.

As you will learn in Civil Procedure, anything submitted to the court must also be provided to all the other parties in the lawsuit. An attorney for one party may not communicate with the court *ex parte*, that is, without providing notice and copies to the other parties in the suit. This is a basic tenet of law, and as the paralegal, you are responsible for ensuring that anything your attorney submits to the court is submitted to all the parties involved in the suit. Correspondence among the parties, on the other hand, does not necessarily have to be provided to the court.

In addition to correspondence to attorneys' offices, you also will draft correspondence to clients, witnesses, and potential clients. When corresponding with clients and witnesses, there are a number of things you need to consider when drafting your letter; these are discussed later in the chapter. First, though, we will address determining the purpose of the correspondence. Remember that if your letter is requesting or demanding that its recipient perform a specific act, like providing discovery or making a payment, you should state a specific hard deadline for them to meet. Therefore, instead of saying that they should provide the requested item "within two weeks," give a date certain, such as "September 14, 20XX." A firm date is more motivating psychologically, and is more effective if you need to file a motion to compel later.

Note that, as the drafter of the letter, you will place your initials in lower case at the bottom of the letter. In this case, the initials are "pp" for Pat Peters. This allows the drafter of the correspondence to be identified later if needed; it also allows the work to be traced to you, which is another incentive to write the best correspondence you can.

"To inform or notify"

Below are some of the reasons you will draft correspondence.

EXAMPLES

To Inform or Notify

- To notify a client of the next appointment
- To notify a client of the need to make an appointment
- To notify a witness of a scheduled deposition
- To notify opposing counsel of forthcoming discovery
- To notify the court of a change of counsel
- To notify the court of a bankruptcy filing, thus staying any other civil action
- To notify a civil defendant of a complaint, that is, a lawsuit against him or her

To Record

- To deposit a will with the court
- To record a deed, title, or mortgage
- To record a settlement agreement
- To memorialize a discussion, verbal agreement, or an argument

To Describe

- To describe the process of a deposition
- To describe the course of a lawsuit
- To describe the bail process
- To describe how to answer interrogatories and requests for production of documents
- To describe the process of bankruptcy court

To Threaten

- To serve an eviction notice
- To demand payment in a collection action

To Make Someone Act

- To subpoena witnesses, legally compelling appearance at a given time and place
- To demand payment of a debt
- To demand return of discovery requests when opposing counsel delays
- To stop an action, pursuant to a restraining order

To Extract Information

- To submit discovery requests, including interrogatories to other parties

One form of discovery is called Interrogatories. These are a list of questions the lawyer drafts that he or she wants the other party to answer. In many states, the number of discovery questions is limited to forty. In a later chapter, we will discuss the drafting of Interrogatories.

The following examples of correspondence demonstrate a format for a formal letter. Although the law office in which you work may use a slightly different format, this example is one standard form.

EXAMPLE ONE

SMITH & GARCIA, ATTORNEYS AT LAW
123 Main Street
Parkhurst, Ohio, 44XXX

Lowe, Down & Nogud
56 Shyster Lane
Parkhurst, Ohio 44XXX   November 1, 20XX

RE: Doe v. Roe, outstanding discovery requests

Dear Ms. Lowe:

This firm served interrogatories and requests for production of documents on your firm on August 2, 20XX, and to date we have not received either the completed discovery or any other correspondence from your firm explaining the delay in your return of said discovery.

As you are aware, the deadline for depositions in this case is January 10, 20XX. Without discovery, it is impossible to arrange a deposition schedule. Therefore, we request your prompt return of completed discovery by November 15, 20XX.

We appreciate your attention to this matter.

Yours truly,

Bradley Smith, Esq.
123 Main Street
Parkhurst, Ohio 44XXX
Attorney Number XXXXXXX

pp

EXAMPLE TWO

You are a paralegal who works for Smith & Garcia. Sheila Kowalski has requested Ana's help in getting hot water to her apartment, which the landlord has refused to provide. By refusing to provide hot water to the apartment, the landlord has materially breached the terms of the lease. The landlord had been uncooperative with Sheila, saying that she had insisted on moving into the model unit, and that he had not breached the rental contract.

SMITH & GARCIA, ATTORNEYS AT LAW
123 Main Street
Parkhurst, Ohio, 44XXX

October 12, 20XX

Martin J. Boyle
666 Shady Lane
Parkhurst, Ohio 44XXX

RE: Landlord's breach of Kowalski lease

Dear Mr. Boyle:

This firm represents Sheila Kowalski in the matter of the material breach to the lease for the apartment located at 140 Maple Drive, Apt. 306, Parkhurst, Ohio, 44XXX. As Ms. Kowalski informed you by certified mail on October 5, 20XX, her unit does not have hot water. It is now over 30 days since you received that letter, and Ms. Kowalski still does not have hot water. You have materially breached the terms of the lease, and effective immediately Ms. Kowalski will be depositing her rent with the court and moving for the court to order you to rectify the situation.

Sincerely yours,

Ana Garcia, Esq.
123 Main Street
Parkhurst, Ohio 44XXX
Attorney Number XXXXXXX

pp

cc: Sheila Kowalski

The purpose of the above letter is to make someone act, i.e. to make the landlord provide the tenant with hot water.

EXERCISE

Determine the purpose of the letters from the following choices. Were these letters written to inform or notify, to record, to describe, to get information, or to make someone act?

LETTER ONE

SMITH & GARCIA, ATTORNEYS AT LAW
123 Main Street
Parkhurst, Ohio, 44XXX

Mr. Thomas Williams, Sr.
65 Maple Drive
Parkhurst, Ohio 44XXX

RE: Appointment on October 16, 20XX

Dear Mr. Williams:

Thank you for responding to our request for information we need to assist you with your legal situation. As we discussed on the telephone today, your appointment is on *Tuesday, October 16, 20XX at 2:00 pm*. In order to better assist you in this matter, please bring the following items with you:

1. The name and address of the owner of the truck used to move the refrigerator.
2. If possible, photocopies of the registration and title for the truck.
3. A list of the regulars at the Dew Drop Inn who might have overheard the alleged conversation that is the subject of the blackmail threat.
4. Your driver's license and social security card.
5. Your auto insurance policy that was in effect at the time of the alleged incident.
6. A copy of any other insurance you might have, such as umbrella coverage.

It is important that you do not discuss the incident that is the subject of the blackmail threat or the threat itself with anyone. Please assist us in limiting the potential damage you may incur.
Please call if you have any questions or concerns.

Sincerely,

Brad Smith, Esq.
123 Main Street
Parkhurst, Ohio 44XXX
Attorney Number XXXXXXX

pp

(continued)

LETTER TWO

SMITH & GARCIA, ATTORNEYS AT LAW
123 Main Street
Parkhurst, Ohio, 44XXX

Jeremy Hunter, M.D.
Parkhurst Hospital
200 Healthcare Drive
Parkhurst, OH 44XXX

RE: Doe v. Parkhurst

Dear Dr. Hunter:

Your deposition in the above captioned matter is scheduled for *Wednesday, November 7, 20XX at 9:00 am* in the law offices of Smith & Garcia. In order to prepare you for this deposition, Ms. Garcia will need to meet with you several days prior to the scheduled deposition. Please call this office at your earliest convenience to schedule an appointment for this purpose. Ms. Garcia can be available to meet in the evening or on a weekend if your schedule so necessitates.

Please call 216-555-1234 to schedule the appointment.

Sincerely,

Ana Garcia, Esq.
123 Main Street
Parkhurst, Ohio 44XXX
Attorney Number XXXXXXX
pp

In a lawsuit, the attorneys for the opposing sides obtain information they need from the other side or sides through discovery. There are several forms of discovery, which will be discussed later in the book, and the paralegal might draft a cover letter for discovery requests that are sent to opposing counsel. Below is a cover letter sent with interrogatories.

LETTER THREE

SMITH & GARCIA, ATTORNEYS AT LAW
123 Main Street
Parkhurst, Ohio, 44XXX

October 12, 20XX

Lowe, Downe & Nogud
56 Shyster Lane
Parkhurst, Ohio 44XXX

RE: Doe v. Parkhurst

Dear Ms. Nogud:

Enclosed please find the Interrogatories for plaintiff to answer in the above captioned case. We appreciate your prompt attention to these.

We received your Interrogatories for Dr. Hunter in Friday's mail, and we will be meeting with him for his responses shortly.

Do not hesitate to call with any questions or concerns.

Yours truly,

Ana Garcia, Esq.
123 Main Street
Parkhurst, Ohio 44XXX
Attorney Number XXXXXXX
pp

Enclosure

(*continued*)

LETTER FOUR

SMITH & GARCIA, ATTORNEYS AT LAW
123 Main Street
Parkhurst, Ohio, 44XXX

John Jones   January 26, 20XX
17 West Circle
Parkhurst, Ohio 44XXX

RE: Jones v. Jones

Dear Mr. Jones:

This is the fourth notice this firm has sent you concerning your outstanding balance due. We successfully represented you in the above captioned matter six months ago. To date, we have received no payment beyond the token retainer from the beginning of our professional relationship. To avoid formal collection proceedings, you must make a minimum partial payment of $250 by February 16, 20XX.

Yours truly,

Bradley Smith, Esq.
123 Main Street
Parkhurst, Ohio 44XXX
Attorney Number XXXXXXX

pp

(*continued*)

LETTER FIVE

SMITH & GARCIA, ATTORNEYS AT LAW
123 Main Street
Parkhurst, Ohio, 44XXX

Honorable Matthew Goode
1 Main Street
Common Pleas Court
Parkhurst, Ohio 44XXX

RE: State v. Williams   September 7, 20XX

Dear Judge Goode:

This firm just received notice of the pretrial you have set for November 16, 20XX in the above captioned case. We respectfully request a change in the pretrial date in the above captioned matter. Both of the counsel for this firm have previous trials scheduled for November 16, 20XX. Ms. Garcia is scheduled in Judge X X's courtroom in Lakeland Municipal Court. This trial has been scheduled for over a month. Mr. Smith is scheduled for trial in Judge YY's courtroom in Parkhurst Common Pleas Court. This trial was set on August 5, 20XX. This trial is anticipated to last three days, and Mr. Smith is available upon completion of this trial.

Thank you for your consideration of this request.

Sincerely yours,

Bradley Smith, Esq.
123 Main Street
Parkhurst, Ohio 44XXX
Attorney Number XXXXXX

Ana Garcia, Esq.
123 Main Street
Parkhurst, Ohio 44XXX
Attorney Number XXXXXX

pp

CERTIFICATE OF SERVICE

A copy of this letter has been sent by regular United States mail on this _____ day of _____, 20XX to the Prosecutor, Brian Kategoros, 3 Courthouse Square, Parkhurst, Ohio 44XXX.

Bradley Smith XXXXXX
Attorney for the Defendant,
Thomas Williams, Sr.
123 Main Street
Parkhurst, Ohio 44XXX
(216) 555-5555

(continued)

LETTER SIX

SMITH & GARCIA, ATTORNEYS AT LAW
123 Main Street
Parkhurst, Ohio, 44XXX

Martin J. Boyle
140 Maple Drive, Manager's Office
Parkhurst, Ohio 44XXX

RE: Kowalski v. Landlord   August 25, 20XX

Dear Mr. Boyle:

This firm represents Sheila Kowalski in the above captioned matter. As a person with knowledge of this matter, you are summoned to be deposed at the law offices of Smith & Garcia on **September 15, 20XX at 2:00 pm**. As noted in the attached subpoena duces tecum, you are ordered to bring with you any documents, voice mails, emails, or other evidence that relates to this matter. Please feel free to call this office with any questions or concerns.

Sincerely,

Ana Garcia, Esq.
123 Main Street
Parkhurst, Ohio 44XXX
Attorney Number XXXXXXX

pp

Enclosure: subpoena duces tecum

(*continued*)

LETTER SEVEN

SMITH & GARCIA, ATTORNEYS AT LAW
123 Main Street
Parkhurst, Ohio, 44XXX

Clerk of Courts, Probate Division
1 Main Street
Common Pleas Court
Parkhurst, Ohio 44XXX

RE: Jeremiah Gray, Last Will and Testament   July 21, 20XX

Dear Clerk of Probate Court:

Enclosed please find the original and official Last Will and Testament of Jeremiah Gray for filing with the Court.

Sincerely,

Bradley Smith, Esq.
123 Main Street
Parkhurst, Ohio 44XXX
Attorney Number XXXXXXX

pp

Enclosure

(*continued*)

LETTER EIGHT

SMITH & GARCIA, ATTORNEYS AT LAW
123 Main Street
Parkhurst, Ohio, 44XXX

Lowe, Downe & Nogud
56 Shyster Lane
Parkhurst, Ohio 44XXX

RE: Thompson v. Brett discovery   October 27, 20XX

Dear Mr. Downe:

As per our telephone conversation of today, October 27, 20XX, at 1:30 pm, your office will hand deliver, by close of business on November 10, 20XX, your responses to Interrogatories and the copies of the documents requested in our Request for Production of Documents for the above captioned case. Additionally, you acknowledged receipt of our responses to all your discovery requests to date.

Further, you will produce your client for deposition on or before November 30, 20XX at a mutually agreeable time and date.

I look forward to an efficient course of discovery in this matter.

Sincerely yours,

Bradley Smith, Esq.
123 Main Street
Parkhurst, Ohio 44XXX
Attorney Number XXXXXXX

pp

(continued)

LETTER NINE

OPPOSING COUNSEL, ATTORNEYS AT LAW
456 Prospect Street
Parkhurst, Ohio, 44XXX

Ana Garcia, Esq.
123 Main Street
Parkhurst, Ohio 44XXX

Dear Ms. Garcia

RE: Thompson v. Brett   November 10, 20XX

I regret to notify you that my client will not be able to be deposed on the previously scheduled date, December 14, 20XX. She has just informed me that she will be out of the country on vacation beginning today until the day before our scheduled trial.

I hope this does not present any difficulties for you.

Sincerely yours,

Peter Entraver, Esq.
456 Prospect Street
Parkhurst, Ohio 44XXX
Attorney Number XXXXXXX

(*continued*)

LETTER TEN

SMITH & GARCIA, ATTORNEYS AT LAW
123 Main Street
Parkhurst, Ohio, 44XXX

Peter Entraver, Esq
456 Prospect Street
Parkhurst, Ohio 44XXX

RE: Thompson v. Brett   November 15, 20XX

Dear Mr. Entraver:

I have attached a copy of my October 27, 20XX letter memorializing our discovery agreement, a copy of your correspondence confirming the date and time of your client's deposition on December 14, 20XX, and a copy of your letter canceling said deposition.

Deposing your client is necessary for me to effectively represent my client in this matter. Therefore, by this letter, I am confirming that she will attend the scheduled deposition or be in contempt of court. In accordance with Civil Rule 45, at 10:00 am today, November 20, 20XX, your client was served at her home by a process server with a subpoena compelling her attendance at the deposition. A copy of his proof of service is also attached for your convenience.

I look forward to seeing you at your client's deposition on the scheduled date and time.

Sincerely yours,

Ana Garcia
123 Main Street
Parkhurst, Ohio 44XXX
Attorney Number XXXXXXX

pp

cc: Honorable Judge Matthew Goode

Enclosures

EXERCISE

Read the following five fact patterns and the accompanying letter. Revise each letter so that it is appropriately professional in tone and grammatically correct.

FACT PATTERN ONE

Brad Smith has asked you, the firm's paralegal, to obtain a police report for an automobile accident that occurred on Saturday October 11, 20XX, at State Route 50 and Connors Avenue at 11:30 pm. The cars involved were a 20XX Chevy Malibu with the license number ABC 123, and a 1999 Toyota Camry with the license number XYZ 890. The police department is located at 5000 Concourse Parkway, Parkhurst OH 44XXX.

LETTER ONE

Dear Records Clerk,

I need a copy of a police report for an accident that happened. It happened on Saturday October 11, 20XX. There were two cars involved, and one was a beater! It was a 1999 Toyota Camry. Who would drive an old granny car like that? The other car was a Chevy. The accident happened at 11:30 pm. The license plate numbers on the cars were ABC 123 and XYZ 890.

I almost forgot! The accident happened at State Route 50 and Connors Avenue.

Thanks! ☺

Pat Paralegal

FACT PATTERN TWO

Ana Garcia has asked you to send a letter to Sheila Kowalski asking her to come to an appointment next Tuesday at 4:00 pm and to bring a copy of the advertisement she answered about the apartment she had leased, and anything else that she might consider relevant.

LETTER TWO

Dear Sheila;

Ana wants you to come to an appointment next Tuesday. Bring your copy of the lease with you. Bring a copy of the ad from the paper or Internet that you used to find the apartment. If you think of anything else, bring it too.

Pat

FACT PATTERN THREE

Brad Smith has asked you to write a letter to opposing counsel requesting possible dates for him to depose their client. He told you that he will be available on September 16, 20XX all day, on September 19, 20XX after 1:00 pm, and the entire week of September 25, 20XX. The opposing counsel represents Jacob Smith, and the counsel representing him is Peter Entraver, Esq., whose office is located at 456 Prospect Street, Parkhurst, Ohio 44XXX.

LETTER THREE

Dear Pete——

Mr. Smith wants to depose your client and he can do it on September 19, 20XX after 1:00 pm. If that doesn't work, he can do it anytime on September 16th or anytime during the week of September 25, 20XX. Surely you and your client are available at one of those times. Call me and let me know which time works so I can book our conference room and the court reporter.

See ya then . . . .

Pat Paralegal

FACT PATTERN FOUR

Ana Garcia has asked you to send to Mrs. Brown a draft copy of the will she wrote for her. Ana also wants you to ask Mrs. Brown to make an appointment to sign the will. Mrs. Brown lives in the Assisted Living facility at 65 Oak Circle, Parkhurst, Ohio 44XXX. Ana wanted you to be sure that Mrs. Brown knows that Ana will come to her if Mrs. Brown cannot get a ride to the office.

(continued)

LETTER FOUR

Dear Mrs. Brown

Ana axed me to send U this copy of the will she wrote for U. She also axed me to have U call us to make an appointment so U can sign the will. Call me, afternoons are better, but I suppose U can call in the morning if U have to, so I can schedule the appointment. Just so U know, Ana is usually crabbier on Mondays, so I wouldn't schedule it on a Monday if I were U.

TTYL,

ParalegaL

FACT PATTERN FIVE

After counsel for both sides has chosen September 16, 20XX at 2:00 pm for the deposition, you have arranged the court reporter. The court reporter and Mr. Smith are set up in the conference room by 1:45 pm, sipping coffee. You are waiting at your desk, ready to welcome the attorney and his client when they arrive. Much to everyone's surprise, they do not show up. At 4:00 pm, you place a call to opposing counsel's office, but the phone rolls over into voicemail.

Mr. Smith asks you to draft a letter for him to send to opposing counsel rescheduling the deposition.

LETTER FIVE

Mr. Entraver!

How rude! I can't believe you didn't at least call and let me know that you weren't planning to show up for your client's deposition! You owe me for the court reporter- they aren't cheap, you know.
Don't think you can play games with me just because Judge X refuses to get involved in discovery disputes. I can still report you to the County Bar Association for malfeasance. You'd better call my paralegal with a date and time for the deposition in the week of September 25th if you don't want me to report you to the ethics committee.

Not Sincerely Yours,

P-

obo

Attorney

■ IDENTIFY THE AUDIENCE

The next question to ask is, who is my target audience? The style, wording, and format of your letter will vary according to its intended recipient. For example, if your letter is being written to a client to inform him or her of documents and items the attorney needs the client to provide, your choice of language will include more basic English and fewer legal terms than a letter to opposing counsel would contain. If your client is not well-educated, your choice of words and the length of your sentences will accommodate for that, without talking down to the client. Similarly, if your client's first language is not English, your choice of vocabulary will accommodate for that.

On the other hand, if your letter is intended for opposing counsel, you will be able to use legal terminology, but you will have to be more cautious in your wording, because the attorney receiving the letter is on the other side. Anything you write to opposing counsel can be used against your client.

Some of the points you should consider before you begin drafting your correspondence are the recipient's:

- **Education.** If the person to whom you are writing is highly educated, you will be able to use more complex sentence structures and sophisticated vocabulary. You will be able to discuss more abstract concepts in your writing. On the other hand, if the recipient lacks a high school diploma, you probably will need to use simpler words and use a shorter sentence structure to explain your logic. It is important not to "talk down" to a person whose education level is limited. Lack of education does not equate to lack of intelligence. It is possible that circumstances have prevented that person from completing his or her education. You might even find that the person is better read than you or a more highly educated person might be. Nonetheless, it is preferable to err on the side of simple, plain language; intimidating the client is counterproductive.
- **Reading ability.** A person's reading ability is often commensurate with his or her level of education. It is important to remember, however, that even highly educated people can have dyslexia or another impediment to reading ability. Again, it is preferable to err on the side of simplicity while avoiding condescension.
- **Native language.** When English is a person's second language, writing a clear, unambiguous letter to him or her can be even more challenging than writing to a native English speaker with limited education. It is difficult to be able to place yourself inside the mind of the non-native speaker. Idioms, colloquialisms, and alternative word meanings that are second nature to the native speaker can confuse, or worse, mislead the person whose English is limited. Even non-native speakers whose English is very good might not catch concepts or references that a native speaker would catch. Think, for example, of the word "brief." The native speaker knows that this word has at least three very different meanings. It can refer to a length of time that is short. It can refer to an article of men's underclothing. Or, in the legal context, it can refer to a document drafted for the court. Using this word in a complex sentence could confuse the non-native speaker. Try to place yourself in the recipient's mind and view the letter through his or her eyes.
- **Physical problems.** The recipient of your letter might have vision problems, have difficulty with manipulating things, or have difficulty walking. Having to alter the format of your writing for a person with limited vision is obvious. Less obvious is the need to make sure your correspondence to a person with limited manual dexterity, perhaps as a result of arthritis, is organized in such a way that the person can keep the documents together and handle them most easily. Although limitations in walking will not affect the person's ability to read the letter, if you are writing a letter to arrange an appointment, it is important to remember to alert the person to any impediment he or she may encounter trying to reach the office. In other words, it is important to

keep the whole person in mind, not just the legal problem associated with him or her.

- **Age.** Although age itself is not necessarily a limiting factor, an older client might have limited vision. Also, it is important to avoid using any current cultural references that might not be familiar to the older client. If the client is a very young adult, it is important to remember that person's limited life experience, particularly in areas of adult responsibility. This client might require more guidance with basic facets of dealing with a legal issue.

- **Profession.** The vocabulary you use in your correspondence might depend on the profession of the recipient. If you are writing to a medical professional, you will be able to use more sophisticated terms than if the client is a patient. If the person is an insurance agent, you can use terms that are specialized to the insurance industry. If the person is a real estate agent, you can use language that a real estate professional would be familiar with and that you would not use with a lay person.

- **Familiarity with legal language.** If the person you are writing to is a legal professional or has a comfortable familiarity with legal terminology, you will be able to use language that more precisely expresses your meaning. Using that language with a lay person, however, would serve only to confuse and perhaps annoy or intimidate the recipient.

- **Attitude.** You may have to take your client's attitude into consideration when writing your letter. For example, your client may be a person who takes offense easily when no offense is intended. You will have to word the letter carefully to avoid alienating the client. Some clients are very timid or easily intimidated, and your letter will have to be more reassuring to those clients. Some clients are aggressive and negative, and you will want to be sure that the tone of your letter does not trigger a counterproductive response.

- **Personal concerns.** Few people consult an attorney for happy reasons. Usually, the person has a problem and needs an attorney's help in handling it. The scale of the client's response is often proportionate with the severity of the legal issue involved, but this is not always the case. Consider, for example, a lawsuit over an amount of money. An average person being sued for $10,000 would be very upset at the prospect of having to pay this amount. A wealthy person, on the other hand, might not consider this amount more than an annoyance. The president of a large corporation might consider this amount beneath his notice. If the person being sued is a physician, and the suit alleges medical malpractice, you can be certain that the doctor will be extremely upset. The doctor's distress will result not from the amount of money at issue but from what he or she perceives as a personal attack on his or her professional ability and reputation. Similarly, many of the parties in divorce cases allow their emotional distress to affect their response to even minor situations. It is very important to remember the mental state of the recipient of your correspondence.

EXERCISE

Read the following twelve client descriptions and name the recipient's qualities and limitations that should be considered when writing correspondence.

1. Arnold Skiba stormed into the office demanding to speak with Brad immediately. He told Brad that he was sick and tired of hunters trespassing on his land. A stray bullet from one hunter had killed Mr. Skiba's favorite dog yesterday. Despite numerous "no trespassing" signs, Mr. Skiba continued to find deer stands in his trees and spent cartridges on the ground. He is very concerned that a stray bullet might hit one of his young children next time.

2. James Hess, the president of the local bank and ranking golf champion at Parkhurst Country Club, has asked Brad to represent him in a suit against his home builder. Mr. Hess had a prominent architect draw up the plans for his new home, and he contracted with Connolly Homes of Parkhurst to build it. The house is only half finished, but the leaking roof has caused mold to start growing on the inside walls of several rooms. Additionally, the builder apparently failed to anchor the foundation in bedrock, and the entire house has shifted, causing large cracks in the basement walls. Mr. Hess pointed out to Brad that his bank handled most of the local mortgages, and the builder was being foolish to aggravate him. He also stated that a man of his position and stature was not accustomed to being treated in this way.

3. Dr. Alberts has consulted Ana to represent him in the dissolution of the medical practice he has with Dr. Reyes. Each doctor is accusing the other of not carrying his fair share of the work, of pilfering money and supplies from the office, and of stealing patients.

4. Angelo Gallo has consulted Brad for legal defense after he was arrested for assaulting a man at the local tavern. The man he hit had put his arm around Angelo's girlfriend, and even after she tried to push him away, he had laughed and held her tighter. Angelo had warned him to leave her alone, but the man just laughed harder. Angelo had been bullied all of his life for being "stupid" because he was dyslexic. When the man who was holding his girlfriend laughed at him, Angelo had punched him. Although the man was not injured, an off-duty police officer had witnessed the altercation. When the man insisted on pressing charges against Angelo, the officer had to admit what he had witnessed.

5. Eighteen-year-old Matthew Kovach has sought Brad's help with a ticket he received for driving while intoxicated. He and his friends had gone out to celebrate their high school graduation. Matt had drunk far too much and was stopped almost as soon as he drove out of the bar's parking lot. The legal drinking age in the state is 21.

6. George Pappas, CEO of online pharmaceuticals, has asked Ana to defend him in an action the FDA is taking against his website. He assured Ana that he only sold properly manufactured drugs that he had obtained from Canadian wholesalers. Mr. Pappas is a high school drop out who is brilliant with computers. He had been diagnosed with Asperger's disorder and never looked directly at Ana's eyes when he spoke to her. He is concerned that if the FDA shuts down his website, he could be liable for criminal prosecution as well as multiple lawsuits from dissatisfied (or opportunistic) former customers.

7. Mr. and Mrs. Harper, a couple in their twenties, have met with Ana concerning a potential medical malpractice suit against the obstetrician who delivered their son. The baby is in a stroller, and even at less than a year old, he clearly has significant brain injury. Mr. Harper is an auto mechanic, and Mrs. Harper cleans houses for a company that provides maids.

8. Jane Barber, a paralegal with another law firm in Parkhurst, has consulted Ana to represent her in her divorce. She has taken their children and moved out of the family home into a shelter. She has a black eye, and her jaw has been wired because it is broken. Additionally, her arm is in a cast.

9. Mrs. Schroeder, the ninety-year-old mother of the parish priest, has asked Brad to meet with her in her hospital room. She slipped and fell on water from a malfunctioning freezer at the local supermarket. She now has a broken hip and may end up having to live the rest of her life in a nursing home. Prior to the accident, she had lived with her son in the parish rectory.

(continued)

10. Mrs. Suarez, a friend of Ana's grandmother, has come in to the office to revise her will. Mrs. Suarez speaks limited English, and she is 84 years old. Because her vision is limited, her daughter brought her to the office. Mrs. Suarez is changing her will because she is angry at her son, who has left his wife for a younger woman. She wants to write her son out of the will and leave his share to his children.

11. Tamara, who works at the local sheltered workshop for the developmentally disabled and had been a special education student through high school, has consulted Ana for assistance in dealing with her landlord. Tamara had just moved into her apartment when she noticed she was being bitten by some sort of insect. After reading an article in the newspaper, she went into her bedroom with the lights off, pulled back the sheets, and shone a flashlight on the mattress. Appalled, she realized that the apartment had bed bugs. When she notified the landlord, he blamed her for bringing the pests into the building and told her she was responsible for the cost of extermination. Additionally, he removed all her furniture and belongings from the apartment and burned them. Tamara has difficulty with maintaining focus and organization. (Be sure to have the exterminator in immediately after she leaves. Burn the office furniture and rip out the carpet!)

12. Mr. Stephan Januwicz came to Ana in tears, begging her help in preventing Sunny Acres Nursing Home from discharging his wife. An immigrant from Eastern Europe, he had a limited grasp of English. He had worked as a tailor and never had the opportunity to finish his schooling. Nonetheless, Ana was able to determine that Mrs. Januwicz had suffered a stroke and had been at Sunny Acres for over a year. The couple had run out of money to pay for her care, and Sunny Acres had put a lien on the family home. Now that the cost of her care exceeded the value of the home, the nursing home is threatening to discharge her. In interviewing him, Ana suspected he might be in the early stages of dementia because he repeated the same questions over and over. At one point during the interview, he stared into space and was startled when Ana spoke. He appeared confused and took a little time figuring out where he was.

As the above exercises demonstrate, knowing the characteristics of the recipient of your letter should influence the way you write it. Keeping in mind all the various characteristics demonstrated in the examples, you will apply the following list to the format of your letter.

Sentence length: Long versus short
Word choice: Sophisticated versus simple
Style: Technical versus basic
Emphasis: Color, bold, italicize, underline, and/or bullet point
Font size: Large versus regular.

If the recipient is visually impaired, elderly, or otherwise would have difficulty with a standard 12 point font, it will be necessary to increase the font size to 14 or even 16. For court documents, however, consult the local and state rules for the required font size.

After you have written the correspondence, review it and ask yourself whether it accomplishes your goal.

EXERCISE

Using one or more of the client descriptions in the previous exercises, draft a letter or letters to the selected clients informing the client that he or she is required to attend a deposition to be taken by opposing counsel on December 10, 20XX at 10:00 am EST at 14 Courthouse Square, Suite 1600, Parkhurst, Ohio 441XX.

■ MAINTAIN PROFESSIONAL TONE

As electronic communication has become more prevalent, the tone of writing has become more casual. Fewer people have experience in writing a formal communication, whether a letter, other correspondence, or electronic communication. Nonetheless, it is important to maintain a professional tone in all legal correspondence.

Earlier in the chapter, we provided one format of a letter. The format in the office you work in may be somewhat different, but the overall concepts are universal. You must include the date, first and foremost. This is your proof that your office sent the correspondence and the time that you sent it. You must include the party to whom you are sending the correspondence, and the subject matter of it.

After the formalities of the format have been laid out, and you have determined the audience and purpose of the correspondence, you next focus on the tone of the letter or electronic communication. Even if the letter is being sent to an uneducated person, the tone must be professional and respectful.

Similarly, when sending electronic communications, your message should be grammatically correct, well-organized, and as formal as it would be if it were printed as a letter. This means you use a formal greeting, "Dear Mr. Jones." It means you do not use slang: "Hey," emoticons, smiley faces, and texting abbreviations such as IMHO, U, or LOL are all unacceptable.

The tone of your communication must be respectful and not be too familiar. The client is not a friend, neighbor, or family member. The client will find a professional tone in correspondence reassuring; it will let the client know that you are taking the case seriously and will present the issues to the court appropriately.

EXAMPLE OF POOR ELECTRONIC COMMUNICATION

Hey there, Mr. Jones, I forgot to tell you 2 bring your car registration when U come to our office. Oh, and you'll need any pictures you took of the accident. Shoot me an email if you have any questions. BTW, bring any medical bills you got because of being treated for the MVA. See you then! TTYL!! ☺ Pat

EXAMPLE OF GOOD ELECTRONIC COMMUNICATION

Dear Mr. Jones,

When you come to the office on January 5, 20XX at 2:00 pm, please bring the following items:

1. Your car registration
2. Your auto insurance policy
3. Pictures of the accident
4. Any medical bills you have incurred.

We look forward to meeting with you.

Sincerely,

Pat Peters, Paralegal for

Brad Smith, Esq.

You will notice that this electronic communication appears very similar to what you would write in a letter sent through the United States mail. It should.

You should also be sure to populate the subject line in any email you send. If you do not summarize the subject matter of the email, the reader may assume it is spam/junk mail, or the reader may decide it is unimportant. For this communication, you might say, "Items to bring to your meeting at Attorney Brad Smith's office." The subject line should be concise but thorough and accurate.

EXERCISE

Examine the above example of a poor electronic communication on page 89 and identify each unprofessional word, expression, or other communication in it. Next to each unprofessional item you have selected, explain why it is unprofessional.

SUMMARY

- Written communication, whether to clients, witnesses, or other law offices, is an essential part of the paralegal's duties.

- Traditionally, communication consisted of letters and documents, along with occasional telephone calls.

- More recently, electronic communications have become more prevalent in legal communication.

- Whatever form communication takes, the paralegal has to consider the same factors when communicating on behalf of the attorney and the law office: a professional tone and correct grammar and punctuation are essential.

- In addition to a professional tone and correct grammar and punctuation, paralegals must identify the purpose of the communication and the characteristics of its recipients.

- Paralegals must consider the recipient's education, profession, reading ability, familiarity with legal language, age, physical limitations, attitude, and personal concerns.

- Before paralegals begin drafting their correspondence, therefore, they must both determine the purpose of the writing as well as its audience.

- The correspondence must be tailored in style, wording, and format that the recipient can understand.

- Paralegals should reread correspondence before sending it to ensure that it conveys the intended message and achieves its purpose.

- Using a professional tone is imperative in legal correspondence. A professional tone will reassure anxious clients that their selected counsel is competent and professional.

ASSIGNMENTS

I. Read the following client fact pattern, and then compose a letter to the client according to the instructions contained in the fact pattern. Remember to apply all the information you have learned in previous chapters as well as in this chapter. First, draft an outline of the letter, and then write the final letter.

You are the paralegal working for Brad and Ana. A new client, Mrs. Janet Lemon, has retained Ana to represent her in a lawsuit against the company she hired to paint the outside of her house. Ana has asked you to write a letter to Mrs. Lemon reminding her that she has an appointment on Thursday, August 12, 20XX at 2:30 pm. Ana wants you to remind Mrs. Lemon to bring the contract with the painting company, pictures of her house before they started painting and as it looks now, the tape from her answering machine on which the owner of the painting company left a nasty voice message, and a copy of the canceled check she gave the company as a down payment on the work.

II. Read the following client fact pattern, and then compose a letter to the client according to the instructions contained in the fact pattern. Remember to apply all the information you have learned in previous chapters as well as in this chapter. First, draft an outline of the letter, and then write the final letter.

Brad has asked you to write a letter for him to send to Norton Russell telling Mr. Russell that the firm will not represent him in his case against his neighbor. Mr. Russell admitted to Brad that the fence he built impinged on his neighbor's property, and Mr. Russell wanted Brad to help him prove that the neighbor had given him permission for the fence to sit partially on the neighbor's property. Mr. Russell had no proof that the neighbor had agreed, and in fact, Mr. Russell had shown Brad a letter the neighbor had sent demanding the removal of the fence. Brad can see no legal ground for Mr. Russell's action.

III. Read the following client fact pattern, and then compose a letter to the client according to the instructions contained in the fact pattern. Remember to apply all the information you have learned in previous chapters as well as in this chapter. First, draft an outline of the letter, and then write the final letter.

Ana has asked you to write a letter to Carrie Thomas, a woman who had gone to school with Ana until Ms. Thomas had been placed in a special education classroom in second grade. Ana had not had much contact with Ms. Thomas since second grade, except to see her in the grocery store or at church. Ms. Thomas, who lives in government subsidized housing, had been very upset about a letter she had received concerning changes in the management structure of the housing project. She did not understand the letter and had asked Ana to explain it to her. After studying the letter, researching the law, and discussing the letter with the housing authorities, Ana now understands that none of the changes will directly affect Ms. Thomas. Rather, all the residents had received the letter so they would know which person to call for different situations.

The letter had been poorly written and confusing. Ana wants you to write a letter telling Ms. Thomas clearly what she needs to do for various situations. If her power goes out, she is to call Mr. Jackson at 216-555-3333. If the water leaks or the toilet will not flush, she is to call Mr. Williams at 216-555-4444. If she wants to complain about loud noise, she is to call Ms. Roberts at 216-555-5555. If she sees any pests, insects, or other vermin, she is to call Ms. Shapiro at 216-555-1111. For all other problems, she is to call Mr. Angelotti at 216-555-7777. Ana wants you to make this letter very clear and easy for Ms. Thomas to understand.

IV. Read the following client fact pattern, and then compose a letter to the client according to the instructions contained in the fact pattern. Remember to apply all the information you have learned in previous chapters as well as in this chapter. First, draft an outline of the letter, and then write the final letter.

Mr. Maxamed Xamdi, an immigrant from Somalia, has consulted with Ana concerning harassment he is enduring from his supervisor. Ana has asked you to write a letter to Mr. Xamdi instructing him to keep a journal of everything his supervisor says or does to him that is harassment, including the time, date, and any witnesses to the incident. Mr. Xamdi speaks limited English, and his education ended in eighth grade, after his father died. He and his mother were permitted to enter the country legally when Mr. Xamdi was seventeen. He has since obtained his U.S. citizenship. Nonetheless, he has informed Ana that his supervisor continually threatens to report him to the immigration officials. Ana has asked you to list the types of things that constitute harassment, including name calling, threats, taunts, insults, etc.

V. Read the following client fact pattern, and then compose a letter to the client according to the instructions contained in the fact pattern. Remember to apply all the information you have learned in previous chapters as well as in this chapter. First, draft an outline of the letter, and then write the final letter.

Jeff Fisher, a 36-year-old worker at the auto plant, has asked Brad to represent him in his divorce. Mr. Fisher's wife has decided that she no longer wants to be married. She has decided, he told Brad, that she can make more money than he can and does not want to share her earnings with him. He believes that because he supported her throughout her education, which is the reason she can now make so much money, that he should be awarded the house, the cars, and all their possessions except her clothing. He also strongly believes that she should return all the jewelry and gifts he gave her during the course of the marriage, because she obtained them under false pretense, i.e., that she was a faithful and loving wife. Brad has tried to explain to Mr. Fisher that Parkhurst is in a no-fault state for divorce, and that the court will require a fair distribution of marital assets. Although Brad did not address it in their meeting, he wants the letter you draft to include the information that Mrs. Fisher is entitled to half the value of any pension he earned during the marriage. Brad mentions that Mr. Fisher is dyslexic and is a high school dropout.

LEARNING OBJECTIVES

1. Construct a persuasive, formal written document

2. Analyze the difference between passive and active voice

3. Differentiate when to use passive voice versus active voice for persuasive writing

4. Apply parallelism, effective paragraph structure, and varied appearance for persuasive writing

5. Alter spoken language practices for formal written documents

6. Refrain from inadvertent plagiarism when incorporating legal research into documents

Persuasive Writing

CHAPTER 5

■ FORMAL WRITING GUIDANCE

Formal writing does not mean boring or unpersuasive writing. In this chapter we explain several principles and techniques that will help to make your writing, while formal and correct, also effective. Additionally, we have included several points that are important but defy categorization.

Persuasive Writing

Formal writing does not mean boring or unpersuasive writing. In fact, most legal writing should be persuasive. Certainly documents written on your client's behalf for the court or opposing counsel have to be persuasive, that is, written in a light that is most favorable to your client. That does not mean, however, that you can omit, twist, or invent facts to enhance your client's case. Persuasive writing is a fine art that requires careful crafting and emphasis. Persuasive writing is not aggressive or offensive; as tempting as it may be, writing aggressively or offensively will alienate, not persuade, your reader.

So how do you write persuasively? It takes practice, but one way to think about it is to remember a time before you were an adult when you had done something to get yourself in trouble with your parents or guardians. How did you tell them about what had happened?

EXAMPLE

Say you had been at fault in a driving accident. You would not have said,

> "Dad, I was fooling around with my buddies while I was driving and didn't see the car in front of me had suddenly stopped. I wrecked the car through my carelessness."

Instead, you might have said,

"Dad, I was in an accident. The car in front of me stopped suddenly, and I was not able to stop in time. I'm sorry, but the car is damaged."

Notice how the second example does not assign blame to you until the third independent clause. The first sentence sets out the situation, but in a way that states that the accident occurred, not who caused the accident. The first clause of the second sentence, while truthful, has the other car performing the first causative action; the car stopped suddenly. It is not until your next independent clause that you place any blame upon yourself. You have to admit that you hit the car in front of you, because that is the truth. You do not have to disclose that your inattentiveness caused you to hit the car in front of you. Notice also in the last sentence, you again have removed yourself from the action. Instead, you have made a factual statement about the condition of the car.

It is imperative in your legal writing to be truthful. You cannot omit any facts that are essential to your client's case. The facts in this situation were that the car in front of you stopped suddenly, and you did not stop in time to avoid hitting it. As a result the car you were driving has damage. At this point, the Dad in this scenario probably asked whether you were fooling around or otherwise not paying proper attention to the road. This is the role your opposing counsel will take in writing or at a trial. But you do not have to give away the case, although you cannot omit the facts.

You have a number of tools at your disposal to assist you to craft a persuasive document. Among those are the limited, intentional use of the passive voice, parallelism, and paragraph structure. The appearance of your document also influences the readers' reactions.

First we will address a tool that most writers do not realize exists and many cannot recognize when they write or read it: passive voice.

PASSIVE VOICE

Although passive voice usually is not persuasive, it is a good way to de-emphasize negative facts in your case. Unfortunately, although the passive voice can be an effective tool when used properly, new (and sometimes experienced) writers too often use the passive voice inadvertently, thereby weakening their writing, diminishing the persuasive power of their writings.

So how do you recognize the passive voice? When a sentence is written in the passive voice, the actor is not identified. In that last sentence, the dependent introductory clause, "When a sentence is written in the passive voice" is a perfect example of the passive voice. Who is the person doing the writing? That person is not identified. When you want to diminish the attention to the actor, as Brad would in Mr. Williams' case, you use the passive voice.

Many, many years ago, one of us learned from a linguistics teacher the easiest way to remember the passive voice. This example is part of history to many of you, but President Nixon always taped the conversations he had in the Oval Office. When President Nixon was embroiled in the Watergate scandal, the prosecutors wanted to listen to those tapes, which were evidence. The tapes were mysteriously blank when the prosecutor received them. The newspapers had headlines that read "The Tapes Were Erased." The sentence, "The tapes were erased" is truthful, but evasive. We probably will never know the answer to the question that that sentence leaves hanging; who erased the tapes? Note also the ethics breach in that situation. Destruction of evidence is a serious breach of legal ethics, and attorneys who are found guilty of doing so may find themselves in prison.

A more contemporary version of this passive voice example would be, "The train station was bombed." This is a truthful yet incomplete statement, because it does not disclose who performed the bombing.

Passive voice can seriously weaken your argument when you are trying to be persuasive. If you want the readers to focus on a fact that is important to persuade them to your point of view, you must write it in the active voice. You sacrifice much of the persuasive power of your writing if you use passive voice ineffectively.

For example, compare these two different sentences from one of our fact patterns:

EXAMPLE OF PASSIVE VOICE WEAKENING AN ARGUMENT

The apartment lacked hot water, despite the landlord's receipt of written notice of the problem.

EXAMPLE OF ACTIVE VOICE STRENGTHENING AN ARGUMENT

Despite the tenant's having sent written notice that her apartment lacked hot water, the landlord had failed, in fact refused, to provide it.

The first example, while truthful and accurate, is weak. It fails to identify the actor who failed to provide the hot water. The second sentence, conversely, puts the landlord at the center of the action, making it clear to the reader that the landlord is responsible for the situation. This sentence is far more effective in persuading the readers that Sheila's situation is the fault of the landlord. This is the version that Sheila's counsel would use.

If you were writing the fact pattern for the landlord, on the other hand, you might want to use the passive voice version of the facts, because they lessen the focus on the landlord and his failure to act. To be useful in your writing, therefore, passive voice must be used selectively. In writing the trial brief for Mr. William's case, Brad might say, "The refrigerator fell off the truck. It was placed back into the truck, which then drove away" rather than saying, "Mr. Williams and his friend put the refrigerator back into the truck and left." The passive voice is truthful but de-emphasizes Mr. William's culpability in reloading the refrigerator into the truck and leaving the scene.

Even when using the active voice, the omission of certain words, as long as they do not change the truth of the writing, can be effective. Notice how omitting the last section of the following sentence is less harmful to the case: "Mr. Williams and his friend put the refrigerator back into the truck and left *the scene of the accident.*" Brad does not want to highlight the fact of the accident or the fact that his client broke the law by leaving the scene of the accident. By omitting the clause "the scene of the accident," he is not denying that the accident occurred; he is merely avoiding repeated mention of it. You can be sure that the prosecutor will provide more than enough emphasis of that fact, both because it is central to convicting Mr. Williams and because it is persuasive to the jury.

EXERCISE _____

Rewrite the following paragraphs from passive voice to active voice.

1. The church was robbed on Monday morning, with the collection from the previous day taken. Edgar White was seen running from the church yard on Monday morning, and proof could be made by the police that the robbery had been committed by Edgar. Unfortunately, the money could not be found even after the search of Edgar's apartment. Investigation was done by the senior detective on the police force. Nonetheless, surveillance was placed on Edgar.

2. Shortly after Pat was employed by Brad and Ana's firm, some of what had been taught in school became useful to Pat. A complaint had been filed with the court by Pat. It also had been written by Pat, although it was approved by Ana. A couple of changes had been made to it after proofreading, but pride was felt by Pat, nonetheless.

3. The answer to the complaint was filed quickly. Deception was evident in some of the answers, making them suspicious to Ana.

EXERCISE _____

Rewrite the following paragraph from active voice to passive voice.

1. Johnny bullied Patrick on the schoolyard, and the teachers did nothing to stop him. As he grew up, Johnny got bolder and meaner in his bullying, until everyone was afraid of him. Johnny came to believe that his behavior was acceptable and that his bullying would never cause him any problems. In the end, however, he bullied someone to suicide, and the school expelled him.

2. The woman had tripped on the two inch deep pothole in the sidewalk, and she suffered serious injuries. She required an ambulance to take her to the hospital, where she was diagnosed with a fractured nose, broken teeth, and a broken arm. Although the landowner had noticed the pothole, he had taken no action to fix it.

3. Despite the nurse's warnings at the end of the surgery that a sponge was missing, the doctor chose to ignore her and finished the surgery without an x-ray. Two months later, the patient had a serious infection in his abdomen, and a different doctor operated on him and found the sponge, which had caused the infection.

PARALLELISM

Another important technique for persuasive writing is parallelism. Accomplished speakers and writers use this rhetorical technique to great effect. Parallelism is a way of constructing a series of phrases, clauses, sentences, or even paragraphs so that the structures are similar. With parallelism, the like parts of speech are in the same form.

Parallelism is best explained with examples.

EXAMPLE OF LACK OF PARALLELISM

The judge instructed the jury to refrain from discussing the case, not to read the newspaper, and not research the Internet.

Instead of keeping all the phrases in the gerund form, "discussing," "reading," and "researching," this example includes a gerund, a participle, and an infinitive. This lack of parallelism weakens the impact of the sentence, and it distracts the reader because it is jarring.

EXAMPLE OF PARALLELISM

The judge instructed the jury to refrain from discussing the case, reading the newspaper, and researching the Internet.

Notice how in this version of the sentence, the series of actions the jury was instructed to avoid are all in the same form. Each of the verbs ends in –ing, creating cohesion. Notice how pleasing it is to the ear, and therefore to the eye. Many people "hear" words when they read them, and in the version of this sentence that is not parallel, it is jarring to the reader.

Properly used, parallelism can be astonishingly persuasive. Consider the excerpts from the following famous speech, President John F. Kennedy's Inaugural Speech. Notice how parallelism is used for contrast as well as continuity.

All examples of parallelism in the speech are highlighted; however, examples of parallelism emphasizing contrast are underlined, and examples of parallelism emphasizing continuity or commonality are italicized. Parallelism that is pivotal to the speech is bolded. For example, notice the use of the clause "we pledge." This repetition, which is parallelism, provides unity to the speech. Also notice later in the speech, how President Kennedy begins each new paragraph with "Let both sides." And toward the end of the speech, you might recognize the famous quote from this brief speech, which is made more effective by the use of parallelism.

We have provided a table summarizing how each use of parallelism is identified within the speech.

Table 5.1 Parallelism

Concept	Emphasis
Parellelism	**Highlight**
Parellelism emphasizing contrast	<u>Underlined</u>
Parellelism emphasizing continuity or commonality	*Italicized*
Parellelism pivotal to the speech	**Bolded**

EXAMPLE

"My fellow Americans, <u>**ask not what your country can do for you. Ask what you can do for your country**</u>."

By using parallel clauses, that contain the same words, the President provided a brief, memorable sentence that defined his view of his presidency.

1. We observe today <u>not a victory of party, but a celebration of freedom</u> - symbolizing an end, as well as a beginning -signifying renewal, as well as change. For I have sworn before you and Almighty God the same solemn oath our forebears prescribed nearly a century and three quarters ago.
2. The world is very different now. For man holds in his mortal hands the power to <u>abolish all forms of human poverty and all forms of human life</u>. And yet the same revolutionary beliefs for which our forebears fought are still at issue around the globe, the belief that <u>the rights of man come not from the generosity of the state, but from the hand of God</u>.
3. We dare not forget today that we are the heirs of that first revolution. Let the word go forth from this time and place, to friend and foe alike, that the torch has been passed to a new generation of Americans - *born in this century, tempered by war, disciplined by a hard and bitter peace, proud of our ancient heritage*-and unwilling to witness or

permit the slow undoing of those human rights to which this Nation has always been committed, and to which we are committed today at home and around the world.

4. Let every nation know, whether it wishes us well or ill, that *we shall pay any price, bear any burden, meet any hardship, support any friend, oppose any foe, in order to assure the survival and the success of liberty.*

5. This much **we pledge**, and more.

6. *To those old allies* whose cultural and spiritual origins we share, **we pledge** the loyalty of faithful friends. United, there is little we cannot do in a host of cooperative ventures. Divided, there is little we can do, for we dare not meet a powerful challenge at odds and split asunder.

7. *To those new States* whom we welcome to the ranks of the free, **we pledge** our word that one form of colonial control shall not have passed away merely to be replaced by a far more iron tyranny. We shall not always expect to find them supporting our view. But we shall always hope to find them strongly supporting their own freedom, and to remember that, in the past, those who foolishly sought power by riding the back of the tiger ended up inside.

8. *To those peoples in the huts and villages* across the globe struggling to break the bonds of mass misery, **we pledge** our best efforts to help them help themselves, for whatever period is required - not because the Communists may be doing it, not because we seek their votes, but because it is right. If a free society cannot help the many who are poor, it cannot save the few who are rich.

9. *To our sister republics south of our border*, **we** offer a special **pledge** to convert our good words into good deeds in a new alliance for progress, to assist free men and free governments in casting off the chains of poverty. But this peaceful revolution of hope cannot become the prey of hostile powers. Let all our neighbors know that we shall join with them to oppose aggression or subversion anywhere in the Americas. And let every other power know that this Hemisphere intends to remain the master of its own house.

10. *To that world assembly of sovereign states*, the United Nations, our last best hope in an age where the instruments of war have far outpaced the instruments of peace, we renew our pledge of support to prevent it from becoming merely a forum for invective, to strengthen its shield of the new and the weak, and to enlarge the area in which its writ may run.

11. Finally, *to those nations who would make themselves our adversary*, we offer not a pledge but a request: that both sides begin anew the quest for peace, before the dark powers of destruction unleashed by science engulf all humanity in planned or accidental self-destruction.

12. We dare not tempt them with weakness. For only when our arms are sufficient beyond doubt can we be certain beyond doubt that they will never be employed.

13. But neither can two great and powerful groups of nations take comfort from our present course, both sides overburdened by the cost of modern weapons, both rightly alarmed by the steady spread of the deadly atom, yet both racing to alter that uncertain balance of terror that stays the hand of mankind's final war.

14. So let us begin anew, remembering on both sides that civility is not a sign of weakness, and sincerity is always subject to proof. Let us never negotiate out of fear. But let us never fear to negotiate.

15. *Let both sides* explore what problems unite us instead of belaboring those problems which divide us.

16. *Let both sides*, for the first time, formulate serious and precise proposals for the inspection and control of arms, and bring the absolute power to destroy other nations under the absolute control of all nations.

17. *Let both sides* seek to invoke the wonders of science instead of its terrors. Together let us explore the stars, conquer the deserts, eradicate disease, tap the ocean depths, and encourage the arts and commerce.

18. *Let both sides* unite to heed in all corners of the earth the command of Isaiah, to "undo the heavy burdens . . . and to let the oppressed go free."

19. And if a beachhead of cooperation may push back the jungle of suspicion, *let both sides* join in creating a new endeavor, not a new balance of power, but a new world of law, where the strong are just and the weak secure and the peace preserved.

20. All this will not be finished in the first 100 days. Nor will it be finished in the first 1,000 days, nor in the life of this Administration, nor even perhaps in our lifetime on this planet. But let us begin.

21. In your hands, my fellow citizens, more than in mine, will rest the final success or failure of our course. Since this country was founded, each generation of Americans has been summoned to give testimony to its national loyalty. The graves of young Americans who answered the call to service surround the globe.

22. Now the trumpet summons us again, not as a call to bear arms, though arms we need; not as a call to battle, though embattled we are, but a call to bear the burden of a long twilight struggle, year in and year out, "rejoicing in hope, patient in tribulation," a struggle against the common enemies of man: tyranny, poverty, disease, and war itself.

23. Can we forge against these enemies a grand and global alliance, North and South, East and West, that can assure a more fruitful life for all mankind? Will you join in that historic effort?

24. In the long history of the world, only a few generations have been granted the role of defending freedom in its hour of maximum danger. I do not shrink from this responsibility, I welcome it. I do not believe that any of us would exchange places with any other people or any other generation. The energy, the faith, the devotion which we bring to this endeavor will light our country and all who serve it, and the glow from that fire can truly light the world.

25. And so, my fellow Americans, ask not what your country can do for you. Ask what you can do for your country.

26. My fellow citizens of the world, ask not what America will do for you, but what together we can do for the freedom of man.

27. Finally, whether you are citizens of America or citizens of the world, ask of us the same high standards of strength and sacrifice which we ask of you. With a good conscience our only sure reward, with history the final judge of our deeds, let us go forth to lead the land we love, asking His blessing and His help, but knowing that here on earth God's work must truly be our own.

This carefully crafted speech used parallelism to its best advantage. The exact repetition of key phrases and clauses drew attention to the speech's message. The parallel contrasts emphasized the disparities that the President planned to address. Whether or not you agree with the political message it expresses, the speech's effectiveness cannot be denied.

Some of the parallelism in this speech is subtler; for example, in the third paragraph, notice the parallelism of the phrases used to describe the "new generation of Americans." Each of the first three phrases begins with the same tense of an active verb: born, tempered, and disciplined. Each verb is modified by a prepositional phrase.

a new generation of Americans - *born in this century, tempered by war, disciplined by a hard and bitter peace, proud of our ancient heritage*

In the fourth paragraph notice the parallelism of the compound verb, along with the repeated use of the adjective "any" modifying the direct objects of each of the compound verbs.

we shall pay any price, bear any burden, meet any hardship, support any friend, oppose any foe, in order to assure the survival and the success of liberty.

In the eight paragraph, notice again the parallelism of the subordinate clauses, with two of them beginning with "not because," and the final clause beginning with "but because." The parallelism of the three clauses emphasizes the contrast between the reasons discarded in the first two clauses and the chosen reason in the last clause.

not because the Communists may be doing it, not because we seek their votes, but because it is right

The ninth paragraph provides a far more understated example of parallelism in its compound direct object. Each direct object is modified by the same adjective, "good."

convert our good words into good deeds

The tenth paragraph also contains strong parallelism in describing the pledge of support: "to prevent," "to strengthen," to enlarge."

we renew our pledge of support to prevent it from becoming merely a forum for invective, to strengthen its shield of the new and the weak, and to enlarge the area in which its writ may run.

In the thirteenth paragraph, again the parallelism draws attention to the similarities of the two sides on the cold war, which was a serious issue at the time of this speech. The repeated use of the word "both" followed by a common description provides an emphasis that a plain sentence would lack. Notice how much weaker this section would be if it were written, "both sides are overburdened by the cost of modern weapons and are rightly alarmed by the steady spread of the deadly atom. They are racing to alter that uncertain balance of terror that stays the hand of mankind's final war."

both sides overburdened by the cost of modern weapons, both rightly alarmed by the steady spread of the deadly atom, yet both racing to alter that uncertain balance of terror that stays the hand of mankind's final war.

In the fourteenth paragraph, the use of parallel independent clauses, each using the same linking verb after a noun that stands for a positive quality again provides emphasis and fluidity to the speech.

that civility is not a sign of weakness, and sincerity is always subject to proof

In the seventeenth paragraph, the compound verbs and their direct objects are parallel, providing continuity and fluidity.

> let us explore the stars, conquer the deserts, eradicate disease, tap the ocean depths, and encourage the arts and commerce.

The nineteenth paragraph contains two subtle examples of parallelism. The first provides contrast: the subject and its modifying prepositional phrase, "beachhead of cooperation" contrasts with the direct object that is in the same format, "jungle of suspicion." The second example of parallelism in this paragraph is found in the last sentence: "strong are just and the weak secure."

> And if a beachhead of cooperation may push back the jungle of suspicion, *let both sides* join in creating a new endeavor, not a new balance of power, but a new world of law, where the strong are just and the weak secure and the peace preserved

In the twenty-second paragraph, notice that the "common enemies of man" are in parallel form, all nouns.

> common enemies of man: tyranny, poverty, disease, and war itself.

Finally, in the twenty-seventh paragraph, notice the use of parallel prepositional phrases to introduce the sentence.

> With a good conscience our only sure reward, with history the final judge of our deeds,

PARAGRAPH STRUCTURE

Additionally, persuasive writing requires appropriate paragraph structure. If your paragraphs are too long, the readers' eyes tire, and they lose interest. Conversely, if your paragraphs are too short, your writing becomes too choppy to engage the reader. Nonetheless, you can use paragraph length and structure to enhance your persuasiveness.

If you have a fact that you must include, but that you wish to de-emphasize, you might consider burying it in the middle of a long paragraph. That way, you have not ignored the fact, but you also have not made it stand out to the reader in any way.

If what you have to say takes only one sentence, it probably can be incorporated into one of the paragraphs preceding or following it. The primary exception to this rule is when the one sentence paragraph is used for emphasis. One sentence paragraphs should be used very sparingly, or they lose their strength.

BAD EXAMPLE

Brad's closing statement emphasized Mr. Williams' generosity in helping his friend move the refrigerator, and downplayed the fact that he had left the scene of an accident. The prosecutor's closing statement emphasized exactly the reverse; it focused on the irresponsibility of leaving the scene of an accident that Mr. Williams had caused, and it highlighted the severity of the victim's injuries.

The prosecutor reminded the jury that Mr. Williams had left the victim, whom he had blinded through his irresponsibility.

You could incorporate the second paragraph into the first one for continuity and to prevent choppiness.

> ### GOOD EXAMPLE ONE
>
> Brad's closing statement emphasized Mr. Williams' generosity in helping his friend move the refrigerator, and downplayed the fact that he had left the scene of an accident. The prosecutor's closing statement emphasized exactly the reverse; it focused on the irresponsibility of leaving the scene of an accident that Mr. Williams had caused, and it highlighted the severity of the victim's injuries. The prosecutor reminded the jury that Mr. Williams had left the victim, whom he had blinded through his irresponsibility.

However, for emphasis, and remember that this technique is only effective when used very sparingly, you might write the following:

> ### GOOD EXAMPLE TWO
>
> Brad's closing statement emphasized Mr. Williams' generosity in helping his friend move the refrigerator, and downplayed the fact that he had left the scene of an accident. The prosecutor's closing statement emphasized exactly the reverse; it focused on the irresponsibility of leaving the scene of an accident that Mr. Williams had caused, and it highlighted the severity of the victim's injuries.
>   Mr. Williams had recklessly blinded the man and then had run away.

In this example, the single sentence paragraph highlights the most persuasive portion of the prosecutor's case. This technique is used rarely and only for great emphasis. As a rule, you will not write one sentence paragraphs until you are a far more sophisticated legal writer.

APPEARANCE

Finally, when writing for the court or opposing counsel, as well as for your attorney or the attorney's client, remember to look at the document and ensure it has enough "white space" to be readable. This will make the document less psychologically daunting and more inviting to read. Avoid overly long paragraphs and give the readers a chance to mentally catch their breath. White space also provides the reader with points of reference on the page and allows them time to reflect on what you have written.

Persuasive writing requires close attention to the focus of your document. You must be sure to emphasize the facts that help your case, and downplay those that do not. Nonetheless, you always must be honest and not omit material facts. Use active voice for favorable facts, and use the passive voice selectively to de-emphasize harmful facts. But never omit a material fact. If you do, you may be certain that the opposing side will seize upon your omission and make it more damaging than the admission ever would have been. More importantly, your attorney's reputation is of supreme importance in his or her ability to practice law. One instance of dishonesty will ruin the attorney's reputation for the rest of his or her career. Think of it as breaking a precious vase; once it is broken, it is broken forever. Without credibility, the attorney will lose the respect of the court and his or her peers, and the courts will not trust the attorney's word. Additionally, it will not help your chances of getting another job when the attorney fires you for ruining his or her reputation. The legal community is small and tight-knit, even in a large city. Your lack of ethics and its effect on your reputation will follow you throughout your career. Persuasive writing is effective, but it also must be honest.

You have additional tools to make your writing more persuasive. Use parallelism for emphasis and continuity, and craft your paragraphs to the most effective length. Be sure to provide sufficient white space on your pages, so you do not fatigue your readers' eyes.

■ SPOKEN LANGUAGE VERSUS WRITTEN LANGUAGE

New legal writers often have difficulty recognizing language that is correct when spoken but incorrect when written. While we use contractions regularly in speaking, they have no place in a formal legal document. Similarly, colloquial and slang terms do not belong in formal legal writing. While a colloquialism might not be significant to readers who live in the area where the colloquialism commonly is used, it certainly will jar and perhaps even confuse readers from other areas.

Another problem new legal writers encounter is using the wrong spelling of a word that sounds the same when spoken as the word they mean to use. These words are called homonyms, and while some are confused consistently throughout the country, others are limited to certain geographic areas or dialects.

Similarly, when we speak a number, it has only one spoken form. In formal writing, however, there are specific places where the number is written out in letters and others where the Arabic numeral is used.

Additionally, modern life is rife with acronyms, and when you use an acronym in your writing, you must introduce it properly. We might look at a smokestack spewing smelly pollution and say, "Why doesn't the EPA do something about that?" In writing, however, we would have to introduce the acronym "EPA" properly, the Environmental Protection Agency (EPA).

Another area in which we compensate in speech and in informal writing is the absence of a gender-neutral third person plural pronoun. When the gender of a person being discussed is not known, we often refer to the person as "they," although we may be referencing only one person. If the unknown person could also be referred to as multiple unknown persons, try to use the plural. So if you are discussing a situation involving students, begin referring to "the students" rather than "the student." That way, when you have to refer back to your subject, the use of the plural pronoun "they" will be correct. If you specifically are referencing an individual whose gender is unknown, it is correct to refer to the person as "he or she," although that sounds more stilted.

No Contractions

An important point to remember when writing a formal document is to write out verbs and not use contractions. A contraction is the combination of a verb with either the negative or another verb. The verb "cannot" is the proper form of the contraction "can't." The verbs "would have" are the proper form of the contraction "would've." Contractions are never appropriate in formal writing, unless the writer is quoting another person.

Because contractions are so ingrained in our speaking pattern, this point bears repeating; do not use contractions in formal writing. Despite that caveat, a surprising number of students include contractions in their written assignments. These same students tell us that they looked for contractions when they proofread their documents, but because they are so ingrained in our speech, the students did not recognize them.

BAD EXAMPLE

The judge instructed the jury that it couldn't take notes during the trial.

GOOD EXAMPLE

The judge instructed the jury that it could not take notes during the trial.

BAD EXAMPLE

One of the jurors didn't understand why he could not take notes.

GOOD EXAMPLE

One of the jurors did not understand why he could not take notes.

BAD EXAMPLE

It wasn't that hard to remember what the witnesses said.

GOOD EXAMPLE

It was not that hard to remember what the witnesses said.

EXERCISE

Identify the errors in the following sentences and correct them. The errors are not limited to the material in this chapter, but also include grammar and punctuation.

1. I'll research that topic and won't stop until I have all the law on it.
2. The judge can't give another extension of time unless she doesn't remember her ruling that she wouldn't give any more extensions before trial.
3. The plaintiff has to realize they do not have a valid legal claim.
4. The juror is sworn not to discuss the trial until they are through with the trial.
5. A lawyer takes an oath of office; he or she has to remind him or herself of it from time to time.
6. Brad had joined the ABA when he graduated from law school, and one of his fraternity brothers, who had taken a different path in life, joined the PGA.

EXERCISE

Read the following paragraph and change the spoken language mode to formal written language.

When Ana's paralegal, Pat, began her paralegal studies, she was in a class with a student that snapped their gum incessantly. Pat couldn't tune out the annoying snapping, but she'd have had to confront the annoying student, and they were known to be mean and vindictive. She asked the SGA president about how they would handle the problem, but they said, "I'm the student government association president. Where in SGA does it include 'advice columnist?'" Pat wondered how such a nasty woman could be elected to student government, but she realized that she would have to deal with the man and his gum or learn to tune it out. She wondered whether the president of the ABA had better manners, or if they were just SGA presidents who moved up in the legal world.

Colloquial and Slang Words

In formal legal writing, you should not use any colloquial or slang terms. A word or expression is colloquial when it is appropriate for informal conversation but not for formal writing. For example, one friend greeting another might say, "How ya doing?" In a formal situation, one person will say to another, "How are you?" The slang version of this greeting might be "What's up?" or "What's happening?"

Many colloquialisms are regional, so that a person from one part of the country or another country would not grasp the speaker's meaning. For example, in New England, a milkshake is called a frappe. In parts of Ohio, soda is called pop; in Massachusetts, it is called tonic. In Pennsylvania, to clear away clutter is to "red up" or "rid up."

Other regional colloquialisms are comprehensible to others, but they sound unusual or wrong. A Northerner might say, "It gets tiresome;" a Southerner might say, "It gets old." A Midwesterner might say, "That ice cream is really good;" a New Englander would say it was "wicked good." Although the pervasiveness of television and social media has reduced the differences in speech patterns around the country, charming examples still exist.

Slang words and expressions are forms of colloquialisms that may be specific to a certain group, often young people as a way of separating them from the older generation. As slang becomes adopted by the mainstream, it loses its appeal to the group that started it, and that group, or the next group of young people, will create new expressions to confound the older generation. In legal writing, your goal is to communicate clearly. Slang, by its very nature, is intended to be exclusive to a certain group; it therefore has no place in writing that is meant to convey information to all groups of people.

Colloquial and slang language is not inherently wrong. In fact, in the proper context, it is appropriate. It becomes a problem when it is used in the wrong context, which is usually a more formal situation. As social media become more prevalent, people are having trouble discerning the difference between formal and informal communications, and they are having trouble even knowing proper language for formal situations. The country is becoming more casual, but in a legal setting, formality is still obligatory.

Remember that in this course you are expected to use language that is appropriate for the legal setting. Even your e-mails to your professors should be written as formally as a letter to the court would be. Informal or colloquial writings make you look unprofessional, thereby hurting your chances for a good job after you complete your paralegal studies. Just as you would not appear in court in shorts and a tee shirt, you should not communicate in a legal context in similarly casual language.

Many people are so accustomed to casual language that they are not aware that they are using slang or colloquialisms. For example, would you realize that some of the language in the following paragraph was colloquial?

> Mrs. Pritchett, an elderly retired school teacher, sought Brad's counsel concerning a contract she had signed to have the roof replaced on her house. Brad quickly realized that Mrs. Pritchett had been conned in a scam. Clearly, the salesman who dealt with her was very sharp; she was nobody's fool. Because her ownership of her home was at issue, Brad realized that the situation was intense. Mrs. Pritchett had been Brad's third grade teacher, and Brad began to get steamed at the person who had swindled her.

There are eight colloquialisms in that paragraph. How many can you identify?

Mrs. Pritchett, an elderly retired school teacher, sought Brad's counsel concerning a contract she had signed to have the roof replaced on her house. Brad quickly realized that Mrs. Pritchett had been <u>conned</u> in a <u>scam</u>. Clearly, the salesman who <u>dealt</u> with her was very <u>sharp</u>, because she was <u>nobody's fool</u>. Because her ownership of her home was at issue, Brad realized that the situation was <u>intense</u>. Mrs. Pritchett had been Brad's third grade teacher, and Brad began to get <u>steamed</u> at the person who had <u>swindled</u> her.

EXAMPLES

- Con is slang for deceive.
- Scam is slang for a plan to cheat.
- Dealt is slang for contracted with.
- Sharp is slang for clever, quick, or skilled.
- Nobody's fool is slang for an intelligent person.
- Intense is slang for very serious.
- Steamed is slang for became angry.
- Swindled is slang for defrauded.

Sometimes you have to think about what the appropriate word or expression would be for a situation.

EXAMPLES

Colloquial

Get: I don't get the math homework.

Standard

Understand: I don't understand the math homework.

Colloquial

Flaky: How can she be a judge? She is so flaky.

Standard

Scattered, unreliable: How can she be a judge? She is so unreliable.

Colloquial

Eat the cost: He will never pay the bill. The firm will have to eat the cost.

Standard

Absorb, write off: He will never pay the bill. The firm will have to absorb the cost.

Colloquial

Glitch: There is a glitch in this computer program.

Standard

Flaw: There is a flaw in this computer program.

Colloquial

An earful: The client gave Brad an earful after she lost her case.

Standard

Speech: The client gave Brad a stern speech after she lost her case.

Colloquial

Meltdown: Upon cross examination, the witness had a meltdown.

Standard

Lost control: Upon cross examination, the witness lost control.

Colloquial

Airhead: That attorney is a real airhead.

Standard

Scattered, stupid: That attorney is very scattered and stupid.

Colloquial

Action: Tonight, I am going to find a party with some action.

Standard

Fun activity: Tonight, I am going to find a party with some fun activities.

Colloquial

Bent out of shape: That client really got bent out of shape when she lost.

Standard

Upset: That client really got upset when she lost.

Colloquial

Cushy: That paralegal thinks this will be a cushy job.

Standard

Easy: That paralegal thinks this will be an easy job.

Colloquial

Damage: Ana shopped and did some damage.

Standard

Spent a lot of money: Ana shopped and spent a lot of money.

Colloquial

Knock: I could not believe the judge knocked the settlement we reached.

Standard

Criticized: I could not believe the judge criticized the settlement we reached.

Colloquial

Awesome: Ana gave an awesome opening statement.

Standard

Impressive: Ana gave an impressive statement.

Colloquial

Chewed out: After opposing counsel lied, the judge really chewed him out.

> *Standard*
>
> Scolded: After opposing counsel lied, the judge really scolded him.
>
> *Colloquial*
>
> Deep pockets: A good corporate defendant has deep pockets.
>
> *Standard*
>
> Resources to pay a judgment: A good corporate defendant has the resources to pay a judgment.

Note that this last slang is common in legal offices. The opposite is a defendant who is "judgment-proof," meaning he does not have any money to pay a judgment.

EXERCISE

Compare documents A and B. Which one is more formal? Which is informal? Circle the colloquial and slang words and phrases in the informal letter.

Version one:

Memorandum

To: Ana Garcia

From: Pat Paralegal

Re: Potential client Tanya Geddings

Ms. Geddings, a distraught woman in her early twenties, requested an appointment with you to discuss her divorce action against her husband. Ms. Geddings appeared to be a possible victim of domestic violence; she had a black eye and her arm was in a cast. She was frightened and timid. She asked if she could meet with you in a room without windows. I scheduled her for an appointment on Wednesday, November 6th, when she was certain her husband would be at work.

Version two:

Hey Ana,

Tanya Geddings stopped by for an appointment today. She's young, but she was all beat up and got spooked real easy. She was so shaken up that she wanted her appointment in a room without windows! She wants to divorce her husband, and he sounded like a real dirt ball. She is so freaked out that she kept looking over her shoulder. Her appointment is for next Wednesday when her old man will be working.

EXERCISE

Identify the words or phrases that are appropriate for legal communications.

1. Run the complaint to the clerk.
   File the complaint with the Clerk of Courts.
2. Lose the attitude and get moving on the discovery.
   Get serious and prepare the answers to discovery.
3. Grab the file and straighten it out.
   Get the file and organize it clearly.
4. Buzz the other side and set up a depo of their guy.
   Call opposing counsel and schedule a deposition of their client.
5. Run a check on this guy and see if it's worth taking the case.
   Research the potential defendant's assets to see whether he could pay any judgment against him.

EXERCISE

Correct the following letter by replacing any colloquial word and slang with formal words.

Dear Opposing Counsel;

On October 16, 20XX, this firm sent your firm discovery requests for Gedding v. Gedding. Please get on the stick and return the completed discovery before we have to run to tell the Judge that you are blowing off your duties. We expect you to get your act together, even though we know that your client is a loser. If you are too lame to pin him down to complete discovery, we will have to file a motion to compel. Our client is hot to get this thing done, and she is not going to fritter away any more time on him.

Thank you for getting it together and returning the completed discovery.

Ciao,

Brad

EXERCISE

Read the paragraph below, an excerpt of the first draft of Brad's trial brief, and then change the incorrect details of formal writing or information to create a well written and accurate document. Then rewrite it from the prosecutor's point of view.

On the day in question, Mr. Williams was doing a favor for a friend, helping him move a refrigerator. While in transit to the friend's home, an untoward situation occurred. Mr. Williams can't remember much of what happened, but he feels awful about what took place. Because the refrigerator was not damaged, Mr. Williams assumed that no significant damage was done to the car behind the truck. Certainly, if he had known there was a problem, he would have helped. PPD Officer Blackstone did not stop at the friend's house until six months later, and that was the first time that Mr. Williams realized there might be trouble. Six months later, as you may well imagine, his memory of one day is certainly dimmed. The Parkhurst Police Department, PPD, can't expect someone to remember that far back.

Confusing/Misused Word Pairs

Confusing word pairs present a common problem in writing in English. It is important for you as the paralegal to be able to recognize when a document contains the wrong word, so you can avoid making your attorney look unprofessional. As we will discuss later, spell check misses these kinds of errors most of the time, so you cannot rely on spell check to catch them. Some confusing word pairs are a result of homonyms, words that sound the same but are spelled differently. Notice how many of the examples contain this type of confusion.

EXAMPLES

A: This is the indefinite article that precedes a word beginning with a consonant.
An: This is the indefinite article that precedes a word beginning with a vowel.

The judge gave the defendant a long sentence.
The defendant's attorney made an objection to the long sentence.

Accept: Accept means to believe, or to take something as given.
Except: Except means a thing is excluded.

Brad accepted the fact that he would never be a corporate attorney.
Ana was happy to accept the diamond engagement ring Brad gave her.
Despite the snow storm, we all made it in to the office except the secretary.

Advice: Advice is a noun that means to give guidance to another.
Advise: Advise is a verb that means to give counsel or advice to someone.

"Let me give you a piece of advice," the judge told the litigant.
The officer advised the driver to slow down if he did not want a ticket.

The following is one of the most common word pairs causing confusion in formal writing.

Affect: Affect is a verb meaning to influence or change.
Effect: Effect is a noun that means a result or consequence.

The defendant's testimony certainly will affect the jury's verdict.
The defendant's testimony had a negative effect on his case.

There are exceptions to the rule concerning affect and effect. In psychology, the word affect is used as a noun to describe a person's demeanor. A psychologist might describe a depressed patient as having a flat affect.

Similarly, the word effect is in rare instances used as a verb. "Each candidate for office promised to effect change in the tax structure."

For the most part, however, affect will be used as a verb and effect will be used as noun.

A lot: Means many, a large number.
A lot: Means a parcel of real estate.
Allot: Means to apportion or assign part of something.

Brad noticed the firm had received a lot of traffic cases that month.
One of the clients wanted assistance with buying a lot next to his home.
When Sheila was charge nurse, she was careful to allot an equal amount of work to each nurse.

The next example occurs in certain dialects and areas of the country. For some readers, the confusion will be unclear. Other readers, though, will recognize this error. We have received papers with this error from our students.

Ask: To inquire, to question.
Ax: A sharp implement used to chop wood.

"I will ask Pat to draft a letter for me," Ana thought.
Brad was appalled that the murder weapon was an ax.

Assure: Means to promise or to guarantee.
Insure: Means to indemnify or cover.
Ensure: Means to guarantee or make certain.

The salesman had assured Mrs. Pritchett he would do a good job.
Brad called his agent to insure Ana's ring as soon as possible.

Ana filed the complaint against the salesman in person to ensure it was filed properly.

Note that in some legal situations, insure and ensure are interchangeable.

Bad: An adjective, that can modify only a noun or pronoun.
Badly: An adverb, that can modify verbs, adjectives, and other adverbs.

The salesman had done a bad job on Mrs. Pritchett's roof.
Ana very badly wanted to make the salesman return Mrs. Pritchett's money.

Bare: Means naked, exposed, unadorned.
Bear: Means to tolerate or put up with. It also can mean to carry.
Bear: A large mammal with fur. (We are not likely to use this version.)

Brad's law school apartment had been bare except for a bed and a desk.
Ana had not understood how he could bear to live so simply.
The Second Amendment gives citizens the right to bear arms.

Between: Describes the relationship of two things.
Among: Describes the relationship of more than two things.

The paralegal's work was evenly assigned between Brad and Ana.
The paralegal had been among the four top students in the class.

Capital: Refers to the city that is a seat of government, or to assets or resources.
Capitol: Refers to the actual building where the government meets.

Brad planned a trip to the nation's capital, Washington, D.C.
He was especially eager to see the Capitol Building.

Complimentary: Means flattering or approving.
Complementary: Means corresponding or balancing, or to make complete.

Brad received jury feedback that was complimentary.
Brad's quiet nature and Ana's gregariousness were complementary.

Comprise: Means to consist of, to include or encompass.
Compose: Means to create or write. It also means to collect oneself.
Consist: Means to be made up of.

The firm's clients comprise a spectrum of society.
Ana sat down to compose a Motion for Summary Judgment.
After testifying, the nervous witness composed herself.
The Court's dockets consist of half civil and half criminal cases.

Confidant: Is a person who is a sounding board, a close friend, or who shares secrets or private thoughts.
Confident: Means secure, positive, self-assured.

Since grade school, Carolyn and Ana had been confidants.
After many trials, Brad was more confident of his skills.

Counsel: To advise or to warn.
Council: A committee, board, or elected body.

Brad was careful to counsel all his clients to behave ethically.
Brad declined to run for City Counsel, fearing it would take away from his law practice.

Ethics: Moral principles or philosophies.
Ethnic: Of a certain group, culture, tribe, or ancestry.

Legal Ethics is the most important course you will take.
Ana's ethnic background was Puerto Rican.

Fair: Just, reasonable, or of pale complexion, or a seasonal community gathering.
Fare: a price for a mode of travel, or, how one does in a venture.

Brad was pleased to have his case assigned to a fair judge.
The witness described the suspect as tall and fair.
Growing up, Ana had always enjoyed the County Fair.
The plane fare was too high, so the witness drove to the trial.
The defendant expected to fare well in the trial.

Few: Describes a quantity that can be counted, represents a specific number.
Less: Describes a volume or mass that cannot be counted by number.

Their first month in practice, they had only a few clients: three to be precise.
They still had less work than they wanted but knew they had to be patient.

Foul: Means unclean, stinking, disgusting, or, unfair/out-of bounds, or, to taint.
Fowl: Means poultry, a bird domesticated for consumption.

The fish scraps left in the trash over the weekend gave the office a foul smell.
At the baseball game, Brad nearly was hit by a foul ball.
Ana smiled when opposing counsel fouled up his closing statement.
Ana was cooking fowl, specifically, turkey, for Thanksgiving.

Hi: A greeting upon seeing another, the informal version of "hello."
High: Elevated, lofty, above many things, noble, the opposite of low.

"Hi," Tommy said to the receptionist when he came to see Brad.
The Supreme Court is the high court of the land.
Ana could not reach the books high on the top shelf.

Illicit: Means illegal, criminal.
Elicit: Means to extract, to draw out.

Brad warned Mr. Williams not to engage in any illicit behavior.
Brad knew the prosecutor would try to elicit a confession.

Lie: To recline, to become supine, to be in a horizontal position.
NOTE: lie does not take a direct object.
Lay: To place, to set down. NOTE: Lay takes a direct object—an object is placed, laid down.

After a week of trials, Ana could not wait to go home and lie down.
"Please lay the book on my desk," Ana asked the paralegal.

Passed: Approved, went ahead of, to approve of, to skip a turn.
Past: Before the present, already completed.

The legislature barely passed the tax bill.
Brad passed opposing counsel in the hall of the courthouse.
Ana passed on using a challenge for juror number three.
Brad was glad his first trial was in the past.

Principal: Means primary, key, or major.
Principle: Means a standard, rule, or law.

Keeping Mr. Williams out of jail was Brad's principal goal.
Nonetheless, he would not compromise his principles to do so.

Set: To place, position, or lay down.
Sit: To take a seat, to be seated.

The paralegal had to set down her pen to shake the client's hand.
The client appeared glad to have a chance to sit down.

Shirk: To evade, avoid, or get out of doing a duty.
Shrink: To become smaller.

Brad suspected that Mr. Williams was going to shirk his duties.
The nervous witness seemed to shrink as he sunk into the chair.

The next confused word pair is limited to certain parts of the country. One of your authors has encountered it frequently when teaching in a specific geographic area.

Specific: Particular, precise, the exact one.
Pacific: The ocean between Asia and the west coast of the Americas.

Brad had a specific point he wanted to get across to the jury.
Ana's family lived in the northern part of Puerto Rico, so she had seen the Atlantic but not the Pacific ocean.

Stationary: Static, still, staying in one place, not moving.
Stationery: Paper used for letters.

Although they wanted to rearrange the office, Ana and Brad discovered that the receptionist's desk was stationary.
Ana was excited when the firm got their letterhead stationery.

Suppose: Presume, understand, or believe.
Supposed: Hypothetical, theoretical, or obligated.
Opposed: Conflicting, on opposite sides.

Brad asked Ana, "Do you suppose Mr. Williams can get probation?"
She answered, "Jail is supposed to be a punishment, but so is probation."
The prosecutor opposed a sentence of probation because Mr. Williams had left the scene of the accident.

Then: Subsequently, after, in that case, at a specific moment.
This: A pronoun referring to a closer or certain object, as opposed to another.
Than: A conjunction that introduces the second part of a comparison.

First, Ana had to pass the bar. Then she could practice law.
After the interviews, Brad and Ana knew they wanted this paralegal.
They found Pat to be more professional than the other applicants.

Their: The plural possessive, indicating group ownership or characteristic.
There: A pronoun indicating a place, or, indicating proximity.
They're: A contraction combining the pronoun "they" with the verb "are." This is not used in formal writing.

Tommy Williams was their first client.
"Please sit there, in the comfortable chair," Brad invited Tommy.
At 5:30 pm, they're leaving for the day.

To: Toward, in the direction of.
Too: In addition, also.
Two: A number more than one and less than three.

After picking up the briefs, Ana went to court.
When she saw Brad, she waited, because he was coming too.
The two of them walked over to the courthouse together.

Which: A pronoun introducing a non-essential part of a sentence, set off by a comma.
That: A pronoun introducing an essential part of a sentence. It is not set off by a comma.

NOTE: In English, the word "that" is often implied and not actually spoken or written. Law was the career she had chosen. The word "that" is implied: Law was the career <u>that</u> she had chosen.

Tommy always paid his father's legal bills on time, which pleased Brad.
The crime that Mr. Williams committed was quite serious.
The crime Mr. Williams committed was quite serious. (implied)

Who: The subjective case of this pronoun. Use it when it is the subject of the clause.
Whom: The objective case of this pronoun. Use it when it is the direct object or the object of a preposition.

"Who do you suppose will hear this case?" Brad asked.
"To whom will it be assigned?" he wondered.
Whom did the jury select for foreman?

Whose: A pronoun indicating ownership by an unspecified person.
Who's: The contraction of the pronoun "who" and the verb "is" or "has."
This is not used in formal writing.

Ana wondered whose boots were in the reception area of the firm.
Brad told her, "They belong to a client who's meeting with me."

Your: The pronoun indicating the second person possessive.
You're: The contraction of the pronoun "you" and the verb "are.
This is not used in formal writing.

"The prosecutor hopes your testimony will convict your father," Brad told Tommy.
Brad warned Tommy, "You're going to be called as a witness by the prosecution."

EXERCISE

Read the following paragraphs and correct the misused words which were explained in this chapter. Be careful: some of them are used correctly.

Mr. Williams set in Brad's office. He and Brad were discussing the case among themselves. Brad again counciled Mr. Williams to say nothing to anyone, especially to his son Tommy, whom knew nothing about the incident with the refrigerator. "Who's business is it, anyway?" Brad axed him. "The pacific point is the prosecutor is going to try to cry fowl because you left the scene. He will argue that it is the principal of the matter that counts. He will make it sound like that is more important then the fact that it was a accident." Mr. Williams agreed. "There going to want to hang me, that am for sure." Nonetheless, Mr. Williams was confidant that he would fair well with Brad as his council. Brad had always gotten him out of jams in the passed. He knew Brad's skills would have the same affect, accept he was not sure how good the prosecutor was. Brad's advise was to sit tight and keep his mouth shut, and he planned to stay stationery in his home, talking to no one. He would lay on his couch and remember the ethnics Brad had taught him: be honest, but only answer what their asking, and no more.

EXERCISE

Read the following paragraph and correct any errors of any kind, including misused words, grammar, and punctuation. Retype the paragraph with the errors corrected.

Mr. Williams takes Brads advise and when his son Tommy axed him questions, he would not answer. Tommy did not take it personal, he knew his father had an good reason to avoid a issue. Tommy excepted his fathers silence. Knowing Brad as he does, Tommy figured there was some principal involved. Besides, Tommy would never comprise his fathers case. He suppose his father had a better chance of winning with Brad and Ana than with any other firm. Among Brad and Ana, Tommy could not even decide witch were the better attorney. He just knew that Brad will have a good affect on the jury. If anyone could illicit sympathy for his father, Brad could. He just hoped that the case was assigned to a fare judge. His father would not even tell Tommy whose the judge on the case.

EXERCISE

Brad has asked Pat to summarize the prosecutor's opening statement to assist him during trial in focusing on areas the prosecutor emphasized. Read the following paragraph and correct the misused words. Then draft a summary of the prosecutor's opening statement in a form that would be useful to the attorney.

In her opening statement, the prosecutor illicited allot of the jury's interest. She pointed out how by leaving the scene of the accident, Mr. Williams engaged in elicit behavior. "Whose going to be confidant in his testimony, when he acted so bad at the time of the accident?" she axed the jury. "He has already shown that he had no intention of acting ethnically. The bear truth is, he was willing to let the person he hurt set there with the shattered windshield lie in his lap. I insure you, he is not a nice person." She went on to describe Mr. Williams' fowl play when he shrinked his duty to report the accident. She pointed out that if Mr. Williams had not confided in his confident, who then tried to blackmail him, his actions would never have been known. "Your going to decide whether society is willing to except this heinous behavior. Imagine if the person who he blinded was you're loved one. This badly behavior must be punished." She concluded that the judge would advice them on the law, but she hoped he would not get a sentence of less than five years in prison. She offered them some advise; "Think about what is fare. Discuss it between yourselves. You have two choices to pick among. You can set there and think, well this is all in the passed, so we will let it go. Or you can sit your minds on doing the right thing and punish him. Live up to you're principals."

Correct Form of Numbers

A detail that often confuses new writers is how to write numbers in a formal document. Should you use Arabic numerals, or should you write the number out? Although different sources provide varying answers to this question, the general rule in law, as indicated in the *The Bluebook: A Uniform System of Citation* (Columbia Law Review Ass'n et al. eds., 19th ed. 2013), is to spell out numbers up to ninety-nine and to use numerals for higher numbers. If, however, the number starts the sentence, then it is always spelled out. Thus, you would write, "One hundred and fifty friends of the victim arrived at the courthouse," not "150 friends of the victim arrived at the courthouse." If the numbers are in a series, for the sake of clarity, they are written out. Thus, you would write, "The prosecutor and Brad asked the witness 15, 24, and then 13 questions respectively." But you would write, "The prosecutor asked the witness fifteen questions, and Brad asked the witness twenty-four questions. Then the prosecutor asked the witness thirteen questions on re-examination."

When writing numbers that indicate a date, always use numerals for the date and year, and spell out the month completely. Thus, you would write, "The Declaration of Independence was signed on July 4, 1776," not "The Declaration of Independence was signed on 7/4/1776," and not "The Declaration of Independence was signed on July fourth, one thousand, seven hundred and seventy-six."

Notice in this last example that when writing a number over twenty that requires two words, you put a hyphen between the two numbers. Thus, "He finished college when he was twenty-one years old," not "He finished college when he was twenty one years old." This does not hold true for numbers with three digits: you would write "One hundred and twenty-two" or "One hundred twenty-two," not "one hundred-twenty-two."

Acronyms

Acronyms are inherently confusing, but unfortunately, their use is widespread, and they often appear in formal writing. Especially when referring to government agencies and professional organizations, the use of acronyms is common. The first time you refer to an organization or agency that commonly uses its acronym in your document, you write out the name of the organization or agency, and then indicate the acronym in parentheses immediately after it. For your readers' convenience, if you reuse an acronym after not using for several pages, you might repeat the full title that the acronym abbreviates.

An example of a common acronym is "Ana had to go to the Bureau of Motor Vehicles (BMV) to renew her driver's license." The use of quotation marks around the acronym in the parentheses is a matter of your attorney's preference, although the trend in legal writing is toward simplicity and omitting the quotation marks. But it is not incorrect to write, "Ana had to go the Bureau of Motor Vehicles ("BMV") to renew her driver's license." Some attorneys might prefer the older method of indicating the abbreviation, which was "Ana had to go the Bureau of Motor Vehicles (hereinafter, "BMV") to renew her driver's license." Although this form is falling out of favor, you will write the way your employer prefers.

As we saw earlier, people use the acronym "EPA" in speech, and they rarely refer to the agency as the Environment Protection Agency. Although the speakers and listeners know what the EPA does, in a formal written document, unlike in speech, you write out the full name the first time you use the acronym.

■ ETHICAL AND ACCURATE WRITING

For legal writing to achieve its purpose, to persuade, it must be honest and accurate. Honesty involves more than telling the truth and not omitting salient facts. It also means never presenting someone else's work as your own. Doing so constitutes plagiarism.

Accuracy requires the use of the correct word at the correct time and writing a grammatically correct document. Earlier, we addressed the confused/misused word pairs that sound the same or very similar. Misusing any of these words is a disservice to your client, because they will distract or even confuse the readers. We have alluded to the fact that you cannot rely on spell and grammar check, and we will discuss this fact more fully below, with multiple examples of errors spell check has missed, and worse, "corrections" it has suggested that would have turned correct text into grammatically incorrect text.

First, we will discuss the serious matter of plagiarism.

Plagiarism

Being absolutely certain that what you have written as your own text is entirely your own original material is essential to legal writing. Equally important is properly setting off the text you take from someone else's writing in quotation marks and properly attributing the quote to the exact source. Be aware, also, that you can plagiarize concepts that are unique to a source, even when you do not use the same words as the source. If a physicist reworded Albert Einstein's theory of relativity without citing to the source of the idea, the physicist would have plagiarized.

Although this concept should be obvious to everyone, nonetheless, famous authors have, either by honest mistake or by intentional deception, plagiarized portions of dissertations and even published works.

These breaches of integrity have ruined the reputations and careers of the authors who plagiarized. Some authors have lost prestigious teaching positions. Some have had advanced degrees withdrawn. All have lost the most valuable resource an intellectual or professional can have: reputation.

It can be difficult for new writers to recognize when they inadvertently have plagiarized their material. For example, at the beginning of each new semester, your authors give their students a syllabus quiz. This forces the students to actually read the syllabus. The syllabus always contains a definition of plagiarism, and we always spend time discussing it in the first class. Despite this discussion, and the express warning to not copy the definition of plagiarism verbatim, when the students answer the quiz question asking them to define plagiarism, 90 percent of the students copy the definition verbatim from the syllabus without using quotation marks or citing the source.

Experts differ in their opinions concerning the number of consecutive words that may be copied from another source before something constitutes plagiarism. Some experts consider using three consecutive words from another source to be plagiarism. Other experts put the number at five words and others ten words. However, some terms of art like "a breach of contract" or "meeting of the minds" are so commonly used that repeating them verbatim could not constitute plagiarism. We recommend that if you are unsure whether you have used too many words verbatim from your source, you should put those words in quotation marks and cite the source.

So, although there is not a set number of words that constitutes plagiarism, it is sometimes necessary to use the exact words someone else wrote, either for clarity or efficiency. Also, some attorneys prefer to have their paralegals quote from a source rather than paraphrasing. When you quote directly, you must make sure that you quote accurately and include inside your quote all the words you have taken from the source. Some students make the mistake of leaving part of the quoted material in their text outside the quotation marks, which results in plagiarism. Occasionally, a student will miscopy the quote, inadvertently changing its meaning, particularly when they are omitting nonessential portions of the quote.

If you are quoting 50 or more words from another source, the quote is set off in block quotes. Block quotes are single spaced and indented five places on each side and do not have quotation marks.

As a rule, when in doubt regarding whether you need to put text into a quotation, err on the side of caution. It is better to place something in a quote than to risk plagiarizing.

Spell and Grammar Check

Spell and grammar check give a writer a false sense of security that everything in the document is spelled correctly and that the grammar is correct. Unfortunately, this is too often not the case. Spell check often does not recognize when a homonym is used mistakenly if one of the correct spellings of the word is used.

In the first exercise in the section of this chapter titled Misused/Confused Word Pairs, the paragraph contained twenty one errors. Grammar and spell check pointed out only five errors. Additionally, it found an "error" that was not incorrect.

Grammar check will often underline something and offer a "correction" that is wrong, while what you had will be correct. In that same exercise, grammar check wanted to change, "There going to want to hang me, that's for sure" to "There going to want to hang me, that am for sure." Grammar check wanted to change the verb tense to an incorrect form. Spell check also failed to identify the misuse of the form of "there," which should have been "they're."

After it made this "correction," grammar check then wanted to remove the comma between "want to hang me, that am for sure," while ignoring the use of the wrong verb that it had suggested. Underlined below are the words or portions that grammar and spell check caught.

EXAMPLE ONE

Mr. Williams set in Brad's office. He and Brad were discussing the case among themselves. Brad again <u>counciled</u> Mr. Williams to say nothing to anyone, especially to his son Tommy, whom knew nothing about the incident with the refrigerator. "<u>Who's</u> business is it, anyway?" Brad axed him. "The pacific point is the prosecutor is going to try to cry fowl because you left the scene. He will argue that it is the principal of the matter that counts. He will make it sound like that is more important then the fact that it was <u>a</u> accident." Mr. Williams agreed. "There going to want to hang <u>me, that</u> am for sure." Nonetheless, Mr. Williams was confidant that he would fair well with Brad as his council. Brad had always gotten him out of jams in the passed. He knew Brad's skills would have the same affect, accept he was not sure how good the prosecutor was. Brad's <u>advise</u> was to sit tight and keep his mouth shut, and he planned to stay stationery in his home, talking to no one. He would <u>lay</u> on his couch and remember the ethnics Brad had taught him: be honest, but only answer what their asking, and no more.

Similarly, in the second exercise, excerpted below, grammar and spell check caught six errors out of seventeen. In this example, it did not suggest changing something that was correct.

EXAMPLE TWO

Mr. Williams takes Brads <u>advise</u> and when his son Tommy axed him questions, he would not answer. Tommy did not take it personal; he knew his father had <u>an</u> good reason to avoid a issue. Tommy <u>excepted</u> his fathers silence. Knowing Brad as he did, Tommy figured there was some principal involved. Besides, Tommy would never comprise his <u>fathers</u> case. He <u>suppose</u> his father had a better chance of winning with Brad and Ana than with any other firm. Among Brad and Ana, Tommy could not even decide witch were the better attorney. He just knew that Brad would have a good affect on the jury. If anyone could illicit sympathy for his father, Brad could. He just hoped that the case was assigned to a fare judge. His father would not even tell Tommy <u>whose</u> the judge on the case.

In the next exercise, excerpted below, spell and grammar check noted five errors out of nine, a better average than usual. Unfortunately, it also found three "errors" that were not wrong. In two cases, it ignored or did not recognize the implied subordinating "that" in a sentence with two clauses. In the other case, grammar check wanted to insert a coordinating conjunction between two subordinate clauses. Granted, the second subordinate clause had an implied "then" that subordinated it. Nonetheless, to have added the coordinating conjunction would have changed the sentence. The original sentence read, "She pointed out that if Mr. Williams had not confided in his confident, who then tried to blackmail him, his actions would never have been known." Grammar check wanted to change this sentence to "She pointed out that if Mr. Williams had not confided in his confident, who then tried to blackmail him, AND his actions would never have been known."

Grammar check wanted to insert the word "and," which would have changed the sentence to the point that it did not make sense.

EXAMPLE THREE

In her opening statement, the prosecutor <u>illicited</u> allot of the jury's interest. She pointed out how by leaving the scene of the accident, Mr. Williams engaged in elicit behavior. "Whose going to be confidant in his testimony, when he acted so bad at the time of the accident?" she axed the jury. "He has already shown that he had no intention of acting ethnically. The bear truth is, he was willing to let the person he hurt set there with the shattered windshield lie in his lap. I insure <u>you,</u> he is not a nice person." She went on to describe Mr. Williams' fowl play when he <u>shrinked</u> his duty to report the accident. She pointed out that if Mr. Williams had not confided in his confident, who then tried to blackmail him, his actions would never have been known. "<u>Your</u> going to decide whether society is willing to except this heinous behavior. Imagine if the person who he blinded was you're loved one. This badly behavior must be punished." She concluded that the judge would advice them on the law, but she hoped he would not get a sentence of less than five years in prison. She offered them some <u>advise</u>; "Think about what is fare. Discuss it between yourselves. You have two choices to pick among. You can set there and think, well this is all in the passed, so we will let it go. Or you can sit your minds on doing the right thing and punish him. Live up to you're principals."

Brad's grandfather, who had been a judge, in addition to collecting old law books, enjoyed language. He often would read the newspaper with Brad when Brad was a young boy. Whenever the judge found mistakes in the paper, he would point them out to Brad. Brad would copy the mistakes into his computer, and he was amazed to discover that spell and grammar check did not catch many of the errors.

He email this list to Ana when they were dating, and she too was surprised at how few of the mistakes the computer recognized.

EXAMPLE FOUR

According to the government, the move will curtain overuse of MRIs, CT scans, and other imaging tests.

Spell and grammar check did not see anything wrong with this sentence, despite the fact that the verb "curtail," is mistyped as "curtain."

EXAMPLE FIVE

When Jerry got pulled over for speeding he was very upset he knew this new ticket would result in his drivers license being suspended now he would have no way to get to see his girlfriend she lived twenty miles away Im in deep trouble he thought his first impulse had been to try to outrun the police car but he knew his little Geo Metro would never beat a Crown Victoria when he thought back on the ticket later that night he was very glad he had fought the urge to run away he could not afford to spend time in jail besides jail was a scary place.

This public interest story was in a school newspaper the judge had read. Brad noticed that spell and grammar check caught only one error in this paragraph:

the lack of an apostrophe in the contraction "I'm." The computer did not recognize the fused sentences, lack of punctuation, run-on sentences, or the lack of possessive.

EXAMPLE SIX

After the new paralegal was introduced to everyone in the office and assigned her desk. Tom, whose desk was next to hers, introduced himself. She told him her name was Jennifer Smith but everyone called her Jenny. The attorney she was assigned to work for. Ms. Thachett fit her name. Because she had a thatch of hair that looked like the roof of a thatched hut. Ms. Thachett assigned Jenny a task immediately she had to file a complaint at the courthouse immediately.

The judge had shown this memo from his former legal secretary. Brad discovered that grammar check caught only one of the errors in this paragraph, a sentence fragment. It also noted the spelling of the attorney's name, Ms. Thachett.

EXAMPLE SEVEN

1. Having won the election after a long race.
2. Sam and Joan made up after their argument.
3. Upon learning his daughter had eloped with the rock star.

Brad found also that spell and grammar check did not see any problem with the incomplete sentences of one and three.

EXAMPLE EIGHT

At the continuing education seminar. Angela Simmons and "Butch" Mason sat together. Discussing Judge Jones and the lecture she had given them. They were glad the problem had not hurt either of their clients but it had not helped their reputations with the judges. They knew they could never lose their tempers in trial again they would have to be sure to be polite to everyone. Which meant not talking while the speaker at the seminar was lecturing. Even though he was the most boring speaker they had heard in a long time. After the seminar was finally over. They met some other attorneys for a cocktail, "This is the best part of day," Angela thought. Taking a cab home because she had too much to drink. After the evening was over.

Again, grammar check caught four of the errors but missed five others.

EXAMPLE NINE

The two thieves, one of whom got caught, was bold committing the crime in daylight.

Grammar check did not catch this error. The subject of the sentence, thieves, is plural, but the verb, was, is singular.

EXAMPLE TEN

If my neighbor hadn't been on vacation, she'd of called me, but she weren't there and didn't see the garage sale.

Grammar check missed both the errors in this sentence. Instead of using the word "have" in the first independent clause, the computer had no problem with using the word "of." The subject of the second independent clause, "she," is singular, but the verb "were" is plural.

> **EXAMPLE ELEVEN**
>
> Surprisingly, this rule is very difficult for students to remember, even when they are specifically warned to proof read for contractions and correct them.

Brad noticed that despite the fact that the word "when" subordinated the clause that followed it, grammar check wanted to put a semicolon after the word "remember."

> **EXAMPLE TWELVE**
>
> Judge Smith's will said that Brad could have his law book collection as long as Brad was alive.

In this sentence, grammar check wanted to change the word "said" to "say." It could not recognize that the word "will" was being used as a noun and not a helping verb.

In the following exercise, some of the confused/misused word pairs are used in the same sentence. Spell and grammar check did not recognize any of the misused words as incorrect in the sentence.

EXERCISE _____

Read and select the correct version of the sentence and explain why your choice is correct.

Choices

1. **a.** A week before Mr. Williams' trial, Brad axed Ana to sit second chair.
    b. A week before Mr. Williams' trial, Brad asked Ana to sit second chair.

2. **a.** He hoped she would be able to ensure he made no mistakes.
    b. He hoped she would be able to assure he made no mistakes.

3. **a.** Also, he thought her presence might elicit some subconscious sympathy from the jury.
    b. Also, he thought her presence might illicit some subconscious sympathy from the jury.

4. **a.** He also hoped the jury would comprise open minded people.
    b. He also hoped the jury would compose open minded people.

5. **a.** He knew the assigned judge was fare.
    b. He knew the assigned judge was fair.

6. **a.** Nonetheless, he was not as confident in this case as he had been in many others.
    b. Nonetheless, he was not as confidant in this case as he had been in many others.

7. **a.** As he prepared for trial, he knew that in addition to hard work, he would need some luck two.
    b. As he prepared for trial, he knew that in addition to hard work, he would need some luck too.

8. **a.** He knew he needed to develop a pacific strategy and be consistent.
    b. He knew he needed to develop a specific strategy and be consistent.

9. **a.** Ana was able to advice him.
    b. Ana was able to advise him.

10. **a.** They discussed allot of matters.
    b. They discussed a lot of matters.

EXERCISE

Rewrite the following document by correcting the ten mistakes in it. Note that spell check failed to identify nine of the ten errors.

Brad felt more confident when he received the prosecutor's trial brief. The body of the brief contained the following paragraph.

The defendant, Mr. Williams, should receive a prison term for his crime. The People expect the State to assure an outcome that satisfies they're sense of justice. The State respectfully requests this honorable Court to make a pacific example of Mr. Williams' total lack of ethnics. Not only did the defendant fail to assist an innocent person who he had seriously injured, but he also took the time to retrieve the refrigerator that had caused the injury. If only on principal, this honorable Court must make an example of Mr. Williams. The State is confidant of a conviction; no jury could except Mr. William's heinous behavior. Between this honorable Court, the prosecution, and the jury, the State is certain that Justice will bare its burden when Mr. Williams is convicted and sentenced to the maximum prison term.

SUMMARY

- Good legal writing is persuasive while being honest.

- Good legal writing is formal, and it uses techniques that enhance its effectiveness.

- The passive voice must be used consciously; writers must be able to recognize and avoid using the passive voice when it would weaken their writing.

- Parallelism is an effective tool in legal writing that can provide unity and emphasis.

- Carefully structured paragraphs that provide sufficient white space on the page make writing more appealing to the reader.

- Too short or overly long paragraphs and poor layout distract the reader.

- Written English differs from spoken English, and new writers must learn to avoid being too casual in the tone of their correspondence.

- Contractions, colloquialisms, and slang have no place in legal writing, and new writers must learn to recognize and avoid them in legal writing.

- English contains many homonyms or words that sound very similar to each other but have different meanings. New writers must be certain they are using the correct word.

- Knowing when to write out a number and when to use the Arabic numeral is also a problem for new writers.

- When using acronyms, writers must write the full title of the organization so that the reader understands what the acronym means.

- Writers must never present someone else's writing as their own; plagiarism is a serious offense.

- Writers must always credit the source of their material, whether a direct quote or a concept.

- All quoted material must be placed either in quotation marks or in a block quote if the quotation is long.

- Writers cannot rely on spell and grammar check. Many, many times, these programs will advise writers to make mistakes.

- Writers must learn the correct rules of grammar so that they will not be tricked by spell and grammar check into changing correct writing into incorrect writing.

- Writers must learn the proper use of words that sound alike or similar to avoid using the wrong word.

ASSIGNMENTS

I. Read the following fact pattern and rewrite it, correcting the colloquial and misused words.

The person who was blinded when the refrigerator smashed his windshield has also filed a civil suit against Mr. Williams. Unfortunately, Mr. Williams did not return his answers to Interrogatories until the day they were due to be served. Brad has given them to you and asked you to reword them into proper formal English so that they can be served on opposing counsel by the end of the day. Below is the answer Mr. Williams provided to the first interrogatory.

Interrogatory #1. Explain your location and activities for the entire day of the incident that is the subject of this lawsuit.

Answer: I lay down to sleep just before the sun come up I had crashed late. After I got up, around noon, I set in front of the TV and watched some football on the tube. Then I called my son to see how he was. He axed me to meet him for some chow, but I couldn't except because I had other plans. Turning him down don't effect things between us he knows he's my main man. So he did not feel badly that I said no. Then I went to see a friend I hang with allot and we decided to get some liquid refreshment. We got to the Dew Drop Inn around dusk, I think, then we had a few brews. I quit drinking by early though, cause I was driving my 'Stang, my pride and joy aside from my son a course. I get home that night around midnight I reckon. Then I watched more tube, threw back a few more beers, and caught some rack time.

II. Using proper language only, with no colloquial or slang terms or words, write a letter to your future employer explaining five of your character traits that would make you a good employee for him or her. Be sure to incorporate legal ethics into your letter.

III. You are a paralegal working for Smith & Garcia. Brad asks you to write a draft summary of the Williams case. Although this document is privileged, because it is for in-office use only, Brad will use it as the base for his Trial Brief. It is important, therefore, that it be well organized, grammatically correct, and written in court-appropriate language. Be sure to proof read your draft for slang or colloquial terms, misused words, spelling errors, and any grammatical or punctuation errors. Your draft should be two pages, double-spaced, with one inch margins, and 12 point font.

IV. Read the following facts, and then read the summary that follows. Identify and correct the passive voice, incorrect writing details, and misrepresentations that breach ethical standards that are contained in the summary. Also, include parallelism where appropriate and correct any errors in the summary. Rewrite the summary in your own words so it is persuasive on behalf of the plaintiff, the executor of Judge Smith's estate, who wants Brad to take the law books and still get an equal share of the judge's remaining assets.

- The retired Judge Smith had collected many rare law books. He had searched for these books throughout his career.
- Many of these books were old.
- Some were written in other languages than English.
- Some were European.
- African law books also were in the collection.
- Even law books from Asia were included.
- Judge Smith had a will.
- Judge Smith's will said that Brad could have his law book collection as long as Brad was alive.
- Once Brad had died, the law book collection was going to be donated to the law school where Brad went and where his grandfather had gone.
- Judge Smith's will split his assets equally among his grandchildren.
- After Judge Smith died, Brad's cousins complained that it was not fair for Brad to get the law book collection.
- At least five of the Arabic language books were worth over $5,000 each.
- They said Judge Smith's assets had to be divided equally.
- Brad said he did not own the books.
- Brad said the books belonged to the law school.

Judge Smith collected law books. It was his hobby. He searched all over for old law books. Some of his books weren't even in English some were in strange African languages. He even had law books from old Arabian countries. Judge Smith's will said that his grandson, Brad Smith, could keep these books until Brad died. Then the law school Judge Smith and Brad went to got to have the books. All his assets were going to equally be split between the grandchildren. Brad's cousins and him were gonna split everything.

Then Judge Smith died. His cousins said no fair about Brad getting to have the books. 5 of the books were worth five thousand dollars. Apiece! Why should Brad get something that valuable? The will said the assets were going to be split equally between the grandchildren. That wasn't equal!

But wait! Brad told them that he didn't own them. He was just keeping them for the law school. He couldn't sell them the will didn't say that. The law school would receive the books from Brad. His cousins were just <u>wrong</u>. This was not what their grandpa wanted. If his cousins got some of the law books, they'd sell them for sure. Keeping the books safe is what Brad was supposed to do.

LEARNING OBJECTIVES

1. Identify citations within documents

2. Describe correct citation format for case law and statutes

3. Compare the differences in citation formats

4. Select correct citation for legal material

Citations

CHAPTER 6

■ CITATIONS

Citations tell the reader of legal documents where to find the case law, statute, or secondary source that the writer has referenced or quoted. You will see citations being used in Chapter 8 of this book, and then it will become clearer how citation format is applied. Use of citations will be an integral part of your paralegal career. This chapter is an introduction to citation format, but you will study it in more depth in your legal research class.

Citing cases in the prescribed format is important in order to maintain consistency for readers. People who read legal documents often need to consult the original source material that the writers are discussing. If each writer decided to invent his or her own format for citing legal materials, the readers would find it challenging to locate the sources being referenced or quoted.

In order to establish and maintain consistency in the format of these citations, the Law Reviews of several prestigious law schools collaborate and publish a volume called *The Bluebook: A Uniform System of Citation* (Columbia Law Review Ass'n et al. eds., 19th ed. 2013). Other citation systems exist as well, for example, *The Maroonbook: The University of Chicago Manual of Legal Citation* (University of Chicago Law Review, eds., 3d ed. 2009). Additionally, individual states may have a legal citation system for use in their own courts. Nevertheless, *The Blue Book* is by far the most commonly used citation system, and it is well-worth having among your personal desk references, along with a good legal dictionary.

The Blue Book is updated frequently, and it is important to ensure that the citation format you are using is current. Fortunately, many of these law schools have websites that provide current information. Nonetheless, *The Blue Book* is essential for any legal writer. If you work in a larger firm, the firm's librarians will have copies you can consult. Even a sole practitioner, though, will need to have access to a current version of *The Blue Book*.

Keep in mind that your employer will rely on you to use the correct citation format in legal memoranda. You also may be expected to correct the citations in your attorney's documents. Your responsibility to your attorney and the client includes accurate citations in all legal documents you handle.

Accurate, correct citation format requires meticulous attention to detail, and courts can be demanding regarding correct citation format. Use of incorrect citations frustrates the reader who is attempting to locate and examine your source material, reflects very badly on the attorney, and, therefore, could adversely affect the client's case. Submitting documents that contain incorrectly formatted citations demonstrates lack of professionalism.

As noted above, although *The Blue Book* is the general authority on citation format, some jurisdictions have established their own citation formats. If the jurisdiction in which you are working has a different format for citations, then your documents should use that format. For example, in the following chapters you will see that we sometimes cited to Ohio cases. The Ohio Supreme Court has adopted its own citation system and style manual, which it most recently updated in 2013. Thus, any citations we have made to Ohio cases are formatted the way the Ohio Supreme Court requires. Fortunately, *The Blue Book* contains a table of citation formats, T1, for various jurisdictions.

However, in addition to consulting the rules of your jurisdiction for any format requirements, if your attorney works in several counties or parishes, you will need to consult the local rules of each for documents filed in each particular county. Because jurisdictions occasionally change their rules, you should check the jurisdiction's website for the current appropriate citation format for your document.

New legal writers will find that legal citations use words that are new to them, and citations use familiar words in discretely unique ways. Most of the words that may be new to you are derived from Latin. Some of these words are discussed in the box called Citations Derived from Latin.

Note that most of these words are usually italicized or underlined, the same way that the title of the case is italicized or underlined. Names of cases are discussed below. It is important to determine which form your jurisdiction uses. Also, remember that the italicizing or underlining includes the period after "*Id.*" Thus, in a jurisdiction that underlines instead of italicizing, it would be written as follows: "<u>Id.</u>" Note that the punctuation that is not part of the citation, in this case a quotation mark, is not underlined.

Citations Derived from Latin

Id.—This word is an abbreviation of *Idem*. When citing to the source most recently cited in the document, it is not necessary to repeat the name of the source. Instead, *id.* to let the readers know what source you are discussing.

At—When citing to the page number on which the law being discussed is found, citations use the word "at" instead of referencing page or "p." Thus, if you were referencing page 100 of the most recent document you cited, instead of repeating the name of the case, you would write "*Id.* at 100."

Supra—*Supra* is Latin for "above." If your document referred to a publication that was not a statute, case, or constitution, you would write "the last name of the author of the work, followed by a comma and the word '*supra.*'" *The Blue Book.* at 74.

See—When the point you are trying to make is supported by more than one case, you may discuss the most important case and then refer the reader to another case or cases that support the proposition you are arguing. To do this, use the word "*See*" followed by the citation for the case. Note that there is not a comma after the word "*See.*"

See also—When there are several cases supporting your point, use "*See also*" to direct readers to additional sources supporting the argument.

But see—If there are cases that do not support your position, you must point out these cases as well. "*But see*" directs readers to the cases that are contrary to your position. Note that including these citations is an ethical obligation.

The Blue Book contains far too much information to be summarized here, and students are strongly encouraged to consult its clear and comprehensive introductory Bluepages for a more complete discussion of the particulars and details of citation to various sources. This chapter will be limited to a basic introduction to case law and statutory citations.

Case Law Citations

A surprising realization for new legal writers is the fact that the courts rely to a large extent on previous court decisions addressing the same issue of law in making their decisions. This is known as "case law." People who are unfamiliar with the workings of the legal process often assume that the "law" means laws passed by a legislative body, for example, statutes.

In reality, however, many court decisions are based upon decisions written by previous courts. Thus, when you read court decisions, you will discover that much of the law the courts cite to and rely on comes from earlier cases. Similarly, in documents submitted to the courts, attorneys cite to and/or quote case law that addresses the issues they are discussing.

Since there is an enormous amount of case law that has been written, it is important for the readers to be able to find the case easily if they want to consult it. Further, for ease in locating the source, uniformity in the way the case is referenced is essential. Fortunately, *The Blue Book* is a uniformly recognized and accepted authority on correct citation format.

In order to understand case law citation, you need to understand the way court decisions are published or issued. Many court decisions are published in compilations called "reporters." As *The Blue Book* clearly explains,

> A reporter is a series of books collecting the published cases within a given jurisdiction or set of jurisdictions. Typically, a case citation will tell the reader where the case can be found by listing: (1) the volume number of the reporter in which the case is published; (2) the abbreviated name of the reporter (listed by jurisdiction in table T1); and (3) the page on which the case report begins.

Id. at 9.

Many states have their own reporters in which their court decisions are compiled. Additionally, however, state court decisions are also included in regional reporters, which, as the name implies, include cases from a number of states within a region. For example, Ohio cases are published in the Northeaster reporter, which is abbreviated "N.E." After a regional reporter, or a state reporter for that matter, has published a large amount of material in its reporter, it will start over with the second version of the reporter. Thus, more recent cases from Ohio courts will be in the "N.E.2d." Note that there is not a space between the E. and the 2. Spacing in citations is very specific and not necessarily clear to new writers, and you would be well advised to study *The Blue Book* as you write documents during your paralegal courses and later during your career. *Id.* at 11.

While all this can sound quite intimidating, as in many things in life, it will become second nature to you after you have used it for a while. Think back to when you learned to print letters. At that time, you never could have written in complete sentences and paragraphs. Similarly, with citations, it is hard to believe that you will be so familiar with them that writing and checking them will be no more difficult than writing is to you now.

Each case also has a name, however, and the name of the case consists of the parties who are involved in the case. The citation begins with the name of the case, and is followed by the state reporter that has published the case. When writing the reporter in a case citation, the volume number of the reporter precedes the name of the reporter, and the page on which the case starts follows the name of the reporter. This will become clear with example below. For now, though, we have inserted two examples of case citations so you can see what we are discussing. Both the citations in the example are formatted the way *The Blue Book* instructs writers to format.

EXAMPLES

Curry v. Meijer, Inc., 286 Mich. App. 586, 780 N.W.2d 603 (2009).
Bruce Farms v. Coupe, 219 Va. 287, 289, 247 S.E.2d 400, 402 (1978).

After the state reporter, the citation lists the regional reporter that published the case, again with the volume number preceding the name of the regional reporter and the page the case begins after the name of the regional reporter.

After the regional reporter, the year the case was published is included in parentheses. The date of the decision is important, because writers must cite the most recent controlling law on an issue.

Thus, you have four essential elements to a full case citation: Please see Table 6.1.

Table 6.1 Elements for Case Citation

#	CASE CITATION
1.	The name of the case.
2.	The state reporter in which the case is published, with the volume number before and the page number after the name of the reporter.
3.	The regional reporter in which the case is published, with the volume number before and the page number after the name of the reporter.
4.	The date the decision was published, in parentheses.

EXAMPLE

Curry v. Meijer, Inc., 286 Mich. App. 586, 780 N.W.2d 603 (2009).

1. *The name of the case: Curry v. Meijer, Inc.* In this citation, the plaintiff, that is, the person initiating the lawsuit, is named Curry. The defendant, the person or entity being sued, is Meijer, Inc. *The Blue Book* recommends underlining in legal practice, but some states use italicizing instead of underlining. You will have to consult your own state's system when you cite to cases. In our experience, more courts use italics, which we have chosen to do here.

2. *The state reporter*: 286 Mich. App. 586. Note that the first number, 286, is the volume number in which the case is published. Thus, this case is in the 286th volume of this reporter. Each state has its own abbreviation, which you can find in *The Blue Book*. Here, the abbreviation for the State of Michigan is "Mich." The abbreviation "App." tells us that the reporter contains decisions from appellate courts. The number 586 tells us the page on which this decision begins in the reporter.

3. *The regional reporter*: 780 N.W.2d 603. As with the state reporter, the volume number precedes the name of the reporter. The case is published in the 780th volume of this regional reporter. The name of the reporter is always abbreviated. In this case, the reporter is the

Northwestern Reporter, which is abbreviated "N.W." Because many reporters have published so many cases, they often begin a second edition and restart numbering at one for the new edition. In this case, the Northwestern Reporter started a second edition. This case is published in the second edition, so the reporter's abbreviation indicates that with the "2d" after the "N.W." Thus, the regional reporter's name is abbreviated "N.W.2d" for this case. Notice that there is not a space between the letters, nor is there a space between the letters and the number. Also, there is not a period after "2d" in the reporter citation.

4. *The year of publication:* (2009). Notice that there is no punctuation between the page number of the regional report and the parenthesis preceding the year, 2009. Including the year the decision was written is important; the court may have changed its position on an issue, and providing the year of the decision informs the readers how old the case is. If a case is older, it is important to check and be certain that it is still "good law," that is, has not been overruled or changed.

Pinpoint Citations

If the actual text of the case that the writer is referencing is not the first page of the case, the writer indicates the page on which that part of the case is found in a pinpoint cite. The pinpoint cite is written immediately after the page on which the decision starts in the volume.

A pinpoint citation provides the reader with the specific page in the case that contains the law you are referencing. It is imperative to include pinpoint citations in your documents because opposing counsel and the court may want to review the section of the decision that you are discussing. *The Blue Book* at 9.

Therefore, if the writer was discussing something the court had written that was located on page 590 of the Michigan Reporter and page 606 of the Northwestern Reporter, the writer would include those page numbers in the citation. The citation would look like this:

EXAMPLES

Curry v. Meijer, Inc., 286 Mich. App. 586, 590, 780 N.W.2d 603, 606 (2009).
Another example is seen below:
Narkeeta, Inc. v. McCoy, 247 Miss. 65, 70, 153 So.2d 798, 800 (1963).

This is the accepted way of telling the readers on what page they can find the exact part of the decision the writer is discussing. In the Michigan Reporter, the *Curry* decision begins on page 586, and the part of the case the writer is referencing in found on page 590. Similarly, in the Northwestern Reporter, the case begins on page 603, and the part of the case the writer is referencing in found on page 606.

For the second citation, the law in the *Narkeeta* decision that is being discussed is on page 70 of the Mississippi Reporter and on page 800 of the Southern Reporter.

Short Form Citations

This citation, *Curry v. Meijer, Inc.*, 286 Mich. App. 586, 780 N.W.2d 603 (2009), is called a full citation. You will provide the full cite to a case the first time you reference it. Because it would be redundant and take up so much space, the full citation is used only the first time the case is cited in a document.

Further references to the case will be made in the short citation form "so long as (1) it will be clear to the reader from the short form what is being referenced; (2) the earlier full citation falls in the same general discussion; and (3) the reader will have little trouble quickly locating the full citation." *The Blue Book* at 13 (emphasis in original). Generally, when using the short citation form, you will include the name of the first party and the volume and page numbers for reporters in which the case is published.

If the name of the first party would not make the identity of the case clear, however, you will use the name of the defendant in the short form of the citation. For example, if the name of the case is *State Farm Mutual Automobile Insurance v. Perry*, calling the case *State Farm* would not help readers to identify it from among the many cases involving the insurance company. Therefore, the case would be called *Perry* in the short format.

Using our previous example, in which the full citation is *Curry v. Meijer, Inc.*, 286 Mich. App. 586, 590; 780 N.W.2d 603, 606 (2009), we will see that the short form of this citation is *Curry*, 286 Mich. App. 586, 590; 780 N.W.2d 603, 606. If your discussion references a case that was cited immediately before this discussion, you would use *Id.* Thus, the citation would look like this:

Id. at 590, 606.

> **EXAMPLE**
>
> In a document discussing law found in the case *Bruce Farms v. Coupe*, 219 Va. 287, 289, 247 S.E.2d 400, 402 (1978), the short citation would be *Bruce Farms*, 219 Va. 287, 289, 247 S.E.2d 400, 402.
>
> If the *Bruce Farms* case had been the most recent case cited, the short citation would be *id.* at 289, 402.

So how do writers know how the name of the state is abbreviated? If the court that wrote the decision you are citing is not the United States Supreme Court, then you will abbreviate the name of the court in parentheses the way it is written in table T10 of *The Blue Book. Id.* at 10.

Not all cases are published in reporters, however, and these cases are known as, logically, "unreported cases." *Id.* at 11-12. Citation format for unreported cases is beyond the scope of this text, but it is important to know whether the case on which you are relying is unreported because, in some jurisdictions, unreported cases are not considered to be as important or persuasive as reported cases.

> **BAD EXAMPLE**
>
> *Allen v.* Marriott Worldwide Corp., 2011, 961 A.2d 1141, 1146, (183 Md. App. 460, 469).

> **GOOD EXAMPLE**
>
> *Allen v. Marriott Worldwide Corp.*, 183 Md. App. 460, 469, 961 A.2d 1141, 1146 (2011).

> **BAD EXAMPLE**
>
> (Id.1989), 116 Idaho 228, 775 P.2d 120 *Griggs v. Nash.*

> **GOOD EXAMPLE**
>
> *Griggs v. Nash*, 116 Idaho 228, 775 P.2d 120 (1989).

EXERCISE

Read the excerpt from an Oregon Appellate Court decision below and write down all the citations that you see.

> To determine whether a challenged rule exceeds the agency's statutory authority, we may consider only "the wording of the rule itself (read in context) and the statutory provisions authorizing the rule." *Wolf v. Oregon Lottery Commission*, 344 Or 345, 355, 182 P3d 180 (2008) (citing ORS 183.400(3)(a), (b)). Based on those sources, we consider whether the agency's adoption of the rule exceeded the authority granted by statute and, further, whether the agency "departed from a legal standard expressed or implied in the particular law being administered, or contravened some other applicable statute." *Planned Parenthood Assn. v. Dept. of Human Res.*, 297 Or 562, 565, 687 P.2d 785 (1984). In making that determination, we seek to discern the legislature's. intent by examining the text and context of the relevant statutes and, if useful to the analysis, pertinent legislative history. *See State v. Gaines*, 346 Or 160, 171–72, 206 P3d 1042 (2009) . . . .

> *Oregon Association of Acupuncture and Oriental Medicine v. Board of Chiropractic Examiners*, 260 Or. App. 676, 677 (2014).

EXERCISE

Read the quoted section from an Arkansas case below and write down all the citations that you see.

> We have frequently held that we will not decide the merits of an appeal when the order appealed is not a final order. *Schueck Steel, Inc. v. McCarthy Bros. Co.*, 289 Ark. 436, 711 S.W.2d 820 (1986) and supplemental opinion on rehearing, 289 Ark. 436, 717 S.W.2d 816 (1986). For an order to be final, it must dismiss the parties from the court, discharge them from the action, or conclude their rights to the subject matter in controversy. *Roberts Enters., Inc. v. Arkansas State Highway Comm'n*, 277 Ark. 25, 638 S.W.2d 675 (1982); Ark.R.App.P. 2. Even if neither party raises the issue of the finality of the judgment, the appellate court should raise it on its own. *Cigna Ins. Co. v. Brisson*, 294 Ark. 504, 744 S.W.2d 716 (1988) and supplemental opinion on rehearing 294 Ark. 506-A, 746 S.W.2d 558 (1988). The order vacating the judgment in this case does not dismiss or discharge the parties from the court, nor does it conclude their rights to the subject matter in controversy. Rather, the order vacating the judgment places both of the parties back in the position they were in before the judgment was entered, *see Hawkeye Tire & Rubber Co. v. McFarlin*, 146 Ark. 491, 225 S.W. 632 (1920), and it is clear that neither party had a right to appeal before the judgment was entered.

> *Lamb v. JFM, Inc.*, 311 Ark. 89, 842 S.W.2d 10 (1992).

Public Domain Format

Many states are changing their citation formats to what is known as the public domain format. In the public domain format, the case citation includes "the case name, the year of the decision, the state's two-character postal code . . . , the court abbreviation . . . , [and] the sequential number of the decision . . . ." *The Blue Book* at 96. When citing to a specific section of a case in a public domain citation, refer to the paragraph number, as shown in the second example below. Ideally, you also would include the page number in the regional reporter, here the Pacific Reporter, as well.

> **EXAMPLE**
>
> *Wilson v. State ex rel. State Election Bd.*, 2012 OK 2, 270 P.3d 155.
>
>   When citing or quoting a specific passage, include the paragraph number as below:
>
>   *Wilson v. State ex rel. State Election Bd.*, 2012 OK 2, ¶ 4, 270 P.3d 155.

Statutory Citations

Although much of your legal writing will cite to case law, you also will cite to statutory law. Unfortunately, each state has its own format for citing to statutes, so you will have to consult *The Blue Book* T1 to find the correct way to cite them.

> **EXAMPLES**
>
> For example, Michigan's statutory citation format is "Mich, Comp. Laws § x.x (year). *Id.* at 247.
>
>   Virginia's citation statutory format is "Va. Code Ann. § x.x (year)." *Id.* at 271.
>
>   Wisconsin's statutory citation format is "Wis. Stat. § x.x (year)." *Id.* at 273.
>
>   Ohio's statutory format, according to *The Blue Book*, includes the name of the publisher in addition to the year. Its format is "Ohio Rev. Code Ann. § x.x (LexisNexis year)" or "Ohio Rev. Code Ann. § x.x (West year)." *Id.* at 260. However, the courts when referencing the statute in a decision may refer to "section 5321.04 of the Revised Code" or "R.C. 5321.04."

You may find variation in the way the courts in your state cite to statutes in the body of decisions. When in doubt, either check your state's website or follow the form found in *The Blue Book* Table 1 (T1).

SUMMARY

- Citations provide a consistent, convenient way to inform readers how to locate the source of material cited in a document.

- *The Blue Book* is the accepted source for citation format.

- Each jurisdiction, however, can have its own citation format, so writers should verify the correct format for citation in that jurisdiction.

- Each state has its own format for citing to statutes. *The Blue Book*, T1, provides the format for each state. Writers may find, nonetheless, that the courts in those jurisdictions may have a different way of citing to statutes.

- Case citations have four essential elements: the name of the case, the state reporter, the regional reporter, and the year the decision was issued.

- Pinpoint cites direct readers to the page number in the decision that contains the law being discussed.

- Short citations are used after the long citation has been used first in a document.

- Citations use words derived from Latin, including *Id.* and *supra*.

- Citations also use regular words in particular ways, including *See, See also* and *But see*.

- The word "at," which is used to designate the exact page on which a citation is found, is not italicized or underlined.

ASSIGNMENTS

I. Read the section from the Ohio criminal case below and write down all the citations that you see.

{¶ 9} The state asks us to clarify the effect of *Johnson* on the standard for determining whether "the same conduct by defendant can be construed to constitute two or more allied offenses of similar import" under R.C. 2941.25(A). We hold that while *Johnson* abandoned a portion of the test for determining whether offenses share a "similar import," it did not change the test for determining whether those offenses resulted from the "same conduct."

Multiple Punishments, Legislative Intent, and R.C. 2941.25

{¶ 10} The Fifth Amendment's Double Jeopardy Clause "protects only against the imposition of multiple criminal punishments for the same offense, * * * and then only when such occurs in successive proceedings." (Emphasis deleted.) *Hudson v. United States,* 522 U.S. 93, 99, 118 S.Ct. 488, 139 L.Ed.2d 450 (1997); *State v. Raber,* 134 Ohio St.3d 350, 2012-Ohio-5636, 982 N.E.2d 684,¶ 24. Whether multiple punishments imposed in the same proceeding are permissible is a question of legislative intent. *Missouri v. Hunter,* 459 U.S. 359, 365, 103 S.Ct. 673, 74 L.Ed.2d 535 (1983).

{¶ 11} Absent a more specific legislative statement, R.C. 2941.25 is the primary indication of the General Assembly's intent to prohibit or allow multiple punishments for two or more offenses resulting from the same conduct. *State v. Childs,* 88 Ohio St.3d 558, 561, 728 N.E.2d 379 (2000). We have described the statute as an attempt to codify the judicial doctrine of merger, *State v. Logan,* 60 Ohio St.2d 126, 131, 397 N.E.2d 1345 (1979), the penal philosophy that " 'where one crime necessarily involves another, * * * the offense so involved is merged in the offense of which it is a part,' " *State v. Botta,* 27 Ohio St.2d 196, 201, 271 N.E.2d 776 (1971), fn. 1, quoting 21 American

Jurisprudence 2d 90 (1965). In its entirety, R.C. 2941.25 provides:

(A) Where the same conduct by defendant can be construed to constitute two or more allied offenses of similar import, the indictment or information may contain counts for all such offenses, but the defendant may be convicted of only one.

(B) Where the defendant's conduct constitutes two or more offenses of dissimilar import, or where his conduct results in two or more offenses of the same or similar kind committed separately or with a separate animus as to each, the indictment or information may contain counts for all such offenses, and the defendant may be convicted of all of them.

{¶ 12} R.C. 2941.25(A) identifies two conditions necessary for merger: the offenses must (1) result from the "same conduct" and (2) share a "similar import." R.C. 2941.25(A); *see also Logan* at 128 ("In addition to the requirement of similar import * * *, the defendant, in order to obtain the protection of R.C. 2941.25(A), must show that the prosecution has relied upon the same conduct to support both offenses charged"). Restated in the negative, offenses do not merge if they were "committed separately" or if the offenses have a "dissimilar import." R.C. 2941.25(B) In addition to these restrictions, R.C. 2941.25(B) identifies another bar to merger for offenses committed "with a separate animus as to each." *See State v. Bickerstaff,* 10 Ohio St.3d 62, 66, 461 N.E.2d 892 (1984) (describing the three bars to merger as "disjunctive in nature").

State v. Washington, 137 Ohio St.3d 427, 2013-Ohio-4982

II. Answer the following questions.

1. What is a citation?

2. Why is it important to cite to cases in the pre-scribed format?

3. Is citation to court decisions (cases) the same in the entire country?

4. How do I cite to a statute?

5. Where can I find the proper way to cite to a statute for any given state in *The Blue Book?*

6. What are the four elements of a case citation?

7. Why is it important to know the year a case was decided?

8. How do I find out how the name of a state is abbreviated for citations?

9. What is a pinpoint citation?

10. What does *"id."* mean?

III. Match the correct citation to the source and fill in the blank with the corresponding number.

1. Michigan statutory citation

2. Wisconsin statutory citation

3. Oklahoma statutory citation

4. South Dakota statutory citation

5. Nebraska statutory citation

6. Colorado

7. statutory citation

8. Montana

_____ S.D. Codified Laws § x-x-x (year) Id. at 266.

_____ Okla. Stat. tit, x(year) Id. at 261.

_____ Va. Code Ann. § x.x (year). Id. at 271.

_____ Neb. Rev. Stat. § x-x (year) Id. at 250.

_____ Mich. Cop. Laws § x.x. (year). Id at 247.

_____ Colo. Rev. Stat. § x-x-x (year) Id. at 233.

_____ Wis. Stat. § x.x (year)." Id. at 273.

_____ Mont. Code Ann. § x-x-x (year) Id. at 250.

LEARNING OBJECTIVES

1. Define IRAC formatting

2. Memorize the IRAC sequence

3. Recognize the appropriate question for the issue statement in IRAC

4. Detect the correct issue in a fact pattern

5. Create a succinct, correct statement of the issue in a given fact pattern

CHAPTER 7

IRAC - Issue

■ IRAC FORMATTING

Formatting is the way a document is organized and arranged. The document is structured in a manner that both achieves the writer's purpose and makes the document clear and easy to follow for the reader.

Writing from an outline is one form of formatting that you have learned in an earlier chapter. We saw how writing is more logical and understandable if it is well organized.

Readers expect certain types of documents to be organized in certain patterns. Without these patterns, the writing is more difficult to follow, and thereby less effective.

For example, in the chapter on letter writing, we saw that the page has the firm's name and address at the top, the name and address of the recipient on the left margin, the date of the letter on the right margin, the subject line, and then the greeting. Clients and other counsel will expect letters to be organized this way, and a letter that lacks the proper organization will be less effective.

Similarly, when you read a news story, the headline summarizes the content, and the first paragraph or two answer the most important questions: who, what where, when, and why. Less important details are placed later in the article. The reader expects a news story to follow this format, and the reader does not expect to have to read through the whole story to find out the highlights.

In law, the format we use is called IRAC, which is an acronym for Issue, Rule, Analysis, and Conclusion. When legal arguments, memoranda, or other documents do not follow this format, they lose effectiveness and are not persuasive to the reader. This format, or slight variations of it, is used throughout legal documents, from memoranda for attorneys to Appellate Court decisions.

Because you will be writing for other legal professionals, it is important that you follow this writing format.

Defining IRAC

So what is IRAC formatting? It lays out the legal problem in a useful pattern. The ISSUE, although brief, is one of the more difficult parts of the outline. Defining your issue is essential for an effective legal document. It establishes the parameter of the legal research and the analysis that apply to the fact pattern of the case.

If your issue is not correctly drafted, your legal research will not focus on the correct law, and your analysis will not address the necessary legal aspects of the case.

The RULE section of the IRAC format is exactly what it sounds like; it encapsulates the result of research of the law that applies to the issue. Once you know what your issue is, you will research and find the law, regulation, or precedent that applies. We will discuss the rule in detail in the next chapter.

The ANALYSIS is the heart of your document, but without a properly focused issue and the correct applicable rule, the analysis is worthless. Even with a properly focused issue and the appropriate rule, however, an inadequate analysis renders the entire document ineffective. We will discuss the analysis at length in the chapter 9 after the rule chapter 8.

The CONCLUSION consists of a restating of the issue in the affirmative or the negative. We will discuss the conclusion in the chapter 10 following the analysis in chapter 9.

When the legal reader sees an issue and a law or rule stated, he or she expects to see that rule applied to the set of facts that created the issue. Right now this is probably clear as mud to you, but the following exercises and examples should help clarify this process. Nonetheless, clear and effective writing is essential to a successful paralegal career. IRAC is a major tool for achieving that essential part of your skill set.

EXERCISE _____

As you read this chapter, fill in the worksheet below.

1. The issue is probably the hardest and _____ segment of the _____ document.

2. A _____ issue negatively affects the effectiveness of the rest of the document.

3. Traditionally, the issue is limited to _____ sentence(s).

4. The issue should contain _____ _____ to make the precise issue clear.

5. Spotting the issue takes _____.

6. Name two characteristics of the issue: _____ and _____.

7. It is very important to rely only on the _____ you have.

8. The issue is the _____ or _____ between the parties that they want the court to settle.

9. The issue is the _____ of any case. It is the _____ point on which everything else in the case hinges.

10. _____ the issue often is the most difficult and the most important part of writing a legal document.

■ I = ISSUE

The issue is probably the hardest and most important segment of the IRAC document. Writers sometimes make the mistake of underestimating its importance, but a poorly focused issue negatively affects the effectiveness of the rest of the document. It is important to note that, traditionally, the issue is limited to one sentence. Also, note that, traditionally, an issue had to begin with the word "whether," thereby posing the issue as a question. Paradoxically, issue statements beginning with the word "whether" end with a period and not a question mark, although they are considered questions.

In addition to the aberrant punctuation, this traditional method creates an inherent grammatical error: by starting the issue with "whether," it makes the clause that follows a dependent clause, and therefore a sentence fragment.

Perhaps for that reason, some attorneys are moving away from this tradition. Nonetheless, it is still standard in many legal settings, so it is important to learn to write an issue beginning with "whether." However, because many attorneys are moving away from the traditional method of starting the issue with "whether," we also will provide examples of the same issues worded as a question. The distinct advantage of wording the issue as a question is that it avoids creating a sentence fragment or punctuation anomaly. Your instructor may decide to teach only the grammatically correct form of the issue. If you later work for an attorney who requires the use of issues beginning with "whether," you can refer back to this chapter for guidance.

An issue rarely contains the names of the parties. Rather, the parties are referenced by the roles they play in the facts. Thus, in a case between a car owner and his mechanic, the issue would not refer to Mr. Jones and Mr. Smith. It would reference the car owner and the mechanic. Additionally, the attorneys are not referred to in the issue, unless the issue involves the attorney's actions. Instead, the issue focuses solely on the parties, or in cases in which only the interpretation of a point of law is at issue, to the law.

The issue should contain only as many facts as necessary to make the precise issue clear. For example, taking the car owner and the mechanic, let us say that after picking up the car from the repair shop, the car owner discovers that his good winter coat is missing from the trunk. The issue would not include the name of the repair shop, the color of the coat, or the nature of the repair on the car. Instead, it would focus on what level of responsibility the mechanic had for the personal property contained in the vehicles he repaired.

That issue might be worded as follows:

> **EXAMPLE**
>
> Whether an auto repair shop is liable for the loss of valuable personal property left in vehicles entrusted to it for repairs.

In the newer issue form, the issue might be worded as follows:

> **EXAMPLE**
>
> Is an auto repair shop liable for the loss of valuable personal property left in vehicles entrusted to it for repairs?

Notice that the issue is generic in one sense; it could apply to any car owner and any auto repair shop encountering a loss of personal property from the car owner's vehicle. The focus is the liability for personal property, not what specific property was missing.

If we knew that the owner of the auto repair shop had a large sign informing car owners that it did not take responsibility for any lost items, the wording of the issue would include this fact.

Then the issue might be worded as follows:

> **EXAMPLE**
>
> Whether an auto repair shop that expressly informs customers that it is not responsible for lost property can be held liable for the loss of valuable personal property left in vehicles entrusted to it for repairs.

In the newer issue form, the issue might be worded as follows:

> **EXAMPLE**
>
> When an auto repair shop expressly informs customers that it is not responsible for lost property, can it be held liable for the loss of valuable personal property left in vehicles entrusted to it for repairs?

The second versions of the issue presume that we are writing the issue on behalf of the auto repair shop.

If we represented the customer, we might reword the issue as follows:

> **EXAMPLE**
>
> Whether an auto repair shop is liable for loss of valuable personal property left in vehicles entrusted to it for repairs, when the only notice of its disclaimer of responsibility is a sign on the wall of the shop.

In the newer issue form, the issue might be worded as follows:

> **EXAMPLE**
>
> When the only notice of its disclaimer of responsibility is a sign on the wall of the shop, is an auto repair shop liable for loss of valuable personal property left in vehicles entrusted to it for repairs?

Spotting the issue takes practice. It also takes experience and an understanding of the law. It is important to craft the issue with precision, however, because the issue will clarify the fulcrum, the pivotal point, upon which the case rests. In other words, the issue defines the heart of the case.

The issue is the statement of the question or disagreement between the parties that they want the court to settle. It includes enough of the fact pattern and the law to make the question comprehensible to the reader, but does not include so much that it muddles the issue.

What Are the Characteristics of the Issue?

The Issue Is

- The first segment of the IRAC statement
- A separate section of its own
- A section that consists of one sentence
- A sentence that identifies the legal issue/question at hand
- A sentence that is succinct, thorough, and to the point
- A sentence that provides the most important points in the case

Important

- The issue must be concise.
- The issue must be precise.
- The issue must be clear.
- The issue should not include detailed facts; those belong in the analysis.

Points to Ponder

What happens if:

- The issue contains too many facts? The reader gets confused.
- The sentence is too complex? The issue is not clear.

EXAMPLE OF THE ISSUE

■ **LANDLORD-TENANT**

You are a paralegal who works for Smith & Garcia. Ana already helped Sheila Kowalski when she had difficulty gaining access to the specific apartment she had leased. Unfortunately, Sheila has had ongoing issues with her landlord, and Sheila again is requesting Ana's help with dealing with her landlord.

After Ana had sent the landlord a letter pointing out that he was in material breach of the lease, he had relented and allowed Sheila to move into the apartment she had specified in the lease. After she moved in, though, Sheila discovered that the apartment did not have hot water. When she complained to the landlord, he responded by reminding her that she had insisted on having this specific apartment. Because it was the model, he said, it had never been connected to the hot water tank. He told her that she had gotten just what she had asked for—that specific apartment. Sheila is now consulting Ana for recourse concerning the lack of hot water.

How might we frame the issue in this case?

EXAMPLE

1. Whether a landlord of residential properties is required under law to provide hot water to the tenants of such property.
   Is a landlord of residential properties required under law to provide hot water to the tenants of such property?
2. Whether a tenant has recourse against a landlord who refuses to provide hot water to the leased premises.
   Does a tenant have recourse against a landlord who refuses to provide hot water to the leased premises?
3. Whether the landlord is responsible for the pneumonia the tenant contracted after she was forced to take weeks of cold showers.
   Is the landlord responsible for the pneumonia the tenant contracted after she was forced to take weeks of cold showers?
4. Whether the landlord should be required to cover the cost of the gym membership the tenant had to buy so she could have access to hot showers.
   Should the landlord be required to cover the cost of the gym membership the tenant had to buy so she could have access to hot showers?

Each of these issues focuses on a different aspect of the question at hand, while still addressing the client's problem. Some are good issues, and some are not. The first issue deals solely with forcing the landlord to provide hot water to the tenant's apartment. This issue is well focused.

The second issue approaches the fact pattern from a different perspective. It addresses what actions the tenant can take in response to the landlord's refusal to provide hot water. It is also well focused.

Both of these issues are valid and appropriate.

The third issue expands the scope of the question beyond the fact pattern into damages that do not exist in the fact pattern. Nothing in the facts states that the tenant caught pneumonia at all, much less from taking cold showers. This is not a good issue.

Similarly, the fourth issue creates facts that are not before us. While joining a gym to have access to a hot shower might be a sensible move, the available facts do not state that Sheila did so. This also is not a good issue.

A surprising number of paralegal students invent facts in an attempt to create a more persuasive argument. It is very important to rely only on the facts you have. Inventing facts jeopardizes your, and in turn your attorney's, credibility. Once a legal professional loses credibility, especially with the court, his or her reputation in the legal community is irrevocably ruined.

EXERCISE

Identify what is wrong with the following issue statement.

1. Whether the attorney can help the client with her housing problem.
   - Can the attorney help the client with her housing problem?
2. Whether the client was foolish not to check for hot water before she signed the lease.
   - Should the client have checked the apartment for hot water before signing the lease?
3. Whether, because the tenant insisted on renting an apartment that was not hooked up to the hot water when the landlord tried to give her an apartment that did have hot water, all this is the tenant's fault.
   - Since the tenant insisted on renting an apartment that was not hooked up to the hot water when the landlord tried to give her an apartment that did have hot water, is this problem all the tenant's fault?
4. Whether the amount the attorney could make off this case makes it worth bothering to take.

- Will the attorney make enough money from this case to make it worth bothering to take?

5. Whether the landlord has pulled a bait and switch on other tenants so that the client can get a class action suit against the landlord for fraud because the client talked to three other people who live in the apartment complex and were promised the same unit as Sheila when the landlord knew that there was not hot water in the unit although he promised the unit to all these residents so that many residents of the apartment building are really, really angry at the landlord and want to see him lose.
   - Has the landlord pulled a bait and switch on other tenants so that the client can get a class action suit against the landlord for fraud because the client talked to three other people who live in the apartment complex and were promised the same unit as Sheila when the landlord knew that there was not hot water in the unit although he promised the unit to all these residents so that many residents of the apartment building are really, really angry at the landlord and want to see him lose?

■ MOTOR VEHICLE ACCIDENT (MVA) ▥

On a still, dark winter morning, Cherelle Jackson was driving to her boutique to get an early start on inventory. Because the roads were slippery, she was driving 35 mph in a 50 mph zone. A large van that had been driving behind her passed when they reached a long straight stretch of road. The van hit a patch of ice, turned around totally, and then slid into Cherelle's car. Fortunately, Cherelle's seat belt and airbag prevented her from serious injury. Nonetheless, her car was damaged beyond repair. The van was one of a fleet of rental vehicles owned by Efficiency Car and Truck Rental Company. The driver of the van was cited for failure to control his vehicle and failure to maintain a safe speed for road conditions. Cherelle's auto insurance company paid her for the value of her car, and the insurance company now is seeking compensation from both the driver of the van as well as the Efficiency Car and Truck Rental Company.

EXERCISE

Explain why the following issue statements are incorrect.

1. Whether Cherelle was at fault for the accident for driving 15 miles below the speed limit.
    - Was Cherelle at fault for the accident because she was driving 15 miles below the speed limit?
2. Whether Cherelle had to pay out-of-pocket expenses to cover the difference between the insurance payment and the cost of her new car.
    - Did Cherelle have to pay out-of-pocket expenses to cover the difference between the insurance payment and the cost of her new car?
3. Whether the driver of the van can be held liable for the value of the car destroyed in the accident.
    - Can the driver of the van be held liable for the value of the car that was destroyed in the accident?

4. Whether the rental company can hold the driver liable if it is held responsible for the damages to the destroyed car.
    - Can the rental company hold the driver liable if it is held responsible for the damages to the destroyed car?
5. Whether the driver of the destroyed car has partial liability for contributing to the accident by driving below the speed limit and causing the driver of the van to need to pass and thereby causing him to lose control of his vehicle.
    - Is the driver of the destroyed car partially liable for contributing to the accident by driving below the speed limit and causing the driver of the van to need to pass and thereby causing him to lose control of his vehicle?

In the following exercise, the numbered sets of issues are written in the traditional "Whether" issue format. The lettered sets of issues consist of the same issues written in the newer question format. Depending on the instructor's preference, both versions may be assigned for the student to do, or the instructor may decided to use only the sets written in the "Whether" format, or alternatively, only the sets in the question format.

Efficiency Car and Truck Rental Company is also suing the driver of the van for the damages to the van from the accident.

EXERCISE

Compare and differentiate between the following issue statements and determine which of the following is correct.

1. Whether a driver of a rental vehicle can be held liable for damages to the rental vehicle from an accident after the driver was cited for failure to control his vehicle and failure to maintain a safe speed for road conditions during that accident.
2. Whether a vehicle rental company has a cause of action for damages to its vehicle caused by a driver who was passing on icy roads in the dark.

A. Can a driver of a rental vehicle be held liable for damages to the rental vehicle from an accident after the driver was cited for failure to control his vehicle and failure to maintain a safe speed for road conditions during that accident?
B. Does a vehicle rental company have a cause of action for damages to its vehicle caused by a driver who was passing on icy roads in the dark?

Meanwhile, the driver of the van is suing Efficiency Car and Truck Rental Company, claiming the tires on the van were bald and caused the accident.

(continued)

3. Whether the driver of the van is lying when he says the tires on the van were bald.
4. Whether the rental company met its duty to provide a safe vehicle to the driver.

   C. Is the driver of the van being truthful when he says the tires on the van were bald?
   D. Did the rental company meet its duty to provide a safe vehicle to the driver?

The accident between the rental van and Cherelle's car had blocked the road in both directions for most of the morning. One of the drivers who had been delayed by the accident had been on his way to the airport to fly to the west coast for a job interview. The delay resulted in his missing his plane. As a result, he did not get the job. He is now suing Cherelle, the driver of the van, and Efficiency Car and Truck Rental Company, claiming that but for the accident, he would have gotten the job.

5. Whether damages to other drivers resulting from delays due to an unintentional accident are the responsibility of the drivers involved in the accident.

6. Whether blaming the drivers in an accident for a lost job opportunity because a person missed his plane to the job interview is too remote because they did not plan to get into an accident and they were inconvenienced almost as much if not more than the person who missed his interview who has no proof he would have gotten the job even if he had gotten to the interview.

   E. Are damages to other drivers resulting from delays due an unintentional accident the responsibility of the drivers involved in the accident?
   F. Is blaming the drivers in an accident for a lost job opportunity because a person missed his plane to the job interview is too remote because they did not plan to get into an accident and they were inconvenienced almost as much if not more than the person who missed his interview who has no proof he would have gotten the job even if he had gotten to the interview.

■ REAL ESTATE

EXERCISE _____

Compare and make a distinction between the following issue statements. Which of the two is correct, and why? The incorrect issue statement will be too vague, too wordy, or focus on something other than the issue.

EXERCISE _____

Antoine Taylor was a realtor in Parkhurst, Ohio. In November, Antoine had represented the seller in the sale of a home. The home passed the buyers' inspection, and the sellers had signed the disclosure statement attesting that they had no knowledge of any material defects in the house. The April after the property transferred, however, the buyers woke up one warm, sunny morning and discovered the basement had four feet of water in it. When they discussed this with the neighbors, the neighbors told them that the basement of the home had flooded six years earlier, while the sellers of the home lived in and owned it. The neighbors told the new owners that the sellers had been told that the house had been built directly over a natural stream, and that

(continued)

when the snows melted in the spring, the stream could overflow if there were a rapid snow melt.

The new owners are suing Antoine Taylor for misrepresentation and demanding he compensate them for the amount it will cost to reroute the stream from underneath the home, as well as for the cost of repairs to the basement.

Compare and distinguish between the following issue statements. Which of the two is correct, and why? The incorrect issue statement will be too vague, too wordy, or focus on something other than the issue.

1. Whether the realtor representing the seller is responsible for compensating the buyers for the damage to their home resulting from an undisclosed, hidden defect that was unknown to the realtor.

2. Whether a realtor is responsible for damages to a home when he did not represent the buyers and it was the responsibility of the buyers to discover any defects in the property and they had an inspection so they should sue the inspector who missed this flaw.

   A. Is the realtor representing the seller responsible for compensating the buyers for the damage to their home resulting from an undisclosed, hidden defect that was unknown to the realtor?

   B. Is a realtor responsible for damages to a home when he did not represent the buyers and it was the responsibility of the buyers to discover any defects in the property and they had an inspection so they should sue the inspector who missed this flaw?

3. Whether the new owner's problem is really the sellers' fault.

4. Whether the seller can be held accountable for failing to disclose a known hidden defect to the buyers.

   C. Is the new owner's problem really the sellers' fault?

   D. Can the sellers be held accountable for failing to disclose a known hidden defect to the buyers?

5. Whether a realtor who represented the sellers has recourse against them after their failure to disclose a known, hidden defect resulted in the buyers suing the realtor.

6. Whether a realtor can go after the sellers he represented when those sellers failed to disclose a defect that they were aware of and now he is being sued because they moved out of the country and the new owners cannot reach them but the realtor knows their employers and can get their wages garnished.

   E. Does a realtor who represented the sellers have recourse against them after their failure to disclose a known, hidden defect resulted in the buyers suing the realtor?

   F. Can a realtor go after the sellers he represented when those sellers failed to disclose a defect that they were aware of and now he is being sued because they moved out of the country and the new owners cannot reach them but the realtor knows their employers and can get their wages garnished?

■ MEDICAL MALPRACTICE (MED MAL)

Dr. Jeremy Hunter, a general surgery resident at Parkhurst Hospital, had assisted Dr. Patel, an attending surgeon, when she operated on an assault victim. During a fight, the man had been struck in the face with a baseball bat, which had broken his jaw in several places. The two doctors spent the better part of two hours wiring the man's jaw together to stabilize the fractures. They also did reconstructive work to the skin where the bat had broken it open.

During the surgery, when Dr. Patel was cutting one of the wires, it flew into the patient's eye. Because the anesthesiologist had placed a protective gel in the patient's eyes, it did not appear that the eye sustained any damage. Nonetheless, when Dr. Hunter wrote the operative report, he mentioned the incident.

Six months later, Dr. Hunter saw the patient to remove the wires. The patient had a patch over his eye. When asked, the patient told Dr. Hunter that his eye must have been damaged during the fight in which his jaw had been broken.

Several weeks later, both Dr. Patel and Dr. Hunter received notices in the mail from an attorney representing the patient. It alleged that the patient's jaw had not healed properly because they had not reduced the fracture adequately. It also alleged that the patient has unnecessary scarring on his face where they had repaired the laceration.

During the discovery phase of the lawsuit, Dr. Hunter received a subpoena to be deposed. To prepare for this deposition, he went to the medical records department to request his handwritten notes. He had found that the computerized copy that Dr. Patel had signed differed significantly from what he remembered writing in the post operative note.

When he looked at his handwritten notes in the paper file, he discovered that his reference to the wire striking the patient's eye had been marked out with a black marker, so that it was not able to be seen at all. Dr. Patel happened upon Dr. Hunter as he discovered this alteration, but she refused to meet his eye and ignored his attempts to speak with her. Instead, she hurried out of the department and did not respond to his attempts to reach her.

Dr. Hunter has now been named as a defendant in a medical malpractice case, along with Dr. Patel.

EXERCISE

Compare and differentiate the following issue statements and determine which of the following is correct.

1. Whether Dr. Hunter can be sued because he is only a resident.
2. Whether a surgical resident physician's liability for a patient's alleged injuries is limited by his subordinate role in the surgery.

   A. Can Dr. Hunter be sued because he is only a resident?

   B. Is a surgical resident physician's liability for a patient's alleged injuries limited by his subordinate role in surgery?

3. Whether the attending physician destroyed evidence when she obliterated portions of the surgical resident's handwritten operative report.
4. Whether, because they are being sued for nonunion of the patient's jaw and the quality of the laceration repair, the attending physician's altering the medical record does not matter anyway.

   C. Did the attending physician destroy evidence when she obliterated portions of the surgical resident's handwritten operative report?

   D. Does the attending physician's alteration of the medical record matter, since the doctors are being sued for nonunion of the patient's jaw and the quality of the laceration repair?

5. Whether the surgical resident should not have mentioned the wire hitting the patient in the eye because doctors should cover for each other, not get each other in trouble.
6. Whether the surgical resident has any liability for the attending physician's altering of the medical record after receiving notice of the lawsuit.

   E. Should the surgical resident not mention the wire that hit the patient's eye because doctors should cover for each other, not get each other in trouble?

   F. Does the surgical resident have any liability for the attending physician's altering of the medical record after receiving notice of the lawsuit?

■ CONTRACT BREACH

Marcus Johnson, whose father, Henry, owned Parkhurst Industries, married his long-time girlfriend, Brianna Jones. As a wedding present, Marcus's father Henry paid for Marcus and Brianna to have a custom built home constructed for them on a plot of land adjacent to homes other family members owned. Marcus's father wanted to keep his family near him to enhance family ties.

Marcus, Henry, and Brianna met with a number of builders before selecting Connolly Homes of Parkhurst to build the home. Connolly agreed to follow the plans their architect had drawn up and to give Marcus and Brianna a choice of all finishes and colors. Henry, Marcus, and Brianna all signed the construction contract. Henry put the funds for the cost of construction into a separate checking account so that either Marcus or Brianna could write checks as construction proceeded.

Connolly began construction shortly before Brianna and Marcus's wedding. Marcus and Brianna went on a month-long honeymoon after the wedding. Although Marcus's father had intended to visit the construction site regularly, a strike at one of Parkhurst Industries' primary suppliers required Henry to locate and contract with a substitute supplier. This prevented him from overseeing the construction as he had planned.

When Marcus and Brianna returned from their honeymoon, the home construction was far more complete than they had expected. The roof was on, the outside walls were up, and the drywall was in place in almost all of the rooms. The architect had monitored the layout of the construction, and the room sizes and placements were consistent with the plans.

Brianna and Marcus moved in a month later, after the cabinets, countertops, and fixtures they had selected were installed. On their first night in the new home, however, Marcus discovered that the water faucets in the master bathroom were reversed, so that the cold water tap ran hot, and the hot water tap ran cold. Over the course of the next few days, they realized that five electrical outlets did not work, and within a month, they saw water damage on the family room vaulted ceiling.

As they discovered these defects, they complained to Connolly, who promised to repair them. For each repair appointment, Brianna waited at home for the repairman to come to fix a defect; however, no one showed up. When she or Marcus called Connolly, one of the company's representatives always had an excuse and scheduled a new appointment. Each rescheduled appointment resulted in failure to appear. Finally, after nine months of broken appointments, Brianna sent written complaints to the builder, the Better Business Bureau, and the Secretary of State for the State of Ohio. Even after she sent several certified letters listing all the problems with the home, Connolly failed to fix them.

After the first year, Connolly began responding to the phone calls by saying that the one-year warranty on the home had expired, and because Marcus and Brianna had failed to put their complaints in writing, they could not prove that Connolly had notice of their alleged defects before the warranty expired.

Marcus and Brianna consulted with Brad, Marcus's college fraternity brother, to see what recourse he had against Connolly. Brianna told Brad that she had filed complaints with the Better Business Bureau and the State Attorney General, and that she had sent written complaints by certified mail to Connolly describing each of the defects. She gave the Post Office's return receipt slips to Brad.

In the following exercise, the first version of the issue is written in the traditional "Whether" format, and the second in the newer question format.

EXERCISE

Revise and correct the issue in the following exercises based on this fact pattern.

1. Whether Brianna and Marcus should sue Connolly Homes of Parkhurst.
   - Should Brianna and Marcus sue Connolly Homes of Parkhurst?

2. Whether the builder ever got the certified letters complaining of the defects in the house.
   - Did the builder ever receive the certified letters buyer sent complaining of defects in the house?

3. Whether buyers should be worried about the rest of the wiring and plumbing in the home if they have found so many problems and Henry, Marcus's father, did not supervise the installations because he was too busy arranging for replacement widgets after his widget maker went on strike so all the wiring and plumbing could be substandard and even dangerous.
   - Should the buyers be worried about the rest of the wiring and plumbing in the home if they have found so many problems and Henry, Marcus's father, did not supervise the installations because he was too busy arranging for replacement widgets after his widget maker went on strike so all the wiring and plumbing could be substandard and even dangerous.

4. Whether buyer can sue builder for her lost time spent waiting for the repair people who never came when promised.
   - Can the buyer sue the builder for her lost time spent waiting for repair people who never came when promised?

5. Whether the one-year warranty Connolly Homes of Parkhurst claims has expired is the only recourse Marcus and Brianna have against the company because the company clearly did not do a good enough job on the house and so Marcus and Brianna should get some of the money they paid for the house back along with having all the wiring and plumbing replaced, which means they would have to move into a hotel until the house was fully repaired so Connolly should pay for the cost of their hotel, too.
   - Is the one-year warranty Connolly Homes of Parkhurst claims has expired the only recourse Marcus and Brianna have against the company because the company clearly did not do a good enough job on the house and so Marcus and Brianna should get some of the money they paid for the house back along with having all the wiring and plumbing replaced, which means they would have to move into a hotel until the house was fully repaired so Connolly should pay for the cost of their hotel, too?

■ PRODUCT LIABILITY

When they were still in college, Brad and Antoine had been fraternity brothers. During a party at their fraternity house, the gas stove in the kitchen had exploded. Although no one was hurt, the fraternity house burned to the ground, and the students who lived in the house lost their all their belongings. The fire department's investigation determined that the explosion was a result of a flaw in either the stove or the gas line to the stove.

Their attorney, Ms. Walker, had found, through her paralegal's research, that the stove they had bought at the big box store had been recalled prior to the date the fraternity brothers bought it. Although the store denied knowing about the recall, it had sold the stove at cost. The paralegal also discovered that the manufacturer of the stove had gone bankrupt and could not be sued.

EXERCISE

Identify the issue for the product liability fact pattern, then draft the most concise and thorough issue that you can. This exercise should take you at least 30 to

45 minutes, because you will need to refine, revise, and reword the issue repeatedly to make it as succinct yet complete as it should be.

SUMMARY

- Legal writers use a pattern called IRAC to organize their arguments.

- The first letter in the acronym IRAC stands for the Issue.

- The issue is the statement of the question or disagreement between the parties that they want the court to settle.

- The issue includes enough of the fact pattern and the law to make the question comprehensible to the reader, but does not include so much that it muddles the issue.

- Identifying the correct issue is essential.

- The issue is the fulcrum of any case. It is the pivot point on which everything else in the case hinges.

- If the issue is not precisely and concisely written, the rest of the document will be ineffective and lack adequate focus.

- Framing the issue often is the most difficult and the most important part of writing a legal document.

ASSIGNMENTS

I. Read the fact pattern below and select the correct issue.

A decade ago, Henry Johnson had bought property in Wisconsin that he hoped to turn into a family vacation compound. He then got distracted by business matters, and when he returned to the property after Marcus and Brianna were married, he discovered that what had once been a quiet, wooded property on a pristine lake was now surrounded by condominiums, gated communities, and a large shopping mall. Although Henry's property was still wooded, it was no longer quiet. The lake was abuzz with jet skis and motor boats. Because his dream of a quiet vacation compound was no longer feasible, Henry decided to sell the property.

When he got an appraisal of the property, he was pleased to discover that the surrounding development had caused his property to increase in value ten-fold. He quickly entered into a sales contract, selling it to a developer. The contract specifically provided that if one of the parties failed to perform, that is, to uphold its side of the contract, the other side could demand specific performance. [See note] The developer had been insistent on including this clause, because it realized that the property would increase in value, and it wanted to be certain that Henry did not decide to sell it to someone else for a higher price.

When the sale was scheduled to close, however, the developer informed Henry that it had not obtained financing yet. After an additional six month delay, Henry hired local counsel to sue the buyer for specific performance. After a trial, the court awarded a verdict for Henry and ordered the developer to complete the purchase of the property. The developer appealed, claiming that Henry should have sought other legal remedies rather than specific performance.

[Note: Specific performance is a contract term that applies to the sale of real property. Specific performance requires the buyer to complete the purchase of the property even if the buyer changes its mind and decides it does not want the property. Similarly, if a seller tries to renege on the sale of a specific property, the buyer also can sue for specific performance, forcing the seller to transfer the property to the buyer. The courts allow specific performance in a real estate contract to be enforced because each piece of real estate is considered to be unique and not able to be substituted.]

Which of the following issue statements is correct?

1. Whether a developer can be forced to complete a property purchase when it does not have the money to buy the property.

   Can a developer be forced to complete a property purchase when it does not have the money to buy the property?

2. Whether a seller is required to pursue legal remedies before enforcing a specific performance clause in the sales contract.

   Is a seller required to pursue legal remedies before enforcing a specific performance clause in the sales contract?

3. Whether a seller can sell the property to another developer who offered him more money now that the first developer has backed out of the deal.

   Can a seller sell the property to another developer who offered him more money now that the first developer has backed out of the deal?

4. Whether Henry can sue the realtor who sold him the property as a pristine, quiet vacation site because the realtor should have known that the area was about to be developed.

   Can Henry sue the realtor who sold him the property as a pristine, quiet vacation site because the realtor should have known that the area was about to be developed?

II. Read the fact pattern below and reword the issue more concisely.

Antoine and Cherelle were visiting her Aunt Denise in Boston. They had adopted a small mixed breed dog from the pound a month earlier. They wryly had named the dog Spike, because it was so timid and shy. Because Spike suffered from separation anxiety when he was away from Cherelle, Aunt Denise graciously had told them that the dog was welcome to visit, too. Fortunately, the dog was housebroken and well trained, and the visit was proceeding pleasantly. Cherelle and Aunt Denise took the dog for a walk in the park. Cherelle was careful to keep Spike on a leash, even though she was certain that he would never let her out of his sight.

Suddenly, a large dog ran up from behind Cherelle and snatched Spike up in its jaws. Cherelle and Aunt Denise both shouted at the large dog and beat on it, trying to get it to let go of Spike. A park ranger arrived, and despite his best efforts, could not loosen the large dog's jaws. The park ranger finally shot the attacking dog through the heart. The ranger then rescued Spike from the dead dog's mouth. Spike was bleeding profusely and was barely conscious.

Another ranger drove Cherelle, Aunt Denise, and Spike to the nearest veterinary hospital, where the veterinarian spent five hours operating on him. To everyone's surprise, Spike recovered almost completely, and Cherelle and Antoine took him home a week later.

When the bill arrived for Spike's emergency medical treatment, Cherelle was appalled to find that she owed the veterinarian $5,000. She was even more distraught when the owner of the large dog filed a lawsuit against her in Massachusetts for the loss of his AKC registered dog. The large dog's owner was suing her for loss of income, claiming that he often made several thousand dollars each year breeding the dog.

Brad and Ana gave Cherelle and Antoine the name of a law school classmate who was practicing law in Boston, and the classmate countersued for the veterinary bills incurred in Spike's treatment.

III. The following issue addresses Cherelle's position concerning the cost of the veterinary bills, but it is poorly stated. Reword it more concisely. If your instructor prefers the issue to be stated beginning with "whether," reword your concise issue in that form.

"When a dog who was not provoked attacks a dog that was minding its own business and injures the other dog so that the other dog needs a lot of medical treatment and that medical treatment turns out to have been very extremely expensive does the owner of the dog that attacked the dog that was minding its own business have to pay the veterinarian bills the owner racked up for the dog's surgery and other treatments?"

IV. Read the fact pattern below and state the issue from Jeremy's point of view.

While he was doing a one year internship at a large university medical center in upstate New York, Jeremy found that jogging helped clear his mind and helped him sleep—not that he had much opportunity to sleep. He and a classmate were jogging in late October in the classmate's home town, Trumansburg, New York, a quaint little town near the large medical center. After running up a short but steep hill off the main road, they turned left onto McLallen Street, which had charming pre-Civil War homes. Some of the homes had the original slate sidewalks, and the wet leaves were slicked onto the sidewalks.

Jeremy slipped on moss that was hidden by the leaves and fell, breaking his right hand. Because he planned to be a surgeon, he was quite distressed by this injury. One of the professors at the law school that was affiliated with the university offered to represent him in a lawsuit against the homeowners whose sidewalk was the location of his fall. He told Jeremy that the homeowners should have cleared the slippery moss and wet leaves off their sidewalk.

V. Adding to the fact pattern in Assignment IV, read the following paragraph and state the issue from the homeowner's point of view.

After the homeowners received Jeremy's complaint alleging that they were responsible for his fall on the mossy, leaf covered sidewalk in front of their home, they argued that by running on slate sidewalks, which were known to be slippery when wet, and by running on these wet slate sidewalks that were covered by wet leaves, Jeremy had assumed the risk of his injury. The homeowners argued that they were not liable for the slippery sidewalk. They also argued that by running on wet leaves without knowledge of the surface under the leaves, Jeremy had negligently contributed to his own injury.

LEARNING OBJECTIVES

1. Identify IRAC formatting

2. Explain where Primary and Secondary sources originate

3. Recognize the correct content that is needed for the Rule segment in IRAC

4. Write the rules in direct quotes, weaving, and paraphrasing accurately

5. Judge whether the rule applies to the current fact pattern that is being researched

6. Compose excellent, succinct summaries, and interpretations of the rule for the document

IRAC - Rule

CHAPTER 8

■ DEFINE IRAC

This book is not intended to teach you how to research the law, only how to write in a legally appropriate manner. Your legal research class will go into the art of finding the applicable law. In this chapter, we provide you with law from various states that is applicable to the fact patterns introduced in the chapter preceding this one discussing the issue and demonstrate how to state the law. In the next chapter discussing the analysis, we show you how to apply the law to the facts of the case.

The rule is the second element in IRAC. The rule is the law that applies to the case. The law consists of primary sources that include the Constitution, statutes, regulations, ordinances, and case law. Primary sources are the most important and most reliable form of law. Secondary sources of law consist of Treatises, Restatements, AmJur, and other scholarly books written to be the guide and outline areas of law. Secondary sources serve to supplement and complement the primary sources, but they are used only in conjunction with primary sources. This chapter will apply only primary sources of law; however, it will briefly explain secondary sources while focusing on primary sources. Following the exercise below is discussion of the primary sources of law.

EXERCISE _____

As you read this chapter on the rule, fill in the worksheet below.

1. The second segment/section of an IRAC statement is the _____.
2. The rule is the _____ that _____ to the case.
3. Primary sources include: _____ _____.

4. Primary sources are the most _____ and most _____ form of law.
5. Secondary sources are _____ and _____ on the primary sources of law.
6. An example from your reading of a secondary source is _____ (Wikipedia does not count as a secondary source.)

(continued)

7. If the court incorporates part of a secondary source decision then _____ becomes the law.

8. If you do not have good law or a primary source to rely on what should you do? _____ _____

9. Remember only quoting secondary sources makes _____ than it would be with primary sources.

10. A state's constitution shall not contradict anything in _____.

■ SOURCES

As noted above, earlier, there are various sources of law that lawyers and judges use. New legal writers need to learn what the different sources of law are and how to use them correctly. When most people think of the law, they think of statutes that legislators pass. Often, people think of the law as primarily a form of criminal control, like the laws against murder or robbery. They also think of traffic laws, like the laws against speeding or running a red light. As you will learn in this chapter and the rest of your paralegal education, however, there are many sources of law.

By learning about the actual sources of law used by lawyers and the courts, new legal writers will be able to identify which laws and which types of laws are applicable to their cases. Paralegals will learn to analyze case law and apply it to the arguments in their documents. Below is a brief summary of the various types of law that are enforced in the United States.

Primary Sources

The Constitution

The supreme law of the land is the United States Constitution. All statutes and case law interpret and apply the law set forth in the Constitution. Each state also has its own Constitution, but a state's Constitution shall not contradict anything in the U.S. Constitution. In the case of a conflict, the U.S. Constitution prevails.

Statutes

The first form of law we will address is statutory law. Statutes are laws passed by Congress to more specifically enforce the Constitution. Laws enforcing the United States Constitution are enacted by the Congress and Senate in Washington, D.C. Each state or commonwealth has its own legislative body that enacts legislation for its Constitution. Statutes or ordinances are laws created not only by a legislative body like Congress, but also by a City or a County Council (which may refer to them as ordinances). Because the United States has both federal and state governments, there are federal statutes that are enforceable throughout the United States. State statutes, as you can surmise, are enforceable only in the state whose legislature passed the law. Similarly, a City or County ordinance is enforceable only in the relevant city or county. This diversity of laws can cause confusion for the novice.

Note that it is improper to begin a sentence with an abbreviation or an Arabic numeral. Thus, when discussing a case or statute, be careful not to begin the sentence with the abbreviation for that statute. Instead, write out the proper title of the statute. This will become clearer when we begin quoting and citing to statutes.

Regulations

Because a statute can encompass such an enormous area of law, the statute might mandate the creation of an agency to promulgate regulations that more specifically guide people and corporations. Regulations are rules that more specifically interpret a statute. On a federal level, the Environmental Protection Agency (EPA) is an example of an agency created to draft specific regulations to enforce the statutes Congress passed to protect the environment. On a state level, the State Medical Board or the State Nursing Board establishes regulations controlling the practice of medicine and nursing within the state. Many states also have their own versions of an EPA. Regulations have the force of law, and violating a regulation subjects the violator to penalties, just as violating a statute does. A doctor violating a regulation, for example, might not be held criminally liable, but he or she could lose the medical license that allows him or her to practice medicine. Regulations have the same force as a statute.

Case Law

The form of law that is most difficult to understand for a person new to the law is case law. United States law is modeled after the British legal system. Initially, a case is heard by the trial court. This is the court usually depicted in legal shows on television. If the losing party chooses, he, she, or it (in the case of a corporation or other non-human party) can appeal the case to an appellate court. Once an Appellate Court makes its ruling and issues a decision, the decision is the controlling law for that issue, unless the Supreme Court agrees to hear the case. The highest court to rule on the case's decision is the one that controls, or is final. This controlling decision is called "precedent." When the same issue arises in a later case, that precedent is the law that other courts in that jurisdiction will follow. For example, if an appellate court decides that a homeowner is not responsible for the ice on the sidewalk outside the homeowner's house during an ice storm, the trial courts in that jurisdiction will follow that rule when someone sues a homeowner for an injury resulting from ice on the homeowner's sidewalk during an ice storm.

Courts are reluctant to overturn precedent, because it is important for citizens to be able to rely on the law. If each panel of judges decided to ignore what the other judges had done before them, the citizens would have no clear guidance about their legal rights and obligations.

Sometimes courts in different jurisdictions reach contradictory conclusions on an issue. When this happens, one of the parties in the cases can appeal to a higher court for resolution of the conflict of law. When the highest court of the jurisdiction – the United States Supreme Court for federal cases – makes a ruling, that is, issues a decision on an issue, that decision is the law of the land. Occasionally, a subsequent Supreme Court might overturn a prior decision, and when that happens, it can have significant societal repercussions. This occurred in 1954, when the US Supreme Court overturned longstanding precedent established in 1896 in *Plessy v. Ferguson*, 163 U.S.537, 16 S. Ct. 1138, 41 L. Ed. 256, 1896 U.S. 3390.[1] The *Plessy* Court had held that people of different races could be assigned to separate railway cars, and that people of one race could be fined for trying to

---

[1] Note that although we discussed citation format in the citation chapter, the system for citing to cases has evolved over time and continues to evolve. Some citations contained in this and other chapters, therefore, might differ somewhat from strict *The Blue Book* format.

ride in the car assigned to the other race. The Court's decision was in large part a product of its time, less than 50 years after the Civil War. The Court stated, "[t]he distinction between laws interfering with the political equality of the negro (sic) and those requiring the separation of the two races in schools, theatres and railway carriages has been frequently drawn by this court." The Court held that separate but equal accommodations could be enforced within a state.

The concept of "separate but equal" remained the law of the land until 1954, when the US Supreme Court overruled *Plessy* in *Brown v. Board of Education of Topeka*, 347 U.S. 483, 74 S. Ct. 686, 98 L. Ed. 873 (1954). The *Brown* Court said, "We come then to the question presented: Does segregation of children in public schools solely on the basis of race, even though the physical facilities and other 'tangible' factors may be equal, deprive the children of the minority group of equal educational opportunities? We believe that it does."

After the US Supreme Court decided *Brown v. Board of Education*, *Plessy* was no longer "good law." Although it is unlikely that you will be involved in a case of the magnitude of *Brown*, it will be important for your clients for you to make sure any case you quote or rely on is still good law, that is, has not been overturned.

To summarize a long explanation of what comprises the rule in IRAC, the rule is the statute, regulation, ordinance, or case law that controls the issue in the case.

As we discussed in the definition of the rule, case law applies the statute to a specific case and decides the rights and obligations of the parties. Case law consists of a decision made by an appellate court; after the trial court has had a trial or otherwise ruled on the case, any party involved at the trial court level may then appeal.

Thus, case law consists of the courts' interpretation and application of statutes to real life situations. Case law applies the statute to a specific case and decides the rights and obligations of the parties.

Although this textbook includes a chapter addressing citation format, for students whose Instructors do not cover that chapter, we have included a brief explanation of citation format here. For students whose Instructors did cover this chapter, the following will serve as a refresher.

The recognized standard for citation format is *The Bluebook: A Uniform System of Citation* (Columbia Law Review Ass'n et al. eds., 19th ed. 2013). Nonetheless, as Internet sources of case law become more prevalent, individual states are adopting new formats to reference the online locations of their decisions. It is important, therefore, to follow the format for the jurisdiction in which your document will be submitted.

Nonetheless, the standard format has been to state in what state volume number a case was published, then the title of the state reporter, and then the page number on which the case started. Next, the citation states the volume of the regional reporter, followed by the name of the regional reporter, followed by the page number on which the case begins in the regional reporter. Before the Internet became a primary vehicle for exchanging information, the cases from a geographic region were (and still are) also published together in a Reporter. The Reporters are grouped geographically, so that Ohio cases are published in the Northeastern Reporter, and Michigan cases are published in the Northwestern Reporter. Florida cases are reported in the Southern Reporter, and California cases are reported in the Pacific Reporter. Note that many, but not all, states also have their own Reporters. Additionally, not all cases reported in state reporters are included in regional reporters. A Michigan Court of Appeals case we will use later in this chapter is cited as follows: *Curry v. Meijer, Inc.*, 286 Mich. App. 586, 780 N.W.2d 603 (2009).

This citation tells us first the title of the case, in italics or underlined, depending on the jurisdiction's preference. The next item, a number, tells us that the case was published in volume 286 of the Michigan reporter and that the case begins on page 586. The next number, 780, tells us that the case is printed in volume 780 of the Northwestern Reporter, which is abbreviated N.W.2d. The number after N.W.2d tells us the page number on which the case begins in that volume. Finally, the number in parentheses at the end of the citation tells us what year the decision was issued.

Sometimes you will see a case cited with a second number after the number indicating the page on which the case begins. This second number indicating pagination tells the reader the page on which the citation is located. Notice that in the different Reporters, the pagination is different, as is the volume number. If we were citing to page 591 in the Michigan reporter and page 606 in the Northwestern Reporter, the citation would be *Curry v. Meijer, Inc.*, 286 Mich. App. 586, 591, 780 N.W.2d 603, 606 (2009)

Many states continue to use this citation format. Several states though, including the State of Ohio,[2] have been using a different format for case citation. Some of these states identify the case by the year it was published, the name of the state, and the unique, individual case number. The norm once was that some cases were published, and these were considered to be "good law," that is, reliable sources upon which to rely. Unpublished cases, on the other hand, were those that had been decided by the courts but were not included in bound volumes. They were not considered to be precedential. Legal writers cited to unreported cases only when they could not find a reported case that supported their arguments. Now that many states are including all decisions online, some states, including Ohio, no longer make the distinction between reported and unreported cases. All cases are considered to be good precedent.

Because, unlike the bound volumes of case law, the online cases did not have assigned page numbers, the states using the online format began numbering the paragraphs in each decision and designating the part of the decision being referenced by its paragraph number. That way, people reading the decision would be able to locate the reference, regardless of the volume or electronic site they were using. Still, as you are researching law online, you will notice the page numbers for the printed volumes inserted into the text corresponding to the page numbers in the various reporters.

The electronic information revolution is changing the way most data are communicated. Only time will tell what legal citation format will look like in the future. For now, however, we will use the citation format of each state whose law we use, as found in the *Blue Book*, or on the state's website.

The case we cite to throughout the Landlord-Tenant fact pattern is an unreported case. But because it an Ohio case, it is good law, because Ohio does not differentiate between unreported and reported cases for precedential value. Note that for unreported cases, the state district and county are included, along with the number the case had in that district. Different states will have different methods of citing to online cases, but this is an example of how one state does it.

Thus, the Ohio citation for a case we will be citing is *Gammarino v. Smith*, 1st Dist. Hamilton No. C-060636, 2007-Ohio-4073. In the Landlord-Tenant section below, you will see a cite from this case from paragraph 19. In the text, the

---

[2] The search index can be accessed at http://www.sc.ohio.gov/ROD/docs/. *See also* Supreme Court of Ohio, Published for the Supreme Court of Ohio, A Guide to Citations, Style, and Judicial Opinion Writing, effective July 1, 2013, Second edition; http://www.supremecourt.ohio.gov/ROD/manual.pdf, at 5.

paragraph number is included in brackets. Other states may indicate the paragraph number differently.

{19} A tenant may escrow rent with the municipal court when (1) the landlord fails to abide by R.C. 5321.04, the rental agreement, or local health and safety laws; (2) the tenant notifies the landlord in writing of the defects in his property; and (3) the landlord fails to remedy the defects within the sooner of "a reasonable time" or 30 days.

Gammarino at ¶ 19.

Secondary Sources

As noted above, this chapter will not apply any secondary sources of law, but you need to be aware of them and how they are used. In law, there are primary sources and secondary sources. Primary sources are the actual statutes, regulations, and court decisions (case law). Secondary sources are commentaries and interpretations on the primary sources of law. For example, Black's Law Dictionary, which was first published in 1891, is considered to be the most respected source for definitions of legal terms. Nonetheless, it is not the law, but a secondary source that defines legal terms. In tort law, the Restatement of Torts is sometimes a source that the courts quote in a decision. Still, it is not law unless the court incorporates part of it into its decision. Then only the decision is the law.

Because primary sources of law are the only ones that provide controlling, or legally enforceable law, you should rely only on primary sources for a legal argument whenever it is available. If you do not have any good law to rely on, then citing to a secondary source may be your only option. Keep in mind, though, that secondary sources make your argument much weaker than it would be with primary sources. Using a secondary source to bolster an argument that relies on good primary law is fine. Still, avoid using secondary sources without a good primary source whenever possible.

When you are quoting the law, it must be quoted exactly. If you bold, italicize, or underline any portion for emphasis, you must state so at the end of the sentence by saying (Emphasis added). If the Court has used one of these in the original, at the end of the sentence, you should add (Emphasis in original).

Finally, remember that Internet searches, unless they lead you to an official site, are not reliable. Never quote, rely on, or use Wikipedia, except as a guide to the real law.

■ REVIEW-ISSUE

The issue summarizes the legal question being addressed in the document. When writers craft the issue of a case, they establish the parameters of their legal research and the subsequent analysis that will apply to the case. Correctly defining the issue is essential for an effective legal document.

■ R = RULE

After the issue has identified the area in dispute, legal writers focus their research on the law that applies to the case. The law is comprised of several different sources. Primary law is the controlling law for the case, and it consists of constitutions, but more commonly, case law and statutes. Secondary sources of law are learned treatises and other scholarly analyses of the law, and although they are not controlling, because they are highly respected, they are persuasive.

When courts make a decision regarding a dispute in a lawsuit, they apply the law that exists that applies to the question that the issue raises. When attorneys try to persuade the court that their clients' point of view is correct and should prevail, the attorneys cite to and compare the same law to their clients' situations. Every court relies on the law to guide it in making its judgments.

What Are the Characteristics of the Rule?

The Rule Is

- The second segment of the IRAC document
- A summary, paraphrase, or quotation of the applicable law- only the relevant law
- A separate paragraph or paragraphs

Important

- Discuss all applicable rules; do not wait to add them later in other sections.
- Do not discuss rules that do not apply.

Points to Ponder

What happens if:

- We give a rule that does not apply? The IRAC statement is incorrect.
- We give law that has been overturned? The IRAC statement is incorrect.
- We do not state the rule clearly? The reader becomes confused.

So how do you insert the law into your writing? There are several ways to state the law in your document.

Direct Quote

You can quote the law directly, either in full or selecting only the pertinent part. If the law you are referencing is succinct or requires very specific wording, this might be the best choice.

Weaving

You can also weave the law into a sentence or paragraph with the quoted portion interwoven into your text. As with simply quoting the law, it is important to make sure that when you omit inapplicable portions, you do not make any changes to the meaning of the law.

Paraphrasing

In addition to quoting or interweaving the law, you can paraphrase it. The attorney you work for might not allow you to paraphrase the law for fear you might misinterpret it. Some practicing attorneys are reluctant to paraphrase for this reason. Nonetheless, paraphrasing can be the most fluid and coherent way to include the law in your document. If you learn to paraphrase accurately, your document can be more persuasive because it can be clearer. Even if you do not use paraphrasing in your final document, by paraphrasing the law for yourself, you can gain a greater understanding of the concept and scope of the law you are applying. Paraphrasing will also assist you in seeing how the law applies to the facts of your client's case.

We provide examples of how to directly quote, weave, and paraphrase the law into your writing later in the chapter, when we address the law that applies to our fact patterns, specifically, in the sections addressing landlord-tenant law and contract breach law.

■ JURISDICTIONAL VARIATIONS IN LAW

As we discussed briefly in the section addressing statutes, above there are different levels of jurisdiction in the United States. Federal law applies to all the states, but it is limited to areas of law that are granted to the authority of the federal government by the United States Constitution. Federal statutes apply equally in all fifty states, and Federal case law is controlling in the same areas.

The Constitution reserves many powers to the individual states, however, and each state has its own set of statutes and case law. Note that Louisiana's legal structure differs from the structures in the other 49 states, in that Louisiana follows the civil law system instead of the common law system. The civil law system is used in most of Europe, and relies on statutes for deciding disputes rather than relying on case law, as England and the United States do. However, those differences are beyond the scope of this text. Also, several states are organized as Commonwealths instead of States, but the Commonwealths' legal systems generally are organized in similar ways to the States.

Although each state has statutes drafted by its legislature, and each has a court system for interpreting and enforcing those statutes, the names of the courts vary from state to state. Thus, a Supreme Court may be the highest court in one state, but the court titled the Supreme Court in another state may be a lower level court.

Because each state enforces its own laws, we have included law from several different states in the IRAC sections of this text. The majority of paralegals will work in jobs that apply state, and not Federal, law, so you will have to learn how to navigate the legal structure of your state. We are providing a sampling to demonstrate the differences and similarities of law from state to state. All the fact patterns and IRAC analyses in the text include Ohio law, because the action of each fact pattern occurs in Ohio.

Many corporations that do business in more than one state, however, include a forum selection clause in their contracts. A forum selection clause is a choice of law provision that requires those doing business with the company to apply the law of the state where the company is incorporated to any dispute or legal action. Thus, even when the situation that gives rise to a lawsuit occurs in one state, a forum selection clause may require the litigation to apply the law of another state, where one of the parties is incorporated.

Further discussion of forum selection is beyond the scope of this text. We mention it only because the paralegal in these fact patterns is researching law from various jurisdictions depending on the location of the corporate offices of the companies involved in each lawsuit.

■ LANDLORD–TENANT

Sheila has hired Ana Garcia to represent her in her problem with the landlord who is not providing hot water to the apartment that Sheila rented. Sheila has left messages and even sent a certified letter to the landlord informing the landlord that the apartment does not have hot water. To date, the landlord has merely laughed at Sheila, telling her she got exactly what she bargained for by insisting on taking possession of that specific apartment when it was the model apartment. The landlord also told Sheila that the company that owned the apartment building was headquartered in Florida, and the lease she signed stated that Florida law would apply to any disputes the tenant had.

Ana determined that Sheila's best option might be to deposit her rent with the Court until the landlord has provided the basic legal requirements. Ana has asked the paralegal to research the law in both Ohio and Florida concerning a landlord providing hot water to a residential tenant and the recourse the tenant has when the landlord fails to do so, and the paralegal has discovered the following:

■ OHIO STATUTORY LAW

Note, in Ohio, the statute is abbreviated as R.C. when referred to in text, as required by the Ohio Supreme Court *Writing Manual*. When quoting fifty or more words, the quote must be single spaced and indented five spaces on both the left and right margins.

EXAMPLE

Ohio Revised Code: R.C. § 5321.04 **Landlord obligations.**

(A) A landlord who is a party to a rental agreement shall do all of the following:

. . . .

(6) Supply running water, reasonable amounts of hot water, and reasonable heat at all times . . . .

. . . .

EXAMPLE

Ohio Revised Code: R.C. § 5321.07 **Failure of landlord to fulfill obligations - remedies of tenant.**

> (A) If a landlord fails to fulfill any obligation imposed upon him by section 5321.04 of the Revised Code . . . the tenant may give notice in writing to the landlord, specifying the acts, omissions, or code violations that constitute noncompliance. The notice shall be sent to the person or place where rent is normally paid.
>
> (B) If a landlord receives the notice described in division (A) of this section and after receipt of the notice fails to remedy the condition within a reasonable time considering the severity of the condition and the time necessary to remedy it, or within thirty days, whichever

is sooner, and if the tenant is current in rent payments due under the rental agreement, the tenant may do one of the following:

(1) Deposit all rent that is due and thereafter becomes due the landlord with the clerk of the municipal or county court having jurisdiction in the territory in which the residential premises are located;

(2) Apply to the court for an order directing the landlord to remedy the condition. As part of the application, the tenant may deposit rent pursuant to division (B)(1) of this section, may apply for an order reducing the periodic rent due the landlord until the landlord remedies the condition, and may apply for an order to use the rent deposited to remedy the condition. In any order issued pursuant to this division, the court may require the tenant to deposit rent with the clerk of court as provided in division (B)(1) of this section.

(3) Terminate the rental agreement.

Above is a statute. (Notice that in subsection (A), we have used ellipses to indicate that we deleted a portion of the statute that did not pertain to our fact pattern.)

As the landlord told Sheila, the company that owns the apartment complex is headquartered in Florida. After reviewing the lease that Sheila signed, Ana verified that it indicates that Florida law controls in any dispute concerning the rental property. Therefore, the paralegal also researched Florida law on this issue and found a similar statute for the State of Florida that states the following:

■ FLORIDA STATUTORY LAW

The Florida statutes governing landlords and tenants differ from those in Ohio in several ways, as a review of the following statutes reveals:

EXAMPLE

Florida statutes are abbreviated as follows: Fla. Stat. § 83.51 (2012).
   Landlord's obligation to maintain premises.—

(1) The landlord at all times during the tenancy shall:

(a) Comply with the requirements of applicable building, housing, and health codes; or

(b) Where there are no applicable building, housing, or health codes, maintain the roofs, windows, screens, doors, floors, steps, porches, exterior walls, foundations, and all other structural components in good repair and capable of resisting normal forces and loads and the plumbing in reasonable working condition. . . . .

(2) (a) Unless otherwise agreed in writing, in addition to the requirements of subsection (1), the landlord of a dwelling unit . . . shall, at all times during the tenancy, make reasonable provisions for:

5. Functioning facilities for heat during winter, running water, and hot water.

EXAMPLE

Florida Statute: Fla. Stat. § 83.44 (2014)   **Obligation of good faith.—**

Every rental agreement or duty within this part imposes an obligation of good faith in its performance or enforcement.

EXAMPLE

Florida Statute: Fla. Stat. § 83.55 (2014)   **Right of action for damages.—**

If either the landlord or the tenant fails to comply with the requirements of the rental agreement or this part, the aggrieved party may recover the damages caused by the noncompliance.

EXAMPLE

Florida Statute: Fla. Stat. § 83.56 (2014) **Termination of rental agreement.—**

(1) If the landlord materially fails to comply with s. 83.51(1) or material provisions of the rental agreement within 7 days after delivery of written notice by the tenant specifying the noncompliance and indicating the intention of the tenant to terminate the rental agreement by reason thereof, the tenant may terminate the rental agreement. If the failure to comply with s. 83.51(1) or material provisions of the rental agreement is due to causes beyond the control of the landlord and the landlord has made and continues to make every reasonable effort to correct the failure to comply, the rental agreement may be terminated or altered by the parties, as follows:

(a) If the landlord's failure to comply renders the dwelling unit untenantable and the tenant vacates, the tenant shall not be liable for rent during the period the dwelling unit remains uninhabitable.

(b) If the landlord's failure to comply does not render the dwelling unit untenantable and the tenant remains in occupancy, the rent for the period of noncompliance shall be reduced by an amount in proportion to the loss of rental value caused by the noncompliance.

. . . .

EXAMPLE

Florida Statute: Fla. Stat. § 83.60 (2014) **Defenses to action for rent or possession; procedure.—**

1. In an action by the landlord for possession of a dwelling unit based upon nonpayment of rent or in an action by the landlord under s. 83.55 seeking to recover unpaid rent, the tenant may defend upon the ground of a material noncompliance with s. 83.51(1) [F.S. 1973], or may raise any other defense, whether legal or equitable, that he or she may have, including the defense of retaliatory conduct in accordance with s. 83.64.

> The defense of a material noncompliance with s. 83.51(1) [F.S. 1973] may be raised by the tenant if 7 days have elapsed after the delivery of written notice by the tenant to the landlord, specifying the noncompliance and indicating the intention of the tenant not to pay rent by reason thereof. Such notice by the tenant may be given to the landlord, the landlord's representative as designated pursuant to s. 83.50(1), a resident manager, or the person or entity who collects the rent on behalf of the landlord. A material noncompliance with s. 83.51(1) [F.S. 1973] by the landlord is a complete defense to an action for possession based upon nonpayment of rent, and, upon hearing, the court or the jury, as the case may be, shall determine the amount, if any, by which the rent is to be reduced to reflect the diminution in value of the dwelling unit during the period of noncompliance with s. 83.51(1) [F.S. 1973]. After consideration of all other relevant issues, the court shall enter appropriate judgment.
>
> 2. In an action by the landlord for possession of a dwelling unit, if the tenant interposes any defense other than payment, the tenant shall pay into the registry of the court the accrued rent as alleged in the complaint or as determined by the court and the rent which accrues during the pendency of the proceeding, when due. The clerk shall notify the tenant of such requirement in the summons. Failure of the tenant to pay the rent into the registry of the court or to file a motion to determine the amount of rent to be paid into the registry within 5 days, excluding Saturdays, Sundays, and legal holidays, after the date of service of process constitutes an absolute waiver of the tenant's defenses other than payment, and the landlord is entitled to an immediate default judgment for removal of the tenant with a writ of possession to issue without further notice or hearing thereon. In the event a motion to determine rent is filed, documentation in support of the allegation that the rent as alleged in the complaint is in error is required. . . . .

You will notice that although the formats are slightly different, the organization of the statutes is similar. You also will notice that Florida law does not provide the tenant with the option of depositing the rent with the Court until after the landlord has taken action to evict the tenant. Ohio law provides stronger protections to tenants, in that it gives tenants the means to force the landlord to correct a violation while allowing the tenant to stay in the home. The Florida law, on the other hand, provides the tenant the option of vacating the rental unit or staying without paying rent, but it does not provide an express vehicle for forcing the landlord to make the repairs. Also, it does not provide the option of depositing the rent with the court until after the landlord has initiated eviction proceedings.

As noted at the beginning of the chapter, in addition to statutory law, case law is a primary source of law. You will rely extensively on case law in your legal writing, and incorporating it into your documents requires the methods we addressed earlier in the chapter: directly quoting from the case, weaving the quotes into your text, and paraphrasing the substance of the case law in your text.

To enhance the flow of their writing, many good legal writers weave or paraphrase the law, rather than just relying on quotes, particularly block quotes of extensive sections of law. Although directly quoting the law is the safest and easiest method for incorporating the law into your text, it can be tedious, distracting, or awkward. It is important, therefore, to learn to weave and paraphrase accurately. Doing so has the added advantage of forcing you to be sure that you clearly understand the law.

The two paragraphs below are examples of weaving case law, and case law citing to statutory law, into the text.

EXAMPLE OF WOVEN LAW

Ohio Case Law

The *Gammarino* Court went on to say that a "landlord may apply to the court for the release of the escrowed rent if (1) the defects have been remedied, (2) the tenant was not current on his rent when he began escrowing rent, or (3) there was no violation of R.C. 5321.04, the rental agreement, or local health and safety laws. The Sixth Circuit has upheld the constitutionality of this statutory scheme." (Citations omitted.) *Id.* at ¶20.

The Court concluded that "[d]epriving a tenant of air conditioning breaches the landlord's duty under R.C. 5321.04 and warrants damages.26 Smith had suffered through three summers without air conditioning." *Id.* at ¶ 34. The Court then allowed an abatement of the tenant's rent.

Gammarino v. Smith, 1st Dist. Hamilton No. C-060636, 2007-Ohio-4073, ¶¶ 20, 34.

EXAMPLE OF ORIGINAL LAW

Ohio Case Law

{¶20} And the landlord may apply to the court for the release of the escrowed rent if (1) the defects have been remedied, (2) the tenant was not current on his rent when he began escrowing rent, or (3) there was no violation of R.C. 5321.04, the rental agreement, or local health and safety laws. The Sixth Circuit has upheld the constitutionality of this statutory scheme.

. . . .

{¶34} Depriving a tenant of air conditioning breaches the landlord's duty under R.C. 5321.04 and warrants damages. Smith had suffered through three summers without air conditioning. No doubt the trial court took judicial notice of the semi-tropical conditions that often prevail during Cincinnati summers in finding that Gammarino had violated R.C. 5321.04. Smith presented correspondence with his landlord and testified to the conditions in his home. (footnotes omitted)

Gammarino v. Smith, 1st Dist. Hamilton No. C-060636, 2007-Ohio-4073, ¶¶ 20, 34.

The examples above show how both case law and statutory law apply. Although the case is not "on all four corners," meaning the fact pattern is not identical to the facts in Sheila's case, it is analogous enough to apply. Both Sheila's and

Gammarino's problems arose from the landlord's refusal to provide the basic necessities or to provide the services and amenities bargained for in the rental contract.

Note that the term "escrowing" is synonymous with depositing in this situation. The abatement the Court allowed meant the amount of rent the tenant had to pay was reduced by the reduction in value of the premises without the expected and bargained for amenities.

EXAMPLE

Florida Case Law

In a similar Florida case, *Ralston v. Miller*, 357 So.2d 1066 (Fla. 1978)[3], the landlord failed to repair a leaky roof after receiving notice of the problem.

> The [appellant tenants] alleged that the [landlord] failed to maintain the roof and exterior of the premises and failed to maintain the structure in good repair and condition; that the building and the leased premises were permitted to fall into such a state of disrepair that the City of Opa Locka declared the building unsafe and ordered the tenants to remove themselves; that the appellants were evicted by the City by reason of the failure of the appellee to maintain the structure. Damages were claimed for loss of value of improvements, loss of profits, loss of leasehold rights, and other damages resulting from the breach.

Id. at 1068.

. . . .

> The rule in Florida is that any disturbance of the possession of a tenant by the landlord that renders the premises unfit for occupancy, for the purposes for which they were demised or that deprives the tenant of the beneficial enjoyment of the premises, amounts to a constructive eviction. (citation omitted). A constructive eviction has the effect of essentially depriving the tenant of the beneficial enjoyment of the leased premises as where they are rendered unsafe, unfit, or unsuitable for occupancy in whole or in substantial part for the purposes for which leased. *Hankins v. Smith*, 103 Fla. 892, 138 So. 494 (1931).

Id. at 1069.

. . . .

> A constructive eviction may occur if the landlord does any wrongful act or is guilty of any default or neglect whereby the leased premises are rendered unsafe, unfit, or unsuitable for occupancy in whole or in substantial part, for the purposes for which they were leased . . . . . [The tenants] were, after a six (6) month period of constructive eviction, then, actually evicted by order of the City premised on the [landlord]'s failure to maintain the premises in a safe, suitable, and useable condition.

Id. at 1070.

---

[3] The Florida Reporter published cases until 1948. *The Blue Book* at 237. Since then, Florida decisions are cited with the Southern Reporter with the state included in the parentheses before the year. *The Blue Book* at 237.

EXERCISE

Identify whether the following statements of law are paraphrased, quoted directly, or woven together.

1. "If a landlord fails to fulfill any obligation imposed upon him by section 5321.04 of the Revised Code . . . the tenant may give notice in writing to the landlord, specifying the acts, omissions, or code violations that constitute noncompliance." R.C. § 5321.04(A)(6).

2. If the landlord does not fulfill all the obligations imposed by law, the tenant may deposit the rent after providing the landlord with the statutorily required notice. R.C. § 5321.07(A).

3. The Court held that if the tenant's rent was not current at the time he deposited the rent with the court, the landlord is entitled to receive the rent that was deposited with the court. *Gammarino* at ¶ 19.

4. After having provided the required notices to the landlord, the tenant may "[d]eposit all rent that is due and thereafter becomes due the landlord with the clerk of . . . court . . . " until the landlord fixes the defect described in the notice. R.C. § 5321.07(B)(1).

5. The Court held that failing to provide "air conditioning breaches the landlord's duty under R.C. 5321.04 and warrants damages." The failure to provide hot water breaches the duty to provide an even more basic necessity, and certainly therefore warrants damages. *Gammarino* at ¶ 34.

6. "If the landlord's failure to comply renders the dwelling unit untenantable and the tenant vacates, the tenant shall not be liable for rent during the period the dwelling unit remains uninhabitable." Fla. Stat. § 83.56 (2014).

IMPORTANT: Notice in question number 4 that we have changed the first word of the quote. The quote was the beginning of a sentence, and thus the word "Deposit" was capitalized. In legal writing, when interweaving a quote into text, the capital letter that began the quoted material is replaced with a lower case letter, and the change is signaled by the placing of brackets around the letter with the changed case. This is standard, and you will have to ignore spell-check's attempts to change it.

EXAMPLE

Identify what is wrong with the following rule statements.

1. "If a landlord receives the notice described in division (A) of this section and after receipt of the notice fails to remedy the condition . . . within thirty days . . . the tenant may do one of the following . . . ." R.C. § 5321.07(B).

2. After the tenant deposits the rent with the court, the landlord has 60 days to fix the problem the tenant addressed. R.C. § 5321.07(B).

3. If the tenant ends the lease because the landlord would not fix a problem, the tenant is liable for the rent due for the balance of the lease. R.C. § 5321.07(B)(3).

(continued)

4. If a tenant in Ohio applies "to the court for an order directing the landlord to remedy the condition," the tenant never has to deposit the rent with the court. R.C. § 5321.07(B)(2).

5. The Florida statute gives the landlord 15 days to repair a major problem before the tenant can break the lease. Fla. Stat. § 83.56(1) (2014).

6. "The rule in Florida is that any disturbance of the possession of a tenant by the landlord that renders the premises unfit for occupancy" does not amount to constructive eviction. *Ralston v. Miller*, 357 So.2d 1066, 1069 (Fla. 1978).

■ MOTOR VEHICLE ACCIDENT (MVA)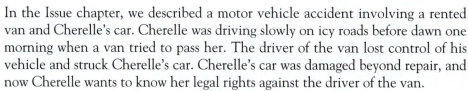

In the Issue chapter, we described a motor vehicle accident involving a rented van and Cherelle's car. Cherelle was driving slowly on icy roads before dawn one morning when a van tried to pass her. The driver of the van lost control of his vehicle and struck Cherelle's car. Cherelle's car was damaged beyond repair, and now Cherelle wants to know her legal rights against the driver of the van.

Because each state has its own traffic laws, and these laws are easily accessible through a simple Internet search, your instructor either will provide you with your state's applicable law or will have you research it yourself.

■ OHIO STATUTORY LAW

EXAMPLE

Ohio Revised Code § 4511.21 **Speed limits - assured clear distance.**

> (A) No person shall operate a motor vehicle, trackless trolley, or streetcar at a speed greater or less than is reasonable or proper, having due regard to the traffic, surface, and width of the street or highway and any other conditions, and no person shall drive any motor vehicle, trackless trolley, or streetcar in and upon any street or highway at a greater speed than will permit the person to bring it to a stop within the assured clear distance ahead.

EXAMPLE

Ohio Revised Code § 4511.202 **Operation without being in reasonable control of vehicle, trolley, or streetcar.**

> (A) No person shall operate a motor vehicle, trackless trolley, streetcar, . . . on any street, highway, or property open to the public for vehicular traffic without being in reasonable control of the vehicle, trolley, streetcar . . . .
>
> (B) Whoever violates this section is guilty of operating a motor vehicle . . . without being in control of it, a minor misdemeanor.

As we discuss in the punctuation unit in the Legal Writing Handbook, the way to omit unnecessary portions of a quote is using ellipses. When quoting from statutes, it is often necessary to omit portions in order to make the section you need clear to your reader. Remember, though, it is imperative that you are accurate when omitting sections: you must not change the meaning of what you are quoting in any way. We have seen students do this in their early paralegal papers because they are so intent on being persuasive. But any inaccuracy, in addition to being dishonest, significantly harms your case.

So looking at the Ohio law concerning the need to maintain a safe speed and to leave enough distance to stop safely, R.C. § 4511.21, we notice that much of the statute does not apply to the fact pattern in our case. By using ellipses to eliminate the words we do not need, the law is more readable and effective in our argument.

The statute reads,

EXAMPLE

Ohio Revised Code § **4511.21 Speed limits - assured clear distance.**

> (A) No person shall operate a motor vehicle, trackless trolley, or streetcar at a speed greater or less than is reasonable or proper, having due regard to the traffic, surface, and width of the street or highway and any other conditions, and no person shall drive any motor vehicle, trackless trolley, or streetcar in and upon any street or highway at a greater speed than will permit the person to bring it to a stop within the assured clear distance ahead.

For our purposes, we will quote the statute as follows:

EXAMPLE

Ohio Revised Code § 4511.21 **Speed limits - assured clear distance.**

> (A) No person shall operate a motor vehicle . . . at a speed greater or less than is reasonable or proper, having due regard to the traffic, surface, and width of the street or highway and any other conditions, and no person shall drive any motor vehicle . . . in and upon any street or highway at a greater speed than will permit the person to bring it to a stop within the assured clear distance ahead.

The fact pattern does not include a trackless trolley or a streetcar, and the law reads more clearly with those words omitted. Note that the meaning of the statute is the same. Beware of inadvertently omitting any word or words that are essential for maintaining the meaning of whatever you are quoting.

◼ OHIO CASE LAW

As you may imagine, there are a number of cases involving motor vehicle accidents (abbreviated "MVA.") Below is a section from a seminal Ohio case.

EXAMPLE

Ohio case law has consistently held that a person violates the assured clear distance ahead statute if "there is evidence that the driver collided with an object which (1) was ahead of him in his path of travel, (2) was stationary or moving in the same direction as the driver, (3) did not suddenly appear in the driver's path, and (4) was reasonably discernible."

Pond v. Leslein, 72 Ohio St. 3d 50, 52, 647 N.E.2d 477, 478 (1995).

EXERCISE

Explain why the following rule statements are incorrect or inapplicable.

1. "No person shall operate a . . . trackless trolley . . . on any . . . property open to the public . . . without being in reasonable control of the . . . trolley . . . ." R.C. § 4511.202(A).

2. If a driver did not see the obstruction ahead of him because he was had dropped ketchup from his French fry in his lap, he is not liable for failing to maintain an assured clear distance. *Pond* at 52.

3. The assured clear distance law does not apply unless a streetcar or trackless trolley was also involved in the accident. R.C. § 4511.21.

4. Because the statute states that "no person shall drive any motor vehicle . . . in and upon any street or highway at a greater speed than will permit the person to bring it to a stop within the assured clear distance ahead," a driver is not liable if the car strikes a pedestrian on the sidewalk, because the sidewalk is not a street or highway. R.C. § 4511.21.

5. When the driver struck a motorcyclist during a lane change, he did not violate the statute because the motorcyclist had not been "ahead of him in his path of travel" when the driver had been in the lane he was leaving. Also, the driver did not see the motorcyclist, so the motorcyclist was not "reasonably discernible." R.C. § 4511.21.

6. *Pond* does not apply to the van that struck Cherelle's car because at the time the van hit her car, it was traveling the opposite direction and hit her head on. *Id.* at 50, 52, 647 N.E.2d at 478.

■ REALTOR'S LIABILITY

Realtor Antoine Taylor represented the sellers who failed to disclose a material defect, a basement with significant water issues, in the home they sold. Despite Antoine's direct questions regarding defects in the home, including water issues, the sellers denied knowledge of any problems. The sellers had been aware of an underground stream that ran directly below the house and caused the basement to flood during spring thaw after winters with heavy snows. The buyers of the property are now suing Antoine for misrepresentation and demanding he compensate them for the amount it will cost to reroute the stream from underneath the home, as well as for the cost of repairs to the basement. Note that the Ohio law refers to the realtor as a licensee, that is, one who holds a license to sell real estate. So when you are reading the law, the licensee is the realtor. Similarly, the transferor is the seller of the property. The transferee is the buyer.

    The buyers of the property had moved to Parkhurst, Ohio from California, where they both had been realtors. They were, therefore, well versed in California real estate law. They had decided to represent themselves in the lawsuit. For that reason, the paralegal researched California real estate law as well as Ohio real estate law, so the attorney could compare the law of the two states and be prepared for arguments the buyers might raise.

■ OHIO STATUTORY LAW

Below are two Ohio statutes addressing the realtor's duty to a buyer of property.

EXAMPLE

Ohio Revised Code § 4735.67 **Disclosures to purchaser**.

(A) A licensee shall disclose to any purchaser all material facts of which the licensee has actual knowledge pertaining to the physical condition of the property that the purchaser would not discover by a reasonably diligent inspection, including material defects in the property, environmental contamination, and information that any statute or rule requires be disclosed. For purposes of this division, actual knowledge of such material facts shall be inferred to the licensee if the licensee acts with reckless disregard for the truth.

(B) A licensee is not required to discover latent defects in the property or to advise on matters outside of the scope of the knowledge required for real estate licensure, or to verify the accuracy or completeness of statements made by the seller, unless the licensee is aware of information that should reasonably cause the licensee to question the accuracy or completeness of such statements.

(C) Nothing in this section limits any obligation of a seller to disclose to a purchaser all material facts known by the seller pertaining to the physical condition of the property, nor does it limit the obligation of the prospective purchaser to inspect the physical condition of the property.

(D) Nothing in this section limits any obligation of a purchaser to disclose to a seller all material adverse facts known by the purchaser pertaining to the purchaser's financial ability to perform the terms of the transaction.

(E) No cause of action shall arise on behalf of any person against a licensee for disclosing information in compliance with this section, unless the information is materially inaccurate and the disclosure by the licensee was made in bad faith or was made with reckless disregard for the truth.

EXAMPLE

Ohio Revised Code § 4735.68 **Liability for false information.**

(A) A licensee is not liable to any party for false information that the licensee's client provided to the licensee and that the licensee in turn provided to another party in the real estate transaction, unless the licensee had actual knowledge that the information was false or acted with reckless disregard for the truth.

(B) No cause of action shall arise on behalf of any person against a client for any misrepresentation a licensee made while representing that client unless the client had actual knowledge of the licensee's misrepresentation.

(C) Knowledge of or information contained in a brokerage or an affiliated or past licensee's transaction records of any current or previous defect, adverse condition, or repair in real property shall not be imputed to that broker or to other licensees affiliated with that broker. No cause of action based on imputed knowledge shall accrue on behalf of any person against a broker or affiliated licensee for failure to disclose such defects, adverse condition, or repair.

Note that being aware of the date the statute took effect will be important in your practice a paralegal. You can apply only the law that was in effect at the time the events at issue occurred, so it is important to ascertain the date that the law you have researched was in effect.

■ CALIFORNIA STATUTORY LAW

The corresponding California statutes regarding the duties of a realtor are found in sections of the California Civil Code Sections 1102-1102.18 and Civil Code Sections 2079-2079.24. Note that the statutes refer to this section as "this article." The following portions are applicable in this case:

EXAMPLE

California Civil Code § 1102.4.

(a) Neither the transferor nor any listing or selling agent shall be liable for any error, inaccuracy, or omission of any information delivered pursuant to this article if the error, inaccuracy, or omission was not within the personal knowledge of the transferor or that listing or selling agent, was based on information timely provided by public agencies or by other persons providing information as specified in subdivision (c) that is required to be disclosed pursuant to this article, and ordinary care was exercised in obtaining and transmitting it.

EXAMPLE

California Civil Code § 1102.5.

> If information disclosed in accordance with this article is subsequently rendered inaccurate as a result of any act, occurrence, or agreement subsequent to the delivery of the required disclosures, the inaccuracy resulting therefrom (*sic*) does not constitute a violation of this article. If at the time the disclosures are required to be made, an item of information required to be disclosed is unknown or not available to the transferor, and the transferor or his or her agent has made a reasonable effort to ascertain it, the transferor may use an approximation of the information, provided the approximation is clearly identified as such, is reasonable, is based on the best information available to the transferor or his or her agent, and is not used for the purpose of circumventing or evading this article.
>
> . . . .

EXAMPLE

California Civil Code § 1102.12.

> (a) If more than one licensed real estate broker is acting as an agent in a transaction subject to this article, the broker who has obtained the offer made by the transferee shall, except as otherwise provided in this article, deliver the disclosure required by this article to the transferee, unless the transferor has given other written instructions for delivery.
> (b) If a licensed real estate broker responsible for delivering the disclosures under this section cannot obtain the disclosure document required and does not have written assurance from the transferee that the disclosure has been received, the broker shall advise the transferee in writing of his or her rights to the disclosure.

A licensed real estate broker responsible for delivering disclosures under this section shall maintain a record of the action taken to effect compliance in accordance with Section 10148 of the Business and Professions Code.

EXAMPLE

California Civil Code § 1102.13.

> No transfer subject to this article shall be invalidated solely because of the failure of any person to comply with any provision of this article. However, any person who willfully or negligently violates or fails to perform any duty prescribed by any provision of this article shall be liable in the amount of actual damages suffered by a transferee.

EXAMPLE

California Civil Code § 1102.14. (b)

> As used in this article, "selling agent" means selling agent as defined in subdivision (g) of Section 1086, exclusive of the requirement that the agent be a participant in a multiple listing service as defined in Section 1087.

Another segment of California statutory law that applies in this situation, Cal. Civil Code §§ 2079-2079.24, is the following:

EXAMPLE

California Civil Code § 2079.

> (a) It is the duty of a real estate broker or salesperson, licensed under Division 4 (commencing with Section 10000) of the Business and Professions Code, to a prospective purchaser of residential real property comprising one to four dwelling units, or a manufactured home as defined in Section 18007 of the Health and Safety Code, to conduct a reasonably competent and diligent visual inspection of the property offered for sale and to disclose to that prospective purchaser all facts materially affecting the value or desirability of the property that an investigation would reveal, if that broker has a written contract with the seller to find or obtain a buyer or is a broker who acts in cooperation with that broker to find and obtain a buyer.
>
> . . . .

EXAMPLE

California Civil Code § 2079.5.

> Nothing in this article relieves a buyer or prospective buyer of the duty to exercise reasonable care to protect himself or herself, including those facts which are known to or within the diligent attention and observation of the buyer or prospective buyer.
>
> . . . .

EXAMPLE

California Civil Code § 2079.14.

> Listing agents and selling agents shall provide the seller and buyer in a real property transaction with a copy of the disclosure form specified in Section 2079.16, and, except as provided in subdivision (c), shall

obtain a signed acknowledgment of receipt from that seller or buyer, except as provided in this section or Section 2079.15, as follows:

(a) The listing agent, if any, shall provide the disclosure form to the seller prior to entering into the listing agreement.

(b) The selling agent shall provide the disclosure form to the seller as soon as practicable prior to presenting the seller with an offer to purchase, unless the selling agent previously provided the seller with a copy of the disclosure form pursuant to subdivision

(a).

. . . .

(d) The selling agent shall provide the disclosure form to the buyer as soon as practicable prior to execution of the buyer's offer to purchase, except that if the offer to purchase is not prepared by the selling agent, the selling agent shall present the disclosure form to the buyer not later than the next business day after the selling agent receives the offer to purchase from the buyer.

. . . .

EXAMPLE

California Civil Code § 1102.6

Effective July 1, 2014, pursuant to Cal. Civil Code § 1102.6 (West July 1, 2014), sellers of residential real estate in California were required to provide a new disclosure form. The disclosure form that sellers are required to provide to buyers reads in part:

THIS STATEMENT IS A DISCLOSURE OF THE CONDITION OF THE ABOVE DESCRIBED PROPERTY IN COMPLIANCE WITH SECTION 1102 OF THE CIVIL CODE AS OF _____, 20 _____. IT IS NOT A WARRANTY OF ANY KIND BY THE SELLER(S) OR ANY AGENT(S) REPRESENTING ANY PRINCIPAL(S) IN THIS TRANSACTION, AND IS NOT A SUBSTITUTE FOR ANY INSPECTIONS OR WARRANTIES THE PRINCIPAL(S) MAY WISH TO OBTAIN.

. . . .

II

Seller's Information

The Seller discloses the following information with the knowledge that even though this is not a warranty, prospective Buyers may rely on this information in deciding whether and on what terms to purchase the subject property. Seller hereby authorizes any agent(s) representing any principal(s) in this transaction to provide a copy of this statement to any person or entity in connection with any actual or anticipated sale of the property.

THE FOLLOWING ARE REPRESENTATIONS MADE BY THE SELLER(S) AND ARE NOT THE REPRESENTATIONS OF THE AGENT(S), IF ANY. THIS INFORMATION IS A DISCLOSURE

AND IS NOT INTENDED TO BE PART OF ANY CONTRACT BETWEEN THE BUYER AND SELLER:

. . . .

B. Are you (Seller) aware of any significant defects/malfunctions in any of the following?

__Yes __No. If yes, check appropriate space(s) below.
__Interior Walls __Ceilings __Floors __Exterior Walls __Insulation __Roof(s)
__Windows __Doors __Foundation __Slab(s) __Driveways __Sidewalks __Walls/Fences __Electrical Systems __Plumbing/ Sewers/Septics __Other

Structural Components (Describe)

....

....

If any of the above is checked, explain. (Attach additional sheets if necessary):

....

....

III

Agent's Inspection Disclosure

(To be completed only if the Seller is represented by an agent in this transaction.)
THE UNDERSIGNED, BASED ON THE ABOVE INQUIRY OF THE SELLER(S) AS TO THE CONDITION OF THE PROPERTY AND BASED ON A REASONABLY COMPETENT AND DILIGENT VISUAL INSPECTION OF THE ACCESSIBLE AREAS OF THE PROPERTY IN CONJUNCTION WITH THAT INQUIRY, STATES THE FOLLOWING:

Agent notes no items for disclosure.

Agent notes the following items:

....

....

A previous version of the Code required the following on the disclosure form:

EXAMPLE

California Civil Code § 2079.16.

The disclosure form required by Section 2079.14 shall have Sections 2079.13 to 2079.24, inclusive, excluding this section, printed on the back, and on the front of the disclosure form the following shall appear:

DISCLOSURE REGARDING

REAL ESTATE AGENCY RELATIONSHIP

(As required by the Civil Code)

When you enter into a discussion with a real estate agent regarding a real estate transaction, you should from the outset understand what type of agency relationship or representation you wish to have with the agent in the transaction.

SELLER'S AGENT

A Seller's agent under a listing agreement with the Seller acts as the agent for the Seller only. A Seller's agent or a subagent of that agent has the following affirmative obligations:

To the Seller:

A fiduciary duty of utmost care, integrity, honesty, and loyalty in dealings with the Seller.

To the Buyer and the Seller:

(a) Diligent exercise of reasonable skill and care in performance of the agent's duties.

(b) A duty of honest and fair dealing and good faith.

(c) A duty to disclose all facts known to the agent materially affecting the value or desirability of the property that are not known to, or within the diligent attention and observation of, the parties.

An agent is not obligated to reveal to either party any confidential information obtained from the other party that does not involve the affirmative duties set forth above.

. . . .

EXAMPLE

California Civil Code § 2079.24.

> Nothing in this article shall be construed to either diminish the duty of disclosure owed buyers and sellers by agents and their associate licensees, subagents, and employees or to relieve agents and their associate licensees, subagents, and employees from liability for their conduct in connection with acts governed by this article or for any breach of a fiduciary duty or a duty of disclosure.

■ OHIO REGULATORY LAW

As we discussed at the beginning of this chapter, it is not always possible to include all the necessary details in a statute. In those situations, the legislature will include provisions in the statute for the establishment of a board or agency to issue regulations that further explain the requirements needed to enforce the intent of the statute. While California delineated the requirements of the disclosure form in Cal.

Civil Code § 2079.16, Ohio established regulations to expound on its real estate statutes.

Below is a regulation that states the required method in Ohio for a seller to disclose any known defects in a property. Note that O.A.C. stands for Ohio Administrative Code. The Administrative Code comprises regulations established to provide details for the statute.

EXAMPLE

Ohio Administrative Code §1301:5-6-10

> In accordance with division (D) of section 5302.30 of the Revised Code, the attached residential property disclosure form is prescribed by the director of commerce to permit transferors of residential real estate to disclose material matters relating to the physical condition of the property to be transferred, including, but not limited to, the source of water supply to the property; the nature of the sewer system serving the property; the availability of information relating to the sewage treatment system; the condition of the structure of the property, including the roof, foundation, walls, and floors; the presence of hazardous materials or substances, including lead-based paint, asbestos, urea-formaldehyde foam insulation, and radon gas; and any material defects in the property that are within the actual knowledge of the transferor.

EXAMPLE

Ohio Administrative Code § 1301:5-6-10 Residential property disclosure form.

Taking this code section and weaving it into a paragraph gives us the following:

> In the case of disclosure of defects in real property, OAC § 1301:5-6-10 contains a section that includes "the attached residential property disclosure form" which "is prescribed by the director of commerce" for the seller of the property requiring the seller . . . to disclose material matters relating to the physical condition of the property to be transferred, including, but not limited to, the source of water supply to the property; the nature of the sewer system serving the property; the availability of information relating to the sewage treatment system; the condition of the structure of the property, including the roof, foundation, walls, and floors; the presence of hazardous materials or substances, including lead-based paint, asbestos, urea-formaldehyde foam insulation, and radon gas; and any material defects in the property that are within the actual knowledge of the transferor.

O.A.C. § 1301:5-6-10

EXAMPLE

Ohio Case Law

The type of situation Antoine's clients encountered has been litigated numerous times in the courts. In a similar situation, the buyers of a home sued the realtor for failing to tell them that the garage was in poor condition. In the following Ohio case *Moreland v. Ksiazek*, 8th Dist. Cuyahoga No. 83509, 2004-Ohio-2974, the buyers in this case were the Morelands and the realtor representing the seller was Lenz. Jaworski was the realtor representing the buyers, the Morelands.

{¶41} Moreland claims that Lentz committed fraud by failing to disclose to Jaworski that he had never seen the interior of the garage and that he had no idea of its condition. He further claims that this nondisclosure misled Jaworski into believing that there was nothing wrong with the garage. These claims are legally and factually unfounded.

{¶42} Lentz statutorily must disclose all material facts concerning the property to which he had actual knowledge, and he is not required to discover latent defects or to advise on matters outside the scope of his knowledge. R.C. 4735.67. It is uncontroverted that Lentz did not inspect the garage and, thus, he did not have actual knowledge of the condition of the garage. Thus, Lentz was not required to disclose that he never viewed the garage. Additionally, there is nothing in the record to indicate that Jaworski was misled by Lentz into believing that there was nothing wrong with the garage.

{¶43} During deposition, Moreland admitted that he never had any conversations with anyone from ERA Lentz. Because he did not have any conversations with Lentz, Davis or ERA Lentz, no misrepresentation could occur. "Absent a demonstration of misrepresentation, a cause of action for fraud does not arise." *Kossutich*, supra, citing *Hibbett v. Cincinnati*, 4 Ohio App. 3d 128 (1982).

{¶47} The record reveals that Lentz did not conceal the condition of the garage. The padlock was already on the garage and Lentz did not place it there. It is clear from the record that he never went inside the garage, so he did not know its condition. Additionally, he stated that he went to the house only one time after he listed the property, just to remove the lockbox.

. . . .

{¶51} We find that Moreland has failed to present evidence demonstrating genuine issues of material fact as to whether Lentz made material misrepresentations to Moreland about the condition of the property. Therefore, the trial court properly granted summary judgment in favor of Lentz . . . .

Id. at ¶¶ 41-43, 47. 51.

■ CALIFORNIA CASE LAW

A California case law interpreting its statutes similarly outlines the seller's real estate agent's duties to the buyer. In the case *Robinson v. Grossman*, 57 Cal.App.4th 634, 67 Cal. Rptr. 2d 380 (1997), the Court provided extensive background concerning the responsibilities and duties of a selling agent to the buyer of residential real estate. In *Robinson*, the seller had built and lived in the home that the buyer purchased. The seller told his realtor that cracks in the walls were a result of the type of finish used on the walls and could be corrected by using a certain product. The seller also told his real estate agent that the water damage visible in various places on the walls and ceiling were the result of leaks that had been repaired. The realtor relied on the seller's representations and indicated on the disclosure form that the cracks and water damage, according to the seller, were not structurally significant. This information was not accurate, and the buyer later sued the seller and the realtor.

EXAMPLE

We find no support for the [buyer's] argument section 2079's disclosure duty includes a duty to independently verify or disclaim the accuracy of the seller's representations, and we do not interpret section 2079 in that manner. To the contrary, in enacting section 2079, the Legislature sought to foster availability of professional negligence insurance by eliminating the implication . . . that a seller's agent could have negligence 644*644 liability for relying in good faith upon the seller's representations or failing to discharge a vague obligation to obtain professional inspections or reports to confirm those representations. In other words . . . once the sellers and their agent make the required disclosures, it is incumbent upon the potential purchasers to investigate and make an informed decision based thereon. In making the required disclosures, the sellers' agent is required only to act in good faith and not convey the seller's representations without a reasonable basis for believing them to be true . . . .

Robinson at 643-644.

EXERCISE

Compare and make a distinction between the following rule statements. Which of the two is correct, and why? The incorrect rule statement will contain an inaccurate statement of the law. Review the example below before starting the exercise.

EXAMPLE

1. According to R.C. § 4735.67(B), the realtor shall not "advise on matters outside of the scope of the knowledge required for real estate licensure," and therefore Antoine cannot be responsible for informing the buyers about engineering issues, even if he is aware of them.

2. According to R.C. § 4735.67(B), the realtor "is not required to discover latent defects in the property . . . or to verify the accuracy or completeness of statements made by the seller, unless the licensee is aware of information that should reasonably cause the licensee to question the accuracy or completeness of such statements."

(continued)

Example one is incorrect. If the realtor is aware of a defect in the property that would be an engineering issue, for example if the foundation has horizontal cracking that was covered by new paneling, the realtor is required by law to inform the prospective buyer of the problem.

1. The realtor is not responsible for discovering hidden defects in the property, and the seller does not have to reveal them. The buyer has an obligation "to inspect the physical condition of the property." R.C. § 4735.67(C)
2. Although the realtor representing the seller is not liable for discovering hidden defects in the property, the law does not limit "any obligation of a seller to disclose to a purchaser all material facts known by the seller pertaining to the physical condition of the property." R.C. § 4735.67(C).

3. In California, according to Cal. Civil Code § 1102.4, only the seller is liable "for any error, inaccuracy, or omission of any information delivered pursuant to this article" if the seller knew about the defect, even if the real estate agent also knew of the defect and did not disclose it.
4. In California, according to Cal. Civil Code § 1102.4, both the seller and the seller's agent are liable "for any error, inaccuracy, or omission" if the seller knew about the defect, and if the real estate agent also knew of the defect and did not disclose it.

5. The realtor is not responsible for repeating his client's statements, even when those statements turn out to be false, unless the realtor knew at the time he or she repeated the statements that they were not true, according to R.C. § 4735.68(A).
6. The realtor can provide whatever information the client gives him, pursuant to R.C. § 4735.68(A), because it is the seller's obligation to tell the truth, not the realtor's obligation to make the seller be honest.

7. Pursuant to Cal. Civil Code § 2079, the seller's real estate agent may not ignore an issue on the property that could potentially be a defect, even when the seller does not disclose it.
8. Pursuant to Cal. Civil Code § 2079, the seller's real estate agent may ignore an issue on the property that could potentially be a defect as long as the seller does not disclose it.

9. The code OAC §1301:5-6-10 requires the seller to inform the buyer of any problems with the water supply that are in the seller's knowledge.
10. The code OAC §1301:5-6-10 does not require the seller to inform the buyer of problems with the water supply.

11. Pursuant to *Moreland v. Ksiazek,* 8th Dist. Cuyahoga No. 83509, 2004-Ohio-2974, the realtor is not required to look for defects that are not readily apparent.
12. Pursuant to *Moreland v. Ksiazek,* 8th Dist. Cuyahoga No. 83509, 2004-Ohio-2974, the realtor is liable for any defects, even if he or she was not aware of them.

■ MEDICAL MALPRACTICE (MED MAL)

Dr. Jeremy Hunter has asked Brad to represent him in defending against the medical malpractice suit involving non-union of the jaw of the patient who had been hit with the baseball bat. The patient had been assaulted with a baseball bat, and Dr. Hunter had been the surgical resident who assisted the attending, Dr. Patel, with wiring the patient's broken jaw so it could heal. During the surgery, a piece of wire accidentally had hit the patient's eye, and Dr. Hunter had documented that in his operative note. Dr. Patel later had altered the note and redacted that section. Dr. Hunter is concerned about Dr. Patel's actions in changing his medical record.

The laws controlling medical malpractice suits vary from state to state, but because this form of litigation is so prevalent, the student will be able to locate law from his or her state that would apply to this fact pattern. Further, the students should make themselves familiar with the rules regarding preservation of evidence and the penalty for violating those rules.

Brad has asked you to research the Ohio law on altering medical records in anticipation of a lawsuit for Dr. Hunter. You have found the following case.

■ OHIO CASE LAW

EXAMPLE

The Ohio Supreme Court addressed the issue of altering medical records in *Moskovitz v. Mt. Sinai Med. Ctr.*, 69 Ohio St.3d. 638, 635 N.E.2d 331 (1994). (The Ohio Supreme Court provided the following prior history of the case.)

The facts giving rise to this appeal involve the conduct of Dr. Harry E. Figgie III, appellee, who failed to timely diagnose and treat a malignant tumor on Moskovitz's left leg and altered certain records to conceal the fact that malpractice had occurred.

. . . .

On October 2, 1986, Moskovitz visited Dr. Figgie's office, complaining of a lump on her leg. Figgie examined Moskovitz and detected "a small calcified lesion along the tendo Achilles." Figgie did not recommend a biopsy of the lesion and reassured Moskovitz that nothing was wrong. Figgie was aware that tumors had been removed from Moskovitz's left leg in 1978 and 1984. On November 3, 1986, Moskovitz was admitted to University Hospitals for a right knee revision. Prior to surgery, Moskovitz was examined by Rick Magas, a registered nurse. Magas's written report of the examination, signed by Dr. Figgie, noted the existence of a firm nodule measuring one centimeter by one centimeter on Moskovitz's left Achilles tendon. Figgie performed the right knee revision on November 5, 1986. Following surgery, Moskovitz was examined on Figgie's behalf by Dr. G. Balourdas, a resident physician at University Hospitals. A discharge summary prepared by Balourdas (and signed by Figgie) noted the existence of a "[l]eft Achilles tendon mass, [1] x 1 cm. nodule." The report indicated that the mass had been present for some time.

Moskovitz continued to see Dr. Figgie through November 1987. On November 10, 1987, Figgie finally removed the mass that had been growing on Moskovitz's left leg. On November 13, 1987, the tumor was found to be an epithelioid sarcoma, a rare form of malignant soft-tissue cancer. A bone scan revealed that the cancer had metastasized to Moskovitz's shoulder and right femur.

. . . .

Immediately following the diagnosis of cancer, Moskovitz's care was transferred to Figgie's partner at University Orthopaedic, Dr. John T. Makley, an orthopedic surgeon specializing in oncology. At that time, Makley received Figgie's original office chart, which contained seven pages of notes documenting Moskovitz's course of treatment from 1985 through November 1987. Makley thereafter referred Moskovitz to radiation therapy at University Hospitals. Apparently, in November 1987, without Figgie's knowledge, Makley sent a copy of page seven of Figgie's office notes to the radiation department at University Hospitals.

In December 1987, Figgie or someone on his behalf requested that Dr. Makley return Figgie's office chart pertaining to the care of Moskovitz. In December 1987, Makley was Moskovitz's primary treating physician and Figgie was no longer directly involved in Moskovitz's care and treatment. On December 14, 1987, Makley's secretary forwarded the chart to Figgie's office. Figgie's secretary then sent a copy of the chart to Dr. Zev Ashenberg, Moskovitz's psychologist. The copy was received by Ashenberg sometime between December 14 and 18, 1987. In January 1988, Makley's secretary requested that Figgie's office return the chart to Makley. At this time, it was discovered that the original chart had mysteriously vanished, never to be seen again.

In February 1988, Makley amputated Moskovitz's left leg. . . . .

On December 5, 1988, Moskovitz died as a result of the cancer. Prior to her death, Moskovitz's testimony was preserved by way of videotaped deposition. Makley was deposed on January 30, 1989. At his deposition, Makley produced a copy of page seven of Figgie's office chart. (That copy was identical to the copy ultimately recovered by plaintiff's counsel from the radiation department records at University Hospitals.) The copy produced by Makley contained a typewritten entry dated September 21, 1987, which states: "Mrs. Moskovitz comes in today for her evaluation on the radiographs reviewed with Dr. York. He was not impressed that this [the mass on Moskovitz's left leg] was anything other than a benign problem, perhaps a fibroma. We [Figgie and York] will therefore elect to continue to observe." However, the photostatic copy revealed that a line had been drawn through the sentence "We will therefore elect to continue to observe." The copy further revealed that beneath the entry, Figgie had interlineated a handwritten notation: "As she does not want excisional Bx [biopsy] we will observe." The September 21, 1987 entry was followed by a typewritten entry dated September 24, 1987, which states: "I [Figgie] reviewed the x-rays with Dr. York. I discussed the clinical findings with him. We [Figgie and York] felt this to be benign most likely a fibroma. He [York] said that we could observe and I concur." At some point, Figgie had also added to the September 24, 1987 entry a handwritten notation, "see above," referring to the September 21 handwritten notation that Moskovitz did not want an excisional biopsy.

Figgie was deposed on March 2, 1989. At his deposition, Figgie produced records, including a copy of page seven of his office chart. As his original chart had been lost in December 1987 or January 1988, Figgie had had this copy made from the copy of the chart that had been sent to Ashenberg in December 1987. The September 21, 1987 entry in the records produced by Figgie did not contain the statement "We will therefore elect to continue to observe." Apparently, that sentence had been deleted (whited-out) on the original office chart from which Ashenberg's copy (and, in turn, Figgie's copy) had been made, in a way that left no indication on the copy that the sentence had been removed from the original records.

. . . .

During discovery, another copy of page seven of Figgie's office chart (identical to the copy produced by Makley during his deposition) was recovered from the radiation department records at University Hospitals. This copy had been received by the radiation department in November 1987, when Moskovitz was referred to radiation therapy by Dr. Makley. Therefore, it became apparent that the final sentence in the September 21, 1987 entry had been deleted (whited-out) from Figgie's original office chart sometime between November 1987 (when the radiation department obtained a copy of the record) and mid-December 1987, when Ashenberg received a copy of the record from Figgie's office. Presumably, that alteration occurred in December 1987 while the original chart was in the possession of Dr. Figgie.

All versions of the September 21, 1987 entry obtained during discovery contained the handwritten notation by Figgie "As she does not want excisional Bx [biopsy] we will observe." That sentence clearly suggested that it was Moskovitz's choice not to have the tumor biopsied during the course of her treatment with Figgie, whereas the typewritten text as it originally appeared in the September 21, 1987 entry indicated that it was Figgie's decision to observe the growth because the tumor was thought to be benign.

Eventually, Figgie's entire office chart was reconstructed from copies obtained through discovery. The reconstructed chart contains no indication that a workup or biopsy was recommended by Figgie and refused by Moskovitz at any time prior to August 10, 1987. Entries in the reconstructed chart for October 2, 1986, February 23, 1987 and May 7, 1987, refer to the mass, but do not mention a suggested biopsy or the refusal of a biopsy.

The Ohio Supreme Court then provided legal analysis, including the following:

. . . .

Figgie's alteration of records exhibited a total disregard for the law and the rights of Mrs. Moskovitz and her family. Had the copy of page seven of Figgie's office chart not been recovered from the radiation department records at University Hospitals, appellant would have been substantially less likely to succeed in this case. The copy of the chart and other records produced by Figgie would have tended to exculpate Figgie for his medical negligence while placing the blame for his failures on Moskovitz. We find that the evidence adduced at trial fully supported an award of punitive damages . . . .

Id. at 652, 343.

. . . .

An intentional alteration, falsification or destruction of medical records by a doctor, to avoid liability for his or her medical negligence, is sufficient to show actual malice, and punitive damages may be awarded whether or not the act of altering, falsifying or destroying records directly causes compensable harm. However, we reiterate that the purpose of punitive damages is to punish and deter. The jury's reaction in awarding $3 million in punitive damages may be understandable, given its findings of Figgie's activities, but it is wrong.

Punishment does not mean confiscation. . . . . .

Id. at 653, 344.

■ OHIO STATUTORY LAW

EXAMPLE

The statute provides guidance to someone in Dr. Hunter's position:

> The [state medical] board, by an affirmative vote of not fewer than six members, shall, to the extent permitted by law, limit, revoke, or suspend an individual's certificate to practice, refuse to register an individual, refuse to reinstate a certificate, or reprimand or place on probation the holder of a certificate for one or more of the following reasons:
>
> . . . .
>
> (18) . . . violation of any provision of a code of ethics of the American Medical Association, the American Osteopathic Association, the American Podiatric Medical Association, or any other national professional organizations that the oard specifies by rule. The State Medical Board shall obtain and keep on file current copies of the codes of ethics of the various national professional organizations.

R.C. § 4731.22(B).

The American Medical Association's Code of Ethics includes its Principles of Medical Ethics, which it states "are not laws, but standards of conduct which define the essentials of honorable behavior for the physician." They include:

> II. A physician shall uphold the standards of professionalism, be honest in all professional interactions, and strive to report physicians deficient in character or competence, or engaging in fraud or deception, to appropriate entities.

> III. A physician shall respect the law . . . .

EXERCISE _____

Compare and differentiate each of the following pairs of rule statements and choose which of the two is correct.

1. "An intentional alteration, falsification or destruction of medical records by a doctor, to avoid liability for his or her medical negligence, is sufficient to show actual malice, and punitive damages may be awarded whether or not the act of altering, falsifying or destroying records directly causes compensable harm."

2. "An intentional alteration, falsification or destruction of medical records by a doctor, to avoid liability for his or her medical negligence, is sufficient to show actual malice, and punitive damages may be awarded [when] the act of altering, falsifying or destroying records directly causes compensable harm."

Moskovitz v. Mt. Sinai Med. Ctr. (1994), Ohio St.3d. 638, 653, 635 N.E.2d 331, 344.

3. Dr. Figgie would have escaped blame for Mrs. Moskovitz's death if he had done a better job of changing the records.

(continued)

4. The fact that Dr. Figgie would have escaped blame for Mrs. Moskovitz's death if he had done a better job of changing the records motivated the Court to allow punitive damages for doing so.

Moskovitz v. Mt. Sinai Med. Ctr. (1994), Ohio St.3d. 638, 653, 635 N.E.2d 331, 344.

5. The Ohio State Medical Board may revoke a physician's license to practice medicine if the physician violates the code of ethics of the American Medical Association. R.C. § 4731.22(B).

6. The Ohio State Medical Board only may reprimand a physician for violating the AMA code of ethics. R.C. § 4731.22(B).

7. Dr. Hunter has a legal obligation to report Dr. Patel for possibly altering the medical record. R.C. § 4731.22(B).

8. Because he has no proof that she changed his medical record, and because the AMA code of Medical Ethics states that the Principles of Medical Ethics are not laws, Dr. Hunter has no legal obligation to report his suspicions that Dr. Patel altered the medical record. R.C. § 4731.22(B).

■ CONTRACT BREACH

After Marcus and Brianna Johnson consulted with Brad concerning the faulty construction of their new home and Connolly Homes of Parkhurst's failure to correct the defects, Brad has instructed you, the firm's paralegal, to research Ohio law regarding home construction. Because the builder is headquartered in Virginia, and the contract the Johnson's signed stated that any disputes would be tried using Virginia law, Brad also instructed you to research Virginia law on this issue. Below is the Ohio law, and following Ohio law is the Virginia law.

■ OHIO STATUTORY LAW

EXAMPLE

Ohio Revised Code § 1312.01 Definitions.

As used in this chapter:

(A) "Construction defect" means a deficiency that arises directly or indirectly out of the construction or the substantial rehabilitation of a residential building. "Substantial rehabilitation" includes the addition of a room and the removal or installation of a wall, partition, or portion of the structural design.

(B) "Dwelling action" means any civil action in contract or tort for damages or indemnity brought against a residential contractor for damages or the loss of use of real property caused by a construction defect.

(C) "Owner" means an owner or a prospective owner of a residential building or a dwelling unit in a residential building who enters into a contract with a residential contractor for the construction or substantial rehabilitation of that residential building or unit.

(D) "Residential building" means a structure that is a one-family, two-family, or three-family dwelling house or a dwelling unit within that structure, any accessory structures incidental to that dwelling house, and a unit in a condominium development in which the owner holds title to that unit. "Residential building" includes any structure that is used as a model to promote the sale of a similar dwelling house.

(E) "Residential contractor" means a person or entity who, for pay, enters into a contract with an owner for the construction or the substantial rehabilitation of a residential building and who has primary responsibility for the construction or substantial rehabilitation of a residential building.

EXAMPLE

Ohio Revised Code § 1312.03 **Notice of contractor's right to resolve alleged defects.**

Upon entering into a contract for the construction or the substantial rehabilitation of a residential building, a residential contractor shall provide the owner with notice of the contractor's right to offer to resolve any alleged construction defect before the owner may commence a dwelling action or arbitration proceedings against the contractor. The contractor may include the notice in the contract or provide the notice as a separate document delivered at the time the owner signs the contract. The notice shall be conspicuous and in substantially the following form:

OHIO LAW CONTAINS IMPORTANT REQUIREMENTS YOU MUST FOLLOW BEFORE YOU MAY FILE A LAWSUIT OR COMMENCE ARBITRATION PROCEEDINGS FOR DEFECTIVE CONSTRUCTION AGAINST THE RESIDENTIAL CONTRACTOR WHO CONSTRUCTED YOUR HOME. AT LEAST SIXTY DAYS BEFORE YOU FILE A LAWSUIT OR COMMENCE ARBITRATION PROCEEDINGS, YOU MUST PROVIDE THE CONTRACTOR WITH A WRITTEN NOTICE OF THE CONDITIONS YOU ALLEGE ARE DEFECTIVE. UNDER CHAPTER 1312 OF THE OHIO REVISED CODE, THE CONTRACTOR HAS AN OPPORTUNITY TO OFFER TO REPAIR OR PAY FOR THE DEFECTS. YOU ARE NOT OBLIGATED TO ACCEPT ANY OFFER THE CONTRACTOR MAKES. THERE ARE STRICT DEADLINES AND PROCEDURES UNDER STATE LAW, AND FAILURE TO FOLLOW THEM MAY AFFECT YOUR ABILITY TO FILE A LAWSUIT OR COMMENCE ARBITRATION PROCEEDINGS. (Total capitalization in original)

EXAMPLE

Ohio Revised Code § 1312.04 Notice to contractor of alleged defects prior to action.

(A) No owner shall commence arbitration proceedings or file a dwelling action against a residential contractor unless, at least sixty days before commencing the proceedings or filing the action, the owner provides the contractor with written notice of the construction defect that would be the basis of the arbitration proceedings or the dwelling action. The notice shall be in writing and mailed, sent by telegram, delivered in person, or sent by any means the contractor has indicated communications may be sent, including facsimile transmission and electronic mail. The notice shall substantially comply with the requirements set forth in division (B) of this section.

(B) Any notice that an owner provides to a contractor pursuant to this section shall substantially do all of the following:

(1) Assert a claim involving a construction defect by itemizing and describing those construction defects;

(2) Include or attach a copy of any documentation concerning the construction defects prepared by a person who inspected the residential building for the owner;

(3) Include the name, address, and telephone number of the owner and the contractor and the address of the building that is the subject of the claim.

(C) After receiving a notice of defects, a contractor may request an owner to provide a description of the cause of the defects and the nature and extent of repairs necessary to remedy the defects. An owner may provide this information if the owner has knowledge of the cause of the defects and the repairs necessary to remedy those defects.

(D) If a contractor files a mechanics lien or commences any type of arbitration proceedings or legal action against an owner, this chapter does not apply, and the owner immediately may counterclaim, commence arbitration proceedings, or file a dwelling action against the contractor . . .

EXAMPLE

Ohio Revised Code § 1312.07 **Commencement of arbitration or action by owner.**

Unless otherwise indicated in this chapter, an owner has complied with this chapter and may commence arbitration proceedings or file a dwelling action sixty days after the owner mails, delivers, sends by facsimile transmission or electronic mail, or otherwise provides the residential contractor with a defect notice pursuant to division (A) of section <u>1312.04</u> of the Revised Code.

EXAMPLE

Ohio Revised Code § 1312.08 **Tolling of statutes of limitation and repose - dismissal - application of chapter.**

(A) All applicable statutes of limitation or repose are tolled from the time the owner sends a notice of defect to a contractor pursuant to section <u>1312.04</u> of the Revised Code until the owner has complied with this chapter.

(B) If an owner files a dwelling action or commences arbitration proceedings without having complied with this chapter, the court or arbitrator shall dismiss that action or those proceedings without prejudice. The owner may again file a dwelling action or commence arbitration proceedings after complying with this chapter.

EXAMPLE

Consumer Safety Protection Act (CSPA)

Ohio Statutory Law

Ohio Revised Code § Sec. 4722.01. As used in this chapter:

(A) "Home construction service" means the construction of a residential building. "Home construction service" does not include construction performed on a structure that contains four or more dwelling units, except for work on an individual dwelling unit within that structure, or construction performed on the common area of a condominium property.

(B) "Home construction service contract" means a contract between an owner and a supplier to perform home construction services, including services rendered based on a cost-plus contract, for an amount exceeding twenty-five thousand dollars.

(C) "Home construction service supplier" or "supplier" means a person who contracts with an owner to provide home construction services for compensation and who maintains in force a general liability insurance policy in an amount of not less than two hundred fifty thousand dollars.

(D) "Owner" means the person who contracts with a home construction service supplier. "Owner" may include the owner of the property, a tenant who occupies the dwelling unit on which the home construction service is performed, or a person the owner authorizes to act on the owner's behalf to contract for a home construction service, and any other person who contracts for a home construction service.

(E) "Residential building" means a one-, two-, or three-family dwelling and any accessory construction incidental to the dwelling. . . . .

EXAMPLE

Ohio Revised Code § Sec. 4722.08.

For a violation of Chapter 4722. of the Revised Code, an owner has a cause of action and is entitled to relief as follows:

(A) Where the violation was an act prohibited by section 4722.02, 4722.03, or 4722.04 of the Revised Code, the owner may, in an individual action, rescind the transaction or recover the owner's actual economic damages plus an amount not exceeding five thousand dollars in noneconomic damages.

(B) In any action for rescission, revocation of the transaction must occur within a reasonable time after the owner discovers or should have discovered the ground for it and before any substantial change in condition of the subject of the transaction.

(C) Any owner may seek a declaratory judgment, an injunction, or other appropriate relief against an act or practice that violates this chapter.

(D) The court may award to the prevailing party a reasonable attorney's fee limited to the work reasonably performed, if either of the following apply:

(1) The owner complaining of the act or practice that violated this chapter has brought or maintained an action that is groundless, and the owner filed or maintained the action in bad faith;

(2) The home construction service supplier has knowingly committed an act or practice that violates this chapter.

(E) As used in this section, "actual economic damages" means damages for direct, incidental, or consequential pecuniary losses resulting from a violation of Chapter 4722. of the Revised Code and does not include damages for noneconomic loss as defined in section 2315.18 of the Revised Code.

(F) Nothing in this section shall preclude an owner from also proceeding with a cause of action under any other theory of law.

■ VIRGINIA STATUTORY LAW

In the Virginia statute, the party selling the home is the vendor, and the party buying the home is the vendee. The Virginia statutes are abbreviated as Va. Code Ann.

EXAMPLE

Virginia Code Annotated § 55-70.1 (2011) **Implied warranties on new homes.**

(A) In every contract for the sale of a new dwelling, the vendor shall be held to warrant to the vendee that, at the time of the transfer of record title or the vendee's taking possession, whichever occurs first, the dwelling with all its fixtures is, to the best of the actual knowledge of the vendor or his agents, sufficiently (i) free from structural defects, so as to pass without objection in the trade, and (ii) constructed in a workmanlike manner, so as to pass without objection in the trade.

(B) In addition, in every contract for the sale of a new dwelling, the vendor, if he is in the business of building or selling such dwellings, shall be held to warrant to the vendee that, at the time of transfer of record title or the vendee's taking possession, whichever occurs first, the dwelling together with all its fixtures is sufficiently (i) free from structural defects, so as to pass without objection in the trade, (ii) constructed in a workmanlike manner, so as to pass without objection in the trade, and (iii) fit for habitation.

(C) The above warranties implied in the contract for sale shall be held to survive the transfer of title. Such warranties are in addition to, and not in lieu of, any other express or implied warranties pertaining to the dwelling, its materials or fixtures. A contract for sale may waive, modify or exclude any or all express and implied warranties and sell a new home "as is" only if the words used to waive, modify or exclude such warranties are conspicuous (as defined by subdivision (b)(10) of § 8.1A-201), set forth on the face of such contract in capital letters which are at least two points larger than the other type in the contract and only if the words used to waive, modify or exclude the warranties state with specificity the warranty or warranties that are being waived, modified or excluded. If all warranties are waived or excluded, a contract must specifically set forth in capital letters which are at least two points larger than the other type in the contract that the dwelling is being sold "as is."

(D) If there is a breach of warranty under this section, the vendee, or his heirs or personal representatives in case of his death, shall have a cause of action against his vendor for damages; provided, however, for any defect discovered after July 1, 2002, such vendee shall first provide the vendor, by registered or certified mail at his last known address, a written notice stating the nature of the warranty claim. Such notice also may be hand delivered to the vendor with the vendee retaining a receipt of such hand delivered notice to the vendor or its authorized agent. After such notice, the vendor shall have a reasonable period of time, not to exceed six months, to cure the defect that is the subject of the warranty claim.

(E) The warranty shall extend for a period of one year from the date of transfer of record title or the vendee's taking possession, whichever occurs first, except that the warranty pursuant to clause (i) of subsection B for the foundation of new dwellings shall extend for a period of five years from the date of transfer of record title or the vendee's taking possession, whichever occurs first. Any action for its breach shall be brought within two years after the breach thereof. For all warranty claims arising on or after January 1, 2009, sending the notice required by subsection D shall toll the limitations period for six months.

(F) As used in this section, the term "new dwelling" shall mean a dwelling or house that has not previously been occupied for a period of more than 60 days by anyone other than the vendor or the vendee or that has not been occupied by the original vendor or subsequent vendor for a cumulative period of more than 12 months excluding dwellings constructed solely for lease. The term "new dwelling" shall not include a condominium or condominium units created pursuant to Chapter 4.2 (§ 55-79.39 et seq.) of this title.

(G) The term "structural defects," as used in this section, shall mean a defect or defects that reduce the stability or safety of the structure below accepted standards or that restrict the normal use thereof.

. . . .

■ OHIO CASE LAW

EXAMPLE

Jones v. Centex Homes, 132 Ohio St.3d 1, 2012-Ohio-1001, 967 N.E.2d 1199.

{¶10} We conclude that in Ohio, a duty to construct houses in a workmanlike manner using ordinary care is imposed by law on all home builders.

. . . .

{¶14} We conclude that the duty to construct a house in a workmanlike manner using ordinary care is the baseline standard that Ohio home buyers can expect builders to meet. The duty does not require builders to be perfect, but it does establish a standard of care below which builders may not fall without being subject to liability, even if a contract with the home buyer purports to relieve the builder of that duty. Accordingly, we conclude that a home builder's duty to construct a house in a workmanlike manner using ordinary care is a duty imposed by law, and a home buyer's right to enforce that duty cannot be waived.

Id. at ¶¶ 10, 14.

EXAMPLE

In a more recent Ohio case, an Ohio Court expands on the Ohio Supreme Court's ruling in *Centex*: *Landis v. William Fannin Builders, Inc.*, 2011-Ohio-1489; 193 Ohio App. 3d 318.

{¶2} In 2004, Landis and his wife, Weidman, decided to build a custom home on land that Landis owned in Pleasantville, Ohio. After interviewing three builders, they chose Fannin Builders to construct their home. On May 4, 2004, appellees signed a contract with Fannin Builders, in which Fannin Builders agreed to construct appellees' home in accordance with the plans and specifications attached to the contract for $356,750.

{¶3} The specifications for appellees' home called for T1-11 exterior siding covered with two coats of stain in a color of appellees' choice. T1-11 siding is a plywood siding with one-inch deep vertical grooves spaced 11 inches apart. Appellees chose T1-11 siding for their home because it provided a more natural, rustic look than other types of siding. Before signing the construction contract, appellees sought, and received, assurances from Fannin Builders that it had experience with installing and staining T1-11 siding.

. . . .

{¶5} Fannin Builders subcontracted with 84 Lumber for the procurement and installation of the T1-11 siding. Unfortunately, 84 Lumber underestimated the amount of siding needed to completely clad appellees' home by 19 sheets. Consequently, the company 84 Lumber hired to stain the T1-11 siding, Precision Applied Coating Enterprises ("PACE"), stained the 19 additional sheets separately from the majority of the siding. Although PACE stained both batches of siding with Cabot semi-transparent, allagash stain, one batch of siding turned out a noticeably darker hue than the other batch.

. . . .

{¶7} When installing the siding, 84 Lumber did not attempt to group same-colored siding together. Instead, 84 Lumber placed darker and lighter siding at random intervals around the perimeter of the house and unattached garage. As a result, appellees' home acquired a striped or patchwork appearance.

. . . .

{¶11} Contrary to Klinger's earlier assurances, the second coat of stain did not improve the patchwork appearance of the siding.1 Appellees and Fannin Builders discussed various ways in which to fix the patchwork appearance.

. . . .

{¶19} Ultimately, on April 11, 2007, appellees filed suit against Fannin Builders, alleging claims for breach of contract, breach of the express limited warranty, and violation of the Ohio Consumer Sales Practices Act ("OCSPA"). Fannin Builders, in turn, filed a third-party complaint against 84 Lumber, alleging claims for breach of contract and indemnification. With the trial court's leave, Fannin Builders also later amended its answer to add a counterclaim against appellees for breach of contract and unjust enrichment. In the counterclaim, Fannin Builders alleged that appellees still owed it $3,908.98 for the construction of appellees' home.

. . . .

{¶21} In its decision, the trial court found in appellees' favor on their breach of contract claim and against appellees on their claims for breach of the express limited warranty and violation of the OCSPA. Additionally, the trial court found in Fannin Builders' favor on its counterclaim for breach of contract and against Fannin Builders on its third-party claims for breach of contract and indemnity. The trial court determined that appellees' damages amounted to $66,906.24, and after setting off the $3,908.98 that appellees owed Fannin Builders under the construction contract, the trial court awarded appellees $62,997.26. The trial court reduced its decision to judgment on May 18, 2010.

. . . .

{¶23} By its first assignment of error, Fannin Builders argues that the trial court erred in ruling that it breached its contract with appellees when it provided siding that did not meet appellees' approval. Fannin Builders misinterprets the trial court's ruling. The trial court actually held that Fannin Builders breached the construction contract because it failed to provide appellees "siding with a uniform shade of oil-based Cabot semi-transparent stain." (Decision, at 13.) (Emphasis added.) Thus, the patchwork appearance of the siding, not appellees' dissatisfaction with the siding, constitutes the breach of contract.

{¶24} Contracts for the future construction of a residence include a duty, implied by law, that the builder must perform its work in a workman-like manner. *Kishmarton v. William Bailey Constr., Inc.*, 93 Ohio St.3d 226, 228-29, 2001-Ohio-1334; *Jones v. Centex Homes*, 189 Ohio App.3d 668, 2010-Ohio-4268, ¶9, appeal accepted for review, 127 Ohio St.3d

1531, 2011-Ohio-376. "This implied duty 'requires a construction professional to act reasonably and to exercise that degree of care which a member of the construction trade in good standing in that community would exercise under the same or similar circumstances.' " *Jarupan v. Hanna*, 173 Ohio App.3d 284, 2007-Ohio-5081, ¶19 (quoting *Seff v. Davis*, 10th Dist. No. 03AP-159, 2003-Ohio-7029, ¶19). In determining whether a builder has breached its implied duty to perform in a workmanlike manner, a fact finder must assess whether the builder used proper materials and workmanlike skill and judgment. *Gilham v. Stasiulewicz*, 7th Dist. No. 09 JE 25, 2010-Ohio-6407, ¶48.

{¶25} In the case at bar, the parties do not dispute that the evidence establishes that Fannin Builders fell below local industry standards in constructing a house with siding of such disparate color. Fannin admitted that the siding is unacceptable under industry standards. The BIA report states that the color variance in the siding "does not comply with professional standard's [sic] in the residential construction industry." (Exhibit 73, decision of the BIA Professional Standards Committee.) Finally, appellees' expert witness testified that the patchwork appearance of the siding does not meet industry standards. Given this evidence, we conclude that the trial court did not err in finding that Fannin Builders' failure to provide siding in a uniform color amounted to a breach of contract. Because the siding does not conform to industry standards, Fannin Builders breached its implied duty to perform in a workmanlike manner.

{¶26} Fannin Builders, however, contends that the color variance could not constitute a breach because Fannin Builders provided appellees replacement siding was uniform in color. Essentially, Fannin Builders argues that its belated performance under the contract vitiated its earlier defective performance. We disagree. Under contract law, a breach occurs when a party fails, without legal excuse, to perform a promise that forms a whole or part of a contract. *Natl. City Bank v. Erskine & Sons, Inc.* (1953), 158 Ohio St. 450, paragraph one of the syllabus. Here, Fannin Builders breached the contract when it constructed appellees' house with mismatched siding, and thus, failed to perform its promise to construct the house in a workmanlike manner. Fixing defective work may eliminate a non-breaching party's injury, but it cannot negate the breach itself.

. . . .

{¶28} By its second assignment of error, Fannin Builders argues that appellees cannot recover for breach of the contract because they refused to allow Fannin Builders to cure the breach. Fannin Builders bases its right to cure on a provision of the one-year limited warranty, which reads:

The Builder warrants * * * that the construction was completed in accordance with the Quality Standards for the construction of a single family home as adopted by the Building Industry Association of Central Ohio, Inc.

Within one year from the date of closing or occupancy by the Buyer, whichever is first to occur, the Builder will repair or replace, at Builder's option, any defects in material or workmanship as determined by the application of the above-referenced Quality Standards and as otherwise limited by the terms and conditions of this Limited Warranty.

According to Fannin Builders, because appellees prevented it from carrying out the promise to repair or replace contained in the limited warranty, appellees cannot take advantage of Fannin Builders' nonperformance. In other words, Fannin Builders contends that appellees' rejection of the sole remedy offered in the limited warranty precludes them from recovering damages for the mismatched siding.

{¶29} Although Fannin Builders depends upon a term of the limited warranty for its right to cure, the trial court concluded that no breach of the limited warranty occurred. Fannin Builders breached the duty of workmanlike conduct implicit in the construction contract, not the limited warranty requiring it to satisfy the BIA's Quality Standards. Consequently, the limited warranty does not apply to this case, and thus, it does not prevent appellees' recovery of damages. Accordingly, we overrule Fannin Builders' second assignment of error.

Id. at ¶¶ 2-3, 5, 7, 11, 19. 21, 23-26, 28-29.

EXAMPLE

The paralegal found another Ohio residential construction case that addressed a similar problem:

Estate of Cattano v. High Touch Homes, Inc., 6th Dist. Erie No. E-01-022, 2002-Ohio-2631.

{¶12} In 1995, Lamont Cattano executed a written contract with High Touch Homes to purchase a modular home. The home was delivered by Redman Homes, Inc. The parties dispute who was responsible for the setup of the home. After he moved into the home, Cattano complained about deficiencies in the home. . . . .

{¶13} Cattano . . . asserts that the home did not meet the standard of quality required under the contract because: 1) it did not include galvanized floor-joist hangers as required under the contract; 2) it was not of the same quality and did not have the same amenities as the model shown to Cattano; and 3) it was not constructed in a professional and workmanlike manner. Cattano . . . asserted claims of fraud, breach of contract, breach of workmanlike performance, and violation of several sections of the Consumer Sales Practices Act. The fraud claim was later dismissed by the court. . . . .

{¶14} At trial, the following evidence was presented. Angelo Mularoni, who had been in the construction industry for forty-eight years and a general contractor of custom-built houses for thirty years, testified that he examined the home at issue and found various defects. He found that the service door to the garage was not plumb and level causing gaps in the fittings; a six-foot span of the floor sagged from the exterior wall to the supporting wall; the drywall corners were not installed correctly; there were cracks along the ceiling; the cabinets had not been set properly; there were stress cracks in the drywall due to the sagging floor; the drywall had been poorly taped; the formica counters had been improperly glued; and either the floor joists were too short or the marriage beam was not installed properly because the nailing of the joists did not hold. He attributed the wall and floor problems to improper nailing and to the fact that the floor joist and beam configuration were not up to industry standard. However, Mularoni testified that he was not familiar with modular homes and did not know the industry standards to evaluate them.

He did expect, however, that a modular home should not be of lesser quality than a custom built home.

. . .

{¶27} Following a jury trial, Cattano's estate was awarded $25,000 on the breach of contract claim and $20,000 for violating the Consumer Sales Practices Act.

. . . .

{¶42} The Consumer Sales Practices Act prohibits unfair or deceptive acts and unconscionable acts or practices by suppliers in consumer transactions. *Einhorn v. Ford Motor Co.* (1990), 48 Ohio St.3d 27, 29. By enacting this legislation, the General Assembly intended to give the consumer protections he lacked under common law by eliminating the need to prove intent or knowledge to deceive to establish unfair or deceptive practices. *Karst v. Goldberg* (1993), 88 Ohio App.3d 413, 417-418, citing *Thomas v. Sun Furniture and Appliance Co.* (1978), 61 Ohio App. 2d 78, 81-82. The Consumer Sales Practices Act also provides consumers with additional remedies for the same conduct that might not be available under other statutes or at common law. R.C.1345.13.

. . . .

{¶52} A consumer establishes a claim under the Act by proving facts that establish an act or practice described in R.C. *Gatto v. Frank Nero Auto Lease, Inc.* (Apr. 8, 1999), Cuyahoga App. No. 74894 at 11. We find that there was sufficient evidence in this case from which the jury could find that the home Cattano purchased did not meet the standards of the model that he was shown. While appellant did offer to remedy the problems with the home, there was also evidence from which the jury could conclude that the repairs appellant intended to make were insufficient to remedy the problems with the home.

Id. at ¶¶ 12-14, 27, 42, 52.

■ VIRGINIA CASE LAW

EXAMPLE

The Virginia Supreme Court also addressed the warranty requirements for builders of new homes in *Davis v. Tazewell Place Associates*, 254 Va. 257, 260, 492 S.E.2d 162, 164 (1997).

At common law, a purchaser did not acquire an implied warranty associated with the sale of a new dwelling. *See Bruce Farms v. Coupe*, 219 Va. 287, 289, 247 S.E.2d 400, 402 (1978). Code §§ 55-70.1(B) and (E), which changed the common law, create certain statutory warranties, provide a warranty period of one year from the date of transfer or possession, and prescribe a statute of limitations of two years from the date of the breach of the warranty. If the buyer notifies the builder of any defects covered by the statutory warranty within the one-year statutory warranty period, and the builder fails to remedy such defects, then the builder has breached its statutory duty, and the buyer is entitled to file an action for damages against the builder within two years from the date that the buyer notified the builder of the defect.

Id. at 260, 164.

In the landlord-tenant case earlier in the chapter, we saw examples of the law being woven into the text. Below are further examples incorporating direct quotes, weaving, and paraphrasing law into text for the home construction case, with the actual text of the original law provided underneath the example, except for those examples in which we already have used the direct quote. Notice how we have used paraphrasing and weaving to integrate the law into the narrative.

EXAMPLES

Paraphrased Text

1. Pursuant to R.C § 1312.01(c) and (d), Brianna and Marcus's home qualifies as a residential property, and Connolly Homes of Parkhurst qualifies as a contractor.

Original Text

(C) "Owner" means an owner or a prospective owner of a residential building or a dwelling unit in a residential building who enters into a contract with a residential contractor for the construction or substantial rehabilitation of that residential building or unit.

(D) "Residential building" means a structure that is a one-family, two-family, or three-family dwelling house or a dwelling unit within that structure, any accessory structures incidental to that dwelling house, and a unit in a condominium development in which the owner holds title to that unit. "Residential building" includes any structure that is used as a model to promote the sale of a similar dwelling house.

Ohio Revised Code § 1312.01(c) and (d).

Direct Quote

2. The Ohio Revised. Code § 1312.04(A) states in pertinent part, "No owner shall commence arbitration proceedings or file a dwelling action against a residential contractor unless, at least sixty days before commencing the proceedings or filing the action, the owner provides the contractor with written notice of the construction defect that would be the basis of the arbitration proceedings or the dwelling action. The notice shall be in writing . . . ."

WOVEN TEXT

3. The Consumer Safety Protection Act allows the court to "award to the prevailing party a reasonable attorney's fee" under limited circumstances.

Direct Quote

(D) The court may award to the prevailing party a reasonable attorney's fee limited to the work reasonably performed, if either of the following apply:

(1) The owner complaining of the act or practice that violated this chapter has brought or maintained an action that is groundless, and the owner filed or maintained the action in bad faith;

(2) The home construction service supplier has knowingly committed an act or practice that violates this chapter. R.C. § 4722.08.

PARAPHRASED TEXT

4. The Ohio Supreme Court has ruled that although construction does not have to be perfect, builders are required to build residential properties in a manner that is workmanlike and that uses ordinary care. The court found that this is a duty that the buyer cannot waive. *Jones v. Centex Homes*, 132 Ohio St.3d 1, 2012-Ohio-1001 ¶ 14, 967 N.E.2d 1199.

Direct Quote

{¶14} We conclude that the duty to construct a house in a workmanlike manner using ordinary care is the baseline standard that Ohio home buyers can expect builders to meet. The duty does not require builders to be perfect, but it does establish a standard of care below which builders may not fall without being subject to liability, even if a contract with the home buyer purports to relieve the builder of that duty. Accordingly, we conclude that a home builder's duty to construct a house in a workmanlike manner using ordinary care is a duty imposed by law, and a home buyer's right to enforce that duty cannot be waived.

Jones v. Centex Homes, 132 Ohio St.3d 1, 2012-Ohio-1001 ¶ 14, 967 N.E.2d 1199.

WOVEN TEXT

5. The Virginia statute imposes a requirement on builders of new homes to warrant that the home was "constructed in a workmanlike manner, so as to pass without objection in the trade." Va. Code Ann. § 55-70.1(A).

Direct Quote

(A) In every contract for the sale of a new dwelling, the vendor shall be held to warrant to the vendee that, at the time of the transfer of record title or the vendee's taking possession, whichever occurs first, the dwelling with all its fixtures is, to the best of the actual knowledge of the vendor or his agents, sufficiently (i) free from structural defects, so as to pass without objection in the trade, and (ii) constructed in a workmanlike manner, so as to pass without objection in the trade.

Va. Code Ann. § 55-70.1.

PARAPHRASED TEXT

6. The Virginia statute also gives the buyer a five-year warranty on the foundation of a newly built home. The warranty begins the first of the following: either when the title buyer receives to the home or when the buyer takes possession of the new home. Va. Code Ann. § 55-70.1(E).

Direct Quote

The warranty shall extend for a period of one year from the date of transfer of record title or the vendee's taking possession, whichever occurs first, except that the warranty pursuant to clause (i) of subsection B for the foundation of new dwellings shall extend for a period of five years from the date of transfer of record title or the vendee's taking possession, whichever occurs first. Any action for its breach shall be brought within two years after the breach thereof. For all warranty claims arising on or after January 1, 2009, sending the notice required by subsection D shall toll the limitations period for six months. Va. Code Ann. § 55-70.1(E).

WOVEN QUOTE

7. The Virginia Supreme Court ruled that "[i]f the buyer notifies the builder of any defects covered by the statutory warranty within the one-year statutory warranty period, and the builder fails to remedy such defects, then the builder has breached its statutory duty, and the buyer is entitled to file an action for damages against the builder within two years from the date that the buyer notified the builder of the defect." *Davis v. Tazewell Place Associates*, 254 Va. 257, 260, 492 S.E.2d 162, 164 (1997).

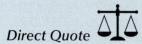

Direct Quote

At common law, a purchaser did not acquire an implied warranty associated with the sale of a new dwelling. See *Bruce Farms v. Coupe*, 219 Va. 287, 289, 247 S.E.2d 400, 402 (1978). Code §§ 55-70.1(B) and (E), which changed the common law, create certain statutory warranties, provide a warranty period of one year from the date of transfer or possession, and prescribe a statute of limitations of two years from the date of the breach of the warranty. If the buyer notifies the builder of any defects covered by the statutory warranty within the one-year statutory warranty period, and the builder fails to remedy such defects, then the builder has breached its statutory duty, and the buyer is entitled to file an action for damages against the builder within two years from the date that the buyer notified the builder of the defect.

Davis v. Tazewell Place Associates, 254 Va. 257, 260, 492 S.E.2d 162, 164 (1997).

PARAPHRASED

8. The warranty builders must give to buyers of newly constructed homes includes the actual structure as well as the fixtures. Va. Code Ann. § 55-70.1.

Direct Quote

(A) In every contract for the sale of a new dwelling, the vendor shall be held to warrant to the vendee that, at the time of the transfer of record title or the vendee's taking possession, whichever occurs first, the dwelling with all its fixtures is, to the best of the actual knowledge of the vendor or his agents, sufficiently (i) free from structural defects, so as to pass without objection in the trade, and (ii) constructed in a workmanlike manner, so as to pass without objection in the trade.

Va. Code Ann. § 55-70.1.

EXERCISE

Revise and correct the rule in the following exercises.

1. In your memo to Brad regarding the law that applies to Marcus and Brianna's home, you should include the following portion of the statute: "'Construction defect' means a deficiency that arises directly or indirectly out of the construction or the substantial rehabilitation of a residential building. 'Substantial rehabilitation' includes the addition of a room and the removal or installation of a wall, partition, or portion of the structural design."

2. In your memo to Brad, you should be sure to point out that an action under CSPA, R.C. § 4722.08(D) always includes attorney fees, so he does not have to worry about collecting his fees.

3. When the homeowner signed the contract to have a new home constructed, the contract included a written warranty that states "that the builder must perform its work in a workmanlike manner." *Landis v. William Fannin Builders, Inc.*, 2011-Ohio-1489 , ¶ 24, 193 Ohio App. 3d 318. Without this writing, the homeowner has no recourse against the builder for defects the homeowner discovers.

4. If the homeowner tells the builder in writing that the owner will not hold the builder responsible for any defects in the house if the builder completes it by a certain date, then the homeowner cannot go back and sue the builder when the homeowner discovers defects, no matter how serious. *Jones v. Centex Homes*, 132 Ohio St.3d 1, 2012-Ohio-1001, ¶ 14.

5. To be held liable for violating the CSPA, the builder must have intended to be dishonest and to deceive the homeowner. Otherwise, the homeowner is limited to the remedies available to him under common law. *Estate of Cattano v. High Touch Homes, Inc.*, 2002-Ohio-2631, ¶ 42.

6. Because Marcus and Brianna waited until after a year to contact a lawyer, under Virginia law, they waived their right to sue for a violation of the home warranty. Va. Code Ann. § 55-70.1(E).

7. "If the buyer notifies the builder of any defects covered by the statutory warranty within the one-year statutory warranty period, . . . the builder [shall] remedy such defects . . . ." *Davis v. Tazewell Place Associates*, 254 Va. 257, 260, 492 S.E.2d 162, 164 (1997).

8. The Virginia statute expressly excludes any defect in the fixtures in the home, so the only issue the builder has to repair is the leaky roof. The warranty applies only to the structure, and not to the fixtures like the electrical outlets and the water faucets. Va. Code Ann. § 55-70.1(A) and (B).

■ PRODUCT LIABILITY

You will recall the fraternity house's stove explosion from earlier chapters:

When they were still in college, Brad and Antoine had been fraternity brothers. During a party at their fraternity house, the gas stove in the kitchen had exploded. Although no one was hurt, the fraternity house burned to the ground, and the students who lived in the house lost their all their belongings. The fire department's investigation determined that the explosion was a result of a flaw in either the stove or the gas line to the stove.

Their attorney, Ms. Walker, had found, through her paralegal's research, that the stove they had bought at the big box store had been recalled prior to the date the fraternity brothers bought it. Although the store denied knowing about the recall, it had sold the stove at cost. The paralegal also discovered that the manufacturer of the stove had gone bankrupt and could not be sued.

The attorney had informed the paralegal that the big box store where Brad and Antoine bought the fraternity house gas stove that exploded during the party is headquartered in Texas, and it has a forum selection clause stating that all purchasers must use Texas law for litigation over products bought at its stores.

The bankrupt manufacturer was headquartered in Michigan, so the attorney asked the paralegal to research both Texas and Michigan law. The attorney also noted that the Ohio CSPA law the paralegal had found for the Johnson's case against the home builder also applied to other merchandise, including "white goods" like stoves, refrigerators, washers, and dryers.

■ TEXAS STATUTORY LAW

The Texas statute differs significantly from the Ohio statute. Although if we were to apply Ohio law, we would use the CSPA cited above in the home building section, here we will apply Texas and Michigan law. In Texas, a seller's liability for damages resulting from a defective product is limited. You will use the Texas law cited below for exercises in future chapters, so make note of the pages on which this law is contained, and save the work you do in this chapter; you will build on it in the upcoming chapters. Texas Civil Practice & Remedies Code, Chapter 82, Products Liability, which is abbreviated Civ. Prac. & Rem., states the following:

EXAMPLE

Texas Civil Practice & Remedies Code § 82.001.

DEFINITIONS. In this chapter:

(1) "Claimant" means a party seeking relief, including a plaintiff, counterclaimant, or cross-claimant.

(2) "Products liability action" means any action against a manufacturer or seller for recovery of damages arising out of personal injury, death, or property damage allegedly caused by a defective product whether the action is based in strict tort liability, strict products liability, negligence, misrepresentation, breach of express or implied warranty, or any other theory or combination of theories.

(3) "Seller" means a person who is engaged in the business of distributing or otherwise placing, for any commercial purpose, in the stream of commerce for use or consumption a product or any component part thereof.

(4) "Manufacturer" means a person who is a designer, formulator, constructor, rebuilder, fabricator, producer, compounder, processor, or assembler of any product or any component part thereof and who places the product or any component part thereof in the stream of commerce.

EXAMPLE

Texas Civil Practice & Remedies Code § 82.002.

MANUFACTURER'S DUTY TO INDEMNIFY. (a) A manufacturer shall indemnify and hold harmless a seller against loss arising out of a products liability action, except for any loss caused by the seller's negligence, intentional misconduct, or other act or omission, such as negligently modifying or altering the product, for which the seller is independently liable.

. . . .

(e) The duty to indemnify under this section:

(1) applies without regard to the manner in which the action is concluded; and

(2) is in addition to any duty to indemnify established by law, contract, or otherwise.

(f) a seller eligible for indemnification under this section shall give reasonable notice to the manufacturer of a product claimed in a petition or complaint to be defective, unless the manufacturer has been served as a party or otherwise has actual notice of the action. (g) a seller is entitled to recover from the manufacturer court costs and other reasonable expenses, reasonable attorney fees, and any reasonable damages incurred by the seller to enforce the seller's right to indemnification under this section.

EXAMPLE

Texas Civil Practice & Remedies Code § 82.003.

LIABILITY OF NONMANUFACTURING SELLERS. (a) A seller that did not manufacture a product is not liable for harm caused to the claimant by that product unless the claimant proves:

(1) that the seller participated in the design of the product;

(2) that the seller altered or modified the product and the claimant's harm resulted from that alteration or modification;

(3) that the seller installed the product, or had the product installed, on another product and the claimant's harm resulted from the product's installation onto the assembled product;

(4) that:

(A) the seller exercised substantial control over the content of a warning or instruction that accompanied the product;

(B) the warning or instruction was inadequate; and

(C) the claimant's harm resulted from the inadequacy of the warning or instruction;

(5) that:

(A) the seller made an express factual representation about an aspect of the product;

(B) the representation was incorrect;

(C) the claimant relied on the representation in obtaining or using the product; and

(D) if the aspect of the product had been as represented, the claimant would not have been harmed by the product or would not have suffered the same degree of harm;

(6) that:

(A) the seller actually knew of a defect to the product at the time the seller supplied the product; and

(B) the claimant's harm resulted from the defect; or

(7) that the manufacturer of the product is:

(A) insolvent; or

(B) not subject to the jurisdiction of the court.

Fortunately for the purchaser of the stove, evidence exists that shows that the seller of the stove knew about the defect. Further, the attorney has obtained two expert witness reports confirming that the defective stove was the actual cause of the purchaser's damage. Additionally, the Texas statute states "[a] seller that did not manufacture a product is not liable for harm caused to the claimant by that product unless the claimant proves . . . .that the manufacturer of the product is . . . insolvent . . . ." *Id.* In this case, the manufacturer declared bankruptcy shortly after the stoves were recalled.

When you research case law, you might encounter a fact pattern for which there is no case law on point. In that situation, you will have to use the closest case and explain how the situation in your client's case differs from the case law, or you might have to analogize as closely as possible to the existing case law.

Texas case law does not address a situation in which a manufacturer had gone bankrupt. It does, however, have case law that addresses the manufacturer's obligation to indemnify the seller of its products. This means that if the seller is found liable for the injuries, the manufacturer has to reimburse the seller for the amount of the judgment against it.

EXAMPLE

Texas Case Law

The following Texas Supreme Court case, *Owens & Minor v. Ansell Healthcare Products*, 251 SW 3d 481 (2008), is not "on all fours," that is, "on all four corners:" it does not fit our fact pattern as well as we would want. Sometimes you have to use the law that you can find and do your best to make an argument with it. You will see how we do this in the analysis chapter that follows this one.

[A] manufacturer that offers to defend or indemnify a distributor for claims relating only to the sale or alleged sale of that specific manufacturer's product fulfills its obligation under Section 82.002.

Id. at 482.

. . . .

But it is unmistakable that the duty under Section 82.002 is premised on a nexus between a given manufacturer and its product. This nexus is inherent in the statute that requires a "manufacturer" to hold a seller harmless against loss arising out of a products liability action. TEX. CIV. PRAC. & REM.CODE § 82.002(a). Section 82.001(4) defines the term "manufacturer" for purposes of chapter 82 as "a person who is a designer, formulator, constructor, rebuilder, fabricator, producer, compounder, processor, or assembler of any product or any component part thereof and who places the product or any component thereof in the stream of commerce." Id. § 82.001(4). Thus, Ansell and Becton can be "manufacturers" under Section 82.002 only with respect to their own products. On at least two prior occasions, we have implied that requiring a manufacturer to defend or indemnify a seller against claims related to the products of its competitors is an absurd result that cannot have been the intent of the Legislature.

Id. at 485.

. . . .

Section 82.002 was designed to remedy the fundamental unfairness inherent in a scheme that holds an innocent seller liable for defective products manufactured by another by requiring the manufacturer to indemnify the seller unless the seller is independently liable for negligence, intentional misconduct, or any other act or omission. TEX. CIV. PRAC. & REM.CODE § 82.002(a).

Id. at 487.

In an earlier case, *Meritor Automotive, Inc. v. Ruan Leasing*, 44 SW 3d 86 (2001), the Texas Supreme Court analyzed the application of the statute in conferring liability on the seller rather than the manufacturer when the seller's independent actions caused the injury:

EXAMPLE

Texas Products Liability Statute

The Texas Products Liability Act describes the manufacturer's indemnity duty as follows:

A manufacturer shall indemnify and hold harmless a seller against loss arising out of a products liability action, except for any loss caused by the seller's negligence, intentional misconduct, or other act or omission, such as negligently modifying or altering the product, for which the seller is independently liable.

Tex.Civ.Prac. & Rem.Code § 82.002(a). This section requires a manufacturer to indemnify an innocent seller for certain damages and litigation expenses arising out of a products liability action, but requires sellers to bear the damages and expenses for losses they cause. *Fitzgerald v. Advanced Spine Fixation Sys., Inc.*, 996 S.W.2d 864, 867 (Tex.1999). (Internal citation altered in form only).

Id. at 88.

. . . .

Whether or not the Manufacturers' position is fair, it is simply not what the statute provides. In describing the manufacturer's duty, section 82.002(a) provides that the manufacturer must indemnify the seller except when the loss is "caused by the seller's negligence [or other independent culpable conduct]." Section 82.002(e)(1) then further elaborates on the manufacturer's duty to indemnify, stating that it "applies without regard to the manner in which the action is concluded." Thus, under (e)(1), it is the manufacturer's "duty to indemnify" that applies regardless of outcome, and plaintiff's pleadings are accordingly sufficient to invoke that duty. But for the Manufacturers to implicate section 82.002(a)'s exception to that duty, it must be established that seller's conduct "caused" the loss. In this instance, the statute's plain language indicates that the plaintiff's pleadings are not sufficient to invoke the exception. Legislative history further confirms that the exception applies only upon a finding that the seller was independently liable.

. . . .

This analysis goes on to explain that under the exception, "Retailers would still be held responsible if they were truly negligent, engaged in intentional misconduct or altered a product." (Internal citation omitted). And while the manufacturer's duty to indemnify the seller is invoked by the plaintiff's pleadings and joinder of the seller as defendant, the exception to that duty is established by a finding that the seller's independent conduct was a cause of the plaintiff's injury.

Id. at 88-89.

EXAMPLE

Michigan Statutory Law

You will notice similarities and differences between Texas's law and Michigan's. Michigan's statutes are abbreviated Mich. Comp. Laws.

Michigan Compiled Laws § 600.2947 Product liability action; liability of manufacturer or seller.

(1) A manufacturer or seller is not liable in a product liability action for harm caused by an alteration of the product unless the alteration was reasonably foreseeable. Whether there was an alteration of a product and whether an alteration was reasonably foreseeable are legal issues to be resolved by the court.

(2) A manufacturer or seller is not liable in a product liability action for harm caused by misuse of a product unless the misuse was reasonably foreseeable. Whether there was misuse of a product and whether misuse was reasonably foreseeable are legal issues to be resolved by the court.

(3) A manufacturer or seller is not liable in a product liability action if the purchaser or user of the product was aware that use of the product created an unreasonable risk of personal injury and voluntarily exposed himself or herself to that risk and the risk that he or she exposed himself or herself to was the proximate cause of the injury. This subsection does not relieve a manufacturer or seller from a duty to use reasonable care in a product's production.

(4) Except to the extent a state or federal statute or regulation requires a manufacturer to warn, a manufacturer or seller is not liable in a product liability action for failure to provide an adequate warning if the product is provided for use by a sophisticated user.

(5) A manufacturer or seller is not liable in a product liability action if the alleged harm was caused by an inherent characteristic of the product that cannot be eliminated without substantially compromising the product's usefulness or desirability, and that is recognized by a person with the ordinary knowledge common to the community.

(6) In a product liability action, a seller other than a manufacturer is not liable for harm allegedly caused by the product unless either of the following is true:

(a) The seller failed to exercise reasonable care, including breach of any implied warranty, with respect to the product and that failure was a proximate cause of the person's injuries.

(b) The seller made an express warranty as to the product, the product failed to conform to the warranty, and the failure to conform to the warranty was a proximate cause of the person's harm.

EXAMPLE

Michigan Compiled Laws § 600.2948 Death or injury; warnings as evidence.

(1) Evidence is admissible in a product liability action that, before the death of the person or injury to the person or damage to property, pamphlets, booklets, labels, or other written warnings were provided that gave notice to foreseeable users of the material risk of injury, death, or damage connected with the foreseeable use of the product or provided instructions as to the foreseeable uses, applications, or limitations of the product that the defendant knew or should have known.

(2) A defendant is not liable for failure to warn of a material risk that is or should be obvious to a reasonably prudent product user or a material risk that is or should be a matter of common knowledge to persons in the same or similar position as the person upon whose injury or death the claim is based in a product liability action.

(3) In a product liability action brought against a manufacturer or seller for harm allegedly caused by a failure to provide adequate warnings or instructions, a manufacturer or seller is not liable unless the plaintiff proves that the manufacturer knew or should have known about the risk of harm based on the scientific, technical, or medical information reasonably available at the time the specific unit of the product left the control of the manufacturer.

(4) This section does not limit a manufacturer's or seller's duty to use reasonable care in relation to a product after the product has left the manufacturer's or seller's control.

EXAMPLE

Michigan Case Law

Just as Texas law differed materially from Ohio law, so too, Michigan law differs from both Texas and Ohio law.

For example, note the law in *Greene v. AP Products, Ltd.*, 475 Mich. 502, 717 N.W.2d 855 (2006):

> In this case we consider the scope of a manufacturer's or seller's duty to warn of product risks under MCL 600.2948(2). We conclude that the statute imposes a duty to warn that extends only to material risks not obvious to a reasonably prudent product user, and to material risks that are not, or should not be, a matter of common knowledge to persons in the same or a similar position as the person who suffered the injury in question.
>
> . . . .
>
> Super 7 Beauty Supply argued that plaintiff failed to establish that it, as a nonmanufacturing seller, had independently breached an express or implied warranty or was independently negligent. It further argued that plaintiff failed to show that the product was not fit for its ordinary uses or for a particular purpose.
>
> . . . .
>
> Before 1995, a manufacturer's or seller's duty to warn of material risks in a product-liability action was governed by common-law principles. Tort reform legislation enacted in 1995, however, displaced the common law. MCL 600.2948, in chapter 29 of the Revised Judicature Act, now governs a defendant's duty to warn of an obvious danger in a product-liability action. It states, in relevant part:
> A defendant is not liable for failure to warn of a material risk that is or should be obvious to a reasonably prudent product user or a material risk that is or should be a matter of common knowledge to persons in the same or similar position as the person upon whose injury or death the claim is based in a product liability action. [MCL 600.2948(2).]
>
> . . . .
>
> Accordingly, we hold that defendants owed no duty to warn plaintiff that her son's ingestion and inhalation of the Wonder 8 Hair Oil posed a material risk. Moreover, defendants owed no duty to warn of the potential injuries that could arise from ingesting and inhaling the product. The plaintiff also pleaded breach of implied warranty under MCL 600.2947(6)(a) and breach of implied warranty of merchantability under MCL 440.2314(2)(e) with respect to the nonmanufacturing seller, Super 7 Beauty Supply. Plaintiff claimed that, in the absence of a warning, the oil was not properly labeled. Because no warning was required, however, these claims are without merit. Defendants are therefore entitled to judgment as a matter of law.

Greene v. AP Products, Ltd., 475 Mich. 502, 504, 506, 507-508, 513, 717 N.W.2d 855, 857-859, 862 (2006).

EXAMPLE

Similarly, see how the Michigan Court applies this law in *Curry v. Meijer, Inc*, 286 Mich. App. 586, 780 N.W.2d 603 (2009),:

> Before 1996, it was settled in Michigan that a plaintiff was not required to establish negligence to recover under a breach of implied warranty theory. *Piercefield v. Remington Arms Co., Inc.*, 375 Mich. 85, 96, 133 N.W.2d 129

(1965). Rather, at common law, a plaintiff need only show that a product was sold in a defective condition and the defect caused the plaintiff's injury. *Id.* at 96-97, 133 N.W.2d 129. However, tort reform legislation effective in 1996 displaced application of the common law in certain products liability actions. *Greene v. A.P. Products, Ltd.*, 475 Mich. 502, 507-508, 717 N.W.2d 855 (2006). Thus, MCL 600.2947(6), contained within the Revised Judicature Act, now governs the liability of a nonmanufacturing seller in breach of implied warranty cases. That section provides:

In a product liability action, a seller other than a manufacturer is not liable for harm allegedly caused by the product unless either of the following is true:

(a) The seller failed to exercise reasonable care, including breach of any implied warranty, with respect to the product and that failure was a proximate cause of the person's injuries.

(b) The seller made an express warranty as to the product, the product failed to conform to the warranty, and the failure to conform to the warranty was a proximate cause of the person's harm. [MCL 600.2947(6).]

Id. at 590, 606.

In sum, MCL 600.2947(6)(a) requires a plaintiff to establish that a nonmanufacturing seller failed to exercise reasonable care in addition to establishing proximate cause to prevail on a products liability claim based on breach of implied warranty.

Id. at 599, 610.

EXERCISE

Applying the law you just read to the fact pattern, in which the fraternity brothers bought a stove that they did not know was defective, but the seller knew or should have known was defective, compose the rule for the rule section of the IRAC statement. Use the law from whichever state your instructor chooses. First, cite and quote the applicable law regarding a seller's potential liability and the limitations on the seller's liability. Second, cite and quote the applicable case law regarding this liability. Third, interweave the scope of a non-manufacturer seller's duty to those to whom it sells products. Fourth, interweave the law as stated in the case your instructor selects. Fifth, paraphrase the law regarding the seller's liability for all three states, being sure to be clear in explaining which law applies to which state.

SUMMARY

- The acronym IRAC stands for Issue, Rule, Analysis, and Conclusion.

- The rule is the second element in IRAC.

- The rule is the law that applies to the case.

- The law consists of primary sources that include statutes, regulations, ordinances, and case law. Primary sources are the most important and most reliable form of law.

- The supreme law of the land in the United States is the United States Constitution. All statutes and case law interpret and apply the law set forth in the Constitution.

- Each state also has its own Constitution, but a state's Constitution shall not contradict anything in the U.S. Constitution. In the case of a conflict, the U.S. Constitution would prevail.

(continued)

- Statutes are laws passed by Congress to more specifically enforce the Constitution. Statutes or ordinances are laws created by a legislative body like Congress or a City or County Council (which may refer to them as ordinances).

- Because the United States has both a federal and state governments, there are federal statutes that are enforceable throughout the United States.

- State statutes are enforceable only in the state whose legislature passed the law.

- A City or County ordinance is enforceable only in the relevant city or county.

- Because a statute can encompass such an enormous area of law, the statute might mandate the creation of an agency to promulgate regulations that more specifically guide people and corporations. Regulations are rules that more specifically interpret a statute.

- Case law is the ruling issued by a court when a conflict of interpretation of law arises and is litigated, or when a person violates a statute, regulation, or ordinance.

- If the losing party in a criminal or civil case chooses, he can appeal the case to an appellate court.

- Precedent is an appellate court's ruling on the same issue of law in a previous case.

- Once an Appellate Court makes its ruling and issues a decision, the decision is the controlling law for that issue.

- Appellate courts rarely overturn their jurisdiction's precedent.

ASSIGNMENTS

I. Read the fact pattern below and select the correct rule.

[Note to students: Specific performance is a contract term that applies to the sale of real property. Specific performance requires the buyer to complete the purchase of the property if the buyer changes its mind and decides it does not want the property. Similarly, if a seller tries to renege on the sale of a specific property, the buyer also can sue for specific performance, forcing the seller to transfer the property to the buyer. The courts allow specific performance in a contract to be enforced because each piece of real estate is considered to be unique and not able to be substituted.]

A decade ago, Henry Johnson had bought property in Wisconsin that he hoped to turn into a family vacation site. He then got distracted by business matters, and when he returned to the property after Marcus and Brianna were married, he discovered that what had once been a quiet, wooded property on a pristine lake was now a surrounded by condominiums, gated communities, and a large shopping mall. Although Henry's property was still wooded, it was no longer quiet. The lake was abuzz with jet skis and motor boats. Because his dream of a quiet vacation site was no longer feasible, Henry decided to sell the property.

When he received an appraisal of the property, he was pleased to discover that the surrounding development had caused his property to increase in value ten-fold. He quickly entered into a sales contract, selling it to a developer. The contract specifically provided that if one of the parties failed to perform, that is, to uphold its side of the contract, the other side could demand specific performance. The developer had been insistent on including this clause, because it realized that the property would increase in value, and it wanted to be certain that Henry did not decide to sell it to someone else.

When the sale was scheduled to close, however, the developer informed Henry that it had not obtained financing yet. After a six-month delay, Henry hired local counsel to sue the buyer for specific performance. After a trial, the court awarded a verdict for Henry and ordered the developer to complete the purchase of the property. The developer appealed, claiming that Henry should have sought other legal remedies rather than specific performance. Henry's Wisconsin attorney cited the following case in the Appellate Brief responding to the developer's appeal.

[In the following case, the petitioner is the buyer of the property, and Ash Park, LLC is the seller. The circuit court is the trial court. Summary Judgment is an action the trial court takes deciding a case before trial. Summary Judgment will be discussed in the Motions chapter.]

WISCONSIN CASE LAW

The petitioner, Alexander & Bishop, Ltd., seeks review of a published decision of the court of appeals affirming the orders of the circuit court. After Alexander & Bishop breached a contract to purchase a parcel of real estate from Ash Park, LLC, the circuit court granted summary judgment in favor of Ash Park and ordered specific performance of the contract. It also imposed interest on the purchase price.

. . . .

The contract provides that specific performance is an available remedy, and neither the contract nor Wisconsin law requires Ash Park to demonstrate that a legal remedy would be inadequate as a precondition to relief. Further, although impossibility is a defense to specific performance, Alexander & Bishop failed to present evidence that performance would be impossible in the proceedings before the circuit court.

Ash Park, LLC v. Alexander & Bishop, Ltd., 2010 WI 44, ¶4, 324 Wis.2d 703, 710, 783 N.W.2d 294, 297.

Which of the following statements of law is correct?

1. Pursuant to *Ash Park*, Henry should have tried to find another buyer rather than forcing the developer to complete the purchase of the vacation property.
2. Wisconsin law does not allow a seller to force the buyer to complete the deal if the buyer does not have the funds.
3. Wisconsin law allows a seller to enforce a contract clause requiring specific performance without the seller first pursuing other options.

4. The realtor who sold Henry the vacation property breached his fiduciary duty to Henry by selling him property in a developing area.

II. Read the fact pattern below and paraphrase the rule as it is stated in the case provided.

Antoine and Cherelle were visiting her Aunt Denise in Boston. They had adopted a small mixed breed dog from the pound a month earlier. They wryly had named the dog Spike, because it was so timid and shy. Because Spike suffered from separation anxiety when he was away from Cherelle, Aunt Denise graciously had told them that the dog was welcome to visit, too. Fortunately, the dog was housebroken and well-trained, and the visit was proceeding pleasantly. Cherelle and Aunt Denise took the dog for a walk in the park. Cherelle was careful to keep Spike on a leash, even though she was certain that it would never let her out of his sight.

Suddenly, a large dog ran up from behind Cherelle and snatched Spike up in its jaws. Cherelle and Aunt Denise both shouted at the large dog and beat on it, trying to get it to let go of Spike. A park ranger arrived, and despite his best efforts, could not loosen the large dog's jaws. The park ranger finally shot the attacking dog through the heart. The ranger then rescued Spike from the dead dog's mouth. Spike was bleeding profusely and was barely conscious.

Another ranger drove Cherelle, Aunt Denise, and Spike to the nearest veterinary hospital, where the veterinarian spent five hours operating on him. To everyone's surprise, Spike recovered almost completely, and Cherelle and Antoine took him home a week later.

When the bill arrived for Spike's emergency medical treatment, Cherelle was appalled to find that she owed the veterinarian $5,000. She was even more distraught when the owner of the large dog filed a lawsuit against her in Massachusetts for the loss of his AKC registered dog. The large dog's owner was suing her for loss of income, claiming that he often made several thousand dollars each year breeding the dog.

Brad and Ana gave Cherelle and Antoine the name of a law school classmate who was practicing law in Boston, and the classmate countersued for the veterinary bills incurred in Spike's treatment. The Boston attorney found the following case and included it in his court documents.

MASSACHUSETTS CASE LAW

An unprovoked attack by the defendants' unleashed German shepherd caused the plaintiffs' Bichon Frisé severe internal injuries, external bruising, and wounds to the head, neck, abdomen, and chest. Emergency surgery was successful but expensive, with veterinary costs ultimately amounting to over $8,000. After a bench trial, a District Court judge found those costs to be both reasonable and necessary and awarded them in full.

The judgment was affirmed by the Appellate Division. The sole issue on appeal is whether damages should be capped at the market value of the dog, regardless of the reasonableness of the veterinary costs necessary to treat the dog's injuries. We affirm.

The plaintiffs sued under G.L. c. 140, § 155, as amended by St.1934, c. 320, § 18, which since 1791 has imposed strict liability for damage caused by dogs:

"If any dog shall do any damage to either the body or property of any person, the owner or keeper . . . shall be liable for such damage, unless such damage shall have been occasioned to the body or property of a person who, at the time such damage was sustained, was committing a trespass or other tort, or was teasing, tormenting or abusing such dog."

. . . .

Although the statute imposes strict liability for "any damage" caused by a dog, it is silent as to how to measure such damage. We turn, accordingly, to the common law.

. . . .

reasonableness is the touchstone for determining whether, and to what extent, veterinary costs can be recovered. If it is reasonable in the circumstances presented to incur the veterinary costs at the time they are undertaken, then the owner of the injured animal may recover them. . . . . Our reading of the common law leads us, therefore, to conclude that reasonable veterinary costs that are reasonably incurred can be recovered under G.L. c.

140, § 155, even if they exceed the market value or replacement cost of an animal injured by a dog.

. . . .

Although the owner's affection for the animal may be considered in assessing the reasonableness of the decision to treat the animal, the owner cannot recover for his or her own hurt feelings, emotions, or pain. Nor is the owner entitled to recover for the loss of the animal's companionship or society.

Irwin v. Degtiarov, 85 Mass. App. Ct. 234, 234-239; 8 N.E.3d 296, 298-302 (2014).

III. Read the fact pattern below and state the issue and correct rule as it is stated in the case provided.

While he was doing a one-year internship at a large university medical center in upstate New York State, Jeremy found that jogging helped clear his mind and helped him sleep– not that he had much opportunity to sleep. He and a classmate were jogging in late October in the classmate's home town, Trumansburg, New York, a quaint little town near the large medical center. After running up a short but steep hill off the main road, they turned left onto McLallen Street, which had charming pre-Civil War homes. Some of the homes had the original slate sidewalks, and the wet leaves were slicked onto the sidewalks.

Jeremy slipped on moss that was hidden by the leaves and fell, breaking his right hand. Because he planned to be a surgeon, he was quite distressed by this injury. One of the professors at the law school that was affiliated with the university offered to represent him in a lawsuit against the homeowners whose sidewalk was the location of his fall.

The homeowners argued that by running on slate sidewalks, which were known to be slippery when wet, and by running on these wet slate sidewalks that were covered by wet leaves, Jeremy had assumed the risk of his injury. The homeowners argued that they were not liable for the slippery sidewalk. They also argued that by running on wet leaves without knowledge of the surface under the leaves, Jeremy had negligently contributed to his own injury.

Jeremy's attorney countered that because sidewalks were designed for people to traverse, the homeowner had a duty to clean the slippery moss off of the sidewalk. Jeremy's attorney further alleged that the homeowners had a duty to clear the wet leaves off the sidewalk, because they knew the leaves would be slippery on the slate walk.

The attorney found the following case concerning contributory negligence and assumption of the risk:

NEW YORK CASE LAW

In this case involving a plaintiff who fell and sustained injuries while rollerblading, we conclude that the doctrine of 86*86 primary assumption of the risk does not preclude her common-law negligence claim against the landowner defendants. We therefore affirm the Appellate Division order reinstating the complaint.

. . . .

Our analysis begins with CPLR 1411, which the Legislature adopted in 1975 to abolish contributory negligence and assumption of the risk as absolute defenses in favor of a comparative fault regime. CPLR 1411 provides:

"In any action to recover damages for personal injury, injury to property, or wrongful death, the culpable conduct attributable to the claimant or to the decedent, including contributory negligence or assumption of risk, shall not bar recovery, but the amount of damages otherwise recoverable shall be diminished in the proportion which the culpable conduct attributable to the claimant or decedent bears to the culpable conduct which caused the damages."

. . . .

Since the adoption of CPLR 1411, we have generally restricted the concept of assumption of the risk to particular athletic and recreative activities in recognition that such pursuits have "enormous social value" even while they may "involve significantly heightened risks" (*Trupia*, 14 NY3d at 395). Hence, the continued application of the doctrine "facilitate[s] free and vigorous participation in athletic activities" (*Benitez*, 73 NY2d at 657), and fosters these socially beneficial activities by shielding coparticipants, activity sponsors or venue owners from "potentially crushing liability" (*Bukowski*, 19 NY3d at 358).

. . . .

In contrast, in Trupia we recently declined to apply the assumption of the risk doctrine to a child who was injured while sliding down a bannister at school. Based on the tension that exists between assumption of the risk and the dictates of CPLR 1411, we clarified that the doctrine "must be closely circumscribed if it is not seriously to undermine and displace the principles of comparative causation" (*Trupia*, 14 NY3d at 395). We noted that the injury-causing activity at issue in *Trupia* — horseplay — did not render the school worthy of insulation from a breach of duty claim, as it was "not a case in which the defendant solely by reason of having sponsored or otherwise supported some risk-laden but socially valuable voluntary activity has been called to account in damages" (*id.* at 396).

Guided by these principles, we conclude that assumption of the risk does not apply to the fact pattern in this appeal, which does not fit comfortably within the parameters of the doctrine. As a general rule, application of assumption of the risk should be limited to cases appropriate for absolution of duty, such as personal injury claims arising from sporting events, sponsored athletic and recreative activities, or athletic and recreational pursuits that take place at designated venues. In this case, plaintiff was not rollerblading at a rink, a skating park, or in a competition; nor did defendants actively sponsor or promote the activity in question.

Moreover, extension of the doctrine to cases involving persons injured while traversing streets and sidewalks would create an unwarranted diminution of the general duty of landowners — both public and private — to maintain their premises in a reasonably safe condition. As we explained in an earlier case, assumption of the risk "does not exculpate a landowner from liability for ordinary negligence in maintaining a premises" (*Sykes*, 94 NY2d at 913). The exception would swallow the general rule of comparative fault if sidewalk defects or dangerous premises conditions were deemed "inherent" risks assumed by non-pedestrians who sustain injuries, whether they be joggers, runners, bicyclists or rollerbladers (see *Ashbourne v City of New York*, 82 AD3d 461, 463 [1st Dept 2011]; *Cotty v Town* of 90*90 Southampton, 64 AD3d 251, 257 [2d Dept 2009]). We therefore decline to expand the doctrine to cover the circumstances presented here.

Custodi v. Town of Amherst, 20 N.Y.3d 83, 85-86, 89-90; 980 N.E.2d 933, 957 (2012).

IV. Read the fact pattern below and state the issue and correct rule as it is stated in the case provided.

Ana asked the paralegal to do some legal research for her as a personal favor. She told the paralegal that her twenty-two-year old cousin, Guadalupe, had been earning college money by waiting tables. Her cousin was living and working in Kansas, and she called Ana to tell her that despite numerous requests for her credit card tips, her employer refused to pay her not only her tips, but also her base salary. Her manager, Ted, refused to believe that Guadalupe was an American citizen, and he withheld money from all the staff members who were in the United States illegally. He knew that they would be too afraid of being deported to report him.

Because she was a native-born American citizen, Guadalupe complained about her boss to the Kansas Department of Labor. When she reported to work a few days later, he fired her. He claimed that he had fired her for being an illegal alien, but she noticed that he had not fired any of the workers that she knew were in the country illegally. Ana asked the paralegal to research the Kansas law regarding this issue and write up a summary of the law for her. The paralegal found the following 2011 case from the Supreme Court of Kansas:

KANSAS CASE LAW

Robert L. Campbell was an at-will employee with Husky Hogs, L.L.C., for about 1 year when he filed a complaint with the Kansas Department of Labor (KDOL) alleging Husky Hogs was not paying him as required by the KWPA [Kansas Wage Payment Act]. Campbell was fired 1 business day after KDOL acknowledged receiving his claim. Campbell filed this lawsuit in Phillips County District Court alleging Husky Hogs terminated him for pursuing his statutory rights under the KWPA. Husky Hogs denied the allegation.

. . . .

The company also filed a . . . motion for judgment on the pleadings. It argued Kansas had not previously recognized a retaliatory discharge claim for alleging KWPA violations and no public policy reasons existed for allowing such a claim now.

. . . .

The district court granted Husky Hogs' motion. It held Campbell's termination did not violate Kansas public policy, even though it was required to assume the discharge resulted from filing the disputed wage claim.

. . . .

Kansas historically adheres to the employment-at-will doctrine, which holds that employees and employers may terminate an employment relationship at any time, for any reason, unless there is an express or implied contract governing the employment's duration. [Citation omitted] But there are specific statutory exceptions to this rule, such as terminations based on race, gender, or disability.

. . . .

There are also exceptions recognized by Kansas courts through our case law. Over the past 30 years, exceptions to the at-will doctrine created a common-law tort for retaliatory discharge. These exceptions gradually eroded the general terminable-at-will rule 4*4 when an employee is fired in contravention of a recognized state public policy.

. . . .

To date, this court has endorsed public policy exceptions in four circumstances: (1) filing a claim under the Kansas Workers Compensation Act, K.S.A. 44-501 et seq; (2) whistleblowing; (3) filing a claim under the Federal Employers Liability Act (FELA), 45 U.S.C. § 51 (2006) et seq.; and (4) exercising a public employee's First Amendment right to free speech on an issue of public concern.

. . . .

. . . Kansas courts permit the common-law tort of retaliatory discharge as a limited exception to the at-will employment doctrine when it is necessary to protect a strongly held state public policy from being undermined.

. . . .

We have stated that courts tasked with determining whether a public policy exists are faced with three situations: (1) The legislature has clearly declared the state's public policy; (2) the legislature enacted statutory provisions from which public policy may reasonably be implied, even though it is not directly declared; and (3) the legislature has neither made a clear statement of public policy nor can it be reasonably implied.

. . . .

The KWPA was enacted in 1973. L. 1973, ch. 204, secs. 1-16. It is an expansive and comprehensive legislative scheme that is broad in its scope and the rights created for Kansas workers to secure unpaid wages earned from their labors. See K.S.A. 44-313 et seq. It is applicable to most Kansas employers. See K.S.A. 44-313(a). It requires, among various other provisions, that employers promptly pay wages and benefits (K.S.A. 2010 Supp. 44-314 K.S.A. 44-315). It also permits specific damages awards for willful nonpayment (K.S.A.44-315); controls and limits wage withholdings (K.S.A. 2010 Supp. 7*7 44-319); prohibits waivers of the rights created (K.S.A.44-321); and mandates that the Secretary of Labor enforce and administer the KWPA's provisions through administrative proceedings, compulsory process to compel witness attendance and document production, and permits application to the district courts for citations in contempt (see K.S.A. 44-322; K.S.A. 2010 Supp. 44-322a).

The Secretary of Labor is expressly authorized to adopt such rules and regulations as are deemed necessary to accomplish the KWPA's purposes. K.S.A. 44-325.

. . . .

This court has recognized retaliatory discharge claims in different circumstances, including those in which employees are discharged for exercising a statutory right.

. . . .

That principle is applicable to the KWPA. We hold the KWPA embeds within its provisions a public policy of protecting wage earners' rights to their unpaid wages and benefits. And just as we found a common-law retaliatory discharge claim when an injured worker is terminated for exercising rights under the Workers Compensation Act, we find such a cause of action is necessary when an employer fires a worker who seeks to exercise KWPA rights by filing a wage claim. To do otherwise would seriously undermine the public policy and the protections afforded by the KWPA.

Campbell v. Husky Hogs, LLC, 292 Kan. 225, 225-227, 230, 233-234; 255 P.3d 1, 3-4, 6-7 (2011).

LEARNING OBJECTIVES

1. Review previous IRAC sections of Issue and Rule

2. Outline by organizing IRAC analysis statements

3. Combine Fact + Rule with transitions for smooth analysis

4. Assess incorrect IRAC analysis statements

5. Revise incorrect IRAC analysis statements

6. Create correct IRAC analysis statements using correct components

CHAPTER 9

IRAC - Analysis

■ DEFINE IRAC

The IRAC organization of legal writing lays out the legal problem in a useful pattern. The letters in the acronym IRAC stand for the issue, which narrows and defines the legal question that is at issue in the case. The R stands for rule, which is the law that governs the issue in the case. The A stands for analysis, which applies the rule to the facts of the case. The C stands for conclusion, which answers the question presented in the issue.

■ APPLY-ISSUE

The issue summarizes the legal question being addressed in the document. When writers craft the issue of a case, they establish the parameters of their legal research and the subsequent analysis that will apply to the case. Correctly defining the issue is essential for an effective legal document.

■ APPLY-RULE

The rule is the law that applies to the case. The primary sources of law most frequently consist of case law and statutes, but primary sources also include regulations and ordinances. Secondary sources of law are not controlling, but they provide guidance to lawyers and judges. Secondary sources of law consist of Treatises, Restatements, AmJur, and other scholarly books written to be the guide and outline areas of law.

EXERCISE

As you read this chapter, fill in the worksheet below.

1. The analysis is the third segment of the _____ document.
2. Why is the analysis the longest section? _____.
3. The analysis must address both the _____ and _____ salient facts of your case.
4. The more you _____ the _____ of your case to the law the more effective your argument will be.
5. Name three errors of new writers.

a. _____.
b. _____.
c. _____.

6. Another error is that a writer is so familiar with the case that _____.
7. Describe the function of a transitional word in an analysis sentence. _____
8. Do not _____ the law because it would better support your facts.
9. What happens if the analysis is not clearly written? _____.
10. What happens if the analysis is not fully developed? _____.

■ A = ANALYSIS

The analysis must be precise and explicit. The more specifically you correlate the facts of your case to the law, the more effective your argument will be. The more parallels you point out between your case and the law, the more persuasive your argument will be.

New legal writers tend to make several common errors. One of the most glaring errors they make is failing to include the actual analysis in the analysis section. Instead, they state their facts and the law, and do not include the actual application of the facts of their case to the law they have stated. Sometimes the new writers omit this, thinking that how this law applies to their facts is obvious. Others erroneously include the actual analysis in the next section, the conclusion, where it does not belong. We will address this second form of error in the next chapter. Our examples will illustrate these errors.

Another common error in new legal writers' work is failing to draw the parallels between the law and the facts of their case. Just because something is clear in your mind, you cannot assume that it is clear in the readers' minds.

Also, new legal writers, in their zeal to be as persuasive as possible, tend to invent facts that strengthen their case. Sometimes new legal writers will reach a presumption that is based on some of the facts but that assumes other facts that are not in evidence. Other times, new legal writers will attribute thoughts and motives to people involved that are not supported by the facts. These presumed thoughts and motives potentially could be true, but writers cannot guess about things which cannot be proved. You may be sure that if you have embellished your facts with inferences, conjecture, or outright invention, the opposing side will focus on this and attack the credibility of your side. Again, our examples will illustrate this type of error.

As an experienced attorney once advised a new lawyer, "Don't tell me what you know; tell me what you can prove."

Finally, even experienced legal writers, including attorneys, forget what the reader does not know about the case, or in specialized areas of law, the law of that specialty. You will find that you have been so immersed in your case that you will forget that the reader is not similarly immersed. But first, we will take a fact pattern and the law that applies to it and explain how to implement and apply the facts and law in the analysis.

Here is how we go about deciding how to apply this law to our facts, the first step in writing the analysis. We begin by finding all the things our facts have in common with the facts in the law. Then we find all the things that differ between our facts and the facts in the law. Next, we establish why the differences are not important to how that law applies to our facts. Finally, we decide how to organize our comparison of the similarities and the differences so that our analysis is most persuasive to the reader.

What Are the Characteristics of the Analysis?

The Analysis Is

- The analysis is the third and most important portion of the IRAC document.
- The analysis consists of separate paragraphs.
- The analysis is the longest portion of the IRAC document, because it involves stating the facts of your case, the law, and how that law applies to the facts of your case.
- The analysis requires analogizing how the facts in the case law align with the facts of your case, thus making the ruling in the case applicable to your case, or how the statute applies to the facts of your case.
- The analysis must address all the salient facts in your case, both positive and negative.
- The analysis points out the similarities of the law to your case.
- The analysis explains why the differences between your facts and the law are not relevant.
- The analysis distinguishes, or explains the difference between the facts of the case and your case, if the case works against yours.
- The analysis is precise and explicit.
- The analysis persuades the reader that the law supports your position.

Important

- Avoid being too conclusive.
- Remember how little your reader knows about your case: do not omit necessary facts or law.
- Do not draw unsupported conclusions or embellish your facts.
- Do not misconstrue the law because it would better support your facts.

Points to Ponder

What happens if:

- The analysis is not clearly written? The reader will become confused.
- The analysis is not fully developed? The reader will not be persuaded.

EXAMPLE

Let us apply this process to the facts and law below.

Negligence

First, we consider our issue

"Is the city liable for an injury to a person who, while using a city-owned recreational facility, is injured by another person who is using the recreational facility in a legal and intended manner?"

The facts in this case are as follows

Jared Williams and his cousin Tommy were swimming in the reservoir, which was part of the park that the City of Parkhurst owned. The city allowed recreational use of the reservoir, including swimming and boating in boats without motors. The reservoir was popular with sailors, who often held sailing competitions on windy days. On a windy day in July 20XX, a sailboat hit Jared when he was swimming. Jared was knocked unconscious but was rescued by a fellow swimmer. Jared sued the city for negligence in failing to separate the swimmers from the boaters using the reservoir.

Ohio Law

The law we are applying to this case is below

In Ohio, when someone is on a premises for recreational purposes, the owner of that premises has no duty to keep the premises safe for the recreational user. In *Pauley v. Circleville*, 137 Ohio St.3d 212, 2013-Ohio-4541, the plaintiff, Pauley, was injured when he was sledding and struck a hill of dirt the city had created near the sledding hill. As the Ohio Supreme Court has held in the following quoted portion of decision:

> {21} Under R.C. 1533.181(A)(1), "[n]o owner owes any duty to a recreational user to keep the premises safe for entry or use." . . . A duty is "[a] legal obligation that is owed or due to another and that needs to be satisfied." *Black's Law Dictionary*, 580 (9th Ed.2009). Generally speaking, "[i]f there is no duty, no liability can follow." *Collins v. Sabino*, 11th Dist. Trumbull No. 96-T-5590, 1997 WL 531246, * 4, fn. 5 (Aug. 29, 1997). Consequently, an owner cannot be held liable for injuries sustained during recreational use "even if the property owner affirmatively created a dangerous condition." *Erbs v. Cleveland Metroparks Sys.*, at *2, citing *Milliff v. Cleveland Metroparks Sys.*, 8th Dist. Cuyahoga No. 52315, 1987 WL 11969 (June 4, 1987); see also *Phillips v. Ohio Dept. of Natural Resources*, 26 Ohio App.3d 77, 79, 498 N.E.2d 230, X (10th Dist.1985) (property owner not liable to recreational user for willful and wanton failure to warn of dangerous condition); *Press v. Ohio Dept. of Natural Resources*, Ct. of Cl. No. 2005-100004-AD, 2006-Ohio-1025, 2006 WL 538.

> {22} In this case, appellants admitted that Pauley was a recreational user within R.C. 1533.181, as he clearly was. He entered the park, free of charge, to go sledding. Thus, the city owed him no duty to keep the premises safe, and the city's alleged creation of a hazard on the premises does not affect its immunity.

Pauley v. Circleville 137 Ohio St.3d 212 (2013), 2013-Ohio-4541. ¶¶ 21–22.

■ ANALYSIS

Now we begin our analysis, applying the law to the facts of our case.

First, we look for similarities between our facts and the facts in the case law.

The commonalities between our fact pattern and the fact pattern in the law begin with the fact that the plaintiff in our case, Jared Williams, and the plaintiff in the Ohio Supreme Court case, Pauley, both were using recreational facilities. The second commonality is the fact that both Jared Williams and Pauley were injured while using the recreational facility. Third, both were injured by a dangerous condition created by the owner of the recreational facility. Fourth, neither person paid to use the recreational facility. As we formulate our argument, we will decide which similarities are legally significant and which are not.

Next, we must search carefully for the differences between our facts and those in the law. If we fail to address these, we leave a huge opening for our opponents to amplify the differences to weaken our argument. By acknowledging the differences and then explaining why they are not pertinent to our case, we are proactive in diffusing their significance. In some situations, when the law hurts a party's case, focusing on the differences can enhance the party's position.

The differences between the Jared Williams fact pattern and the Pauley fact pattern in the Ohio Supreme Court case begin with the type of recreational activity each was engaged in when he was hurt. Jared Williams was swimming, and Pauley was sledding. For each difference, we examine the differences between the two activities and decide which differences are legally significant and which are not. For example, it might be legally significant to determine whether swimming was a less inherently dangerous activity than sledding. It is not legally significant that swimming occurs in the summer and sledding in the winter. It is not legally significant that the water Pauley was sledding on was frozen and the water Jared Williams was swimming in was not.

Another difference between the two fact patterns is that the hill of dirt Pauley struck was a fixed, inanimate object. On the other hand, the boater who struck Jared Williams was an entity that the city could have, but did not, control. The city could have designated separate areas for the swimmers and sailors. At first blush, this looks like a powerful argument. But we have to look at the conclusion the Supreme Court reached before we get too involved in pursuing this line of thinking.

The Supreme Court reached the conclusion that the city was not legally responsible for Pauley's injury when his sled struck the hill of dirt. The Court held that "the city owed him no duty to keep the premises safe, and the city's alleged creation of a hazard on the premises does not affect its immunity." *Id.*

The Court held that the city had no duty to keep a recreational premises safe for those choosing to use that facility. Even though the sailor whose boat struck and injured Jared Williams was not under the direct control of the city, Jared is suing the city, not the sailor. Jared is claiming that the city should have delineated separate areas in the lake for swimmers and boaters. Even when the argument is not as strong as we would like, however, we have to make the best case we can with what we have.

As you can see, with this law and these facts, the lawyer for the city has a much easier brief to write. Jared Williams' lawyer, on the other hand, has a challenging case to make. That leads us to our next step in drafting the analysis: how to organize the analysis.

Deciding how to organize the analysis requires weighing the strengths and weaknesses of the similarities against the strengths and weaknesses caused by the differences. In a case in which law seems to work against the party seeking relief, focusing on differences can provide the strongest argument.

Sometimes using the compare and contrast method is effective. Frequently, it is better to start with the second strongest argument, bury the weakest argument and the differences in the middle, and end with the strongest argument. Each case will have different facts and law, so each will require its own assessment.

Remember: in every case, both sides are working with the same facts and the same law. You cannot invent facts that would bolster your case, and you cannot misrepresent the law so that it fits better with what you need for your case. Your argument must remain within the confines of the truth, no matter how difficult that makes it to write a persuasive brief.

So the similarities between our facts and the case law are:

1. Both persons used recreational facilities
2. Both persons were injured while using recreational facilities
3. Both persons were injured by a dangerous condition created by the owner of the facility.
4. Neither person paid to use the facilities.

The differences are:

1. One person was swimming and one was sledding
2. One person was on frozen water and one on liquid water
3. One person struck a fixed object, the hill, and one was struck by a moving object, a boat.
4. The city controlled/created the hill, and it did not control the sailor of the boat.

EXAMPLE OF CITY'S ANALYSIS

We noted earlier that the city's lawyer has the easier job in writing a persuasive argument. Here is how that lawyer might write the analysis:

> Although Jared was swimming and not sledding, both he and Pauley were using public premises for recreational purposes. Despite that fact that the reservoir was water and not land, it nonetheless qualifies as a premises under the law. Both the swimming and the sledding occurred in a city park. Both swimming and sledding are recreational activities, and both Jared and Pauley were injured while engaging in recreational activities on city property, in city-owned recreational facilities.

> In this case, Jared claimed that the city was negligent in failing to separate the recreational activities it allowed on the lake. In Pauley's case, he claimed that when the city had constructed the pile of dirt that he had struck while sledding, the city had created a hazard.

> This distinction renders Jared's case even weaker than Pauley's; Pauley claimed that the city had affirmatively created the hazard that caused his injury. Jared claims only that the city failed to prevent the situation that caused his injury. If a city, as the owner of premises used for recreational activities, is not liable for injuries caused by its own "alleged creation of a hazard," certainly it cannot be held liable for failing to meet the lesser standard of preventing a potential hazard from occurring to a recreational user. Clearly, under the Pauley standard, the city cannot be held legally responsible for Jared Williams' injuries, because it has no liability to users of its recreational facilities, even when it affirmatively created the very hazard complained of that caused the injury.

Notice how the city's lawyer started by explaining away one of the differences between Jared's facts and those in the case law. The lawyer quickly categorized both as recreational activities in the city's recreational facilities. The lawyer also dismissed any differences between the nature of the activities by noting that regardless of whether the activity occurred on land or in water, both occurred on the city's recreational property.

The city's lawyer then proceeded to use the differences between the circumstances of each injury to emphasize the greater weakness in Jared's argument, pointing out that the city had not created the hazard when the sailor struck Jared with the boat, whereas the city had put the hill of dirt by the sledding hill. The lawyer expounded on this difference by noting that the city had not placed the boater and Jared on the collision course, thereby emphasizing the greater weakness of Jared's case.

How then, would Jared's lawyer write the brief arguing that the city should be held liable for his injury? Remember, the lawyer has to use the same facts and law while trying to persuade the court that the city was responsible and should pay for Jared's injury.

To review:

The similarities are:

1. Both used recreational facilities
2. Both were injured while using recreational facilities
3. Both were injured by a dangerous condition created by the owner of the facility
4. Neither paid to use the facilities.

The differences are:

5. One was swimming and one was sledding
6. One was on frozen water and one on liquid water
7. One struck a fixed object, the hill, and one was struck by a moving object, a boat
8. The city controlled/created the hill, and it did not control the sailor of the boat

EXAMPLE OF JARED'S ANALYSIS

Here is how Jared's attorney might write the analysis:

Jared Williams was enjoying a summer day swimming in the city's lake, a popular recreational facility enjoyed by many Parkhurst citizens. The lake hosts a variety of activities, including swimming and sailing. Jared was injured when a sailor struck him with his sailboat.

Ohio law has held that the owner of a recreational facility is not liable for injuries occurring to users of those facilities. In *Pauley*, the Ohio Supreme Court held that the city did not owe a duty to a sled rider who was injured when he hit a hill of dirt the city had created near the sledding hill. The Court held that the city was not liable, even though it had allegedly created the hazard near its sledding hill. The city "owed him no duty to keep the premises safe, and the city's alleged creation of a hazard on the premises does not affect its immunity."

The situation in *Pauley* differs significantly, however, from Jared's situation. The city owns the recreational facility, the lake, but the city also determines the rules for users of its recreational facilities. In Pauley, the plaintiff was not injured when a snowmobiler struck him; he was injured when he steered his sled into a stationary hill of dirt. While placing the hill of dirt so close to the sledding hill may have been a poor decision, the city did not steer Pauley's sled into the hill.

Jared, on the other hand, did not swim into the sailboat that injured him. Rather, he was using the city's recreational facility in the anticipated manner; he was swimming. The city knew that swimmers used the lake, and it knew that sailors held races on the lake. When Pauley sledded into the stationary hill, he affirmatively chose to approach the hazard and caused the unsafe situation in which he was injured. Conversely, Jared's injury did not result from his engaging in an unsafe activity.

Even though the city does not owe a duty to the users of its facilities to keep a premises safe, it arguably owes a duty to regulate the use of its facilities so that they are used in a reasonably safe manner. Just as the city would not have allowed snowmobiling in the same area as the sledding hill, so, too, it should not have allowed sailboats to race in the same area where people were swimming. It is one thing to not have a duty to keep a premises safe; it is an entirely different thing to avoid affirmatively creating dangerous situations for unwitting participants of otherwise safe recreational activities.

Jared's situation is distinguishable from Pauley's; Pauley was or should have been in control of his sled when it struck the stationary hill. Additionally, Pauley did not argue that the hill was not present and visible when he started down the sledding hill. Jared, on the other hand, was not in control of the sailor whose boat struck him. In *Pauley*, the sledding hill arguably was unsafe. But sledding was the only activity taking place on the hill. Pauley did not face the risk of larger, faster moving objects competing for the same recreational space.

In Jared's situation, he is not claiming that the city had made the lake unsafe for swimmers; he alleges that the city, by failing to properly regulate the activities on the lake, caused an unforeseen dangerous situation that it could have, but chose not to, control. By failing to separate the sailboats from the swimmers, the city allowed a situation that was the equivalent of snowmobilers competing with sled riders for space. The law in *Pauley* is not controlling in the situation of the present case. The city had an affirmative duty to regulate the safe use of its premises.

In this case, the city has the stronger argument, but depending on the court, the argument Jared's attorney made might gain some traction. Notice how the analysis by Jared's attorney puts the law that one would think would defeat Jared's case right at the beginning. By acknowledging the weakest point in the argument upfront, the writer "clears the air" and frees up the remaining argument for persuading the reader that this law does not control in Jared's case. Then the writer proceeds to distinguish between the facts in the Supreme Court decision and those in Jared's case.

Jared's case is not a strong one, with this case as the controlling law regarding recreational facilities, but sometimes the courts want to reinterpret or narrow the scope of how a statute is applied. Carefully argued to a receptive court, Jared's case could succeed.

You might be wondering about the similarities and differences that one or both attorneys failed to address in their analyses. Neither mentioned the similarity that the recreational facilities Pauley and Jared had used were free. Because the fact that the facilities were free of charge did not have legal significance in this case, both attorneys left it out of their analyses.

Also, the city's attorney ignored the fact that the city did not have control over the sailor who struck Jared, while Jared's attorney relied on this difference as the fulcrum of the argument in the analysis.

The city's attorney was not dishonest in omitting this difference. The attorney did not deny its existence, only ignored it. It is important to distinguish between an omission in which the writer does not dwell on a point that does not support his or her argument and an omission that dishonestly omits a legally significant fact or point of law.

For example, it would have been a dishonest omission if Jared's attorney had tried to quote the case law as follows:

BAD EXAMPLE ⚖️

> Thus, the city owed him . . . [a] duty to keep the premises safe, and the city's alleged creation of a hazard on the premises . . . affect[s] its immunity."

By comparing the quote that dishonestly omitted essential words with the actual quote below, you can see what the attorney did unethically.

GOOD EXAMPLE ⚖️

> {¶ 22} In this case, appellants admitted that Pauley was a recreational user within R.C. 1533.181, as he clearly was. He entered the park, free of charge, to go sledding. Thus, the city owed him no duty to keep the premises safe, and the city's alleged creation of a hazard on the premises does not affect its immunity.
> *Pauley v. Circleville* 137 Ohio St.3d 212, 2013-Ohio-4541 ¶ 22.

Deleting the negatives in the quote changes its meaning to the opposite of what the law actually says. Amazingly, one of your writers has seen attorneys do this in briefs they submitted to the court. While this dishonest omission is obvious, less blatant, but equally dishonest examples abound, unfortunately, in the briefs of a few dishonest attorneys. More frequently, in their zeal, otherwise good attorneys "stretch the truth" to support their cases.

Regardless of the form of dishonesty, it must be avoided. It is essential to maintain strict accuracy. Once an attorney's reputation for truthfulness is lost, it can never be regained.

Still, a well-crafted analysis can minimize points that weaken the argument and expound on those that strengthen it.

The IRAC Analysis Formula

The analysis section can be one of the most challenging parts of legal writing. Your authors have found the following mathematical style formula to be very helpful to new legal writers. This formula helps the writer to glue fact to rule or rule to fact in the analysis. By applying this formula to your analyses, you can ensure that you do not overlook the actual analysis.

Our initial examples are oversimplified so that you can understand the concept. In a real IRAC document that you would be drafting for an attorney, your analysis section would be longer and contain more discussion. In a real IRAC document, your analysis should contain a sub-conclusion.

The sub-conclusion is the final sentence in the paragraph and summarizes the assessment contained in your application of the law to the facts of your case. A writer or a reader can look at the sub-conclusion and quickly assess what the conclusion segment of the IRAC statement will contain.

The Table 9.1 below provides a snapshot of the formula for analysis in IRAC. Tables 9.2 and 9.3 provide examples of the formula being applied. Many good legal writers instinctively use this formula, or apply a similar one, when drafting the analysis. As you begin learning to write the analysis section of your IRAC, you can refer to this formula until it becomes second nature to you.

Table 9.1 Formula for Analysis Sentence Structure

Formula for Analysis Sentence Structure
Facts + **R**ule = **A**nalysis
For short,
F + R = A
The facts and the rule may be reversed:
R + F = A

One of the most important parts of this formula is the equal sign. The equal sign should be a transitional word or words that lead into your application of the law to the facts of your case. Transitional words, phrases, or clauses are necessary for the reader to segue from the explanation of the law to the concept of how the law applies to the specific facts of the case. Conjunctive adverbs are one form of transition. (Refer to composing a paragraph from an outline, which addresses unity and coherence for a list of conjunctive adverbs.) For simpler ideas, a conjunctive adverb may be all you need. For more complex concepts, you may require a phrase or a clause. At the end of your analysis, you should summarize what you have stated into a sub-conclusion. The sub-conclusion is similar to the summary sentence in a writing. As we mentioned, too often new legal writers end their analysis before it actually begins: the use of the equal sign and the "A" portion of the formula helps prevent this common oversight. Read the following examples. After the examples we list some commonly used transitions.

We demonstrate how to apply the formula in the following eight examples. These examples use Ohio law. Ohio's statutes are called the Ohio Revised Code, which is abbreviated R.C.

EXAMPLE ONE

Table 9.2 Fact + Rule = Analysis (F + R = A)

Original		Abbreviation
Fact	is	F
Transitional element	is	+
Rule	is	R
Transitional Word(s)	is	=
Analysis	is	A

The first analysis uses a single transitional word.

    (Fact)   **+**   **(Rule)**

Mr. Williams' blood alcohol level was twice the legal limit. The statute, R.C. § 4511.19(A)(1)(b), prohibits driving with a blood alcohol concentration above eight-hundredths of one percent.

(Transitional Word)   **(Analysis)**

   =

Since Mr. Williams' blood alcohol level exceeded the legal limit for driving, he violated the statute.

EXAMPLE TWO

Table 9.3 Rule + Fact = Analysis (R + F = A)

Original Word		Abbreviation
Rule	is	R
Transitional Element	is	+
Fact	is	F
Transitional Word(s)	is	=
Analysis	is	A

This analysis also uses a single transitional word.

(Rule)
|

Ohio law prohibits driving with a blood alcohol concentration above eight-hundredths of one percent. R.C. § 4511.19(A)(1)(b)

+

(Fact)
|

At the time of his traffic stop, Mr. Williams' blood alcohol level was twice the legal limit.

(Transitional Word)　　　**(Analysis)**
　=　　　　　　　　　　　　　|

Therefore, Mr. Williams violated R.C. § 4511.19(A)(1)(b) when he drove with a blood alcohol level of double the legal limit.

Transitions are not limited to one word; a phrase or a clause also may be a transition. For example, the same analysis might use phrases for transitions rather than clauses.

EXAMPLE THREE

F + R = A

Here is a transition that is a phrase, using the same fact pattern.

(Fact)
|

At the time of his traffic stop, Mr. Williams' blood alcohol level was twice the legal limit.

+　　　　　　　　　**(Rule)**
　　　　　　　　　　　　|

In the State of Ohio, the statute, R.C. § 4511.19(A)(1)(b) prohibits driving with a blood alcohol concentration above eight-hundredths of one percent.

(Transitional phrase)   **(Analysis)**

=

|

With a blood alcohol twice the legal limit, Mr. Williams' blood alcohol level exceeded the legal limit for driving, so he violated the statute.

EXAMPLE FOUR

R + F = A

Here is a transition that is a clause, using the same fact pattern.

(Rule)

|

The law clearly states, in R.C. § 4511.19(A)(1)(b), that it is illegal to drive with a blood alcohol concentration above eight-hundredths of one percent.

+

(Fact)

|

At the time of the traffic stop, Mr. Williams' blood alcohol level was twice the legal limit.

(Transitional clause)

=

Because Mr. Williams was driving with a blood alcohol level that exceeded the legal

(Analysis)

|

limit for driving, he violated the statute.

EXAMPLE FIVE

F + R = A

Here is an example of the use of a transitional word.

(Fact)

|

Brianna's dog got loose from her fenced yard and bit a boy on his way home from middle school.

+

(Rule)

|

The owner, keeper, or harborer of a dog is liable in damages for any injury, death, or loss to person or property that is caused by the dog, unless the injury, death, or loss was caused to the person or property of an individual who, at the time, was committing or attempting to commit criminal trespass or another criminal offense. . . .

R.C.§ 955.28(B).

(Transitional word) (Analysis)

= |

Consequently, Brianna is liable for the boy's dog bite injuries.

EXAMPLE SIX

F + R = A

Here is an example of the use of a transitional phrase.

(Fact)

|

Brianna's dog got loose from her fenced yard and bit a boy on his way home from middle school.

+

(Rule)

|

The owner, keeper, or harborer of a dog is liable in damages for any injury, death, or loss to person or property that is caused by the dog, unless the injury, death, or loss was caused to the person or property of an individual who, at the time, was committing or attempting to commit criminal trespass or another criminal offense. . . .

R.C.§ 955.28(B)

(Transitional phrase)   (Analysis)

= |

As the owner of the dog, Brianna is liable for the boy's dog bite injuries.

EXAMPLE SEVEN

R + F = A

Here is an example of the use of a transitional clause.

(Rule)

|

The law expressly makes the owner of a dog responsible for injuries the dog causes:

The owner, keeper, or harborer of a dog is liable in damages for any injury, death, or loss to person or property that is caused by the dog, unless the injury, death, or loss was caused to the person or property of an individual who, at the time, was committing or attempting to commit criminal trespass or another criminal offense . . . .

R.C. § 955.28(B)

+

(Fact)

|

Brianna's dog got loose from her fenced yard and bit a boy on his way home from middle school.

(Transitional phrase)   **(Analysis)**

= |

Since it was her dog that bit the boy, Brianna is liable for the boy's dog bite injuries.

EXAMPLE EIGHT

F + R = A

Here is an example of an analysis with a sub-conclusion.

(Fact)

|

Brianna's dog got loose from her fenced yard and bit a boy on his way home from middle school.

+

(Rule)

|

The owner, keeper, or harborer of a dog is liable in damages for any injury, death, or loss to person or property that is caused by the dog, unless the injury, death, or loss was caused to the person or property of an individual who, at the time, was committing or attempting to commit criminal trespass or another criminal offense . . . .

R.C.§ 955.28(B)

(Transitional phrase)   **(Analysis)**

= |

Since Brianna was the owner of the dog that bit the boy, the statute applies to her. As the dog's owner, she is liable for any injuries her dog caused to the boy, unless the boy was committing a crime or trespassing or was trying to commit a crime or to trespass. When the dog bit the boy, he was not on Brianna's property. The boy therefore could not have been committing criminal trespass on Brianna's property. Further, nothing in the facts suggests that the boy was committing or trying to commit a crime or trying to trespass.

(Sub-conclusion)

|

Since none of the exceptions that would prevent her from being liable for the injuries her dog caused when it bit the boy, Brianna is liable for the boy's dog bite injuries.

Using transitions serves to make writing more persuasive, because it clarifies the relationship between the ideas that are being connected. Table 9.4 is a chart with examples of transitions and how they help illustrate the point the writer is trying to make.

Table 9.4   Persuasive Transitions

Intention	Examples
Between ideas that agree with each other	therefore, thus, additionally, also, similarly, equally, moreover, and furthermore
Between ideas that do not agree with each other	unlike, distinctly, contrasting, conversely, and alternatively
Transitional phrases between contrasting ideas	"in contrast," "on the other hand," "on the contrary," "quite the opposite," "contrary to popular opinion," and "having disproven the theory offered by the opposing side"
Transitional clauses between like ideas	"as the previous discussion demonstrates," "since the law holds," "because the evidence demonstrates," and "since the facts support"
Transitional clauses between contrasting ideas	"because the facts of this case differ," "although initially the law appears to apply to these facts," and "since the elements required in the statute are not met in this case"

EXERCISE

Read the following analysis sections from IRAC analyses. Identify each piece by marking (F) above the fact, (R) above the rule, (=) above the transition word(s), (A) for the arrived upon analysis.

1. Jeremy drove through a red light without stopping. It is illegal to disobey a traffic control device. R.C.§ 4511.12. Since Jeremy did not obey the traffic control device, the red light, he broke the law.

2. The customer took a bracelet from the boutique without paying for it. It is illegal to take another's property without the owner's consent. R.C. § 2913.02. Therefore, when the customer took the bracelet without the boutique owner's consent, the customer violated the law.

3. During an argument, the patron at the Dew Drop Inn became angry and hit the man next to him and broke his nose. In Ohio, it constitutes assault to knowingly or recklessly hurt someone. Assault is illegal. R.C. § 2903.13. By hitting the man and breaking his nose, the patron knowingly hurt him, thereby violating the law.

4. The boutique owner prevented the customer from leaving the store until the police arrived. Pursuant R.C. 2935.041, the store owner "who has probable cause to believe that items offered for sale . . . have been unlawfully taken by a person, may . . . detain the person in a reasonable manner for a reasonable length of time" inside the store. Because the store owner suspected that the customer had taken the bracelet without paying for it, the store owner had a legal right to detain the customer.

5. Antoine Taylor's dog bit his friend Brad while Brad was visiting. The Ohio Supreme Court cited to R.C. § 955.28 and stated that a dog owner is strictly liable for any injury that the dog causes to a person. *Beckett v. Warren*, 124 Ohio St.3d 256, 2010-Ohio-4, ¶ 10. As the owner of the dog that bit Brad, Antoine is strictly liable for any of Brad's injuries that his dog caused.

6. Brad repeatedly had asked opposing counsel to provide the discovery he requested. Still, even after six months in which Brad had sent weekly requests, opposing counsel had failed to respond. At pretrials, when Brad raised the issue of the missing discovery, opposing counsel stated that he had almost finished it and wanted to wait until he was sure it was complete before sending it. Initially, the Judge ordered the attorneys to work out the discovery dispute between themselves. Finally, Brad filed a Motion to Compel with the Court. In his motion, Brad noted that in a similar case, the Ohio Supreme Court had held that the attorney's "lack of diligence in responding to requests for discovery is the equivalent of obstructing discovery." The Ohio Supreme Court determined that the attorney had "engaged in evasive conduct that was prejudicial to the administration of justice." *Disciplinary Counsel v. Stafford* 128 Ohio St.3d 446, 2011-Ohio-1484 ¶ 56.

(continued)

Analogizing his case to the *Stafford* case, Brad argued that opposing counsel was obstructing discovery by failing to cooperate in discovery. Brad noted the similarities in the behavior of the two attorneys. Opposing counsel in Brad's case continually provided excuses for failing to provide discovery, while the attorney in *Stafford* also failed to provide discovery over an extended period of time. Brad concluded that opposing counsel's conduct was unprofessional, unethical, and "prejudicial to the administration of justice." *Id.*

7. Dr. Hunter had assisted on a surgery to wire a patient's broken jaw. While the attending surgeon was clipping one of the wires, it accidentally flew into the patient's eye, causing injury. When Dr. Hunter saw the patient for a follow up several months after the surgery, he told the patient that he was sorry that the patient's eye was injured. The patient proceeded to sue Dr. Hunter, claiming that his apology constituted an admission of guilt in causing the eye injury. The Ohio Supreme Court addressed this issue in a case in which the doctor expressly acknowledged responsibility for the patient's injury. The Court excluded evidence of the apology, stating, "[t]he General Assembly, in enacting R.C. 2317.43, prohibited the introduction of any sympathetic statements and gestures made by a healthcare provider in any civil action 'brought' by an alleged victim of an unanticipated outcome of medical care." *Estate of Johnson v. Randall Smith, Inc.,* 135 Ohio St.3d 440, 2013-Ohio-1507, ¶ 14. When he sympathized with the patient concerning the eye injury, Dr. Hunter did not even say that he was responsible for the injury. Nonetheless, even if Dr. Hunter had told the patient that he had caused the injury, that statement would not be admissible against Dr. Hunter in a lawsuit. Here, Dr. Hunter merely sympathized generally and never addressed the question of responsibility. Dr. Hunter's sympathetic statements fall under the evidentiary exclusion that the Supreme Court discussed in *Johnson.*

8. Mr. Williams knew that he had injured another driver when the refrigerator fell off his truck and struck the other driver's car. Nonetheless, Mr. Williams put the refrigerator back into his truck and drove away without calling for help for the injured driver. Ohio law requires motorists who are involved in a collision or an accident to stay at the scene until the drivers of all the vehicles involved have exchanged the requisite information. If any person is injured in the accident such that he or she cannot exchange information, the other driver must notify the police and remain at the scene until the police arrive, unless that person is taken away by ambulance. R.C. § 4549.02(A). By leaving the scene of an accident he was involved in, Mr. Williams violated the statute in three different ways. First, he failed to attempt to exchange information with the other driver, as required under the law. Second, he failed to contact the police and inform them of the other driver's injuries. Third, he failed to remain at the scene of the accident.

EXERCISE

Read the following paragraphs that purport to include the law and analysis sections of IRAC. Explain why each paragraph is incorrect. Some of the sections are missing facts, some are missing the rule, and some are missing the transition required for the analysis. Some are missing the actual analysis.

1. The law prohibits driving through a stop sign without stopping and ensuring that the driver's route of travel is clear. R.C. § 4511.12. Because the client ran the stop sign, the officer rightly issued him a ticket.

2. The store next to Cherelle's boutique closed unexpectedly. Cherelle notified the landlord that the store was empty, and the door was unlocked. The landlord responded that he was glad, because he would not have to provide

(continued)

services to the tenants but could still collect the rent. The landlord should have tried to re-rent the store to another tenant.

3. Antoine, a real estate agent, was driving back to his office after an open house late one winter afternoon. It was cloudy and getting dark. Because one of his headlights was burned out, Antoine did not see the deer running into the road and struck it. Antoine is liable for the accident because his headlight was not working.

4. Mrs. Crocker, an elderly client of Brad and Ana's, had signed a contract to have her driveway paved after a door-to-door salesman informed her that it had deteriorated and that the city would fine her for its poor condition. After Mrs. Crocker's son inspected the driveway the next day, he told her that the driveway was fine and to cancel the contract. Mrs. Crocker mailed her cancellation of the contract by certified mail to the address on the contract the next day, but it came back unclaimed. When the contractors showed up two weeks later and tried to break up the driveway, she stopped them. They informed her that because she had signed the contract, she was responsible for paying for the work, whether they replaced her driveway or not. Ohio law allows consumers who sign a contract to cancel the contract by notifying the seller in writing within three business days of having signed the contract. The law also requires the person who made the home solicitation to include the name and address of the company or person making the contract. R.C. § 1345.23. The driveway company has to let Mrs. Crocker cancel the contract.

5. Ana went to vote on Election Day and was about to open the door of the school that was her designated polling place. Her path was blocked, however, by a supporter of a specific candidate for the school board. Ana politely told the man that she had made up her mind regarding her chosen candidates and asked him to let her by him. He refused and continued to press his case for his candidate. In Ohio, R.C. § 3501.35(A)(2) prohibits anyone from hindering or delaying a voter from "reaching or leaving the place fixed for casting the [voter]'s ballot."

6. A client consulted Brad concerning retaining Brad to replace the client's current attorney. The client told Brad that he had given the attorney a large retainer of $5,000, but the attorney had failed to do more than file the case. Because the attorney had not returned the client's phone calls or emails, the client wanted his retainer back and wanted the attorney to withdraw from the case.

> {¶ 21} While the Rules of Professional Conduct permit an attorney to deem a fee earned upon receipt, Prof.Cond.R. 1.5(d)(3) prohibits an attorney from entering into an arrangement for, charging, or collecting fees that are "earned upon receipt," "nonrefundable," or similarly designated "unless the client is simultaneously advised in writing that if the lawyer does not complete the representation for any reason, the client may be entitled to a refund of all or part of the fee based upon the value of the representation pursuant to division (a) of this rule."

Cleveland Metro. Bar Assn. v. Gruttadaurio, 136 Ohio St.3d 283, 2013-Ohio-3662 ¶ 21.

7. Mrs. Crocker had given a substantial deposit to the salesman who had told her that her driveway required replacement. The next day, her son inspected the driveway and realized it was in good condition. On her son's advice, Mrs. Crocker canceled the contract the day after she had signed it. Although Brad had succeeded in making the company honor Mrs. Crocker's cancellation of the contract, a month later, she had not received a refund of her deposit. The contract contained the statutorily required language:

"If you cancel, . . . any payments made by you under the contract or sale . . . will be returned within ten business days following receipt by the seller of your cancellation notice. . . ."

Because Mrs. Crocker canceled the contract within three business days, she legally canceled the contract within the law. [See exercise 4 above.] The law requires a company to return a deposit on a legally canceled consumer contract within ten days of receiving the cancellation notice. The company violated the statute by not returning Mrs. Crocker's down payment within the statutorily mandated ten days.

EXERCISE

Read the following analysis sentences in an IRAC analysis and compare. Which of the two is correct?

SET ONE

i. The Ohio Supreme Court had suspended Attorney Green's license to practice law because he had failed to pay the court-ordered child support for his three children. The Supreme Court previously had ordered an attorney to be suspended when he failed to pay child support. *Cuyahoga Cty. Bar Assn. v. Chandler,* 81 Ohio St.3d 491 (1998).

ii. The Ohio Supreme Court had suspended Attorney Green's license to practice law because he had failed to pay the court-ordered child support for his three children. The Supreme Court previously had ordered an attorney to be suspended when he failed to pay child support. *Cuyahoga Cty. Bar Assn. v. Chandler,* 81 Ohio St.3d 491 (1998). As in the *Chandler* case, suspending an attorney who failed to pay child support was an appropriate course of action.

SET TWO

i. Although the block on which she parked had a sidewalk and also had a crosswalk half a block away, Cherelle jaywalked after parking her car across the street from her destination because she was late for an appointment. A police officer witnessed her jaywalking and gave her a ticket. Jaywalking violates an Ohio statute: "Where a sidewalk is provided and its use is practicable, it shall be unlawful for any pedestrian to walk along and upon an adjacent roadway." R.C. § 4511.50 (A). By walking across the roadway when she crossed the street, Cherelle violated the prohibition against walking in the road. Therefore, the police officer properly ticketed Cherelle for the offense of jaywalking.

ii. Because she was late for an appointment, Cherelle jaywalked after parking her car across the street from her destination. A police officer witnessed her jaywalking and gave her a ticket. "Where a sidewalk is provided and its use is practicable, it shall be unlawful for any pedestrian to walk along and upon an adjacent roadway." R.C. § 4511.50 (A).

SET THREE

i. The owner of a nightclub in the next town has come to Brad and Ana's law office to seek legal guidance. He had held a Halloween party for his customers, and those who arrived in costume received a discount on their cover charge. In the spirit of the season, the nightclub owner had erected a floor-to-ceiling maze of cornstalks. The customers had to work their way through the maze to find the bar, the food, and the music. He had held this party night in the same way for several years, and it was immensely popular. This past year, he had had to make people wait for someone to leave before he could allow customers to enter, because the Code limited the occupancy of the room.

Despite the ban on smoking in public places, one of the customers in the maze had lit a cigarette and caught the cornstalk maze on fire. Although no one was killed in the ensuing blaze, one woman had been seriously burned when her flammable costume caught fire. She is suing the nightclub owner because she had not been able to find an exit during the fire. She claims that the cornstalks had obstructed her view of the signs. The nightclub owner informed Brad and Ana that not having the cornstalks would not have helped her see the signs; he had turned the illumination off because they ruined the atmosphere he was setting with the maze and dry ice.

The Ohio Building Code requires clearly marked and lit exit signs. It states that "[e]xits and exit access doors shall be marked by an approved exit sign readily visible from any direction of egress travel." The Code further requires that the "[e]xit sign placement shall be such that no point in an exit access corridor or exit passageway is more than 100 feet (30 480 mm) or the listed viewing distance for the sign, whichever is less, from the nearest visible exit sign." Ohio Adm. Code 1301:7-7-10(K) [B] Section 1011.1. Further, the signs must be illuminated. *Id.* at 1011.2.

Because the signs were properly placed, the nightclub owner had not violated the code. The code does not address obstructing the signs, only their placement.

ii. The owner of a nightclub in the next town has come to Brad and Ana's law office to seek legal guidance. He had held a Halloween party for

(continued)

his customers, and those who arrived in costume received a discount on their cover charge. In the spirit of the season, the nightclub owner had erected a floor-to-ceiling maze of cornstalks. The customers had to work their way through the maze to find the bar, the food, and the music. He had held this party night in the same way for several years, and it was immensely popular. This past year, he had had to make people wait for someone to leave before he could allow customers to enter, because the Code limited the occupancy of the room.

Despite the ban on smoking in public places, one of the customers in the maze had lit a cigarette and caught the cornstalk maze on fire. Although no one was killed in the ensuing blaze, one woman had been seriously burned when her flammable costume caught fire. She is suing the nightclub owner because she had not been able to find an exit during the fire. She claims that the cornstalks had obstructed her view of the signs. The nightclub owner informs Brad and Ana that not having the cornstalks would not have helped her see the signs; he had turned the illumination off because they ruined the atmosphere he was setting with the maze and dry ice.

The Ohio Building Code requires clearly marked and lit exit signs. It states that "[e]xits and exit access doors shall be marked by an approved exit sign readily visible from any direction of egress travel." The Code further requires that the "[e]xit sign placement shall be such that no point in an exit access corridor or exit passageway is more than 100 feet (30 480 mm) or the listed viewing distance for the sign, whichever is less, from the nearest visible exit sign." Ohio Adm. Code 1301:7-7-10(K) [B] Section 1011.1. Further, the signs must be illuminated. *Id*. S1011.2.

The nightclub owner not only had obstructed the customers' ability to see the exit signs, but he also had turned off the lights in the signs. Exit signs are required to be "readily visible from any direction of egress travel." *Id*. By obstructing the customers' view of the exit signs, the nightclub owner had violated Ohio Adm.Code 1301:7-7-10(K) [B] Section 1011.1. The nightclub owner is liable for violating the Code requiring exit signs to be visible to people in the building.

Additionally, the nightclub owner had intentionally turned off the lighting that illuminated the exit signs. Because the Code requires exit signs to be illuminated, the nightclub owner violated this section of the code when he turned off the illumination. The nightclub owner is also liable for intentionally disobeying the Code by turning off the illumination to the exit signs. The nightclub owner broke the building code in two ways: he did not have clearly visible exit signs, and he did not have the exit signs properly illuminated.

EXERCISE

Read the following fact patterns, law, and analyses. Identify the errors in the analyses and correct them. Note: because you will be writing new versions of the analyses, there is no one correct wording that you need to use, as long as your analysis is accurate and well written.

1. Here is the first analysis that you must identify and correct.

FACT PATTERN

Larry Fromm was an executive with a food manufacturing company. Mr. Fromm took his work seriously, and the food preparation areas at all the company's manufacturing facilities were spotless. Mr. Fromm made surprise inspections at each of the plants. During one of these inspections, Mr. Fromm noticed an employee drop a utensil on the floor, and rather than place it in the washer, as company policy required, he started to stir the food with it without even rinsing it off. Mr. Fromm immediately took the man off the production line and escorted him to the supervisor's office, where he fired the worker. The worker is now suing for wrongful discharge because he did not believe in the germ theory. The worker claims that his right to his beliefs was violated when he was fired.

LAW

The Ohio Revised Code concerning wrongful discharge is R.C. § 4112.02, unlawful discriminatory practices. It states in pertinent part:

> It shall be an unlawful discriminatory practice:
>
> (A) For any employer, because of the race, color, religion, sex, military status, national origin, disability, age, or ancestry of any person, to discharge without just cause, to refuse to hire, or otherwise to discriminate against that person with respect to hire, tenure, terms, conditions, or privileges of employment, or any matter directly or indirectly related to employment.

ANALYSIS

Mr. Fromm had no right to terminate the worker just because his beliefs conflicted with company policy.

2. Here is the second analysis that you must identify and correct.

FACT PATTERN

The worker later amended his complaint to add a cause of action for age discrimination, because the worker had turned forty a few days before he was fired.

LAW

An Ohio Court addressed age discrimination by explaining the employer's burden of proof after an employee has shown that he meets one of the protected groups, which include a person over the age of forty. The Court noted that after the worker had established that he was a member of the protected group, the burden of proof shifted to the employer. "If the employer establishes a nondiscriminatory reason for termination, the employee then bears the burden of showing that the employer's proffered reason was a pretext for impermissible discrimination."

Davidson v. Ziegler Tire & Supply Co., 5th Dist. Stark No. CA 00165, 2013-Ohio-2655, ¶22.

ANALYSIS

Even though Mr. Fromm had no idea that the worker was over the age of forty, he had a duty to ascertain whether the man was a member of a protected class.

3. Here is the third analysis that you must identify and correct.

FACT PATTERN

A woman who attended the same church as Mr. Fromm approached him and asked him whether he might have a job for her son, Wayne, who was mentally challenged. She told Mr. Fromm that although Wayne was a good worker and had worked for free at several places, those prospective employers had told her that the other employees were uncomfortable working with Wayne because

(continued)

his facial features and other deformities that had resulted from the genetic problem that had affected his ability to learn. Mr. Fromm told the woman to have Wayne come to the office on Monday and ask for him personally. Mr. Fromm knew Wayne from church and knew he was hardworking, honest, and likeable.

LAW

The same statute of Ohio Revised Code, R.C. §4112.02(A), applies to wrongful discharge applies to discrimination in hiring.

> It shall be an unlawful discriminatory practice:
>
> (A) For any employer, because of the race, color, religion, sex, military status, national origin, disability, age, or ancestry of any person, to discharge without just cause, to refuse to hire, or otherwise to discriminate against that person with respect to hire, tenure, terms, conditions, or privileges of employment, or any matter directly or indirectly related to employment.

R.C. § 4112.02(A).

ANALYSIS

Mr. Fromm should not hire Wayne even though he is handicapped because he has to respect the sensitivities of the people who already work for him.

4. Here is the fourth analysis that you must identify and correct.

FACT PATTERN

After Mr. Fromm hired Wayne, he would stop by to see how Wayne was doing from time to time. Wayne mentioned to Mr. Fromm that he and his mother were looking for another apartment because the one they were living in had been deemed unsafe. They were having problems finding a landlord who would rent to them because of Wayne's appearance that was part of his disability. Mr. Fromm talked to Brad at church and discussed the situation with him. Brad sent Mr. Fromm a copy

of the following portion of the discrimination statute:

LAW

> It shall be an unlawful discriminatory practice:
>
> . . .
>
> For any person to do any of the following:
>
> (1) Refuse to sell, transfer, assign, rent, lease, sublease, or finance housing accommodations, refuse to negotiate for the sale or rental of housing accommodations, or otherwise deny or make unavailable housing accommodations because of race, color, religion, sex, military status, familial status, ancestry, disability, or national origin. . . .

R.C. § 4112.02(H).

ANALYSIS

Because Wayne's mother, and not Wayne, is the person who would sign the lease, the landlords can refuse to rent to Wayne's mother. After all, Wayne's mother is not handicapped.

5. Here is the fifth analysis that you must identify and correct.

FACT PATTERN

In addition to working at Mr. Fromm's company, Wayne attended classes to help him eventually learn to be independent. His special education teacher, Jessica, worked very hard with Wayne to help him to learn to use public transportation, open a bank account, and keep house. Jessica was well-loved by all her students, and most of the parents also appreciated all the help she gave to her students. The father of one student, however, was angry at Jessica because she could not make his son "normal." At a parent-teacher conference, the man became enraged when Jessica informed him that his son was unlikely to ever be able to become a good golfer. The man lost control of his temper and hit Jessica, giving her a black eye.

(continued)

LAW

The law in Ohio concerning assault states, "[n]o person shall recklessly cause serious physical harm to another or to another's unborn." R.C. § 2903.13(B).

ANALYSIS

Because Jessica was not pregnant, the angry parent could not have harmed her unborn child. Therefore, he is off the hook.

EXERCISE

Read the following fact pattern and law and create your own formula for the analysis section of your IRAC statement. Double space and in each sentence identify above the appropriate section (F) for fact, (R) for the rule, (T) for the transitional word(s), and (A) for the analysis. Also include the plus sign (+) and the equal sign (=) in your equation.

Cherelle sold a beautiful gown to a new customer. Although she usually did not accept personal checks, the woman told Cherelle that she had left her credit card in her other purse and that she needed the gown for an event that evening. Cherelle knew that the Parkhurst Junior Women's League had a black tie ball scheduled that night, and she had seen the woman park a very expensive car. The woman was wearing several expensive rings as well as a full-length mink coat. Cherelle decided that accepting the woman's check was probably safe.

When she tried to deposit the check at her bank the next day, however, the bank refused to accept it. Unfortunately for Cherelle, the check was not drawn on any bank, but rather was a very convincing forgery. Cherelle immediately reported this to the police, who told her that a similar crime had occurred twenty miles away at another small store. A week later, the police caught the woman, and she was charged with forgery and uttering.

The Eighth District Court of Appeals in Ohio addressed the crimes of forgery and uttering R.C. § 2913.31, explaining that the accused must intend to defraud her victim:

> {¶ 35} The first necessary element of the crime is an intent to defraud, which is defined in R.C. 2913.01(B): "'Defraud' means to knowingly obtain, by deception, some benefit for oneself or another, or to knowingly cause, by deception, some detriment to another." In order to defraud someone, therefore, the defendant must have used deception. Deception is also defined in R.C. 2913.01(A): "'Deception' means *knowingly deceiving* another or causing another to be deceived by any false or misleading representation, by withholding information, by preventing another from acquiring information, or by any other *conduct*, act, or omission that *creates*, confirms, or perpetuates *a false impression in another, including a false impression as to law, value, state of mind, or other objective or subjective fact.*" (Emphasis added.)

State v. Lutz, Cuyahoga App. No. 80241, 2003-Ohio-275 ¶ 35.

After completing the exercises above, you have a good idea of what constitutes an analysis. We will take the first issue of our first fact pattern, Sheila's problem with her landlord refusing to provide her with hot water, and we will write an analysis applying the law we referenced in the Rule chapter of IRAC analysis.

LANDLORD-TENANT

Let us revisit Sheila Kowalski's problem with her landlord. Sheila had signed a lease for a specific apartment, but the landlord tried to move her into an inferior unit. When Sheila insisted on being moved into the model apartment she had toured and had specified on the lease, she was able to move in, but then discovered it had no hot water. Rather than address Sheila's problem, the landlord informed her that the model unit had never been connected to hot water because it was not meant for habitation. He indicated that he did not intend to connect hot water to the apartment. The landlord also told Sheila that the company that owned the apartment building was headquartered in Florida, and the lease she signed stated that Florida law would apply to any disputes the tenant had.

Ana believed that Sheila should deposit her rent with the Court, but then the paralegal's research revealed that Florida law did not allow that option. Nonetheless, Ana determined that because the property was located in Ohio, the landlord would not be able to evict Sheila without following Ohio law.

Still, Ana asked the paralegal to write two IRAC analyses, one of which applied Ohio law and one that applied Florida law.

We have formulated our issues for this fact pattern chapter 7. We will be discussing the method for addressing more than one issue in chapter 12; therefore, we will discuss only the first issue for this fact pattern here.

Issue: Whether a landlord of residential properties is required under law to provide hot water to the tenants of such property.

We found pertinent law in the previous chapter, the chapter discussing the rule.

OHIO STATUTORY LAW

The Ohio statutory law answered the question raised in our first issue. R.C. § 5321.04 stated that "[a] landlord who is a party to a rental agreement shall do all of the following: . . . [s]upply . . . reasonable amounts of hot water . . . at all times . . . ." R.C. § 5321.04(A)(6).

OHIO LAW EXAMPLE

Our first issue is whether a landlord of residential properties is required under law to provide hot water to the tenants of such property. We have cited the law that applies to this question. Now we will apply that law to our facts: the analysis.

The tenant moved into the multi-unit complex after she signed the lease. However, the tenant has not had hot water in her apartment since she moved into the unit. Ohio law requires a landlord to provide hot water to any residential rental unit, pursuant to R.C. § 5321.04, which states that "[a] landlord who is a party to a rental agreement shall . . . [s]upply . . . reasonable amounts of hot water . . . at all times. . . ." R.C. § 5321.04(A)(6). The landlord admitted to the tenant that the unit she has rented does not have hot water. Further, the landlord has stated that he does not intend to provide hot water to that unit. Therefore, the landlord has violated Ohio law by failing and refusing to provide hot water to the tenant.

Note that we have focused the analysis solely on question raised in the issue: whether or not the landlord is required by law to provide the tenant with hot water.

The discussion does not need to include the fact that the landlord tried to change the terms of the lease by putting the tenant into a lesser quality apartment, or that the tenant insisted on leasing this particular unit. While those facts may speak to the landlord's motives for refusing to provide the tenant with hot water, they are not relevant to the simple fact that by law, he is required to provide hot water to any apartment he leases.

Notice also that this analysis includes the application of the law to the facts. The last sentence states, "Therefore, the landlord has violated Ohio law by failing and refusing to provide hot water to the tenant." Often new legal writers place that sentence in the Conclusion rather than actually applying the law to their facts in the analysis section. It is important to actually apply this law to your facts in the analysis. Otherwise, your analysis is incomplete.

Notice also that the sentence has a transition from one idea to the next: the word "therefore." Transitional words are essential for the flow of your analysis. They provide clues to the readers regarding the direction the analysis is taking, and they make the writing flow more smoothly.

> The Florida statutory law stated that the landlord was required to "make reasonable provisions for: . . . hot water." Fla. Stat. § 83.51 (2012).

FLORIDA LAW EXAMPLE

Our issue is whether a landlord of residential properties is required under law to provide hot water to the tenants of such property. We have cited the law that applies to this question. Now we will apply that law to our facts: the analysis.

> The tenant moved into the multi-unit complex after she signed the lease. However, the tenant has not had hot water in her apartment since she moved into the unit. Florida law requires the landlord "make reasonable provisions for: . . . hot water." Fla. Stat. § 83.51 (2012). The landlord admitted to the tenant that the unit she has rented does not have hot water. Further, the landlord has stated that he does not intend to provide hot water to that unit. Therefore, the landlord has violated Florida law by failing and refusing to provide hot water to the tenant.

■ ANALYSIS OF LAW

Each of the following analyses applying landlord-tenant law is drafted incorrectly.

EXERCISE _____

Identify what is wrong with the following analyses.

1. The tenant in this case is a nurse at the local hospital. She spent a long time searching for the perfect apartment, and when she found it, she signed a lease for that specific unit. The landlord tried to pull a bait-and-switch on her and tried to move her into an inferior apartment for the same amount of money. After she insisted on moving into the apartment she had toured and had specified in the lease, she found out that the apartment did not have hot water. After she complained to the landlord, he told her that she had refused an apartment that had hot water and insisted on having this one. He was rude and sarcastic with her, and he sneered at her when he told her she would never ever get hot water from him. That will show her, he thought.

(continued)

2. The landlord in this case must provide the tenant with all the statutorily required necessities. The statute states that the landlord "Maintain in good and safe working order and condition all electrical, plumbing, sanitary, heating, ventilating, and air conditioning fixtures and appliances, and elevators, supplied or required to be supplied by the landlord." R.C. § 5321.04(A)(4).

3. The tenant in this case has suffered needlessly due to the callous revenge her landlord seeks to impose on her. Just because she insisted on renting the apartment they agreed on, he is maliciously denying her a basic right: hot water. We know that this is a basic right because R.C. § 5321.04 says so.

4. The tenant has not had hot water in her apartment since she moved in. The court in *Gammarino* said the tenant could deposit the rent with the clerk of courts when the landlord did not supply air conditioning. The tenant here has not said anything about air conditioning. Therefore, *Gammarino* does not apply to this case.

5. The tenant in this case should deposit her rent with the clerk of courts. The landlord can argue, however, that she was not current with her rent and demand the court to release the money to him.

6. If a residential rental unit in Florida does not include running water, the landlord is excused from the requirement of providing hot water, because there is no water to heat Fla. Stat. § 83.56 (2014).

7. In Florida, if the landlord decides not to supply the tenant with hot water, she can take him to court and sue him. Fla. Stat. § 83.56 (2014).

8. The tenant in Florida may not terminate the lease even if the landlord does not provide her with hot water seven days after she has given the landlord a letter complaining about the lack of hot water. Fla. Stat. § 83.56 (2014)

9. If the landlord tries to evict the tenant for not paying the rent, even after she gave him written notice that she did not have hot water, the landlord cannot evict her because he is at fault. Fla. Stat. § 83.60 (2014).

10. The tenant has no choice but to move out of the apartment, because even if she pays the overdue rent to the registry of the court, the landlord can still evict her. Fla. Stat. § 83.60 (2014).

■ MOTOR VEHICLE ACCIDENT (MVA)

Now we will look at our second fact pattern, Cherelle's automobile accident. On a dark, icy morning Cherelle was driving slowly to avoid losing control of her car on the ice. A van tried to pass her, spun out of control, and hit her car. Cherelle's car was damaged beyond repair, and the van driver was cited for failure to control his vehicle. After her insurance company paid her for the value of her car, the insurance company seeks to recover that cost from the driver of the rented van.

Here is the issue we formulated in the chapter 7 discussing the issue:

> Issue: Whether the driver of the rental van who was cited for causing an accident can be held liable for damages to the car he hit when he lost control of the van.

The law for this fact pattern found in the preceding chapter discussing the rule was as follows:

■ OHIO LAW

R.C. §4511.21 Speed limits - assured clear distance.

(A) No person shall operate a motor vehicle, trackless trolley, or streetcar at a speed greater or less than is reasonable or proper, having due regard to the traffic, surface, and width of the street or highway and any other conditions, and no person shall drive any motor vehicle, trackless trolley, or streetcar in and upon any street or highway at a greater speed than will permit the person to bring it to a stop within the assured clear distance ahead.

For our purposes, we will quote the statute as follows:

(A) No person shall operate a motor vehicle . . . at a speed greater or less than is reasonable or proper, having due regard to the traffic, surface, and width of the street or highway and any other conditions, and no person shall drive any motor vehicle . . . in and upon any street or highway at a greater speed than will permit the person to bring it to a stop within the assured clear distance ahead.

The following Ohio Supreme Court case also applies.

Ohio case law has consistently held that a person violates the assured clear distance ahead statute if "'there is evidence that the driver collided with an object which (1) was ahead of him in his path of travel, (2) was stationary or moving in the same direction as the driver, (3) did not suddenly appear in the driver's path, and (4) was reasonably discernible.'"

Pond v. Leslein, 72 Ohio St. 3d 50, 52, 1995-Ohio-193, 647 N.E.2d 477, 478.

■ **ANALYSIS OF LAW**

Each of the following analyses applying the motor vehicle law is drafted incorrectly.

EXERCISE

Explain why the following analysis statements are incorrect.

1. The driver of the rented van lost control of his vehicle on an icy road and hit another driver's car. The car he hit was ahead of him on the road, and he wanted to go faster than it was going, so he tried to pass it. The car the van driver struck was not repairable and had to be replaced. The statute R.C. § 4511.21 says that a driver must not drive "at a greater speed than will permit the person to bring it to a stop within the assured clear distance ahead."

2. A van hit a car when it was trying to pass the car. The driver of the van had been forced to drive at a speed that was "or less than is reasonable or proper" because the driver of the car was going fifteen miles slower than the speed limit. R.C. § 4511.21(A). Therefore, the driver of the car is at fault for causing the accident.

3. The driver of the car owned a boutique and was going to the store early so she could take inventory. She knew the roads were icy, so she was driving very slowly. She had seen accidents where people lost control of their cars on the ice, and she did not have time for an accident! Suddenly, headlights appeared in her rear view mirror. They were approaching very quickly! Before she knew what had happened, a large vehicle that later turned out to be a van hit her. She was upset, at first because she knew she would not get to her store on time. When she found out that her car was totaled, she was even more upset. Fortunately, the police cited the driver of the van for hitting her. Now she can sue him.

4. The driver of the van that hit the car lost control of his van. The car was ahead of the van. The van driver knew the car was there because he tried to pass the car. But when the van hit the car, it had spun around, so it was no longer "or moving in the same

(continued)

direction as the driver." *Pond* at 52. The statute does not apply to this case.

5. The driver of the van was cited for failure to control his vehicle. The case of *Pond* is not applicable, however, because the facts do not say that he was still behind the car he struck when he hit it. He was cited in error, and he should fight the ticket.

■ REAL ESTATE

Next, let us consider the case of Antoine Taylor. As you will recall, realtor Antoine Taylor represented the sellers who failed to disclose a material defect, a basement with significant water issues, in the home they sold. The buyers of the property are now suing Antoine for misrepresentation and demanding he compensate them for the amount it will cost to reroute the stream from underneath the home, as well as for the cost of repairs to the basement. Note that the Ohio law refers to the realtor as a licensee, that is, one who holds a license to sell real estate. So when you are reading the law, the licensee is the realtor. Similarly, the transferor is the seller of the property.

> Issue: Whether the realtor representing the seller is responsible for compensating the buyers for the damage to their home resulting from an undisclosed, hidden defect that was unknown to the realtor.

We found three types of law for Ohio governing this issue: statutes, regulations, and case law.

■ OHIO LAW

The applicable statute from the Ohio Revised Code, R.C. § 4735.67(B), states in pertinent part: "A licensee is not required to discover latent defects in the property or to advise on matters outside of the scope of the knowledge required for real estate licensure." Nor is the realtor required to "verify the accuracy or completeness of statements made by the seller, unless the licensee is aware of information that should reasonably cause the licensee to question the accuracy or completeness of such statements." Id.

The regulation that applies here is Ohio Administrative Code, Ohio Adm. Code 1301:5-6-10, which requires the seller of the property to disclose any know defects in the property. The regulation provides a form the seller has to complete that informs potential buyers of defects including "any material defects in the property that are within the actual knowledge of the" seller. Id.

The case law is Moreland v. Ksiazek, 8th Dist. Cuyahoga No. 83509, 2004-Ohio-2974, which involves an allegation of fraud against a realtor for failing to tell the buyer that the padlocked garage on the property was in poor condition. In Moreland, the realtor had never been inside the garage and had no knowledge of its condition.

■ ANALYSIS WITH OHIO LAW

EXERCISE

Compare the following analyses, and determine which of the two is correct. Explain why the correct analysis is correct and why the incorrect analysis is incorrect.

SET ONE

i. The defendant in this case is a realtor who represented the sellers when they sold their house. The realtor gave the sellers the property disclosure form and had them fill it out. He trusted them to tell the truth. They did not say anything on the disclosure form about water problems in the basement.

The regulation requires the sellers to reveal any defects, and it specifically asks about water problems. Ohio Adm.Code 1301:5-6-10. Further, the statute says that the realtor is not responsible for making sure the sellers were truthful on the disclosure form. R.C. § 4735.67(B). Additionally, the statute says that the realtor does not have to look for problems on the property if they are not apparent. The realtor is also not supposed to give advice about things that are not part of what he needs to know to be a licensed realtor. R.C. § 4735.67(B).

ii. The defendant in this case is a realtor who represented the sellers when they sold their house. The realtor gave the sellers the property disclosure form and had them fill it out. He trusted them to tell the truth. They did not say anything on the disclosure form about water problems in the basement.

The regulation requires the sellers to reveal any defects, and it specifically asks about water problems. Ohio Adm.Code 1301:5-6-10. Further, the regulation says that the realtor is not responsible for making sure the sellers were truthful on the disclosure form. R.C. § 4735.67(B). Additionally, the statute says that the realtor does not have to look for problems on the property if they are not apparent. The realtor is also not supposed to give advice about things that are not part of what he needs to know to be a licensed realtor. R.C. § 4735.67(B).

The realtor in this case had no way of knowing that the basement had been flooded years earlier.

His clients did not tell the truth about the water problems they had experienced, and the walls of the basement were paneled. The realtor did not have any way of finding out that the basement was flooded. The realtor should not be held responsible for the seller's dishonesty.

SET TWO

i. When the realtor gave the seller's the property disclosure form, he told them they had to be truthful when they answered it. They promised him they would, but they lied anyway. He even asked them if they ever had problems with water. They bold-face lied and told him they had not. How can a realtor stay in business when his clients leave him holding the bag like this? If they were in the jurisdiction, the realtor should sue them! Anyway, now the buyers are suing the realtor, like he had any way of knowing about the flooding that happened years ago, probably before he was even a realtor.

The law says the sellers had to tell the truth on the disclosure form. The law even says it is not the realtor's problem if the sellers lie on the form. This realtor should not even be sued.

ii. The sellers in this case filled out the property disclosure form, and they did not indicate that the house had experienced any water problems. The realtor was not aware of any water problems, so he could not disclose what he did not know.

The sellers had a legal obligation to divulge any and all problems they were aware of with the property, including water problems. They had to reveal "any material defects in the property that are within [their] actual knowledge." Ohio Adm. Code 1301:5-6-10. In a similar case, the court did not hold the realtor representing the seller responsible for not revealing the condition of the garage on a property. *Moreland v. Ksiazek*, 8th Dist. Cuyahoga No. 83509, 2004-Ohio-2974. In *Moreland*, the garage had been padlocked, and the realtor did not know the condition of the inside of it. Similarly here, the realtor could not see the walls of the basement, because they were paneled. He could not know whether the

(continued)

basement had ever flooded. Just as in the *Moreland*, the realtor was not responsible for divulging information that he did not have. The realtor could not reasonably have suspected that a water problem with the basement existed, just as the realtor in *Moreland* did not suspect that the interior of the padlocked garage had problems.

The realtor in this case was not responsible for his clients' failure to disclose a material defect in the property that was hidden and that he did not know existed.

SET THREE

i. The realtor representing the sellers in this case sold the property to the buyers. The realtor did not withhold any information from the buyers, and he did not know that the sellers had experienced flooding in the basement while they owned the home. The sellers had not revealed this fact on the disclosure form, nor had the disclosed it to the realtor representing them. The buyers of the property sued the seller's realtor for failing to disclose this defect prior to the sale.

It is without question that the sellers of the property legally were required to reveal this defect. Ohio Adm.Code 1301:5-6-10. The realtor representing those sellers, however, is not required to discover latent defects in the property or to advise on matters outside of the scope of the knowledge required for real estate licensure." R.C. § 4735.67(B). The realtor may rely on the statements the sellers make on the disclosure form unless the realtor has a reason to doubt "question the accuracy or completeness of such statements." *Id.*

In the case *Moreland v. Ksiazek,* 8th Dist. Cuyahoga No. 83509, 2004-Ohio-2974, the buyers of a property sued the seller's realtor for failing to tell them that the garage was in poor condition. The garage in question, however, was padlocked, and the seller's realtor had never been inside the garage. The *Moreland* Court held that the realtor lacked any actual knowledge of the condition of the inside of the garage and therefore was not liable to the buyers for failing to inform them of it.

Similarly here, the seller's realtor had no knowledge that the basement of the seller's home had experienced flooding. The sellers had not reported the flooding on the property disclosure form. They had not informed the realtor that they had ever had flooding in the basement. The buyers had not noticed anything wrong in the basement because the sellers had paneled it, and no water marks were visible. Because the buyers could not see any evidence of flooding, it is reasonable to presume that the seller's realtor also did not see any evidence of flooding. He cannot, therefore, be held liable for failing to inform the buyers that the basement had flooding issues.

ii. The realtor representing the sellers in this case sold the property to the buyers. The realtor did not ask the sellers if the basement had ever flooded, but he knew that they did not say anything about flooding on the property disclosure form. He did not look too closely; it is in a realtor's best interest not to look for problems with a property he is trying to sell. Why would he look for problems? He noticed that the basement was paneled, and he knew that paneling could hide problems, but he figured that was for the buyers' inspector to investigate. The paneling simply gave him the chance to advertise the home as having a finished basement. The buyers of the property should be suing the inspector, not the realtor.

The regulation says the sellers have to write any defects they know about the property on the disclosure form. The regulation does not say the realtor representing the sellers has to interrogate them to be sure that they told the truth on it. Ohio Adm.Code 1301:5-6-10. After all, the realtor representing the sellers cannot afford to offend them; they are his clients. Besides, the realtor "is not required to discover latent defects in the property or to advise on matters outside of the scope of the knowledge required for real estate licensure." R.C. § 4735.67(B). The realtor may rely on the statements the sellers make on the disclosure form unless the realtor has a reason to doubt "question the accuracy or completeness of such statements." *Id.*

In the case *Moreland v. Ksiazek*, 8th Dist. Cuyahoga No. 83509, 2004-Ohio-2974, the buyers of a property sued the seller's realtor for failing to tell them that the garage was in poor condition. The garage in question, however, was padlocked, and the seller's realtor had never

(continued)

been inside the garage. The *Moreland* case is different from this case because in this case, the realtor even saw the basement and did not notice any problems.

Thus, the seller's realtor had no knowledge that the basement of the seller's home had experienced flooding. The sellers had not reported the flooding on the property disclosure form. They had not informed the realtor that they had ever had flooding in the basement. The realtor was not a mind reader, so he had no way of knowing the basement had ever flooded. The realtor should win this case and sue the buyers for making him have to hire an attorney!

Next, let us consider the case of Antoine Taylor applying California law. As you will recall, realtor Antoine Taylor represented the sellers who failed to disclose a material defect, a basement with significant water issues, in the home they sold. The buyers of the property are now suing Antoine for misrepresentation and demanding he compensate them for the amount it will cost to reroute the stream from underneath the home, as well as for the cost of repairs to the basement. The buyers of the home had been real estate agents in California, and they had informed Antoine that they were well-versed in real estate law. The paralegal had researched California real estate law.

The issue in this case is whether the realtor representing the seller is responsible for compensating the buyers for the damage to their home resulting from an undisclosed, hidden defect that was unknown to the realtor.

■ ANALYSIS WITH CALIFORNIA LAW

EXERCISE

Compare the following analyses, and determine which of the two is correct. Explain why the correct analysis is correct and why the incorrect analysis is incorrect.

SET ONE

i. The defendant in this case is a realtor who represented the sellers when they sold their house. The realtor gave the sellers the property disclosure form and had them fill it out. He trusted them to tell the truth. They did not say anything on the disclosure form about water problems in the basement.

The regulation requires the sellers to reveal any defects in the property to the buyers. Cal. Civil Code § 1301:5-6-10. Further, the law says that the realtor is not responsible for making sure the sellers were truthful on the disclosure form.

Cal. Civil Code § 1102.4. (a). The real estate agent must "conduct a reasonably competent and diligent visual inspection of the property offered for sale" and tell the buyers of any problems the real estate agent dicovers. Cal. Civil Code § 2079(a).

The realtor in this case had no way of knowing that the basement had been flooded years earlier. His clients did not tell the truth about the water problems they had experienced, and the walls of the basement were paneled. The realtor did not have any way of finding out that the basement was flooded. The realtor should not be held responsible for the seller's dishonesty.

ii. The defendant in this case is a realtor who represented the sellers when they sold their house. The realtor gave the sellers the property disclosure form and had them fill it out. He trusted them

(continued)

to tell the truth. They did not say anything on the disclosure form about water problems in the basement.

The regulation requires the sellers to reveal any defects in the property to the buyers. Cal. Civil Code § 1301:5-6-10. Further, the law says that the realtor is not responsible for making sure the sellers were truthful on the disclosure form. Cal. Civil Code § 1102.4. (a). The real estate agent must "conduct a reasonably competent and diligent visual inspection of the property offered for sale" and tell the buyers of any problems the real estate agent dicovers. Cal. Civil Code § 2079(a).

SET TWO

i. When the realtor gave the seller's the property disclosure form, he told them they had to be truthful when they answered it. They promised him they would, but they lied anyway. He even asked them if they ever had problems with water. They bold-face lied and told him they had not. How can a realtor stay in business when his clients leave him holding the bag like this? If they were in the jurisdiction, the realtor should sue them! Anyway, now the buyers are suing the realtor, like he had any way of knowing about the flooding that happened years ago, probably before he was even a realtor.

The law says the sellers had to tell the truth on the disclosure form. The law even says it is not the realtor's problem if the sellers lie on the form. This realtor should not even be sued.

ii. The sellers in this case filled out the property disclosure form, and they did not indicate that the house had experienced any water problems. The realtor was not aware of any water problems, so he could not disclose what he did not know. As the Court noted, "the sellers' agent is required only to act in good faith and not convey the seller's representations without a reasonable basis for believing them to be true. . . ." *Robinson v. Grossman,* 57 Cal.App.4th 634, 643–644; 67 Cal. Rptr. 2d 380 (1997).

The realtor could not have known about the water problems, even with a competent visual inspection. The realtor in this case was not responsible for his clients' failure to disclose a material defect

in the property that was hidden and that he did not know existed.

SET THREE

i. The realtor representing the sellers in this case sold the property to the buyers. The realtor did not withhold any information from the buyers, and he did not know that the sellers had experienced flooding in the basement while they owned the home. The sellers had not revealed this fact on the disclosure form, nor had the disclosed it to the realtor representing them. The buyers of the property sued the seller's realtor for failing to disclose this defect prior to the sale. The buyers claimed that it was the selling agent's duty to make sure that everything the sellers stated on the disclosure form was correct and true.

In *Robinson*, the Court expressly held that the selling agent does not have "a duty to independently verify or disclaim the accuracy of the seller's representations . . . ." The selling agent is not liable "for relying in good faith upon the seller's representations" when the sellers have failed to disclose a hidden defect. *Robinson v. Grossman,* 57 Cal.App.4th 634, 643–644; 67 Cal. Rptr. 2d 380 (1997).

The seller's realtor had no knowledge that the basement of the seller's home had experienced flooding. The sellers had not reported the flooding on the property disclosure form. They had not informed the realtor that they had ever had flooding in the basement. The buyers had not noticed anything wrong in the basement because the sellers had paneled it, and no watermarks were visible. Because the buyers could not see any evidence of flooding, it is reasonable to presume that the seller's realtor also did not see any evidence of flooding. He cannot, therefore, be held liable for failing to inform the buyers that the basement had flooding issues.

ii. The realtor representing the sellers in this case sold the property to the buyers. The realtor did not ask the sellers if the basement had ever flooded, but he knew that they did not say anything about flooding on the property disclosure form. He did not look too closely; it is in a realtor's best interest not to look for problems with a property he is trying to sell. Why would he look

(continued)

for problems? He noticed that the basement was paneled, and he knew that paneling could hide problems, but he figured that was for the buyers' inspector to investigate. The paneling simply gave him the chance to advertise the home as having a finished basement. The buyers of the property should be suing the inspector, not the realtor.

The California Court even said that the selling agent does not have to double check everything the seller writes on the disclosure form. *Robinson v. Grossman,* 57 Cal.App.4th 634, 643–644; 67 Cal. Rptr. 2d 380 (1997). After all, the agent is not a professional inspector, and if the agent is any good, they will have a lot more listings to keep track of.

The statute does not say that the selling agent has to go to extremes to find any flaws in the property; it says that the agent has to exercise "ordinary care . . . in obtaining and transmitting" the disclosure form, as long as the agent does not know there are errors in it. Cal. Civil Code § 1102.4.

The seller's realtor had no knowledge that the basement of the seller's home had experienced flooding. The sellers had not reported the flooding on the property disclosure form. They had not informed the realtor that they had ever had flooding in the basement. The realtor was not a mind reader, so he had no way of knowing the basement had ever flooded. The realtor should win this case and sue the buyers for making him have to hire an attorney!

■ MEDICAL MALPRACTICE (MED MAL)

Dr. Jeremy Hunter has asked Brad to represent him in defending him against the medical malpractice suit involving non-union of the jaw of the patient who had been hit with the baseball bat. Dr. Hunter is concerned about Dr. Patel's actions in changing his operative report.

■ OHIO LAW

There is an Ohio Supreme Court case that addresses this issue, *Moskovitz v. Mt. Sinai Med. Ctr.* (1994), Ohio St.3d. 638, 635 N.E.2d 331. In *Moskovitz,* The Court held:

> An intentional alteration, falsification or destruction of medical records by a doctor, to avoid liability for his or her medical negligence, is sufficient to show actual malice, and punitive damages may be awarded whether or not the act of altering, falsifying or destroying records directly causes compensable harm.

Id. at 653, 344.

The statute provides guidance to someone in Dr. Hunter's position:

> The [state medical] board, by an affirmative vote of not fewer than six members, shall, to the extent permitted by law, limit, revoke, or suspend an individual's certificate to practice, refuse to register an individual, refuse to reinstate a certificate, or reprimand or place on probation the holder of a certificate for one or more of the following reasons:
>
> . . .
>
> (18) . . . violation of any provision of a code of ethics of the American medical association, the American osteopathic association, the American podiatric medical association, or any other national professional

organizations that the board specifies by rule. The state medical board shall obtain and keep on file current copies of the codes of ethics of the various national professional organizations.

R.C. § 4731.22(B).

The American Medical Association's Code of Ethics includes its Principles of Medical Ethics, which it states "are not laws, but standards of conduct which define the essentials of honorable behavior for the physician." They include:

II. A physician shall uphold the standards of professionalism, be honest in all professional interactions, and strive to report physicians deficient in character or competence, or engaging in fraud or deception, to appropriate entities.

III. A physician shall respect the law. . . .

■ ANALYSIS OF THE LAW

Below are several different analyses for the medical malpractice case for you to review in this exercise.

EXERCISE

Compare and differentiate the following Analyses, and determine which of the two is correct.

SET ONE

i. Dr. Hunter had assisted Dr. Patel in a surgery to wire the patient's broken jaw. During the surgery, a wire that had been cut accidentally struck the patient's eye. When he wrote the operative note, Dr. Hunter mentioned this accident. He later discovered that Dr. Patel had altered his note and deleted the portion that described this incident. The patient has sued both doctors for malpractice, complaining that his jaw did not heal correctly.

In *Moskovitz v. Mt. Sinai Med. Ctr.* (1994), Ohio St.3d. 638; 635 N.E.2d 331, the doctor had altered his medical record to hide his failure to diagnose cancer. This was an ethical violation, and the medical board had the authority to suspend or revoke his license. R.C. § 4731.22(B). The AMA Principles of Medical Ethics includes honesty as a requirement for doctors. These Principles also require physicians to "respect the law." *Id.*

Dr. Patel violated the Principles of Ethics, and thereby could be sanctioned by the Ohio State Medical Board for altering the patient's records. As the *Moskovitz* Court held, the court in her case also could impose punitive damages against her.

ii. Dr. Hunter had assisted Dr. Patel in a surgery to wire the patient's broken jaw. During the surgery, a wire that had been cut accidentally struck the patient's eye. When he wrote the operative note, Dr. Hunter mentioned this accident. He later discovered that Dr. Patel had altered his note and deleted the portion that described this incident. The patient has sued both doctors for malpractice, complaining that his jaw did not heal correctly.

Although a doctor who altered records in another case, *Moskovitz v. Mt. Sinai Med. Ctr.* (1994), Ohio St.3d. 638; 635 N.E.2d 331, had to pay punitive damages for changing the records, that case is different. In *Moskovitz*, the doctor changed the record concerning something that was the subject of the lawsuit. The doctors here are not being sued for hurting the patient's eye, so it does not matter if the doctor changed the record about that. They are only being sued for the jaw, and there is no need for the patient to know that they hurt his eye.

SET TWO

i. Dr. Hunter had assisted Dr. Patel in a surgery to wire the patient's broken jaw. During the surgery, a wire that had been cut accidentally struck the

(continued)

patient's eye. When he wrote the operative note, Dr. Hunter mentioned this accident. He later discovered that Dr. Patel had altered his operative note and deleted the portion that described this incident. The patient has sued both doctors for malpractice, complaining that his jaw did not heal correctly.

The Ohio Supreme Court held that a doctor purposely altering a medical record shows malice and "punitive damages may be awarded whether or not the act of altering, falsifying or destroying records directly causes compensable harm." *Moskovitz v. Mt. Sinai Med. Ctr.* (1994), Ohio St.3d. 638; 635 N.E.2d 331. Further, the State Medical Board will revoke a doctor's medical license for ethical violations. R.C. § 4731.22(B). Ethical violations are defined by the American Medical Association, and include requirements that doctors be honest and show respect for the law. The American Medical Association's Code of Ethics Principles of Medical Ethics.

In *Moskovitz*, the doctor changed a portion of the medical record that showed that he had failed to diagnose the malignancy that caused the patient's death. In this case, not only did the error Dr. Patel deleted from the record not cause a death, it is not even the subject of the lawsuit. Nonetheless, the Ohio statute mandates that the State Medical Board must take action against physicians who violate the ethical standards set forth in the American Medical Association's Code of Ethics.

Dr. Patel acted dishonestly and unethically when she altered the medical records to avoid being found liable for malpractice. Because Dr. Hunter is bound by the same ethical rules that bind all licensed doctors in Ohio, if he were questioned under oath concerning the alteration in the medical record, he would be compelled to tell the truth about the original record. Although Dr. Hunter cannot be held liable for the spoliation of evidence, he cannot protect Dr. Patel from the consequences of her action in spoliating the medical record.

ii. When Dr. Patel was wiring the patient's jaw, Dr. Hunter was helping her. A wire accidentally flew into the patient's eye, but since the anesthesiologist had put a large amount of ointment in his eye, the wire probably did not cause any damage.

Although the Court in a case discussing spoliation of evidence found that the doctor who altered the medical record could be held liable for punitive damages for changing the record, because no other set of records exists in this case, Dr. Patel does not need to worry about getting caught. Therefore, *Moskovitz v. Mt. Sinai Med. Ctr.* (1994), Ohio St.3d. 638; 635 N.E.2d 331 does not apply in this case.

SET THREE

i. Dr. Hunter, who assisted Dr. Patel in wiring the patient's fractured jaw, wrote the original operative report. Although the surgery was restricted to the patient's jaw, he included the information that a wire had struck the patient's eye by mistake. When Dr. Patel realized that Dr. Hunter had added this unnecessary information in the operative report, she redacted it. Now that they are both being sued for a poorly healed jaw, Dr. Hunter is afraid he might get into trouble because he knows that Dr. Patel changed the medical record.

The Ohio State Medical Board requires honesty and respectfulness of the law in doctors, and it can punish them by suspending or revoking their medical licenses. R.C. § 4731.22(B). The Ohio Supreme Court addressed a case in which a doctor had changed a medical record after he was sued for failing to diagnose cancer in a patient. *Moskovitz v. Mt. Sinai Med. Ctr.* (1994), Ohio St.3d. 638; 635 N.E.2d 331. Because the information concerning the patient's eye did not belong in the operative report, Dr. Patel was correct to remove it. Dr. Hunter should know that physicians must stick together and protect each other's professional reputations. Dr. Patel did the right thing in correcting the record.

ii. Dr. Hunter had assisted Dr. Patel in a surgery to wire the patient's broken jaw. During the surgery, a wire that had been cut accidentally struck the patient's eye. When he wrote the operative note, Dr. Hunter mentioned this accident. He later discovered that Dr. Patel had altered his note and deleted the portion that described this incident. The patient has sued both doctors for malpractice, complaining that his jaw did not heal correctly.

The Ohio Supreme Court held that a doctor purposely altering a medical record shows malice and "punitive damages may be awarded whether or not the act of altering, falsifying or destroying records directly causes compensable harm."

(continued)

Moskovitz v. Mt. Sinai Med. Ctr. (1994), Ohio St.3d. 638; 635 N.E.2d 331. Further, the State Medical Board will revoke a doctor's medical license for ethical violations. R.C. § 4731.22(B). Ethical violations are defined by the American Medical Association, and include requirements that doctors be honest and show respect for the law. The American Medical Association's Code of Ethics Principles of Medical Ethics. The Principles of Ethics also states that physicians "shall . . . strive to report physicians deficient in character or competence, or engaging in fraud or deception, to appropriate entities." *Id.*

Dr. Hunter is aware that Dr. Patel altered a medical record. He suspects that she altered the record so the cause of the patient's eye injury would not be discovered. The Principles of Ethics, which are incorporated by reference into the statute, require physicians to "strive to report" other physicians who engage "in fraud or deception, to appropriate entities." *Id.* Although Dr. Hunter has no proof of Dr. Patel's motives for changing the record, ethically, he should report her changing his operative report to the appropriate entity. The consequences for Dr. Patel could be severe, as described in *Moskovitz*, but Dr. Hunter should not participate in her dishonesty by concealing it.

■ CONTRACT BREACH

Marcus and Brianna Johnson consulted with Brad concerning the faulty construction of their new home and Connolly Homes of Parkhurst's failure to correct the defects. In your research, you found law that applied to their case. Now you have written an analysis of your research for Brad.

■ OHIO LAW

The Ohio law you have found is Pursuant to R.C. § 1312.01(c) and (d), Brianna and Marcus's home qualifies as a residential property, and Connolly Homes of Parkhurst qualifies as a contractor.

1. R.C. § 1312.04(A) states in pertinent part, "[n]o owner shall commence arbitration proceedings or file a dwelling action against a residential contractor unless, at least sixty days before commencing the proceedings or filing the action, the owner provides the contractor with written notice of the construction defect that would be the basis of the arbitration proceedings or the dwelling action. The notice shall be in writing. . . ."
2. The Consumer Safety Protection Act (CSPA), R.C. § Sec. 4722, allows the court to "award to the prevailing party a reasonable attorney's fee" under limited circumstances.
3. The Ohio Supreme Court has ruled that although construction does not have to be perfect, builders are required to build residential properties in a manner that is workmanlike and that uses ordinary care. The court found that this is a duty that the buyer cannot waive. *Jones v. Centex Homes*, 132 Ohio St.3d 1, 2012-Ohio-1001 ¶ 14.
4. A limited warranty does not preclude the owner of a residential property from recovering damages for construction that fails to meet workmanlike quality, which is implied in every construction contract. *Landis v. William Fannin Builders, Inc.*, 193 Ohio App. 3d 318, 2011-Ohio-1489 ¶29.

■ ANALYSIS OF THE LAW

Each of the following analyses for breach of contract is drafted incorrectly.

EXERCISE

Revise and correct the Analyses in the following exercises.

1. Connolly Homes of Parkhurst built a home for Brianna and Marcus. When they moved in, they discovered several defects, including reversed hot and cold water faucets and non-working electrical outlets. Within a month of moving into the home, they saw water damage on the family room vaulted ceiling. The home came with a one-year warranty.

   A homeowner cannot start arbitration proceedings against the builder unless the homeowner gives the builder written notice "at least sixty days before commencing the proceedings." R.C. § 1312.04(A). Pursuant to R.C. § 1312.01(c) and (d), Brianna and Marcus's home qualifies as a residential property, and Connolly Homes of Parkhurst qualifies as a contractor. Even though the warranty has expired, every contract has an implied warranty that the builder "meet workmanlike quality *Landis v. William Fannin Builders, Inc* 193 Ohio App. 3d 318, 2011-Ohio-1489 ¶ 29.

2. Marcus Johnson, whose father Henry owned Parkhurst Industries, married his long-time girlfriend, Brianna Jones. As a wedding present, Marcus's father Henry paid for Marcus and Brianna to have a custom-built home constructed for them on a plot of land adjacent to homes other family members owned. Marcus's father wanted to keep his family near him to enhance family ties.

   When Marcus and Brianna returned from their honeymoon, the home construction was far more complete than they had expected. The roof was on, the outside walls were up, and the drywall was in place in almost all of the rooms. The architect had monitored the layout of the construction, and the room sizes and placements were consistent with the plans. Brianna and Marcus moved in a month later, after the cabinets, countertops, and fixtures they had selected were installed. On their first night in the new home, however, Marcus

discovered that the water faucets in the master bathroom were reversed, so that the cold water tap ran hot, and the hot water tap ran cold. Over the course of the next few days, they realized that five electrical outlets did not work, and within a month, they saw water damage on the family room vaulted ceiling.

The builder qualifies as a contractor, and the home in question qualifies as a residential property. R.C. § 1312.01(c) and (d). Brianna provided 60 days written notice of the defects to the builder, as required under R.C. § 1312.04(A). The builder is liable because the Ohio Supreme Court has ruled that although construction does not have to be perfect, builders are required to build residential properties in a manner that is workmanlike and that uses ordinary care. The court found that this is a duty that the buyer cannot waive. *Jones v. Centex Homes*, 132 Ohio St.3d 1, 2012-Ohio-1001 ¶ 14. The builder's reliance on the expired warranty is a red herring because a limited warranty does not preclude the owner of a residential property from recovering damages for construction that fails to meet workmanlike quality, which is implied in every construction contract. *Landis v. William Fannin Builders, Inc* 193 Ohio App. 3d 318, 2011-Ohio-1489 ¶ 29.

3. Brianna and Marcus contracted with Connolly Homes of Parkhurst to build their home. Brianna and Marcus knew when they signed the contract that the home came with a one-year warranty. After they moved in, they discovered several defects, including reversed hot and cold water faucets and nonworking electrical outlets. Within a month of moving into the home, they saw water damage on the family room vaulted ceiling. After a year, the builder did not have to fix any of the things they complained about because the warranty had expired.

4. Brianna and Marcus contracted with Connolly Homes of Parkhurst to build their home. Brianna and Marcus knew when they signed the contract that the home came with a one-year

(continued)

warranty. After they moved in, they discovered several defects, including reversed hot and cold water faucets and nonworking electrical outlets. Within a month of moving into the home, they saw water damage on the family room vaulted ceiling. Brianna notified the builder in writing and specifically detailed each of the problems. Connolly stalled in making the repairs for a year, and then told her that the warranty had expired. The company stated that they no longer had an obligation to fix anything on the property.

A limited warranty does not preclude the owner of a residential property from recovering damages for construction that fails to meet workmanlike quality, which is implied in every construction contract. *Landis v. William Fannin Builders, Inc*193 Ohio App. 3d 318, 2011-Ohio-1489 ¶ 29.

5. Brianna and Marcus contracted with Connolly Homes of Parkhurst to build their home. Brianna and Marcus knew when they signed the contract that the home came with a one-year warranty. After they moved in, they discovered several defects, including reversed

hot and cold water faucets and nonworking electrical outlets. Within a month of moving into the home, they saw water damage on the family room vaulted ceiling. Brianna notified the builder in writing and specifically detailed each of the problems.

The CSPA allows the court to "award to the prevailing party a reasonable attorney's fee" under limited circumstances. Brad should take this case, because the research shows that the builder failed to meet the standards of workmanlike quality as required in *Jones v. Centex Homes*, 132 Ohio St.3d 1, 2012-Ohio-1001 ¶ 14. Also, Brad knows that the expiring of the warranty will not hurt the case because a limited warranty does not preclude the owner of a residential property from recovering damages for construction that fails to meet workmanlike quality, which is implied in every construction contract. *Landis v. William Fannin Builders, Inc.*, 193 Ohio App. 3d 318, 2011-Ohio-1489 ¶ 29.

Brianna fulfilled the notice requirements of R.C. § 1312.04(A) when she sent the certified letters to the builder. Brad is sure he can win this case.

■ CONTRACT BREACH CONTINUED

Marcus and Brianna Johnson consulted with Brad concerning the faulty construction of their new home and Connolly Homes of Parkhurst's failure to correct the defects. In your research, you found the Virginia law that applied to their case, because the builder is headquartered in Virginia, and the contract the Johnson's signed stated that any disputes would be tried using Virginia law. Now you have written an analysis of your research for Brad.

Note that the buyer is called the vendee and the builder is called the vendor.

■ VIRGINIA LAW

The Virginia law you have found is as follows:

1. Under Virginia law, Brianna and Marcus's home qualifies as a "new dwelling." Va. Code Ann. § 55-70.1(F). "In every contract for the sale of a new dwelling, the vendor shall be held to warrant to the vendee that . . . the dwelling with all its fixtures is, to the best of the actual knowledge of the vendor or his agents" free from structural defects. Va. Code Ann. § 55-70.1(A)

2. When the vendor breaches the warranty of a newly built house, the vendee has to provide the vendor with a written notice, sent by certified or

registered mail, informing the vendor that the defect exists, and the vendee has to allow the vendor to "have a reasonable period of time, not to exceed six months, to cure the defect that is the subject of the warranty claim." Va. Code Ann. § 55-70.1(D)

3. Every new home has an implied warranty that it is "(i) free from structural defects, so as to pass without objection in the trade, and (ii) constructed in a workmanlike manner, so as to pass without objection in the trade." Va. Code Ann. § 55-70.1(A)

4. The statutory warranty period for new homes is one year, but if the buyer has informed the builder of the defect or defects within that one-year period, and the builder had not fixed the defects, then they buyer can file a lawsuit "against the builder within two years from the date that the buyer notified the builder of the defect." *Davis v. Tazewell Place Associates*, 254 Va. 257, 260, 492 S.E.2d 162, 164 (1997).

5. The Virginia statute defines a structural defect as "a defect or defects that reduce the stability or safety of the structure below accepted standards or that restrict the normal use thereof." Va. Code Ann. § 55-70.1(G)

■ ANALYSIS OF THE LAW

The analyses for breach of contract applying Virginia law in the following exercise are drafted incorrectly.

EXERCISE

Revise and correct the Analyses in the following exercises.

1. Connolly Homes of Parkhurst built a home for Brianna and Marcus. When they moved in, they discovered several defects, including reversed hot and cold water faucets and non-working electrical outlets. Within a month of moving into the home, they saw water damage on the family room vaulted ceiling. The home came with a one-year warranty.

Brianna sent a certified letter to Connolly Homes of Parkhurst detailing each of the defects. Pursuant to Va. Code Ann. § 55-70.1(D), Connolly has six months to fix the defects that are in breach of the warranty. After six months, however, Connolly had not fixed the defects, so Brianna and Marcus were out of luck. They were stuck with the flaws in their new home.

2. Marcus Johnson, whose father Henry owned Parkhurst Industries, married his long-time girlfriend, Brianna Jones. As a wedding present, Marcus's father Henry paid for Marcus and Brianna to have a custom built home constructed for them on a plot of land adjacent to homes other family members owned. Marcus's father wanted to keep his family near him to enhance family ties.

When Marcus and Brianna returned from their honeymoon, the home construction was far more complete than they had expected. The roof was on, the outside walls were up, and the drywall was in place in almost all of the rooms. The architect had monitored the layout of the construction, and the room sizes and placements were consistent with the plans.

Brianna and Marcus moved in a month later, after the cabinets, countertops, and fixtures they had selected were installed. On their first night in the new home, however, Marcus discovered that the water faucets in the master bathroom were reversed, so the cold water tap ran hot, and the hot water tap ran cold. Over the course of the next few days, they realized that five electrical outlets did not work, and within a month, they saw water damage on the family room vaulted ceiling.

The statute requires a new dwelling to be built in such a way that it meets the trade's definition of workmanlike construction. Va.

(continued)

Code Ann. § 55-70.1(A). Because neither Brianna nor Marcus is a member of the trades, they have no knowledge of what constitutes workmanlike construction. They cannot prove that the problems that they are experiencing with their home are the result of failure of the builder to construct the home in compliance with workmanlike construction.

3. Brianna and Marcus contracted with Connolly Homes of Parkhurst to build their home. They discovered that some of the electrical outlets did not work, the hot and cold water faucets were reversed, and the roof was leaking in the family room.

    The Virginia statute provides a definition of a structural defect as one that reduces the home's safety or stability "below accepted standards or that restrict[s] the normal use thereof." Va. Code Ann. § 55-70.1(G).

    Connolly Homes of Parkhurst argues that neither the nonfunctioning outlets nor the reversed water taps causes any reduction in the stability or safety of the home. They also argue that a leaking roof is not unsafe, and it does not make the home unstable. Rather, it is merely inconvenient.

4. Despite sending several certified letters to Connolly Homes of Parkhurst, Brianna has not had any satisfaction in her requests for repairs of the defects in the home.

    Virginia law requires a vendor to provide a statutory warranty for every new dwelling it sells. That warranty includes the fixtures. Va. Code Ann. § 55-70.1(A). Brianna and Marcus's home qualifies as a "new dwelling." Va. Code Ann. § 55-70.1(F).

    Connolly can sue the company that sold it the fixtures, even though it was Connolly's workers who put them in backwards. The fixtures did not say "left side" and "right side" on them, and the manufacturers should know that not every construction worker is a brain trust.

5. Brianna and Marcus contracted with Connolly Homes of Parkhurst to build their home. Brianna and Marcus knew when they signed the contract that the home came with a one-year warranty. After they moved in, they discovered several defects, including reversed hot and cold water faucets and nonworking electrical outlets. Within a month of moving into the home, they saw water damage on the family room vaulted ceiling. Brianna notified the builder in writing by certified mail and specifically detailed each of the problems. Because almost a year has passed since she sent the certified letter, Brianna has sought Brad to represent her in a lawsuit against Connolly.

6. According to the case *Davis v. Tazewell Place Associates*, 254 Va. 257, 260, 492 S.E.2d 162, 164 (1997), a homeowner has a one year warranty period to notify the builder of any defects. If the builder does not repair the defects within the warranty period, then the homeowner has two years from the time she notified the builder of the defects to file a lawsuit.

    Brianna should not have to wait until a lawsuit is completed to get her home fixed. Connolly should have built it properly, and she should not have to give them an entire year to get around to fixing it. Also, Connolly should keep in mind that Brianna's father-in-law is probably the most important person in Parkhurst, and if it wants any more business, it had better straighten up and correct the problems in her home.

■ PRODUCT LIABILITY

You will recall the fraternity house's stove explosion from earlier chapters:

When they were still in college, Brad and Antoine had been fraternity brothers. During a party at their fraternity house, the gas stove in the kitchen had exploded. Although no one was hurt, the fraternity house burned to the ground, and the students who lived in the house lost all their belongings. The fire department's investigation determined that the explosion was a result of a flaw in either the stove or the gas line to the stove.

Their attorney, Ms. Walker, had found, through her paralegal's research, that the stove they had bought at the big box store had been recalled prior to the date the fraternity brothers bought it. Although the store denied knowing about the recall, it had sold the stove at cost. The paralegal also discovered that the manufacturer of the stove had gone bankrupt and could not be sued.

The attorney had informed the paralegal that the big box store where Brad and Antoine bought the fraternity house gas stove that exploded during the party is headquartered in Texas, and it has a forum selection clause stating that all purchasers must use Texas law for litigation over products bought at its stores. The bankrupt manufacturer was headquartered in Michigan, so the attorney asked the paralegal to research both Texas and Michigan law. The attorney also noted that the Ohio CSPA law the paralegal had found for the Johnson's case against the home builder also applied to other merchandise, including "white goods" like stoves, refrigerators, washers, and dryers.

■ TEXAS LAW

EXERCISE _____

Refer back to the previous chapter discussing the rule for the law for the product liability fact pattern. Using this law, compose an analysis portion of the IRAC for this fact pattern using Texas law. This law is located in the section immediately preceding the Summary.

■ OHIO LAW

EXERCISE _____

Refer back to the previous chapter discussing the rule for the law for the product liability fact pattern. Using this law, compose an analysis portion of the IRAC for this fact pattern using Ohio law. Your Instructor will provide you with the Ohio CSPA law and other law that applies.

■ MICHIGAN LAW

EXERCISE _____

Refer back to the previous chapter discussing the rule the rule chapter for the law for the product liability fact pattern. Using this law, compose an analysis portion of the IRAC for this fact pattern using Michigan law. This law is located in the section immediately preceding the Summary.

ANALYSIS OF THE LAW

The analysis is to be composed for the following states from the exercise above:
Texas, Ohio, and Michigan.

SUMMARY

- The analysis portion of the IRAC is the heart of the process.

- The analysis applies the law to the specific facts of your case and demonstrates why your client's point of view is legally correct, or why the opposing side's point of view is not legally defensible.

- Drafting the analysis begins with finding the similarities and the differences between the law and the facts in the case at hand.

- The next step of the analysis is determining which similarities and/or differences support the case, and which hurt it.

- After determining what supports and what harms the case, the writers then organize the material in conjunction with the facts of the case.

- Writers will emphasize the parts of the law that support their argument and distinguish the differences between the case and the parts of the law that hurt their argument.

- Even when the law makes it difficult for writers to support an argument, however, they must apply the law honestly in their analysis.

ASSIGNMENT

I. Using the fact pattern and law below, write a cogent analysis applying the law to the facts. Be sure to cite only the pertinent law and to focus on the pivotal facts.

A decade ago, Henry Johnson had bought property in Wisconsin that he hoped to turn into a family vacation site. He then got distracted by business matters, and when he returned to the property after Marcus and Brianna were married, he discovered that what had once been a quiet, wooded property on a pristine lake was now a surrounded by condominiums, gated communities, and a large shopping mall. Although Henry's property was still wooded, it was no longer quiet. The lake was abuzz with jet skis and motor boats. Because his dream of a quiet vacation site was no longer feasible, Henry decided to sell the property.

When he got an appraisal of the property, he was pleased to discover that the surrounding development had caused his property to increase in value ten-fold. He quickly entered into a sales contract, selling it to a developer. The contract specifically provided that if one of the parties failed to perform, that is, to uphold its side of the contract, the other side could demand specific performance. [See note] The developer had been insistent on including this clause, because it realized that the property would increase in value, and it wanted to be certain that Henry did not decide to sell it to someone else for a higher price.

When the sale was scheduled to close, however, the developer informed Henry that it had not obtained financing yet. After an additional six-month delay, Henry hired local counsel to sue the buyer for specific performance. After a trial, the court awarded a verdict for Henry and ordered the developer to complete the purchase of the property. The developer appealed, claiming that Henry should have sought other legal remedies rather than specific performance.

[Note: Specific performance is a contract term that applies to the sale of real property. Specific performance requires the buyer to complete the purchase of the property even if the buyer changes its mind and decides it does not want the property. Similarly, if a seller tries to renege on the sale of a specific property, the buyer also can sue for specific performance, forcing the seller to transfer the property to the buyer. The courts allow specific performance in a real estate contract to be enforced because each piece of real estate is considered to be unique and not able to be substituted.]

In the following case, the petitioner is the buyer of the property, and Ash Park, LLC s the seller. The circuit court is the trial court. Summary Judgment is an action the trial court takes deciding a case before trial. We will discuss Summary Judgment later in the chapter addressing motions.

WISCONSIN CASE LAW

The petitioner, Alexander & Bishop, Ltd., seeks review of a published decision of the court of appeals affirming the orders of the circuit court. After Alexander & Bishop breached a contract to purchase a parcel of real estate from Ash Park, LLC, the circuit court granted summary judgment in favor of Ash Park and ordered specific performance of the contract. It also imposed interest on the purchase price.

. . . .

The contract provides that specific performance is an available remedy, and neither the contract nor Wisconsin law requires Ash Park to demonstrate that a legal remedy would be inadequate as a precondition to relief. Further, although impossibility is a defense to specific performance, Alexander & Bishop failed to present evidence that performance would be impossible in the proceedings before the circuit court.

Ash Park, LLC v. Alexander & Bishop, Ltd., 2010 WI 44, ¶4, 324 Wis.2d 703, 710; 783 N.W.2d 294, 297.[1]

II. Using the fact pattern and law below, write a cogent analysis applying the law to the facts. Be sure to cite only the pertinent law and to focus on the pivotal facts.

Antoine and Cherelle were visiting her Aunt Denise in Boston. They had adopted a small mixed breed dog from the pound a month earlier. They wryly had named the dog Spike, because it was so timid and shy. Because Spike suffered from separation anxiety when he was away from Cherelle, Aunt Denise graciously had told them that the dog was welcome to visit, too. Fortunately, the dog was housebroken and well trained, and the visit was proceeding pleasantly. Cherelle and Aunt Denise took the dog for a walk in the park. Cherelle was careful to keep Spike on a leash, even though she was certain that he would never let her out of his sight.

Suddenly, a large dog ran up from behind Cherelle and snatched Spike up in its jaws. Cherelle and Aunt Denise both shouted at the large dog and beat on it, trying to get it to let go of Spike. A park ranger arrived, and despite his best efforts, could not loosen the large dog's jaws. The park ranger finally shot the attacking dog through the heart. The ranger then rescued Spike from the dead dog's mouth. Spike was bleeding profusely and was barely conscious.

Another ranger drove Cherelle, Aunt Denise, and Spike to the nearest veterinary hospital, where the veterinarian spent five hours operating on him. To everyone's surprise, Spike recovered almost completely, and Cherelle and Antoine took him home a week later.

When the bill arrived for Spike's emergency medical treatment, Cherelle was appalled to find that she owed the veterinarian $5,000. She was even more distraught when the owner of the large dog filed a lawsuit against her in Massachusetts for the loss of his AKC registered dog. The large dog's owner was suing her for loss of income, claiming that he often made several thousand dollars each year breading the dog.

Brad and Ana gave Cherelle and Antoine the name of a law school classmate who was practicing law in Boston, and the classmate countersued for the veterinary bills incurred in Spike's treatment. The Boston attorney found the following case and included it in his court documents.

MASSACHUSETTS CASE LAW

An unprovoked attack by the defendants' unleashed German shepherd caused the plaintiffs' Bichon Frisé severe internal injuries, external bruising, and wounds to the head, neck, abdomen, and chest. Emergency surgery was successful but expensive, with veterinary costs

---

ultimately amounting to over $8,000. After a bench trial, a District Court judge found those costs to be both reasonable and necessary and awarded them in full.

The judgment was affirmed by the Appellate Division. The sole issue on appeal is whether damages should be capped at the market value of the dog, regardless of the reasonableness of the veterinary costs necessary to treat the dog's injuries. We affirm.

The plaintiffs sued under G.L. c. 140, § 155, as amended by St.1934, c. 320, § 18, which since 1791 has imposed strict liability for damage caused by dogs:

"If any dog shall do any damage to either the body or property of any person, the owner or keeper . . . shall be liable for such damage, unless such damage shall have been occasioned to the body or property of a person who, at the time such damage was sustained, was committing a trespass or other tort, or was teasing, tormenting or abusing such dog."

. . . .

Although the statute imposes strict liability for "any damage" caused by a dog, it is silent as to how to measure such damage. We turn, accordingly, to the common law.

. . . .

[R]easonableness is the touchstone for determining whether, and to what extent, veterinary costs can be recovered. If it is reasonable in the circumstances presented to incur the veterinary costs at the time they are undertaken, then the owner of the injured animal may recover them. . . . Our reading of the common law leads us, therefore, to conclude that reasonable veterinary costs that are reasonably incurred can be recovered under G.L. c. 140, § 155, even if they exceed the market value or replacement cost of an animal injured by a dog.

. . . .

Although the owner's affection for the animal may be considered in assessing the reasonableness of the decision

to treat the animal, the owner cannot recover for his or her own hurt feelings, emotions, or pain. Nor is the owner entitled to recover for the loss of the animal's companionship or society.

Irwin v. Degtiarov, 85 Mass. App. Ct. 234, 234–239; 8 N.E.3d 296, 298–302 (2014)

III. Using the fact pattern and law below, write a cogent analysis applying the law to the facts. Be sure to cite only the pertinent law and to focus on the pivotal facts.

While he was doing a one-year internship at a large university medical center in upstate New York State, Jeremy found that jogging helped clear his mind and helped him sleep – not that he had much opportunity to sleep. He and a classmate were jogging in late October in the classmate's home town, Trumansburg, New York, a quaint little town near the large medical center. After running up a short but steep hill off the main road, they turned left onto McLallen Street, which had charming pre-Civil War homes. Some of the homes had the original slate sidewalks, and the wet leaves were slicked onto the sidewalks.

Jeremy slipped on moss that was hidden by the leaves and fell, breaking his right hand. Because he planned to be a surgeon, he was quite distressed by this injury. One of the professors at the law school that was affiliated with the university offered to represent him in a lawsuit against the homeowners whose sidewalk was the location of his fall. He told Jeremy that the homeowners should have cleared the slippery moss and wet leaves off their sidewalk.

The homeowners argued that by running on slate sidewalks, which were known to be slippery when wet, and by running on these wet slate sidewalks that were covered by wet leaves, Jeremy had assumed the risk of his injury. The homeowners argued that they were not liable for the slippery sidewalk. They also argued that by running on wet leaves without knowledge of the surface under the leaves, Jeremy had negligently contributed to his own injury.

Jeremy's attorney countered that because sidewalks were designed for people to traverse, the homeowner had a duty to clean the slippery moss off of the sidewalk. Jeremy's attorney further alleged that the homeowners had a duty to clear the wet leaves off the sidewalk, because they knew the leaves would be slippery on the slate walk.

The attorney found the following case concerning contributory negligence and assumption of the risk:

NEW YORK CASE LAW

In this case involving a plaintiff who fell and sustained injuries while roller-blading, we conclude that the doctrine of 86*86 primary assumption of the risk does not preclude her common-law negligence claim against the land-owner defendants. We therefore affirm the Appellate Division order reinstating the complaint.

. . . .

Our analysis begins with CPLR 1411, which the Legislature adopted in 1975 to abolish contributory negligence and assumption of the risk as absolute defenses in favor of a comparative fault regime. CPLR 1411 provides:

"In any action to recover damages for personal injury, injury to property, or wrongful death, the culpable conduct attributable to the claimant or to the decedent, including contributory negligence or assumption of risk, shall not bar recovery, but the amount of damages otherwise recoverable shall be diminished in the proportion which the culpable conduct attributable to the claimant or decedent bears to the culpable conduct which caused the damages."

. . . .

Since the adoption of CPLR 1411, we have generally restricted the concept of assumption of the risk to particular athletic and recreative activities in recognition that such pursuits have "enormous social value" even while they may "involve significantly heightened risks" (*Trupia*, 14 NY3d at 395). Hence, the continued application of the doctrine "facilitate[s] free and vigorous participation in athletic activities" (*Benitez*, 73 NY2d at 657), and fosters these socially beneficial activities by shielding coparticipants, activity sponsors or venue owners from "potentially crushing liability" (*Bukowski*, 19 NY3d at 358).

. . . .

In contrast, in Trupia we recently declined to apply the assumption of the risk doctrine to a child who was injured while sliding down a bannister at school. Based on the tension that exists between assumption of the risk and the dictates of CPLR 1411, we clarified that the doctrine "must be closely circumscribed if it is not seriously to undermine and displace the principles of comparative causation" (*Trupia*, 14 NY3d at 395). We noted that the injury-causing activity at issue in *Trupia* — horseplay — did not render the school worthy of insulation from a breach of duty claim, as it was "not a case in which the defendant solely by reason of having sponsored or otherwise supported some risk-laden but socially valuable voluntary activity has been called to account in damages" (*id.* at 396).

Guided by these principles, we conclude that assumption of the risk does not apply to the fact pattern in this appeal, which does not fit comfortably within the parameters of the doctrine. As a general rule, application of assumption of the risk should be limited to cases appropriate for absolution of duty, such as personal injury claims arising from sporting events, sponsored athletic and recreative activities, or athletic and recreational pursuits that take place at designated venues. In this case, plaintiff was not rollerblading at a rink, a skating park, or in a competition; nor did defendants actively sponsor or promote the activity in question.

Moreover, extension of the doctrine to cases involving persons injured while traversing streets and sidewalks would create an unwarranted diminution of the general duty of landowners — both public and private — to maintain their premises in a reasonably safe condition. As we explained in an earlier case, assumption of the risk "does not exculpate a landowner from liability for ordinary negligence in maintaining a premises" (*Sykes*, 94 NY2d at 913). The exception would swallow the general rule of comparative fault if sidewalk defects or dangerous premises conditions were deemed "inherent" risks assumed by non-pedestrians who sustain injuries, whether they be joggers, runners, bicyclists or rollerbladers (see *Ashbourne v City of New York*, 82 AD3d 461, 463 [1st Dept 2011]; *Cotty v Town* of 90*90 Southampton, 64 AD3d 251, 257 [2nd Dept 2009]). We therefore decline to expand the doctrine to cover the circumstances presented here.

Custodi v. Town of Amherst, 20 N.Y.3d 83, 85–86, 89–90; 980 N.E.2d 933, 957 (2012).

IV. Adding to the fact pattern in III, read the following paragraph and use the same facts and law to argue the case from the homeowner's point of view.

After the homeowners received Jeremy's Complaint alleging that they were responsible for his fall on the mossy, leaf covered sidewalk in front of their home, they argued that by running on slate sidewalks, which were known to be slippery when wet, and by running on these wet slate sidewalks that were covered by wet leaves, Jeremy had assumed the risk of his injury. The homeowners argued that they were not liable for the slippery sidewalk. They also argued that by running on wet leaves without knowledge of the surface under the leaves, Jeremy had negligently contributed to his own injury.

V. Using the fact pattern and law below, write a cogent analysis applying the law to the facts. Be sure to cite only the pertinent law and to focus on the pivotal facts.

Ana asked the paralegal to do some legal research for her as a personal favor. She told the paralegal that her twenty-two-year old cousin, Guadalupe,

had been earning college money by waiting tables. Her cousin was living and working in Kansas, and she called Ana to tell her that despite numerous requests for her credit card tips, her employer refused to pay her not only her tips, but also her base salary. Her manager, Ted, refused to believe that Guadalupe was an American citizen, and he withheld money from all the staff members who were in the United States illegally. He knew that they would be too afraid of being deported to report him.

Because she was a native born American citizen, Guadalupe complained about her boss to the Kansas Department of Labor. When she reported to work a few days later, he fired her. He claimed that he had fired her for being an illegal alien, but she noticed that he had not fired any of the workers that she knew were in the country illegally. Ana asked the paralegal to research the Kansas law regarding this issue and write up a summary of the law for her. The paralegal found the following 2011 case from the Supreme Court of Kansas:

KANSAS CASE LAW

Robert L. Campbell was an at-will employee with Husky Hogs, L.L.C., for about 1 year when he filed a complaint with the Kansas Department of Labor (KDOL) alleging Husky Hogs was not paying him as required by the KWPA [Kansas Wage Payment Act]. Campbell was fired 1 business day after KDOL acknowledged receiving his claim. Campbell filed this lawsuit in Phillips County District Court alleging Husky Hogs terminated him for pursuing his statutory rights under the KWPA. Husky Hogs denied the allegation.

. . . .

The company also filed a . . . motion for judgment on the pleadings. It argued Kansas had not previously recognized a retaliatory discharge claim for alleging KWPA violations and no public policy reasons existed for allowing such a claim now.

. . . .

The district court granted Husky Hogs' motion. It held Campbell's termination did not violate Kansas public policy, even though it was required to assume the discharge resulted from filing the disputed wage claim.

. . . .

Kansas historically adheres to the employment-at-will doctrine, which holds that employees and employers may terminate an employment relationship at any time, for any reason, unless there is an express or implied contract governing the employment's duration. [Citation omitted] But there are specific statutory exceptions to this rule, such as terminations based on race, gender, or disability.

. . . .

There are also exceptions recognized by Kansas courts through our case law. Over the past 30 years, exceptions to the at-will doctrine created a common-law tort for retaliatory discharge. These exceptions gradually eroded the general terminable-at-will rule 4*4 when an employee is fired in contravention of a recognized state public policy.

. . . .

To date, this court has endorsed public policy exceptions in four circumstances: (1) filing a claim under the Kansas Workers Compensation Act, K.S.A. 44-501 et seq; (2) whistleblowing; (3) filing a claim under the Federal Employers Liability Act (FELA), 45 U.S.C. § 51 (2006) et seq.; and (4) exercising a public employee's First Amendment right to free speech on an issue of public concern.

. . . .

. . . Kansas courts permit the common-law tort of retaliatory discharge as a limited exception to the at-will employment doctrine when it is necessary to protect a strongly held state public policy from being undermined.

. . . .

We have stated that courts tasked with determining whether a public policy

exists are faced with three situations: (1) The legislature has clearly declared the state's public policy; (2) the legislature enacted statutory provisions from which public policy may reasonably be implied, even though it is not directly declared; and (3) the legislature has neither made a clear statement of public policy nor can it be reasonably implied.

. . . .

The KWPA was enacted in 1973. L. 1973, ch. 204, secs. 1-16. It is an expansive and comprehensive legislative scheme that is broad in its scope and the rights created for Kansas workers to secure unpaid wages earned from their labors. See K.S.A. 44-313 et seq. It is applicable to most Kansas employers. See K.S.A. 44-313(a). It requires, among various other provisions, that employers promptly pay wages and benefits (K.S.A. 2010 Supp. 44-314 K.S.A. 44-315). It also permits specific damages awards for willful nonpayment (K.S.A.44-315); controls and limits wage withholdings (K.S.A. 2010 Supp. 7*7 44-319); prohibits waivers of the rights created (K.S.A. 44-321); and mandates that the Secretary of Labor enforce and administer the KWPA's provisions through administrative proceedings, compulsory process to compel witness attendance and document production, and permits application to the district courts for citations in contempt (see K.S.A. 44-322; K.S.A. 2010 Supp. 44-322a). The Secretary of Labor is expressly authorized to adopt such rules and regulations as are deemed necessary to accomplish the KWPA's purposes. K.S.A. 44-325.

. . . .

This court has recognized retaliatory discharge claims in different circumstances, including those in which employees are discharged for exercising a statutory right.

. . . .

That principle is applicable to the KWPA. We hold the KWPA embeds within its provisions a public policy of protecting wage earners' rights to their unpaid wages and benefits. And just as we found a common-law retaliatory discharge claim when an injured worker is terminated for exercising rights under the Workers Compensation Act, we find such a cause of action is necessary when an employer fires a worker who seeks to exercise KWPA rights by filing a wage claim. To do otherwise would seriously undermine the public policy and the protections afforded by the KWPA.

Campbell v. Husky Hogs, LLC, 292 Kan. 225, 225–227, 230, 233–234; 255 P.3d 1, 3–4, 6–7 (2011).

LEARNING OBJECTIVES

1. Recognize the appropriate content for the conclusion

2. Differentiate which content does not belong in the conclusion

3. Recognize incorrect conclusions

4. Analyze the Issue, Rule, and Analysis to write an accurate Conclusion statement

5. Compose a well written conclusion

6. Combine previous work of Issue, Rule, and Analysis to your Conclusion statement for a strong IRAC structure

IRAC - Conclusion

CHAPTER 10

DEFINE IRAC

Legal writers use the IRAC method of organization because it lays out the legal problem they are addressing into a practical, clear, and widely recognized pattern. The issue is the first element of IRAC; the issue defines the legal question and narrows the focus of the case. The rule identifies the law that controls in the case. The analysis is the heart of the IRAC document, because it applies the law to the facts of the case. The conclusion, which we will discuss in greater length here, states the results of applying the law to the case and answers the question raised in the issue.

APPLY-ISSUE

The issue crystallizes the legal question being addressed in the document. A correctly crafted issue is essential for the rest of the IRAC document. If the issue is defined correctly and narrowly, it will clarify the parameters of the legal research and will eliminate unnecessary effort. Correctly defining the issue is essential for an effective legal document. An overly vague or unfocused issue severely hampers writing an effective legal document.

APPLY-RULE

After the issue has identified the area in dispute, legal writers focus their research on the law that applies to the case. The law is comprised of several different sources. Primary law is the controlling law for the case, and it consists of constitutions, but more commonly, case law and statutes. Secondary sources of law are learned treatises and other scholarly analyses of the law, and although they are not controlling, because they are highly respected, they are persuasive.

APPLY-ANALYSIS

The analysis is the core of the IRAC document. In the analysis, legal writers describe the pertinent facts of the case in a way that demonstrates the relation of those facts to the issue they have written. Then they explain how the rule that they have found applies to the facts of the case. Sometimes, legal writers argue that the facts of their case are similar to the law, and therefore their clients should prevail. Other times, when the law seems to hurt their clients' cases, legal writers will explain in the analysis why the facts of their clients' cases are different from the situation addressed in the law, and that therefore the law should not apply to their clients' situation.

EXERCISE

As you read this chapter, fill in the worksheet below.

1. The conclusion restates the _____.

2. The conclusion _____ the question that has been raised in the Issue section.

3. The conclusion is the _____ segment in the IRAC statement.

4. The conclusion does not contain the _____ or the _____.

5. A separate _____ is written for the conclusion.

6. Is the conclusion a long or short paragraph?

7. Is new information added in the conclusion?

8. To help your case, is it acceptable to make up facts?

9. A question that you must ask yourself while writing the conclusion is, "Does your conclusion _____ _____ __ _____ raised in the issue?"

10. A second question that you must ask yourself while writing the conclusion is, "Does your conclusion give an _____ _____ of the analysis?"

■ C = CONCLUSION

The conclusion restates the issue in the affirmative or the negative. It answers the question raised in the issue based on the results you have reached through the application of the law to the facts in your analysis. It does not contain any portion of the analysis. Although the concept of the conclusion is simple, its execution often is fraught with errors. Frequently, in the course of their research and analysis, legal writers lose focus on the initial issue they framed at the beginning of the IRAC process. It is imperative, therefore, to go back and examine the issue you initially drafted. The conclusion should answer the question asked in the issue. Rarely should the conclusion include anything more that the issue restated in the affirmative or the negative.

What Are the Characteristics of the Conclusion?

The Conclusion Is

- The fourth and last segment of the IRAC structure.
- A restatement of the issue in the affirmative or negative.
- A separate paragraph.
- A short paragraph– a restatement of the issue in the affirmative or negative.
- A statement that answers the question raised in the issue based on the application of the facts of the case to the law.

Important

- Do not add new information in the conclusion.
- Do not make the mistake of including portions of your analysis in the conclusion.

Points to Ponder

What happens if:

- The conclusion does not answer the question presented in your issue?
- The reader does not know the resolution of the issue.
- Information has been added to the conclusion that belongs in the analysis?
- The analysis is incomplete and fails to adequately apply the law to the facts.
- The conclusion does not encompass all the points raised in the issue?
- Some of the issues needed to address the client's legal position are left unanswered.
- The conclusion is not an accurate representation of the analysis?
- The reader will be misled.

■ LANDLORD-TENANT

In our first fact pattern, we drafted two issues:

1. Whether a landlord of residential properties is required under law to provide hot water to the tenants of such property.
2. Whether a tenant has recourse against a landlord who refuses to provide hot water to the leased premises.

Worded in the more contemporary manner, the same issues can be stated as follows:

1. Is a landlord of residential properties required under law to provide hot water to the tenants of such property?
2. Does a tenant have recourse against a landlord who refuses to provide hot water to the leased premises?

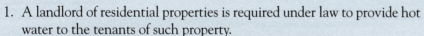

EXAMPLES OF THE CONCLUSION

1. A landlord of residential properties is required under law to provide hot water to the tenants of such property.
2. A tenant has recourse against a landlord who refuses to provide hot water to the leased premises.

Note that the above two conclusions are verbatim restatements of the issue in the affirmative. For the beginning legal writer, this is the safest way to phrase the conclusion. It allows the writer to reassess whether the analysis has addressed the question or questions raised in the issue. It accurately summarizes the results of the analysis.

The conclusion may be reworded somewhat from the issue to include specific facts ascertained in the analysis. For example, the conclusion below narrows the conclusion to Ohio law, because the rental property in question is located in Ohio, and therefore is governed by Ohio law.

EXAMPLES OF THE CONCLUSION
NARROWED TO OHIO LAW

1. A landlord in Ohio is required by law to provide hot water to tenants of residential property.

In the issue asking about whether a tenant has recourse against the landlord who refused to provide hot water, we can add more specifics to the conclusion:

2. A tenant in Ohio has several options for recourse against a landlord who refuses to provide hot water: she may deposit her rent with the court after proper notice of the problem to the landlord, she can ask the court to apply the deposited rent to the repairs, or she can terminate the lease.

Taking the same issues and stating their conclusions under Florida law, we reach the following conclusions:

EXAMPLE OF THE CONCLUSION NARROWED TO FLORIDA LAW

1. A landlord in Florida is required by law to provide hot water to tenants of residential property.

You will recall from the chapter discussing the rule that the Florida law, Fla. Stat. § 83.51, required the landlord to supply hot water to the tenant of a residential property. However, the conclusion to the second issue regarding recourse the tenant has against a landlord who refuses to provide hot water is different when we apply Florida law:

2. A tenant in Florida has recourse against a landlord who refuses to provide hot water to the leased premises: the tenant may terminate the lease if the landlord fails to repair the lack of hot water within seven days after being given written notice by certified mail.

EXERCISE

Identify which of the following are proper conclusion statements.

OHIO LAW CONCLUSIONS

1. The landlord should give the tenant hot water.
2. The tenant has the option of terminating the lease when the landlord fails to provide hot water.
3. The tenant does not have hot water. Ohio law requires the landlord to provide hot water, so he is in violation of the law. He has to provide the tenant with hot water.
4. The tenant could deposit her rent with the court, but the landlord might get nasty and retaliate against her.
5. The landlord cannot evict the tenant for depositing the rent with the court.

FLORIDA LAW CONCLUSIONS

6. The landlord should give the tenant hot water.
7. The tenant has the option of terminating the lease when the landlord fails to provide hot water.
8. The tenant does not have hot water. Florida law requires the landlord to provide hot water, so he is in violation of the law. He has to provide the tenant with hot water.
9. If the landlord tries to evict the tenant for refusing to pay rent because the landlord will not provide hot water within seven days of receiving a certified letter notifying the landlord of the problem, the tenant may pay the rent that is due to the registry of the court.
10. The tenant should quit whining and just move somewhere else. The landlord will be a problem as long as she lives there.

■ MOTOR VEHICLE ACCIDENT (MVA)

On a dark, icy morning Cherelle was driving slowly to avoid losing control of her car on the ice. A van tried to pass her, spun out of control, and hit her car. Cherelle's car was damaged beyond repair, and the van driver was cited for failure to control his vehicle. After her insurance company paid her for the value of her car, the insurance company seeks to recover that cost from the driver of the van.

The Issue for this case is:

Whether the driver of the rental van who was cited for causing an accident can be held liable for damages to the car he hit and damaged when he lost control of the van.

The applicable Ohio statutory law is:

(A) No person shall operate a motor vehicle . . . at a speed greater or less than is reasonable or proper, having due regard to the traffic, surface, and width of the street or highway and any other conditions, and no person shall drive any motor vehicle . . . in and upon any street or highway at a greater speed than will permit the person to bring it to a stop within the assured clear distance ahead.

R.C. § 4511.21 Speed limits - assured clear distance.

Applicable Ohio case law is:

Ohio case law has consistently held that a person violates the assured clear distance ahead statute if " 'there is evidence that the driver collided with an object which (1) was ahead of him in his path of travel, (2) was stationary or moving in the same direction as the driver, (3) did not suddenly appear in the driver's path, and (4) was reasonably discernible.'"

Pond v. Leslein, 72 Ohio St. 3d 50, 52, 1995-Ohio-193, 647 N.E.2d 477, 478.

EXERCISE

Use the issue and motor vehicle accident fact pattern above, and applying them to the law provided above, write the analysis for this IRAC. Then draft the conclusion for this IRAC document.

EXERCISE

Explain why the following conclusion statements are incorrect.

1. Whether the driver of the rental van who was cited for causing an accident can be held liable for damages to the car he hit and damaged when he lost control of the van.

2. The driver of the van was not liable because Cherelle's tires were bald, and that was why she was driving so slowly, not because it was icy.

3. The driver of the van did not know the road was icy, so he did not violate the statute that says a person has to drive according to the road surface. Therefore, *Pond v. Leslein*,

(continued)

72 Ohio St.3d 50, 53, 1995-Ohio-193, 647 N.E.2d 477 is not applicable in this case. Cherelle's insurance company cannot collect from him.

4. The driver of the van is appealing the ticket so Cherelle cannot prove he was at fault in the accident. Whether she was in front of him or not is his word against hers.

5. The driver of the van is not liable because it was dark, so Cherelle's car was not "reasonably discernible," and he cannot be held responsible. She will have to deal with the increase in her insurance rates when her insurance company raises them because she was in an accident that cost them a lot of money.

■ REAL ESTATE

Can Antoine, who sold a house that unbeknownst to him had significant water problems, be held liable for the buyers' damages when the house flooded?

The Issue for this case is:

1. Whether the realtor representing the seller is responsible for compensating the buyers for the damage to their home resulting from an undisclosed, hidden defect that was unknown to the realtor.

The applicable Ohio law is a summary of legal sources, statutory, code, and case law.

The sellers of the property legally were required to reveal this defect. Ohio Adm. Code 1301:5-6-10. The realtor representing those sellers "is not required to discover latent defects in the property or to advise on matters outside of the scope of the knowledge required for real estate licensure." R.C. 4735.67(B). The realtor may rely on the statements the sellers make on the disclosure form unless the realtor has a reason to doubt "question the accuracy or completeness of such statements." *Id*.

In the case *Moreland v. Ksiazek*, 8th Dist. Cuyahoga No. 83509, 2004-Ohio-2974, the buyers of a property sued the seller's realtor for failing to tell them that the garage was in poor condition. The garage in question, however, was padlocked, and the seller's realtor had never been inside the garage. The *Moreland* court held that a realtor who lackes any actual knowledge of the condition that constitutes a defect is not liable to the buyers for failing to inform them of it.

Moreland v. Ksiazek, 8th Dist. Cuyahoga No. 83509, 2004-Ohio-2974.

The applicable California law is:

The regulation requires the sellers to use ordinary care in providing information regarding defects in the property they are selling. Cal. Civil Code § 1102.4(a). Further, the law says that the realtor is not responsible for making sure the sellers were truthful on the disclosure form. Cal. Civil Code § 1102.4(a). The real estate agent must "conduct a reasonably competent and diligent visual inspection of the property offered for sale" and tell the buyers of any problems the real estate agent dicovers. Cal. Civil Code § 2079(a).

Further, the Cal. Civil Code § 1102.4(a) states that the listing agent is not "liable for any error, inaccuracy, or omission of any information delivered pursuant to this article if the error, inaccuracy, or omission was not within the personal knowledge of . . . that listing . . . agent . . . and ordinary care was exercised in obtaining and transmitting it."

EXERCISE

Use the issue and real estate fact pattern above, and applying them to the law provided above, write the analysis for this IRAC. Then draft the conclusion for this IRAC document.

EXERCISE

Compare and differentiate the following conclusion statements; which of the two is correct, and why?

OHIO LAW CONCLUSIONS

SET ONE

i. Whether the realtor representing the seller is responsible for compensating the buyers for the damage to their home resulting from an undisclosed, hidden defect that was unknown to the realtor.

ii. The realtor representing the seller is not responsible for compensating the buyers for the damage to their home resulting from an undisclosed, hidden defect that was unknown to the realtor.

SET TWO

i. The realtor representing the seller is not responsible for compensating the buyers for the damage to their home resulting from an undisclosed, hidden defect that was unknown to the realtor because he fulfilled his duties to the buyers according to the law, which states a realtor is not responsible for defects that he reasonably could not have discovered.

ii. The realtor representing the seller is responsible for compensating the buyers for the damage to their home resulting from an undisclosed, hidden defect that was unknown to the realtor.

SET THREE

i. The realtor who represented the sellers will be liable to the buyers for the undisclosed water problems with the property because the sellers are out of the country and the realtor assumes liability when the buyers cannot get payment from the sellers.

ii. The realtor who represented the sellers of a home that had a hidden, undisclosed defect is not responsible for failing to advise the buyers of latent defects that were unknown to him and which the sellers hid from both the realtor and the buyers.

CALIFORNIA LAW CONCLUSIONS

SET FOUR

i. Whether the realtor representing the seller is responsible for compensating the buyers for the damage to their home resulting from an undisclosed, hidden defect that was unknown to the realtor.

ii. The realtor representing the seller is not responsible for compensating the buyers for the damage to their home resulting from an undisclosed, hidden defect that was unknown to the realtor.

SET FIVE

i. The realtor representing the seller is not responsible for compensating the buyers for the damage to their home resulting from an undisclosed, hidden defect that was unknown to the realtor because he fulfilled his duties to the buyers according to the law, which states a realtor is not responsible for defects that he reasonably could not have discovered.

ii. The realtor representing the seller is responsible for compensating the buyers for the damage to their home resulting from an undisclosed, hidden defect that was unknown to the realtor.

(continued)

SET SIX

i. The realtor who represented the sellers will be liable to the buyers for the undisclosed water problems with the property because the sellers are out of the country and the realtor assumes liability when the buyers cannot get payment from the sellers.

ii. The realtor who represented the sellers of a home that had a hidden, undisclosed defect is not responsible for failing to advise the buyers of latent defects that were unknown to him and which the sellers hid from both the realtor and the buyers.

■ MEDICAL MALPRACTICE (MED MAL)

Dr. Jeremy Hunter has asked Brad to represent him in defending against the medical malpractice suit involving non-union of the jaw of the patient who had been hit with the baseball bat. Dr. Hunter is concerned about Dr. Patel's actions in changing his medical record.

The Issue for this case is:

1. Whether Dr. Hunter has any liability for Dr. Patel's altering of the medical record after receiving notice of the lawsuit.

The applicable Ohio case law is: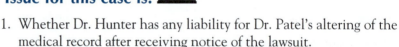

An intentional alteration, falsification or destruction of medical records by a doctor, to avoid liability for his or her medical negligence, is sufficient to show actual malice, and punitive damages may be awarded whether or not the act of altering, falsifying or destroying records directly causes compensable harm.

Moskovitz v. Mt. Sinai Med. Ctr. (1994), Ohio St.3d. 638; 635 N.E.2d 331.

The applicable Ohio statutory law is:

The [state medical] board . . . shall, to the extent permitted by law, limit, revoke, or suspend an individual's certificate to practice . . . or reprimand or place on probation the holder of a certificate for . . .

. . . .

. . . .

(18) . . . violation of any provision of a code of ethics of the American medical association . . . .

R.C. § 4731.22(B).

The applicable American Medical Association Principles of Ethics are:

II. A physician shall uphold the standards of professionalism, be honest in all professional interactions, and strive to report physicians deficient in character or competence, or engaging in fraud or deception, to appropriate entities.

III. A physician shall respect the law . . . .

EXERCISE

Use the issue and medical malpractice fact pattern above, and applying them to the law provided above, write the analysis for this IRAC. Then draft the conclusion for this IRAC document.

EXERCISE

Compare and differentiate the following conclusion statements; which of the two is correct, and why?

SET ONE

i. The resident physician is liable for the attending physician's altering of the medical record after receiving notice of the lawsuit because he wrote something irrelevant in the operative report, so she had to correct it.

ii. The resident physician does not have liability for the attending physician's altering of the medical record after receiving notice of the lawsuit.

SET TWO

i. Whether the resident physician has any liability for the attending physician's altering of the medical record after receiving notice of the lawsuit.

ii. The resident physician has no liability for the attending physician's altering of the medical record after receiving notice of the lawsuit.

SET THREE

i. Although the resident physician is not liable for the attending physician's alteration of the medical record, if questioned under oath, he is bound to tell the truth; further, the Principles of Ethics state that he should "strive to report" a doctor who has engaged "in fraud or deception."

ii. Not only is the resident physician not liable for the attending physician's alteration of the medical record, he cannot prove that she was the one who changed it and he should cover for her in case she did because his reputation among doctors would be ruined and no one would send him patients if he destroyed her career.

CONTRACT BREACH

Marcus and Brianna Johnson consulted with Brad concerning the faulty construction of their new home and Connolly Homes of Parkhurst's failure to correct the defects.

The Issue for this case is:

Whether Brianna and Marcus have recourse against the builder for defects in their newly constructed home despite the fact that the warranty has expired.

The applicable Ohio statutory law is

1. R.C. § 1312.04(A) states in pertinent part, "No owner shall commence arbitration proceedings or file a dwelling action against a residential contractor unless, at least sixty days before commencing the proceedings or filing the action, the owner provides the contractor with written notice of the

construction defect that would be the basis of the arbitration proceedings or the dwelling action. The notice shall be in writing . . . ."

2. The Consumer Safety Protection Act (CSPA), R.C. § 4722, allows the court to "award to the prevailing party a reasonable attorney's fee" under limited circumstances.

3. The Ohio Supreme Court has ruled that although construction does not have to be perfect, builders are required to build residential properties in a manner that is workmanlike and that uses ordinary care. The court found that this is a duty that the buyer cannot waive. *Jones v. Centex Homes*, 132 Ohio St.3d 1, 2012-Ohio-1001 ¶ 14.

4. A limited warranty does not preclude the owner of a residential property from recovering damages for construction that fails to meet workmanlike quality, which is implied in every construction contract. *Landis v. William Fannin Builders, Inc.*, 193 Ohio App. 3d 318, 2011-Ohio-1489, ¶29.

The applicable Virginia law is: ⚖

5. Under Virginia law, Brianna and Marcus's home qualifies as a "new dwelling." Va. Code Ann. § 55-70.1(F). "In every contract for the sale of a new dwelling, the vendor shall be held to warrant to the vendee that . . . the dwelling with all its fixtures is, to the best of the actual knowledge of the vendor or his agents" free from structural defects. Va. Code Ann. § 55-70.1(A)

6. When the vendor breaches the warranty of a newly built house, the vendee has to provide the vendor with a written notice, sent by certified or registered mail, informing the vendor that the defect exists, and the vendee has to allow the vendor "a reasonable period of time, not to exceed six months, to cure the defect that is the subject of the warranty claim." Va. Code Ann. § 55-70.1(D)

7. Although a new dwelling does not have to be flawless,, every new home has an implied warranty that it is "(i) free from structural defects, so as to pass without objection in the trade, and (ii) constructed in a workmanlike manner, so as to pass without objection in the trade." Va. Code Ann. § 55-70.1(A)

8. The statutory warranty period for new homes is one year, but if the buyer has informed the builder of the defect or defects within that one-year period, and the builder had not fixed the defects, then the buyer can file a lawsuit "against the builder within two years from the date that the buyer notified the builder of the defect." *Davis v. Tazewell Place Associates*, 254 Va. 257, 260, 492 S.E.2d 162, 164 (1997).

EXERCISE

Use the issue and breach of contract fact pattern above, and applying them to the law provided above, write the analysis for this IRAC. Then draft the conclusion for this IRAC document.

EXERCISE

Using Ohio law, revise and correct the conclusions in the following exercises based on this fact pattern.

1. Connolly Homes of Parkhurst built a home for Brianna and Marcus. When they moved in, they discovered several defects, including reversed hot and cold water faucets and non-working electrical outlets. Within a month of moving into the home, they saw water damage on the family room vaulted ceiling. The home came with a one-year warranty. That warranty expired, so Brianna and Marcus are out of luck.

2. Brianna and Marcus do not have recourse against the builder for defects in their newly constructed home because the warranty has expired.

3. Whether Brianna and Marcus have recourse against the builder for defects in their newly constructed home despite the fact that the warranty has expired.

4. Although Ohio law protects buyers from implied warranties, in this case, the warranty was express, and it has expired. Therefore, Brianna and Marcus do not have recourse against the builder for the defects in the home.

5. The fact that the one-year warranty that Connolly Homes of Parkhurst claims has expired is the only recourse Marcus and Brianna have against the company because the company clearly did not do a good enough job on the house and so Marcus and Brianna should get some of the money they paid for the house back along with having all the wiring and plumbing replaced, which means they would have to move into a hotel until the house was fully repaired so Connolly should pay for the cost of their hotel, too. A limited warranty does not preclude the owner of a residential property from recovering damages for construction that fails to meet workmanlike quality, which is implied in every construction contract. *Landis v. William Fannin Builders, Inc.*, 2011-Ohio-1489, 29.

6. Brad Smith should accept this case because his fraternity brother Marcus will not even have to pay his attorney fees under CSPA.

Using Virginia law, revise and correct the conclusions in the following exercises based on this fact pattern.

7. Connolly Homes of Parkhurst built a home for Brianna and Marcus. When they moved in, the discovered several defects, including reversed hot and cold water faucets and non-working electrical outlets. Within a month of moving into the home, they saw water damage on the family room vaulted ceiling. The home came with a one-year warranty. That warranty expired, so Brianna and Marcus are out of luck.

8. Brianna and Marcus do not have recourse against the builder for defects in their newly constructed home because the warranty has expired.

9. Whether Brianna and Marcus have recourse against the builder for defects in their newly constructed home despite the fact that the warranty has expired.

10. Although Virginia law protects buyers from implied warranties, in this case, the warranty was express, and it has expired. Therefore, Brianna and Marcus do not have recourse against the builder for the defects in the home.

11. The fact that the one-year warranty that Connolly Homes of Parkhurst claims has expired is the only recourse Marcus and Brianna have against the company because the company clearly did not do a good enough job on the house and so Marcus and Brianna should get some of the money they paid for the house back along with having all the wiring and plumbing replaced, which means they would have to move into a hotel until the house was fully repaired so Connolly should pay for the cost of their hotel too. The warranty period is two years after the buyers complained in writing and they did that less than two years ago.

12. Marcus and Brianna cannot prove that the problems result from lack of workmanlike construction, so they lose.

■ PRODUCT LIABILITY

You will recall the fraternity house's stove explosion from earlier chapters:

When they were still in college, Brad and Antoine had been fraternity brothers. During a party at their fraternity house, the gas stove in the kitchen had exploded. Although no one was hurt, the fraternity house burned to the ground, and the students who lived in the house lost their all their belongings. The fire department's investigation determined that the explosion was a result of a flaw in either the stove or the gas line to the stove.

Their attorney, Ms. Walker, had found, through her paralegal's research, that the stove they had bought at the big box store had been recalled prior to the date the fraternity brothers bought it. Although the store denied knowing about the recall, it had sold the stove at cost. The paralegal also discovered that the manufacturer of the stove had gone bankrupt and could not be sued.

The attorney had informed the paralegal that the big box store where Brad and Antoine bought the fraternity house gas stove that exploded during the party is headquartered in Texas, and it has a forum selection clause stating that all purchasers must use Texas law for litigation over products bought at its stores. The bankrupt manufacturer was headquartered in Michigan, so the attorney asked the paralegal to research both Texas and Michigan law. The attorney also noted that the Ohio CSPA law the paralegal had found for the Johnson's case against the home builder also applied to other merchandise, including "white goods" like stoves, refrigerators, washers, and dryers.

EXERCISE

Using the issue and analysis incorporating Texas law for this products liability fact pattern that you wrote in the previous chapters, draft the conclusion for this IRAC document. These assignments were the last assignments before the summary in each chapter.

EXERCISE

Using the issue and analysis incorporating Ohio law for this products liability fact pattern that you wrote in the previous chapters, draft the conclusion for this IRAC document. These assignments were the last assignments before the summary in each chapter.

EXERCISE

Using the issue and analysis incorporating Michigan law for this products liability fact pattern that you wrote in the previous chapters, draft the conclusion for this IRAC document. These assignments were the last assignments before the summary in each chapter.

SUMMARY

- The conclusion restates the issue in the affirmative or negative.

- The conclusion only summarizes the legal conclusions you have reached in your analysis.

- The conclusion does not contain any analysis; that belongs in the analysis section.

- The conclusion only answers the question presented in the issue.

- Although most conclusions merely restate the issue and answer it, occasionally the conclusion may be reworded somewhat from the issue to include specific facts ascertained in the analysis.

- New legal writers often make the mistake of including analysis in their conclusions: it is imperative that the conclusion not include analysis.

ASSIGNMENT

I. Using the issue, rule, and analysis you drafted for Assignment I at the end of the issue, rule, and analysis chapters, combine them into an IRAC document. Complete the document by drafting a correct and appropriate conclusion.

II. Using the issue, rule, and analysis you drafted for Assignment II at the end of the issue, rule, and analysis chapters, combine them into an IRAC document. Complete the document by drafting a correct and appropriate conclusion.

III. Using the issue, rule, and analysis you drafted for Assignment III at the end of the issue, rule, and analysis chapters, combine them into an IRAC document. Complete the document by drafting a correct and appropriate conclusion.

IV. Using the issue, rule, and analysis you drafted for Assignment IV at the end of the issue, rule, and analysis chapters, combine them into an IRAC document. Complete the document by drafting a correct and appropriate conclusion.

LEARNING OBJECTIVES

1. Identify the specific role that each segment serves in the IRAC structure

2. Analyze how each segment relies upon the others for correct content and flow

3. Arrange the IRAC segments in the correct order

4. Merge the four IRAC segments into a document using transitional words and phrases

5. Compose well written and well organized IRAC documents

CHAPTER 11

IRAC as a Whole

IRAC

STRATEGIES FOR WRITING IRAC

The IRAC method of organizing legal documents provides a clear and logical means of addressing legal questions and the law that applies to them. Nonetheless, approaching your first IRAC document may seem daunting. One way of approaching the task is to assess your facts. By reviewing the facts the client has presented, you can identify the area of law that applies. In earlier IRAC chapters, we saw fact patterns that included motor vehicle accidents, medical malpractice, breach of contract, and landlord-tenant problems. After you have identified the area of law involved in your case, you can craft the discrete issue that those facts raise. The issue will guide your legal research, and you will be able to draft the rule section of your IRAC document based on that. Applying the law you have found to the facts of your case will comprise the largest portion of the IRAC document, but this is the heart of the document. Finally, your analysis should guide you to your logical conclusion, which must restate the issue in the affirmative or negative.

THE IRAC STRUCTURE

The IRAC structure provides a well recognized pattern. We have addressed each IRAC section in its own chapter, but now it is time to view it as a complete whole. When you write your legal document, it will look something like this:

ISSUE: You will state your issue here.

RULE: You will provide the law, including any statutory law and case law that you have found that applies to your case. You may quote the law directly, weave it into a narrative, or paraphrase it. You will organize it logically so that it flows into your analysis.

ANALYSIS: You will summarize only the pertinent facts of the case, and then you will explain how the law you found either is similar to the facts of your case, or how the facts of your case are different, so that this law does not apply. Your analysis should be concise, but thorough. Be sure to step away from the analysis and reread it to verify that it is logical and flows smoothly.

CONCLUSION: You will restate your issue in the affirmative or negative for the conclusion. You will be sure not to include any analysis in the conclusion, and you will be sure that it squarely addresses the issue you have stated at the beginning of the document.

IRAC

I=ISSUE

R=RULE

A=ANALYSIS

C=CONCLUSION

Now that we have examined each of the elements of the IRAC structure individually, it is time to put them together into a complete document, in the way you will use them in your paralegal career. Although each discreet section of the IRAC pattern is essential, each is only as useful as the whole IRAC analysis of which it is a part.

To show how each element of the IRAC structure fits into the whole, we will take an element from each chapter and put them together. Initially, we might find that they do not flow together as well as they should, but after some revision and the addition of some transitions, they will flow smoothly.

In the analysis chapter 9, we touched on the importance of transitions. Transitions can be small, as in a one word transition like the word "however" or the word "therefore." Transitions also can be phrases, as in "on the other hand" or "as noted above." Transitions also can be full sentences, as in a topic sentence at the beginning of a new paragraph.

You will, therefore, use transitions between concepts within a paragraph, between paragraphs, and between sections of your IRAC document. Transitions not only remind us to include all the sections of the IRAC structure, but they also aid the readers in identifying the patterns in the argument and following the evolution of the discussion toward its logical and persuasive conclusion.

Assembling your document will be similar to assembling a jigsaw puzzle in some ways. Initially, the pieces of the jigsaw puzzle look like a jumble of unrelated items. Upon closer scrutiny and analysis, however, you can see where certain parts fit together. As the pieces begin to form the picture that the puzzle depicts, more and more of the pieces fit into place.

Similarly, as you begin to organize your IRAC document, you will begin to see how some of the parts fit together, and eventually you will be able to see "the big picture" that your document conveys. Also, just as a properly assembled jigsaw

Figure 11.1

puzzle is seamless when it is completed, so too, should your document flow smoothly from one section to the next (Figure 11.1). The jigsaw puzzle does not contain any holes, and your IRAC analysis should not contain any holes in its argument.

On pages 287–288 we listed some examples of introductions and transitions that might help to get you started until you have a little practice.

■ STEPS TO WRITING WITH IRAC

- Organize your thoughts
- Create an outline
- Determine your issue
- Research the law that applies to the issue
- Apply the law to the facts of your case
- State the issue as the conclusion in the affirmative or the negative
- Write the topic sentence of each segment and proceed to complete the paragraph logically
- Review your draft
- Correct grammatical and punctuation errors
- Assess your analysis with backward outlining
- Evaluate your style, legal accuracy, and flow
- Submit your IRAC statement

What Are the Characteristics of the IRAC Structure?

The IRAC Structure Is

- Always consistent
- Inherently logical
- Structurally coherent
- Easily grasped by the reader and the writer

Important

- Narrowly focus the issue for each legal question. Avoid being too broad or vague
- Specifically tailor your law to allow for a smooth flow into the analysis
- Carefully check your analysis: be sure you have applied the law to the facts of your case
- Limit your conclusion to a restatement of your issue in the affirmative or the negative

Points to Ponder

- Is my issue sufficiently focused?
- Have I crafted my issue in such a way that it addresses the true matter the case presents?
- Have I included all the pertinent law and eliminated extraneous portions that do not apply?
- Have I crafted my statement of the law to provide a smooth transition into the analysis?
- Have I thoroughly applied the law to the facts of my case?
- Have I provided a sub-conclusion to my analysis?
- Is my conclusion limited to a restatement of my issue in the affirmative or the negative?

Benefits of IRAC

- Reader can easily follow
- Reader can easily scan
- Reader knows where the key features are located
- Writer can assemble all the information systematically

■ BENEFITS OF IRAC

By perfecting your grasp on drafting persuasive IRAC documents now, you will be well prepared for your career as a paralegal. You most likely will have to provide writing samples to prospective employers, and if you have an excellent IRAC document that you have written during your paralegal courses, you will have an advantage over other applicants who have not mastered this material. Additionally, you will be able to be productive from the beginning of your career, which provides a satisfying transition from being a student.

EXERCISE

The four IRAC segments are listed at the left. In the right column are points, descriptions, and characteristics that fit in each segment. Note: Some points may apply to more than one segment. Please select all of the letters that relate to each IRAC segment. An example is provided.

EXAMPLE X:

2., 3. QUOTES STATUTORY LAW

1. ISSUE

_____ A. First segment of the IRAC structure

_____ B. Separate paragraph

_____ C. Discuss the legal rules that apply to the issue

_____ D. Third segment of the IRAC statement

_____ E. Usually the longest segment

_____ F. The number of this paragraph is unsure because of the flexibility of the analysis statement

2. RULE

_____ G. Succinct and to the point

_____ H. Gives important facts for initial formatting

_____ I. Construct an outline

_____ J. Apply the rules to the facts of the case through analytical reasoning

3. ANALYSIS

_____ K. Consider all the facts

_____ L. Apply the rules that are relevant to the issue

_____ M. Fourth segment of the IRAC statement

_____ N. Short paragraph

4. CONCLUSION

_____ O. Paragraph is generally only one sentence

_____ P. Construct a sound analysis

_____ Q. Use transitional words

_____ R. Most important paragraph

_____ S. Use thesis sentences to begin each paragraph

■ TRAFFIC VIOLATION

EXERCISE _____

Identify each IRAC section and label it in the left-hand margin next to each paragraph. Use I for Issue, R for Rule, A for Analysis, and C for Conclusion.

> Pursuant to R.C. 4511.12, a driver must obey the traffic signal unless a traffic officer directs otherwise, or unless the sign or signal is not in its proper position and legible enough for an ordinary person to observe it.

> Whether the client violated the law by running the red light.

> The client admitted that he did not see the red light because he was unfamiliar with the area and was looking at the directions on his electronic device. The statute does not, however, allow discretion when the traffic signal is clearly visible and has not been superseded by a traffic officer's direction.

> The client violated the law by running the red light.

> The law does not hold a driver liable if the traffic signal or sign is not visible.

> In this case, the driver's view of the stop sign was obscured by a bush that had grown higher than the stop sign. When the driver pointed this fact out to the officer who performed the traffic stop, the officer was not persuaded and proceeded to give the driver a ticket. Fortunately, the driver took a picture of the bush, the stop sign, and the intersection. Applying the statute, the driver should not be held liable for failing to obey a traffic sign that was not able to be seen by the ordinarily observant driver.

> The driver did not violate the traffic control device statute when he ran a stop sign that was not visible.

> Whether a driver violated the traffic control device statute by running a stop sign that was obscured by a tall bush that covered it.

Below we listed some examples of introductions and transitions for IRAC sections that might help to get you started until you have a little practice. Notice that the only transitions needed for the issue and the conclusion are the actual titles, ISSUE and CONCLUSION.

EXAMPLES OF RULE TRANSITIONS

The Ohio courts have considered the question of the legality of detaining a shoplifter . . .

When addressing the issue of a shopkeeper detaining a suspected shoplifter, one court held . . . .

A review of the controlling statute provides guidance concerning this issue . . . .

In a similar situation involving detention of a shoplifter, the court held . . .

EXAMPLES OF ANALYSIS TRANSITIONS

Although the facts in the case law above differ somewhat from those in the case at bar, these differences are not legally significant because . . . .

The situation in the case law is on all fours with that of the defendant in this case . . . .

Despite the apparent similarities between the case law and the facts in this case, they can be distinguished in several ways. First, ...

The statute expressly and clearly delineates the controlling law in this case . . . .

■ RESIDENTIAL CONSTRUCTION CONTRACT

EXERCISE

Read the fact pattern below and compose an IRAC document appropriately using transitions both between the IRAC sections and within your document.

Carol and Ricky Gardner had a new home built in North Carolina. They had saved for years to build their dream home and were very excited. They had worked closely in developing the plans and selecting the finishes for their home and yard.

The home was built on a hill, so that the front of the home was at street level, and the back of the home was one story above the back yard. Because the lot sloped down toward the back, it had a partial walk-out basement, and the family room at the back of the home was above the garage. The family room had a deck off of it with stairs to the back yard. Underneath the deck was a patio.

The garage was directly below the family room. There was a fireplace in the corner of the family room, and there was an outdoor gas grill attached to the outside of the house on the patio, sharing a chimney with the family room fireplace. This meant that the lowest portion of the chimney was in the garage.

When the builders were constructing the chimney, Carol noticed that the portion of the chimney that was in the garage had a corner that protruded into the garage. The plans called for this portion of the chimney to be flat, so that it did not compromise the space in the garage. Carol brought this problem to the attention of the foreman of the job, and she also called the home office of the builder's company. Both the foreman and the company representative assured her that the chimney would be rebuilt according to specifications.

The builder made small modifications to the chimney, but it did not construct the portion of the chimney that was in the garage in compliance with the plans. As a result, the Gardners

were able to park only one car in what the plans labeled a two-car garage.

The Gardners sued the builder, demanding that the builder tear out and reconstruct the portion of the chimney that was in the garage according to the plans, so they could park both their cars in the two-car garage. The builder claimed that the fact that the chimney encroached on the garage space did not constitute a major or a hidden defect, and therefore did not breach the implied warranty of habitability.

You, the paralegal for the Gardners' attorney, found a very similar case, *Lapierre v. Samco Development Corporation, d/b/a Americraft Builders*, 103 N.C. App. 551 406 S.E.2d 646 (1991), portions of which are quoted below:

NORTH CAROLINA CASE LAW

Defendant argues that the implied warranty of habitability applies only to "hidden, major defects which affect the 'essential utility' of the residence." Defendant contends that the plaintiffs had an opportunity to see the garage before closing and that the Lapierres should have known the size of the garage. Here, the evidence indicates that Mr. Lapierre expressed his concern to the builder about the effect of the steps extending into the garage. The salesman told him "[D]on't worry about it. We'll take care of it." Additionally, plaintiffs had no opportunity to try to park their car in the garage until after they had closed on the house. Defendant also argues that there is no allegation that the garage was "structurally unsound or unusable" . . . .

The implied warranty of habitability means both that "the dwelling, together with all its fixtures, is sufficiently free from major structural defects" and that it "is constructed in a work-manlike manner, so as to meet the standard

(continued)

of workmanlike quality then prevailing at the time and place of construction." *Hartley v. Ballou*, 286 N.C. 51, 62, 209 S.E.2d 776, 783 (1974). In *Lyon v. Ward*, 28 N.C. App. 446, 450, 221 S.E.2d 727, 729 (1976), this Court held that *Hartley* "stand[s] for the proposition that a builder-vendor impliedly warrants to the initial purchaser that a house and all its fixtures will provide the service or protection for which it was intended under normal use and conditions." Additionally, the Supreme Court has said, "The test of a breach of an implied warranty of habitability in North Carolina is not whether a fixture is an 'absolute essential utility to a dwelling house.' The test is whether there is a failure to meet the prevailing standard of workmanlike quality." *Gaito v. Auman*, 313 N.C. 243, 252, 327 S.E.2d 870, 877 (1985).

Here, plaintiffs put on evidence that the garage was not constructed in a manner that conformed to standards of workmanlike quality. Plaintiffs presented the testimony of two witnesses who were experts in residential construction. One expert testified that the standard width for a single-car garage was 12 feet of usable space excluding obstructions such as steps. The other expert testified that the stairway leading from the garage into the kitchen violated the North Carolina Building Code. The Building Code requires a minimum width of thirty-six inches for platforms at building entrances. The Lapierres' garage had a usable width of 11 feet, one inch and the stoop in the garage was only 26 and one-half inches wide. The plaintiff testified that once his car was parked in the garage, he had to pull to the back wall of the garage to have enough room to open the door and had to "squeeze" between the side of the car and the stairway to reach the kitchen. Plaintiff also testified that because the stoop was so narrow, the kitchen door could only be opened to a 60 degree angle. From this evidence, we conclude that the jury did not err when it concluded that Americraft breached the implied warranty of habitability by failing to conform to workmanlike standards in constructing the garage.

. . . .

Here, the jury found that the defendant breached the implied warranty of habitability in its construction of the . . . garage. The garage cost $ 4,500 to build and plaintiffs estimate that it will cost $ 21,477.24 to repair. Without the repairs, the garage is virtually useless for its intended purpose . . . . As to the garage . . . claim[], we cannot say that the cost of repair is disproportionately high when compared to the loss in value without the repair.

Lapierre v. Samco Development Corporation, d/b/a Americraft Builders, 103 N.C. App. 551, 555–556, 560; 406 S.E.2d 646, 648, 650–651 (1991).

EXERCISE

Read the fact pattern below and compose an IRAC document appropriately using transitions between the IRAC sections and within your document.

In addition to the problems that Carol and Ricky Gardner had with the chimney in their garage in their newly built home, which were described in the previous exercise, they also had problems with the patio underneath their deck. As noted above, the home was built on a hill, so that the front of the home was at street level, and the back of the home was one story above the back yard. Because the lot sloped down toward the back, it had a partial walk out basement, and the family room at the back of the home was above the garage. The family room had a deck off of it with stairs to the back yard. Underneath the deck was the patio.

The home had been completed in late November, so the family did not have a chance to use the deck until the following spring. When they hosted their first cookout on the patio, however, they discovered that the dimensions of the patio were much smaller than had been stated on the plans. They also realized that instead of being slate, as the plans had called for, the patio was stamped concrete. Additionally, they found that

(continued)

the patio had not been sloped properly, so that water pooled on it. Their first winter in the home had been especially severe, so the water on the patio had frozen and thawed a number of times, causing it to crack and heave. It even had a pothole in the middle of it. The patio was unusable, and when Ricky Gardner contacted the builder, the builder insisted that the patio substantially complied with the plans, and that because the patio was underneath the deck, the only way to regrade the slope would be to tear down the deck so heavy equipment could move the land, or to have workers hand dig and change the slope. With either method, the builder insisted, it would cost too much to regrade the land. The builder offered to reimburse them the $2,000 they had paid for the patio upgrade.

You, the paralegal for the Gardners' attorney, found a very similar case, *Lapierre v. Samco Development Corporation, d/b/a Americraft Builders*, 103 N.C. App. 551 406 S.E.2d 646 (1991), portions of which are quoted below:

NORTH CAROLINA CASE LAW ⚖️

[2] Defendant next argues that the trial court erred in finding that defendant had engaged in unfair and deceptive trade practices in construction of the deck. We disagree.

Defendant contends that the evidence was insufficient to establish that it had engaged in any unfair or deceptive conduct. In *Marshall v. Miller* the Supreme Court said:

Whether a trade practice is unfair or deceptive usually depends upon the facts of each case and the impact the practice has in the marketplace. A practice is unfair when it offends established public policy as well as when the practice is immoral, unethical, oppressive, unscrupulous, or substantially injurious to consumers. As also noted in *Johnson*, under Section 5 of the FTC Act, a practice is deceptive if it has the capacity or tendency to deceive; proof of actual deception is not required. . . . [S]tate courts have generally ruled that the consumer need only show that an act or practice possessed the tendency or capacity to mislead, or created the likelihood of deception, in order to prevail under the states' unfair and deceptive practices act.

Marshall v. Miller, 302 N.C. 539, 548, 276 S.E.2d 397, 403 (1981) (citations omitted in original).

Here, the evidence was sufficient to support the trial court's conclusion that defendant engaged in unfair and deceptive trade practices concerning the deck. Defendant Americraft's brochure provided a picture showing the location of the deck and gave its exact dimensions. Americraft's salesman told the plaintiff that the deck would be built according to the description in the brochure. Americraft's vice president testified that because of the location of the ash clean-out door on the chimney, it was impossible to locate the deck where the salesman and the brochure had represented that it would be built. Plaintiffs' expert witness testified that building the deck as represented would have created a fire hazard. Additionally, the model home blueprints or plans for the house indicated that the deck would be built to certain dimensions and in a certain location. Although here plaintiff did not see the plans before the lawsuit was instituted, it is not necessary to show that plaintiff was actually deceived but only that the tendency or capacity to mislead exists. *Marshall v. Miller*, 302 N.C. 539, 276 S.E.2d 397 (1981).

Here, defendant represented through its salesman, sales brochures, and blueprints that it would build the deck in a certain location and to certain dimensions. Defendant knew that it was impossible to build the deck in that location. Defendant relocated the site for the deck and built the deck smaller than represented. We think that these representations have the capacity to mislead consumers. Accordingly, we hold that the trial court did not err in finding that defendant violated G.S. 75-1.1.

[3] Next, defendant contends that the trial court erred because it did not instruct the jury to calculate damages based on diminution of fair market value. Defendant argues that it was inappropriate to instruct the jury on repair value only because here substantial destruction and waste are involved in making the repairs. We find appellant's argument unpersuasive. Plaintiffs here brought an action for unfair and deceptive trade practices under Ch. 75 and for breach of the implied warranty of habitability. We do not think that

(continued)

the trial court erred in instructing the jury on damages under either theory of recovery.

G.S. 75-16 provides:

[I]f any person shall be injured . . . such person, firm or corporation so injured shall have a right of action on account of such injury done, and if damages are assessed in such case judgment shall be rendered in favor of the plaintiff and against the defendant for treble the amount fixed by the verdict.

"An action for unfair or deceptive acts or practices is 'the creation of . . . statute. It is, therefore, sui generis. It is neither wholly tortious nor wholly contractual in nature . . . .'" *Bernard v. Central Carolina Truck Sales, Inc.*, 68 N.C. App. 228, 230, 314 S.E.2d 582, 584 (quoting *Slaney v. Westwood Auto, Inc.*, 366 Mass. 688, 704, 322 N.E.2d 768, 779 (1975)), *disc. review denied*, 311 N.C. 751, 321 S.E.2d 126 (1984). This Court has also noted that "[t]he statute merely refers to the person being 'injured' and does not state the method of measuring damages. Consequently, there is confusion as to the proper measure of damages in an unfair or deceptive act or practice case." *Id.* at 231, 314 S.E.2d at 585. The Court has also said that an action for unfair or deceptive acts or trade practices is a distinct action apart from fraud, breach of contract, or breach of warranty. Since the remedy was created partly because those remedies often were ineffective, it would be illogical to hold that only those methods of measuring damages could be used. "To rule otherwise would produce the anomalous result of recognizing that although G.S. 75-1.1 creates a cause of action broader than traditional common law actions, G.S. 75-16 limits the availability of any remedy to cases where some recovery at common law would probably also lie.

The measure of damages used should further the purpose of awarding damages which is "to restore the victim to his original condition, to give back to him that which was lost as far as it may be done by compensation in money."

Id. at 232, 314 S.E.2d at 585 (citations omitted). Here, plaintiffs were promised a ten-foot by sixteen-foot deck in the location shown on the "Mayberry" brochure and building plans. In our view, awarding plaintiffs the

cost of building the deck they bargained for puts them in their original position and "gives back to [them] that [***16] which was lost as far as it may be done by compensation in money." Accordingly, we hold that the trial court's instruction on damages for the deck was proper.

In *Griffin v. Wheeler-Leonard & Co.*, 290 N.C. 185, 225 S.E.2d 557 (1976), the Supreme Court said that where there is a breach of the implied warranty of habitability the measure of damages is either the difference between the reasonable market value of the subject property as impliedly warranted and its reasonable market value in its actual condition or the amount required to bring the property into compliance with the implied warranty. In *Kenney v. Medlin Construction and Realty Co.*, 68 N.C. App. 339, 344–45, 315 S.E.2d 311, 314–15, *disc. review denied*, 312 N.C. 83, 321 S.E.2d 896 (1984) (citations omitted), this Court said:

Our courts have adhered to the general rule that the cost of repair is the proper measure of damages unless repair would require that a substantial portion of the work completed be destroyed. In such case, the diminution in value method may be the better measure of a party's damages.

The policy underlying this general rule recognizes the need to avoid economic waste and undue hardship to the defendant contractor when, although the building substantially conforms to the contract specifications, a minor defect exists that does not substantially lower its value.

. . . . While the diminution in value method can avoid economic waste, when the cost of repair does not involve an imprudent expense, the cost of repair method may best ensure the injured party of receiving the benefit of his or her bargain, even if repair would involve destroying work already completed. When defects or omissions in construction are so major that the building does not substantially conform to the contract, then the decreased value of the building constructed justifies the high cost of repair.

Lapierre v. Samco Development Corporation, d/b/a Americraft Builders, 103 N.C. App. 551, 557–560; 406 S.E.2d 646, 649–651(1991).

The transitions from one IRAC segment to another in the following examples are italicized. Additionally, all the transitions within the examples are italicized. Notice that the use of transitions is not limited to movement between major sections, but also to assist the evolution within sections to move the narrative of the evaluation along.

■ RESTRAINT OF SHOPLIFTER

EXAMPLE

ISSUE: Is it legal in Ohio for a merchant to detain a suspected shoplifter until law enforcement officers arrive, or does such detention constitute kidnapping?

RULE: *Under certain circumstances*, restraining a person against his or her will constitutes kidnapping. The Ohio Revised Code definition of kidnapping includes using of force or threat to "restrain the liberty of the other person" for certain purposes, including for ransom, as a hostage of as a shield, for committing a felony or for fleeing after a felony, for terrorizing or inflicting serious physical harm, for engaging in non-consensual sexual activity, for obstructing a government function, or for involuntary servitude. R.C. 2905/01(A).

On the other hand, pursuant R.C. 2935.041, a store owner "who has probable cause to believe that items offered for sale . . . have been unlawfully taken by a person, may . . . detain the person in a reasonable manner for a reasonable length of time" inside the store.

ANALYSIS: Cherelle Taylor, the owner of a boutique in Parkhurst, noticed a female customer examining a bracelet that was part of a display. *Instead of returning the bracelet to the display or bringing it to the cash register for purchase*, the woman instead tucked the bracelet in her purse and began to walk toward the door of the store. Cherelle quickly stepped between the woman and the door while another clerk phoned the police. Cherelle prevented the woman from leaving, and the woman accused Cherelle of kidnapping her. The woman informed Cherelle indignantly that she worked in a law office, and she knew what Cherelle was doing was illegal. She threatened to prosecute Cherelle for kidnapping if she was not permitted to leave the store immediately. Cherelle politely informed her that all the activities that occurred in the store were video and sound recorded, and that Cherelle would be glad to provide a copy of the recording to the woman's attorney at the appropriate time.

After the police arrived and questioned the woman, she became agitated and pushed one of the officers away. At that point, the officers arrested her and took her to the police station. *During the search of her belongings at the police station*, they discovered the bracelet with the boutique's price tag and security tab still on it. The woman was charged with attempted theft and with assault on an officer.

Despite having been charged with stealing the bracelet, the woman proceeded to sue Cherelle for kidnapping. She claimed that Cherelle had forcibly blocked the doorway of the boutique, thereby restraining her by use of force.

To qualify as kidnapping, the restraining of another against her will through the use of force or threat must be done for one of the statutorily listed reasons. *To have committed the crime of kidnapping*, Cherelle would have to had restrained the woman for the purpose of collecting a ransom, using her as a hostage or a shield, committing a felony, fleeing after committing a felony, terrorizing her, inflicting serious physical harm, engaging in sexual activity against the woman's will, or keeping her for involuntary servitude. R.C. 2905/01(A). Cherelle's purpose for restraining the woman, *however*, was to prevent her from stealing a bracelet from the boutique. This purpose does not meet the requirements of the statute for qualifying as kidnapping. *Thus*, Cherelle's restraining of the woman does not meet the statutory requirements for kidnapping.

Further, a close reading of the statutory law regarding shoplifters reveals that as a merchant, Cherelle had a legal right to detain the woman until the police arrived, as long as she detained the customer "in a reasonable manner." *Since Cherelle's detention of the woman does not qualify as kidnapping under the Ohio statute*, the remaining question is whether Cherelle's manner of detaining the woman was reasonable Nothing in the record suggests that Cherelle ever actually touched the woman. *Rather*, she blocked the exit from the boutique to prevent the woman from leaving. Although the woman insisted that she had the right to leave and that Cherelle was breaking the law by restraining her, the woman was not injured or harassed in any way during the detention. *In fact*, Cherelle had been careful to treat the woman with extreme courtesy and to maintain a calm, polite tone of voice. *Therefore*, the means Cherelle used to keep the woman she suspected of trying to steal a bracelet in the store until the police arrived were reasonable.

CONCLUSION: It is legal in Ohio for a merchant to detain a suspected shoplifter until law enforcement officers arrive, or does such detention constitute kidnapping.

Students always tell us that they wish they had more time to study and practice writing IRAC structures. This chapter provides that opportunity after it gives ample examples of IRAC as applied to the fact patterns used in the IRAC formatting chapters of this book.

You will recall the dilemma of Brad and Ana's client, Sheila Kowalski, the nurse who rented an apartment that turned out to lack hot water. We have italicized the transitions in this IRAC and have italicized the transitions between sections.

■ LANDLORD-TENANT

EXAMPLE

Issue

We framed the issue in the previous issue chapter 7. Note that the issue is written in two ways; the first is the more contemporary version written in the form of a question, and the second is the traditional "whether" format.

ISSUE: Is the landlord of a residential property required to provide hot water to tenants of the property?

Or

Whether a landlord of residential properties is required under law to provide hot water to the tenants of such property.

We found the pertinent statutory rules in the previous rule chapter 8.

Florida Statute

RULE: In the State of Florida, a landlord has a statutory duty to provide the tenants of residential property with hot water:

Fla. Stat. § 83.51

(2)(a) Unless otherwise agreed in writing, . . . the landlord of a dwelling unit . . . shall, at all times during the tenancy, make reasonable provisions for:

. . . .

5. Functioning facilities for heat during winter, running water, and hot water.

Fla. Stat. § 83.55

Right of action for damages.—If either the landlord or the tenant fails to comply with the requirements of the rental agreement or this part, the aggrieved party may recover the damages caused by the noncompliance.

Fla. Stat. §83.56   Termination of rental agreement.—

(1) If the landlord materially fails to comply with s. 83.51(1) or material provisions of the rental agreement within 7 days after delivery of written notice by the tenant specifying the noncompliance and indicating the intention of the tenant to terminate the rental agreement by reason thereof, the tenant may terminate the rental agreement. If the failure to comply with s. 83.51(1) or material provisions of the rental agreement is due to causes beyond the control of the landlord and the landlord has made and continues to make every reasonable effort to correct the failure to comply, the rental agreement may be terminated or altered by the parties, as follows:

(a) If the landlord's failure to comply renders the dwelling unit untenantable and the tenant vacates, the tenant shall not be liable for rent during the period the dwelling unit remains uninhabitable.

(b) If the landlord's failure to comply does not render the dwelling unit untenantable and the tenant remains in occupancy, the rent for the period of noncompliance shall be reduced by an amount in proportion to the loss of rental value caused by the noncompliance.

. . . .

Fla. Stat. § 83.51(1). After consideration of all other relevant issues, the court shall enter appropriate judgment.

(2) In an action by the landlord for possession of a dwelling unit, if the tenant interposes any defense other than payment, the tenant shall pay into the registry of the court the accrued rent as alleged in the complaint or as determined by the court and the rent which accrues during the pendency of the proceeding, when due. The clerk shall notify the tenant of such requirement in the summons. Failure of the tenant to pay the rent into the registry of the court or to file a motion to determine the amount of rent to be paid into the registry within 5 days, excluding Saturdays, Sundays, and legal holidays, after the date of service of

process constitutes an absolute waiver of the tenant's defenses other than payment, and the landlord is entitled to an immediate default judgment for removal of the tenant with a writ of possession to issue without further notice or hearing thereon.

Analysis with Florida Law /

ANALYSIS: The tenant moved into the multi-unit complex after she signed the lease. *However*, the tenant has not had hot water in her apartment since she moved into the unit. Florida law requires the landlord "make reasonable provisions for: . . . hot water." Fla. Stat. § 83.51. The landlord admitted to the tenant that the unit she has rented does not have hot water. *Further*, the landlord has stated that he does not intend to provide hot water to that unit. *Therefore*, the landlord has violated Florida law by failing and refusing to provide hot water to the tenant.

Florida Conclusion

CONCLUSION: A landlord of residential properties is required under law to provide hot water to the tenants of such property.

EXAMPLE

Issue

We framed the issue in the issue chapter 12 earlier:

ISSUE: Is the landlord of a residential property required to provide hot water to tenants of the property?

Or

Whether a landlord of residential properties is required under law to provide hot water to the tenants of such property.

We found the pertinent statutory rules in the rule chapter earlier:

Ohio Statutory Law

RULE: *The State of Ohio provides clear guidance regarding the provision of hot water to tenants of residential property.* The controlling law states,

(A) A landlord who is a party to a rental agreement shall do all of the following:

. . . . .

(6) Supply running water, reasonable amounts of hot water, and reasonable heat at all times . . . .

R.C. § 5321.04

Then we found case law that interpreted the statute:

Ohio Case Law

In interpreting the landlord's duty to provide basic services to residential tenants, one Ohio court held:

The Court held that failing to provide "air conditioning breaches the landlord's duty under R.C. 5321.04 and warrants damages." *Gammarino v. Smith*, 1st Dist. Hamilton No. C-060636, 2007-Ohio-4073, ¶ 34.

We analyzed how the rule applied to the facts of Sheila's case:

Analysis With Ohio Law

ANALYSIS: *After the tenant signed the lease and moved into her apartment,* she discovered that the unit did not have hot water. *Despite the tenant's conversations with the landlord requesting hot water,* he has refused to provide it. The tenant has several statutorily provided options for dealing with this situation. Pursuant to R.C. 5321.07, the tenant must give the landlord written notice of the defect and allow "a reasonable time considering the severity of the condition and the time necessary to remedy it," not exceeding thirty days. R.C. 5321.07(B)

Ohio courts have applied this statute in cases, including *Gammarino v. Smith*, 1st Dist. Hamilton No. C-060636, 2007-Ohio-4073. *In Gammarino,* the Court held that the landlord breached its duty to the tenant by failing to provide conditioning. In this case, the tenant lacks an even more basic necessity: hot water. Just as the *Gammarino* court found the failure to provide air conditioning a violation of the statute, so too here, the failure to provide hot water is a clear violation of the statute.Finally, we drafted a conclusion:

Ohio Conclusion

CONCLUSION: A landlord of residential properties is required under law to provide hot water to the tenants of such property.

■ FOOD POISONING

EXERCISE

Read the fact pattern below and compose an IRAC document appropriately using transitions between the IRAC sections and within your document.

Brianna and Marcus Johnson celebrated their first wedding anniversary by dining at Parkhurst's finest restaurant, the Pinnacle. The lighting was low, and although Brianna noted that her chicken cordon bleu was chewier than she expected, it was not until she had nearly finished it that she realized it was undercooked. Marcus reported the problem to the server, but because this was a celebration, he did not wish to make a scene complaining to the manager.

Two days later, Brianna developed a high fever, severe gastrointestinal symptoms including bleeding, and significant light-headedness. Marcus took her to the emergency department at Parkhurst Hospital, and laboratory tests confirmed that she had Campylobacter, a food-borne bacterial infection commonly transmitted through undercooked chicken. Brianna was hospitalized for a week, receiving several powerful intravenous antibiotics.

Marcus telephoned to speak to the manager at the Pinnacle, but instead his call was returned by the Pinnacle's insurance company. Because Marcus and his family had patronized this restaurant for several decades, Marcus was offended by the manager's lack of concern and communication.

(*continued*)

OHIO STATUTORY LAW

The director of agriculture and the director of health have the exclusive power in this state to adopt rules regarding retail food establishments and food service operations. The rules adopted under this chapter shall be applied uniformly throughout this state.

R.C. § 3717.04, **Rules regarding retail food establishments and food service operations**

Ohio's directors of agriculture and of health are mandated by R.C. § 3717.05(A) to establish an "Ohio uniform food safety code, which shall be used by the licensors of retail food establishments and food service operations in ensuring the safe handling of food in this state."

The Ohio Administrative Code, Ohio Adm.Code 3717-1-03.3(A)(1)(c), addressing preparation of raw meats for public consumption, states,

. . . raw animal foods such as eggs, fish, meat, poultry, and foods containing these raw animal foods, shall be cooked to heat all parts of the food to a temperature and for a time that complies with one of the following methods based on the food that is being cooked: . . . One-hundred sixty-five degrees Fahrenheit (seventy-four degrees Celsius) or above for fifteen seconds for poultry . . . .

■ ANIMAL OWNER'S LIABILITY

EXERCISE

Read the fact pattern below and compose an IRAC document appropriately using transitions between the IRAC sections and within your document. Use the law of whichever state, Connecticut or Ohio, your instructor prefers.

One Sunday, as Antoine was preparing to hold an open house for one of his fellow realtors, he parked his car across the street from the home, so that prospective buyers could park freely in the short driveway. Suddenly, he felt a stabbing pain in his leg and heard growling. He looked down to see a large dog's jaws clamped on his leg and blood running down his pants. A man ran over from the home's driveway and struck the dog in the head.

The man apologized and explained that he thought his wife had put the dog in the car already. The man informed Antoine that the family was planning to visit family in Connecticut, and that they had planned to be out of the house before the realtor arrived for the open house. The man then took the dog, got in his car, and drove away.

Realizing that he needed medical attention, Antoine phoned the realty office and arranged for another realtor to handle the open house. He then drove himself to the Emergency Department of Parkhurst Hospital, where the physician asked him about the current location of the dog that had bit him. Antoine explained what the owner had told him, and the physician became perturbed.

"The law requires a dog that bit a person to be quarantined for fourteen days!" the doctor exclaimed. Within minutes, a police officer entered the cubicle where Antoine was sitting and began to question him. Antoine provided the officer with all the information then he had, and the he asked the officer whether it really was illegal for the owner to prevent the dog from being quarantined. The officer confirmed that it was illegal. After receiving treatment and being instructed to follow up with his personal physician the next day, Antoine went home and called his friend Brad Smith, the attorney. Brad found the statute on his computer:

(continued)

CONNECTICUT STATUTE ⚖

(c) If such officer finds that the complainant has been bitten or attacked by such dog, cat or other animal when the complainant was not upon the premises of the owner or keeper of such dog, cat or other animal the officer shall quarantine such dog, cat or other animal in a public pound or order the owner or keeper to quarantine it in a veterinary hospital, kennel or other building or enclosure approved by the commissioner for such purpose. When any dog, cat or other animal has bitten a person on the premises of the owner or keeper of such dog, cat or other animal, the Chief Animal Control Officer, any animal control officer, any municipal animal control officer or regional animal control officer may quarantine such dog, cat or other animal on the premises of the owner or keeper of such dog, cat or other animal. The commissioner, the Chief Animal Control Officer, any animal control officer, any municipal animal control officer or any regional animal control officer may make any order concerning the restraint or disposal of any biting dog, cat or other animal as the commissioner or such officer deems necessary. Notice of any such order shall be given to the person bitten by such dog, cat or other animal within twenty-four hours. The owner of such animal shall pay all fees as set forth in section 22–333. On the fourteenth day of such quarantine the dog, cat or other animal shall be examined by the commissioner or someone designated by the commissioner to determine whether such quarantine shall be continued or removed. Whenever any quarantine is ordered under the provisions of this section, notice thereof shall be given to the commissioner and to the person bitten or attacked by such dog, cat or other animal within twenty-four hours. Any owner or keeper of such dog, cat or other animal who fails to comply with such order shall be fined not more than two hundred fifty dollars or imprisoned not more than thirty days or both.

Conn. Gen. Stat. § 22–358 (2012).

OHIO STATUTE ⚖

(A) (1) No person shall remove a dog that has bitten any person from the county in which the bite occurred until a quarantine period as specified in division (B) of this section has been completed.

. . . .

(B) The quarantine period for a dog that has bitten any person shall be ten days or another period that the board of health for the district in which the bite occurred determines is necessary to observe the dog for rabies.

R.C. § 955.261

▪ NEGLIGENT ENTRUSTMENT 🏛

EXERCISE

Read the fact pattern below and compose an IRAC document appropriately using transitions between the IRAC sections and within your document. Use the law of the state, either Ohio or Indiana, that your instructor prefers.

Tommy Williams was in his apartment watching a football game with his father one Sunday afternoon. Tommy's father, Mr. Williams, had encountered various legal problems in the past, and currently was under a driving suspension for driving while intoxicated. At half time, Tommy went into the kitchen to make them both a sandwich. When he returned to the living room, his father was gone. Although

(continued)

Tommy was annoyed, he was not surprised. His father had a habit of disappearing unexpectedly, and Tommy had gotten used to it. Because his father lived just around the block, Tommy assumed he had gone home to get a drink of alcohol, which he knew Tommy would not give him.

After the game had ended and Tommy's father had not returned, Tommy sighed. He suspected that his father had indulged a bit more than he intended and was unable to navigate his way back to Tommy's apartment. Later that evening, Tommy received a phone call from the police, who informed him that his father had been in an automobile accident in the neighboring state of Indiana. "He's not allowed to drive!" Tommy responded. "I disabled his car and took his keys so that he couldn't drive." The officer then informed Tommy that the car that had been destroyed in Mr. Williams' accident was Tommy's. The officer also told Tommy that a passenger in the car was in critical condition in an Indiana hospital. Tommy sunk into a chair and put his head in his hands. He called Brad and asked him what the legal ramifications of this situation were. Because the accident occurred in Indiana, Brad researched both Ohio and Indiana law.

Brad again did an Internet search and found this:

OHIO STATUTE

(A) No person shall permit a motor vehicle owned by the person or under the person's control to be driven by another if any of the following apply:

(1) The offender knows or has reasonable cause to believe that the other person does not have a valid driver's or commercial driver's license or permit or valid nonresident driving privileges.

(2) The offender knows or has reasonable cause to believe that the other person's driver's or commercial driver's license or permit or nonresident operating privileges have been suspended or canceled under Chapter 4510. or any other provision of the Revised Code.

R.C. § 4511.203

INDIANA CASE LAW

The Indiana Court of Appeals held:

In order to support a claim of negligent entrustment regarding a vehicle, a plaintiff must demonstrate that another: "(1) entrusted her car; (2) to an incapacitated person or one who is incapable of using due care; (3) with actual and specific knowledge that the person is incapacitated or incapable of using due care at the time of the entrustment; (4) proximate cause; and (5) damages." *Davidson v. Bailey*, 826 N.E.2d 80, 88 (Ind.Ct.App.2005).

. . . .

. . . . Indiana does not recognize a cause of action for negligent entrustment brought by a voluntarily intoxicated adult entrustee, and . . . even if it did; the evidence in this case is insufficient to support a finding that [the car's owner] actually knew Bailey was incapacitated, we necessarily conclude that the trial court did not abuse its discretion in denying Bailey's motion to conform the pleadings to the evidence.

Bailey v. State Farm Mutual Automobile Insurance Company, 881 N.E.2d 996, 1001, 1005 (2008).

To recap, IRAC is a method of structured legal writing that allows for logical development of the analysis of a legal issue. It provides a framework for concisely summarizing the legal issue, spelling out the applicable law, and applying that law to the facts of the situation.

Some tips for making your IRAC writing as effective as possible include creating a smooth flow to your writing. You can do this by presenting the information in a logical, often chronological, way. It is also important to be clear and concise, to vary your sentence lengths, to have strong sentence structure, to choose your words carefully and precisely, and to use appropriate transitional words and phrases. It is especially important to proofread your work, preferably after stepping away from it for a period of time.

The steps to writing an IRAC analysis begin with formulating the issue in the case, then determining what the applicable law is, and applying that law to your facts. Remember to organize your thoughts and outline your material. Be aware that after you have worked with applying the law to your facts, the thesis sentence may change.

After you have organized your material through an outline, you will proceed to complete the paragraphs sequentially. Clearly, you cannot write the analysis section of the IRAC until you know what the applicable law is. You cannot research the law until you know what the issue is that you need to research. Focusing your issue to pinpoint accuracy is essential for you to write an effective IRAC analysis. Once you have determined the issue, you progress to researching the law that applies and ensuring that it is still in effect and fits the issue. (You will learn more about this in your legal research class.) Only then can you apply the facts of your case to the law you have found and either draw the necessary parallels or distinguish the law from the facts of your case.

After you have written your first draft, step away from it, if only to get a drink of water. Then proofread your draft, correcting grammatical and punctuation errors as you proceed. Construct a backward outline of the writing to be sure that it accomplishes your aim. Then proofread the draft again, this time for style and flow. Finally, your IRAC analysis is ready to submit.

Although you may be tempted to try to take shortcuts in your legal analysis, you will find that IRAC is the most workable system for legal writing: it is easy to follow and easy to scan quickly, both of which are important for the attorney. The reader knows where to locate the key features, and it provides you, the writer, with a predetermined system for assembling your information.

SUMMARY

- The IRAC structure is a widely used format for legal analysis.

- IRAC provides writers with a framework for determining the legal issue presented to them, establishing the law that applies to the issue presented by the client's case, and applying that law to the unique facts of their client's case.

- A well-written analysis, one that explains how the law supports the client's case and that distinguishes law that does not support the client's case, is one of the most persuasive tools in the legal writer's inventory.

- Writing in the IRAC format forces writers to narrow their focus, sift through the facts of their client's case to sort out the legally pertinent facts of the case, and logically and cohesively examine and articulate how the law applies to those facts.

- The logical approach that IRAC provides allows writers to complete sound legal reasoning that is lucid and coherent.

ASSIGNMENTS

I. Read the fact pattern below and compose an IRAC document appropriately using transitions between the IRAC sections and within your document.

After Antoine had been bitten by the dog at the home where he was trying to hold an open house, the doctor in the Emergency Department treated him. Additionally, Antoine had to see his own doctor the next day, and his injuries prevented him from working for two weeks. As a realtor, Antoine was dependent on his ability to show and sell houses for his income. Additionally, he had to replace the suit he had been wearing, because the dog had torn it when it bit Antoine. Finally, Antoine had received medical bills for his Emergency Department treatment and his doctor's visit. Antoine asked Brad whether he could sue the dog's owner for his monetary losses.

Brad was researching the law when he found this case:

OHIO CASE LAW

Ohio Supreme Court interpreted the statute and held, "in an action for damages under R.C. 955.28, the plaintiff must prove (1) ownership or keepership [or harborship] of the dog, (2) that the dog's actions were the proximate cause of the injury, and (3) the damages." *Beckett v. Warren*, 124 Ohio St. 3d 256, 2010-Ohio-4, 921 N.E.2d 624, ¶ 11.

II. Read the fact pattern below and compose an IRAC document appropriately using transitions between the IRAC sections and within your document.

At the time that Mr. Williams crashed Tommy's car, his blood alcohol was well over the legal limit for driving. The officer arrested him, but Mr. Williams complained that the officer had no right to charge him. Mr. Williams insisted that it was his right to drive a car regardless of whether he had been drinking or not.

Brad knew the Ohio law on this subject: R.C. § 4511.19, Operating vehicle under the influence of alcohol or drugs – OVI, states in pertinent part:

(A)(1) No person shall operate any vehicle, streetcar, or trackless trolley within this state, if, at the time of the operation, any of the following apply:

(a.) The person is under the influence of alcohol, a drug of abuse, or a combination of them.

Because Mr. Williams was arrested in Indiana, though, Brad also researched the statute for Indiana.

INDIANA STATUTE

(a) A person who causes serious bodily injury to another person when operating a motor vehicle:

(1) with an alcohol concentration equivalent to at least eight-hundredths (0.08) gram of alcohol per:

(A) one hundred (100) milliliters of the person's blood; or

(B) two hundred ten (210) liters of the person's breath;

(2) with a controlled substance listed in schedule I or II of IC 35-48-2 or its metabolite in the person's body; or

(3) while intoxicated;

commits a Class D felony. However, the offense is a Class C felony if the person has a previous conviction of operating while intoxicated within the five (5) years preceding the commission of the offense.

(b) A person who violates subsection (a) commits a separate offense for each person whose serious bodily injury is caused by the violation of subsection (a).

(c) It is a defense under subsection (a)(2) that the accused person consumed the controlled substance under a valid prescription or order of a practitioner (as defined in IC 35-48-1) who acted in the course of the practitioner's professional practice.

Ind. Code § 9-30-5-4 (2004).

III. Read the fact pattern below and compose an IRAC document appropriately using transitions between the IRAC sections and within your document.

When Tommy's father was in the motor vehicle accident with Tommy's car, the driver of the car Mr. Williams hit was injured. He sued Tommy for negligent entrustment, that is, allowing Mr. Williams to drive his car when Mr. Williams had a suspended license. Brad checked the case law for rulings on the liability of owners whose cars were used without their knowledge. Because the accident had occurred in Indiana, he also considered the Indiana case law quoted below the Ohio case.

OHIO CASE LAW

Although the case he found was not as current as he wanted, Brad did find *Brown v. Harrison*, No. 23108, 9th Dist. Summit No. 2006-Ohio-6231, in which the Court had held that

{¶6} To prevail on a claim of negligent entrustment, a party must establish that the owner of the vehicle "knowingly, either through actual knowledge or through knowledge implied from known facts and circumstances, entrusts its operation to an inexperienced or incompetent operator whose negligent operation results in the injury." *Pfund v. Ciesielczyk* (1992), 84 Ohio App.3d 159, 163–64, quoting *Gulla v. Straus* (1950), 154 Ohio St. 193, 193–194 at paragraph three of the syllabus. Further, "[i]n an action against the owner of a motor vehicle for injury arising from its entrustment for operation, the burden is upon the plaintiff to establish that the motor vehicle was driven with the permission and authority of the owner; that the entrustee was in fact an incompetent driver; and that the owner knew at the time of the entrustment that the entrustee had no driver's license, or that he was incompetent or unqualified to operate the vehicle, or had knowledge of such facts and circumstances as would imply knowledge on the part of the owner of such incompetency." *Gulla*, 154 Ohio St. 193, at paragraph five of the syllabus.

Id. at ¶ 6.

INDIANA CASE LAW

The Indiana Court of Appeals held:

In order to support a claim of negligent entrustment regarding a vehicle, a plaintiff must demonstrate that another: "(1) entrusted her car; (2) to an incapacitated person or one who is incapable of using due care; (3) with actual and specific knowledge that the person is incapacitated or incapable of using due care at the time of the entrustment; (4) proximate cause; and (5) damages." *Davidson v. Bailey*, 826 N.E.2d 80, 88 (Ind.Ct.App.2005).

. . . .

. . . . Indiana does not recognize a cause of action for negligent entrustment brought by a voluntarily intoxicated adult entrustee, and . . . even if it did; the evidence in this case is insufficient to support a finding that [the car's owner] actually knew Bailey was incapacitated, we necessarily conclude that the trial court did not abuse its discretion in denying Bailey's motion to conform the pleadings to the evidence.

Bailey v. State Farm Mutual Automobile Insurance Company 881 N.E.2d 996, 1001, 1005 (2008).

IV. Read the fact pattern below and compose an IRAC document appropriately using transitions between the IRAC sections and within your document.

Cherelle made an appointment to consult with Brad to defend her in a lawsuit that had been filed against her by a customer of her boutique. Because both Brad and Ana were in trial, Cherelle spoke with Pat, their paralegal.

"I received this Complaint in the mail yesterday. I remember this customer; she had parked in the lot that I rent behind the boutique. She came in and shopped. She told me she was doing the last of her Christmas shopping, and we talked about how it looked like we weren't going to have a white Christmas. While she was shopping, it began to rain. The temperature dropped suddenly, as it does sometimes here in Ohio, and the rain froze. It could not have been raining long, because one of my regular customers had come in about five minutes before this customer left. My regular customer said she had heard a weather forecast on the radio saying the temperature was supposed to drop. My regular customer was dry, so I know it was not raining when she came in.

"Anyway, when the customer who filed this lawsuit left, she must have slipped on ice from the freezing rain. We heard her shouting, and we called an ambulance right away. I heard later that the customer had broken her hip and spent Christmas in the hospital. I felt bad for her and sent her flowers.

"This Complaint seems to say that I was negligent in not putting salt on the parking lot when I knew it was going to get cold. But I didn't know it was going to rain, and anyway, I could not have had time to put salt down between the time the freezing rain began and the time she fell. I hope you guys can help me here."

After the interview was over and Cherelle had left, Pat did some research on this subject. She found the following case, *Allen v. USA Parking Sys.* 7th Dist. Mahoning No. 10 MA 175 2011-Ohio-6642:

OHIO CASE LAW

> {¶ 2} Allen fell on a natural accumulation of ice caused by the freeze and thaw cycle due to temperature change. The record contains no evidence that USA Parking did anything to cause an unnatural accumulation of ice to form. Further, there is no evidence in the record that Allen fell on loose concrete; this argument is mere speculation. Finally, Allen knew that the lot was sloped and that snow can melt and refreeze into ice in wintertime. The condition of the lot was an open and obvious danger such that USA Parking owed no duty to warn Allen of it. Accordingly, the judgment of the trial court is affirmed.

Id. at ¶ 2.

V. Read the fact pattern below and compose an IRAC document appropriately using transitions between the IRAC sections and within your document. When applying the Montana law, you will find that

the law does not provide you with an easy analysis. Nonetheless, a well-crafted analysis can minimize points that weaken the argument and expound on those that strengthen it.

Because Brad was busy in court, he asked Pat to continue to research the issue of negligent entrustment of an automobile. By coincidence, a client had come in requesting Brad's representation in a case involving the client's teenaged son. The client had been so upset with the situation that he was unclear regarding whether the accident had occurred in Ohio or in Montana, where his son was in going to school, but what was clear was that the client had allowed his son to use the family car to take his girlfriend to a school dance, even though the son's driver's license had been suspended. The son had gotten several speeding tickets, and he had lost his license after he had hit a fire hydrant because he was looking at his electronic device while he was driving and missed a curve in the road. The son was allowed to drive to his part-time job after school, but he was not allowed to drive to school or for any personal activities.

The father had been strict with the son regarding restricting his driving only to his part time job, but the suspension was scheduled to end a week after the dance, so the father relented and allowed the son to use the car. The father did not realize that the son and his friends would consume alcohol, so when the police officer arrived at the father's door and asked him to come down to the police station, the father was shocked to learn that his son had been arrested for driving under the influence of alcohol. It was not until the father arrived at the police station that he learned that his son had totaled not only his own car, but also had totaled an expensive Corvette that had been loaned to another student for the dance.

Now the owner of the Corvette was suing the client, the father of the student with the suspended license, for the damages to the expensive sports car. The client is concerned to know what his responsibility in this situation is.

After Pat had researched the Ohio law and found a similar case, Brad asked her to also research the law in Montana, so he could be prepared in case the client had meant that the accident occurred there.

OHIO CASE LAW

> {¶ 19} In Gulla v. Straus (1950), 154 Ohio St. 193, 198, 93 N.E.2d 662, the Ohio

Supreme Court set forth the elements of negligent entrustment: "It is a well settled rule of law that the owner of a motor vehicle may be held liable for an injury to a third person resulting from the operation of the vehicle by an inexperienced or incompetent driver, upon the ground of negligence, if the owner knowingly, either through actual knowledge or through knowledge implied from known facts and circumstances, entrusts its operation to such a driver."

. . .

{¶ 23} At the time of the accident, Mustafa was 20 years old and driving under a suspended license. This was his second driving license suspension. Prior to the accident, Mustafa had multiple speeding tickets and other driving infractions, including a conviction for operating a motor vehicle while intoxicated. Abe testified that he knew about his son's "traffic problems," including the license suspensions.

Page 9

{¶ 24} As a result of the accident, Mustafa was cited for speeding and driving under a suspended license. Westlake Police Officer Keenan Cook testified that at the scene of the accident, Mustafa stated that he had been driving 45 miles per hour. The speed limit in this area is 35 miles per hour. Officer Cook's "Traffic Crash Report" from the accident states that "witnesses stated [Mustafa] was traveling at a high rate of speed [and] struck [Gereby's car], sending it approximately 83 ft. east."

. . . .

{¶ 25} One eyewitness testified that she saw Mustafa "traveling extremely fast" on Center Ridge Road, then heard the impact of the accident seconds later. A second eyewitness testified that she was stopped in traffic on Center Ridge Road when she heard Mustafa's car "coming behind me going very fast." She saw Gereby's car trying to turn left, and thought that because Mustafa was driving so fast, Gereby would not be able to see him coming. She then saw Mustafa's car hit Gereby's car. Asked how fast Mustafa was driving, this witness testified, "I mean, he was going very fast. I would say he was

going highway speeds because I could hear him behind me before he ever even passed me. I could hear the noise of him coming."

{¶ 26} It is undisputed that the car was in Abe's name at the time of the accident. As to whether Abe gave Mustafa permission to use the car, Abe testified at trial as follows:

{¶ 27} "Q: And regarding the automobile, he was driving — he drove that car as well as you did. Whenever he needed this car, he drove the car, correct?

Page 10

{¶ 28} A: No, sir.

{¶ 29} Q: Do you remember my taking your deposition on August 21, 2008 when you came to my office with Mr. McGown, and I asked you a series of questions?

{¶ 30} A: Yes, sir.

{¶ 31} Q: Okay. And I asked you the question, line 16: And how was it that your son happened to be driving the car that night?

{¶ 32} Your answer: He drove the car as well as I did. Whoever needed the car drove the car, period.

{¶ 33} Correct, sir?

{¶ 34} A: Yes, sir. Not without my permission, though. See, sir, it was his car. I put it in my name so I can control him. I can't take his license away.

{¶ 35} THE COURT: Wail 'til the next question.

{¶ 36} THE WITNESS: Yes, sir.

{¶ 37} Q: Mr. Ayad, you know at the time this accident happened that your son had received some speeding tickets before the accident?

{¶ 38} A: That's why the car was in my name, yes, sir."

{¶ 39} Abe's trial testimony was inconsistent with his prior statement that Mustafa routinely drove the car as needed. This prior statement is an admission by a party opponent and is allowed as evidence at trial. Evid. R. 801(D)(2). In addition, Gereby presented evidence that during Mustafa's June 2, 2008

Page 11

deposition, Mustafa stated that his father owned the car that was involved in the accident, but that he typically drove the vehicle with his father's permission.

{¶ 40} This evidence is sufficient to show that Mustafa was an incompetent driver; Abe knew of his son's incompetence; Abe allowed Mustafa to drive the car; and Mustafa was driving negligently — if not recklessly — when he hit Gereby's car. As these are the elements that Gereby must show to succeed on her negligent entrustment claim, we find no error in the court's denial of Abe's motion for a directed verdict.

. . . .

{¶ 66} Additionally, there is ample evidence in the record to show that Mustafa was negligent when he hit Gereby's car, including: his admission that he was driving ten miles over the posted speed limit; that his driver's license was suspended at the time of the accident; that he received traffic citations for speeding and driving under a suspended license at the scene of the accident; and the testimony of two witnesses who saw and heard him driving extremely fast when he crashed into Gereby's car.

{¶ 67} Accordingly, there is competent, credible evidence in the record to prove the elements of negligent entrustment, thus the judgment is not against the manifest weight of the evidence. Abe's third assignment of error is overruled.

Ayad v. Gereby, 8th Dist. Cuyahoga No. 92541, 2010-Ohio-1415.

MONTANA CASE LAW

¶ 16 Generally, a parent is not liable for the tortious acts of his or her child, except under limited statutory circumstances. *Crisafulli v. Bass*, 2001 MT 316, ¶ 16, 308 Mont. 40, 38 P.3d 842. That said, a parent can be liable, *not for the tortious acts of his or her child*, but for the parent's *own* failure to exercise reasonable care. *Crisafulli*, ¶¶ 22, 27 (emphasis added). In other words, the parent is not liable for the alleged tortious act of the child— negligent entrustment is a standalone tortious act of the parent. For liability to be imposed under this limited circumstance, the parent must (1) "know that he or she has the ability to control the child[;]" (2) "the parent understands the necessity for doing so[;]" and (3) the parent's failure to exercise reasonable care "under these circumstances create[s] an *unreasonable* risk of harm to a third person." *Crisafulli*, ¶ 22 (emphasis in original).

¶ 17 negligent entrustment requires more than simply allowing a young person to 1234*1234 operate a vehicle. *McGinnis v. Hand*, 1999 MT 9, ¶ 29, 293 Mont. 72, 972 P.2d 1126; *Smith v. Babcock*, 157 Mont. 81, 88–89, 482 P.2d 1014, 1018 (1971). In *McGinnis*, we concluded that even evidence showing that a driver was "underage for driving purposes or that she was not licensed to drive" would "be insufficient[,]" without more, "to establish lack of competence" as a reasonable and prudent driver. *McGinnis*, ¶ 29.

Styren Farms, Inc. v. Roos, 2011 Mont. 299, 265 P. 3d 1230, 1233–1234, (2011).

LEARNING OBJECTIVES

1. Identify when a case presents multiple issues

2. Outline future document for multiple issues

3. Insert relevant facts of the case into outline format

4. Arrange facts of the case using smooth transitions between multiple IRAC sections

5. Write a logically organized, concise, fluid document with multiple IRAC sections

6. Revise the multiple IRAC document to ensure an effective, excellent document

IRAC - Multiple Issues

CHAPTER 12

■ OTHER IRAC FORMATS

We have discussed the standard IRAC formula, but you need to be aware of some variations that exist. One is IFRAC: I = Issue, F = Fact, R = Rule, A = Analysis, C = Conclusion. In this version of the formula, the added fact section, the "F," summarizes the facts of the case that is being addressed before discussing the applicable law.

Another variation on the IRAC formula is ICRA: is I = Issue, C = Conclusion, R = Rule, and A = Analysis. This format provides the final answer to the analysis up front so that the reader knows in advance what the final conclusion is. If the reader wants only the question and the answer, this saves time. The reader then can go on to read the rest of the document if desired.

■ MULTIPLE ISSUES FORMAT OF IRAC

Many legal situations contain more than one issue, and you will have to write memoranda and briefs that address each of the issues in the case. Although this may sound challenging, addressing multiple issues simply requires writing individual IRAC analyses for each issue. As always, outlining provides you with the framework you need to organize and prioritize your questions and your material.

First, determine what issues the facts of your case present. A simple set of columns with headings for different issues might help you to organize the facts. Keep in mind that some facts will relate to more than one issue, so you will need to place those facts in as many columns as are appropriate.

After you have sorted the relevant facts into the various issues, draft an issue for each of the columns. Once you have drafted the issues, assess the most effective order for addressing them in your document. Be aware that your research may cause you to rethink this initial order, and if it does, you will need to be flexible and rearrange the different issues.

You almost certainly will be working on a computer, so you might organize your files with the case itself being the primary file, and each issue having its own subfile within the case's file. These individual issue subfiles will have their own subfiles, including the files for the law, the drafts of the issue, and the drafts of the analysis.

A hard-learned lesson we would like to pass on to you is this: when you name your documents, always date them, so you know which is the most recent version. If you have several versions throughout the day, name them with the time that you stopped working on them.

As you research the law, you may find that a case addresses more than one of your issues. Either label this case carefully with the issues it addresses, or save it into each of the subfiles that address the issues contained in the case. While this may seem excessive, if you do not do this, you often will find yourself searching your computer for a case you know you have seen but cannot locate.

Once you have completed your research, briefly review it and decide whether your initial order of addressing the issues is still the best approach. If it is, you can move on to the next step. If it is not, carefully consider the most effective way to organize the document.

Once you have determined the order in which you plan to address your issues, outline each section of the document. Include the various legal citations and the order in which you plan to cite them. Then reassess the issues you have drafted and make sure they still state the question accurately and concisely.

Only after you have performed these steps are you ready to begin drafting the document. For the sake of clarity, address each issue and its corresponding law individually. Before you move from your first IRAC section to the next, however, determine how you plan to transition from one legal concept to the next. Your document should flow from idea to idea.

Repeat these steps for the remaining issues, and then step away from the document. Go to lunch, go home if it is the end of the day, or at least walk down the hall for a drink of water.

Then approach your document with a fresh eye, and study it to see whether it is clear, it flows smoothly, and it makes the point you want it to make. After you have proofread the document, revise it and make any necessary changes. If you have the luxury of time, repeat these last two steps.

It is important for the attorney for whom you work to know that your writing is thorough, organized, and clear. The better writer you are, the better paralegal you will be. Writing is the heart of the paralegal's job.

Mirroring

Whichever format you use, you must remain consistent and use the same format for each individual IRAC section in your document. This format is known as mirroring. Thus, if you decide to use the IFRAC format and include the facts of your case before the rule, you must repeat that format for each issue you address in your document. Clearly, you would not need to repeat all the facts for each analysis, but you would need to include the facts that pertained to that issue. At the beginning, however, you would have to include all the pertinent facts to provide the reader with sufficient information to understand each analysis and the interrelationship among them.

EXAMPLE ONE OF IRAC FORMAT FOR MULTIPLE ISSUES

First format

Issue 1:

Rule 1:

Analysis 1:

Conclusion 1:

Issue 2:

Rule 2:

Analysis 2:

Conclusion 2:

Issue 3:

Rule 3:

Analysis 3:

Conclusion 3:

Some practitioners alter this format slightly, as shown below titled "Second format," that states all the issues at the beginning, then cites the law that applies to each issue in the same order as the issues are stated. After that, the writer will write the analysis for each issue in the same order that the issue and the rule have been stated. Finally, all the conclusions will be stated at the end of the document. (Note that most courts prefer the first format, rather than the format outlined below, in documents submitted to them.)

Notice the difference between the format in example one and the format in example two. Ask yourself what is different between the two systems, and what is the same. The attorney for whom you work will determine which format you use, although in your authors' experience, example one's format is the standard one.

EXAMPLE TWO OF IRAC FORMAT FOR MULTIPLE ISSUES

<u>Second format</u>

Issue 1:

Issue 2:

Issue 3:

Rule 1:

Rule 2:

Rule 3:

Analysis 1:

Analysis 2:

Analysis 3:

Conclusion 1:

Conclusion 2:

Conclusion 3:

Almost always, addressing each issue through to its conclusion, the first format, provides a clearer explanation for the readers, who otherwise are forced to juggle several concepts at the same time. This can distract them from focusing on the argument you are presenting. Occasionally, however, your issues are so interrelated, while still requiring separate analysis, that this second format is more effective. Deciding which format will serve your argument best will be done on a case by case basis.

Your first task when approaching a case with multiple issues is determining what those issues are. As you recall from chapter 7 addressing issues, formulating the most precise and concise issue is essential for an effective argument. This step takes a surprisingly long time and amount of effort. After you have clarified and refined your issues, you then will research the law for each of them.

So when you are writing a document with multiple issues, your first step is to identify each issue. Do not be alarmed if at some point in your writing you realize that you have missed an important issue or misframed one of the issues. As you research and work on your arguments, your understanding of the case and how it fits the law for your jurisdiction will become clearer.

The following paragraphs explain the differences between approaching writing a single issue IRAC and writing a multiple issue IRAC. The process does not merely consist of repeating the process for each discrete issue.

STEP 1: IDENTIFY THE ISSUE(S)

Think of all the ideas or problems that arise from the client's situation that are important then list the issues. Frequently, your issues will consist of different aspects of the same problem, each of which requires independent analysis and argument. Sometimes, the issues will be discrete from each other, but you must keep the cohesiveness of your document in mind when drafting the individual sections.

STEP 2: RESEARCH APPLICABLE LAW FOR THE RULE

Often, because your issues will be related, you will find that your legal research applies to more than one issue in your case. Although this is not always the case, you would be wise to keep all your issues in mind as you pursue your research.

STEP 3: WRITE THE ANALYSIS

After you have compiled your research and determined how the law applies to each of your issues, you will decide how to address the arguments in each issue so that they augment or build upon each other. Because you are writing one document that addresses more than one issue, the analyses of each IRAC should be a cohesive part of the whole; otherwise, your readers will be jolted from one section to the next. Your goal is to write a series of seamless arguments that convince your reader of the correctness of your point of view as a whole.

STEP 4: STATE THE CONCLUSION

Sometimes, you may become so absorbed in your analysis that when you are ready to draft your conclusion and you go back and review your issue, you realize that you have strayed from the issue you were addressing. Or, you may realize that the conclusion your argument has reached conflicts with the conclusion you had hoped to reach for another issue. Ensuring that your conclusion both answers the question presented in the issue and is supported by your analysis is a critical step in your IRAC drafting.

In chapter 11 on IRAC as a whole, we provided different formulas for you to follow in organizing your IRAC documents.

We have repeated the formula for your analysis; this formula applies to all your IRAC analyses. Remembering the formula will help prevent you from writing an incomplete analysis. The analysis section for each issue requires a statement of the relevant facts, a statement of the law that applies to those facts, and an analysis of how that law applies to the relevant facts. It ends with a subconclusion summarizing how the law applies to the facts of the specific case. The formula is repeated for each issue you address in a multi-issue IRAC document:

EXAMPLE

Analysis:

1. F + R = Analysis with Subconclusion

2. F + R = Analysis with Subconclusion

3. F + R = Analysis with Subconclusion

Table 12.1 IRAC analysis formula for multiple issues

IRAC Analysis Formula for Multiple Issues
Analysis:
1. _____
_____F + R = Analysis_____.
Subconclusion_____
2. _____
_____F + R = Analysis_____.
Subconclusion_____.
3. _____
_____F + R = Analysis_____
Subconclusion_____.

When you reach the analysis section for each of your issues, refer back to this formula to be sure that you have included all the necessary elements of the analysis.

EXAMPLE

Landlord-Tenant

Now we will take one of our earlier fact patterns, the landlord-tenant lack of hot water case, and apply both formats to it. Recall that because the landlord company was headquartered in Florida, the paralegal has researched both Florida and Ohio law. Because the laws of the two states differ, each state requires its own IRAC analysis. We will complete the entire document applying Florida law, and then we will repeat the process using Ohio law. That way you will be able to see how the finished document is completed.

As you recall, the format below is the more frequently used IRAC format:

EXAMPLE ONE OF IRAC FORMAT FOR MULTIPLE ISSUES

Florida Law

<u>First format</u>

Issue 1:

Rule 1:

Analysis 1:

Conclusion 1:

Issue 2:

Rule 2:

Analysis 2:

Conclusion 2

I. ISSUE NUMBER ONE

Step 1: Identify the Issues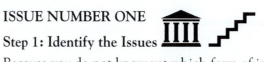

Because you do not know yet which form of issue your future employer will want you to use, we have written the issue both as a question and in the more traditional "whether" form.

In this case, the first issue is

Issue

1. Is the landlord of a residential property required to provide hot water to tenants of the property?

2. Whether a landlord of residential properties is required under law to provide hot water to the tenants of such property.

STEP 2: RESEARCH APPLICABLE RULE FOR THE LAW

Florida Law

Rule

> The Florida statutory law stated that the landlord was required to "make reasonable provisions for: . . . hot water."

Fla. Stat. § 83.51.

STEP 3: WRITE THE ANALYSIS

Analysis

  (Facts)   **+**   **(Rule)**

The landlord refuses to provide the tenant hot water. Florida law requires the landlord "make reasonable provisions for: . . . hot water." ****83.51.

=   **(Analysis)**

The landlord admitted to the tenant that the unit she has rented does not have hot water. Further, the landlord has stated that he does not intend to provide hot water to that unit. As a landlord, he is required to comply with the law and to provide hot water to the tenant, and he is violating the law by refusing to do so.

(Subconclusion)

Therefore, the landlord has violated Florida law by failing and refusing to provide hot water to the tenant.

STEP 4: STATE THE CONCLUSION

Conclusion

The landlord of a residential property is required to provide hot water to tenants of the property.

II. ISSUE NUMBER TWO

STEP 1: IDENTIFY THE ISSUES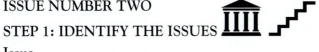

Issue

In this case, the second issue is

2. Does a tenant have legal recourse against a landlord who refuses to provide hot water to the leased premises?

2. Whether a tenant has recourse against a landlord who refuses to provide hot water to the leased premises.

STEP 2: RESEARCH
APPLICABLE RULE FOR THE LAW

Florida Law

Rule

Florida law provides limited recourse in the event of a breach of a rental contract. It allows either the tenant or the landlord to recover any damages incurred by the other party's failure to comply with the requirements in the lease. Fla. Stat. § 83.55. For a tenant, one of the limited number of recourses available is found Fla. Stat. § 83.56:

> (1) If the landlord materially fails to comply with s. 83.51(1) or material provisions of the rental agreement within 7 days after delivery of written notice by the tenant specifying the noncompliance and indicating the intention of the tenant to terminate the rental agreement by reason thereof, the tenant may terminate the rental agreement.

The statute goes on to release the tenant from responsibility for the rent for "the period the dwelling unit remains uninhabitable." *Id.* If the dwelling unit is not totally uninhabitable, then the tenant has the option of staying in the unit and reducing the amount of rent the tenant pays by the amount that the value of the property is diminished as a result of the landlord's noncompliance. *Id.*

The Court addressed a similar situation, in *Ralston v. Miller*, 357 So.2d 1066 (1978), where the landlord failed to repair a leaky roof after receiving the statutorily required notice of the problem. In *Ralston* the leak had forced the city to condemn the building. The city evicted the tenants, who sued the landlord for the money they lost in improvements that they had put into the premises as well as other losses they had incurred due to the landlord's breach.

The Court held that because the landlord had failed to maintain a habitable premises, the landlord had constructively evicted the tenant. The Court defined constructive eviction as occurring when "the landlord . . . is guilty of any . . . neglect whereby the leased premises are rendered unsafe, unfit, or unsuitable for occupancy in whole or in substantial part, for the purposes for which they were leased . . . ." *Id.* at 1068–1070.

STEP 3: WRITE THE ANALYSIS

Analysis

(Facts)

|

After the she signed the lease and moved into her apartment, the tenant discovered that the unit did not have hot water. Despite the tenant's conversations with the landlord requesting hot water, he has refused to provide it. The tenant sent the landlord a certified letter detailing the problem, and he had failed to respond.

+

(Rule)

|

The tenant has several statutorily provided options for dealing with this situation. Pursuant to Fla. Stat. § 83.56,

> [i] f the landlord materially fails to comply with . . . material provisions of the rental agreement within 7 days after delivery of written notice by the tenant specifying the noncompliance and indicating the intention of the tenant to terminate the rental agreement by reason thereof, the tenant may terminate the rental agreement.

=   #### (Analysis)

|

The tenant's first legal option, therefore, is to find another place to live and terminate her lease. This option places the burden of finding a new place to live and the cost of moving on the tenant. If the unit is not uninhabitable, the tenant might choose to stay and try to force the landlord to rectify the situation.

If the tenant does not choose to terminate and stays in the apartment, she has the option of reducing her rental payment to the actual value of the unit without the requested repairs, in this case without hot water. The landlord might deem this partial payment as a breach of the lease and commence eviction proceedings against the tenant. At that time "if the tenant interposes any defense other than payment, the tenant shall pay into the registry of the court the accrued rent . . . ." Fla. Stat. § 83.60. If the tenant does not pay the rent, as required, within five days into the court registry, then the tenant had waived all defenses apart from paying the rent. If the tenant does not pay the rent, "the landlord is entitled to an immediate default judgment for removal of the tenant with a writ of possession to issue without further notice or hearing thereon." *Id.*

On the other hand, if the tenant pays the rent to the court registry, the landlord may not evict her. The tenant may pursue the request for repairs through the court.

If, on the other hand, the lack of hot water were deemed to render the unit uninhabitable, the tenant would not be liable for any portion of the rent. The tenant would be deemed to have been constructively evicted. In the case of *Ralston v. Miller*, 357 So.2d 1066, 1068-1070 (1978), the Florida Court addressed a case in which the landlord failed to comply with the rental agreement to provide a safe and habitable building. In *Ralston*, the landlord had let the building fall into disrepair. The Court held,

"A constructive eviction may occur if the landlord does any wrongful act or is guilty of any default or neglect whereby the leased premises are rendered unsafe, unfit, or unsuitable for occupancy in whole or in substantial part, for the purposes for which they were leased . . . .."

(Subconclusion)

Thus, the tenant whose landlord refuses to provide her apartment with hot water must send written notice of the lack of hot water. If the landlord fails to provide the tenant with hot water within seven days, then she has the option of terminating the lease. If the tenant does not want to terminate the lease, and instead she opts to remain in the apartment and withhold her rent until the landlord supplies hot water, the tenant has no other recourse until and unless the landlord files an action to evict the tenant for nonpayment of the rent. At that time, the tenant may pay the amount of rent that has accrued into the court registry, pay the accrued rent to the landlord, or be evicted.

STEP 4: STATE THE CONCLUSION

Conclusion

A tenant has limited legal recourse against a landlord who refuses to provide hot water to the leased premises.

Now we will take the same facts, apply Ohio law, and see how the analysis differs, based on the difference in the States' laws.

EXAMPLE ONE OF IRAC FORMAT FOR MULTIPLE ISSUES

Ohio law

First format

Issue 1:

Rule 1:

Analysis 1:

Conclusion 1:

Issue 2:

Rule 2:

Analysis 2:

Conclusion 2:

I. **ISSUE NUMBER ONE**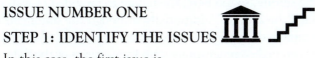

STEP 1: IDENTIFY THE ISSUES

In this case, the first issue is

Issue

1. Is the landlord of a residential property required to provide hot water to tenants of the property?

    OR

1. Whether a landlord of residential properties is required under law to provide hot water to the tenants of such property?

STEP 2: RESEARCH APPLICABLE RULE FOR THE LAW

Ohio Law

Rule

> Ohio law expressly requires a landlord of a residential property to provide hot water: R.C. § 5321.04 states that "[a] A landlord who is a party to a rental agreement shall . . . [s]upply . . . reasonable amounts of hot water . . . at all times . . . ."

R.C. 5321.04(a)(6).

STEP 3: WRITE THE ANALYSIS

Analysis

(Facts)

When the tenant took possession of the apartment, she quickly discovered that it lacked hot water. She contacted the landlord to inform him that the unit did not have hot water, but he verbally informed her that he did not intend to connect hot water to the apartment. The tenant proceeded to send a letter by certified mail informing the landlord that the apartment did not have hot water and requesting that he rectify the situation.

+ (Rule)

According to the statute, R.C. § 5321.07, the tenant had fulfilled her duty by notifying the landlord in writing of the defect she wanted repaired. The tenant also had allowed the landlord "a reasonable time considering the severity of the condition and the time necessary to remedy it," as required by R.C. § 5321.07(B). The statute states that the maximum amount of time the landlord has to fix a deficiency is not to exceed thirty days, and should be shorter depending on the severity of the deficiency.

Ohio courts have applied this statute requiring a landlord to supply basic necessities to tenants. In one case, *Gammarino v. Smith*, 1st Dist. Hamilton No. C-060636, 2007-Ohio-4073, the Court found that the landlord breached its duty to the tenant by failing to provide air conditioning. *Id.* at ¶ 34.

= (Analysis)

In this case, the tenant lacks an even more basic necessity: hot water. Just as the *Gammarino* Court found the failure to provide air conditioning a violation of the statute, so too here, the failure to provide hot water is a clear violation of the statute. Additionally, although the statute allows a landlord a maximum of thirty days to repair a complained of defect, that time limit is shortened commensurate with the severity of the defect. Given that hot water is considered a basic necessity, the tenant reasonably should expect the landlord to fix it in less than thirty days.

(Subconclusion)

Ohio law provides the tenant with several options for forcing her landlord to provide her residential apartment with hot water. After she provides the landlord with written notice of the defect, she may deposit her rent with the Court. If she deposits her rent with the Court, she additionally may ask the Court to order the landlord to provide her with hot water.

STEP 4: STATE THE CONCLUSION

Conclusion

The landlord of a residential property required to provide hot water to tenants of the property.

II. ISSUE NUMBER TWO

STEP 1: IDENTIFY THE ISSUES

1. Does a tenant have legal recourse against a landlord who refuses to provide hot water to the leased premises?

2. Whether a tenant has recourse against a landlord who refuses to provide hot water to the leased premises.

STEP 2: RESEARCH
APPLICABLE RULE FOR THE LAW

Ohio Law

Rule

Ohio law provides significant recourse to a tenant when the landlord breaches the duty of providing the statutorily imposed services. The tenant, must, however, give the landlord proper written notice of the problem. R.C. § 5321.07(A). Additionally, the tenant must allow the landlord a reasonable period of time to correct the problem. The law defines "a reasonable time" as no more than thirty days, and a shorter period depending on "the severity of the condition and the time necessary to remedy it." R.C. § 5321.07(B).

If the landlord fails to correct the problem within a reasonable period of time after having received written notice of the problem, then the tenant "[d]eposit all rent that is due and thereafter becomes due the landlord with the clerk of . . . court . . . " until the landlord fixes the defect described in the notice. R.C. § 5321.07(B)(1).

The Court has interpreted the landlord's duty to provide a habitable premises in *Gammarino v. Smith*, 1st Dist. Hamilton No. C-060636, 2007-Ohio-4073. In *Gammarino*, the landlord had failed to provide air conditioning to the tenant's unit. The Court held that failing to provide "air conditioning breaches the landlord's duty under R.C. § 5321.04 and warrants damages." *Id.* at ¶ 34. The Court further held that the tenant had the right to deposit the rent with the clerk of courts until the landlord provided air conditioning. *Id.*

In *Gammarino*, the Court found just cause for depositing the rent for lack of that the landlord breached its duty to the tenant by failing to provide air conditioning. In this case, the tenant lacks an even more basic necessity: hot water. Just as the *Gammarino* Court found the failure to provide air conditioning a violation of the statute, so too here, the failure to provide hot water is a clear violation of the statute.

STEP 3: WRITE THE ANALYSIS

Analysis

(Facts)

Despite the tenant's serving the landlord with certified mail informing him in writing that her apartment lacked hot water, and requesting the landlord correct that problem, the landlord has failed to act. Not only did the landlord fail to repair the deficiency within a reasonable period of time, considering the severity of the problem, he failed to fix it within the thirty days required by the statute. R.C. § 5321.07(B).

+ (Rule)

The tenant therefore is legally authorized to deposit the rent with the clerk of courts. R.C. § 5321.07(B)(1). The tenant also has the option of asking the court to order the landlord to remedy the situation. R.C. § 5321.07(B)(2). Finally, the tenant also has the option of terminating the lease and moving without obligation. R.C. § 5321.07(B)(3).

An Ohio Court addressed a similar situation in *Gammarino v. Smith*, 1st Dist. Hamilton No. C-060636, 2007-Ohio-4073. The landlord in *Gammarino* refused to fix the air conditioning in the tenant's rental unit. The *Gammarino* Court held that the tenant had the right to deposit the rent with the clerk of courts until the landlord provided air conditioning. *Id.* at {¶19}.

= (Analysis)

If air conditioning, an amenity that has been widely available for less than fifty years, was considered essential, then certainly hot water, an amenity that has been widely available for far longer, is even more essential. The tenant has complied with all the statutorily required actions, and the landlord has not responded. The tenant is well within her legal rights to take one of the options the statute provides.

(Subconclusion)

The tenant's legal situation provides her with three options; she can stay in the apartment and deposit her rent with the court, she can ask the court to order the landlord to provide hot water, or she can terminate the lease and move.

STEP 4: STATE THE CONCLUSION

Conclusion

A tenant has legal recourse against a landlord who refuses to provide hot water to the leased premises.

Notice the differences in the analyses and conclusions when we apply the law from the two different states. It is important to be aware of the law of the jurisdiction that controls in the case you are researching. Clearly, different jurisdictions can have vastly different laws for the same situation.

We are repeating the IRAC analysis formula here that is at the beginning of this chapter to refresh your memory as you read the domestic relations IRAC document below. Refer back to this when you get to the analysis section.

Analysis:

1. F + R = Analysis with Subconclusion

2. F + R = Analysis with Subconclusion

3. F + R = Analysis with Subconclusion

IRAC Analysis Formula

Analysis:

1. _____

   _____F + R = Analysis_____.

   Subconclusion_____

2. _____

   _____F + R = Analysis_____

   _____

   Subconclusion_____.

3. _____

   _____F + R = Analysis_____

   Subconclusion_____.

EXAMPLE

Domestic Relations

After a whirlwind romance, Dr. Jeremy Hunter married Melissa Morrison, a nurse who had moved to Parkhurst. They were blissfully happy in the first year of their marriage, and they welcomed twins, a boy and a girl, on their first anniversary. Although Melissa quit work to stay at home with their children, she kept in touch with the nurses she had worked with at Parkhurst Hospital. When the twins were three years old, one of those nurses reluctantly told Melissa that Jeremy was having an affair with a fellow physician, Dr. Jackie LaSalle.

When Melissa confronted Jeremy with this, he did not deny it. Rather, he informed Melissa that he had no intention of giving up his relationship with Dr. LaSalle, but he wished to remain married to Melissa. He pointed out that his income as a doctor provided her with a standard of living that she never would have been able to afford as a nurse. He also reminded her of how difficult life was for her fellow nurses who were single mothers. He suggested that she would have a very difficult time supporting the children on her salary.

Melissa asked Jeremy to be tested for HIV. Offended, he refused. He shouted that his girlfriend was a respectable physician and would not have been exposed to sexually transmitted diseases. Melissa pointed out that his girlfriend was a surgeon, and as such, had a higher risk of non-sexually transmitted exposure than average.

Jeremy adamantly informed Melissa that if she chose to file for divorce, he would make her life very difficult. The next day, before Melissa had decided what to do, Jeremy visited and retained a law firm with a reputation for filing unnecessary motions, failing to provide timely discovery, and extending the length of the divorce process by requesting multiple continuances.

Melissa also visited an attorney, Ana, to ask her advice and to retain her if she decides she wants a divorce. She has asked Ana to advise her concerning what would happen if she did decide to seek a divorce. She is concerned about losing custody of her children. She is also concerned about supporting her family on a nurse's salary with the necessary expenses related to child care. Melissa has no family in Parkhurst, and she is afraid and feeling very alone. We have provided the outline of this multiple issue IRAC in the second format, but we have not written the final IRAC document.

EXAMPLE TWO FORMAT OF IRAC FORMAT FOR MULTIPLE ISSUES

<u>Second format</u>

Issue 1:

Issue 2:

Issue 3:

Rule 1:

Rule 2:

Rule 3:

Analysis 1:

Analysis 2:

Analysis 3:

Conclusion 1:

Conclusion 2:

Conclusion 3:

STEP 1: IDENTIFY THE ISSUES

ISSUE

Issue I: What is the likelihood that Wife would lose custody of the children in divorce?
Issue II: Is Wife eligible for child support for the children if she initiates the divorce?
Issue III: Can Wife receive spousal support and stay home to raise the minor children?
Once you have focused your issues, you can begin researching the law. Your research might reveal law that looks like the following:

STEP 2: RESEARCH
APPLICABLE RULE FOR THE LAW

Ohio Law

Rule

Because the couple was married and both reside in Ohio, the analyses are limited to Ohio law.

Rule for issue I: Custody

When husband and wife are living separate and apart from each other, or are divorced, and the question as to the parental rights and responsibilities for the care of their children and the place of residence and legal custodian of their children is brought before a court of competent jurisdiction, they shall stand upon an equality as to the parental rights and responsibilities for the care of their children and the place of residence and legal custodian of their children, so far as parenthood is involved.

R.C. § 3109.03 Equality of parental rights and responsibilities.

Another statute that applies is the following:

(A) In any divorce, legal separation, or annulment proceeding and in any proceeding pertaining to the allocation of parental rights and responsibilities for the care of a child, upon hearing the testimony of either or both parents and considering any mediation report filed pursuant to section 3109.052 of the Revised Code and in accordance with sections 3127.01 to 3127.53 of the Revised Code, the court shall allocate the parental rights and responsibilities for the care of the minor children of the marriage. Subject to division (D)(2) of this section, the court may allocate the parental rights and responsibilities for the care of the children in either of the following ways:

(1) If neither parent files a pleading or motion in accordance with division (G) of this section, if at least one parent files a pleading or motion under that division but no parent who filed a pleading or motion under that division also files a plan for shared parenting, or if at least one parent files both a pleading or motion and a shared parenting plan under that division but no plan for shared parenting is in the best interest of the children, the court, in a manner consistent with the best interest of the children, shall allocate the parental rights and responsibilities for the care of the children primarily to one of the parents, designate that parent as the residential parent and the legal custodian of the child, and divide between the parents the other rights and responsibilities for the care of the children, including, but not limited to, the responsibility to provide support for the children and the right of the parent who is not the residential parent to have continuing contact with the children.

(2) If at least one parent files a pleading or motion in accordance with division (G) of this section and a plan for shared parenting pursuant to that division and if a plan for shared parenting is in the best interest of the children and is approved by the court in accordance with division (D)(1) of this section, the court may allocate the parental rights and responsibilities for the care of the children to both parents and issue a shared parenting order requiring the parents to share all or some of the aspects of the physical and legal care of the children in accordance with the approved plan for shared parenting. If the court issues a shared parenting order under this division and it is necessary for the purpose of receiving public assistance, the court shall designate which one of the parents' residences is to serve as the child's home. The child support obligations of the parents under a shared parenting order issued under this division shall be determined in accordance with Chapters 3119., 3121., 3123., and 3125. of the Revised Code.

R.C. § 3109.04, Allocating parental rights and responsibilities for care of children - shared parenting.

Rule for issue II: Child support

> (A)(1) In a divorce, dissolution of marriage, legal separation, or child support proceeding, the court may order either or both parents to support or help support their children, without regard to marital misconduct. In determining the amount reasonable or necessary for child support, including the medical needs of the child, the court shall comply with Chapter 3119 of the Revised Code.
>
> . . . .

R.C. § 3109.05

Rule for issue III: Spousal support

> (A) As used in this section, "spousal support" means any payment or payments to be made to a spouse or former spouse . . . that is both for sustenance and for support of the spouse or former spouse. "Spousal support" does not include any payment made to a spouse or former spouse, or to a third party for the benefit of a spouse or former spouse, that is made as part of a division or distribution of property or a distributive award under section 3105.171 of the Revised Code.
>
> (B) In divorce and legal separation proceedings, upon the request of either party and after the court determines the division or disbursement of property under section 3105.171 of the Revised Code, the court of common pleas may award reasonable spousal support to either party. During the pendency of any divorce, or legal separation proceeding, the court may award reasonable temporary spousal support to either party.
>
> An award of spousal support may be allowed in real or personal property, or both, or by decreeing a sum of money, payable either in gross or by installments, from future income or otherwise, as the court considers equitable.
>
> . . . .
>
> (C) (1) In determining whether spousal support is appropriate and reasonable, and in determining the nature, amount, and terms of payment, and duration of spousal support, which is payable either in gross or in installments, the court shall consider all of the following factors:
>
> (a) The income of the parties, from all sources, including, but not limited to, income derived from property divided, disbursed, or distributed under section 3105.171 of the Revised Code;
> (b) The relative earning abilities of the parties;
>
> . . . .
>
> (e) The duration of the marriage;
> (f) The extent to which it would be inappropriate for a party, because that party will be custodian of a minor child of the marriage, to seek employment outside the home;
> (g) The standard of living of the parties established during the marriage;
> (h) The relative extent of education of the parties;
>
> . . . .
>
> (n) Any other factor that the court expressly finds to be relevant and equitable.

R.C. § 3105.18

Applying the IRAC formula to the issues and the rules, we will draft the analysis to the first issue.

STEP 3: WRITE THE ANALYSIS

Analysis for issue I: Custody

ISSUE What is the likelihood that Wife would lose custody of the children in a divorce?

Rule

> When husband and wife are . . . divorced, and the question as to the parental rights and responsibilities for the care of their children and the place of residence and legal custodian of their children is brought before a court of competent jurisdiction, they shall stand upon an equality as to the parental rights and responsibilities for the care of their children and the place of residence and legal custodian of their children, so far as parenthood is involved.

R.C. § 3109.03 Equality of parental rights and responsibilities.

ANALYSIS

(Facts)   **+ (Rule)**

Melissa and Jeremy are the parents of the twins. In questions of custody of minor children in Ohio, both parents have equal rights as well as equal responsibilities to the children.

=   (Analysis)

Therefore, Jeremy will not have an upper hand in determining the custody of their children. As the mother of the children, Melissa has an equal right to custody to the children.

(Subconclusion)

Melissa's right to custody of the minor children is equal to Jeremy's right.

II. ISSUE NUMBER TWO

Analysis for issue II: Child support

Melissa is also worried about being able to support the children if she decides to divorce Jeremy.

ISSUE Is Wife eligible for child support for the children if she initiates the divorce?

RULE

When a couple divorces, "the court may order either or both parents to support or help support their children, without regard to marital misconduct."

R.C. § 3109.05(A).

ANALYSIS

(Facts)   **+ (Rule)**

Jeremy is the father of the twins. In a family in which the parents divorce, "the court may order either or both parents to support or help support their children, without regard to marital misconduct." R.C. § 3109.05(A)

=   (Analysis)

Although Jeremy implied that Melissa would have sole responsibility, in Ohio the Court may order either parent to contribute to or to entirely support the children. Jeremy can be held liable for child support.

(Subconclusion)

Melissa may be eligible to receive child support from Jeremy for their children.

Analysis for issue III: Spousal support

Finally, Melissa would like to be able to be a stay-at-home mother to the twins. She wonders whether Jeremy can be made to support her while she does this.

ISSUE: Can Wife receive spousal support and stay home to raise the minor children?

RULE:

> Courts will award spousal support for certain lengths of time under certain circumstances. "In divorce and legal separation proceedings, upon the request of either party and after the court determines the division or disbursement of property under section 3105.171 of the Revised Code, the court of common pleas may award reasonable spousal support to either party." Spousal support awards are based upon several factors, including "[t]he relative earning abilities of the parties, . . . [t] duration of the marriage, [t]he extent to which it would be inappropriate for a party, because that party will be custodian of a minor child of the marriage, to seek employment outside the home; [and]
> [t]he standard of living of the parties established during the marriage."

R.C. § 3105.18(C)(1).

ANALYSIS:

(Facts)

Melissa has stayed home since the birth of the twins three years ago. Although she has earning potential as a Registered Nurse, she will never earn as much as Jeremy can as a physician. The marriage has lasted only four years, but Melissa thinks it would be in the best interests of the twins for her to stay at home and raise them.

+ (Rule)

The law allows for spousal support in situations in which one of the parties has a greater earning power, the party with the lower income cannot sustain the standard of living enjoyed during the marriage, and the spouse seeking support would stay at home to raise the minor children. The length of the marriage is also a determining factor in whether the Court chooses to award spousal support.

=   **(Analysis)**

In Melissa's situation, her income will never reach the level that Jeremy's has reached and has the potential to increase. Because the Courts consider a disparity in income ability when determining whether to award spousal support, Melissa's lesser earning power is a significant factor the Court will consider.

(Subconclusion)

This disparity in income capacity weighs in favor of Melissa receiving spousal support to equalize the incomes of the parties.

=   (Analysis)
                                               |

Another factor weighing in Melissa's favor is the standard of living she has enjoyed during the marriage and which she could not achieve on the salary she could earn as a nurse. The Courts consider whether the party with the lesser earning power will be able to maintain the same standard of living that party enjoyed during the marriage.

(Subconclusion)
   |

Because Melissa could never sustain the standard of living she enjoyed during the marriage, the Court might award spousal support on that basis.

   =

(Analysis)
   |

Melissa's strongest motivator for seeking spousal support, however, is her desire to avoid disrupting the children's life. The children have had their mother home with them full-time since they were born, and Melissa believes that it would be harmful to them to start them in daycare at this age, which she would have to do if she returned to work. Without spousal support, Melissa would not have the money she needs to survive. The Courts consider spouse seeking support would stay at home to raise the minor children to be a viable factor weighing in favor of awarding spousal support.

(Subconclusion)
      |

Melissa might be able to receive an award of spousal support to stay home and raise the children.

STEP 4: STATE THE CONCLUSION

Conclusion for issue I: Custody
Parents in a divorce have equal rights to custody of minor children; therefore, wife's likelihood of losing custody of the children in a divorce is unlikely.

Conclusion for issue II: Child support
Wife is eligible for child support for the children if she initiates the divorce.

Conclusion for issue II: Child support
Wife may receive spousal support and stay home to raise the minor children, depending on the individual circumstances of the parties.

EXERCISE

Read the following multiple issue scenario and compose an IRAC statement with all four sections, I-Issue, R-Rule, A-Analysis, C-Conclusion. Use all the strategies discussed in this chapter along with chapters 7 through 11.

Now that she has a better idea of her legal rights, Melissa has decided to file for divorce from Jeremy. She realized that she cannot live in a marriage in which her husband has no intention of remaining faithful. Ana has helped her secure the joint marital assets like the bank accounts and the IRAs. Now Melissa would like to get child support and custody of the children when she files the divorce papers. She has told Ana that Jeremy had moved into a luxury apartment. She showed Ana several articles from the local

(continued)

paper reporting the police having been called to resolve disputes and break up noisy parties at Jeremy's new apartment. Melissa is concerned that if the twins were to stay with Jeremy, they might be exposed to situations that would be inappropriate for young children. She pointed particularly to one article in which Jeremy had been arrested for driving recklessly while the children were in the car. Melissa is still living in the marital home, and she decided not to go back to work because she did not want to disrupt the children's lives any more than they already had been disrupted. Jeremy has refused to give her any money, so she has been supporting herself and the children with money from their inheritance. The Ohio Statutes that apply are Ohio Rev. Code § 3109.04 and 3109.05.

R.C. § 3109.04(B)(1).

> When making the allocation of the parental rights and responsibilities for the care of the children under this section in an original proceeding or in any proceeding for modification of a prior order of the court making the allocation, the court shall take into account that which would be in the best interest of the children. In

determining the child's best interest for purposes of making its allocation of the parental rights and responsibilities for the care of the child and for purposes of resolving any issues related to the making of that allocation, the court, in its discretion, may and, upon the request of either party, shall interview in chambers any or all of the involved children regarding their wishes and concerns with respect to the allocation.

R.C. § 3109.04(B)(1).
and
R.C. § 3109.05 (A)(1).

> In a divorce, dissolution of marriage, legal separation, or child support proceeding, the court may order either or both parents to support or help support their children, without regard to marital misconduct. In determining the amount reasonable or necessary for child support, including the medical needs of the child, the court shall comply with Chapter 3119. of the Revised Code.
>
> . . . .

R.C. § 3109.05.

EXERCISE

Read the following multiple issue scenario and compose an IRAC statement with all four sections, I-Issue, R-Rule, A-Analysis, C-Conclusion. Use all the strategies discussed in this chapter and chapters 7-11.

Melissa and Jeremy's divorce is proceeding, and Jeremy called Melissa and promised her he would provide child support of $100 a week until the court can determine an appropriate amount. Jeremy's attorney was ordered to supply Jeremy's information a month earlier, and not only has the attorney not provided any of Jeremy's income information except his expense vouchers for his work-related expenses, Jeremy has failed to make any of the court-ordered payments. Ana has filed a motion to have the child support payments deducted from Jeremy's paycheck. The following law states which documents Jeremy is required to provide to the court and how a court may deduct the amount of child support owed from the paycheck of person who owes the money (the obligor).

When a court computes the amount of child support required to be paid under a court child support order or a child support enforcement agency computes the amount of child support to be paid pursuant to an administrative child support order, all of the following apply:

(A) The parents' current and past income and personal earnings shall be verified by electronic means or with suitable documents, including, but not limited to, paystubs, employer statements, receipts and expense vouchers related to self-generated income, tax returns, and all supporting documentation and schedules for the tax returns.

R.C. § 3119.05.

(continued)

(1) If the court or the child support enforcement agency determines that the obligor is receiving income from a payor, the court or agency shall require the payor to do all of the following:

(a) Withhold from the obligor's income a specified amount for support in satisfaction of the support order and begin the withholding no later than fourteen business days following the date the notice is mailed or transmitted to the payor under section 3121.035, 3123.021, or 3123.06 of the Revised Code and division (A) (2) of this section or, if the payor is an employer,

no later than the first pay period that occurs after fourteen business days following the date the notice is mailed or transmitted;

(b) Send the amount withheld to the office of child support in the department of job and family services pursuant to section 3121.43 of the Revised Code immediately but not later than seven business days after the date the obligor is paid;

(c) Continue the withholding at intervals specified in the notice until further notice from the court or child support enforcement agency.

R.C. § 3121.03 (A).

SUMMARY

- Many cases involve more than one legal issue.

- In order to write a coherent and complete memorandum or brief with multiple issues, the document must be organized in a logical manner.

- The IRAC formula provides a blueprint for writing an excellent document.

- Also essential for an excellent document are good grammar, smooth transitions, and clear reasoning.

- Begin a multiple issue document by refining and prioritizing the issues.

- After the issues have been crafted carefully, research the law for each issue.

- Remember to save the law in the file for each issue to which it applies.

- Apply the law to the facts of each issue.

- Especially in cases with multiple issues, it is essential to outline the document before beginning to research and before beginning to write.

- Use the outline to decide where to insert transitions that will clarify the meaning and enhance the flow of your document.

ASSIGNMENT

I. Read the fact pattern and law below. Write an IRAC argument first from Henry Johnson's point of view and then from Burto Enterprises' point of view.

[Note: Specific performance is a contract term that applies to the sale of real property. Specific performance requires the buyer to complete the purchase of the property if the buyer changes its mind and decides it does not want the property. Similarly, if a seller tries to renege on the sale of a specific

property, the buyer also can sue for specific performance, forcing the seller to transfer the property to the buyer. The courts allow specific performance in a contract to be enforced because each piece of real estate is considered to be unique and not able to be substituted.]

A decade ago, Henry Johnson had bought property in Wisconsin that he hoped to turn into a family vacation site. He then got distracted by business matters, and when he returned to the property after Marcus and Brianna were married, he discovered that what had once been a quiet, wooded property on a pristine lake was now a surrounded by condominiums, gated communities, and a large shopping mall. Although Henry's property was still wooded, it was no longer quiet. The lake was abuzz with jet skis and motor boats. Because his dream of a quiet vacation site was no longer feasible, Henry decided to sell the property.

When he received an appraisal of the property, he was pleased to discover that the surrounding development had caused his property to increase in value ten-fold. He quickly entered into a sales contract, selling it to a developer. The contract specifically provided that if one of the parties failed to perform, that is, to uphold its side of the contract, the other side could demand specific performance. The developer, Burton Enterprises, had been insistent on including this clause, because it realized that the property would increase in value, and it wanted to be certain that Henry did not decide to sell it to someone else.

When the sale was scheduled to close, however, the developer informed Henry that it had not obtained financing yet. After a six month delay, Henry hired local counsel to sue the buyer for specific performance. After a trial, the court awarded a verdict for Henry and ordered the developer to complete the purchase of the property. The developer appealed, claiming that Henry should have sought other legal remedies rather than specific performance. Henry's Wisconsin attorney cited the following case in the Appellate Brief responding to the developer's appeal.

[In the following case, the petitioner is the buyer of the property, and Ash Park, LLC s the seller. The circuit court is the trial court. Summary Judgment is an action the trial court takes deciding a case before trial. It will be discussed further in chapter 17 discussing motions.]

WISCONSIN CASE LAW

The petitioner, Alexander & Bishop, Ltd., seeks review of a published decision of the court of appeals affirming the orders of the circuit court.[footnote omitted] After Alexander & Bishop breached a contract to purchase a parcel of real estate from Ash Park, LLC, the circuit court granted summary judgment in favor of Ash Park and ordered specific performance of the contract. It also imposed interest on the purchase price.

. . . .

The contract provides that specific performance is an available remedy, and neither the contract nor Wisconsin law requires Ash Park to demonstrate that a legal remedy would be inadequate as a precondition to relief. Further, although impossibility is a defense to specific performance, Alexander & Bishop failed to present evidence that performance would be impossible in the proceedings before the circuit court.

Ash Park, LLC v. Alexander & Bishop, Ltd., 2010 WI 44, 324 Wis.2d 703, 710; 783 N.W.2d 294, 297, ¶4 (2010).

II. Read the fact pattern and law below. Write an IRAC argument first from Cherelle's point of view and then from Mark Kotter's point of view.

Antoine and Cherelle were visiting her Aunt Denise in Boston. They had adopted a small mixed breed dog from the pound a month earlier. They wryly had named the dog Spike, because it was so timid and shy. Because Spike suffered from separation anxiety when he was away from Cherelle, Aunt Denise graciously had told them that the dog was welcome to visit too. Fortunately, the dog was housebroken and well trained, and the visit was proceeding pleasantly. Cherelle and Aunt Denise took the dog for a walk in the park. Cherelle was careful to keep Spike on a leash, even though she was certain that it would never let her out of his sight.

Suddenly, a large dog ran up from behind Cherelle and snatched Spike up in its jaws. Cherelle and Aunt Denise both shouted at the large dog and beat on it, trying to get it to let go of Spike. The dog's owner, Mark Kotter, kicked the dog to try to get it to let go of Spike. A park ranger arrived, and despite his best efforts, could not loosen the large dog's jaws. The park ranger finally shot the attacking dog through the heart. The ranger then rescued Spike from the dead dog's mouth. Spike was bleeding profusely and was barely conscious.

Another ranger drove Cherelle, Aunt Denise, and Spike to the nearest veterinary hospital, where the veterinarian spent five hours operating on him. To everyone's surprise, Spike recovered almost completely, and Cherelle and Antoine took him home a week later.

When the bill arrived for Spike's emergency medical treatment, Cherelle was appalled to find that she owed the veterinarian $5,000. She was even more distraught when the owner of the large dog filed a lawsuit against her in Massachusetts for the loss of his AKC registered dog. The large dog's owner was suing her for loss of income, claiming that he often made several thousand dollars each year breeding the dog.

Brad and Ana gave Cherelle and Antoine the name of a law school classmate who was practicing law in Boston, and the classmate countersued for the veterinary bills incurred in Spike's treatment. The Boston attorney found the following case and included it in his court documents.

MASSACHUSETTS CASE LAW

An unprovoked attack by the defendants' unleashed German shepherd caused the plaintiffs' Bichon Frisé severe internal injuries, external bruising, and wounds to the head, neck, abdomen, and chest. Emergency surgery was successful but expensive, with veterinary costs ultimately amounting to over $8,000. After a bench trial, a District Court judge found those costs to be both reasonable and necessary and awarded them in full.[footnote omitted]

The judgment was affirmed by the Appellate Division. The sole issue on appeal is whether damages should be capped at the market value of the dog, regardless of the reasonableness of the veterinary costs necessary to treat the dog's injuries. We affirm.

The plaintiffs sued [footnote omitted] under G.L. c. 140, § 155, as amended by St.1934, c. 320, § 18, which since 1791[footnote omitted] has imposed strict liability[footnote omitted] for damage caused by dogs:

"If any dog shall do any damage to either the body or property of any person, the owner or keeper . . . shall be liable for such damage, unless such damage shall have been occasioned to the body or property of a person who, at the time such damage was sustained, was committing a trespass or other tort, or was teasing, tormenting or abusing such dog."

. . . .

Although the statute imposes strict liability for "any damage" caused by a dog, it is silent as to how to measure such damage.[footnote omitted] We turn, accordingly, to the common law.[footnote omitted]

. . . .

reasonableness is the touchstone for determining whether, and to what extent, veterinary costs can be recovered. If it is reasonable in the circumstances presented to incur the veterinary costs at the time they are undertaken, then the owner of the injured animal may recover them. [footnote omitted] . . . . Our reading of the common law leads us, therefore, to conclude that reasonable veterinary costs that are reasonably incurred can be recovered under G.L. c. 140, § 155, even if they exceed the market value or replacement cost of an animal injured by a dog.

. . . .

Although the owner's affection for the animal may be considered in assessing the reasonableness of the decision to treat the animal, the owner cannot recover for his or her own hurt feelings, emotions, or pain. Nor is the owner entitled to recover for the loss of the animal's companionship or society. [citation omitted]

Irwin v. Degtiarov, 85 Mass. App. Ct. 234, 234-239; 8 N.E.3d 296, 298-302 (2014).

III. Read the fact pattern and law below. Write two IRACs: argue the case first from Jeremy Hunter's point of view and then from the Smith's point of view.

    Read the fact pattern below and state the issue and correct rule as it is stated in the case provided.

While he was doing a one-year internship at a large university medical center in upstate New York State, Jeremy found that jogging helped clear his mind and helped him sleep- not that he had much opportunity to sleep. He and a classmate were jogging in late October in the classmate's home town, Trumansburg, New York, a quaint little town near the large medical center. After running up a short but steep hill off the main road, they turned left onto McLallen Street, which had charming pre-Civil War homes. Some of the homes had the original slate sidewalks, and the wet leaves were slicked onto the sidewalks.

Jeremy slipped on moss that was hidden by the leaves and fell, breaking his right hand. Because he planned to be a surgeon, he was quite distressed by this injury. One of the professors at the law school that was affiliated with the university offered to represent him in a lawsuit against the homeowners whose sidewalk was the location of his fall.

The homeowners, Darlene and Kenneth Smith, argued that by running on slate sidewalks, which were known to be slippery when wet, and by running on these wet slate sidewalks that were covered by wet leaves, Jeremy had assumed the risk of his injury. The homeowners argued that they were not liable for the slippery sidewalk. They also argued that by running on wet leaves without knowledge of the surface under the leaves, Jeremy had negligently contributed to his own injury.

Jeremy's attorney countered that because sidewalks were designed for people to traverse, the homeowner had a duty to clean the slippery moss off of the sidewalk. Jeremy's attorney further alleged that the homeowners had a duty to clear the wet leaves off the sidewalk, because they knew the leaves would be slippery on the slate walk.

The attorney found the following case concerning contributory negligence and assumption of the risk:

NEW YORK CASE LAW

In this case involving a plaintiff who fell and sustained injuries while rollerblading, we conclude that the doctrine of 86*86 primary assumption of the risk does not preclude her common-law negligence claim against the landowner defendants. We therefore affirm the Appellate Division order reinstating the complaint.

. . . .

Our analysis begins with CPLR 1411, which the Legislature adopted in 1975 to abolish contributory negligence and assumption of the risk as absolute defenses in favor of a comparative fault regime. CPLR 1411 provides:

"In any action to recover damages for personal injury, injury to property, or wrongful death, the culpable conduct attributable to the claimant or to the decedent, including contributory negligence or assumption of risk, shall not bar recovery, but the amount of damages otherwise recoverable shall be diminished

in the proportion which the culpable conduct attributable to the claimant or decedent bears to the culpable conduct which caused the damages."

. . . .

Since the adoption of CPLR 1411, we have generally restricted the concept of assumption of the risk to particular athletic and recreative activities in recognition that such pursuits have "enormous social value" even while they may "involve significantly heightened risks" (*Trupia*, 14 NY3d at 395). Hence, the continued application of the doctrine "facilitate[s] free and vigorous participation in athletic activities" (*Benitez*, 73 NY2d at 657), and fosters these socially beneficial activities by shielding coparticipants, activity sponsors or venue owners from "potentially crushing liability" (*Bukowski*, 19 NY3d at 358).

. . . .

In contrast, in Trupia we recently declined to apply the assumption of the risk doctrine to a child who was injured while sliding down a bannister at school. Based on the tension that exists between assumption of the risk and the dictates of CPLR 1411, we clarified that the doctrine "must be closely circumscribed if it is not seriously to undermine and displace the principles of comparative causation" (*Trupia*, 14 NY3d at 395). We noted that the injury-causing activity at issue in *Trupia* — horseplay — did not render the school worthy of insulation from a breach of duty claim, as it was "not a case in which the defendant solely by reason of having sponsored or otherwise supported some risk-laden but socially valuable voluntary activity has been called to account in damages" (*id.* at 396).

Guided by these principles, we conclude that assumption of the risk does not apply to the fact pattern in this appeal, which does not fit comfortably within the parameters of the doctrine. As a general rule, application of assumption of the risk should be limited to cases appropriate for absolution of duty, such as personal injury claims arising from sporting events, sponsored athletic and recreative activities, or athletic and recreational pursuits that take place at designated venues. [Footnote omitted] In this case, plaintiff was not rollerblading at a rink, a skating park, or in a competition; nor did defendants actively sponsor or promote the activity in question.

Moreover, extension of the doctrine to cases involving persons injured while traversing streets and sidewalks would create an unwarranted diminution of the general duty of landowners — both public and private — to maintain their premises in a reasonably safe condition. As we explained in an earlier case, assumption of the risk "does not exculpate a landowner from liability for ordinary negligence in maintaining a premises" (*Sykes*, 94 NY2d at 913). The exception would swallow the general rule of comparative fault if sidewalk defects or dangerous premises conditions were deemed "inherent" risks assumed by non-pedestrians who sustain injuries, whether they be joggers, runners, bicyclists or rollerbladers (see *Ashbourne v City of New York*, 82 AD3d 461, 463 [1st Dept 2011]; *Cotty v Town* of 90*90 Southampton, 64 AD3d 251, 257 [2d Dept 2009]). We therefore decline to expand the doctrine to cover the circumstances presented here.

Custodi v. Town of Amherst, 20 N.Y.3d 83, 85-86, 89-90; 980 N.E.2d 933, 957 (2012).

IV. Read the fact pattern and law below. Write an IRAC argument first from Guadalupe's point of view and then from the manager Ted's point of view.

Ana asked the paralegal to do some legal research for her as a personal favor. She told the paralegal that her twenty-two-year old cousin, Guadalupe, had been earning college money by waiting tables. Her cousin was living and working in Kansas, and she called Ana to tell her that despite numerous requests for her credit card tips, her employer refused to pay her not only her tips, but also her base salary. Her manager, Ted, refused to believe that Guadalupe was an American citizen, and he withheld money from all the staff members who were in the United States illegally. He knew that they would be too afraid of being deported to report him.

Because she was a native born American citizen, Guadalupe complained about her boss to the Kansas Department of Labor. When she reported to work a few days later, he fired her. He claimed that he had fired her for being an illegal alien, but she noticed that he had not fired any of the workers that she knew were in the country illegally. Ana asked the paralegal to research the Kansas law regarding this issue and write up a summary of the law for her. The paralegal found the following 2011 case from the Supreme Court of Kansas:

KANSAS CASE LAW

Robert L. Campbell was an at-will employee with Husky Hogs, L.L.C., for about 1 year when he filed a complaint with the Kansas Department of Labor (KDOL) alleging Husky Hogs was not paying him as required by the KWPA [Kansas Wage Payment Act]. Campbell was fired 1 business day after KDOL acknowledged receiving his claim. Campbell filed this lawsuit in Phillips County District Court alleging Husky Hogs terminated him for pursuing his statutory rights under the KWPA. Husky Hogs denied the allegation.

. . . .

The company also filed a . . . motion for judgment on the pleadings. It argued Kansas had not previously recognized a retaliatory discharge claim for alleging KWPA violations and no public policy reasons existed for allowing such a claim now.

. . . .

The district court granted Husky Hogs' motion. It held Campbell's termination did not violate Kansas public policy, even though it was required to assume the discharge resulted from filing the disputed wage claim.

. . . .

Kansas historically adheres to the employment-at-will doctrine, which holds that employees and employers may terminate an employment relationship at any time, for any reason, unless there is an express or implied contract governing the employment's duration. [Citation omitted] But there are specific statutory exceptions to this rule, such as terminations based on race, gender, or disability.

. . . .

There are also exceptions recognized by Kansas courts through our case law. Over the past

30 years, exceptions to the at-will doctrine created a common-law tort for retaliatory discharge. These exceptions gradually eroded the general terminable-at-will rule 4 * 4 when an employee is fired in contravention of a recognized state public policy.

. . . .

To date, this court has endorsed public policy exceptions in four circumstances: (1) filing a claim under the Kansas Workers Compensation Act, K.S.A. 44-501 et seq; (2) whistleblowing; (3) filing a claim under the Federal Employers Liability Act (FELA), 45 U.S.C. § 51 (2006) et seq.; and (4) exercising a public employee's First Amendment right to free speech on an issue of public concern.

. . . .

. . . Kansas courts permit the common-law tort of retaliatory discharge as a limited exception to the at-will employment doctrine when it is necessary to protect a strongly held state public policy from being undermined.

. . . .

We have stated that courts tasked with determining whether a public policy exists are faced with three situations: (1) The legislature has clearly declared the state's public policy; (2) the legislature enacted statutory provisions from which public policy may reasonably be implied, even though it is not directly declared; and (3) the legislature has neither made a clear statement of public policy nor can it be reasonably implied.

. . . .

The KWPA was enacted in 1973. L. 1973, ch. 204, secs. 1-16. It is an expansive and comprehensive legislative scheme that is broad in its scope and the rights created for Kansas workers to secure unpaid wages earned from their labors. See K.S.A. 44-313 et seq. It is applicable to most Kansas employers. See K.S.A. 44-313(a). It requires, among various other provisions, that employers promptly pay wages and benefits (K.S.A. 2010 Supp. 44-314 K.S.A. 44-315). It also permits specific damages awards for willful nonpayment (K.S.A.44-315); controls and limits wage withholdings (K.S.A. 2010 Supp. 7*7 44-319); prohibits waivers of the rights created (K.S.A.44-321); and mandates that the Secretary of Labor enforce and administer the KWPA's provisions through administrative proceedings, compulsory process to compel witness attendance and document production, and permits application to the district courts for citations in contempt (see K.S.A. 44-322; K.S.A. 2010 Supp. 44-322a). The Secretary of Labor is expressly authorized to adopt such rules and regulations as are deemed necessary to accomplish the KWPA's purposes. K.S.A. 44-325.

. . . .

This court has recognized retaliatory discharge claims in different circumstances, including those in which employees are discharged for exercising a statutory right.

. . . .

That principle is applicable to the KWPA. We hold the KWPA embeds within its provisions a public policy of protecting wage earners' rights to their unpaid wages and benefits. And just as we found a common-law retaliatory discharge claim when an injured worker is terminated for exercising rights under the Workers Compensation Act, we find such a cause of action is necessary when an employer fires a worker who seeks to exercise KWPA rights by filing a wage claim. To do otherwise would seriously undermine the public policy and the protections afforded by the KWPA. [Citation omitted]

Campbell v. Husky Hogs, LLC, 292 Kan. 225, 225-227, 230, 233-234; 255 P.3d 1, 3-4, 6-7 (2011).

LEARNING OBJECTIVES

1. Recognize the elements of a legal document

2. Memorize the sequence of the elements of a legal document

3. Identify characteristics of the content in each element of a legal document

4. Detect errors in legal documents

5. Differentiate appropriate sections for boilerplate from sections requiring new text

6. Assess boilerplate in each document for necessary edits and additions

Components of a Document

CHAPTER 13

■ ELEMENTS OF A LEGAL DOCUMENT

During your paralegal career, you will write many legal documents. Some of these documents you will have to write from scratch. Others will consist of forms or templates that you will fill in or revise. The format of documents that are submitted to the court, that is, legal documents, may vary somewhat from jurisdiction to jurisdiction, but the basic, underlying concept regarding the format is the same. Regardless of the minor variations from jurisdiction to jurisdiction, therefore, even when you are adapting a template with your client's information, you will use the same jurisdictional format for the caption. What will vary throughout the case will be the title of the document: it may be a motion for summary judgment, a motion to dismiss, or a request for an extension of time, for example. Still, the remaining information in the caption will remain the same.

One important piece of the document that you must remember is to always number your pages. This is a detail that paralegals sometimes forget, and it is an essential requirement in legal documents.

Also, as noted above, the exact format of the caption may vary from jurisdiction to jurisdiction, even within a given state. Thus, a paralegal working for an attorney practicing in different counties in the same state should consult the local rules and be sure that the caption and other details in the document meet the local requirements.

Nonetheless, certain information is essential for the caption of a document submitted to the court. Also, the other elements of legal documents are detailed in Table 13.1.

Certain elements are included in every legal document. Complaints and answers, which are addressed in chapter 15, have additional elements, which are essential to remember. We will address those additional elements at length in chapter 15 later in the book. The Table 13.1, however, contains the elements that are common to every document filed with the court. Figure 13.1 which follows the table is to help you remember the importance of the order of a document.

Table 13.1 Basic Elements of a Legal Document

Elements of a Legal Document	Section
Caption	1st section
Body	2nd section
Signature Block	3rd section
Service Page	4th section

Figure 13.1 and mnemonic table will help you remember the importance of the order of many law documents.

Figure 13.1

<u>C</u>lerks <u>B</u>ring <u>S</u>ummons <u>S</u>wiftly

Key Word	Elements of a Document	Section
<u>C</u>LERKS	<u>C</u>aption	1st section
<u>B</u>RING	<u>B</u>ody	2nd section
<u>S</u>UMMONS	<u>S</u>ignature Block	3rd section
<u>S</u>WIFTLY	<u>S</u>ervice Page	4th section

The Caption

Below is a standard CAPTION. Every court filing must have a caption. The caption for a complaint, which is the first document filed in a civil lawsuit, is slightly different. We will discuss that in the complaint and answer chapter, chapter 15.

The basic elements of a caption are the title of the court, including the jurisdiction, the city or county, and the state. The title of the court is centered, usually at the top of the page. Be aware, however, that some courts have local rules requiring a three-inch margin above the start of the caption. Always consult the local rules of the court in which you are filing a document to ensure that your formatting complies with the local rules.

The title of the court and the jurisdiction will change, depending on the nature of the case. Cases can be filed, depending on various factors, in municipal court, common pleas court, probate court, domestic relations court, juvenile court, an appellate court, or a supreme court. The specifics of what court a case belongs in is covered in your civil procedure class and is outside the purview of this text.

After the title and jurisdiction of the court, the remaining portion of the caption is divided in half vertically. The caption is divided down the middle with some form of marking. Here we used the closing half of the parentheses, but some areas use asterisks. Again, look at a document from the court where you are filing the document to see what the custom is in that court.

On the left hand side of the caption, the parties and their roles in the case are listed. In a Common Pleas case, the plaintiff's name is always listed first, with the defendant's name below it. The plaintiff is the party initiating the lawsuit, or, in a criminal case, the government entity prosecuting the defendant. The defendant is the party being accused of having wronged the appellant, in a civil case, or of having violated a law, in a criminal case. In an appeals case, the person who appealed the decision is called the Appellant, and regardless of whether that party was the plaintiff or the defendant in the lower court case. The party not appealing a decision or verdict is called the Appellee.

Between the parties is some version of the word "versus." In many jurisdictions, it is written "vs." In others, it may be written without the letter s: "v." However it is written, it signifies that these are the parties opposing each other in the case.

On the right hand side of the caption is the case number. It is imperative to include the case number on every document you file with the court (except the complaint, which the Clerk's Office will assign). This ensures that your document is filed with the correct case. Different jurisdictions assign case numbers in different ways. For example, in Cuyahoga County, Ohio, the caption contains only the six digit case number assigned by the clerk. In Medina County, Ohio, on the other hand, the case number includes the year that the case was filed, the court in which it was filed, and then the actual case number. The date is indicated by the last two digits of the year, and the court is indicated by an abbreviation, for example "CR" for criminal and "CV" for civil. As you work as a paralegal, you will become familiar with the way the courts your attorney practices in assigns case numbers.

The right side of the caption also contains the name of the judge who is assigned to the case. (Again, with the complaint, the Clerk's Office will randomly assign a judge to the case.) Including the judge's name on the document ensures that it is routed to the judge for review.

Finally, the last element of the caption of every document, except the complaint and the answer, is the name of the document. We will discuss the additional elements of the caption for the complaint and answer in that upcoming chapter.

Our example states that the document is a Motion to Compel. In a given case, regardless of whether you are filing a Motion to Dismiss, a Request for Extension of Time, a Motion for Summary Judgment, or any other document, this is the only section of the caption that will change. (In rare circumstances, the name of the judge might change, but ordinarily, the same judge stays with a case until its completion.)

IN THE COURT OF COMMON PLEAS
CUYAHOGA COUNTY, OHIO

MELISSA M. HUNTER	)	Case No. XXXXX
	)	
Plaintiff	)	
	)	
vs.	)	JUDGE: LEROY STEINER
	)	
	)	
	)	
	)	
JEREMY HUNTER	)	<u>MOTION TO COMPEL</u>
	)	
Defendant	)	
	)	
	)	
	)	
	)	
	)	

The Body

The BODY of the document will vary depending on the document's purpose. In upcoming chapters, including the chapter on complaint and answer and the chapter on motions, we will examine the types of documents you will be producing. For more discussion of the body of a legal document, please see the discussion of boilerplate below. Be aware, however, that often you will have to write the entire body of the document and will not be able to use any boilerplate.

The Signature Block

The SIGNATURE BLOCK is placed at the end of the document. It has a line on which the attorney will sign his or her name. By signing, the attorney is attesting that the contents of the document are true.

The signature block contains the name and attorney number of the attorney who is signing the document directly under the signature line. It also states which party the attorney represents. After identifying the party, the signature block provides the address of the attorney's office, as well as the attorney's telephone number. The signature block traditionally is single-spaced and aligned along the right margin. It is preceded by a line on which the attorney will sign his or her name.

EXAMPLE

Ana Garcia 000000
Attorney for the Plaintiff,
Melissa Hunter
123 Main Street
Parkhurst, Ohio 44XXX
(216) 555-5555 telephone

The Service Page

The final element of every document filed with the court is the SERVICE PAGE. Note that it is also correct to include the service page at the beginning of the document if the entire first page is taken up by the caption.

The service page is the attorney's proof that all other parties to the lawsuit have received a copy of the document. The attorney must sign the service page; it is his or her attestation that he or she has made sure that service has been made on all parties. Although the exact wording may vary from jurisdiction to jurisdiction, or even from attorney to attorney, the purpose of the service page is for the attorney to swear that he or she has served the document on all parties in the case. If the case involves more than two parties, each party must be served with a copy of every court filing, and that service must be documented on the service page.

The blank lines in the certificate of service allow the attorney to fill in the date and month that he or she signed the certificate. For example, this service page might be completed as follows:

EXAMPLE

CERTIFICATE OF SERVICE

A copy of the foregoing was sent to Gerald Boylston, Attorney for Defendant Jeremy Hunter, XXX Main Street, Suite 4600, Parkhurst, Ohio, 44XXX on 14th day of April , 20XX.

Ana Garcia
Ana Garcia 000000
Attorney for the Plaintiff,
Melissa Hunter
123 Main Street
Parkhurst, Ohio 44XXX
(216) 555-5555

EXERCISE

Fill in the alphabetical blanks from the information discussed above. An example has been provided **"a." Level of Court.**

IN THE COURT OF   a. ___Level of Court___

b. _____

c. _____   )
   _____   )
)   h. ⟋⟋⟋⟋
)
)
d. _____   )
)
)   i. _____
e. _____.   )
)
)
f. _____   )
   _____   )
)
g. _____.   )
)   j. _____
)
)
)
)
)

_____

EXERCISE IN CLASS

One of the best ways to learn information is to teach it to someone else. In the following exercise, two class members will teach each other about the elements of the legal document.

First student: What is the very first thing written on every legal document?
Second Student:
First student: That information is part of what element of the document?
Second student:
First student: What else is contained in the caption?
Second student:
First student: What is the purpose of each of those?

Second student:
First student: What follows the caption?
Second student:
First student: What is the purpose of the body of the document?
Second student:
First student: What follows the body of the document?
Second student:
First student: Why does the document have a signature block?
Second student:
First student: What other information does the signature block contain?

(continued)

Second student:
First student: Is that all that is contained in a legal document?
Second student:

First student: What exactly does the service page show?
Second student:

■ BOILERPLATE

Not every legal document is created from the start every time one is written. Many, if not all, attorneys use prewritten forms or documents, which are called "boilerplate." Boilerplate consists of legal documents and/or forms are partially or almost totally prewritten. For example, the basic layout of the caption is boilerplate, and your attorney or firm will store a copy of this form in your computer's form file. When you need to draft a document to be submitted to the court, you will revise the caption by adding the necessary information specific to the case you are working on, along with completing the rest of the document or form.

While boilerplate saves significant time, and therefore saves the client money, it is important to proofread any document created from a boilerplate form or document, so that you are sure that it includes only information pertaining to the case at hand. Even excellent attorneys can, in their haste, fail to remove information that does not apply to the case at hand. Boilerplate provides a shortcut and a format; it does not provide the information that you have to add. Even more importantly, you must proofread any boilerplate you use to make sure it does not contain information that does not apply to the case for which you are using it.

Many boilerplate documents or forms are specific to the area of law in which your firm or attorney practices. We will address boilerplate forms first, and following the example of a boilerplate form, we will discuss boilerplate documents.

Boilerplate Forms

Many areas of law use boilerplate forms, including bankruptcy, worker's compensation, and domestic relations. For example, if the client is a parent involved in a child support dispute, the state in which your attorney practices may have statutorily mandated child support form that the magistrate, hearing officer, or judge will use. If your client's information is provided to the court on this form, you can expedite the court's calculating the support. It is always best practice to provide the information to the court in a format the court will want to use. Below is an example of the form that the magistrate or judge must use in Ohio to calculate child support. You would need to fill in only the portion for your client.

EXAMPLE

CHILD SUPPORT COMPUTATION WORKSHEET
SOLE RESIDENTIAL PARENT OR SHARED PARENTING ORDER

Name of parties _____

Case No _____

Number of minor children _____

The following parent was designated as residential parent and legal custodian:

_____ mother

_____ father

_____ shared

Column I	Column II	Column III
Father	Mother	Combined

INCOME:

1.a. Annual gross income from employment or, when determined appropriate by the court or agency, average annual gross income from employment over a reasonable period of years. (exclude overtime, bonuses, self-employment income, or commissions) ....

$_____ $_____

1.b. Amount of overtime, bonuses, and commissions (year 1 representing the most recent year)

<u>Father</u>   <u>Mother</u>

Yr. 3 $_____   Yr. 3 $_____
      (Three years ago)   (Three years ago)

Yr. 2 $_____   Yr. 2 $_____
      (Two years ago)   (Two years ago)

Yr. 1 $_____   Yr. 1 $_____
      (Last calendar year)   (Last calendar year)

Average $_____   Average $_____

(Include in Col. I and/or Col. II the average of the three years or the year 1 amount, whichever is less, if there exists a reasonable expectation that the total earnings from overtime and/or bonuses during the current calendar year will meet or exceed the amount that is the lower of the average of the three years or the year 1 amount. If, however, there exists a reasonable expectation that the total earnings from overtime/bonuses during the current calendar year will be less than the lower of the average of the 3 years or the year 1 amount, include only the amount reasonably expected to be earned this year.) ....

$_____ $_____

2. For self-employment income:

2.a. Gross receipts from business ....
$_____ $_____

2.b. Ordinary and necessary business expenses ....
$_____ $_____

2.c. 5.6% of adjusted gross income or the actual marginal difference between the actual rate paid by the self-employed individual and the F.I.C.A. rate.............................
$_____ $_____

2.d. Adjusted gross income from self-employment (subtract the sum of 2b and 2c form 2a) ....
$_____ $_____

3. Annual income from interest and dividends (whether or not taxable) ....
$_____ $_____

4. Annual income form unemployment compensation
$_____ $_____

5. Annual income from workers' compensation, disability insurance benefits, or social security disability/retirement benefits.
$_____ $_____

6. Other annual income (identify) ....
$_____ $_____

7.a. Total annual gross income (add lines 1a, 1b, 2d, and 3-6) ......
$_____ $_____

7.b. Health insurance maximum (multiply line 7a by 5%) ....
$_____ $_____

ADJUSTMENTS TO INCOME:

8. Adjustment for minor children born to or adopted by either parent and another parent who are living with this parent; adjustment does not apply to stepchildren (number of children times federal income tax exemption less child support received, not to exceed the federal tax exemption) ....
$_____ $_____

9. Annual court-ordered support paid for other children ....
$_____ $_____

10. Annual court-ordered spousal support paid to any spouse or former spouse ....
$_____ $_____

11. Amount of local income taxes actually paid or estimated to be paid ...
....
$_____ $_____

12. Mandatory work-related deductions such as union dues, uniform fees, etc. (not including taxes, social security, or retirement) ....
....
$_____ $_____

13. Total gross income adjustments (add lines 8 through 12) ....
$_____ $_____

14.a. Adjusted annual gross income (subtract line 13 from line 7a).

$_____ $_____

14.b. Cash medical support maximum (If the amount on line 7a, Col. I, is under 150% of the federal poverty level for an individual, enter $0 on line 14b, Col. I. If the amount on line 7a, Col. I, is 150% or higher of the federal poverty level for an individual, multiply the amount on line 14a, Col. I, by 5% and enter this amount on line 14b, Col. I. If the amount on line 7a, Col. II, is under 150% of the federal poverty level for an individual, enter $0 on line 14b, Col. II. If the amount on line 7a, Col. II, is 150% or higher of the federal poverty level for an individual, multiply the amount on line 14a, Col. II, by 5% and enter this amount on line 14b, Col. II.) ....

$_____ $_____

15. Combined annual income that is basis for child support order (add line 14a, Col. I and Col. II) .... $_____

16. Percentage of parent's income to total income

16.a. Father (divide line 14a, Col. I, by line 15, Col. III) _____%

16.b. Mother (divide line 14a, Col. II, by line 15, Col. III) _____%

17. Basic combined child support obligation (refer to schedule, first column, locate the amount nearest to the amount on line 15, Col. III, then refer to column for number of children in this family. If the income of the parents is more than one sum but less than another, you may calculate the difference.) ....

$_____

18. Annual support obligation per parent

18.a. Father (multiply line 17, Col. III, by line 16a) ....

$_____

18.b. Mother (multiply line 17, Col. III, by line 16b) ....

$_____

19. Annual child care expenses for children who are the subject of this order that are work-, employment training-, or education -related, as approved by the court or agency (deduct tax credit from annual cost, whether or not claimed) ....

$_____ $_____

20.a. Marginal, out-of-pocket costs, necessary to provide for health insurance for the children who are the subject of this order (contributing cost of private family health insurance, minus the contributing cost of private single health insurance, divided by the total number of dependents covered by the plan, including the children subject of the support order, times the number of children subject of the support order) ....

$_____ $_____

20.b. Cash medical support obligation (enter the amount on line 14b or the amount of annual health care expenditures estimated by the United States Department of Agriculture and described in section **3119.30** of the Revised Code, whichever amount is lower) ....

$_____ $_____

21. ADJUSTMENTS TO CHILD SUPPORT WHEN HEALTH INSUR-
ANCE IS PROVIDED:

Father (only if obligor or shared parenting)
Mother (only if obligor or shared parenting)

21.a. Additions: line 16a times sum of amounts shown
21.b. Additions: line 16b times sum of amounts shown on line 19, Col. II
and line 20a, Col. II on line 19, Col. I and line 20a, Col. I

$_____

$_____

21.c. Subtractions: line 16b times sum of amounts
21.d. Subtractions: line 16a times sum of amounts shown shown on
line 19, Col. I and line 20a, Col. I on line 19, Col. II and line
20a, Col. II

$_____

$_____

22. OBLIGATION AFTER ADJUSTMENTS TO CHILD SUPPORT
WHEN HEALTH INSURANCE IS PROVIDED:

22.a. Father: line 18a plus or minus the difference between line

21a minus line 21c ....

$_____

22.b. Mother: line 18b plus or minus the difference between line

21b minus line 21d ....

$_____

23. ACTUAL ANNUAL OBLIGATION WHEN HEALTH INSUR-
ANCE IS PROVIDED:

23.a. (Line 22a or 22b, whichever line corresponds to the parent...

$_____

23.b. Any non-means-tested benefits, including social security and veterans' benefits, paid to and received by a child or a person on behalf
of the child due to death, disability, or retirement of the parent ....
. . . .

$_____

23.c. Actual annual obligation (subtract line 23b from line 23a)...

$_____

24. ADJUSTMENTS TO CHILD SUPPORT WHEN HEALTH INSUR-
ANCE IS NOT PROVIDED:

Father (only if obigor or shared parenting)
Mother (only if obligor or shared parenting)

24.a. Additions: line 16a times the sum of the amounts
24.b. Additions: line 16b times the sum of the amounts shown on line
19, Col. II and line 20b, Col. II shown on line 19, Col. I and line
20b, Col. I

$_____

$_____

24.c. Subtractions: line 16b times the sum of the

24.d. Subtractions: line 16a times the sum of the amounts shown on line 19, Col. I and line 20b, Col.I amounts shown on line 19, Col. II and line 20b, Col. II

$_____ .

$_____

25. OBLIGATION AFTER ADJUSTMENTS TO CHILD SUPPORT WHEN HEALTH INSURANCE IS NOT PROVIDED:

25.a. Father: line 18a plus or minus the difference between line 24a minus line 24c ....

$_____

25.b. Mother: line 18b plus or minus the difference between line 24b and 24d ....

$_____

26. ACTUAL ANNUAL OBLIGATION WHEN HEALTH INSURANCE IS NOT PROVIDED:

26.a. (Line 25a or 25b, whichever line corresponds to the parent who is the obligor) ....

$_____

26.b. Any non-means-tested benefits, including social security and veterans' benefits, paid to and received by a child or a person on behalf of the child due to death, disability, or retirement of the parent ....

$_____

26.c. Actual annual obligation (subtract line 26b from line 26a ....

$_____

27.a. Deviation from sole residential parent support amount shown on line 23c if amount would be unjust or inappropriate: (see section **3119.23** of the Revised Code.) (Specific facts and monetary value must be stated.)

_____

_____

_____

_____

27.b. Deviation from shared parenting order: (see sections **3119.23** and **3119.24** of the Revised Code.) (Specific facts including amount of time children spend with each parent, ability of each parent to maintain adequate housing for children, and each parents expenses for children must be stated to justify deviation.)

_____

_____

_____

_____

WHEN HEALTH INSURANCE IS PROVIDED   WHEN HEALTH INSURANCE IS NOT PROVIDED

28. FINAL CHILD SUPPORT FIGURE:
(This amount reflects final annual child support obligation; in Col. I, enter line 23c plus or minus any amounts indicated in line 27a or 27b; in Col. II, enter line 26c plus or minus any amounts indicated in line Father/Mother,
   27a or 27b) $_____ $_____
OBLIGOR

29. FOR DECREE: Child support per month (divide obligor's annual share, line 28, by 12) plus any processing charge $_____
    $_____

30. FINAL CASH MEDICAL SUPPORT FIGURE: (this amount reflects the final, annual cash medical support to be paid by the obligor when neither parent provides health insurance coverage for the child; enter obligors cash medical support amount from line 20b $_____

31. FOR DECREE: Cash medical support per month (divide line 30 by 12) $_____

Prepared by:
Counsel: _____
Pro se: _____
       (For mother/father)

CSEA: _____
Other: _____
       Worksheet Has Been Reviewed and Agreed To:

_____
_____
Mother   Date

_____
_____
Father   Date

Boilerplate Documents

Many firms, particularly those that practice in a specialty area, use boilerplate documents. If an attorney or a firm limits its practice to criminal law, for example, it might find that it frequently defends people accused of possession of illicit drugs. Because the same law in the jurisdiction applies to a given crime, for instance, possession of cocaine, the Rule section of a brief might be essentially identical from one case to the next. Similarly, the analysis might share a number of common elements. Rather than "reinventing the wheel," the attorneys and paralegals will borrow sections from previous documents.

In the same way, if your attorney primarily practices in personal injury cases, the office may have boilerplate sections for documents that address the law that applies to personal injury in your state.

Using boilerplate comes with potential hazards, however. For example, you must be certain that the law has not changed since the boilerplate was written. When one of your authors worked in the Court of Appeals, an attorney submitted a brief in a juvenile delinquency case. Upon researching the law that the attorney had relied on, your author discovered that the attorney was relying on a case that was not "good law." The case the attorney cited applied to a Civil Rule that had been changed, and the case no longer applied. So be forewarned: make sure the boilerplate you are using, be it a form or a portion of a brief, is current.

Another risk inherent in using boilerplate is failing to omit law or other material that does not apply to the case at hand. Even very good attorneys occasionally make this mistake, and it is very embarrassing to them when they do. One excellent public defender submitted an appellate brief for a defendant who had been convicted of trafficking in cocaine. The brief she submitted contained a paragraph that discussed LSD, which was not a drug involved in the case. That attorney had taken wording from a similar appeal brief and had failed to proofread the final document adequately before she submitted it to the court. If she had proofread carefully, she would have seen the errant reference to LSD and deleted it.

Additionally, you must ensure that the boilerplate you have selected is the correct one for the facts of your case. Just because something is prewritten does not mean that it applies to your case. Also, you still need to research to ensure that new law has not been issued that would affect your case, even if the new law does not overturn the previous law completely.

Finally, even if you use an excellent boilerplate that perfectly fits the facts of your case, you still need to add language that tailors the boilerplate to your client's unique situation. You cannot merely cut and paste law and analysis and assume that you have provided the client with the service he or she deserves.

Thus, whenever you use boilerplate, remember that it is a starting point, not a completed product. You must ensure that the law you are citing is still good law. You also must be sure that the boilerplate you use fits the facts of your case. You also must proofread your document carefully to make sure that you have deleted extraneous, unrelated material. Lastly, you must add language that applies specifically to your client's case. You will encounter many forms of boilerplate in your paralegal career, and they will save you an enormous amount of time. It is essential, though, to make sure that you have tailored the document sufficiently to the particular client in the case.

EXERCISE

Answer the following questions:

1. How many segments are in a common legal form?
2. Is the caption first?
3. What information is given in the case number?
4. What is boilerplate?
5. Explain what is in the body/allegation section.
6. Describe the service section of a legal form.

EXERCISE _____

Read the following fact pattern and examine the legal document that was based on the fact pattern. Make all necessary corrections to the legal document to make it comply with the formatting we have discussed above.

Ana has filed suit against Sheila's landlord, and his attorney has filed a motion for summary judgment. Ana had asked a paralegal student she is allowing to intern in the office to set up the motion in opposition to the landlord's motion for summary judgment. Ana has now asked you to correct the document the student drafted. The student's draft is below.

CUYAHOGA   COUNTY

Property Management, Inc.	) JUDGE: MICHAEL Martin J. Boyle
	)
Defendant	)
	)
and	)
	)
Sheila Kowalski	)
Plaintiff	)
	)
Case No. 555555	)

Motion in Opposition to Defendant's Motion for Summary Judgment.

COMMON PLEAS COURT.

_____

Ana Garcia 000000

Attorney for the Plaintiff, Melissa Hunter

123 Main Street

Parkhurst, Ohio 44XXX

(216) 555-5555

Plaintiff, Sheila Kowalski, requests this Court to overrule Defendant, Property Management, Inc.'s Motion for Summary Judgment. Issues of material fact exist that preclude a ruling against the Plaintiff.

CERTIFICATE OF SERVICE

A copy of the foregoing was sent to Gerald Boylston, Attorney for Defendant Jeremy Hunter, XXX Main Street, Suite 4600, Parkhurst, Ohio, 44XXX on 20th _____ day of November _____, 20XX.

Ana Garcia

Ana Garcia 000000

Attorney for the Plaintiff, Sheila Kowalski

EXERCISE

Ana wants you to be patient with the paralegal student, and she has asked you to explain to the student what errors existed in the draft Motion in Opposition to Defendant's Motion for Summary Judgment in the previous exercise. Write a memorandum to the student explaining each error and what the correct format is. Explain the purpose of the format to the student.

SUMMARY

- Each section of a legal document is important.

- The caption provides essential information: the court in which the case is being heard; the case number identifying the case; the Judge hearing the case; the parties to the case; and the nature of the document.

- The body of the document is the heart of the document, communicating the attorney's position or information to the court and the other parties.

- The signature block confirms that the attorney is declaring the contents of the body to be true and accurate. It also provides contact information for that attorney.

- The service page is necessary to assure the court that all parties have the same documents before them.

ASSIGNMENT

I. Correct the errors in the following caption.

MOTION TO COMPEL

Plaintiff   vs.   Defendant
)   JEREMY HUNTER
)
MELISSA M. HU)
)   JUDGE: LEROY STEINER
)
)
)
Case No. XXXXX   )
)
)
)
)
)
)
)
)

IN THE COURT OF COMMON PLEAS, CUYAHOGA COUNTY, OHIO

II. Brad has asked you to format a document for a case. He does not need you to write the body of the document. Draft the remaining three portions of the document. The Plaintiff is Arnold Crocker, and the Defendant is Thomas Williams, Sr. The case has been filed in Cuyahoga County Common Pleas Court in Ohio. It has been assigned case number 666666. The Judge assigned to the case is Miriam Harper. Opposing counsel is Gerald Boylston, whose office is located in Parkhurst at 444 Main Street, Suite 4600, Parkhurst, 44XXX.

III. Take the following information and format all but the body of a Motion to Dismiss. Leave a blank space where the body of the document belongs.

Antoine Taylor has come to seek Brad's help with a complaint he received in the mail yesterday. Zoltan Kovach, a buyer of a house in which Antoine had represented the seller, is suing Antoine because he claims that Antoine should have made the sellers reveal on the property disclosure form the fact that the people next door had a dog that barked incessantly. The sellers, Amanda and Peter Fitzgerald, have moved to another country, so Mr. Kovach cannot sue them. Mr. Kovach's attorney is Marvin Hootspah, whose office is in his home at 645 Maple Avenue in Parkhurst, Ohio 44XXX. The case number is 777777.

You have researched the law and have found that a neighbor's barking dog is not a flaw with the structure and does not need to be disclosed on the property disclosure form. Brad has asked you to format the Motion to Dismiss. Brad will enter the body of the motion later, and you will leave a space where he can do that.

LEARNING OBJECTIVES

1. Recognize the importance of an interoffice memorandum

2. Compare inappropriate and appropriate interoffice memoranda

3. Analyze appropriate situations for casual or formal memoranda

4. Compose well-written memoranda

5. Compose professional emails

Interoffice Memoranda | CHAPTER 14

■ INTEROFFICE MEMORANDUM

In almost every professional setting, one way in which staff and management communicate is through interoffice memoranda. Despite the more casual tone found currently in many office settings, memoranda should be written professionally, regardless of their purpose. Many people entering the workforce now lack experience with writing professionally, and it is important to avoid inadvertently making a bad impression on those with whom you work by writing unprofessionally drafted memos.

Why Use an Interoffice Memorandum

Throughout your paralegal career, you will draft many memos for a number of purposes, but a memo's primary purpose is to inform. First, we want to point out that the singular and plural forms of the word "memorandum" differ from the singular and plural forms of English words. Because the word is derived from Latin, its singular and plural forms follow Latin rules. Thus, the singular form of the word is "memorandum" and the plural form of the word is "memoranda." Throughout this chapter, we will refer to these documents either as memos or by their long name of memorandum or memoranda.

When to Use an Interoffice Memorandum

The subject matters of your memoranda may vary from the mundane to the important. You may write a memorandum to the office staff informing them of a policy change or some other office concern. If you work in a large law office, you might write a memorandum to a fellow paralegal delineating the assigning of tasks on a case between you. You may write a memorandum to the attorney providing the information you learned in a client interview. And you probably will write memoranda to attorneys providing legal research and analysis, similar to the ones you read in the IRAC chapters.

Where to Use an Interoffice Memorandum

You will use an interoffice memo for situations that require written evidence of your communication. A legal memo obviously needs to be in writing, because the attorney is going to rely on it and refer to back to it. Although more mundane memos, like the kitchen memo in an example in this chapter, could be conveyed by email or verbally, it is preferable to put policy issues like this in writing. Once you have given someone a written memo about a subject, you have proof that you have provided the information contained in the memo.

For example, most offices have written policies, and updates to those policies are provided to the staff through memos that are circulated throughout the office. Use of Internet policies are common, both because legal search engines often charge based on the amount of time being used, and because employees are supposed to be spending their time doing work for the firm and not attending to personal matters. If one paralegal were discovered to be abusing the Internet research site by using it for personal research rather than office business, he or she could be terminated. If the paralegal then sued for wrongful discharge, that memo informing all the employees of the office's Internet and legal search engine policy would be evidence of the paralegal's advance notice that the excessive use was an issue. If the memo had been written in the way that follows, its author could be very embarrassed on the witness stand. Additionally, an unprofessionally written memo reflects badly on the firm. You may disagree with your bosses, but to the clients and the public, your job is to make them look good.

EXAMPLE OF A BADLY WRITTEN MEMORANDUM

MEMO

TO: All paralegals

DATE: April 5, 20XX

FROM: Office Manager

RE: LoisLaw Account

Our LoisLaw use has doubled in the past month! This site isn't free, you know. I know we charge the time to our clients' accounts, but really. Some of you haven't been charging the clients on your billing sheets, and the office has to eat that expense!

Any paralegal worth the title knows that they should draft their issues BEFORE they log onto the research site. Is it that hard to copy and paste the law you want to read?

Let's get professional, people!

Just as important as the information you include in an interoffice memo is the information you exclude.

EXAMPLE OF A PROPERLY WRITTEN MEMORANDUM

MEMO

TO: All paralegals

DATE: April 5, 20XX

FROM: Office Manager

RE: LoisLaw Account

Our LoisLaw use has doubled in the past month, creating a significant expense for the office. Remember that the time you spend researching is an expense that should be included with your billable hours for the client for whose case you are researching.

Even though we pass the cost of LoisLaw research on to the client, please avoid excessive time on the site. Formulate your research issues before you log into the account, and copy any cases you wish to spend time reviewing. Then review your research after you have logged off the site. It is less expensive to log on twice than it is to leave the site open for an extended period of time.

Thank you for your attention to this matter.

How to Format an Interoffice Memorandum

You will notice that the format of the memo examples above is the same. Although this format may vary somewhat from office to office, the elements contained in a memorandum generally are consistent.

There will be significant and important differences between the non-legal memos you write and the legal memoranda of law. These differences will be discussed within each of the elements of the memorandum format.

Heading

Memos begin with "MEMO" or "MEMORANDUM" centered at the top of the page. If the contents of the memo are privileged or are law firm work product, this must be clearly and definitively stated at the top of the page. Any legal memoranda you write for the attorney will qualify as attorney work product, which protects the other side from obtaining it. Much of the work you do will be protected as attorney work product. Be sure to include the fact that it is privileged in the title to prevent this work from inadvertently falling into the wrong hands.

The next four lines are placed flush against the left margin of the page.

To:

The next element in many memos is the word "TO:" followed by the identity of the intended recipients of the memo. In our example above, the recipients are "all paralegals." If the contents of the memo are sensitive, you might add the words "for your eyes only" or a similar phrase to alert the recipient not to leave the memo sitting where someone else might be able to read it.

Date:

Next in our example is the date line, indicated with the word "DATE:" Far too often, in the immediacy of the moment when a memo is being drafted, its writer fails to include the date on it. In the case of the paralegal who abused the office's legal search engine and Internet policy, if the memo were not dated, its effectiveness in court would be seriously damaged. Without the date, how is the employer to prove that the paralegal employee received it prior to his discharge?

Similarly, in a legal research memo, your analysis may evolve as the case progresses, and if your memorandum of law is not dated, the reader will be confused concerning which version is most recent.

From:

The "FROM" line sometimes is placed below the "TO" line and before the "DATE" line. The order of these two lines is a matter of office custom. The identity of the memo's writer is important for several reasons. Most importantly, it allows the reader to determine the memo's importance. If the memo is from the managing partner, you will read it more quickly than if it is from the planner of the holiday party. Another reason the identity of the memo's author is important is to allow a reader to distinguish between various memos he or she may receive on similar or the same subject.

Re:

The subject line is an essential element of the memo. It summarizes the content or purpose of the memo for the reader. Determining the contents of your subject line, therefore, is an important step in writing an effective memo. It must be brief, able to be read at a glance. It also must clearly inform the reader of the memo's purpose. In the example above, the purpose is to discuss the LoisLaw Account.

If you are writing a memorandum of law, your subject line might include the name of your client, or it might include the names of both parties: "Kowalski v. Property Management, Inc." Many firms have internal identification numbers, and for a memorandum of law that you are writing for an attorney, it might be customary in that firm to include the office's identification number for the case. Alternatively, once a complaint has been filed, you might include the case number that the clerk of courts has assigned to the case.

Body of the Memo

No matter what the subject matter of your memo, whether it is mundane or of utmost importance, it should have a professional tone and be grammatically correct. Just as with emails, once you have issued a memo, you have no control over where it goes or who sees it. What may have seemed clever or cute when you wrote it can be embarrassing when it is read by the firm's founding partner or your immediate supervisor. Always err on the side of being professional.

Notice the difference in tone and professionalism of the bad example below and the corrected example that follows it:

EXAMPLE OF A BADLY WRITTEN MEMORANDUM

MEMO

TO: All Office Staff

DATE: April 5, 20XX

FROM: Managing Partner's Secretary

RE: Turing off Equipment

As I am sure you are aware, the Managing Partner is an environmental fanatic. He loses sleep worrying that someone has left a monitor on and is wasting electricity. So this is fair warning: you will answer to HIM if I find that you have left a monitor or printer running when you are away from the office. That means when you are in court, have gone home for the evening, or, for pity's sake, or when you are on vacation. I am sick and tired of having to hear about who left a monitor running or the fact that the printer in the secretarial pool was on all night.

The drafter of the above memo is far from professional, and by saying negative things about her attorney, she could be putting her job in jeopardy. Although the world is far more casual in the 21st century, the legal field is still quite formal. This formality should carry over into all your communications within the office and with anyone dealing with the office.

Some office memos address extremely mundane subjects, but whenever a group of people work together, issues of this sort arise. No doubt you will encounter this type of situation, and it is important to address it professionally.

EXAMPLE OF A PROPERLY WRITTEN MEMORANDUM

MEMO

TO: All Office Staff

DATE: April 5, 20XX

FROM: Managing Partner's Secretary

RE: Turing off Equipment

Please remember to turn off your printers and monitors when you will be out of the office for any period of time exceeding four hours. It requires less electricity to turn the equipment on after that period of time than it does to leave the equipment running. Before leaving the office for the evening or for vacation, be sure to check that you have turned off all of your equipment.

This law office is committed to energy conservation, not just for reasons of economy, but also for environmental reasons.

Thank you for your cooperation with this directive.

The above memo is professional in tone and explains the purpose for the requested action.

Although it is initially more satisfying and faster to dash off a memo, the example below will demonstrate the ineffectiveness and lack of professionalism that can result.

EXAMPLE OF AN UNPROFESIONAL MEMO

MEMO

TO: Office staff

DATE: April 5, 20XX

FROM: Pat Paralegal

RE: Kitchen etiquette

I am sick and tired of having clean up after you slobs! If you are too stupid to cover your food in the microwave, then clean it up yourself. The rest of us are not your maids (yes, this means you, Don).

And don't put open containers in the fridge. Your pop spilled, Yvonne, and it dried. Now the fridge is sticky. And your open container of fish, Don? Two words: P. U.

So have some consideration for the rest of us, and remember:

YOUR MOTHER DOES NOT WORK HERE!

If this memo is posted in the office kitchen, how will it look to a visiting attorney who may go in there to get a cup of coffee? Also, although the venting was probably satisfying, how seriously do you think the memo's readers will take it?

EXAMPLE OF A PROFESSIONALLY WRITTEN MEMORANDUM

MEMO

TO: Office staff

DATE: April 5, 20XX

FROM: Pat Paralegal

RE: Kitchen etiquette

For the past week, the microwave in the office kitchen has been left with food splatters that one of us has had to clean. Please be courteous and remember to cover your food when warming it and to clean up any messes you make.

Similarly, an open can of cola spilled in the refrigerator and was left to dry. First, please do not place open containers of any liquid or food into the refrigerator. Second, if you do spill something, clean up after yourself.

We all need to be considerate of the others who use the kitchen.

Obviously, not all interoffice memorandums are so mundane. Most memos address more serious matters. In legal memos, in addition to your important writing skills, your analytical skills are essential. Many of your memoranda will be IRAC memoranda to the attorney. We addressed the IRAC method in chapter 7 discussing the IRAC format, but let us format an IRAC memo the way that you would do it for the attorney. Remember, every office has its own format, but what we are demonstrating is a standard upon which other formats are based.

EXAMPLE OF A STANDARD FORMAT

PRIVILEGED AND CONFIDENTIAL

MEMORANDUM OF LAW

TO: Ana Garcia Smith, Esq.

FROM: Pat Paralegal

DATE: November 14, 20XX

RE: Kowalski v. Property Management, Inc., wrongful eviction

ISSUE: Whether landlord complied with Ohio's statutory requirements when he evicted tenant, thereby making the eviction legal.

SHORT ANSWER: Landlord failed to comply with the statutory requirements for a legal eviction.

LONG ANSWER: In Ohio, prior to evicting a tenant, a landlord must present the tenant with a three-day notice that meets the statutorily mandated wording.

RULE: Only after providing this notice may the landlord then begin formal eviction proceedings. RC § 1923.04. Specifically, the landlord's three-day notice must contain the exact wording provided in RC § 1923.04:

> "You are being asked to leave the premises. If you do not leave, an eviction action may be initiated against you. If you are in doubt regarding your legal rights and obligations as a tenant, it is recommended that you seek legal assistance."
> *Id.*

After the tenant has received the three-day notice, the landlord may file a complaint for forcible entry and detainer. Again, the landlord must follow the strict requirements set out in RC §1923.06 by providing the tenant with a summons no later than seven days prior to the hearing on the eviction. The summons must contain exact mandated language:

"A complaint to evict you has been filed with this court. No person shall be evicted unless the person's right to possession has ended and no person shall be evicted in retaliation for the exercise of the person's lawful rights. If you are depositing rent with the clerk of this court you shall continue to deposit such rent until the time of the court hearing. The failure to continue to deposit such rent may result in your eviction. You may request a trial by jury. You have the right to seek legal assistance. If you cannot afford a lawyer, you may contact your local legal aid or legal service office. If none is available, you may contact your local bar association."

Id.

ANALYSIS: Ms. Kowalski, the tenant, has experienced ongoing problems with her landlord. These problems culminated in his evicting her while she was at work on November 4, 20XX. A few days prior to evicting her, the landlord posted a notice on her door when she was out of town. The landlord's notice simply stated, "I hereby am giving you notice that you are being evicted. You have three days to leave this apartment."

Ms. Kowalski sought our counsel after finding this notice. She left our office to report to work at the hospital, where she is a Registered Nurse working in the Intensive Care Unit. When she returned to her apartment in the morning, she found that the landlord had changed the locks. She learned that he had placed her belongings on the curb, but fortunately her family was able to retrieve most of her belongings.

This eviction failed to meet statutory requirements in several different areas: the landlord's three-day notice lacked the requisite language contained in RC § 1923.04. It did not inform Ms. Kowalski of her right to seek legal counsel. It also did not state that the landlord intended to commence an eviction action against her. From the beginning of this eviction, the landlord's actions failed to meet the statutory requirements.

The landlord further violated the statute when he failed to commence a proper eviction action in the court. Rather that filing a complaint, the landlord put Ms. Kowalski's possessions on the curb and changed the locks on November 4, 20XX.

The landlord's actions in evicting Ms. Kowalski violated Ohio statutory requirements in a number of areas. He failed to comply with the prerequisites mandated in RC §§ 1923.04 and 1923.06.

CONCLUSION: Landlord failed to comply with the statutory requirements for a legal eviction.

Although each memo you write should be professional, depending on the subject matter, various memos may be somewhat less formal than others. The memo regarding kitchen etiquette was less formal than the memorandum of law regarding the unlawful eviction.

Nonetheless, each memo should contain information regarding the recipient or recipients, the sender, the subject matter, and the date. Dating anything you write is essential in a law office. Certainly any correspondence must be dated. It is imperative to make it a habit to date anything you write, from a telephone message to a document that will be filed with the court.

If you are working on a project over the course of more than a day, it is a good idea to include the time of each document when you save it. That way you will be sure to begin working on the most recent draft. This is especially important if you are collaborating with another person who is adding or editing the material.

EXERCISE IN CLASS

The class will break up into groups of no more than four students. Each group will collaborate on writing a memo to the office on the following conversation the paralegal had with the attorney.

Attorney   You know, Pat, I have been seeing a lot of careless errors in documents from several of the paralegals. You are the senior paralegal, so I want you to let all the paralegals know that I expect more professionalism from them.

Paralegal   I am sorry to hear about this. Can you give me some specific examples of the types of errors you have seen?

Attorney   Here is one right here. This sentence is supposed to use the possessive word "their," and instead it says "they're." If I do not catch these types of mistakes, I end up being embarrassed in court. The paralegals are relying too much on spell-check, and we both know how reliable that is! (chuckling).

Paralegal   Are there other types of mistakes you are noticing?

Attorney   Yes, there are. Let me find that document I was reading this morning. Here it is. Look at the area I highlighted. The paralegal missed a sentence fragment and wrote, "Because regulations mandate it." This document is going to Judge Bernard, and you know what a stickler he is for grammar. This could distract him from the very good argument contained in this brief.

Paralegal   That is unacceptable. Are those the primary errors you are seeing?

Attorney   Well, there is one more thing. One of the paralegals is far too casual in tone when writing legal documents. Please remind the paralegals that contractions are unacceptable. Also, remind them that exclamation points have no place in legal writing. I think that covers it. Oh, and let me see the memo before you send it out. Thanks.

EXERCISE

Read the scenario provided and then correct the Interoffice Memo and rewrite the assignment.

FROM: Pat Paralegal

RE: heating smelly food in the microwave

TO: Whoever is heating fish!

DATE: forever!!!

I can't believe how selfish and inconsiderate you are, whoever you are that microwaved that stinking, rotten fish in the kitchen where we all have to eat! This is the third time in month that you have done this, and I have talked to everyone in the office. No one admits doing it, but obviously someone is! We don't have an office cat coming in here and eating fish.

Don't be such a self-centered jerk. Stink up your own house with your reeking, foul fish!

EXERCISE

Write an Interoffice Memo based on the following information.

Your office routinely includes a map and directions for driving to the office when it sends correspondence to new clients. Because of road construction, the clients will not be able to follow the instructions to get to the office. When you realized this and mentioned it to the managing partner at 4:30 pm on August 12, 20XX, he asked you to draft a memo to all the paralegals and secretaries providing them with the new, temporary directions. He expects the new instructions to be included in all correspondence beginning tomorrow.

The new directions tell the clients to use the following route:

Main Street is closed between Second Avenue and Thrush Street. Our office is located in the area of the street that is closed, but we have free client parking in a garage located on Locust Street. Locust Street is parallel to Main, and the garage has an entrance into our building. A building receptionist is located at the garage entrance, and he will direct you to the office on the 13th floor.

EXERCISE

Read the following scenario and compose an Interoffice Memo.

The managing attorney has called you into the office and instructed you to draft a memo to the entire office. He was very upset, and he informed you that when he arrived at the office this morning at 5:00 am, the door to the office was unlocked. Not only was the door unlocked, he found a homeless man sleeping on the couch in the reception area. Additionally, someone had rummaged through the refrigerator in the office kitchen and eaten most of the food. Distressing to him personally was the fact that his private supply of Johnny Walker Black had all been drunk. He told you that he was most upset, however, at the potential breach of client confidentiality. He instructed you to include in the memo an order to lock every file cabinet before leaving for the day.

EXERCISE

Read the scenario and compose an Interoffice Memo.

You have interviewed a potential client, Larry Lush, on December 6, 20XX, and now you must write the memo to the attorney informing him or her of what the client told you. Be sure to include only the legally relevant information.

Potential client: Oh man, am I in big trouble now! I got busted – again – and this time I was drunk and high. Because I wrecked my car, I got took to the hospital and they tested my blood. I'm out on bail now cause they know I am too banged up to travel. I'm stuck in this wheelchair cause I busted both legs. I'm full a metal from them fixing my legs.

Anyways, so I tested 0.35, not to mention the coke they found in my blood. The cops said that I was half-way to dead. They don't know what a good liver I got! My license been suspended since last fall when I got busted for driving drunk. They don't understand that I drive better drunk than most people do sober. They ought to stop some of these old geezers who can't see over the steering wheel!

I need a real good lawyer, someone who has an in with the Judge. I sure hope you guys can help me.

EXERCISE

Read the scenario and compose an Interoffice Memo.

A famous actress, Maria Marvelous, has retained an attorney in your office to represent her in her divorce. She has managed to keep knowledge of her marital problems out of the tabloids, and the attorney managed to meet with her without anyone beside you knowing she was in the office. Your attorney, Ana Garcia, has asked you to draft a memo reminding the entire office of the attorney-client privilege. Specifically, she wants you to cite

The Ohio Rules of Professional Conduct, focusing on Rule 1.6: Confidentiality of Information. You are to directly quote the first clause of the first sentence of section (a), which states, "(a) A lawyer shall not reveal information relating to the representation of a client . . . ." The managing partner wants you to emphasize that until an attorney acts publicly on behalf of a client, for example by filing a document with the court, the fact that the attorney represents the client shall not be disclosed.

Interoffice Emails

Many of your communications within the office will be done by email. Drafting professional emails is particularly challenging for people who grew up using the Internet and learned to communicate in the unique shorthand that email, Twitter, and other forms of instant communication use. Abbreviations such as "U" for the word "you" have no place in a professional email.

Similarly, emoticons and emojis are never professionally appropriate.

Remember that you should never put anything in an email that you would not shout out an open window. Once you send an email, you cannot retrieve it, and more importantly, you cannot control who else receives it.

In one law office, an attorney sent a scathing email to the office manager criticizing a member of the secretarial staff. The office manager forwarded the email to the secretarial staff member who was the subject of the email. Because the secretarial staff member was professional, he never allowed the email to affect his interactions with and assistance to the attorney who sent it. But that attorney risked passive-aggressive retribution from the man he had criticized.

By sending an email to the office manager, who was the secretarial staff member's supervisor, the attorney failed to give the man a chance to correct whatever problem the attorney addressed in the email. Additionally, the attorney risked jeopardizing the man's employment. In this situation, the office manager knew the attorney well and knew that he was a difficult personality, so the office manager disregarded the complaint. But the email lowered both the office manager and the secretarial staff member's respect for the attorney.

It is also important to avoid humor in your professional emails. What might be funny to you and to the original recipient may not amuse someone who receives the forwarded email. An attorney sent an otherwise professional email regarding a legal issue to a partner who was working on the case with her. She and the partner had worked together on the case for months, and they had some inside jokes regarding the case. She made a reference to the joke in the email, which the partner forwarded to another attorney for his opinion on the issue discussed in the email, and copied the attorney on the inquiry. She was quite embarrassed at the unprofessional reference to the inside joke that was forwarded with the email.

Another source of email embarrassment in a professional office is the unintentional use of "Reply All." Rarely will all the addressees on a group email care to receive your response to the email, and your response sometimes can create an awkward situation for you. At best, your group reply will annoy the group. At worst, it can get you fired.

It should go without saying that you never, ever, use foul language in a professional email.

Even outside the office setting, you must be cautious in what you post on the Internet. Social media sites have no guarantee of privacy, and posting a negative comment about your employer or a coworker can have serious consequences. We know a professional who learned that one of his employees had complained about hating her job, and naming her employer, on her Facebook page. Another employee brought this to the professional's attention, and the employee was terminated.

EXERCISE

There is a rumor circulating through the office that the managing partner has a new client who is a famous movie star. Wayne Benning's work buddy, Jack, sent an office-wide email saying that he had seen this famous woman in the hall. Wayne quickly responded to Jack's email.

Identify all the errors in the interoffice email below.

From: Wayne Benning

To: entire office

Subject: Fwd: Re: a client

Jack-holy &**^%#**&!! Can you believe we are breathing the same air as Maria Marvelous??!!? She is SO hot. I love her movie "Slow Dancing." I'd slow dance with her anytime! ☺ Let's meet for a drink at the Drunken Donkey after work. I can't wait to talk about this!

Wayne Benning
Docket Clerk
Smith & Garcia, Attorneys at Law
Phone: 000-000-0000
Fax: 000-000-0000

EXERCISE

The managing partner asked a new paralegal to send this interoffice email memorandum for her. The new paralegal is not permitted yet to send office-wide emails without having them be reviewed. She inserted the managing partner's text into the body of the email, and completed the addressee and subject lines. The head paralegal has asked you to review the email memo and to explain to the new paralegal why the errors are wrong. You are then to correct any errors. The head paralegal will then review the email before it is sent.

From: Managing Partner

To: entire office

Subject: Re: a really, really famous client

"I have an appointment today with a client who happens to be a celebrity. I fully expect that every one of you will treat this person in a professional and courteous manner. It goes without saying that you will not solicit autographs or engage this person in unnecessary conversation, and that you will treat her the same way that you treat all of our clients. Additionally, remember that her presence in the office is a matter of attorney-client privilege, and you are not to gossip about it, even among yourselves. I thank you in advance for your professionalism."

EXERCISE

Draft an email addressing the ethical use of email for a new group of paralegals who are starting with the firm on Monday.

SUMMARY

- Paralegals use memoranda for a number of different purposes.

- The purpose of some memos is to inform fellow office staff members of a situation, like the kitchen memos in the examples.

- Even when the subject matter of an interoffice memo is not formal, the tone of your memo must remain professional.

- Paralegals often write memoranda of law for the attorneys.

- Always indicate on memoranda of law that the contents are privileged.

- Always date every memorandum you write.

- If you write multiple drafts of a memorandum of law, always date each version.

- Always clearly identify the recipients of every memo.

- Always identify the sender of every memo.

ASSIGNMENT

I. Read the following scenario and compose a professional memo for the managing partner to send to the office staff. Refer to the chapter on letter writing, chapter 4, to identify your purpose and your audience.

Within minutes of Wayne Benning accidentally hitting "reply all" instead of restricting his email to his coworker Jack, building security and the managing partner escorted him out of the office. Although they took his key to the office, a locksmith changed the locks as a precautionary measure. Each employee received a copy of the new key.

Because you are a mature and trusted employee, the managing partner has asked you to draft a memo for him to send to the staff informing them of Wayne's termination. The memo should inform the staff that Wayne is not permitted in the office, and that any personal belongings he may have left behind will be retrieved and mailed to him by the managing partner's secretary.

Remember, you are ghostwriting this memo, and it will be from the managing partner.

II. Read the following scenario. Draft a memorandum of law to the managing partner explaining how this statute would apply to Wayne's upcoming trial.

Two months after Wayne had been fired, the managing partner arrived at the office at 5:00 am, as he usually did, and found that the door had been kicked in. He immediately called the police, who discovered that a file cabinet in the managing partner's office had been broken into and files

were missing. The managing partner's office was always kept locked, and the door had been taken off the hinges. The fingerprints on the file cabinet belonged to the managing partner, his secretary, and Wayne Benning. The police arrested Wayne and charged him with breaking and entering.

The managing partner has asked you to research the statute addressing breaking and entering. You have found the following statute. Draft a memo to the managing partner explaining how this statute would apply to Wayne's upcoming trial.

LAW

(A) No person by force, stealth, or deception, shall trespass in an unoccupied structure, with purpose to commit therein any theft offense, as defined in section 2913.01 of the Revised Code, or any felony.

(B) No person shall trespass on the land or premises of another, with purpose to commit a felony.

(C) Whoever violates this section is guilty of breaking and entering, a felony of the fifth degree.

RC 2911.13 Breaking and entering.

III. Read the following scenario and compose a professional Interoffice Memo.

Because of your excellent writing skills, the managing partner often asks you to draft his memos instead of asking his secretary. The office is upgrading its computer system, including the office calendar and tickler list. He has asked you to draft a memo instructing all the secretaries to back up their attorneys' calendars and tickler lists in case the transfer to the new program does not go as planned and the calendars and tickler lists are lost in the switch.

IV. Read the following scenario and draft an email to the lead counsel on the case, taking care to avoid writing anything that could be incriminating to the firm or libelous to the attorney you overheard.

While you were in the firm's law library researching, you overheard a conversation that took place on the other side of the stacks. You recognized one of the voices as belonging to an associate attorney who was new to the firm. She was talking on her cell phone and instructing a client to sign an affidavit and mail it to her. She assured the client that she would notarize the affidavit when it arrived.

The lead attorney on that case was out of town taking a deposition, but you felt it was important to inform him of this attorney's conduct as soon as possible. You knew that any falsification could hurt the client's case, in addition to harming the firm's reputation.

You quickly researched the situation and want to incorporate the following case into your email.

Disciplinary Counsel v. Heffter, 98 Ohio St.3d 320, 784 N.E.2d 693 (2003) states in pertinent part:

LAW

> [I]n an effort to speed up the sale of the property, and as a convenience to her client, on August 30, 1999, respondent notarized the limited powers of attorney . . . without witnessing their signatures. . . . . The panel agreed with the parties' stipulation that respondent's conduct of notarizing the signatures . . . outside their presence constituted a violation of DR 1-102(A)(4) (engaging in conduct involving dishonesty, fraud, deceit, or misrepresentation).
>
> . . . .
>
> [R]espondent is hereby suspended from the practice of law for six months, with the entire suspension stayed on the condition that respondent commit no further misconduct.

Id.

LEARNING OBJECTIVES

1. Recognize the function of a pleading in the sequence of a lawsuit

2. Identify the different sections of a complaint

3. Label the different parts of the caption

4. Compile important information from a fact pattern into the complaint format

5. Outline the answer document in response to a complaint

6. Construct correct, well-organized complaints and answers

7. Explain the purpose and timing of affirmative defenses and counterclaims

The Complaint and Answer

CHAPTER 15

PLEADINGS

Pleadings are documents that parties to a suit file with the court that contain statements regarding what each party claims the other party did to injure them and responses to the allegations, including defenses against them. Pleadings notify the opposing parties of what each intends to address in trial.

The complaint is the first pleading that initiates a lawsuit, and it is filed by the plaintiff. The answer is the response to the allegations contained in the complaint, and it is filed by the defendant. The answer also may include affirmative defenses and counterclaims. These will be discussed briefly later in this chapter. You will learn more about affirmative defenses and counterclaims in your Civil Procedure class. We will include pertinent sections of the Federal Civil Rules with each pleading and motion we discuss in this section. Many, but not all, states have Civil Rules that track the Federal Civil Rules. You must be sure to consult the Civil Rules for the state where you work, as well as the Local Rules for the jurisdiction.

THE COMPLAINT

The complaint is the filing that starts a lawsuit. The person who files the complaint is the plaintiff, although in reality, the plaintiff's attorney acts in the plaintiff's place. The complaint differs in several important aspects from other court filings, as we have explained below. Note that the precise format of the complaint will vary from jurisdiction to jurisdiction, but the basic elements are the same. A caveat: be careful to spell "complaint" correctly, because spell check will not recognize writing "compliant" as being an error.

The basic format of a COMPLAINT includes five sections:

Table 15.1 Complaint Sections

Elements	Sections
Caption	1st section
Allegations/Body	2nd section
Prayer for Relief	3rd section
Jury Demand	4th section
Signature Block	5th section
Service	6th section

Federal Civil Rule 10. Form of Pleadings

(a) CAPTION; NAMES OF PARTIES. Every pleading must have a caption with the court's name, a title, a file number, and a Rule 7(a) designation. The title of the complaint must name all the parties; the title of other pleadings, after naming the first party on each side, may refer generally to other parties.

(b) PARAGRAPHS; SEPARATE STATEMENTS. A party must state its claims or defenses in numbered paragraphs, each limited as far as practicable to a single set of circumstances. A later pleading may refer by number to a paragraph in an earlier pleading. If doing so would promote clarity, each claim founded on a separate transaction or occurrence—and each defense other than a denial—must be stated in a separate count or defense.

Rule 8. General Rules of Pleading

(a) CLAIM FOR RELIEF. A pleading that states a claim for relief must contain:

(1) a short and plain statement of the grounds for the court's jurisdiction, unless the court already has jurisdiction and the claim needs no new jurisdictional support;

(2) a short and plain statement of the claim showing that the pleader is entitled to relief; and

(3) a demand for the relief sought, which may include relief in the alternative or different types of relief.

The Caption

The appearance of the caption of a complaint differs in several areas from other legal documents. First, the caption on the complaint will not include the actual name of the Judge: the Clerk of Courts will assign the Judge when the complaint is filed. Therefore, the space for the Judge is blank. Similarly, the Clerk of Courts assigns the case number, so that space also is left blank.

The caption of a complaint contains very important elements not found in other legal documents (except occasionally, the answer): the jury demand. One of your authors has seen at least two paralegals fired for failing to include the jury demand on a complaint. As you will learn in your Civil Procedure class, if the jury demand is not included on the complaint, the right to a jury can be lost. Since a jury is an important factor in winning some cases, failing to include the jury demand, if the attorney wants one, can be an extremely serious error.

Below is an example of the caption of a complaint for one state. Although the precise format of the caption will vary somewhat from jurisdiction to jurisdiction, the contents of the caption will be similar.

EXAMPLE

IN THE COURT OF COMMON PLEAS
PARKHURST COUNTY, OHIO

James Kovach 777 Oak Street Parkhurst, Ohio 44XXX	)))))	Case No. Judge:
Plaintiff	)))	<u>COMPLAINT</u>
vs.	)))	
Thomas Williams, Sr. 847 West Avenue Parkhurst, Ohio 44XXX Defendant	)))	<u>JURY DEMAND</u> <u>ENDORSED HEREIN</u>

Notice that the addresses of the parties are included on the complaint, while they are not included on other legal documents. This is necessary so the Clerk of Courts can serve the complaint on the other parties, and the other parties know the whereabouts of the plaintiff. You will file as many copies of the complaint as the Clerk of Courts will need to serve a copy on each party listed in the caption and have at least one copy left for the Clerk to put into the court's file. Of course, you also need to have a time-stamped copy of the complaint for your office's client file.

Other parts of the complaint also differ from other legal documents. Rather than having a brief or memorandum of law as the body of the document, the complaint has allegations. These allegations may be separated into different counts, which provide different claims related to the issue or event that is the subject of the complaint.

The Allegations/Body

Depending on the jurisdiction, the introduction to the allegations may contain language similar to the following:

> **EXAMPLE**
>
> Now comes Plaintiff, by and through counsel, and as his Complaint against Defendant states the following:

Then the complaint contains as many counts as needed to thoroughly present the plaintiff's demands. For example:

> **EXAMPLE**
>
> <u>**COUNT ONE**</u>
>
> 1. The Plaintiff, James Kovach (Kovach), was and is a resident of Parkhurst County, Ohio at all times relevant to the facts of this complaint.
>
> 2. The Defendant, Thomas Williams, Sr. (Williams), was and is a resident of Parkhurst County, Ohio, at all times relevant to the facts of this complaint.
>
> 3. On or about May 15, 20XX, at approximately 2:00 p.m., Kovach was driving his Ford Fiesta northbound on County Road 15. He was following a blue pickup truck with a refrigerator in the truck bed. At all times, Kovach maintained an assured clear distance from the vehicle in front of him. Kovach was wearing his lap and shoulder belts. The weather was clear, and the roads were dry.
>
> 4. The pickup truck swerved suddenly and the refrigerator that had been on the truck bed bounced out of the truck, landing on Kovach's windshield. The sudden occurrence of the airborne refrigerator prevented Kovach from taking evasive action to protect himself.
>
> 5. The refrigerator struck Kovach in the head, leaving him in a coma for five days.
>
> 6. The broken windshield glass damaged Kovach's eyes, permanently blinding him.
>
> 7. As a proximate result of William's negligence, Kovach has accrued medical expenses, including treatment by surgeons and physicians, hospitalizations, and multiple surgeries.

8. As a proximate result of Williams's negligence, Kovach has been unable to work and has lost income.

COUNT TWO

9. Kovach restates and incorporates all of Count I as if fully rewritten herein.

10. As a result of the damage caused by the refrigerator striking Kovach's automobile, it was damaged beyond repair.

11. As a proximate result of Williams's negligence, Kovach suffered property damage and loss.

The Prayer for Relief

Another element found in a Complaint that is not included in other legal documents is the prayer for relief. In this section of the complaint, the plaintiff states what resolution he or she desires from the lawsuit. Note that some states require this section of the complaint to be supplemented later, and forgetting to update it is also an extremely serious error.

EXAMPLE

WHEREFORE, Plaintiff James Kovach demands judgment against Defendant Thomas Williams, Sr. in an amount in excess of twenty-five thousand dollars ($25,000.00) on Counts I and II for compensation for injuries, loss of income, and property damage, as well as any additional relief this Court deems Plaintiff to be legally entitled, just, and/or equitable, together with the costs of this action.

The Jury Demand

The jury demand must be repeated after the prayer for relief. The exact wording of the jury demand will vary from office to office and jurisdiction to jurisdiction, but it will state something like one of the following:

EXAMPLE

JURY DEMAND

Plaintiff demands a trial by jury on all issues in this action properly triable to a jury.

The Signature Block

The chapter on formatting, chapter 13, explained and provided examples of the signature block.

Both the prayer for relief and the jury demand must be signed by the attorney. It is acceptable to include the full signature block under each signature, or to have the entire block under the prayer for relief and just the attorney's name and his role in the case below the jury demand.

The Service Page

While the Clerk of Courts will serve the defendants by certified mail or other method as prescribed by the Civil Rules in your jurisdiction, if the case had more than one plaintiff, you would have to provide service to the other plaintiff or plaintiffs. All other filings, after the initial Complaint, must be served on all parties to the action, as well, of course, with the Court.

EXAMPLE

INSTRUCTIONS FOR SERVICE

The Clerk of Courts is hereby instructed to serve a copy of this Complaint on all parties at the addresses listed in the caption.

_____
Clarence Dowling 000000
Attorney for the Plaintiff,
James Kovach

A summons is the actual document, like a complaint, that establishes jurisdiction over the other party or parties and initiates the lawsuit. A summons is the copy of the complaint that is presented to the other party or parties informing them of the suit.

Service is the delivery of the document that initiates the suit on the other party or parties to the suit. Additionally, all subsequent motions are served on the other party or parties to the suit. In most cases, all the pleadings and motions following the complaint are served on counsel for the other party or parties, unless the party is *pro se* that is, representing him or herself.

Remembering Each Element: a Mnemonic

Because remembering each element of the complaint is so important, we have created a mnemonic to help you remember them. A mnemonic is a memory trick in which you use the first letters of the words in a phrase, sentence, or list.

<u>C</u>OURTROOMS <u>A</u>RE <u>P</u>ROOF OF <u>J</u>URIES <u>SI</u>TTING <u>S</u>ILENTLY

Table 15.2 Visualizing the Complaint Sections

Picture	Element	Section
Courtrooms	**C**aptions	1st section
Are	**A**llegations/Body	2nd section
Proof of	**P**rayer for Relief	3rd section
Juries	**J**ury Demand	4th section
Sitting	**S**ignature Block	5th section
Silently	**S**ervice	6th section

Close your eyes and picture the figure 15.1, while saying the phrase out loud several times. Then write the phrase several times on a paper. Do not type it; the physical process of writing is essential to committing it to memory.

Figure 15.1 Courtrooms are proof of juries sitting silently

EXERCISE

In the following form write in the box each section by referring to the chart above.

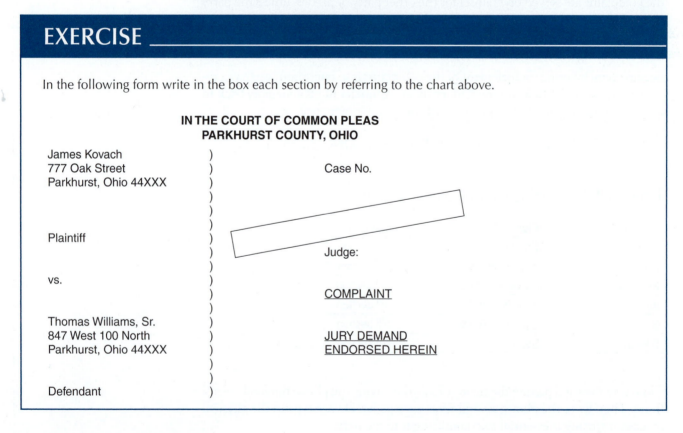

**IN THE COURT OF COMMON PLEAS
PARKHURST COUNTY, OHIO**

James Kovach)   Case No.
777 Oak Street)
Parkhurst, Ohio 44XXX)
)
)
)
Plaintiff)
)   Judge:
vs.)
)   <u>COMPLAINT</u>
)
Thomas Williams, Sr.)
847 West 100 North)   <u>JURY DEMAND</u>
Parkhurst, Ohio 44XXX)   <u>ENDORSED HEREIN</u>
)
)
Defendant)

(continued)

Now comes Plaintiff, by and through counsel, and as his Complaint against Defendant states the following:

COUNT ONE

1. The Plaintiff, James Kovach (Kovach), was and is a resident of Parkhurst County, Ohio at all times relevant to the facts of this complaint.

2. The Defendant, Thomas Williams, Sr. (Williams), was and is a resident of Parkhurst County, Ohio, at all times relevant to the facts of this complaint.

3. On or about May 15, 20XX, at approximately 2:00 pm., Kovach was driving his Ford Fiesta northbound on County Road 15. He was following a blue pickup truck with a refrigerator in the truck bed. At all times, Kovach maintained an assured clear distance from the vehicle in front of him. Kovach was wearing his lap and shoulder belts. The weather was clear, and the roads were dry.

4. The pickup truck swerved suddenly and the refrigerator that had had been on the truck bed bounced out of the truck, landing on Kovach's windshield. The sudden occurrence of the airborne refrigerator prevented Kovach from taking evasive action to protect himself.

5. The refrigerator struck Kovach in the head, leaving him in a coma for five days.

6. The broken windshield glass damaged Kovach's eyes, permanently blinding him.

7. As a proximate result of Williams's negligence, the Kovach has accrued medical expenses, including treatment by surgeons and physicians, hospitalizations, and multiple surgeries.

8. As a proximate result of Williams's negligence, the Kovach has been unable to work and has lost income.

COUNT TWO

9. Kovach restates and incorporates all of Count I as if fully rewritten herein.

10. As a result of the damage caused by the refrigerator striking Kovach's automobile, it was damaged beyond repair.

11. As a proximate result of Williams's negligence, the Kovach suffered property damage and loss.

WHEREFORE, Plaintiff James Kovach demands judgment against Defendant Thomas Williams, Sr. in an amount in excess of twenty-five thousand dollars ($25,000.00) on Counts I and II for compensation for injuries, loss of income, and property damage, as well as any additional relief this Court deems Plaintiff to be legally entitled, just, and or equitable, together with the costs of this action.

Clarence Dowling 000000
Attorney for the Plaintiff, James Kovach
45 Courthouse Square
Parkhurst, Ohio 44XXX
(216) 555-5555 telephone

(continued)

A trial by jury of eight (8) is hereby demanded.

Respectfully Submitted,

_____
Clarence Dowling 000000
Attorney for the Plaintiff, James Kovach
45 Courthouse Square
Parkhurst, Ohio 44XXX
(216) 555-5555 telephone

INSTRUCTIONS FOR SERVICE

The Clerk of Courts is hereby instructed to serve a copy of this Complaint on all parties at the addresses listed in the caption.

_____
Clarence Dowling 000000
Attorney for the Plaintiff, James Kovach

EXERCISE

Fill in the alphabetical blanks as we discuss the information following the chart below. An example has been provided "a." Level of Court and "b." jurisdiction.

IN THE COURT OF

a._____**Level of Court**_____

b._____Jurisdiction_____

c._____   )

d._____   )   j._____

   _____   )

)

)

e._____   )

)   k._____

)

f. _____   )

)

g._____   )

)   l._____

h._____   )

   _____   )

)

i. _____   )

EXERCISE _____

Below is a fact pattern in which the attorney has asked you to draft a complaint for the client, Sheila Kowalski, for constructive eviction, that is, failure to provide her with a habitable property. Using the information above, as well as the information in the formatting chapter 7, format a complaint for Anna to file with the Common Pleas Court. You do not have to write the body of the Complaint, but indicate that it will have three counts. Remember that Anna's last name is Garcia, and her office information 123 Main Street, Parkhurst, Ohio 44XXX, (216) 555-5555. Also, remember that Parkhurst is in the County of Parkhurst, Ohio. Anna is initially requesting an amount "in excess of $25,000."

After Ms. Kowalski began depositing her rent with the Court because the landlord refused to provide her with hot water, the landlord turned off the heat to her apartment. Since it is now November in northern Ohio, temperatures are consistently around forty degrees Fahrenheit. Ms. Kowalski has been forced to stay at her parents' home because her apartment is too cold.

Ms. Kowalski's address is 748 Beech Drive, Suite 14, Parkhurst, Ohio 44XXX. The landlord is a corporation, Property Management, Inc. Its business address is 666 Industrial Parkway, Parkhurst, Ohio, 44XXX. The attorney wants to be sure to demand a jury.

EXERCISE _____

Use the following information and complete the format for a complaint. You do not need to draft the various counts for the complaint, but the attorney wants a jury demand.

The plaintiff is Mary Jane Perkins, and she lives at 14 Maple Drive, Parkhurst, Ohio, 44XXX. She

is suing Donald McLeish, who lives at 21 Maple Drive, Parkhurst, Ohio, 44XXX in Common Pleas Court. Ms. Perkins' attorney is Ana Garcia. Ana Garcia's phone number is (216) 555-5555. Her address is 123 Main Street, Parkhurst, Ohio 44XXX. She is requesting relief in excess of $25,000.

Analyzing Facts for a Complaint

When a client seeks an attorney to file a complaint, the attorney and the paralegal must sift through the facts the client has presented, as well as the evidence they have gathered, to determine which facts are salient to the claims and which are irrelevant.

The attorney and paralegal also must sort these facts into logical sections for each count. In a motor vehicle accident, for example, property damage would go into a separate count from bodily injury.

EXAMPLE

In the following fact pattern, different allegations belong in different counts. Also, some information is not relevant to the suit.

Mary Jones, a red-headed nurse, has sought advice from the attorney concerning an accident in which her car was struck from behind by an inattentive driver in a silver sports utility vehicle at 4:00 pm on June 15, 20XX. Ms. Jones suffered whiplash and a fractured leg, and her blue sedan was damaged beyond repair. She has hospital bills amounting to $15,000 to date, and she still is being treated by a female physical therapist because she was not comfortable working with a male. Ms. Jones informed the attorney that she had been looking in her rearview mirror when the accident occurred, and she saw that the man driving the car was texting. The light was red, and she was stopped at the light. She was on her way home from work and had planned to drive through a fast food restaurant to get dinner, and she did not get to buy the fried chicken she had been looking forward to eating. Instead, she had to eat hospital food. She also missed two months of work, and the doctor she had hoped to date instead started dating another nurse because she was not at work at the hospital.

Ms. Jones, the party filing the suit, is the plaintiff. The driver of the vehicle that hit hers is the defendant.

First, we sort the relevant facts from the irrelevant facts. This can be done informally by having two columns, one titled "relevant facts" and the other titled "irrelevant facts. This way, you are going through the facts once and not repeating the work.

Irrelevant facts:

- The colors of the cars and the color of the plaintiff's hair are irrelevant.
- The plaintiff's destination at the time of the accident is irrelevant.
- The fact that plaintiff did not get to eat the fried chicken that she wanted also is irrelevant.
- The gender of the physical therapist treating the plaintiff and reason for the therapist being that gender is irrelevant.
- The doctor deciding not to date her is irrelevant.

Relevant facts:

- Plaintiff was stopped at a red light.
- The defendant failed to control his vehicle and struck hers.
- The defendant was texting while he was driving.
- Plaintiff suffered bodily injury and will continue to suffer from her injuries incurred in the accident.
- Plaintiff has incurred medical bills totaling $15,000 to date.
- Plaintiff continues to incur medical bills from the injuries sustained in the accident.
- Plaintiff is undergoing physical therapy.
- Plaintiff's car was damaged beyond repair
- The time of day the accident occurred is relevant; it was daytime, so darkness was not an issue in the accident.

Now that we have the relevant facts, we can sort them into the appropriate counts. The first count would include a description of the events that occurred, including the time of day. It would allege recklessness on the part of the defendant because he failed to obey the traffic laws and because he was texting while driving. This count also might contain the bodily injury portion of plaintiff's allegations, asserting the whiplash and broken leg.

The next count could address the plaintiff's lost income.

Another count would address the plaintiff's medical bills.

Another count would address the plaintiff's pain and suffering, both past and future.

Another count would address the property damage to plaintiff's car.

■ WRITING THE COMPLAINT

The actual drafting of the complaint takes practice, but many law offices have "form files" containing examples of complaints that you can use as a pattern for your complaint. Once you have sorted your facts, your different counts should become clear to you.

EXERCISE

Using the facts in the example above, draft the body of the complaint only.

■ THE ANSWER

The Answer is the defendant's response to the plaintiff's complaint. In the answer, the defendant responds specifically to each of the claims that the plaintiff has made in the complaint. It is important to line up the responses in the answer with the allegations in the complaint. Although drafting the answer can seem perfunctory, it is very important to pay close attention to make sure that the answers you provide properly correspond to the number in the complaint. You have to make sure that you do not "admit" to an allegation in error, because it is then considered a fact for the case.

Note that even if the plaintiff has not made a jury demand, the defendant may make a jury demand. The decision to request a jury is a tactical one for an attorney, and a plaintiff's attorney occasionally will decide that a judge would be more objective than a jury in a given case. For example, if the plaintiff is a very difficult personality and would be likely to offend or negatively affect the jury's opinion of his case, the plaintiff's attorney might strategically decide not to request a jury. In that situation, the defendant's counsel might consider it prudent to make a jury demand, because the jury would be more sympathetic to the defendant. Sometimes the defense attorney will include a jury demand even when the plaintiff has done so, in case the plaintiff decides to withdraw the jury demand. The Complaint and the Answer are the only opportunities to make a jury demand, which is why it is so important to remember to include it in the initial pleadings.

Generally, you will draft the answer with the complaint right next to you, so that you are answering each allegation in order.

So let us look at the answer Mr. Williams' attorney drafted in response to Mr. Kovach's complaint.

> **Rule 8. General Rules of Pleading**
> . . . .
> (b) DEFENSES; ADMISSIONS AND DENIALS.
> (1) In General. In responding to a pleading, a party must:
> (A) state in short and plain terms its defenses to each claim asserted against it; and
> (B) admit or deny the allegations asserted against it by an opposing party.
> (2) Denials—Responding to the Substance. A denial must fairly respond to the substance of the allegation.

EXAMPLE

IN THE COURT OF COMMON PLEAS
PARKHURST COUNTY, OHIO

James Kovach	)	Case No. 123456
Plaintiff,	)	
	)	Judge: MICHAEL FLYNN
vs.	)	
	)	
Thomas Williams, Sr.	)	ANSWER
Defendant	)	
	)	
	)	
	)	JURY DEMAND
	)	ENDORSED HEREIN

Now comes the Defendant, by and through counsel, and hereby answers Plaintiff's allegations as follows:

COUNT ONE

1. Deny paragraph one for want of information.

2. Admit paragraph two.

3. Deny paragraph three for want of information.

4. Deny paragraph four for want of information.

5. Deny paragraph five for want of information.

6. Deny paragraph six for want of information.

7. Deny paragraph seven for want of information.

8. Deny paragraph eight for want of information.

COUNT TWO

9. Deny paragraph nine for want of information.

10. Deny paragraph ten for want of information.

11. Deny paragraph eleven.

Wherefore, defendant requests this Court to find these allegations to be without merit.

_____

Bradley Smith 000000
Attorney for the Defendant,
Thomas Williams, Sr.
123 Main Street
Parkhurst, Ohio 44XXX
(216) 555-5555

CERTIFICATE OF SERVICE

A copy of this Answer has been sent by regular United States mail on this

_____day of _____, 20XX to Attorney for the Plaintiff, Clarence Dowling,

to 45 Courthouse Square, Parkhurst, Ohio 44XXX.

_____

Bradley Smith 000000
Attorney for the Defendant,
Thomas Williams, Sr.
123 Main Street
Parkhurst, Ohio 44XXX
(216) 555-5555

Analyzing Complaint Questions to Draft an Answer

It is extremely important to review the complaint carefully when drafting the answer. Any allegation that is answered with "admit" cannot be changed. You do not want to jeopardize your client's case by admitting to something that is an issue of fact. Admitting to something that damages the case comprises legal malpractice.

The other two most common responses are "deny" and "deny for want of information." While these two may sound similar, each must be used appropriately. Looking at some of the relevant facts from our earlier example on pages 375–376, which you no doubt included in the complaint you drafted, we will assess the response to each carefully. Remember that any answer submitted to the court must be the truth to the best of the attorney's knowledge, or the attorney could be liable for sanctions.

- Plaintiff was stopped at a red light.

The defendant does not want to "deny for want of information," because he was driving at the time of the accident. By law, he is responsible for knowing whether the light was red or green. If the defendant admits this, however, he is acknowledging that he drove negligently. If the defendant was cited for failing to stop for a red light because several witnesses told the police that the light was red, however, this might not be a fact he wants to dispute.

- The defendant was texting while he was driving.

If the defendant told the attorney that he was not texting at the time, he can deny this and let it be a fact issue for trial. It is not uncommon for clients to tell the attorney what they want him or her to hear, which is not necessarily the truth. However, if the defendant told the attorney that he was texting, the attorney is ethically obligated to admit that this is true.

- Plaintiff suffered bodily injury and will continue to suffer from her injuries incurred in the accident.

Defendant would deny this allegation for lack of information. He has no knowledge of the plaintiff's medical condition. That is a question of fact to be determined at the trial.

- Plaintiff has incurred medical bills totaling $15,000 to date.

Defendant would deny this allegation for lack of information. He has no knowledge of the plaintiff's medical bills. That is a question of fact to be determined at the trial.

- Plaintiff is undergoing physical therapy.

Defendant would deny this allegation for lack of information. He has no knowledge of the plaintiff's medical treatment. That is a question of fact to be determined at the trial.

- Plaintiff's car was damaged beyond repair.

Defendant also would deny this for lack of information. He had no knowledge of the condition of plaintiff's vehicle.

■ WRITING AN ANSWER

The actual process of writing the answer is straightforward. You simply format the caption, copy the counts and the numbers of the counts, and fill in the appropriate responses. Again, though, it is extremely important to be sure that you have filled in the correct response to each allegation, so you do not admit something you want to deny.

▪ AFFIRMATIVE DEFENSES AND COUNTERCLAIMS

Rule 12. Defenses and Objections:

When and How Presented; Motion for Judgment on the Pleadings; Consolidating Motions; Waiving Defenses; Pretrial Hearing.

. . .

(B) A party must serve an answer to a counterclaim or crossclaim within 21 days after being served with the pleading that states the counterclaim. . . .

Answers may contain more than responses to the allegations in the complaint: they sometimes also have affirmative defenses and/or counterclaims. Affirmative defenses are claims the defendant makes that would absolve him of liability. Counterclaims are allegations the defendant makes against the plaintiff for wrongs the defendant alleges plaintiff committed against the defendant. Note that these counterclaims must arise from the same matter that is the subject of the complaint.

In a case in which the plaintiff sued the railroad when he was hit while walking on the railroad tracks, for example, the railroad company would raise the affirmative defense of assumption of the risk. If a person walks on railroad tracks, he assumes the risk of being hit by a train. This is a known risk, and it could have been avoided if the plaintiff had walked on a sidewalk or beside the tracks.

In a case in which an automobile driver sued an ambulance company whose ambulance ran a red light while its siren and flashing lights were activated and hit the plaintiff's car, the ambulance company would assert a counterclaim for damage to the ambulance resulting from the accident.

Both affirmative defenses and counterclaims must be asserted in the answer. Civ.R 12(B).

EXERCISE

The attorney has asked you to draft an answer to a complaint she has just received. The complaint is below.

Draft the formatting of the answer for the attorney. Notice that the Clerk has added the case number and Judge's name to the original Complaint, which had been blank when submitted to the Clerk.

IN THE COURT OF COMMON PLEAS
PARKHURST COUNTY, OHIO

Amanda Grover 15 Athens Street Parkhurst, Ohio 44XXX	))))	Case No. *123456*
	)	Judge: *Andrew Green*
Plaintiff,	)))	COMPLAINT
vs.	)))	
George Everly 65 West 3rd Street Parkhurst, Ohio 44XXX)	))))	JURY DEMAND ENDORSED HEREIN
Defendant	)	

Now comes Plaintiff, by and through counsel, and as her Complaint against Defendant states the following:

COUNT ONE

1. The Plaintiff, Amanda Grover (Grover), was and is a resident of Parkhurst County, Ohio and a student at Parkhurst College at all times relevant to the facts of this complaint.

2. The Defendant, George Everly (Everly), was and is a resident of Parkhurst County, Ohio, at all times relevant to the facts of this complaint.

(continued)

3. On or about 8:00 am on June 14, 20XX, Grover was jogging on West 3rd Street. When she jogged past 65 West 3rd Street, she was attacked by a vicious dog owned by Everly.

4. Everly was negligent in failing to control his dog.

5. As direct and proximate result of the injuries Everly's Defendant's dog inflicted on Grover, she has incurred medical expenses, and will continue to require reconstructive surgery on her face where the dog bit her.

COUNT TWO

6. Grover restates and incorporates all of Count I as if fully rewritten herein.

7. Grover had been an extremely attractive young woman, and the plastic surgeons have informed her that they will not be able to repair all the disfigurement resulting from her injuries.

8. As a direct and proximate result of the injuries Everly's dog inflicted on Grover, she will be permanently disfigured despite plastic and reconstructive surgery.

COUNT THREE

9. Grover restates and incorporates all of Count I and II as if fully rewritten herein.

10. Prior to the attack by Everly's dog, Grover worked part-time as a model to pay her college tuition.

11. As a direct and proximate result of Everly's negligence in failing to control his dog, Grover will no longer be able to maintain an income.

COUNT FOUR

12. Grover restates and incorporates all of Count I and II as if fully rewritten herein.

13. Grover is a Sustainability and Recycling major and is very concerned with the environmental damage the multiple surgeries she will need to undergo will have on the environment.

14. As a direct and proximate result of Everly's negligence in failing to control his dog, Grover's treatments and surgeries will have a detrimental effect on the environment.

WHEREFORE, Plaintiff Amanda Grover demands judgment against Defendant George Everly in an amount in excess of twenty-five thousand dollars ($25,000.00) on Counts I, II, III, and IV for compensation for injuries, loss of income, and emotional distress, as well as any additional relief this Court deems Plaintiff to be legally entitled, just, and/or equitable, together with the costs of this action.

Clarence Dowling 000000
Attorney for the Plaintiff,
Amanda Grover
45 Courthouse Square
Parkhurst, Ohio 44XXX
(216) 555-5555 telephone

(continued)

A trial by jury is hereby demanded.

—————————————————
Clarence Dowling 000000
Attorney for the Plaintiff,
Amanda Grover

INSTRUCTIONS FOR SERVICE

The Clerk of Courts is hereby instructed to serve a copy of this Complaint on all parties at the addresses listed in the caption.

—————————————————
Clarence Dowling 000000
Attorney for the Plaintiff,
James Kovach

SUMMARY

- Pleadings are the documents that set out the allegations the parties have against each other and any defenses they may have against those allegations.

- The complaint is the initial pleading that begins a lawsuit. The complaint is made up of different counts, each of which alleges a different type of injury arising from the same event.

- In the caption in the complaint, the judge's name and the case number are left blank for the Clerk of Courts to insert.

- The complaint contains a body, which is comprised of the allegations in the various counts.

- The complaint must contain a prayer for relief so that the court knows what plaintiff is demanding in compensation or relief.

- If the attorney wants to have a trial by jury, it is imperative to include the jury demand on the complaint. Otherwise, the client's right to a jury is waived.

- If a plaintiff does not include a jury demand on a complaint, the defendant may include one on the answer.

- The signature block informs the recipient of a complaint of who is representing the party and how to contact that attorney.

- In a complaint, the attorney includes instructions for service, which tell the clerk of courts whom the attorney want to be served with the complaint.

- It is important to be certain that the complaint contains only relevant facts.

- When writing a complaint, each count should be limited to one form of damage, like bodily injury or property damage.

- The answer specifically addresses each and every allegation contained in the complaint.

- It is extremely important to be certain that your answers line up correctly with the allegations in the complaint.

- The answer contains a certificate of service page that states the name and address of each party or party's counsel receiving the answer.

- If a defendant wishes to include affirmative defenses or counterclaims, they must be included in the answer or they are waived.

ASSIGNMENT

I. In one or more pages, explain the purpose of the Complaint and the Answer. Also explain how each is formatted and written. Discuss the relationship between the two documents.

II. Brad and Ana have hired a new legal secretary, and they have asked you to discuss complaints and answers with him. Fill in the paralegal's information in the following dialog. Your answers should total at least three pages, 12-point font, double-spaced, with one-inch margins.

Legal Secretary: I am fairly new to the legal field. Can you explain a few things to me? How does a lawsuit get started?

Paralegal: Sure.

Legal Secretary: Is there a specific way you write a complaint? Please explain it and all the parts to me.

Paralegal:

Legal Secretary: What happens if you forget a part of the complaint?

Paralegal:

Legal Secretary: Why do you have to put on a jury demand?

Paralegal:

Legal Secretary: Does our office get complaints from other offices? If we do, how do we respond?

Paralegal:

Legal Secretary: What form does our response to the complaint take?

Paralegal:

Legal Secretary: Why does the complaint have instructions for service while the answer has a certificate of service?

Paralegal:

III. Read the following fact pattern and draft a complaint that is ready for the attorney, Ana Garcia, to sign.

In her boutique, Cherelle sold an expensive evening gown to Gisele Harrington, a new resident of Parkhurst on April 25, 20XX. Cherelle usually did not accept payment in the form of checks unless she knew the customer well. But because Ms. Harrington's check was drawn on a local bank, Cherelle accepted it. Unfortunately, the check was returned to Cherelle for insufficient funds. Cherelle has politely, and then firmly, asked Ms. Harrington to pay for the gown, but Ms. Harrington has repeatedly put Cherelle off and promised to pay "soon."

Cherelle was out of patience, so she took the returned check to Ana for her help. The check had Ms. Harrington's address on it: 66 Thornbush Lane, Parkhurst, Ohio, 44XXX. Cherelle wishes to sue Ms. Harrington in her business capacity as "Chez Cherelle," 143 Main Street, Parkhurst, Ohio, 44XXX.

Cherelle wants to be reimbursed not only for the cost of the gown, $450.00 (four hundred fifty dollars), but also for the returned check fees of $50.00 (fifty dollars), and for her attorney fees.

Because the gown cost under $15,000, Anna plans to file the suit in Parkhurst Municipal Court, Parkhurst, Ohio. (In Ohio, a Municipal Court may hear a case involving no more than $15,000. RC 1907.01.)

LEARNING OBJECTIVES

1. Define the forms of discovery

2. Compose precisely worded interrogatories that effectively use the limited questions

3. Detect what forms of production of documents are to be requested for a client's case

4. Create letters requesting late discovery responses

5. Identify the appropriate facts to be included in a request for admissions

6. Draft correct affidavits

7. Recognize how to correctly complete a subpoena

8. Complete the proper medical authorization form to obtain medical records

Discovery

CHAPTER 16

■ DISCOVERY

In almost every lawsuit or criminal action, the attorneys will engage in a process known as discovery. In this chapter we will focus solely on civil actions. Through discovery, the attorneys learn what evidence the other side has, and the attorneys learn more about the case to enable them to prepare for settlement or trial. There are several forms of discovery, including subpoenas, depositions, affidavits, and medical record release authorizations. The Federal Civil Rules, as do Civil Rules for many states, require parties to provide needed information even without a discovery request.

Nonetheless, attorneys still need additional formal discovery tools. The most common written forms of discovery will be the focus of this chapter. The Learning Objectives at the beginning of the chapter list various forms of discovery and evidence, but your work will focus primarily on interrogatories ("rogs" in the vernacular) and requests for production of documents ("RPDs" in the vernacular). Requests for admissions are infrequently used, but in certain circumstances they can streamline the process of trial or settlement by narrowing the focus on the actual issues that are important. In rare circumstances, they can win a case.

Each discovery document you send will be accompanied by a cover letter, which will briefly inform the attorney receiving the discovery request of the purpose of the request. For example, if you were sending interrogatories to opposing counsel, your cover letter might look like the following:

Rule 26. Duty to Disclose; General Provisions Governing Discovery

(a) REQUIRED DISCLOSURES.

(1) Initial Disclosure.

(A) In General. Except as exempted by Rule 26(a)(1)(B) or as otherwise stipulated or ordered by the court, a party must, without awaiting a discovery request, provide to the other parties:

(i) the name and, if known, the address and telephone number of each individual likely to have discoverable information—along with the subjects of that information—that the disclosing party may use to support its claims or defenses, unless the use would be solely for impeachment;

(ii) a copy—or a description by category and location—of all documents, electronically stored information, and tangible things that the disclosing party has in its possession, custody, or control and may use to support its claims or defenses, unless the use would be solely for impeachment;

(iii) a computation of each category of damages claimed by the disclosing party—who must also make available for inspection and copying as under Rule 34 the documents or other evidentiary material, unless privileged or protected from disclosure, on which each computation is based, including materials bearing on the nature and extent of injuries suffered; and

(iv) for inspection and copying as under Rule 34, any insurance agreement under which an insurance business may be liable to satisfy all or part of a possible judgment in the action or to indemnify or reimburse for payments made to satisfy the judgment.

EXAMPLE

SMITH & GARCIA, ATTORNEYS AT LAW
123 Main Street, Parkhurst, Ohio 44XXX

Clarence Dowling   March 16, 20XX
45 Courthouse Square
Parkhurst, Ohio 44XXX.

RE: Kovach v. Williams, case number XXXXX

Dear Mr. Dowling,

Enclosed please find the first set of interrogatories for your client in the above captioned case. Please have the client answer each question promptly and completely and sign the oath attesting to their correctness within 45 days. Please return the completed interrogatories to this office by United States mail.

Sincerely,

Pat Paralegal

Paralegal for attorney Bradley Smith, Esq.

Enclosure

CERTIFICATE OF SERVICE

A copy of the foregoing was sent by regular United States mail on this _____ day of _____, 20XX to Attorney for the Plaintiff, Clarence Dowling, to 45 Courthouse Square, Parkhurst, Ohio 44XXX.

_____

Bradley Smith 000000
Attorney for the Defendant,
Thomas Williams, Sr.
123 Main Street
Parkhurst, Ohio 44XXX
(216) 555-5555

Interrogatories

Each party to a lawsuit can submit written questions, which are called interrogatories, to the other parties. All the parties receiving these questions are obliged to answer the questions. This is an important part of the discovery process.

Many states limit to forty the number of interrogatories one side can ask the other. If a case is exceptionally complicated, however, the attorney may file a motion with the Court requesting leave to file additional interrogatories.

Note that if you draft a multipart question, the opposing side will treat it as though each part were an individual question. The civil rules in many jurisdictions allow the attorney to stop answering the questions after he or she has answered forty of them. The wording of your question, therefore, should be drafted in a way that elicits multiple answers while being only one question. For example, in a medical malpractice suit, rather than ask questions regarding each individual doctor, you would request the party to list the names, addresses, and dates of treatment he or she received from all physicians.

> **BAD EXAMPLE**
>
> 1. Who was the doctor who performed the surgery, and which doctor treated you before this doctor and when did that doctor treat you? Who was the anesthesiologist for the surgery?
>
> This question is actually four questions, and opposing counsel will treat it as such.
>
> **GOOD EXAMPLE**
>
> 1. List the names and addresses of each and every physician or other medical practitioner who has treated you for injuries related to the incident that is the subject of this case, including the dates of treatment and the purpose of each treatment.
>
> This is one question, because you have requested a list.

The subject matter of the lawsuit will determine what questions are appropriate for interrogatories. If the case involves a motor vehicle accident ("MVA" in the vernacular), the questions may focus on the opposing side's automobile service record, what automobile insurance coverage he or she has, and what conditions may have led to the accident.

If the lawsuit concerns a dog bite, the plaintiff might ask about the dog's veterinary records, the manner in which the owner had attempted to confine the dog, and the assets the owner has that could compensate the plaintiff. The defendant, on the other hand, would want evidence of the expenses the plaintiff had incurred as a result of the dog bite and would seek a medical records release to verify the treatments the plaintiff received as a result of the bite.

Because the number of permitted interrogatories is limited, it is important to be sure the questions are properly focused, clear, and not overly broad. If opposing counsel believes that a question is broader than it needs to be, he or she will refuse to answer it. You then will have to restate the question and resubmit it to opposing counsel, which delays the development of your case. If the question is unclear, again, counsel will decline to guess at its meaning and answer that it is unclear. If the question asks for material that is not necessary, opposing counsel will refuse to answer it based on lack of relevance. If the question asks for information that

---

Rule 33. Interrogatories to Parties

(a) IN GENERAL.

(1) Number. Unless otherwise stipulated or ordered by the court, a party may serve on any other party no more than 25 written interrogatories, including all discrete subparts. . . .

(b) ANSWERS AND OBJECTIONS.

(1) Responding Party. The interrogatories must be answered:

(A) by the party to whom they are directed; or

(B) if that party is a public or private corporation, a partnership, an association, or a governmental agency, by any officer or agent, who must furnish the information available to the party.

(2) Time to Respond. The responding party must serve its answers and any objections within 30 days after being served with the interrogatories. A shorter or longer time may be stipulated to under Rule 29 or be ordered by the court.

(3) Answering Each Interrogatory. Each interrogatory must, to the extent it is not objected to, be answered separately and fully in writing under oath.

(4) Objections. The grounds for objecting to an interrogatory must be stated with specificity. Any ground not stated in a timely objection is waived unless the court, for good cause, excuses the failure.

is protected by the attorney-client privilege, opposing counsel appropriately will refuse to answer it.

Note that you have to leave space for the person responding to enter the answers to the questions. In this computer age, many parties will create their own document to respond; nonetheless, you still should leave room on the document you send to other parties.

Also, keep in mind that if the rules limit the number of interrogatories you are allowed to ask, the person answering can stop answering when they have reached that question. In Ohio, Civ.R. 33(A)(3) limits interrogatories to forty. In Cuyahoga County, the Local Rules used to limit the number to twenty. Because each sub-question may count as a question, you want to be sure to put your most important questions in the first few interrogatories. These would include the identity of witnesses and the substance of their testimony. That way, if opposing counsel decides that one of your questions actually consists of several questions and refuses to answer some of your last questions because they exceed the limit, you still will have the most important information.

Below is a portion of a sample set of interrogatories. Because of the document's length, the complete set of interrogatories is located at the end of this chapter, after the assignments. You will see that they are quite lengthy, but because interrogatories are an essential discovery tool, it is important that they be thorough to provide the attorney with sufficient evidence to effectively pursue the case.

EXAMPLE

IN THE COURT OF COMMON PLEAS
PARKHURST COUNTY, OHIO

James Kovach	)	Case No. 123456
Plaintiff,	)	
	)	Judge: MICHAEL FLYNN
vs.	)	
	)	
Thomas Williams, Sr.	)	
Defendant	)	INTERROGATORIES
	)	
	)	
	)	

FIRST SET OF INTERROGATORIES PROPOUNDED TO
PLAINTIFF JAMES KOVACH

1. What is your full name, and any other names you have used (including but not limited to maiden name and married names), address, date of birth, social security number, employer's name and address, and citizenship status?
   Answer:

2. Describe in chronological order all of your activities in the 24 hours preceding the incident that is the subject of this suit.
   Answer:

3. Describe chronologically the incident that is the subject of this suit, including any and all details you recall.
   Answer:

4. List any and all physicians or other medical professionals, including their addresses, who have treated you for the injuries you allege resulted from the incident that is the subject of this lawsuit.
   Answer:

5. What is the name and address of each person that you expect to call as an expert witness in the trial of this action? What is the subject matter to which each of these expert witnesses is expected to testify?
   Answer:

6. What is the name and address of each person that you expect to call as a witness (other than expert witnesses) in the trial of this action? What is the subject matter to which each of these other witnesses is expected to testify?
   Answer:

7. List and describe the anticipated testimony of any and all witnesses you plan to call at trial. This question is ongoing and shall be updated with additional witnesses and their anticipated testimony throughout the course of this lawsuit.
   Answer:

8. Describe in detail the injury or injuries you allege you suffered as a result of the incident referred to in the Complaint. Include information concerning the location of any pain suffered, the duration and intensity of such pain and the date, time and place when you first had any pain or significant discomfort from your alleged injury.
   Answer:

9. With respect to the injury allegedly suffered, state the extent and nature of any impairment and whether you suffered any restriction of your normal activities due to the injuries allegedly sustained. If so, describe in detail the nature of such restriction.
   Answer:

10. If you received treatment with respect to the injuries allegedly sustained, state the name and address of each hospital or other facility where you were treated, the dates of treatment, and itemize the charges rendered by each of the facilities listed above.
    Answer:

. . . .

I declare under penalty of perjury that the answers to the foregoing interrogatories are true and accurate to the best of my knowledge, information, and belief.

_____

James Kovach, Plaintiff

_____

Date

CERTIFICATE OF SERVICE

A copy of these Interrogatories has been sent by regular United States mail on this _____ day of _____, 20XX to Attorney for the Plaintiff, Clarence Dowling, to 45 Courthouse Square, Parkhurst, Ohio 44XXX.

_____

Bradley Smith 000000
Attorney for the Defendant,
Thomas Williams, Sr.
123 Main Street
Parkhurst, Ohio 44XXX
(216) 555-5555

See the end of the chapter for the complete set of interrogatories.

EXERCISE

Read the fact pattern and compile fifteen interrogatory questions for the Johnson's attorney to submit to the restaurant, the Pinnacle, where Brianna had eaten the undercooked chicken.

Brianna and Marcus Johnson celebrated their first wedding anniversary by dining at Parkhurst's finest restaurant, the Pinnacle. The lighting was low, and although Brianna noted that her chicken cordon bleu was chewier than she expected, it was not until she had nearly finished it that she realized it was undercooked. Marcus reported the problem to the server, but because this was a celebration, he did not wish to make a scene complaining to the manager.

Two days later, Brianna developed a high fever, severe gastrointestinal symptoms including bleeding, as well as significant light-headedness. Marcus took her to the emergency department at Parkhurst Hospital, and laboratory tests confirmed that she had Campylobacter, a food-borne bacterial infection commonly transmitted through undercooked chicken. Brianna was hospitalized for a week, receiving several powerful intravenous antibiotics.

Marcus telephoned the Pinnacle to speak to the manager, but instead his call was returned by the Pinnacle's insurance company. Because Marcus and his family had patronized this restaurant for several decades, Marcus was offended by the manager's lack of concern and communication.

Brianna incurred significant medical bills during and after her hospitalization for Campylobacter. Because the restaurant's response upset them, the Johnsons decided to sue for the cost of her illness.

EXERCISE

In the previous exercise, you drafted interrogatories for plaintiffs to submit to the defendant restaurant. Using the same fact pattern above, in which Brianna gets food poisoning, draft fifteen interrogatory questions for Defendant, the Pinnacle, to submit to the plaintiffs, the Johnsons.

Requests for Production of Documents

Requests for Production of Documents may be submitted to any other party to the action. The purpose of the request for production of documents is to allow the requesting party to examine, copy, or otherwise inspect any document, item, land, or other physical thing that will further the requesting party's ability to proceed with the suit.

For example, in the Kovach v. Williams case, Plaintiff Kovach may want a copy of any automobile insurance policy that Defendant Williams had in effect at the time of the incident. Plaintiff's attorney would request a copy of the policy in the request for production of documents.

As noted, however, these requests include more than documents. For example, Defendant Williams' attorney may file a request to inspect Plaintiff Kovach's car for the purpose of taking photos in preparation of the defense. The attorney would make this request on a request for production. Similarly, the attorney may ask to inspect and photograph the refrigerator that Plaintiff alleges hit his car.

Although requests for production are often filed at the same time as the interrogatories, the answers to the interrogatories can alert the attorney receiving the answers to items or documents he or she will want to inspect. In the dog bite case, for example, the Defendant dog owner might say in his answers to interrogatories that he kept the dog on a heavy chain that was securely attached to the foundation of his house. At that point, the Plaintiff's attorney may want to inspect and photograph the chain and the way it is attached to the house. Plaintiff's attorney would then submit a request for production to gain access to the property. This could alert the attorney to the fact that the chain had been manufactured defectively, and he might want to include the manufacturer of the chain as a defendant to the suit.

If a lawsuit concerns a piece of land, inspecting that piece of land will be important for both sides. It would, therefore, be the subject of a request for production.

Rule 34. Producing Documents, Electronically Stored Information, and Tangible Things, or Entering onto Land, for Inspection and Other Purposes

(a) IN GENERAL. A party may serve on any other party a request within the scope of Rule 26(b):

(1) to produce and permit the requesting party or its representative to inspect, copy, test, or sample the following items in the responding party's possession, custody, or control:

(A) any designated documents or electronically stored information . . . or

(B) any designated tangible things; or

(2) to permit entry onto designated land or other property possessed or controlled by the responding party, so that the requesting party may inspect, measure, survey, photograph, test, or sample the property or any designated object or operation on it.

EXAMPLE

IN THE COURT OF COMMON PLEAS
PARKHURST COUNTY, OHIO

James Kovach	)	Case No. 123456
Plaintiff,	)	
	)	Judge: MICHAEL FLYNN
vs.	)	
	)	<u>DEFENDANT'S FIRST SET</u>
	)	<u>OF REQUESTS FOR</u>
Thomas Williams, Sr.	)	<u>PRODUCTION</u>
Defendant	)	<u>FROM PLAINTIFF</u>
	)	
	)	

REQUESTS FOR PRODUCTION

Defendant, Thomas Williams, Sr., hereby requests, pursuant to Civil Rule 34 of the State of Ohio, that Plaintiff permit Defendant's counsel to inspect and photograph Plaintiff Kovach's vehicle during daylight hours within the next 45 days.

Defendant further requests Plaintiff produce for inspection and copying at 1:00 p.m. on __, 20XX, at the office of attorney Bradley Smith at 123 Main Street, Parkhurst, Ohio 44XXX, the following documents and records which are in the possession of the Plaintiff or under the control of the Plaintiff:

1. Copies of Plaintiff's automobile and health insurance policies.
2. Written authorizations signed by the Plaintiff before a notary public that authorize the Defendant to obtain copies of all medical records and bills Plaintiff alleges resulted from the incident that is the subject of this complaint. Blank Medical Authorization forms are attached to these requests for production.
3. Property damage estimates for the automobile Plaintiff alleges resulted from the incident.
4. Complete State and Federal income tax returns of the Plaintiff, if a claim for lost wages is being made, for the three (3) years preceding the date the cause of action arose and for all years following the date the cause of action arose.
5. Any written statement or record from the Plaintiff's employer(s) of time lost from work and wages and benefits lost from work due to the injury sustained by the Plaintiff that is described in the Complaint.
6. Copies of any and all bills that the Plaintiff claims are related to the Plaintiff's damages resulting from the accident at issue, including any past or future damages, medical bills, durable medical equipment, and property damage.
7. Copies of all photographs relating to the injury sustained by the Plaintiff that is described in the Complaint and all photographs relating to property damage described in the Complaint.
8. Copies of any and all documents, records, reports, exhibits, photographs, film, video, and objects which the Plaintiff intends to introduce into evidence at the trial or arbitration of this matter, including, but not limited to, bills, medical records, medical reports, accident reports, motor vehicle title and registration, witness statements, expert reports, and curriculum vitae.
9. Copies of any and all medical records and medical reports regarding the injuries the Plaintiff claims the Plaintiff sustained as a result of the subject accident, including the reports of health care providers, doctors, and experts.
10. A copy of the report of any expert witness whom the Plaintiff intends to call as a witness in the trial of this action.
11. Copies of the title and registration of the motor vehicle the Plaintiff was driving at the time of the subject accident.

In lieu of delivering these documents in person, the Plaintiff may mail copies of these documents to the office of the Defendant's Attorney, so long as the documents are mailed early enough to ensure deliver at that office on or before _____, 20XX. This request is continuing with respect to all documents and records that are not currently in the possession of, or under the control of, the Plaintiff, but that subsequently come into the possession of, or under the control of, the Plaintiff after service of this request. Copies of said documents shall be sent to attorney Bradley Smith at 123 Main Street, Parkhurst, Ohio 44XXX

Respectfully submitted,

_____

Bradley Smith 000000
Attorney for the Defendant, Thomas Williams, Sr.
123 Main Street
Parkhurst, Ohio 44XXX
(216) 555-5555

CERTIFICATE OF SERVICE

A copy of these Requests for Production of Documents has been sent by regular United States mail on this _____ day of _____, 20XX to Attorney for the Plaintiff, Clarence Dowling, to 45 Courthouse Square, Parkhurst, Ohio 44XXX.

> Bradley Smith 000000
> Attorney for the Defendant, Thomas Williams, Sr.
> 123 Main Street
> Parkhurst, Ohio 44XXX
> (216) 555-5555

EXERCISE

Draft a request for production of documents based on the following fact pattern. You work for George Everly, the defendant's attorney. Think about all of the evidence the defendant's attorney would need to defend this lawsuit on Mr. Everly's behalf. Be sure to format your requests for production correctly.

Amanda Grover is a client who had been jogging when defendant George Everly's dog got loose and attacked her. She was bitten numerous times on the face, and even after multiple plastic surgeries, she will be disfigured. Amanda had been a model and had been attending Parkhurst College. She has had multiple hospitalizations and surgeries, and she sued Mr. Everly for her lost wages, disfigurement, medical expenses, and emotional distress.

As Attorney Clarence Dowling's paralegal, you are assigned the task of drafting requests for production of documents directed to Ms. Grover. Mr. Dowling has noted that he needs proof that Ms. Grover was enrolled in college, had earned money as a model, etc.

Request for Admissions

In order to limit the number of issues that parties need to argue and prove at trial, or in order to narrow the issues to facilitate settlement, a party may submit requests for admission to the other side. These admissions consist of statements of facts that the submitting party believes that both sides can agree are true. By agreeing to the truth of certain facts, the parties can narrow the number of issues in contention.

Requests for admission are especially useful in cases with multiple issues. Caution: if the attorney receiving the requests fails to respond to them in the designated time period, the court will deem the statements contained in the request for admissions to be true. The attorney who fails to respond to them in a timely manner will have lost the client's case.

As a paralegal, it is your duty to be alert for this type of discovery request and ensure that the attorney submits the response in a timely manner. One of your authors once won a case by submitting requests for admission that the opposition failed to respond to in time. One of the admissions was that their complaint lacked merit.

> **Rule 36. Requests for Admission**
>
> (a) SCOPE AND PROCEDURE.
>
> (1) Scope. A party may serve on any other party a written request to admit, for purposes of the pending action only, the truth of any matters within the scope of Rule 26(b)(1) relating to:
>
> (A) facts, the application of law to fact, or opinions about either; and
>
> (B) the genuineness of any described documents.
>
> . . . .

(3) Time to Respond; Effect of Not Responding. A matter is admitted unless, within 30 days after being served, the party to whom the request is directed serves on the requesting party a written answer or objection addressed to the matter and signed by the party or its attorney. A shorter or longer time for responding may be stipulated to under Rule 29 or be ordered by the court.

(4) Answer. If a matter is not admitted, the answer must specifically deny it or state in detail why the answering party cannot truthfully admit or deny it.

. . . .

(b) EFFECT OF AN ADMISSION; WITHDRAWING OR AMENDING IT. A matter admitted under this rule is conclusively established unless the court, on motion, permits the admission to be withdrawn or amended.

EXAMPLE

Plaintiff Kovach's lawyer sent Brad the following requests for admission:

IN THE COURT OF COMMON PLEAS
PARKHURST COUNTY, OHIO

James Kovach	)	Case No. 123456
Plaintiff,	)	
	)	Judge: MICHAEL FLYNN
	)	
vs.	)	
	)	
Thomas Williams, Sr.	)	REQUEST FOR ADMISSION
Defendant	)	
	)	
	)	

Now comes Plaintiff, James Kovach, by and through counsel, and pursuant to Civ.R. 36, hereby requests the following admissions from Defendant, Thomas Williams, Sr.:

1. The weather on X date was sunny, and the roads were clear.
2. Mr. Williams was driving a pickup truck at X time on X road.
3. Mr. Williams was transporting a refrigerator in the back of the pickup truck.
4. Mr. Williams had failed to secure the refrigerator safely in the truck bed.
5. Mr. Kovach was permanently blinded when the refrigerator fell off the back of the truck and struck his car.

Responses to these requests for admission are due within 28 days, or they will be deemed to have been admitted.

Respectfully submitted,

_____

Clarence Dowling
45 Courthouse Square
Parkhurst, Ohio 44XXX
(216) 555-5555

CERTIFICATE OF SERVICE

A copy of the foregoing Request for Admission was served by regular United States on this _____ day of _____, 20XX to Attorney for the Defendant, Bradley Smith, 123 Main Street, Parkhurst, Ohio 44XXX

Note that Brad would probably agree with the first two requests for admission, but he might respond "neither admit nor deny" to numbers three and four. He might deny number five for lack of information. This set of requests for admission reflects a "fishing expedition" type of request. Since most of the statements consist of facts to be proven at trial, an attorney submitting these would be hoping opposing counsel would be inattentive and miss the response deadline. More often, though, requests for admission are used in complex cases and propose serious agreements of facts that are not at issue.

Below is an example of good faith requests for admission, which would serve to limit the issues for trial.

EXAMPLE

IN THE COURT OF COMMON PLEAS
PARKHURST COUNTY, OHIO

Sheila Kowalski	)	
Plaintiff,	)	Case No. 446551
	)	
	)	
	)	Judge: Michael Flynn
vs.	)	
	)	
	)	
	)	PLAINTIFF SHEILA KOWALSKI'S
Property Management, Inc.	)	REQUESTS FOR ADMISSION
Defendant	)	
	)	

Now comes Plaintiff, Sheila Kowalski, by and through counsel, and pursuant to Civ.R. 36, hereby requests the following admissions from Defendant, Property Management, Inc.:

1. Plaintiff signed the lease for Unit 14 at 748 Beech Drive, Unit 14, Parkhurst, Ohio 44XXX on _____, 20XX.
2. Defendant's representative expressly agreed to lease Unit 14 to Plaintiff.
3. Defendant's representative signed the rental contract and initialed the stipulation that the lease was specifically for Unit 14.
4. Defendant was aware that Unit 14 had never been occupied.
5. Defendant did not inform Plaintiff that Unit 14 had never been occupied at the time the parties signed the lease.
6. Defendant made no effort to verify that Unit 14 met all the legal requirements for a residential unit, including availability of hot water and/or heat prior to Plaintiff taking possession of Unit 14.
7. On the date Plaintiff arrived to take possession of Unit 14, Defendant attempted to compel Plaintiff to move into a different, less desirable unit.
8. Defendant never provided Plaintiff with 24 hours notice of its plans to enter Unit 14 to perform repairs.

Responses to these requests for admission are due within 28 days, or they will be deemed to have been admitted.

Respectfully submitted,

_____

Ana Garcia 000000
Attorney for the Plaintiff,
Sheila Kowalski
123 Main Street
Parkhurst, Ohio 44XXX

CERTIFICATE OF SERVICE

A copy of the foregoing was sent by regular United States mail on this _____ day of _____, 20XX to Attorney for the Defendant, Andrew Adwokat, Esq., to 100 Courthouse Square, Parkhurst, Ohio 44XXX.

_____
Ana Garcia 000000
Attorney for the Plaintiff,
Sheila Kowalsi
123 Main Street
Parkhurst, Ohio 44XXX
(216) 555-5555

EXERCISE

Using the following fact pattern, draft requests for admission for Brad to send to the Pinnacle restaurant. Try to think of admissions that the restaurant actually would agree with so the case might be able to move to settlement.

As you will recall, Brianna and Marcus Johnson had celebrated their anniversary at the Pinnacle restaurant, where Brianna got food poisoning from undercooked chicken. Because the restaurant had not responded in a manner they considered courteous, they have decided to sue the restaurant for Brianna's medical expenses and pain and suffering.

Marcus and Brianna Johnson have provided Brad with a copy of their credit card receipt for the night they ate at the Pinnacle, as well as the slip of paper that came with the bill listing all the items they had ordered, including the bottle of wine, their appetizers, etc., and including the chicken cordon bleu that Brianna had ordered. Brad has supplied copies of these items, along with an affidavit of a friend of the Johnsons who had seen them eating at the Pinnacle on the evening in question. Brad has told you that it would simplify the case if he did not have to prove at trial that the Johnsons had eaten and what they had eaten at the Pinnacle that night.

Affidavits

An affidavit is another form of evidence that you may be asked to draft. An affidavit consists of a written statement or statements of fact that a person swears are true. The person must swear in front of someone with the authority to take an oath or affirmation, like a notary public, that the statements are true. Note that this is one format that your authors have used, but there are various formats for an affidavit. Regardless of the format in which it is written, each affidavit requires a statement sworn before someone with authority to take an oath.

EXAMPLE

IN THE COURT OF COMMON PLEAS
PARKHURST COUNTY, OHIO

James Kovach Plaintiff,	)	Case No. 123456
	)	
	)	Judge: MICHAEL FLYNN
vs.	)	
	)	
Thomas Williams, Sr.	)	<u>AFFIDAVIT OF</u>
Defendant	)	<u>JANE DOE</u>
	)	
	)	
STATE OF OHIO	)	
COUNTY OF PARKHURST	) SS:	
	)	

Jane Doe, being first duly sworn, deposes and says the following:

1. Ms. Doe is a resident of Parkhurst, Ohio in the County of Parkhurst.

2. Ms. Doe lives at 425 County Road 15.

3. Ms. Doe was at home all day on May 15, 20XX.

4. Ms. Doe heard a crashing sound from the road at approximately 2:00 p.m. on MAY 15, 20XX.

5. Ms. Doe went into her front yard to investigate the source of the sound and saw two men putting a refrigerator into the back of a blue pickup truck.

6. The two men got into the pickup truck and drove away at a high rate of speed.

7. A damaged red car with Plaintiff James Kovach in the driver's seat was at the scene.

8. Mr. Kovach was bleeding profusely such that his face was covered with blood.

9. Ms. Doe ran into her home and telephoned 911 for emergency services.

10. Ms. Doe returned to the red car and attempted to assist Mr. Kovach, but she was unable to open either door to the car.

11. The EMS arrived and used the Jaws of Life to extract Mr. Kovach from the car. EMS took Mr. Kovach away in an ambulance.

I declare under penalty of perjury that the foregoing is true and correct to the best of my knowledge, information, and belief.

Further, affiant sayeth naught.

_____
Jane Doe

SWORN TO BEFORE ME and subscribed in my presence this _____ day of May, 20_____.

(Name of person taking the oath with evidence authority)

_____
NOTARY PUBLIC

Rule 45. Subpoena

(a) IN GENERAL.

(1) Form and Contents.

(A) Requirements—In General. Every subpoena must:

(i) state the court from which it issued;

(ii) state the title of the action and its civil-action number;

(iii) command each person to whom it is directed to do the following at a specified time and place: attend and testify; produce designated documents, electronically stored information, or tangible things in that person's possession, custody, or control; or permit the inspection of premises; and

(iv) set out the text of Rule 45(d) and (e).

Subpoenas

A subpoena is used to compel a person to appear at a given place at a given time to give testimony. An attorney may subpoena a witness to appear at a trial or a deposition. In discovery disputes, a *subpoena duces tecum* (Latin for, roughly, come and bring it with you), is useful for compelling someone to provide evidence. If a hospital's medical records department is not responding to discovery requests, for example, an attorney might issue a *subpoena duces tecum* for the medical records director to come to a deposition and bring all of the requested medical records with him or her. This subpoena can include an alternative option of the medical records being provided before the scheduled time for the deposition.

If an attorney is concerned about a potential witness's cooperation in a case, he or she may request the Clerk of Courts to issue a subpoena. The Clerk will give the attorney a subpoena, and the attorney will fill in the blanks with the appropriate information. Below is a blank subpoena. It is followed by a subpoena completed with the specific information for a particular case.

SUBPOENA
PARKHURST COUNTY COMMON PLEAS COURT
Civil Rule 45

PLAINTIFF,

CASE NO. _____
SUBPOENA IN CIVIL CASE

vs.

ATTORNEY: _____
ADDRESS: _____
PHONE: _____

DEFENDANT

SUPREME COURT NO: _____

TO: _____ (NAME)
_____ (ADDRESS)
_____ (CITY, STATE, ZIP)

YOU ARE HEREBY COMMANDED TO

ATTEND AND GIVE TESTIMONY AT A (TRIAL) (HEARING)(DEPOSITION) ON DATE _____, TIME:_____, PLACE:_____

_____

_____

_____ PRODUCE DOCUMENTS, ELECTRONICALLY STORED INFORMATION, OR TANGIBLE THINGS AT TRIAL, HEARING, OR DEPOSITION.

_____ PRODUCE AND PERMIT INSPECTION AND COPYING OF ANY DESIGNATED DOCUMENTS OR ELECTRONICALLY STORED INFORMATION THAT ARE IN YOUR POSSESSION, CUSTODY, OR CONTROL.

_____ PRODUCE AND PERMIT INSPECTION AND COPYING, TESTING, OR SAMPLING OF ANY TANGIBLE THINGS THAT ARE IN YOUR POSSESSION, CUSTODY, OR CONTROL.

_____ PERMIT ENTRY UPON DESIGNATED LAND OR OTHER PROPERTY THAT IS IN THE POSSESSION OR CONTROL OF YOU FOR THE PURPOSES DESCRIBED IN CIV. R. 34(A)(3). DESCRIPTION OF ITEMS TO BE PRODUCED: _____

HEREOF FAIL NOT UNDER PENALTY OF THE LAW

WITNESS MY SIGNATURE AND SEAL OF SAID COURT, THIS _____DAY OF _____, 20 _____

_____
Clerk, Attorney, Notary

_____
Deputy Clerk

Completed subpoena:

SUBPOENA
PARKHURST COUNTY COMMON PLEAS COURT
Civil Rule 45

James Kovach	CASE NO. *123456*
PLAINTIFF,	SUBPOENA IN CIVIL CASE
	ATTORNEY: *Bradley Smith, Esq.*
vs.	ADDRESS: *123 Main Street*
	Parkhurst, Ohio 44XX
Thomas Williams, Sr.	PHONE: *(216) 555-5555*
DEFENDANT	
	SUPREME COURT NO: *000000*

TO: *JANE DOE*
425 County Road 15
Parkhurst, OH 44XXX

YOU ARE HEREBY COMMANDED TO

ATTEND AND GIVE TESTIMONY AT A (~~TRIAL~~)(~~HEARING~~)(DEPO-SITION) ON DATE <u>MAY 7, 20XX</u>, TIME <u>10:00 AM EDT</u>, PLACE <u>123 MAIN STREET, PARKHURST, OHIO 44XXX</u>.

_____
_____

_____ PRODUCE DOCUMENTS, ELECTRONICALLY STORED INFORMATION, OR TANGIBLE THINGS AT TRIAL, HEARING OR DEPOSITION.
_____ PRODUCE AND PERMIT INSPECTION AND COPYING OF ANY DESIGNATED DOCUMENTS OR ELECTRONICALLY STORED INFORMATION THAT ARE IN YOUR POSSESSION, CUSTODY, OR CONTROL.
_____ PRODUCE AND PERMIT INSPECTION AND COPYING, TESTING, OR SAMPLING OF ANY TANGIBLE THING THAT ARE IN YOUR POSSESSION, CUSTODY, OR CONTROL.
_____ PERMIT ENTRY UPON DESIGNATED LAND OR OTHER PROPERTY THAT IS IN THE POSSESSION OR CONTROL OF YOU FOR THE PURPOSES DESCRIBED IN CIV. R. 34(A)(3).
DESCRIPTION OF ITEMS TO BE PRODUCED: _____

_____

HEREOF FAIL NOT UNDER PENALTY OF THE LAW
WITNESS MY SIGNATURE AND SEAL OF SAID COURT, THIS 28TH DAY OF April, 20XX

_____
Bradley Smith, Esq.

RETURN OF SERVICE
Received this Subpoena on the _____ day of _____, 20__, at _____ M, and on the _____ day of _____, 20__, at _____ M, I served the same upon _____ by delivering to _____.
Personally or Residential served a true copy of this subpoena.

_____
Sheriff-Attorney-Process Server-Notary

Medical Authorizations

When we discussed requests for production of documents, we mentioned medical authorization forms. In certain types of cases, including medical malpractice and personal injury cases, you will need to obtain medical authorizations to get copies of the medical records of the person who is claiming injury. There are several variations of this form, but one common version is provided below. Be aware that some major medical centers have their own form and will refuse to honor an authorization that is not on their form. Further, the medical records department will simply ignore any other form, rather than contact the attorney to let him or her know that the form submitted was not the correct form.

EXAMPLE

I, (PATIENT'S NAME HERE), hereby authorize any hospital, medical institution or doctor or medical practitioner to release to the office of Smith & Garcia, LPA, any and all records and written material of any nature whatsoever, pertaining to the hospitalization, examination, treatment, et cetera, of (PATIENT'S NAME HERE), including, but not limited to emergency room records, surgery records, hospitalization records, examination records, x-ray reports, CT scan reports, vision testing, and bills for services rendered at any time starting five years prior to the date of this authorization.

This authorization also includes the release of any psychological and/or psychiatric records, notes, and tests.

I hereby waive and release you from any restrictions imposed by law in disclosing any professional records, observation or communication to the office of Smith & Garcia, LPA.

I also agree that a photocopy of this Authorization may be used in place of the original.

_____
Signature of patient

_____
Date signed

_____
Social Security Number

_____
Date of Birth

SWORN TO BEFORE ME and subscribed in my presence this _____ day of May, 20_____.

_____
Notary Public (or person authorized to take an oath)

EXERCISE-IN CLASS

Now that you have learned about various discovery documents, Brad has asked you to explain them to the new legal secretary. Divide into groups of two and role play for this in-class exercise.

Legal Secretary: I keep hearing people talk about discovery. What is discovery?

Paralegal: Discovery is . . . .

Legal Secretary: Do we use all those different forms of discovery all of the time?

Paralegal:

Legal Secretary: Why would you serve someone with a subpoena?

Paralegal:

Legal Secretary: Which document do you use to get copies of papers the other side has?

Paralegal:

Legal Secretary: How do you draft an affidavit?

Paralegal:

Legal Secretary: What is the purpose of requests for admission?

Paralegal:

Legal Secretary: I noticed that Brad waited to send Requests for Production until he received the responses to the Interrogatories. Why didn't he send them at the same time to be more efficient?

Paralegal:

Legal Secretary: I am getting confused. Explain to me again how Requests for Production and Interrogatories are different?

Paralegal:

SUMMARY

- Discovery is an essential part of any lawsuit that allows each side to prepare the case with the same information.

- Although there are several forms of discovery, the types used most often are interrogatories and requests for production (usually of documents).

- Interrogatories are questions one side submits to the other side to gain important information about the suit.

- Many jurisdictions limit the number of interrogatory questions, so it is important to put the most important questions early in the set of questions. Some questions may be construed as containing more than one question, and opposing counsel may decline to answer them.

- Requests for production usually consist of requests for documents, like medical records in a malpractice suit.

- Requests for production also can address inspecting property that is the subject of the suit for photographing, measuring, or other evaluating.

- Requests for admission are used less frequently, but they are helpful in limiting the amount of facts that need to be proven at trial.

- Affidavits are sworn statements concerning facts that are relevant to the lawsuit.

- Subpoenas are used to command someone to appear to give testimony, or, in the case of a *subpoena duces tecum*, to produce documents for copying.

- Medical authorizations are required when one side wants to obtain medical records concerning the injuries a party is alleging.

ASSIGNMENT

I. Answer the following questions. Information is provided in Chapter 15 and this Chapter 16.

1. Which document is used to initiate a lawsuit?
   a. Interrogatories
   b. Request for Admissions
   c. Answer
   d. Subpoena
   e. Complaint
   f. Request to Produce Documents
   g. Affidavit

2. Which document is used to narrow the number of issues for trial or settlement?
   a. Interrogatories
   b. Request for Admissions
   c. Answer
   d. Subpoena
   e. Complaint
   f. Request to Produce Documents
   g. Affidavit

3. Which document is drafted in response to a Complaint?
   a. Interrogatories
   b. Request for Admissions
   c. Answer
   d. Subpoena
   e. Complaint
   f. Request to Produce Documents
   g. Affidavit

4. Which document seeks answers to questions?
   a. Interrogatories
   b. Request for Admissions
   c. Answer
   d. Subpoena
   e. Complaint
   f. Request to Produce Documents
   g. Affidavit

5. Which document asks another party to the suit to give copies of documents?
   a. Interrogatories
   b. Request for Admissions
   c. Answer
   d. Subpoena
   e. Complaint
   f. Request to Produce Documents
   g. Affidavit

6. Which document legally compels someone to appear to give testimony?
   a. Interrogatories
   b. Request for Admissions
   c. Answer
   d. Subpoena
   e. Complaint
   f. Request to Produce Documents
   g. Affidavit

7. Which document is sworn before a person authorized to take an oath?
   a. Interrogatories
   b. Request for Admissions
   c. Answer
   d. Subpoena
   e. Complaint
   f. Request to Produce Documents
   g. Affidavit

8. Which two documents are most commonly used during discovery?
   a. Interrogatories
   b. Request for Admissions
   c. Answer
   d. Subpoena
   e. Complaint
   f. Request to Produce Documents
   g. Affidavit

9. Which discovery document has a limit to the number of items it may have?

   a. Interrogatories

   b. Request for Admissions

   c. Answer

   d. Subpoena

   e. Complaint

   f. Request to Produce Documents

   g. Affidavit

10. Which document can compel a person to bring something to a certain place at a certain time?

    a. Interrogatories

    b. Request for Admissions

    c. Answer

    d. Subpoena

    e. Complaint

    f. Request to Produce Documents

    g. Affidavit

II. Read the following fact pattern and draft interrogatories for the attorney for Wayne Seller, the van driver, to submit to Cherelle's attorney.

On a still, dark winter morning, Cherelle Jackson was driving to her boutique to get an early start on inventory. Because the roads were slippery, she was driving 35 mph in a 50 mph zone. A large van that had been driving behind her passed when they reached a long, straight stretch of road. The van hit a patch of ice, turned around totally, and then slid into Cherelle Jackson's car. Fortunately, her seat belt and airbag prevented her from serious injury. Nonetheless, her car was damaged beyond repair. The van was one of a fleet of rental vehicles owned by Efficiency Car and Truck Rental Company. The driver of the van was cited for failure to control his vehicle and failure to maintain a safe speed for road conditions. Cherelle Jackson's auto insurance company paid her for the value of her car, and the insurance company now is seeking compensation from both the driver of the van as well as the Efficiency Car and Truck Rental Company. Brad Smith is representing the insurance company, and the lawsuit was filed in Parkhurst County Common Pleas Court.

Ms. Jacksons's insurance company is called Safety First Auto Insurance, and its mailing address is 99 Industrial Drive, Parkhurst, Ohio, 44XXX. Attorney Clarence Dowling, 45 Courthouse Square, Parkhurst, Ohio 44XXX, is the van driver's counsel. The driver of the van, Wayne Sellers, lives at 65773 Indiana Blvd, Chardon, Ohio 44024. Efficiency Car and Truck Rental Company is represented by Vernon McAllister, whose office is at 444 Parkhurst Square, Suite 5000, Parkhurst, Ohio 44XXX.

III. Using the above fact pattern in assignment one, draft all the correct discovery forms for Cherelle Jackson's attorney to sent to the van driver Wayne Seller's attorney.

IV. Read the following fact pattern. Draft all the correct discovery forms for Antoine Taylor's attorney to submit to Mr. and Mrs. Andrew Cappoli.

Antoine Taylor was a realtor in Parkhurst, Ohio. In November, Antoine represented the seller in the sale of a home. The home passed the buyers' inspection, and the sellers signed the disclosure statement attesting that they had no knowledge of any material defects in the house. The April after the property transferred, however, the buyers woke up one warm, sunny morning and discovered the basement had four feet of water in it. When they discussed this with the neighbors, the neighbors told them that the basement of the home had flooded six years earlier, while the sellers of the home lived in and owned it. The neighbors told the new owners that the sellers had been told that the house had been built directly over a natural stream, and that when the snows melted in the spring, the stream could overflow if there was a rapid snow melt.

The new owners are suing Antoine Taylor for misrepresentation and demanding he compensate them for the amount it will cost to reroute the stream from underneath the home, as well as for the cost of repairs to the basement.

Antoine is represented by Bradley Smith, 123 Main Street, Parkhurst, Ohio 44XXX. The buyers, Mr. and Mrs. Andrew Cappoli, are represented by Vernon McAllister, whose office is at 444 Parkhurst Square, Suite 5000, Parkhurst, Ohio 44XXX.

EXAMPLE

Above, we provided you with a sample of interrogatories. Here is the complete set of those interrogatories. You can see that they are extensive. You also can see that the most important questions are at the beginning, in case opposing counsel determines that one of the questions constituted more than a single question. Opposing counsel would then count each part of a multiple question as individual questions. If those individual questions resulted in the interrogatories having more questions than the limit, opposing counsel would refuse to answer the questions that exceeded the limit.

IN THE COURT OF COMMON PLEAS
PARKHURST COUNTY, OHIO

James Kovach	)	Case No. 123456
Plaintiff,	)	
	)	Judge: MICHAEL FLYNN
	)	
vs.	)	
	)	INTERROGATORIES
	)	
Thomas Williams, Sr.	)	
Defendant	)	
	)	
	)	

**FIRST SET OF INTERROGATORIES PROPOUNDED TO PLAINTIFF
JAMES KOVACH**

1. What is your full name, and any other names you have used (including but not limited to maiden name and married names), address, date of birth, social security number, employer's name and address, and citizenship status?
Answer:

2. Describe in chronological order all of your activities in the 24 hours preceding the incident that is the subject of this suit.
Answer:

3. Describe chronologically the incident that is the subject of this suit, including any and all details you recall.
Answer:

4. List any and all physicians or other medical professionals, including their addresses, who have treated you for the injuries you allege resulted from the incident that is the subject of this lawsuit.
Answer:

5. What is the name and address of each person that you expect to call as an expert witness in the trial of this action? What is the subject matter to which each of these expert witnesses is expected to testify?
Answer:

6. What is the name and address of each person that you expect to call as a witness (other than expert witnesses) in the trial of this action? What is the subject matter to which each of these other witnesses is expected to testify?
Answer:

7. List and describe the anticipated testimony of any and all witnesses you plan to call at trial. This question is ongoing and shall be updated with additional witnesses and their anticipated testimony throughout the course of this lawsuit.
Answer:

8. Describe in detail the injury or injuries you alleged you suffered as a result of the incident referred to in the Complaint. Include information concerning the location of any pain suffered and the duration and intensity of such pain and the date, time and place when you first had any pain or significant discomfort from your alleged injury.
Answer:

9. With respect to the injury allegedly suffered, state the extent and nature of any impairment and whether you suffered any restriction of your normal activities due to the injuries allegedly sustained. If so, describe in detail the nature of such restriction.
Answer:

10. If you received treatment with respect to the injuries allegedly sustained, state the name and address of each hospital or other facility where you were treated, the dates of treatment, and itemize the charges rendered by each of the facilities listed above.
Answer:

11. State the name and address of each doctor or medical practitioner of any type whatsoever who examined, treated or conferred with you with respect to the injuries alleged and itemize their charges.
Answer:

12. If you incurred any bills, not yet listed, in connection with the alleged injuries, state the total amount of each bill and the date you received treatment or service.
Answer:

13. State separately each and every act or omission which you claim constituted negligence on the part of the defendant(s) or which you claim constitute grounds for recovery of damages against defendant(s).
Answer:

14. Please provide the names, addresses and telephone numbers of your family doctor(s) for the past ten (10) years.
Answer:

15. Before or after the date of the accident alleged in the present lawsuit, did you ever sustain injury to the part(s) of your body that was/were allegedly injured in the accident which is the subject of this lawsuit?
Answer:

If answer is "yes", then answer the following:

a) What was the nature of the injury and the date, time and place of the injury?
Answer:

b) What is the name and address of each medical provider who treated you for the injury, the part(s) of your body which were injured, and the dates of treatment?
Answer:

c) Give the name and address of each hospital or medical facility where you received treatment or had x-rays taken for injury and the dates of treatment and x-rays.
Answer:

d) Did you make a claim against anyone because of this other injury? If yes, against whom did you make this claim and when did you make the claim? Did you file a lawsuit on this claim?
Answer:

16. Were you under the care of any medical provider immediately prior to receiving the injuries described in this lawsuit? If so, state the nature of the illness or injury for which said medical provider was treating you as well as the medical provider's name and address.
Answer:

17. State the name and address of each hospital or health care facility at which you have ever been admitted as an in-patient, out-patient, or emergency patient, and state the dates and reasons for treatment.
Answer:

18. Were any of the medical bills and/or lost wages incurred as a result of injuries sustained in the present lawsuit paid by any third parties (e.g., employers, insurance companies, workers' compensation, Medicare, Medicaid, or any other similar providers) and, if so, state the amount, name and address of the third party who paid for said expenses and losses.
Answers:

19. Have you ever pled guilty to or have you been convicted of a crime (1) punishable by death or imprisonment in excess of one year; or (2) involving dishonesty or a false statement (including the crime of receiving stolen property) regardless of whether the crime was a misdemeanor offense or a felony?
Answer:

20. At the time of the accident which is the subject of this lawsuit, was there in effect a policy of insurance that provided you with under-insurance coverage or uninsured motorist coverage? If your answer is "yes", provide the name(s) of the insurer(s) and the applicable amount(s) of underinsurance coverage and uninsured motorist coverage.
    Answer:

    Answer:

21. List the names, home and business addresses and home and business telephone numbers of any individuals who witnessed any of the matters involved in this lawsuit.
    Answer:

22. Do you claim any lost time or wages from your business, occupation, or employment as a result of the incident referred to in the complaint? If you answer yes, state with respect to each business, occupation, or employment:
    a) The name, address, and telephone number for each business, occupation, or employer.
       Answer:

    b) The dates, number of days, or total hours lost.
       Answer:

    c) The wages, income, or benefits lost.
       Answer:

    d) The date(s) you resumed your business, occupation, or employment
       Answer:

23. Identify all the exhibits you intend to use at the trial or arbitration of this matter, including the type of document, date, and number of pages.
    Answer:

24. State the name and address of the owner of the motor vehicle you were driving at the time of the subject accident, and state the year, make, and model of the vehicle.
    Answer:

I declare under penalty of perjury that the answers to the foregoing interrogatories are true and accurate to the best of my knowledge, information, and belief.

_____

James Kovach, Plaintiff

_____

Date

CERTIFICATE OF SERVICE

A copy of these Requests for Production of Documents has been sent by regular United States mail on this _____ day of _____, 20XX to Attorney for the Plaintiff, Clarence Dowling, to 45 Courthouse Square, Parkhurst, Ohio 44XXX.

_____

Bradley Smith 000000
Attorney for the Defendant,
Thomas Williams, Sr.
123 Main Street
Parkhurst, Ohio 44XXX
(216) 555-5555

LEARNING OBJECTIVES

1. Define a motion

2. Compare different types of motions

3. Compose a motion to dismiss from a complaint

4. Write an explanation of a motion for summary judgment, support of motion for summary judgment and a brief in opposition of motion for summary judgment

5. Draft a motion to compel

6. Assess knowledge of motions

CHAPTER 17

Motions

■ MOTIONS

After the complaint has initiated the lawsuit, the attorneys may file various motions that attempt to end the suit before trial or to make another party provide discovery. This chapter focuses on the most common types of motions you are likely to encounter in your career as a paralegal. There are additional motions that may be used in a lawsuit, including Motions to Quash and Motions for Protective Orders. These types of motions are used far less frequently and are not discussed in this chapter.

Motions, therefore, are documents submitted to the court to request an action. The first page of a motion brief describes the action the court is requested to take. This is followed by a brief or memorandum in support in which the party explains why the court should take the requested action. The brief or memorandum contains citations to law and explanations of why that law supports the request contained in the brief or memorandum.

Motion to Dismiss

A party may file a Motion to Dismiss in response to a complaint in lieu of filing an answer. As you will learn in Civil Procedure, Rule 12(B) provides several grounds under which a court may dismiss a complaint. The most commonly cited reason for a defendant to file a motion to dismiss is found in Rule 12(B)(6), "failure to state a claim upon which relief can be granted."

If you have not studied Civil Procedure yet, no doubt your head is spinning at this point. Simply stated, a 12(B)(6) Motion to Dismiss argues that the complaint, on its face, lacks any legal grounds on which the plaintiff can win a case.

When one of your authors worked as a paralegal in a medical malpractice firm, part of her job was to answer the phone calls from potential clients to assess whether the clients' complaints met legal requirements. Every Monday morning, after the callers had had the entire weekend to worry about their problems, the firm would receive many, many calls from people complaining about their doctors, hospitals, or other medical experiences. The majority of these callers lacked an actionable claim.

A number of their complaints consisted primarily of objecting to the medical professional's rudeness to them. While one of your authors, having dealt with many medical professionals over the course of a fifteen-year nursing career, believed that the situations about which the callers complained were accurate and true, she would tell the callers, "You cannot sue people for being rude or nasty. If you could, the courts would be overwhelmed with lawsuits."

Federal Civil Rule 7. Pleadings Allowed; Form of Motions and Other Papers

(b) MOTIONS AND OTHER PAPERS.

(1) In General. A request for a court order must be made by motion. The motion must:

(A) be in writing unless made during a hearing or trial;

(B) state with particularity the grounds for seeking the order; and

(C) state the relief sought.

(2) Form. The rules governing captions and other matters of form in pleadings apply to motions and other papers.

Federal Civil Rule 12.

(a) TIME TO SERVE A RESPONSIVE PLEADING.

(1) In General. Unless another time is specified by this rule or a federal statute, the time for serving a responsive pleading is as follows:

(A) A defendant must serve an answer:

(i) within 21 days after being served with the summons and complaint . . . .

(b) HOW TO PRESENT DEFENSES. Every defense to a claim for relief in any pleading must be asserted in the responsive pleading if one is required. . . . .

(6) failure to state a claim upon which relief can be granted . . . .

> A motion asserting any of these defenses must be made before pleading if a responsive pleading is allowed . . . .

Another firm, however, might take the callers' cases, either because the firm saw a potentially actionable claim that your author did not, or the other firm might have been somewhat less scrupulous and have presumed that the defendant might settle the suit to get rid of it. Many potential lawsuits settle even before any complaint is filed because the cost and time involved in defending a suit far exceed the value of defending it.

Nonetheless, if the firm you work for in the future receives a complaint that lacks any legal basis, the attorney will instruct you to draft a Motion to Dismiss pursuant to Civil Rule 12(B)(6). Below are examples of a complaint that lacks any valid legal ground and the opposing sides 12(B)(6) Motion to Dismiss.

Be aware that if the Court denies the 12(B)(6) motion, the defendant then has to file an answer within the time frame stated in Civil Rule 12. Again, you will learn more about these rules in your Civil Procedure class.

EXAMPLE

IN THE COURT OF COMMON PLEAS
PARKHURST COUNTY, OHIO

Winnie Whiner 11 Self Pity Lane Parkhurst, Ohio 44000 　Plaintiff,	))))	Case No. **999999**
	)))	
vs.	)))	Judge: **N. O. Nonsense**
	))	
	)	COMPLAINT
	))	
Rude N. Nasty, M.D. #1 Ego Blvd Parkhurst, Ohio 44XXX	)))	JURY DEMAND ENDORSED HEREIN
	))	
Defendant	)	

Now comes Plaintiff, by and through counsel, and as her Complaint against Defendant states the following:

COUNT ONE

1. The plaintiff, Winnie Whiner ("Whiner"), was and is a resident of Parkhurst County, Ohio at all times relevant to the facts of this complaint.

2. The defendant, Rude N. Nasty, M.D ("Dr. Nasty"), was and is a resident of Parkhurst County, Ohio, at all times relevant to the facts of this complaint.

3. On or about December 20, 20XX, at 5:45 pm., three hours after Whiner's scheduled appointment with Dr. Nasty, Dr. Nasty's office staff informed her that Dr. Nasty would not see her that day and that she would have to reschedule her appointment.

4. Despite Whiner's pleas and arguments concerning her acute medical needs, the staff heartlessly and callously refused to allow Whiner to see Dr. Nasty.

5. Dr. Nasty's office staff informed Whiner that if she felt her medical issue required immediate attention, she should visit an urgent care center or an emergency room.

6. While waiting in the crowded office waiting room, Whiner was exposed to several communicable viruses, and she was infected with one or more of the viruses.

7. As a direct and proximate result of Dr. Nasty's uncivil office staff, and his callous indifference to the well being of his patients, Whiner became seriously ill and missed all the Christmas celebrations that she had scheduled throughout the remaining month of December.

COUNT TWO

8. Whiner restates and incorporates all of Count I as if fully rewritten herein.

9. As a result of the virus(es) Whiner contracted in Dr. Nasty's waiting room while waiting for an appointment Dr. Nasty failed to keep, Whiner was forced to stay in bed with a fever, cough, runny nose, and body aches for over a week.

10. Whiner would not have been exposed to these pathogens but for Dr. Nasty's poor office management and unhygienic office waiting room layout.

11. As a direct and proximate result of Dr. Nasty's uncivil office staff, his callous indifference to the well being of his patients, and his unhygienic office waiting room layout, Whiner endured over a week of suffering and inconvenience.

WHEREFORE, Plaintiff Winnie Whiner demands judgment against Defendant Rude N. Nasty, M.D. in an amount in excess of twenty-five thousand dollars ($25,000.00) on Counts I for injuries, pain and suffering from the viral infections, emotional distress from having missed the most important holidays of the year, as well as any additional relief this Court deems Plaintiff to be legally entitled, just, and/or equitable, together with the costs of this action.

Sue Happy, Esq., 000000
Attorney for the Plaintiff,
Winnie Whiner
75 Shyster Avenue
Parkhurst, Ohio 44XXX
(216) 555-5555

After he finished laughing at the Complaint, Brad instructed Pat Paralegal to draft a 12(b)(6) Motion to Dismiss for Failure to State a Claim upon which Relief Can Be Granted.

Pat Paralegal drafted the following Motion to Dismiss, which Brad proofread and then signed for Pat to file with the Court. As noted above, the first page of the motion informs the court of the action being requested in the motion, and it is supported by a memorandum.

EXAMPLE

IN THE COURT OF COMMON PLEAS
PARKHURST COUNTY, OHIO

Winnie Whiner	)	
11 Self Pity Lane	)	Case No. 999999
Parkhurst, Ohio 44000	)	
Plaintiff,	)	
	)	
	)	
	)	
vs.	)	Judge: N. O. Nonsense
	)	
	)	
	)	
	)	
Rude N. Nasty, M.D.	)	
#1 Ego Blvd	)	**DEFENDANT'S**
Parkhurst, Ohio 44XXX	)	**MOTION TO DISMISS**
	)	
	)	
Defendant	)	

Pursuant to Civ.R. 12(B)(6), Defendant, Rude N. Nasty, M.D. ("Dr. Nasty"), moves this Court to dismiss Plaintiff Winnie Winer's ("Whiner") claims against him because she fails to state a claim upon which relief can be granted.

_____
Bradley Smith 000000
Attorney for the Defendant,
Rude N. Nasty, M.D.
123 Main Street
Parkhurst, Ohio 44XXX
(216) 555-5555

MEMORANDUM IN SUPPORT

Plaintiff Winnie Whiner's Complaint seeks relief in excess of $25,000 for claims that she was exposed to communicable diseases in Defendant Doctor's waiting room, that Dr. Nasty's staff was discourteous to her, and that Dr. Nasty showed callous indifference to the well being of his patients. Plaintiff has alleged no facts that would support a claim entitling her to relief. Therefore, Defendant requests the Court dismiss this Complaint because it fails to state any legal ground on which relief can be granted.

I. Facts

On December 20, 20XX, at 10:00 am, Dr. Nasty was called to Parkhurst Hospital to perform emergency surgery on a victim of a motor vehicle accident. Initially, Dr. Nasty thought the surgery would take approximately an hour, and based on that estimate, he decided not to cancel his office hours for that afternoon. As the surgery proceeded, however, Dr. Nasty discovered several serious internal injuries that required extensive repair. Because he was absorbed in caring for the patient on the operating table, Dr. Nasty did not instruct the operating room supervisor to notify his office.

When the operating room supervisor stepped into the operating room where Dr. Nasty was performing the emergency surgery, he realized that it was after 5:00 pm. He instructed the supervisor to contact his office and tell them to reschedule the patients he had in the waiting room.

Although the above facts are not in evidence, they are provided to the Court as background. Regardless of the cause, Dr. Nasty missed his office hours on the afternoon of December 20, 20XX.

At 5:45 pm on December 20, 20XX, Dr. Nasty's office staff informed the patients in the waiting room that they would have to reschedule their appointments. Most of the patients proceeded to reschedule their appointments. As part of his office policy and procedure, the staff also informed the patients that if they thought their medical situations required immediate attention, they should proceed to an urgent care or an emergency room.

II. Legal Argument

Pursuant to Civ.R. 12(B)(6), a Court shall dismiss a Complaint when it fails to state a legally supportable claim. In reviewing a Motion to Dismiss, the Court must view all the allegations stated in the complaint as true. *Allstate Ins. Co. v. Electrolux Home Prods., Inc.*, 2012-Ohio-90, ¶ 8 (internal citations omitted) Nonetheless, if the Court, after appraising the allegations in the complaint, determines that beyond doubt those allegations fail to assert any facts that would support the claim for relief, the Court will dismiss the complaint. *O'Brien v. Univ. Community Tenants Union, Inc.* 42 Ohio St.2d 242, 327 N.E.2d 753 (1975), citing *Conley v. Gibson* (1957), 355 U. S. 41, 45.

In this case, Whiner alleges that Dr. Nasty's office staff was uncivil, that he maintained an unhygienic layout in his waiting room, and that he was callously indifferent to his patient's well being. Although Dr. Nasty disputes these allegations, even if they were true, none of them states a legally compensable transgression that would entitle Whiner to relief.

Although courtesy is desirable in interactions with others, lack of courtesy is not an actionable offense. Perhaps Dr. Nasty's staff could have alleviated some of Whiner's anger by informing her of the reason for Dr. Nasty not being able to keep her appointment, but they were under no legal obligation to do so. The allegation that Dr. Nasty's staff was discourteous fails to state a claim upon which relief can be granted.

Whiner further alleges that Dr. Nasty's waiting room layout was unhygienic. She does not claim that she was infected by touching contaminated objects in the waiting room or that the waiting room was dangerously dirty. Rather, she argues that sick patients in the waiting room infected her with a virus. The presence of sick people in a physician's waiting room not only is not actionable, it is to be expected. People go to the doctor because they are sick.

Further, the facts as Whiner has stated them do not support the conclusion that she caught the virus in the waiting room, only that may have been exposed to it there. She also could have been exposed to the virus in the grocery store, on the elevator to the doctor's office, on public transportation, or in any other public place. Even if Whiner had caught the virus in the waiting room, being exposed to sick people in a physician's waiting room is not an actionable claim.

Finally, Whiner claims that Dr. Nasty was callously indifferent to his patient's well being. Ignoring the potential libel involved in this allegation, Dr. Nasty's absence from office hours fails to meet the standard of callous indifference. Nor is callous indifference an actionable offense.

Even if the Court takes all Whiner's allegations as true, she has failed to state any claim upon with relief can be granted.

III. Conclusion

For the above stated reasons, Plaintiff Winnie Whiner's complaint should be dismissed for failure to state a claim upon which relief can be granted.

Respectfully submitted,

_____
Bradley Smith 000000
Attorney for the Defendant,
Rude N. Nasty, M.D.
123 Main Street
Parkhurst, Ohio 44XXX
(216) 555-5555

CERTIFICATE OF SERVICE

A copy of the foregoing was sent by regular United States mail on this _____ day of _____, 20XX to Attorney for the Plaintiff, Sue Happy, 75 Shyster Avenue, Parkhurst, Ohio 44XXX, Parkhurst, Ohio 44XXX.

_____
Bradley Smith 000000
Attorney for the Defendant,
Rude N. Nasty, M.D.
123 Main Street
Parkhurst, Ohio 44XXX
(216) 555-5555

EXERCISE

Ana has asked you to read the Complaint below and write a Motion to Dismiss in response to it.

IN THE COURT OF COMMON PLEAS
PARKHURST COUNTY, OHIO

Richard Rage 77 Zorn Street Parkhurst, Ohio 44000 Plaintiff,	)))))	Case No. **838651**
	))	Judge: **N. O. Nonsense**
vs.	))))	
	)	COMPLAINT
Unhöflich Nichtbeachtung **15** Oublieux Place Parkhurst, Ohio 44XXX	))))	JURY DEMAND ENDORSED HEREIN
	))	
Defendant	)	

Now comes Plaintiff, by and through counsel, and as his Complaint against Defendant states the following:

COUNT ONE

1.   The plaintiff, Richard Rage (Rage) was and is a resident of Parkhurst County, Ohio at all times relevant to the facts of this complaint.

2.   The defendant, Unhöflich Nichtbeachtung (Nichtbeachtung), was and is a resident of Parkhurst County, Ohio, at all times relevant to the facts of this complaint.

3.   On or about August 13, 20XX, at 9:30 am at the Parkhurst Stadium parking lot, Rage was in the process of backing his extra large SUV into a parking spot for the purpose of tailgating before the football game. The spot he was maneuvering into was the last large spot left, but numerous small spots remained.

4.   As Rage was backing up his vehicle, Nichtbeachtung darted into the spot in his tiny electronic car.

5.   Rage was unable to see Nichtbeachtung's miniscule car, and his wife, who had been directing him into the parking spot had to alert him to the danger of running over Nichtbeachtung's miniature auto.

6.   As direct and proximate result of Nichtbeachtung's risky and dangerous actions, traffic in the parking lot was obstructed for over half an hour.

COUNT TWO

7.   Plaintiff restates and incorporates all of Count I as if fully rewritten herein.

8.   Although Nichtbeachtung could have parked in another spot and Rage's vehicle could not fit into the remaining spots in the stadium's parking lot, Nichtbeachtung refused to move his vehicle to a more appropriate spot. Instead, Nichtbeachtung berated Rage for the size and low mileage of his SUV.

(continued)

9. As a direct and proximate result of Nichtbeachtung's dangerous and rude actions, Rage had $100 worth of food that spoiled in his SUV because he could not cook it as he had planned and would have done if Nichtbeachtung had not stolen his parking space.

COUNT THREE

10. Plaintiff restates and incorporates all of Counts I and II as if fully rewritten herein.

11. Nichtbeachtung's actions so upset Rage that he was unable to enjoy the tailgating party or the football game, for which he had spent over $300 on tickets.

12. As a direct and proximate result of Nichtbeachtung's actions, Rage suffered economic loss and severe emotional distress.

WHEREFORE, Plaintiff Richard Rage demands judgment against Defendant Unhöflich Nichtbeachtung in an amount in excess of twenty-five thousand dollars ($25,000.00) on Counts I, II, and III for economic losses and emotional distress, as well as any additional relief this Court deems Plaintiff to be legally entitled, just, and or equitable, together with the costs of this action.

Sue Happy, Esq., 000000
Attorney for the Plaintiff,
Richard Rage
75 Shyster Avenue
Parkhurst, Ohio 44XXX
(216) 555-5555

EXERCISE

Commenting that the firm had received more than its share of frivolous complaints that week, Brad handed you another complaint and asked you to draft a motion to dismiss for it.

You will remember that in her boutique, Chez Cherelle, Cherelle had sold an expensive evening gown to Gisele Harrington on April 25, 20XX. Ms. Harrington's check was drawn on a local bank. Unfortunately, the check was returned to Cherelle for insufficient funds. Cherelle has politely, and then firmly, asked Ms. Harrington to pay for the gown, but Ms. Harrington has repeatedly put off Cherelle and promised to pay "soon."

(continued)

Ms. Harrington decided that she was not going to tolerate Cherelle's attempts to collect payment for the dress, so she asked an attorney to file a harassment suit on her behalf. The complaint for this suit is below.

IN THE COURT OF COMMON PLEAS
PARKHURST COUNTY, OHIO

Gisele Harrington	)	
66 Thornbush Lane	)	Case No. **853666**
Parkhurst, Ohio 44000	)	
	)	
	)	
Plaintiff.	)	
	)	Judge: **Michael Flynn**
	)	
vs.	)	
	)	COMPLAINT
	)	
Chez Cherelle, Inc.	)	
143 Main Street	)	JURY DEMAND
Parkhurst, Ohio 44XXX	)	ENDORSED HEREIN
	)	
	)	
Defendant	)	

Now comes Plaintiff, by and through counsel, and as her Complaint against Defendant states the following:

COUNT ONE

1. The Plaintiff, Gisele Harrington (Harrington) was and is a resident of Parkhurst County, Ohio at all times relevant to the facts of this complaint.

2. The Defendant, Chez Cherelle, Inc. was and is a business incorporated in the State of Ohio and the County of Parkhurst, Ohio, at all times relevant to the facts of this complaint.

3. Cherelle Jackson was the owner and operator of Chez Cherelle, Inc., at all times relevant to the facts of this complaint.

4. Plaintiff Harrington purchased a gown at Chez Cherelle, Inc. on April 25, 20XX.

5. Since Harrington April 30, 20XX, Chez Cherelle, Inc., through its owner/operator Cherelle Jackson, has harassed, stalked, and slandered Harrington.

6. As a direct and proximate result of Chez Cherelle's harassment, stalking, and slander, Harrington has suffered severe emotional distress.

COUNT TWO

7. Harrington restates and incorporates all of Count I as if fully rewritten herein.

8. Harrington has suffered embarrassment when visiting her bank because of Chez Cherelle's repeated attempts to negotiate Harrington's check.

(continued)

9. As a direct and proximate result of Chez Cherelle's harassment, stalking, and slander, Harrington has been forced to take her banking business to another financial establishment, causing her great inconvenience.

COUNT THREE

10. Harrington restates and incorporates all of Counts I and II as if fully rewritten herein.

11. Harrington has suffered loss of credibility in the community as a result of Chez Cherelle's slanderous attempt to negotiate the check.

WHEREFORE, Plaintiff Gisele Harrington demands judgment against Defendant Chez Carolyn, Inc. in an amount in excess of twenty-five thousand dollars ($25,000.00) on Counts I, II, and III for emotional distress, loss of valuable time, and loss of reputation, as well as any additional relief this Court deems Plaintiff to be legally entitled, just, and or equitable, together with the costs of this action.

_____

Beau Gusclame, Esq., 000000
Attorney for the Plaintiff,
Gisele Harrington
55 Crooked Lane
Parkhurst, Ohio 44XXX
(216) 555-5555

EXERCISE _____

Read the following complaint and draft a Motion to Dismiss for the Defendant.

Antoine Taylor has come to Brad Smith's law office with a Complaint he received from the buyer of a house in which Antoine had represented the seller. Below is the Complaint.

IN THE COURT OF COMMON PLEAS
PARKHURST COUNTY, OHIO

Karen and Floyd Green Plaintiffs,	)))	Case No. 123456
	)	Judge: MICHAEL FLYNN
vs.	))	
Antoine Taylor Defendant	))))	COMPLAINT JURY DEMAND ENDORSED HEREON

Now comes Plaintiff, by and through counsel, and as his Complaint against Defendant states the following:

COUNT ONE

1. The Plaintiffs, Karen and Floyd Green (the Greens), were and are residents of Parkhurst County, Ohio at all times relevant to the facts of this complaint.

(continued)

2. The Defendant, Antoine Taylor (Taylor), was and is a resident of Parkhurst County, Ohio, at all times relevant to the facts of this complaint.

3. On or about February 3, 20XX, Taylor represented the sellers at 93 Sunset Lane, Parkhurst, Ohio in the sale of said property to the Greens.

4. The sellers of 93 Sunset Lane, Parkhurst, Ohio had completed a Property Disclosure form that Taylor presented to the Greens and represented to the Greens that no other known defects existed in the property.

5. Upon the arrival of warm weather, the Greens opened their windows and heard repeated gunshots coming from an undetermined source.

6. Upon investigating, the Greens discovered that 93 Sunset Lane, Parkhurst, Ohio was adjacent to the Parkhurst Rod and Gun Club's outdoor shooting range.

7. The noise from the shooting range has prevented the Greens from peaceful enjoyment of their home.

8. Taylor had a duty to ensure his clients included the presence of this disturbance adjacent to 93 Sunset Lane, Parkhurst, Ohio in the Property Disclosure form.

9. As a proximate result of Taylor's negligence in ensuring the Property Disclosure form was complete, the Greens have suffered severe emotional distress.

COUNT TWO

10. Plaintiff restates and incorporates all of Count I as if fully rewritten herein.

11. Plaintiff's property values are significantly reduced by the existence of the nuisance presented by the proximity of the Parkhurst Rod and Gun Club.

12. As a proximate result of Taylor's negligence in ensuring the Property Disclosure form was complete, the Greens have suffered severe economic damages in the form of their lost property value.

WHEREFORE, Plaintiffs Karen and Floyd Green demand judgment against Defendant Antoine Taylor in an amount in excess of twenty-five thousand dollars ($25,000.00) on Counts I and II for compensation for injuries, loss of income, and property damage, as well as any additional relief this Court deems Plaintiff to be legally entitled, just, and or equitable, together with the costs of this action.

Clarence Dowling 000000
Attorney for the Plaintiffs,
Karen and Floyd Green
45 Courthouse Square
Parkhurst, Ohio 44XXX
(216) 555-5555

A trial by jury of eight (8) is hereby demanded.

Respectfully Submitted,

Clarence Dowling 000000
Attorney for the Plaintiffs,
Karen and Floyd Green

(continued)

INSTRUCTIONS FOR SERVICE

The Clerk of Courts is hereby instructed to serve a copy of this Complaint on all parties at the addresses listed in the caption.

_____

Clarence Dowling 000000
Attorney for the Plaintiffs,
Karen and Floyd Green
45 Courthouse Square
Parkhurst, Ohio 44XXX
(216) 555-5555

Motion for Summary Judgment

Rule 56. Summary Judgment

MOTION FOR SUMMARY JUDGMENT OR PARTIAL SUMMARY JUDGMENT. A party may move for summary judgment, identifying each claim or defense — or the part of each claim or defense — on which summary judgment is sought. The court shall grant summary judgment if the movant shows that there is no genuine dispute as to any material fact and the movant is entitled to judgment as a matter of law. The court should state on the record the reasons for granting or denying the motion.

TIME TO FILE A MOTION. Unless a different time is set by local rule or the court orders otherwise, a party may file a motion for summary judgment at any time until 30 days after the close of all discovery.

A Motion for Summary Judgment is used when the attorney believes that the evidence that has been gathered demonstrates that the other side cannot prevail at trial. If the Court grants a Motion for Summary Judgment, then the side that filed it wins the case, and the parties and the Court avoid the time and expense of a trial. Courts sometimes grant summary judgment on a portion of the complaint and require trial for another portion of the complaint. For example, in a car accident case, when the evidence overwhelmingly shows that one party caused the accident, the Court may grant summary judgment on liability but still go to trial to determine the amount of damages. For example, in a case in which the driver who caused an accident was jailed for driving under the influence of alcohol or drugs, and video and deposition evidence demonstrates that he was driving the wrong direction on the freeway, it would be a waste of everyone's time to take that issue to trial. Still, the amount of money the guilty driver's insurance company will have to pay the injured parties might be at issue. In that case, the Court would grant summary judgment on liability and go to trial concerning damages: lost wages, medical bills, pain and suffering, etc.

Motions for Summary Judgment usually are filed after discovery is complete. They contain supplementary evidence, including depositions, affidavits, and copies of documents or photographs to support the arguments contained in the brief in support of the Motion. Of course, the other side(s) also has the opportunity to file Briefs in Opposition to Motions for Summary Judgment. These Briefs in Opposition will also contain evidence, and they will attempt to persuade the Court that an issue of material fact exists that precludes the granting of Summary Judgment. You will learn more about the timing and circumstances surrounding motions for summary judgment in your Civil Procedure class.

Your authors would like to raise an important caveat here: in your career as a paralegal, it is imperative that you avoid the unauthorized practice of law (UPL). Writing a Motion for Summary Judgment is part of the practice of law, and it is unlikely that a paralegal would draft one. Nonetheless, the attorney may ask you to research various legal issues and provide memoranda to help him or her to draft the Motion for Summary Judgment. Similarly, if the attorney is drafting a Brief in Opposition to a Motion for Summary Judgment, you may do legal research, draft memoranda, and possibly proofread the draft if you are a good proofreader.

For a paralegal to write a Motion for Summary Judgment could constitute the unauthorized practice of law (UPL), which is a crime in many states. Additionally, attorneys have lost their licenses to practice law for allowing their paralegals to engage in the unauthorized practice of law. Everything you draft for the attorney, from a complaint to a Motion to Compel, must be supervised and approved by the attorney. The attorney is personally required to sign everything submitted to the Court, and the attorney's signature on a document verifies that he or she is the legitimate author of the document or adopts it as his or her own. Attorneys who fail to read and verify the paralegal's work are failing to practice ethically. It is as much the paralegal's job as it is the attorney's job to ensure that the paralegal does not stray into the unauthorized practice of law.

If you are in doubt regarding whether what you are asked to do might constitute the unauthorized practice of law, consult a book written by an expert on the subject, like Deborah K. Orlick's *Ethics for the Legal Profession*.

Below are abbreviated examples of a Motion for Summary Judgment and a Brief in Opposition to the Motion for Summary Judgment. Note that as with all motions, the Motion for Summary Judgment and the Brief in Opposition have briefs in support. As with all pleadings and motions, the title of the motion or pleading, and the title of its brief or memorandum in support, is centered, bolded, and underlined. While the jurisdiction in which you work may have a different method or use only some of these emphasizing formats, the titles will be set off in a way that makes them easily recognizable and clearly alerts the readers to the purpose of the text that follows.

Note that many Motions for Summary Judgment and Briefs in Opposition address multiple issues, cite additional law, and are much longer. That said, sometimes brevity is more effective, when appropriate.

Your authors have included two versions of each document to demonstrate that although the format for each document is similar, different attorneys will draft the same document in different ways. You can be the judge of which versions are more effective.

Brief in support of motion for summary judgment.

EXAMPLE

Version one of Defendant's Motion for Summary Judgment:

IN THE COURT OF COMMON PLEAS
PARKHURST COUNTY, OHIO

Sheila Kowalski	)	
Plaintiff	)	Case No. 446551
	)	
	)	
	)	Judge: Michael Flynn
	)	
vs.	)	
	)	<u>DEFENDANT,</u>
Property Management, Inc.	)	<u>PROPERTY MANAGEMENT, INC'S</u>
Defendant	)	<u>MOTION FOR</u>
	)	<u>SUMMARY JUDGMENT</u>
	)	

Now comes Defendant, Property Management, Inc., by and through counsel, and hereby moves this Court, pursuant to Ohio Civil Rule 56, for summary judgment because there are no genuine issues of material fact upon which Plaintiff can prevail. Defendant thereby is entitled to judgment in its favor as a matter of law.

Andrew Adwokat, Esq., 000000
100 Courthouse Square
Parkhurst, Ohio 44XXX
(216) 555-5555
Attorney for the Defendant,
Property Management, Inc.

BRIEF IN SUPPORT OF DEFENDANT'S MOTION FOR SUMMARY JUDGMENT

I. Introduction and Summary of the Claim

Plaintiff Sheila Kowalski brought this claim alleging constructive eviction from her leased premises at 748 Beech Drive, Suite 14, Parkhurst, Ohio 44XXX. In support of her claim, Plaintiff began depositing her rent with the Court six months prior to filing her Complaint for constructive eviction.

Plaintiff has failed to provide evidence that Defendant has not worked with her to resolve her allegations. In fact, Plaintiff has refused to allow Property Management, Inc. entry into the apartment to perform the requested repairs.

Additionally, because Property Management, Inc. bought the property from the developer who built it, Property Management, Inc. has no liability for latent defects caused by the builder.

II. Statement of Facts

On July 12, 20XX, Property Management, Inc. bought the apartment building at 748 Beech Drive, Parkhurst, Ohio 44XXX from the developer who built it. Property Management, Inc. has owned and operated the building for fifteen years. Plaintiff is the first tenant to deposit rent with the Court because of alleged defects in the property.

Property Management, Inc.'s employee is its rental agent and superintendent for 748 Beech Drive. After touring the property and grounds with Defendant's employee, Plaintiff signed a lease for a unit at 748 Beech Drive, Parkhurst, Ohio 44XXX. Plaintiff insisted on taking possession of the model apartment, despite warnings that it might not be set up for actual habitation. Defendant's employee offered her a unit he believed would be more suitable for her, but Plaintiff adamantly refused to take possession of any unit except number 14, despite warnings that it had never been occupied and might not as suitable as the unit she was offered.

Immediately after she took possession of the premises, Plaintiff's numerous complaints began. Although she had inspected the premises prior to insisting on leasing that particular unit, she quickly found fault with the hot water supply, the heat supply, and various other aspects of the unit.

Property Management, Inc.'s employee has made numerous attempts to gain entry to rectify the issues of which Plaintiff complains, but Plaintiff has refused him entry.

III. Law and Argument

A grant of summary judgment is appropriate only if the moving party can demonstrate all three of the following: first, there are no genuine issues of material fact. Second, the party moving for summary judgment is, as a matter of law, entitled to judgment in its favor. And, third, the only conclusion reasonable minds could reach is, despite construing the evidence most strongly in favor of the party the motion for summary judgment was made against, reasonable minds can reach only one conclusion, in favor of the party moving for summary judgment. Civ.R. 56; *State ex rel. Grady v. State Emp. Relations Bd.*, 78 Ohio St.3d 181, 1997-Ohio-221 (1997).

The party moving for summary judgment has the initial burden, pursuant to Civ.R. 56(C), of providing the trial court with the basis for its motion for summary judgment as well as of pointing to the specific parts of the record that demonstrate that there is no genuine issue of material fact. *Dresher v. Burt*, 75 Ohio St.3d 280, 293, 662 N.E.2d 264 (1996). This burden consists of more than merely asserting that the nonmoving party lacks of evidence to support its claim. Rather, the party moving for summary judgment must demonstrate affirmatively, consistent with Civ.R. 56(C), the absence of requisite evidence to support the nonmoving party's claims. *Id.*; *Vahila v. Hall*, 77 Ohio St.3d 421 1997-Ohio-259, 674 N.E.2d 1164 (1997).

After the party moving for summary judgment has fulfilled this initial burden, a granting of summary judgment in it favor will be appropriate unless the nonmoving party responds in the manner stated in Civ.R. 56 and provides specific facts that demonstrate the existence of genuine issues of material fact warranting a trial. *Dresher* at 293; *Vahila* at 430; Civ.R. 56(E).

A. Inability of Property Management, Inc. to gain entry to make the repairs.

Property Management, Inc.'s employee has scheduled appointments to repair the water and heat issues of which Plaintiff claims. The first time Property Management, Inc.'s employee attempted to execute the repairs, on October 12, 20XX, at 10:00 am, Plaintiff refused the workers entry, stating that she needed to sleep. The second time Property Management, Inc.'s employee attempted to gain entry into the apartment, on November 21, 20XX, Plaintiff refused him and the workers entry because she was not feeling well and did not want to cope with the disturbance. The third and final time Property Management, Inc.'s employee attempted to gain entry into the apartment to perform the requested repairs, on January 30, 20XX, Plaintiff had the chain lock on and refused to answer the door, preventing Property Management, Inc.'s employee from gaining entry and executing the repairs. *See*, attached invoices and work orders; affidavit of Property Management, Inc.'s Property Manager.

It is not disputed that a landlord owes certain duties to a residential tenant. Among those duties is a warranty of habitability. R.C. § 5321.04. Nonetheless, the tenant has a corresponding duty to allow the landlord the opportunity to rectify any problems that arise in the premises. The tenant must allow "the landlord to enter into the dwelling unit in order to inspect the premises, make ordinary, necessary, or agreed repairs . . . ." R.C. § 5321.05(B).

Property Management, Inc. cannot be held liable for failing to rectify alleged defects if the tenant denied it entry to make the requested repairs. Thus, rather than Property Management, Inc. being in violation of R.C. § 5321.04, it is Plaintiff herself who is in violation of R.C. § 5321.05(B) for failing to allow the landlord to make any necessary repairs.

B. Property Management, Inc. is not liable for latent defects that existed in the property prior to its ownership.

Plaintiff alleges that Property Management, Inc. knowingly rented her a defective unit because it lacked hot water and heat. Pursuant to R.C. 5341.04, Property Management, Inc. concedes its obligation to provide both these services. Nonetheless, Plaintiff errs in alleging prior knowledge of these alleged defects.

Certainly Property Management, Inc. would be liable for any defects caused by it or contractors it had hired to perform work on the premises. *Wallace v. Golden Comb, Inc.*, Cuyahoga App. No. 99910, 2013-Ohio-5320. In *Wallace*, the Eighth District Court of Appeals found that the landlord was liable for a faulty handrail installed by a contractor landlord had hired, despite landlord's lack of knowledge of the defect. *Id.*, citing *Strayer v. Lindeman*, 68 Ohio St.2d 32, 36, 42 N.E. 2d 781 (1981).

The Court distinguished this duty, however, from a landlord's liability for a latent defect caused by the builder of the premises prior to landlord's ownership. In *Sikora v. Wenzel*, 88 Ohio St.3d 493, 496, 2000-Ohio-406, 727 N.E. 2d 1277 (2000), the Ohio Supreme Court found that a landlord who purchased a property from the builder was not liable for injuries sustained when the deck, which had been improperly constructed by the builder, collapsed and caused injuries.

Similarly here, Property Management, Inc. bought the apartment building from the developer. As in *Sikora*, the building had passed all requisite inspections. As in *Sikora*, Property Management, Inc. had no notice of any defects in the unit Plaintiff rented.

Further, Property Management, Inc.'s rental agents over the last twenty years have used Unit 14 as the model apartment. Having shown Unit 14 year-around to numerous prospective tenants, none of these rental agents has noted or commented upon lack of heat or hot water. Property Management, Inc. had no prior notice that Unit 14 lacked hot water or heat and cannot be held liable for the alleged preexisting defect.

IV. Conclusion

Plaintiff has failed to cooperate with Property Management, Inc. in its attempts to rectify her complained of issues. Further, Property Management, Inc. had no prior knowledge of any preexisting defects in Unit 14, the apartment Plaintiff rented. Accordingly, no genuine issues of material fact exist in this case, and Property Management, Inc. is entitled to judgment as a matter of law.

Respectfully submitted,

_____
Andrew Adwokat, Esq., 000000
100 Courthouse Square
Parkhurst, Ohio 44XXX
(216) 555-5555
Attorney for the Defendant,
Property Management, Inc.

CERTIFICATE OF SERVICE

A copy of the foregoing was sent by regular United States mail on this _____ day of _____, 20XX to Attorney for the Plaintiff, Ana Garcia, Esq., 123 Main Street, Parkhurst, Ohio 44XXX.

_____
Andrew Adwokat, Esq., 000000
100 Courthouse Square
Parkhurst, Ohio 44XXX
(216) 555-5555
Attorney for the Defendant,
Property Management, Inc.

EXAMPLE

Version Two of Defendant's Motion for Summary Judgment, Applying Florida Law:

IN THE COURT OF COMMON PLEAS
PARKHURST COUNTY, OHIO

Sheila Kowalski Plaintiff	)	Case No. 446551
	)	
	)	
	)	Judge: Michael Flynn
	)	
vs.	)	
	)	DEFENDANT,
Property Management, Inc.	)	PROPERTY MANAGEMENT, INC'S
Defendant	)	MOTION FOR SUMMARY JUDGMENT
	)	

Now comes Defendant, Property Management, Inc, by and through counsel, and hereby moves this Court for summary judgment pursuant to

Florida Civil Rule 56 because there are no genuine issues as to any material fact, and Defendant is entitled to judgment in its favor as a matter of law.

Andrew Adwokat, Esq., 000000
100 Courthouse Square
Parkhurst, Ohio 44XXX
(216) 555-5555
Attorney for the Defendant,
Property Management, Inc.

BRIEF IN SUPPORT OF DEFENDANT'S MOTION FOR SUMMARY JUDGMENT

I. Introduction and Summary of the Claim

Plaintiff Sheila Kowalski's complaint alleges that she was constructively evicted from her leased premises at 748 Beech Drive, Unit 14, Parkhurst, Ohio 44XXX. Plaintiff began depositing her rent with the Court six months before she filed her complaint and has continued as long as this action has been pending.

Plaintiff's complaints concern latent defects created by the builder, ABC Construction Co. ("ABC"). Property Management, Inc. was not aware of these defects when it bought the property from ABC, nor did it learn of them until Plaintiff complained. Therefore, Property Management, Inc. did not knowingly rent Plaintiff a defective apartment. Further, ABC is headquartered in the State of Florida, and the rental contract Kowalski signed agrees that any and all disputes will be resolved applying Florida law.

Property Management, Inc. attempted to work with plaintiff to resolve her complaints, but to no avail. In fact, Plaintiff has refused to allow Property Management, Inc. to enter the apartment to perform the requested repairs. Therefore, Property Management, Inc. cannot be held liable to Plaintiff for failing to make the repairs.

II. Statement of Facts

Property Management, Inc. bought the apartment building at 748 Beech Drive from ABC in 20XX. In the fifteen years that Property Management, Inc. has owned and operated the building, Plaintiff is the only tenant who has ever deposited rent with the Court because of alleged defects in the property.

Plaintiff signed a lease for a unit after touring the property and grounds with the rental agent. Plaintiff insisted on taking possession of the model apartment, despite warnings that the unit was a model and had never been occupied. Property Management, Inc.'s employee offered her another unit, but Plaintiff adamantly refused to take possession of any unit except the model, Unit Number 14.

Immediately after she took possession of the premises, Plaintiff began to complain about the hot water supply, the heat supply, and various other concerns. Because this unit had always been used as a model, it was never occupied by a tenant before Plaintiff, and Property Management, Inc. was not aware of any of these claimed defects before Plaintiff complained. See affidavit of Property Management, Inc.'s Property Manager.

Property Management, Inc. attempted to address Plaintiff's complaints on several occasions, but Plaintiff refused to allow workers entry to the apartment. The first time, on October 12, 20XX, at 10:00 am, Plaintiff refused the workers entry, stating that she needed to sleep. On November 21, 20XX, Plaintiff again denied workers entry because she was not feeling well and did not want to cope with the disturbance. The third and final time, on January 30, 20XX, Plaintiff not only refused to answer the door, but also engaged the security chain on the door, preventing Property Management, Inc.'s employee from gaining entry and executing the repairs. *See*, attached invoices and work orders; affidavit of Property Management, Inc.'s Property Manager.

III. Law and Argument

Summary Judgment is reviewed *de novo*. "Summary judgment is proper if there is no genuine issue of material fact and if the moving party is entitled to a judgment as a matter of law." *Volusia County v. Aberdeen at Ormond Beach, L.P.*, 760 So.2d 126, 130 (Fla. 2000). The review for summary judgment is two pronged; first, the question concerning questions of fact are resolved, and if no question of fact exists, the court addresses whether any questions of law exist. *Id.* at 130-131.

A. Property Management, Inc. acknowledges its duty to supply heat and hot water but asserts that Plaintiff barred its implied right to entry to make needed repairs.

Plaintiff alleges that Property Management, Inc. knowingly rented her a defective unit because Unit 14 lacked hot water and heat. Property Management, Inc. concedes it is obligated to provide hot water and heat pursuant to Fla. Stat. § 83.51 (2012), but denies that it knowingly rented a unit to Plaintiff that did not supply them. Unit 14 has always been used as a model, and Property Management, Inc. was not aware that the unit lacked hot water and heat at the time Plaintiff rented the premises.

Further, Plaintiff has an obligation to allow Property Management access to make the requested repairs to the premises. "Every rental agreement or duty within this part imposes an obligation of good faith in its performance or enforcement." Fla. Stat. § 83.44 (2014).

Plaintiff has failed to cooperate with Property Management, Inc. in its efforts to gain access to Unit 14 to make the requested repairs. Therefore, Property Management, Inc. cannot be held responsible for failing to make repairs unless the tenant demonstrates that she has met her corresponding obligation to allow the landlord access to the premises. Plaintiff cannot meet this burden. As shown by the Property Manager's affidavit, attached as Exhibit B, Plaintiff repeatedly refused to allow workers to enter the apartment to perform the repairs she requested. Therefore, Plaintiff cannot be heard to complain that the repairs were not made.

B. Plaintiff has deposited her rent with the local county in Ohio in violation of Florida law.

Plaintiff had failed to pay her rent over six months. She claims that she has deposited her rent with the Clerk of Courts in the County in which the property is located. Florida law, however, provides only limited situations under which a tenant may deposit rent. The applicable Florida statute delineates the circumstances under which a tenant may deposit rent with the court:

> (2) In an action by the landlord for possession of a dwelling unit, if the tenant interposes any defense other than payment, the tenant shall pay into the registry of the court the accrued rent as alleged in the complaint or as determined by the court and the rent which accrues during the pendency of the proceeding, when due. . . . . Failure of the tenant to pay the rent into the registry of the court or to file a motion to determine the amount of rent to be paid into the registry within 5 days . . . after the date of service of process constitutes an absolute waiver of the tenant's defenses other than payment, and the landlord is entitled to an immediate default judgment for removal of the tenant with a writ of possession to issue without further notice or hearing thereon. . . . . (Emphasis added).

Fla. Stat. § 83.60 (2014)

The landlord in this case, Property Management, Inc., has not initiated an action for possession of the rental unit in question. Plaintiff's right to deposit rent, therefore, has not accrued pursuant to statute. Plaintiff is in violation of Florida law and has an obligation to pay the rent she owes Property Management along with the late penalties specified in the contract, which is included in this motion as exhibit A.

Florida law provides recourse to parties of a rental agreement when one of the parties fails to comply with the rental agreement: Fla. Stat. § 83.55 (2014) states that "[i]f either the landlord or the tenant fails to comply with the requirements of the rental agreement or this part, the aggrieved party may recover the damages caused by the noncompliance." Plaintiff has failed to comply with her obligation to pay the agreed upon rent to the agreed upon rental agent. Plaintiff is, therefore, in violation of Florida Statute: Fla. Stat. § 83.55 (2014).

IV. Conclusion

Plaintiff failed to cooperate with Property Management, Inc. in its attempts to address her complaints. Further, Property Management, Inc. had no prior knowledge of any defects in the model apartment Plaintiff insisted upon renting. Finally, Plaintiff is in violation of Florida law due to her failure to pay her rent in accordance with the rental agreement. Accordingly, no genuine issues of material fact exist in this case, and Property Management, Inc. is entitled to judgment as a matter of law.

Respectfully submitted,

_____

Andrew Adwokat, Esq., 000000
100 Courthouse Square
Parkhurst, Ohio 44XXX
(216) 555-5555
Attorney for the Defendant,
Property Management, Inc.

CERTIFICATE OF SERVICE

A copy of the foregoing Motion was sent by regular U.S. mail on this _____ day of _____, 20XX to Attorney for the Plaintiff, Ana Garcia, Esq., 123 Main Street, Parkhurst, Ohio 44XXX.

_____
Andrew Adwokat, Esq., 000000
100 Courthouse Square
Parkhurst, Ohio 44XXX
(216) 555-5555
Attorney for the Defendant,
Property Management, Inc.

Now it is up to Ms. Kowalski's attorney to draft a brief in opposition to this motion for summary judgment. It is imperative that a Brief in Opposition to Summary Judgment be strong enough to persuade the court that genuine issues of material fact exist that require a trial to resolve.

Brief in opposition of motion for summary judgment.

Although the Brief in Opposition often is organized to correspond to the arguments raised in the Motion for Summary Judgment, some attorneys believe that it is preferable to organize the Brief in Opposition in a way that highlights the strengths of his or her client's case. Although there are good arguments for each approach, after spending years working in the courts, one of your authors notes that the point-for-point response is more effective and more persuasive to the courts.

As with the Motion for Summary Judgment, the purpose of the brief or memorandum is centered, bolded, and underlined for clarity. Again, the jurisdiction in which you work may have a different format, but however it is formatted, the title will be set off enough to provide the readers with the information they need to know the purpose of the text that follows. Also, while the full title of the brief below is "Brief in Opposition to Motion for Summary Judgment," because the full name of the motion, "Plaintiff Sheila Kowalski's Brief in Opposition to Property Management, Inc.'s Motion for Summary Judgment," titling the brief "Brief in Opposition" is acceptable. The readers will not be confused by this title.

EXAMPLE

Version one of Brief in Opposition to Defendant's Motion For Summary Judgment:

**IN THE COURT OF COMMON PLEAS
PARKHURST COUNTY, OHIO**

Sheila Kowalski Plaintiff	)	Case No. 446551
	)	
	)	
	)	Judge: Michael Flynn
	)	
vs.	)	
	)	PLAINTIFF, SHEILA KOWALSKI'S
	)	BRIEF IN OPPOSITION TO
Property Management, Inc.	)	PROPERTY MANAGEMENT, INC.'S
Defendant	)	MOTION FOR SUMMARY JUDGMENT
	)	

Pursuant to Civ.R. 56, Plaintiff Sheila Kowalski opposes Defendant Property Management, Inc.'s Motion for Summary Judgment on the grounds that genuine issues of material fact exist that preclude judgment as a matter of law.

BRIEF IN OPPOSITION

I. Introduction and Summary of the Claim

Plaintiff Sheila Kowalski filed her complaint for constructive eviction from Unit 14 at 748 Beech Drive, Suite 14, Parkhurst, Ohio 44XXX after eight months of tenancy in an apartment that lacked both heat and hot water. As the northeastern Ohio winter approached, these conditions rendered her apartment uninhabitable. Although Ms. Kowalski began depositing her rent within two months of taking possession of the property, Defendant has failed to repair these defects.

Defendant has failed to schedule the entry into Ms. Kowalski's apartment, and the three times defendant appeared, unannounced, to inspect the premises, Ms. Kowalski was unable to allow the workers entry.

Finally, regardless of whether Defendant had prior knowledge of the defects, it has, as it admits, an obligation to correct them and render the living space habitable.

II. Statement of Facts

For as long as Ms. Kowalski can remember, the apartment building at 748 Beech Drive, Parkhurst, Ohio 44XXX has been considered an upscale, desirable place to live. She had visited friends who lived in apartments in the building, however, and she was aware of the discrepancy in quality and desirability of the various apartments in the building. After she toured Unit 14, she decided to rent that apartment because it met all of her needs.

Being aware of the range of quality the apartments in the building had, Ms. Kowalski specifically included the exact unit she agreed to lease, Unit 14. At that time, the property manager made no comment or objection to her explicit choice of unit. It was not until she arrived with her moving van that the property manager attempted a bait-and-switch, trying to persuade Ms. Kowalski to accept a less desirable unit in the building.

Ms. Kowalski reminded the property manager of the terms of the lease, and he grudgingly allowed her to take possession of Unit 14. It was not until that evening, when she prepared to shower, that Ms. Kowalski became aware that the unit lacked hot water. When she notified the property manager, he laughed and told her that she had gotten the apartment she insisted on having.

Despite repeated, documented requests for hot water, and later, heat, Defendant has failed to provide Ms. Kowalski with either. In the eight months since Ms. Kowalski took possession of Unit 14, Defendant has made only three unscheduled attempts to make her apartment habitable.

III. Law and Argument

Summary Judgment may not be granted unless the Court determines that there are no genuine issues of any material fact that remain to be litigated. Additionally, the Court must determine that the party moving for summary judgment is, as a matter of law, entitled to judgment. Finally, the evidence must show that reasonable minds could come to only one conclusion, even when viewing the evidence in a light most favorable to the nonmoving party, and that conclusion is against the nonmoving party and in favor of the moving party. *State ex rel. Zimmerman v. Tompkins*, 75 Ohio St.3d 447, 448, 1996-Ohio-211, 663 N.E.2d 639 (1996) (internal citations omitted.)

A. Failure of Defendant Property Management, Inc. to schedule or make repairs

1. Lack of Notice

Defendant argues that Ms. Kowalski failed to cooperate with its attempts to make the repairs necessary to provide her with heat and hot water. As Defendant concedes, a landlord has statutory obligations, including making needed repairs to "keep the premises in a fit and habitable condition . . . ." R.C. § 5321.05(A)(2). When a landlord needs to enter a residential unit to make needed repairs, however, the law requires the landlord to provide the tenant with reasonable notice that the landlord intends to enter the apartment. The statute defines reasonable notice as twenty-four hours, and it requires the landlord's entry to take place "only at reasonable times." R.C. § 5321.05(A)(8).

At no time has Defendant, despite its claims to the contrary, actually notified Ms. Kowalski of its plans to enter her apartment and make the requisite repairs.

2. Inconvenient Timing of Landlord's Attempted Entries

Defendant argues that Ms. Kowalski barred its workers entry to make the needed repairs each time it attempted to make them.

A tenant must cooperate with the landlord in granting him or her entry into the leased unit so the landlord can make needed repairs; "[t]he tenant shall not unreasonably withhold consent for the landlord to enter into the dwelling unit in order to inspect the premises, make ordinary, necessary, or agreed repairs." R.C. § 5321.05 (B),

Although Defendant may have scheduled the repairs with its workers, it never notified nor attempted to schedule these repairs with Ms. Kowalski. Each of the three times Defendant appeared at Ms. Kowalski's door, it would have been unreasonable for Defendant's workers to enter.

The first time they arrived, on October 12, 20XX at 10:00 am, Ms. Kowalski had worked night shift in the Parkhurst Hospital Intensive Care Unit, where she is employed as a Registered Nurse. Further, she was scheduled to return to work the 3-11 shift five hours later. Despite Defendant's attempts to make her objection to entry sound frivolous, "she needed to sleep," given her rotating shift schedule and lack of notice of the decision to perform the repairs at that time, Ms. Kowalski would have been irresponsible to try to have worked without sleep. If she had been notified in advance of the scheduled work, she would have stayed at her parent's house that day to sleep.

Intensive Care nursing requires alertness and attentiveness, which is not possible when the nurse is sleep deprived.

The second time the workers appeared unexpectedly to make the repairs on November 21, 20XX, Ms. Kowalski was sick in bed with the flu. Her symptoms included dizziness, lightheadedness, and severe coughing. Again, if she had known that Defendant planned to perform the work that day, she could have made alternate sleeping arrangements. But given her illness, she was in no position to suddenly find another place to sleep, much less drive herself to another location. Her dizziness and lightheadedness precluded her driving safely at all.

The third and last time the workers arrived at Ms. Kowalski's apartment, she again had no notice that they were planning to come and do work. That she had no knowledge of their plans was obvious; she had put the chain lock on because she was showering. She could hardly be expected to jump out of the shower when strangers arrived at her home without warning. *See* Deposition of Sheila Kowalski, sworn affidavit of Sheila Kowalski's supervisor regarding her work schedule on October 11-12, 20XX and January 29-30, 20XX, and affidavit of Ms. Kowalski's physician attesting to her severe illness on November 21, 20XX.

Ms. Kowalski was not in violation of RC 5321.05 (B). Each time Defendant's employee arrived unannounced at her doorstep to make repairs, her refusal to allow him and the workers in was reasonable. Defendant failed to notify her of any of its plans, although it scheduled them with its workers. This lack of notice prevented Ms. Kowalski from making alternate plans for sleeping after working night shift, recuperating from a severe case of flu, or showering following a long shift at the hospital.

Defendant is and has continued to violate R.C. § 5321.04 by failing to make the necessary repairs and by failing to notify its tenant, Ms. Kowalski, of plans to enter her unit to make the repairs. Further, Defendant has made only three attempts in eight months to provide Ms. Kowalski with the basic necessities of hot water and heat.

B. Property Management, Inc. Responsibility to Correct Latent Defects Once They Become Known.

Property Management, Inc. protests that because it had never rented Unit 14, it lacked prior knowledge of its lack of hot water and heat. Be that as it may, it does not excuse their failure to rectify those flaws in the eight months since they have become aware of the problems.

As previously noted and noted in Defendant's own Motion, Ohio statutory law requires a landlord to provide the basic necessities, and those basic necessities include heat and hot water. R.C. § 5321.05(A)(2). It its Motion for Summary Judgment, Defendant stated "[p]ursuant to RC 5341.04, Property Management, Inc concedes its obligation to provide both these services [heat and hot water]." Defendant's Motion for Summary Judgment at 5. If Defendant concedes its legal obligation to provide these basic services, why has it not worked with Ms. Kowalski to correct them?

Defendant's artful analysis of liability for latent defects is all well and good, but it avoids the seminal issue contained in Ms. Kowalski's complaint: she still does not have heat or hot water eight months after beginning her tenancy it Defendant's building.

Defendant is and has been aware of its failure to comply with the law. Eight months after receiving notice that Unit 14 lacked hot water, and four months after receiving notice that it lacked heat, Defendant has made no good faith efforts to comply with the law by notifying its tenant of its intent to enter her apartment or by repairing the defects.

Defendant can make this lawsuit go away, not through Summary Judgment, but through fulfilling its basic, statutory obligation to provide its tenant with twenty-four hours notice of its intent to repair the defects in her apartment, and by fulfilling its basic, statutory obligation to provide her with hot water and heat, as required by R.C. § 5321.05.

IV. Conclusion

Defendant has failed to comply with several of a landlord's statutorily imposed obligations. It has failed to notify its tenant of its intent to enter her apartment to make repairs. It has failed to provide its tenant with heat or hot water. Genuine issues of material fact – Defendant's failure to comply with the law – exist. This Court will find that Plaintiff Sheila Kowalski is entitled to judgment as a matter of law against Defendant Property Management, Inc.

Respectfully submitted,

_____

Ana Garcia 000000
123 Main Street
Parkhurst, Ohio 44XXX
(216) 555-5555
Attorney for Plaintiff,
Sheila Kowalski

CERTIFICATE OF SERVICE

A copy of the foregoing was sent by regular United States mail on this _____ day of _____, 20XX to Attorney for the Defendant, Andrew Adwokat, Esq, at 100 Courthouse Square, Parkhurst, Ohio 44XXX.

_____

Ana Garcia 000000
123 Main Street
Parkhurst, Ohio 44XXX
(216) 555-5555
Attorney for Plaintiff,
Sheila Kowalski

EXAMPLE

Version Two of Brief in Opposition To Defendant's Motion For Summary Judgment

IN THE COURT OF COMMON PLEAS
PARKHURST COUNTY, OHIO

Sheila Kowalski	)	
Plaintiff	)	Case No. 446551
	)	
	)	
	)	Judge: Michael Flynn
	)	
vs.	)	
	)	<u>PLAINTIFF, SHEILA KOWALSKI'S</u>
	)	<u>BRIEF IN OPPOSITION TO</u>
Property Management, Inc.	)	<u>PROPERTY MANAGEMENT, INC.'S</u>
Defendant	)	<u>MOTION FOR SUMMARY JUDGMENT</u>
	)	

Now comes Plaintiff, Sheila Kowalski, by and through counsel, and prays that this Honorable Court should deny Defendant Property Management, Inc.'s Motion for Summary Judgment. As explained below, there are genuine issues of material fact for trial.

_____

Ana Garcia 000000
123 Main Street
Parkhurst, Ohio 44XXX
(216) 555-5555
Attorney for Plaintiff,
Sheila Kowalski

BRIEF IN OPPOSITION

I. Introduction and Summary of the Claim

Defendant constructively evicted Plaintiff Sheila Kowalski from her home at 748 Beech Drive, Unit 14, Parkhurst, Ohio 44XXX. Despite Ms. Kowalski's repeated complaints, the apartment she rented from the defendant had neither heat nor hot water from the day she took possession of the premises. It still lacks these basic amenities to this day, more than a year later.

Defendant claims that because the rental agreement mandates that the laws of the State of Florida apply to any and all disputes arising from this agreement, all motions and decisions pertaining to the underlying dispute in this case must comply with the laws of Florida and not Ohio. Defendant fails to support this argument with any law explaining how an Ohio court has jurisdiction to apply the law of another jurisdiction. Nor has defendant provided any reason for failing to remove the case to a Federal court if it alleges that diversity of law applies. Nonetheless, even applying Florida law, defendant cannot prevail. Ms. Kowalski will address the issues as Florida law applies to them.

Ms. Kowalski notified defendant of the obvious defects in the apartment immediately after she took possession of the apartment. Two months later, nothing had been done, so Ms. Kowalski began depositing her rent with the court. Six month after that – with another northeastern Ohio winter approaching – Ms. Kowalski had no choice but to file this suit, as the unheated apartment was uninhabitable.

Defendant concedes that it has a duty to provide Ms. Kowalski with heat and hot water. It further concedes that Ms. Kowalski informed the building manager that the unit lacked these basic services. Consequently, defendant's argument that it was unaware that the unit lacked hot water and heat before Ms. Kowalski complained is irrelevant. There is a genuine issue of fact whether defendant has made reasonable efforts to perform its admitted duty to provide Ms. Kowalski with a habitable apartment. Ms. Kowalski asserts that it did not.

Even if this Court applies Florida law, defendant cannot prevail in its summary judgment motion. First, defendant never once scheduled repairs with Ms. Kowalski. The building manager did appear, unannounced, at Ms. Kowalski's door on a few occasions. However, Ms. Kowalski was not prepared to accommodate workers on such short notice, and she was not reasonably required to do so. Moreover, Appellant failed to make any other attempts to fix the problems within the statutorily mandated seven days.

Therefore, applying the law on which it relies, defendant concedes that it failed to repair the defects in Ms. Kowalski's apartment within the mandated seven day period.

II. Statement of Facts

The attached affidavit of Plaintiff Sheila Kowalski and the documentation appended to it disclose the following facts:

Ms. Kowalski has always considered the apartment building at 748 Beech Drive, Parkhurst, Ohio 44XXX as a desirable place to live. Before she rented the subject apartment, she visited friends who lived there, and she was aware that there were units of different sizes, with different layouts and views. Ms. Kowalski decided to rent the unit she was shown, Unit 14, because that particular apartment met all of her needs.

Ms. Kowalski specifically agreed to lease Unit 14 in the rental agreement. The property manager made no comment or objection to her choice of that specific unit. However, when she arrived with her moving van, the property manager tried to persuade Ms. Kowalski to accept a less desirable unit in the building, an apparent "bait-and-switch" tactic that Ms. Kowalski rejected.

Ms. Kowalski reminded the property manager of the terms of the lease, and he grudgingly allowed her to take possession of Unit 14. When she prepared to shower that evening, however, Ms. Kowalski learned that the unit lacked hot water. She immediately notified the property manager, who laughed and told her that "she had gotten what she asked for."

Despite repeated, documented requests for hot water, and later, heat, Defendant failed to provide Ms. Kowalski with either. In the eight months before Ms. Kowalski filed this suit, Defendant made only three unscheduled attempts to make her apartment habitable.

As the Defendant knows from her rental application, Ms. Kowalski is employed as a Registered Nurse at the Intensive Care Unit at Parkhurst Hospital. She works irregular hours. Her work requires constant alertness and attentiveness, so adequate sleep is critical. The first time Defendant came to her apartment to perform repairs, on October 12, 20XX at 10:00 am,

Defendant made no effort to notify Ms. Kowalski in advance. Ms. Kowalski had worked night shift and was scheduled to return to work at 3:00 p.m., only five hours later. She truly did "need to sleep" to perform her work properly. With prior notice, she could have accommodated Defendant by staying at her parent's house that day.

The second time the workers appeared unexpectedly to make the repairs, on November 21, 20XX, Ms. Kowalski was sick with the flu. She was feverish and lightheaded, and was in no condition to supervise workers in her home. Had the Defendant attempted to schedule the work, she could have warned them off to another time, for both their own health and hers.

The third and last time the workers arrived on January 30, 20XX, Ms. Kowalski did not answer the door because she was showering. She could hardly be expected to jump out of the shower when strangers arrived at her home without warning. The chain lock was engaged as it always is when she is home. Again, Defendant provided her with no notice that it intended to perform the repairs that day.

III. Law and Argument

The applicable standard of review for summary judgment in Florida is stated in a Florida Supreme Court decision:

> Summary judgment is proper if there is no genuine issue of material fact and if the moving party is entitled to a judgment as a matter of law. . . . . Thus, our standard of review is de novo [sic].

Volusia County v. Aberdeen at Ormond Beach, L.P., 760 So.2d 126, 130 (Fla. 2000).

A. Failure of Defendant Property Management, Inc. to schedule or make repairs

Defendant argues that Ms. Kowalski failed to cooperate with its attempts to make the repairs necessary to provide her with heat and hot water. As Defendant concedes, a landlord has the statutory obligation to "at all times during the tenancy, make reasonable provisions for: . . . [f]unctioning facilities for heat during winter, running water, and hot water." Fla. Stat. § 83.51 (2012). Florida law also places a strict time limitation in which the landlord must make the repairs:

> If the landlord materially fails to comply with s. 83.51(1) or material provisions of the rental agreement within 7 days after delivery of written notice by the tenant specifying the noncompliance and indicating the intention of the tenant to terminate the rental agreement by reason thereof, the tenant may terminate the rental agreement.

Fla. Stat. § 83.56 (2014). Defendant concedes in its motion for summary judgment that it made only one attempt during the month of October to make the needed repairs, despite the fact that the Florida law it seeks to apply mandates repairs within seven days. *Id.*

Furthermore, the landlord has "an obligation of good faith" to provide a habitable living unit to Ms. Kowalski. Fla. Stat. § 83.44 (2014). Ms. Kowalski has a right under Florida law to pursue the present cause of action: as defendant itself noted, the statute provides. "[i]f either the landlord or the tenant fails to comply with the requirements of the rental agreement or this part, the aggrieved party may recover the damages caused by the noncompliance." Fla. Stat. § 83.55 (2014).

The Florida court has addressed a similar situation to the one Ms. Kowalski has encountered in *Ralston v. Miller*, 357 So.2d 1066 (Fla. 1978). In *Ralston*, the landlord failed to make necessary repairs to the roof of the rental unit, rendering it uninhabitable. The Florida court found that the landlord had constructively evicted the tenant. "The rule in Florida is that any disturbance of the possession of a tenant by the landlord that renders the premises unfit for occupancy, for the purposes for which they were demised or that deprives the tenant of the beneficial enjoyment of the premises, amounts to a constructive eviction." *Id.* at 1069.

Ms. Kowalski has not been able to live in her apartment for the entire winter because it lacks heat. Instead, she has had to make alternative living arrangements. Ms. Kowalski has been constructively evicted from the premises, and despite defendant's protests of being owed rent, pursuant to *Ralston*, landlord has no right to collect rent where it constructively evicted Ms. Kowalski.

IV. Conclusion

There is a genuine issue of material fact whether Defendant complied with its statutory obligations to provide its tenant, Ms. Kowalski, with basic necessities: heat and hot water. Furthermore, a genuine issue of material fact exists regarding the question of whether Ms. Kowalski owes rent to defendant for the months in which she was constructively evicted, or whether defendant owes damages to Ms. Kowalski pursuant to the very Florida law on which defendant relies. These issues must be tried. Therefore, the court should deny Defendant's motion for summary judgment and should schedule this matter for trial.

Respectfully submitted,

_____
Ana Garcia 000000
123 Main Street
Parkhurst, Ohio 44XXX
(216) 555-5555
Attorney for Plaintiff,
Sheila Kowalski

CERTIFICATE OF SERVICE

A copy of the forgoing was sent by regular United States mail on this _____ day of _____, 20XX to Attorney for the Defendant, Andrew Adwokat, Esq, at 100 Courthouse Square, Parkhurst, Ohio 44XXX.

_____
Ana Garcia 000000
123 Main Street
Parkhurst, Ohio 44XXX
(216) 555-5555
Attorney for Plaintiff,
Sheila Kowalski

EXERCISE

In a three-page paper, define a Motion for Summary Judgment, including how a Brief in Support of Motion for Summary Judgment fits into the Motion for Summary Judgment. Also define a Brief in Opposition of Motion for Summary Judgment and the purpose for each in your own words.

Rule 37. Failure to Make Disclosures or to Cooperate in Discovery; Sanctions

(a) MOTION FOR AN ORDER COMPELLING DISCLOSURE OR DISCOVERY.

(1) In General. On notice to other parties and all affected persons, a party may move for an order compelling disclosure or discovery. The motion must include a certification that the movant has in good faith conferred or attempted to confer with the person or party failing to make disclosure or discovery in an effort to obtain it without court action.

Motion to Compel

Although the Civil Rules require attorneys to provide each other with discovery, unfortunately, during your paralegal career you will encounter the occasional noncompliant attorney. The Courts have the authority to sanction attorneys for failing to respond to discovery requests or for making frivolous objections to valid interrogatories and requests for production, but they are reluctant to exercise this authority. Attorneys are expected to work out discovery disputes among themselves, and the Courts generally are annoyed when they have to intervene between squabbling lawyers.

Therefore, the first step attorneys usually take when opposing counsel fails to provide timely discovery is to send opposing counsel a courteous letter reminding them that discovery is outstanding and requesting its prompt delivery. Of course, as the paralegal, you will be expected to keep a copy of this letter in the client's file.

If opposing counsel is unresponsive to this first reminder, the attorney probably will send a second, more curt letter via certified mail, demanding opposing counsel provide the discovery by a date certain, say ten to fourteen days later. Only after these attempts have failed to elicit a response from opposing counsel will your attorney file a Motion to Compel.

A Motion to Compel is designed to motivate the noncompliant opposing counsel to obey the Civil Rules and provide discovery, as it is required to do. It also puts the Court on notice that opposing counsel is not complying with the rules and is violating professional ethics.

Depending on how much chutzpa opposing counsel has, he or she might file a motion opposing your attorney's Motion to Compel. This may be a valid objection, perhaps over discovery opposing counsel disputes your attorney's right to have, but sometimes it is a stalling technique.

Less than honorable attorneys use noncompliance with discovery as a tool to prevent the other side from having time to prepare its case. The later one side learns of persons it would like to depose, or evidence it would like to obtain, the less chance that side has to complete discovery and effectively prepare its case. The Courts have an obligation to move cases along quickly, and once a Court has set a trial date, it is unlikely to postpone it for a discovery dispute. This tactical technique is an unfortunate tool of unprofessional, and arguably, unethical, attorneys.

So how do you draft a Motion to Compel? First, suppress your frustration and annoyance at the other side, and simply state the facts. Explain to the Court what attempts your attorney has made to obtain discovery, providing exact dates and copies of the letters your attorney has sent. Displays of righteous anger or pique diminish the effectiveness of your document. No one is impressed by a tantrum.

EXAMPLE

You will recall the subpoena that Brad Smith sent to Jane Daugherty, commanding her to attend a deposition. Ms. Daugherty failed to appear at the scheduled deposition, and Brad, working with opposing counsel, rescheduled it. Ms. Daugherty notified opposing counsel that she was unable to attend the deposition at the second time it was scheduled, and Brad rescheduled it again.

On the third date and time the deposition was scheduled, Brad was waiting at the designated location, along with the court reporter he had hired to transcribe the deposition. Ten minutes after the deposition was scheduled to start, Clarence Dowling, Plaintiff's attorney, called Brad to tell him that Ms. Daugherty was out of state visiting her daughter and would not attend the deposition.

Needless to say, Brad was frustrated and annoyed that he had gone to the expense of paying the court reporter. He was also annoyed both at the waste of his time and at the delay in preparing his case. He therefore drafted the following Motion to Compel.

IN THE COURT OF COMMON PLEAS
PARKHURST COUNTY, OHIO

James Kovach	)	Case No. 123456
Plaintiff,	)	
	)	Judge: MICHAEL FLYNN
vs.	)	
	)	
Thomas Williams, Sr.	)	<u>MOTION TO COMPEL</u>
Defendant	)	

Now comes Defendant, Thomas Williams, Sr. (Williams) by and through counsel and respectfully requests the Court to compel Plaintiff, James Kovach (Kovach), to produce his witness, Jane Daugherty, for deposition.

<u>BRIEF IN SUPPORT</u>

I. Introduction

This dispute concerns Kovach's allegations that Williams is responsible for injuries Kovach incurred in an incident that happened on May 15, 20XX, at approximately 2:00 p.m. Kovach's counsel has obtained an affidavit of Jane Daugherty, who states that she witnessed a portion of said incident. Despite being scheduled for deposition three different times, Kovach's counsel has failed to produce Ms. Daugherty for deposition.

II. Law and Argument

With reasonable notice, a party to a lawsuit may take the deposition of any person. Civ.R. 30(A). A person who is served with a subpoena to appear for deposition is required by law to obey said subpoena. Civ.R. 45. When a party to a lawsuit refuses to comply with reasonable discovery requests, the party seeking that discovery may file a motion to compel the noncompliant party to provide the withheld discovery. Civ.R. 37(A).

Kovach has declared Jane Daugherty as his witness and has provided her affidavit of her recollection of the events in question. Scheduling with Kovach's counsel, Williams's counsel has attempted to depose Ms. Daugherty to ascertain her knowledge of these events. One day prior to the both first and second scheduled depositions, Kovach's counsel notified

Williams's counsel that Ms. Daugherty would not be available for deposition at the previously agreed time and place.

Kovach's counsel agreed to a third date and time for Ms. Daugherty's deposition, but at the date and time scheduled, neither Kovach 's counsel nor Ms. Daugherty appeared. Ten minutes after the scheduled start for the deposition, Kovach's counsel telephoned Williams's counsel and informed him that not only would Ms. Daugherty not appear, but also that she was not even in the State of Ohio.

Ms. Daugherty is a crucial fact witness for the Kovach. Without her deposition, Williams's case is severely handicapped. To avoid unfair ambush at trial, Kovach must produce his witness for deposition in a timely manner.

Further, Williams has incurred the expense of the three canceled depositions, including the cost of a court reporter and the cost of preparing this motion.

III. Conclusion

Kovach's counsel has canceled the deposition of his key witness three times for no clear reason. Deposing this witness is crucial to Williams's case. Therefore, Defendant Williams respectfully requests this Court to either grant his motion to compel the deposition of Ms. Daugherty or to bar her testimony at trial. Williams further requests the Court to order Kovach to pay the costs of the court reporter at the canceled deposition and the costs of preparing this motion.

Respectfully submitted,

_____
Bradley Smith 000000
Attorney for the Defendant,
Thomas Williams, Sr.
123 Main Street
Parkhurst, Ohio 44XXX
(216) 555-5555

CERTIFICATE OF SERVICE

A copy of the foregoing Motion to Compel was sent by regular United States mail on this _____ day of _____, 20XX to Attorney for the Plaintiff, Clarence Dowling, to 45 Courthouse Square, Parkhurst, Ohio 44XXX.

_____
Bradley Smith 000000
Attorney for the Defendant,
Thomas Williams, Sr.
123 Main Street
Parkhurst, Ohio 44XXX
(216) 555-5555

EXERCISE

Read the fact pattern below and draft a Motion to Compel.

Unhöflich Nichtbeachtung's counsel, Bradley Smith, Esq., submitted Interrogatories to Richard Rage's counsel on August 15, 20XX. In these Interrogatories, he requested that the Interrogatories be completed and returned by October 1, 20XX. When October 1, 20XX, came and went, Attorney Bradley Smith sent a cordial letter reminding Attorney Sue Happy that discovery was overdue and requesting it be returned no later than November 1, 20XX. It is now the end of November, and Attorney Smith has asked you,

the paralegal, to draft a Motion to Compel discovery and return of the interrogatories.

Below is the signature block from Richard Rage's Complaint. You have created Bradley Smith's signature block in earlier exercises.

_____

Sue Happy, Esq., 000000
Attorney for the Plaintiff,
Richard Rage
75 Shyster Avenue
Parkhurst, Ohio 44XXX
(216) 555-5555 telephone

EXERCISE

Read the fact pattern below and draft a Motion to Compel.

Ana Garcia submitted Requests for Production of Documents to Gisele Harrington's attorney on September 26, 20XX. Despite letters requesting this discovery, as of today, January 14, 20XX, Harrington's counsel has failed to provide the requested documents or to respond in any way to the discovery request. Ana has asked you to draft a Motion to Compel this discovery. Below is the

signature block from Harrington's Complaint. You have created signature blocks for Ana Garcia in previous exercises.

_____

Beau Gusclame, Esq., 000000
Attorney for the Plaintiff,
Gisele Harrington
55 Crooked Lane
Parkhurst, Ohio 44XXX
(216) 555-5555 telephone

EXERCISE

Below are excerpts from various types of the motions we have discussed in this chapter. Identify which type of motion each excerpt represents.

1. Plaintiff has alleged no facts that would support a claim entitling her to relief. Therefore, Defendant requests the Court dismiss this Complaint because it fails to state any legal ground on which relief can be granted.
2. When a party to a lawsuit refuses to comply with reasonable discovery requests, the party

seeking that discovery may file a motion against the noncompliant party to compel that party to provide the withheld discovery. Civ.R. 37(A).
3. Genuine issues of material fact exist that preclude judgment as a matter of law.
4. Even if the Court takes all of Plaintiff's allegations as true, he has failed to state any claim upon with relief can be granted.
5. Defendant is entitled to judgment in its favor as a matter of law.

(continued)

6. There are specific facts that demonstrate the existence of genuine issues of material fact warranting a trial.
7. Accordingly, no genuine issues of material fact exist in this case.
8. Plaintiff further requests the Court to order Defendant to pay the costs of preparing this motion.

9. . . . construing the evidence most strongly in favor of the party opposing the motion, reasonable minds can reach only one conclusion, and that conclusion is in favor of the party . . . .
10. Plaintiff respectfully requests this Court to either grant her motion . . . or to bar introduction of this evidence at trial.

EXERCISE

Brad submitted interrogatories and requests for production of documents to the Greens' attorney on August 15, 20XX, and stated the date for returning completed discovery was October 1, 20XX. Brad has sent several letters to attorney Dowling requesting this discovery to no avail. It is now November 20, 20XX. Brad has asked you to draft a Motion to Compel for him to file with the Court for this discovery. Draft that Motion to Compel.

EXERCISE (IN-CLASS)

The new legal secretary has asked you about the various motions she had filed with the court. She asks you the following questions:

Legal Secretary: I do not understand the difference between the Motion to Dismiss and the Motion for Summary Judgment. When do you file each motion?

Paralegal:

Legal Secretary: When do you file a Motion to Compel?

Paralegal:

Legal Secretary: Why do the attorneys tell you to draft the Motions to Dismiss and not the Motions for Summary Judgment?

Paralegal:

Legal Secretary: You pointed out a Motion for Summary Judgment to Ana the other day and reminded her that she has to answer it by the end of next week. What kind of legal document is she going to write?

Paralegal:

Legal Secretary: What would happen if she filed the document responding to the Motion for Summary Judgment late?

Paralegal:

Legal Secretary: What would happen if she did not respond at all?

Paralegal:

Legal Secretary: Which of these motions and documents has to have a Certificate of Service?

Paralegal:

SUMMARY

- A defendant will file a motion to dismiss in response to a complaint when the defendant believes that the complaint on its face fails to state a claim upon which relief could be granted for the plaintiff.

- Parties to a lawsuit may file one or more motions during the course of the suit.

- Motions for summary judgment argue that even with all the evidence construed in the other party's favor, reasonable minds can reach only one conclusion, and that conclusion is in favor of the party moving for summary judgment.

- The opposing side files a brief on opposition to the motion for summary judgment, arguing that issues of material fact exist that require a trial to decide.

- Ideally, no attorney should have to file a motion to compel discovery. When opposing counsel fails to provide discovery as required by the civil rules, however, after all informal efforts have failed, the party requesting discovery may file a motion to compel.

ASSIGNMENT

I. Based on the Complaint below, draft a Motion to Dismiss.

IN THE COURT OF COMMON PLEAS
PARKHURST COUNTY, OHIO

Jennifer Cabot	)	Case No. 123456
3 Rodeo Lane	)	
Parkhurst, Ohio	)	
Plaintiff	)	Judge: MICHELLE JONES
	)	
vs.	)	
	)	
Chez Carolyn	)	
143 Main Street	)	
Parrkhust, Ohio	)	COMPLAINT
Defendant	)	JURY DEMAND
	)	ENDORSED HEREON
	)	

Now comes Plaintiff, by and through counsel, and as her Complaint against Defendant states the following:

COUNT ONE

1. The Plaintiff, Jennifer Cabot (Cabot), was and is a resident of Parkhurst County, Ohio at all times relevant to the facts of this complaint.

2. The Defendant, Chez Carolyn, was and is a corporation doing business in the City of Parkhurst County, Ohio, at all times relevant to the facts of this complaint.

3. On December 12, 20XX, Cabot had been shopping at Chez Carolyn when she left at or about 4:30 pm.

4. Cabot slipped on ice in the parking over which Chez Carolyn has dominion and control.

5. Chez Carolyn had a duty to make the premises and its parking lot safe for its customers.

6. Chez Carolyn was negligent in failing to apply salt to the parking lot over which it had dominion and control.

7. As a proximate result of Chez Carolyn's negligence, Plaintiff suffered serious injuries.

COUNT TWO

8. Cabot restates and incorporates all of Count I as if fully rewritten herein.

9. Cabot's injuries resulted in her having to cancel all her parties, concerts, and holiday plans for the months of December 20XX, and January 20XX.

10. As a proximate result of Chez Carolyn's negligence, Cabot suffered severe emotional distress.

COUNT THREE

11. Cabot restates and incorporates all of Counts I and II as if fully rewritten herein.

12. As a proximate result of Chez Carolyn's negligence, Cabot has incurred significant medical expenses and will continue to incur additional medical expenses.

WHEREFORE, Plaintiff Jennifer Cabot demands judgment against Defendant Chez Carolyn in an amount in excess of twenty-five thousand dollars ($25,000.00) on Counts I, II, and III for compensation for injuries, emotional distress, and medical expenses, as well as any additional relief this Court deems Plaintiff to be legally entitled, just, and or equitable, together with the costs of this action.

Clarence Dowling 000000
Attorney for the Plaintiff,
Jennifer Cabot
45 Courthouse Square
Parkhurst, Ohio 44XXX
(216) 555-5555

A trial by jury of eight (8) is hereby demanded.

Respectfully Submitted,

Clarence Dowling 000000
Attorney for the Plaintiff,
Jennifer Cabot
45 Courthouse Square
Parkhurst, Ohio 44XXX
(216) 555-5555

INSTRUCTIONS FOR SERVICE

The Clerk of Courts is hereby instructed to serve a copy of this Complaint on all parties at the addresses listed in the caption.

Clarence Dowling 000000
Attorney for the Plaintiff,
Jennifer Cabot
45 Courthouse Square
Parkhurst, Ohio 44XXX
(216) 555-5555

II. Based on the following fact pattern, draft a Motion to Compel.

On May 23, 20XX, Ana Garcia submitted discovery requests to Mr. Dowling on behalf of Chez Carolyn, but Mr. Dowling has not returned the requests despite letters reminding him that the requests were still outstanding. Ana cannot prepare a Motion for Summary Judgment without responses to discovery. It is now September 1, 20XX, and Ana has asked you to draft a Motion to Compel for the Interrogatories and Requests for Production.

III. In the corresponding box in the grid below, write a brief definition of each of the following legal documents:

Legal Document	Description and Use
Interoffice Memorandum	
Complaint	
Answer	
Motion for Discovery	
Interrogatories	
Request for Production	
Request for Admissions	
Affidavit	
Subpoena	
Medical Authorization Release	
Motion to Dismiss	
Motion for Summary Judgment	
Brief in Opposition to Motion for Summary Judgment	
Motion to Compel	

IV. Expanding on your answers in Assignment III. above, write a well-organized, grammatically correct five-page paper explaining the process of a lawsuit and how each of these documents would fit into that process.

V. Based on the fact pattern below, draft an interoffice memo for the attorney, Brad Smith, and then draft a Complaint for Brad to file on behalf of the client. You have interviewed the new client, Mabel Lynch. Your interview with Ms. Lynch follows verbatim. You will have to make sure that you do not incorporate any of the client's grammatical or logic errors into your memorandum.

Paralegal: Good morning, Ms. Lynch. Can I get you a cup of coffee or tea or a bottle of water?

Ms. Lynch: Thank you, kindly, but no. I jist et. I'm full up.

Paralegal: Ok. Please let me know if you need a break during our discussion. So tell me why you are here today.

Ms. Lynch: I ain't never been to no lawyer office afore. This shore is fancy! I cain't hardly think I'm so nerved up.

Paralegal: I understand, Ms. Lynch. Let's start at the beginning.

Ms. Lynch: Okay. I been a waitress all a my life. Now I'm 45, and I finally saved enough money to buy me my own trailer! I was so excited to get my very own home. I'm the first person in my family to own a home. Well, it started out real good and then it got to be a nightmare. I could cry when I think on it.

Paralegal: So you bought a trailer. Who sold it to you, and why is it a problem?

Ms. Lynch: I actually had the trailer builded for me. I picked all the innards- the rug, the counters, the color a the bathroom insert- everthing.

Paralegal: Did you ever move into the trailer?

Ms. Lynch: Oh yeah. It were fine all summer, but then the cold weather come and I about froze to death. The floors and walls all got gaps in em – the wind and cold blow through the place like crazy!

Paralegal: Where is the factory where the trailer was made?

Ms. Lynch: It in southern Ohio, but it get cold down there in the winter too.

Paralegal: It certainly does. Did you ever go down to watch the trailer being made?

Ms. Lynch: No, I work six mornings a week, sometimes seven, at Pancake Palace- you know the place. It's out on Route 6 a ways. We get a lot a truckers and when I worked nights – it's open 24 hours even Christmas- we got a bunch a them college kids who was half drunk. I get to work mornings cause I been there so long.

Paralegal: That sounds challenging. But back to your trailer, when did you first get the trailer and when did you move in? Did you get to inspect it before you took possession of it?

Ms. Lynch: I ain't sure what your meaning by inspect and take possession, but I looked at it when they delivered it and it were real purty. It were the purtiest place I ever seen.

Paralegal: So you didn't see anything wrong with it when you first got it?

Ms. Lynch: Uh uh. It looked perfect. And like I says, it were perfect til it got cold. Then it was an icebox.

Paralegal: It's February now. What have you been doing this winter to stay warm?

Ms. Lynch: Oh, lots a things. I done hung blankets what I bought at Sally Am- you know, that Salvation Army store – and hanged em all over in front a the walls. Then I got big pieces a plastic and taped em over the windows sose I could still get light but not a draft. See, I growed up poor, and I know what I gotta do to keep warm in a drafty place. I done put bails a hay under the trailer to keep the cold from coming up through the floor boards. Well, there ain't no real boards down there, but you know what I mean.

Paralegal: You are very resourceful! What exactly do you want Mr. Smith to make the manufacturer who made your trailer do for you?

Ms. Lynch: I jist want him to make the trailer how it should be. I don't wanna freeze all winter.

Paralegal: That makes sense. Let me write down what you have told me for Mr. Smith, and I will call you in a few days.

Ms. Lynch: Here's the number at Pancake Palace. I cain't afford no phone. I bin saving all my money to pay for my trailer.

Ms. Lynch lives at 14 Daisy Lane, Pinetree Park Estates, Parkhurst, OH 44XXX. The statutory agent for the manufacturer of Ms. Lynch's mobile home is located at 65 Riverview Lane, Suite 25, Worthington, Ohio 44XXX. The name of the manufacturer is Willard's Marvelous Mobile Palaces.

You have researched the law and found the following:

> {6} The duty to construct a house in a workmanlike manner has been imposed by law on all home builders in Ohio since at least 1966. In *Mitchem v. Johnson*, 7 Ohio St.2d 66, 218 N.E.2d 594 (1966), home buyers sought compensation for water damage resulting from their houses having been built in a low portion of a lot with surface-water problems and without a foundation drainage system. Notwithstanding the fact that no warranty covered the alleged defect,

we concluded that the home buyers were entitled to recover damages if they could establish that the home builder had not constructed the house in a workmanlike manner, stating: A duty is imposed by law upon a builder-vendor of a real property structure to construct the same in a workmanlike manner and to employ such care and skill in the choice of materials and work as will be commensurate with the gravity of the risk involved in protecting the structure against faults and hazards, including those inherent in its site. If the violation of that duty proximately causes a defect hidden from revelation by an inspection reasonably available to the vendee, the vendor is answerable to the vendee for the resulting damages. *Id.* at paragraph three of the syllabus.

{7} In determining that a duty to construct a house in a workmanlike manner exists, the court plowed the wide fertile plain between two extreme concepts: caveat emptor and strict liability. *Id.* at 70-72. Without expressly saying so, the court appears to have determined that it would be unfair for it to apply either of these standards. See id. at 70-73. The court also stated that "[t]he Supreme Court of Ohio requirement of workmanlike performance is no more than that which the law imposes upon the builder of a structure on land owned by another, unless, of course, a higher duty may be fairly implied from the terms of the contract itself." Id. at 69, citing 17A

Corpus Juris Secundum, Contracts, Section 515, at 851. The court specifically stated that an implied warranty was not being imposed. *Id.* at paragraph two of the syllabus.

. . . .

{10} We conclude that in Ohio, a duty to construct houses in a workmanlike manner using ordinary care is imposed by law on all home builders.

. . . .

{14} We conclude that the duty to construct a house in a workmanlike manner using ordinary care is the baseline standard that Ohio home buyers can expect builders to meet. The duty does not require builders to be perfect, but it does establish a standard of care below which builders may not fall without being subject to liability, even if a contract with the home buyer purports to relieve the builder of that duty. Accordingly, we conclude that a home builder's duty to construct a house in a workmanlike manner using ordinary care is a duty imposed by law, and a home buyer's right to enforce that duty cannot be waived.

Jones v. Centex Homes, 132 Ohio St.3d 1, 2012-Ohio-1001, 967 N.E.2d 1199 ¶¶ 6-7, 10, 14.

VI. Draft Interrogatories and Requests for Production of Documents for Mabel Lynch's case. The attorney for the manufacturer is Jarrod Carter, and his office is in the same building as the manufacturer. Carter's office is in suite 27.

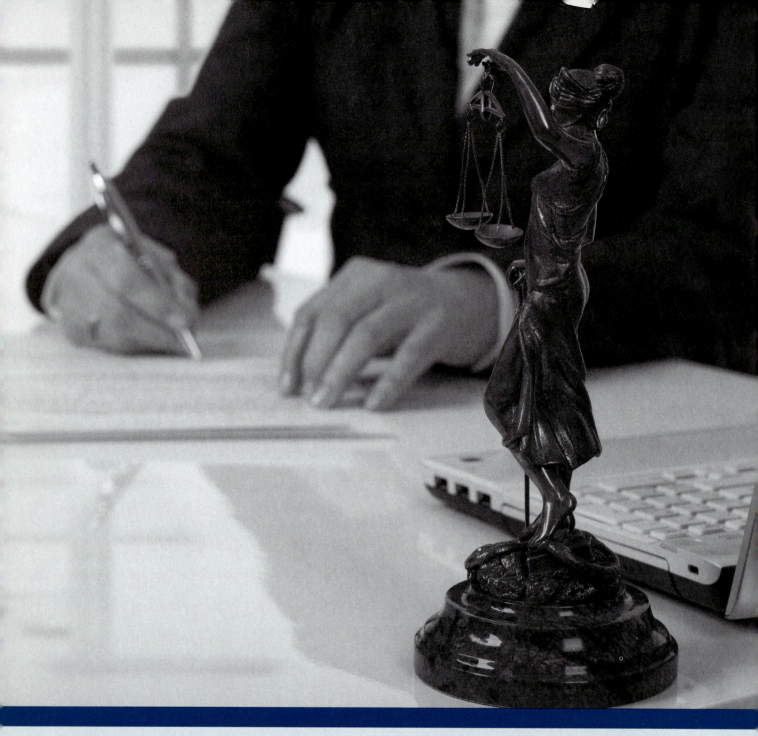

LEARNING OBJECTIVES

1. Detect errors in draft by proofreading

2. Edit errors by correcting the draft

3. Improve writing in legal document

4. Evaluate final writing

Proofreading and Editing | CHAPTER 18

▪ PROOFREADING

Proofreading entails closely reading a document, whether on paper or in electronic form, in order to identify errors, unclear sections, and organizational problems. Actual professional proofreading has its own symbols that indicate, for example, when a letter should be capitalized, when something should be inserted, and when something should be omitted.

Unless you will be doing a large amount of proofreading, however, it will not be necessary for you to learn these symbols. Also, more frequently proofreading now is being done electronically through markup features available in word processing programs.

It is important to be aware that even after electronic edits and comments have been deleted, they can be retrieved by recipients of the documents. This information is stored as metadata, and unless you go through specific steps to delete the metadata, it is still available to anyone possessing the electronic document.[1]

If your attorney practices in a court that accepts electronic filing and you serve opposing counsel with electronic versions of your documents, therefore, it is extremely important to make sure the documents you send are clean of any metadata. Otherwise, you may be providing the other parties with far more information than you intended.

In Unit 7 of the Legal Writing Handbook, we have provided a grid to aid you in proofreading and editing. Be sure to consult this chart often. Eventually, you will learn what types of errors the person whose work you are proofreading and editing, or you yourself are prone to make. At that point, proofreading and editing will be easier for you.

Regardless of how you go about it, proofreading requires strict concentration and a disciplined approach. You cannot thoroughly proofread while you are multitasking.

---

[1] A Federal Court website provides information regarding hidden metadata: "All word-processing programs (such as Microsoft Word, Corel WordPerfect, WordStar, etc.) retain a lot of hidden code (called 'metadata') that can contain revision history and other information. This metadata can reveal anything that was contained in the file at any time, even text that was previously deleted or changed, and even if the file was re-saved. This is a useful tool for tracking revisions, but if this information is not purged from the document, anyone can view this information, even after it has been converted to PDF.

. . . .

"Ink-marking or using semi-translucent tape or paper to cover areas of a document to be scanned can still sometimes show enough information for someone to see what was assumed hidden. Especially if that same data repeats a number of times across a document." This site has procedures to use to eliminate the metadata from electronic documents. You also can consult your IT department if the firm where you work has one." http://www.cadc.uscourts.gov/internet/home.nsf/Content/Guidance%20on%20Redacting%20Personal%20 Data%20Identifiers%20in%20Electronically%20Filed%20Documents/$FILE/ECF%20Redaction%20Guide.pdf

If you are proofreading something that you have written, it is important to put time and distance between writing it and proofreading it. Optimally, you will be able to set the document aside overnight and reread it with fresh eyes the next day. Unfortunately, you will not always have the luxury of this much time between writing and proofreading. If you are working under a deadline – a common occurrence in a law office – at least step away from your desk, get a drink of water, look out the window, or do something to distract your mind from the contents of the writing. Then go back to the document and try to read it as though you were unfamiliar with its subject matter.

Too often, we are so immersed in the details of a case that we forget that our reader is not familiar with these details. This can cause us to omit key facts or to assume knowledge on the part of the reader that the reader does not possess. Needless to say, this renders your writing far less effective. Since the purpose of writing is to convince the reader that your position is the correct one, it is imperative that you proofread what you have written as though you had no knowledge of the case at all.

So what are the specific details you need to identify when you proofread? These proofreading techniques apply when you are proofreading others' work as well when you are proofreading your own.

First, read the document for content: it would be a waste of time to have corrected grammatical errors only to discover that the document required an entire rewrite. After you have determined that the document is organized properly and it correctly states the law, analysis, and conclusions, then look at the details.

If the document is unclear or omits essential facts, note this for the writer, or correct this if you are the document's author. Keep in mind who your audience is; if you are working for a probate law practice, remember that most Appellate Courts are not as familiar with the law in this area than they are with other areas of the law that they see more frequently. Be sure to provide a succinct, but thorough, background in the basic law for the case, even when you have a page limit. Compare the need for this background law to the need for knowledge of basic arithmetic when you are explaining algebra to someone. Without the basic knowledge of arithmetic, your readers will not be able to follow your explanation of algebra.

Once you are satisfied that the document provides the necessary information and is accurate, focus on the details. Look for any grammatical, punctuation, and spelling errors. If you are proofreading an electronic version of the document, remember not to rely on grammar or spellcheck. Eliminate contractions, slang or colloquial terms, and passive voice (unless it is used intentionally).

Avoid using abbreviations and acronyms unless they are widely accepted in the legal community and by the Court. If your document discusses an alleged violation of environmental laws, for example, it would be appropriate to write out Environmental Protection Agency, and then follow that with the widely used acronym for the agency, EPA. Thus, your introduction might appear as follows:

> **EXAMPLE**
>
> The manufacturer received a cease-and-desist letter from the Environmental Protection Agency (EPA) on June 1, 20XX. In response to this EPA communication, the manufacturer shut down the factory in question.

You would not, however, use abbreviations that might be used commonly in the trade but would not be familiar to those outside the trade. For example, if your client referred to toxic waste as TW, you would not use that abbreviation in your document. You would continue to spell out the words toxic waste. The fewer acronyms you use, the clearer your writing will be. You do not want your reader having to backtrack in the document to locate the first use of the term so the reader can identify the meaning of an acronym.

Another item to watch for is overuse of "legalese." Many judges now believe that any use of legalese is too much. Still, some attorneys continue to use many Latin terms in their writing that once were prevalent in legal documents. Perhaps the attorney believes that using these terms makes the document more persuasive by giving it more weight. Too often, though, the contrary is true. The reader has to reach for the legal dictionary to understand what the writer is trying to say, thereby breaking the train of thought and the continuity of the argument being presented. Remember, your goal is clarity. You are not trying to impress the reader with your cleverness; you are trying to persuade the reader that your position is the correct one.

One effective way to determine whether your document flows well is to read it aloud. Obviously, if you work in a cubicle or other open area, this is not always feasible. But if you can take your document somewhere that reading out loud would not disturb others, do so. Although you probably would not use this technique for every document, if what you are writing is important enough, it is worth investing the time. You will recognize phrasing that is awkward when you hear it, even if you did not recognize its awkwardness on the written page.

What type of documents might you be proofreading? Certainly, you always will proofread your own documents. Also, you might proofread the work of another paralegal, or your attorney's work. A smart attorney will be aware of his or her shortcomings and will ask someone to check his or her work for errors. If the attorney you work for has problems with spelling, for example, you may proofread the attorney's documents routinely for spelling errors.

Chapter 5 discusses the folly of relying on spellcheck and grammar check, but since this is such a significant problem, we want to mention it here as well. Your authors have found that perhaps one-third of the time, the error spell and grammar check has identified is a true error. That means that two-thirds of the time, spell and grammar check are wrong. If you follow the program's suggestions, therefore, you will be putting errors into your document intentionally.

EXERCISE

Brad asked the legal secretary to draft a letter for him to send to opposing counsel reminding him that discovery was still outstanding. After Brad looked at the secretary's letter, he realized it needed proofreading. Below is the body of the letter the secretary drafted. Identify the errors in the two paragraphs.

You got my discovery requests on May 16, 20XX I know this because I talked to your secretary to make sure they got there. Why haven't you answered? I'm getting tired of you're stalling I know it is just a way to gain an advantage at trial and I do not appreciate it not one little bit. Don't make me file a motion to compel these documents you know that you are in a heap of trouble as it is with this judge.

Try to be professional I know that is a stretch for you and man up and give me the discovery. If you don't; I will report you to the Ohio Supreme Court or the local bar association.

EXERCISE _____

Because Brad wants the secretary to learn how to write correctly, he has asked that after you proofread the above letter to then explain to the secretary how he wants his correspondence to be written. You will need to be extremely tactful so you do not offend the secretary. Tact is a skill that is necessary in any office setting, but it is particularly important when you are correcting someone else's work.

There are ten errors that consist of grammatical, punctuation, or casual writing. Note that spellcheck did not see a single error in this letter.

In addition to the errors referenced in the previous paragraph, explain to the secretary the tone Brad and Ana prefer to use in professional correspondence.

■ EDITING

While separately defining proofreading and editing might seem like a distinction without a difference, for our purposes, editing includes making the changes that proofreading revealed needed to be changed. In an earlier exercise, you proofread the secretary's letter, but you did not edit it. If you had made the actual changes the letter needed, you would have edited it.

You will edit your own work on a regular basis, and if the attorney for whom you work is comfortable with your editing skills, you may edit the attorney's work as well. As we discussed in the chapter 4 on letter writing, you need to ask yourself several questions when you edit a document. First, you have to determine who your audience is. In the letter in the earlier exercise, the audience was opposing counsel. The language you would be able to use would be more sophisticated in a letter to opposing counsel than the language you would use for a client with limited education.

No matter who your audience is, though, you must maintain a respectful, professional tone. The letter above was far from respectful and not even close to being professional. You will be surprised to see that some attorneys think that these sorts of tactics are effective, but in reality, they merely make the attorney look immature and uncontrolled.

After you have determined your audience, you need to determine what the purpose of your document is. Much legal writing is persuasive; you are trying to convince the reader that your position is correct and that your client deserves to win. If you are writing a memorandum of law for your attorney, however, you will want it to objectively explain not only the strengths of the case but also its weaknesses. The way you address your case's weaknesses in an internal memorandum will differ significantly from the way your attorney will address them in a Motion for Summary Judgment or a Brief in Opposition to a Motion for Summary Judgment.

Another factor to consider in writing is space limitations. We discussed the limitation Civil Rules and Local Rules place on interrogatories. Similarly, Appellate Rules limit the number of pages a brief may be. Even when you do not have a set page limit, brevity is more impressive than verbosity. While you do not want to omit any important arguments, the Court will be most appreciative of a succinctly argued brief. Longer does not equal better, especially to a judge who has to read briefs every day.

A Judge for whom one of your authors worked often said that if she had more time, her decisions would be shorter. An important element of editing is eliminating unnecessary verbiage, tightening your arguments, and providing flow from one argument to another.

Below are two versions of the same document, a memorandum of law the paralegal prepared for Brad concerning Cherelle's potential criminal liability for restraining a shoplifter. Notice how much more effective the second, edited version is.

BADLY EDITED EXAMPLE

ISSUE: Is a merchant liable to be arrested and convicted when she stopped a shoplifter who tries steal from her and is stopping her kidnapping or is it legal?

RULE: Sometime, when you restrained s person which wasn't willing to be restrained, you are guilty of kidnapping! The law calls kidnapping using force or threatening to use force for "restrain the liberty of the other person" like maybe if the person restraining is asking for a ransom, or say you are holding on to the person so they are a shield against the police shooting at him, or even worse you're a terrorist or a rapist. Some kidnappers have held folks to make them slaves, even here in America! This is kidnapping also. I bet a lot of people don't know this can you imagine how many people could be in trouble? RC 2905/01(A).

Anyway, this statute can't apply to the store owner we are rerpesent-ingn cause another statute says she could hold a thieving customer pursuant Ohio Revised Code 2935.041, a store owner "who has probable cause to believe that items offered for sale . . . have been unlawfully taken by a person, may . . . detain the person in a reasonable manner for a reasonable length of time" inside the store.

ANALYSIS: This lady is threatening to prosecute our client, Cherelle Taylor, for kidnapping Cherelle is the owner of a boutique in Parkhurst, saw a woman looking at a bracelet, it looked like rubies but they really are just crystal, and Cherelle was really ticked off when she sees the woman put the bracelet in her purse and high tail to the door! Cherelle's shop has the cutest stuff and it is not at all expensive I just love that store! All this is recorded on the store camera, BTW. Well, Cherelle is quick, and before the thief knew it, Cherelle was blocking the door and another clerk calls the police right away. Doesn't <u>the thieving woman say Cherelle was kidnapping her</u>, for heaven's sake! That woman, THE CROOK!, told Cherelle she knew all about the law cause she worked in a law office and Cherelle would be sorry; if she didn't' let the lady go.

The thief decides she can scare Cherelle off by accusing her of kidnapping. The woman stole from Cherelle, a pretty bracelet I had my eye on. Now I can't buy it because its evidence. **She has some nerve trying to get Cherelle arrested!** Oh, and there is a law that says that Cherelle did right by keeping the thief from leaving it's in another law than the one I pointed to above, you'll find it if you read the whole law and I attached it to this memo you can't just walk out of a store with something you didn't pay for your expected to pay for stuff.

Well this thief was like such a loser that she like pushed a cop so of course she gets arrested to assaulting an officer, duh!, and she got took to jail. Like The cops find the bracelet in her purse and the price tag was still on it. So now like the lady is up for stealing and like for assaulting the cop.

Conclusion: Cherelle is in the clear.

The above document has multiple problems. Note that despite its multiple errors, spell and grammar check found only two misspellings and one grammar error in the entire document above.

First, although the IRAC format is correctly used, the analysis section is poorly organized. Second, the tone of the document is far too casual; it reads like an email one junior high school student would send to another, not like a memorandum of law. Third, the writer shifts frequently from one verb tense to another. Fourth, the writer uses contractions and exclamation points, both of which are unprofessional. The writer also wrote "your" for "you're." Not only has the writer used contractions, which are inappropriate for legal writing, but also the writer used the pronoun and not the verb.

Another problem with the document is the writer inserting him or herself into the document. The first person does not belong in a legal document, nor does the writer's response to the situation belong in the document. Certainly the writer's opinion of the merchandise sold in the store is extraneous to a legal memorandum, unless the type of merchandise is pertinent to the legal analysis.

Also notice that the writer used a common texting and emailing acronym, BTW. These types of abbreviations do not belong in a professional document.

Another major error in this document is the failure of the writer to apply the statute regarding shoplifters in the analysis. Instead, the writer refers the reader to an attached copy of the statute. Also notice the writer's run-on and fused sentences, particularly the last sentence in the middle paragraph of the analysis.

Because it is so badly written and edited, we excerpted one "sentence" from the above example for closer scrutiny:

> **BADLY EDITED EXAMPLE**
>
> The writer wrote:
>
> > Oh, and there is a law that says that Cherelle did right by keeping the thief from leaving it's in another law than the one I pointed to above, you'll find it if you read the whole law and I attached it to this memo you can't just walk out of a store with something you didn't pay for your expected to pay for stuff.

This "sentence" is actually five separate independent clauses, none of which is punctuated correctly. The "sentence" also contains several unrelated ideas without any transition between one idea and another. The writer jumps from the law (which the writer fails to discuss in the analysis) to second person statement about shoplifting.

Other problems in this "sentence" include the use of the interjection "Oh," which is inappropriate in a legal document. The writer also used contractions and the pronoun "I," neither of which has any place in a legal document. The writer also switches from third person when referring to the thief to second person, "you." The writer also used slang in referring to the merchandise as "stuff." The writer used an incorrect predicate with "did right." The writer also used "its" in place of "it's," another contraction that does not belong in legal writing.

Below is an edited version of the memorandum

> **CORRECTLY EDITED EXAMPLE**
>
> ISSUE: Is it legal for a merchant to detain a suspected shoplifter until law enforcement officers arrive, or does such detention constitute kidnapping?

RULE: Under certain circumstances, restraining a person against his or her will constitutes kidnapping. The Ohio Revised Code definition of kidnapping includes using force or threat to "restrain the liberty of the other person" for certain purposes, including for ransom, as a hostage or as a shield, for committing a felony or for fleeing after a felony, for terrorizing or inflicting serious physical harm, for engaging in non-consensual sexual activity, for obstructing a government function, or for involuntary servitude. RC 2905.01(A).

On the other hand, pursuant RC 2935.041, a store owner "who has probable cause to believe that items offered for sale . . . have been unlawfully taken by a person, may . . . detain the person in a reasonable manner for a reasonable length of time" inside the store.

ANALYSIS: Cherelle Taylor, the owner of a boutique in Parkhurst, noticed a female customer examining a bracelet that was part of a display. Instead of returning the bracelet to the display or bringing it to the register for purchase, the woman instead tucked the bracelet in her purse and began to walk toward the door of the store. Cherelle quickly stepped between the woman and the door while another clerk phoned the police. Cherelle prevented the woman from leaving, and the woman accused Cherelle of kidnapping her. The woman informed Cherelle indignantly that she worked in a law office, and she knew what Cherelle was doing was illegal. She threatened to prosecute Cherelle for kidnapping if she was not permitted to leave the store immediately. Cherelle politely informed her that all the activities that occurred in the store were video and sound recorded, and that Cherelle would be glad to provide a copy of the recording to the woman's attorney at the appropriate time.

After the police arrived and questioned the woman, she became agitated and pushed one of the officers away. At that point, the officers arrested her and took her to the police station. During the search of her belongings at the police station, they discovered the bracelet with the boutique's price tag and security tab still on it. The woman was charged with attempted theft and with assault on an officer.

Despite having been charged with stealing the bracelet, the woman proceeded to sue Cherelle for kidnapping. She claimed that Cherelle had forcibly blocked the doorway of the boutique, thereby restraining her by use of force.

To qualify as kidnapping, the restraining of another against her will through the use of force or threat must be done for one of the statutorily listed reasons. To have committed the crime of kidnapping, Cherelle would had to have restrained the woman for the purpose of collecting a ransom, using her as a hostage or a shield, committing a felony, fleeing after committing a felony, terrorizing her, inflicting serious physical harm, engaging in sexual activity against the woman's will, or keeping her for involuntary servitude. RC 2905.01(A). Cherelle's purpose for restraining the woman, however, was to prevent her from stealing a bracelet from the boutique. This purpose does not meet the requirements of the statute for qualifying as kidnapping. Thus, Cherelle's restraining of the woman does not meet the statutory requirements for kidnapping.

Further, a close reading of the statutory law regarding shoplifters reveals that as a merchant, Cherelle had a legal right to detain the woman until the police arrived, as long as she detained the customer "in a reasonable manner." Since Cherelle's detention of the woman does not qualify as kidnapping under the Ohio statute, the remaining question is whether Cherelle's manner of detaining the woman was reasonable Nothing in the record suggests that Cherelle ever actually touched the woman. Rather, she blocked the exit from the boutique to prevent the woman from leaving. Although the woman insisted that she had the right to leave and that Cherelle was breaking the law by restraining her, the woman was not injured or harassed in any way during the detention. In fact, Cherelle had been careful to treat the woman with extreme courtesy and to maintain a calm, polite tone of voice. Therefore, the means Cherelle used to keep the woman she suspected of trying to steal a bracelet in the store until the police arrived were reasonable.

CONCLUSION: It is legal for a merchant to detain a suspected shoplifter until law enforcement officers arrive, and such detention does not constitute kidnapping.

What lessons have we taken away from this example? Table 18.1 contains a list to guide you in proofreading and editing legal documents.

■ REMINDERS AND ADDITIONAL TIPS FOR BOTH EDITING AND PROOFREADING

- Proofread and edit in a quiet environment whenever possible.
- Leave the document and focus on something else, then go back to it.
- Try to be comfortable, well rested, and well fed when you proofread.
- Do not be afraid to reorganize the document, even when you have spent a lot of time on it.
- Look carefully for grammar, punctuation, and spelling errors.
- Omit contractions, slang and colloquial terms, and non-standard abbreviations.
- Avoid passive voice unless its use is intentional.

Table 18.1 Proofreading and Editing Guide

#	Topic
1	Maintain a professional tone.
2	Organize the material logically.
3	Apply the law to the facts of the case.
4	Omit unnecessary and redundant material.
5	Eliminate the author from the document.
6	Avoid using long sentences repeatedly.
7	Be as brief as effectively possible.
8	Write grammatically correctly.
9	Do not switch verb tenses.
10	Do not change from third person to second person, etc.
11	Punctuate correctly.
12	Identify and eliminate passive voice unless used intentionally.

EXERCISE

Brad's client, Mr. Williams, has returned a rough draft of his answers to interrogatories, and Brad has asked you to rewrite them so they are free of errors without changing their meaning. Below are three of Mr. Williams's responses.

1. QUESTION: What is your full name, any other names you have used, your address, your date of birth, and your Social Security number?
ANSWER: I ain't got but one name and its Thomas Williams, Sr. Some folks call me Tom but that ain't my name sose I don't answer to it. I live on Rocky crick lane it ain't really a lane but just a dirt road with a bunch a holes in it. My birthday is august 6, 19XX. The govment says it don't think a person ought a give out your social secirty number so you aint' gittin it.

2. QUESTION: State the name and address of your employers for the past 10 years, including your job titles and the years that you held each job.
ANSWER: Shoot, I cain't hold no job. I do piece work, mow a lawn or such fromtime to time. But no work. Not since Parkhurst Industries canned me no one hires you once they let you go. They got a monpily iin this town.

3. QUESTION: State the year, make, and model of every vehicle you own or have owned in the past 10 years, including the color and license plate numbers of each vehicle.
ANSWER: I don't own nothing anymores. I had bunches of beaters over the years, none of em run much more than a few monthts is all. I cain't bemember all a them. The guy at the junk yard might remember some a them he done towed em all away when they stopped runnin.

EXERCISE

Brad has put together the following notes on an interview he had with a client as well as some basic research he has done on the issues the client presented. He now has asked you to organize the material and write a memorandum of law for him from his notes.

Complaint filed yesterday re slip & fall- parking lot. December 22, 20XX. New customer, regular customer (?identity?) also there. Not raining when regular came in.

Freezing rain.- predicted, per regular customer. But customer (regular) is dry when enters store. So ice Must have just started.

Cherelle leases parking area for customers. New customer leaves- they hear her scream, call ambulance, keep her warm.

Injury = broken hip, hospitalized for Xmas. Claims negligence for not salting icy lot.

Case law-

Allen v. USA Parking Sys. 2011-Ohio-6642

{¶ 2} Allen fell on a natural accumulation of ice caused by the freeze and thaw cycle due to temperature change. The record contains no evidence that USA Parking did anything to cause an unnatural accumulation of ice to form. Further, there is no evidence in the record that Allen fell on loose concrete; this argument is mere speculation. Finally, Allen knew that the lot was sloped and that snow can melt and refreeze into ice in wintertime. The condition of the lot was an open and obvious danger such that USA Parking owed no duty to warn Allen of it. Accordingly, the judgment of the trial court is affirmed.

Id.

SUMMARY

- Any document you or your attorney writes for others or the court to read must be well organized, well expressed, and error-free.

- The only way to achieve the goal of error-free, well expressed, well organized writing is to proofread and edit it.

- Even (or perhaps especially) professional writers, including your authors, proofread and edit their writing scrupulously and often.

- Errors will distract the reader, regardless of the quality of your writing or the strength of your argument.

- Only by consistently proofreading and editing will you learn to improve your writing.

ASSIGNMENTS

I. Ana has jotted down the facts for a Brief in Opposition to a Motion for Summary Judgment. She has asked you to edit this series of facts and reorganize it if necessary. Your goal is to persuade the court that Chez Cherelle was not harassing the Plaintiff and that the Plaintiff still owes Chez Cherelle the money for the gown. (She tells you that she will have you research the law later.)

Chez Cherelle sold a $450 evening gown to Gisele Harrington, whose check bounced. Harrington sued Chez Cherelle for harassment when she tried to collect on the bad check. Harrington repeatedly admitted owing the money and promising to pay Chez Cherelle. Case belongs in Municipal Court because amount is under $15,000. Parkhurst Bank charged Chez Cherelle $50 for the returned check fee.

Harrington claims attempts to collect cost of the gown = harassment. This is a bluff to make Cherelle go away. She claims emotional distress, having to change banks, and lost reputation in her new community. No proof of emotional distress. So what if she had to change banks? No proof of loss of reputation- new to community anyway no one knows her.

II. Brad has drafted a Motion to Compel but realizes it is wordy and repetitive. He has instructed you to edit it so that it is concise and to the point. He has handed you only the body of the brief, so you do not have to create a caption.

Now comes Defendant, Thomas Williams, Sr. (Williams) by and through counsel and respectfully requests the Court to compel Plaintiff, James Kovach (Kovach) to produce answers to Interrogatories submitted to him three months ago.

BRIEF IN SUPPORT

I. Introduction

Plaintiff alleges that Williams is responsible for various injuries, including loss of vision, as well as property damage to his car from an incident that occurred on May 15, 20XX at approximately 2:00 pm. Plaintiff claims his car was totally destroyed, but he has not provided any evidence to date to support either his injures or his property damage. Plaintiff claims that Williams was transporting a refrigerator in the bed of a pickup truck and that the refrigerator fell off the truck and struck his car. Plaintiff claims that he was blinded by the glass from his windshield when the refrigerator hit it. Plaintiff has failed to date to provide even a photograph of the car, much less any medical records substantiating his claimed injuries, or any other evidence.

II. Law and Argument

Pursuant to Civ.R. 33, any party to a lawsuit may propound interrogatories on any other party to the suit. The requesting party may require responses to the interrogatories within a time period greater than 28 days. Parties to a lawsuit are required to provide responses to interrogatories, up to a total of 25 questions.

Williams's counsel served Plaintiff's counsel with interrogatories three months ago. Despite three letters requesting answers to the interrogatories, Plaintiff's counsel has failed to respond.

Without the information contained in the interrogatory responses, Williams's counsel is unable to prepare this case for trial. Plaintiff has had three months to prepare his responses, yet he has to date failed to even respond to letters inquiring about the status of the interrogatories. Williams's counsel has lost three valuable months of trial preparation time, and his case is no further than it had been three months ago. Williams provided discovery responses to Plaintiff's counsel in a timely manner, but Plaintiff's counsel has not provided Williams with the same courtesy. Plaintiff's counsel has ignored three letters reminding him that this discovery is outstanding.

Three months is more than enough time to draft responses to interrogatories, and Williams's requests this Court to compel Plaintiff's counsel to provide responses to interrogatories within the next two weeks. Allowing Plaintiff another two weeks is more than generous after three months have elapsed since Plaintiff's counsel was served with discovery requests. Plaintiff's counsel could not have forgotten about these discovery requests because Williams's counsel sent three letters requesting the responses to interrogatories.

III. Conclusion

Plaintiff's counsel has failed to respond to Williams's discovery requests despite having had three months and three separate letters reminding him of his obligation to provide answers to interrogatories. Williams respectfully requests this Court to order Plaintiff to submit his answers to interrogatories within two weeks from the date of this motion.

III. The office's legal secretary has decided that law office work is too mentally challenging for him and has returned to his old job loading freight. After Brad and Ana placed an ad for a new legal secretary, they received four letters and resumes requesting interviews.

Because they are both busy, they have asked you to review the letters and rate them for quality on a scale of one to ten, with ten being perfect and one being totally unacceptable.

The four letters are below. Rank them according to quality and specifically point to the errors that reduced your ranking for each letter.

Letter Number One

Dear Ms. Garcia and Mr. Smith;

I am applying for the position of legal secretary at your firm Smith & Garcia. I have worked as a secretary in a division of Parkhurst Industries but I recently was laid off. I can provide references for you if you want them I was well liked in my old job.

I am familiar with Word Perfect, Word in Windows 7, and can make an Excel spreadsheet. I am mature hard-working and responsible. I can take dictation and type 80 words a minute. Even though I am not familiar with the legal field I will learn and will put in as much time as I need so I can be a good legal secretary.

Sincerely,

Dotty Conlon

Letter Number Two

Dear Ana and Brad-

Please interview me for you're position of legal secretary. I am a graduate from Parkhurst High and even though I only got Cs in school I am a hard worker and I no how to type and use a computer (some). I can learn quick and will be reliable and show up for work unless the weather is bad or it is really good ha ha.

I am cute two so I can make a good impression on you're clients their going to love coming into the office and having me greet them because I'm real friendly and attractive. Inclosed in a pitcher of me so you know that I am worth an worth an inyerview.

Thanks a ,illion!

Amber Waves

Letter Number Three

Dear Mr. Smith and Ms. Garcia,

I would like to apply for the position of legal secretary with your firm. I have experience as a legal secretary with a firm in Toledo, but I left that position when I moved to Parkhurst twenty years ago. My resume is enclosed. You will notice a gap in my employment history; I am reentering the work force after taking time out to raise my children.

I have taken classes at the library in anticipation of my return to work, and I have spent over forty additional hours practicing on Windows 7, Excel, and word processing on a computer keyboard.

I would appreciate the opportunity to interview with your firm and discuss what I can offer you. I can be reached at 000-555-1111. My email address is nancy.baker@mail.com.

Thank you for considering my application. I hope to meet with you for an interview in the near future. If you have any questions, please do not hesitate to contact me.

Sincerely,

Nancy Baker.

Enclosure

Letter Number Four

Dear Smith & Garcia, LPA-

I am applying four the job for legal secretary. I took keyboarding in school and I have took courses at the community college to. BTW, I am good at Facebook, Twitter, and all them other media who is so important for keeping up with society in this world of today to as well. I can send a letter of reference from one of my professors which liked me in college. I hope U R willing to interview me 4 this job. U won't regret it if you do I am a good worker just ask my boss from Burger Barn.

CU soon, I hope!

Debbie Diztey

IV. Write a brief interoffice memorandum to Ms. Garcia and Mr. Smith explaining the errors you have found in each of the letters in exercise III.

LEARNING OBJECTIVES

1. Differentiate between effective and ineffective documents

2. Review documents for effectiveness

3. Avoid writing pitfalls

4. Establish your personal code of behavior

5. Live in accordance with the paralegal's ethical code

Effective Writing

■ DRAFTING EFFECTIVE DOCUMENTS AND AVOIDING PITFALLS

We have touched on some of the pitfalls that can render a document ineffective, even when the facts and law should allow the party to prevail.

Nothing distracts from your message like ineffective writing. Your writing should be invisible, serving to convey your message. Flashy writing, verbose writing, and especially error-filled writing, at best distract your reader, and at worst, prevent the reader from receiving your message. It bears repeating; your writing should be invisible. Your goal is not to dazzle the reader, nor is your goal to offend the reader. Unfortunately, too many attorneys submit briefs that offend, or worse, inadvertently amuse, the courts and opposing counsel.

Passive Voice

For example, we discussed how writing in passive voice weakens your argument and dulls your narrative. Even good writers prevent themselves from being great writers by failing to recognize and eliminate the passive voice. Chapter 5 discusses the passive voice at greater length.

A sentence is written in passive voice when the actor is not the subject of the sentence. For example, the previous sentence is written in passive voice. The subject of the sentence is "sentence." The verb is "is written." The actual person performing the act of writing is never identified. The sentence did not write itself; it is the recipient of the action of writing, not the actor doing the writing.

In the active voice, the sentence would read, "The author wrote in passive voice because the subject of her sentence was not the person or thing that performed the action of the verb." As you can see, defining passive voice is not easy, but eliminating it once you have learned to recognize it can become easy.

An entire document of passive voice sentences is as weak as a cup of cocoa without the chocolate. The two versions of the same paragraph below, one in passive voice and one in active voice, illustrate this.

EXAMPLE

Passive Voice

The gun was drawn by the defendant after the alarm was sounded. Shots were fired, and both the defendant and the store owner incurred wounds. Bleeding from wounds was copious, and caused the death of the store owner, resulting in the indictment of the defendant.

Sounds kind of namby-pamby, doesn't it? Here is the same story told in active voice:

> **EXAMPLE**
>
> **Active Voice**
>
> The defendant drew his gun after the store owner set off the alarm. Both men fired, and both men were wounded. The store owner was bleeding copiously and subsequently bled to death. The defendant was indicted for his murder.

The best way to recognize passive voice in your writing is to walk away from the piece you are writing and reread it later. If a sentence does not identify the person or thing that acted, that is performed the action of the verb in the sentence, you most likely have a passive voice sentence and should change it.

Grammatically Correct And Well Organized

We have thoroughly addressed the folly of submitting documents with grammatical and punctuation errors, as well as the futility of trying to persuade the reader with a poorly organized brief. Just as the Hippocratic Oath instructs physicians to first do no harm, attorneys and paralegals should have to take an oath that instructs them when writing to first make no errors. Errors are very distracting; if you look at book reviews that readers put on Amazon, one of the most common complaints voiced is the fact that the writing errors distracted the reader from the story. If you find you commit regular errors, consult the Legal Writing Handbook online and work to eliminate your common errors.

While not all Judges are disturbed by these types of errors, some are, and they will focus more on the errors than they will on what you have to say. By failing to eliminate your grammatical and punctuation errors, you will have done your client an enormous disservice.

Concise

We have also explained the necessity of being concise. No one wants to waste precious time reading more words than are needed to convey the message. If the reader has to wade through unnecessary or repetitive verbiage, you will lose the reader's attention. Extraneous material does more than waste the reader's time, though; it robs your writing of effectiveness. Your point is lost in the detritus of superfluous words.

Consider the brief, yet enormously effective, Gettysburg Address. The people who gathered to hear President Lincoln give this speech were stunned at how short it was. Nonetheless, Lincoln's few words have continued to have a profound impact on generations of Americans. If this speech had been longer, it would have been far less effective.

> **EXAMPLE**
>
> Four score and seven years ago our fathers brought forth on this continent, a new nation, conceived in Liberty, and dedicated to the proposition that all men are created equal.
>
> Now we are engaged in a great civil war, testing whether that nation, or any nation so conceived and so dedicated, can long endure. We are met

on a great battle-field of that war. We have come to dedicate a portion of that field, as a final resting place for those who here gave their lives that that nation might live. It is altogether fitting and proper that we should do this.

But, in a larger sense, we can not dedicate—we can not consecrate—we can not hallow—this ground. The brave men, living and dead, who struggled here, have consecrated it, far above our poor power to add or detract. The world will little note, nor long remember what we say here, but it can never forget what they did here. It is for us the living, rather, to be dedicated here to the unfinished work which they who fought here have thus far so nobly advanced. It is rather for us to be here dedicated to the great task remaining before us—that from these honored dead we take increased devotion to that cause for which they gave the last full measure of devotion—that we here highly resolve that these dead shall not have died in vain—that this nation, under God, shall have a new birth of freedom—and that government of the people, by the people, for the people, shall not perish from the earth.

When people write, they feel ownership over their writing and sometimes are reluctant to revise, or heaven forbid, delete some of it. Think of a kindergarten child who becomes upset when his drawing is no longer on the refrigerator or is discarded. Writers tend to be as protective of their prose, regardless of its quality, because they put so much work into it.

A wise Appellate Court Judge told one of our colleagues that the best way to write the facts of your case was to tell the story as though you were explaining the situation to a person over lunch. Obviously you will organize the facts better than that when you write them, but your tone should be informative, and more importantly, you writing should include only the necessary details.

If your client is accused of stealing a woman's purse, and the theft was clearly recorded on a video monitor identifying your client, does the color of the purse matter? No. The fact that it was an expensive designer purse matters, because it may elevate the level of the offense. But does it matter what the woman was wearing, or why the video camera was there? No. So your document would not include those details.

It takes more time to write a succinct document than it takes to write a long document. But the Courts do not appreciate having to wade through unnecessary detritus to discover what your point is. Contrary to the belief of some attorneys, extra length will not distract the reader from a weak argument. It instead will reinforce the weakness of your argument.

Your attorney will ultimately decide what issues are important. Nonetheless, particularly in an appellate brief, limiting the issues to the valid ones is important. One of your authors remembers a defense attorney who routinely filed appellate briefs with fourteen or more issues. While it is important to preserve issues for appeal or for further appeal, this attorney's briefs made it clear that she made no effort to sort out the salient issues for any given case. In fact, it got to the point that when the law clerks were researching this attorney's briefs for the Judges, the law clerks' online law search would consist of the attorney's name and the issue. Then the attorney would cite to the most recent case in which the Court had overruled this issue for this attorney. The tactic of appealing every conceivable issue with the hope that one would cause reversal of the conviction merely diluted the issues with actual merit. It also made this attorney's name a punch line in the Court.

Honest Yet Persuasive

Some cases are hard to defend; that is why the client needs a lawyer. Still, it is possible and necessary to write the facts in a way that casts your client in the most favorable light while avoiding dishonesty or omission.

Take the following fact pattern, for example. The Plaintiff's case is easy to write. She is a sympathetic and blameless victim in this situation.

EXAMPLE

A beautiful, ginger-haired young woman, Mary, was a talented pianist with a promising concert career. She had just been appointed as pianist with a major symphony orchestra and had gone out celebrating with friends over dinner at a local restaurant. As she was walking home after dinner, Josh, a wealthy playboy, turned the corner in his brand new Maserati, driving 80 miles an hour. He lost control of the car, pinning Mary's hands under the wheels of the car. In an instant, her promising piano career was ended.

Mary's brief is easy to write; just telling the facts without any embellishment will persuade the reader that she has been permanently and horrifically damaged. But the temptation is to overwrite it. When you have great facts, let them speak for themselves. Don't get in their way. Too many paralegals would write the facts as follows:

BAD EXAMPLE

Mary, who was an enormously talented pianist and had spent her entire life working toward this moment, had reached the pinnacle of every pianist's career; she had just been appointed to a major, world-renowned symphony orchestra. Overjoyed, she shared delight with her friends over a simple meal. As she ecstatically walked home from the restaurant, Josh recklessly, carelessly, and indifferently drove his exorbitantly expensive car at outrageously excessive speed. His extreme indifference to the safety of others resulted in the car careening out of control and destroying Mary's blossoming future, condemning her to a life of pain and despair.

At this point, your readers have been distracted by your florid prose and are more interested in ending their own pain at reading this.

A persuasive document is not flashy. Your writing should be invisible. Here is a better way to write the facts from Mary's point of view:

GOOD EXAMPLE

Mary was celebrating the best day of her life; she just had been appointed pianist at a major symphony orchestra. She had celebrated her achievement with her friends over dinner, but as she walked home, her life was changed forever. Josh's car struck her at 80 miles per hour. Her hands were pinned under the wheels of the car for 20 minutes until the paramedics could free her. The doctors were unable to repair the damage to her fingers; she will never play piano professionally again. In addition to ending her career, Josh's reckless driving inflicted injuries that will cause Mary pain every day for the rest of her life. Despite Mary's resilience, which saw her using her time ministering to others as a missionary in Mexico, her life was irrevocably diminished.

Notice that everything was understated but true: this was the greatest day of her life. Josh had been reckless. Her life was changed forever. She did face a life of pain, and her career was destroyed. And she did find another direction for her life. But do you see how much more effective this version is? Also notice the irrelevant facts we omitted, Mary's beauty and her hair color.

Now we come to the hard part – writing the story from Josh's point of view. The following is entirely honest, yet it puts Josh in the best possible light:

EXAMPLE

Josh had waited six months for his new car to be ready. He was extremely excited when he finally sat behind the wheel. The salesman assured Josh that this car would corner beautifully at 120 miles per hour. The salesman encouraged Josh to let the car show him what it could do. At first Josh drove slowly, getting the feel for the car and how it handled. Then he decided to see whether what the salesman had told him was true. He took a corner at a speed well above the limit, but he was amazed at how well the car handled. Suddenly though, the car stopped responding to his steering, going unexpectedly and regrettably out of control. A woman was seriously injured, as was Josh.

Notice how this tells the truth yet minimizes the victim's injuries. It does not ignore them, and it also provides a context for what was undeniably reckless behavior.

Just as you should not omit facts that are adverse to your client, you should not omit law that is adverse to your case. In addition to being an ethical violation, you may be sure that opposing counsel will be more than happy to point out the omission and to highlight the adverse law. This hurts your client's case and damages your attorney's credibility.

Even worse is making up facts that are not in evidence. One wise senior partner once said, "Don't tell me what you know. Tell me what you can prove." It irritates judges when your brief embellishes the facts to make your case more appealing, but then you cannot prove those facts. This tactic also hurts the attorney's credibility and strengthens your adversary's case.

One of the worst forms of dishonesty involves a violation of ethics: inventing cases and citations with fraudulent "quotes" to support a case. One of your authors was astounded the first time she read a brief submitted to the Court in which the attorney used this tactic. The case he quoted sounded so good and was so well stated that your author went to the books (this was a number of years ago) and looked for the case. The case did not exist. She checked other volumes, to see whether the submitting attorney had transposed some of the citation numbers, but a subsequent Lexis search revealed that he had made the whole thing up. This is not the way to win a case. The Court will not believe anything else written in the brief. Additionally, the Courts can report this ethical violation to the body governing admission to the practice of law, and the attorney could be sanctioned, suspended, or disbarred. If you were the paralegal who submitted that "law" to the attorney, your paralegal career would be over. If you were a person who would engage in such a serious breach of ethics, however, your loss of career would be the legal field's gain.

Clear

In chapter 18, we addressed the need to eliminate legalese, but it is equally important to avoid other professional jargon, including computer jargon.

Even more important, however, is ensuring that your readers can follow the story and its characters, as well as the role each character is playing in the case. When your case has more than one plaintiff and/or defendant, using the titles plaintiff and defendant will only confuse the reader. While each person may be clear in your mind, your reader is not as familiar with the parties. It is especially important in appellate briefs to avoid referring to your parties as the Appellant and the Appellee. Referring to the parties this way is at best, distracting and, at worst, confusing, because the Appellant can be either the plaintiff or the defendant in a civil case, or the government or the defendant in a criminal case.

Some sources recommend referring to the parties by their names after you have introduced them by their roles, but this can be confusing, too. If the plaintiff's name is Anderson and the defendant Andrews, the reader will get them confused. We found the best way to refer to the parties is by their role in the fact pattern, rather than the legal case. Thus, instead of referring to the surgeon Dr. Andrews and the internist Dr. Anderson treating the patient Mr. Anson, you would refer to the parties as the surgeon, the internist, and the patient. When you define these terms, it gives the reader a point of reference when confused.

This is especially important in those cases with multiple parties. One of your authors worked on a telephone pole case in the Court of Appeals. The city had bought telephone poles, and some of them had not been treated properly with the chemicals that should have made them resistant to weather and rot. Some of the telephone poles were deteriorating and had to be replaced far sooner than they should have.

The wood for the telephone poles had come from various lumberyards, and they had been chemically treated at various processors. These processors in turn had sold the telephone poles to a number of different wholesalers, who in turn sold the poles to various distributors. Each company had corporate names along the lines of Acme products: names that failed to describe adequately what role the company played in the progression of the telephone poles from raw wood to sale to the city. But each company was named as a defendant in the suit.

We had to create a flow chart to keep the parties straight, all of whom had corporate names. It was far less confusing to refer to the Colorado manufacturer, the South Dakota manufacturer, the Minnesota processor, the New York distributor, etc., than to refer to company names.

■ COUNTERPRODUCTIVE OR ANNOYING WRITING TACTICS

Some writers sometimes try so hard to convince their readers that their point of view is correct that they inadvertently damage their cases. The last thing writers who are trying to persuade readers want to do is to annoy, irritate, or amuse their readers. But the following tactics are guaranteed to do just that. Worst of all, though, is that these tactics damage the clients' cases. Never lose sight of the fact that your goal is effective, honest representation of the person who has put his or her trust in the attorney who is your employer.

Irritating, or Worse, Inadvertently Amusing

Misuse of emphasis really, really irritates the courts. Your writing should be persuasive enough to convince the court of the value of your case, and using bolding, underlining, italics, highlighting, or capitalizing will not further your case. Instead, these tactics are the written equivalent of screaming at the court – never an effective tactic.

Occasionally, an attorney will submit briefs with the sections the attorney considers to be important highlighted. This gives the court the impression that the attorney assumes the judge is too stupid to recognize what is important and the attorney has to point it out for him or her. Such tactics do not dispose the judge favorably toward the attorney, and consequently, they hurt the client. No competent attorney wants to insult the judge, but highlighting sections of a brief does just that.

Similarly, other types of emphasis are counterproductive tactics. Too many attorneys submit briefs to the courts with multiple lines bolded, which is the equivalent of screaming at the court. Some attorneys are not satisfied with mere bolding, and they also underline and capitalize the important points. That comes across as screaming with a megaphone. It also makes the writers appear to believe that their cases must be very weak, so they have to resort to shouting. Further, bolding, underlining, and/or capitalizing words or sections implies that the writers do not believe that the judges are intelligent enough to know what is important, and therefore needs the attorneys to point it out to them.

Exclamation points also have no place in legal writing. If the facts of the case are that startling or outrageous, stating them clearly will provide enough emphasis. The exclamation mark will diminish, rather than enhance, their effect on the reader.

If your brief is written clearly and persuasively, the court will recognize and hopefully agree with your arguments. Do not distract the court with unnecessary emphasis.

Notice how annoying the following paragraph is:

EXAMPLE

Josh had waited _six months_ for his new car to be ready. He was **EXTREMELY** excited when he finally sat behind the wheel. The salesman assured Josh that this car would corner beautifully at 120 miles per hour!! The salesman encouraged Josh to let the car show him what it could do. At first Josh drove slowly, getting the feel for the car and how it handled. Then he decided to see whether what the salesman had told him was true. He took a corner at a speed well above the limit, but he was amazed at how well the car handled. Suddenly though, **THE CAR STOPPED RESPONDING** to his steering, going unexpectedly and regrettably out of control. A woman was seriously injured, as was Josh.

Equally ineffective is exaggerating or using hyperbole. In addition to being offensive, hyperbole and bad metaphors may amuse the court. This is the opposite of the writer's intended effect.

Note the exaggeration in the first fact pattern describing the effect of Josh's motor vehicle accident and its effect on Mary. This florid prose diminishes the effect of an otherwise sympathetic fact pattern. The facts of that case, from the plaintiff's standpoint, are so good that they practically write themselves. Do not ruin a good case with bad writing.

Bad analogies and mixed metaphors also provide frequent amusement to the court. Below are paraphrases of briefs one of your authors remembers from nearly twenty years ago.

EXAMPLE

The introductory paragraph of this brief stated something like the following:

> This case is a gross miscarriage of justice – the buyers' rights were ripped from the bloody womb and the contract was viciously aborted . . . .

Regardless of the strength of this attorney's case, she had guaranteed that the rest of the brief would be taken less seriously than hoped.

EXAMPLE

In another case, the attorney had written a brief in opposition to a motion for summary judgment. The plaintiff was arguing that the employer had failed to make the legally required disability accommodation for her client's mental illness. The attorney began the facts in the brief in opposition by saying,

> Harold sat on the side of his bed, moving his handgun from one hand to the other. If it had not been the Fourth of July, his former place of employment would have been open, and he would have gone in and shot his coworkers.

Somehow that was not persuasive in the way the attorney intended.

Carefully Proofread

In addition to the proofreading and editing your new material in a document as discussed in chapter 18, keep in mind that you also must proofread and edit as needed all the boilerplate text you use. It is common practice in many areas of the law, especially in firms that focus on a single area of law, for attorneys and paralegals to cut and paste the standard material and law sections from one brief to another. For example, it would make no sense to rewrite the standard of review for a Motion for Summary Judgment from one case to the next.

When cutting and pasting text and law, however, there is the temptation to skim over the pasted section when proofreading the new document. At best, this can result in jarring transitions from one section of the document to another. At worst, it can result in including sections that do not apply to the case at hand. The court will be puzzled to find law concerning sale of heroin in a brief for a case in which the defendant is charged with possession of cocaine. Even the best attorneys have made this mistake, and it is your job as a paralegal to prevent the attorney from embarrassing himself or herself in this way.

Compliant With the Rules

As we will learn or already have learned in Civil Procedure, any document submitted to the courts must comply with the Rules of that Court, including the Local Rules. The Rules can and do impose page limits on submissions to the Court, and ignoring those limits is hazardous to your client's case. Believe it or not, there are judges who will rip off the pages that exceed the number allowed in the rules and throw the excess pages away. Since we often save our strongest argument for last, you will have wasted your most persuasive opportunity. If absolutely necessary, for example, in an extremely complex case with multiple parties, or in a case appealing conviction on 47 different counts, your attorney may move the court for an extension of the page limit.

Remember that a page limit is not a goal: just because your brief cannot exceed 40 pages does not mean you need to write 40 pages. If you can make your point in

15 pages, there is no need to fill all 40. The Court will be grateful for a refreshingly succinct brief.

The Rules also address formatting, and your authors have seen Courts reject documents that violated the formatting rules. One of your authors remembers an attorney who always submitted his briefs in 14 point font. While she does not remember any of his briefs being rejected outright, the larger font had the effect of making the brief look as though it were written in pencil or crayon. It had at least an unconscious negative impact on the reader.

The Rules also can require certain margin sizes and font sizes in footnotes. One jurisdiction in Ohio used to, and may still, require a three-inch margin at the top of the first page of every document submitted with the court. This allowed the time and date stamp to be clearly legible and not be obstructed by type.

When the case you are working on is filed in a jurisdiction other than the usual jurisdiction where your attorney practices, it is particularly important to consult the local rules and individual requirements that may be unique to that jurisdiction. One of your authors remembers a judge in a smaller county chastising opposing counsel, asking him whether he thought that because he was a "big city" lawyer he was too important to abide by the Local Rules. Irritating the judge did not help the attorney's client.

With the advent of electronic filing, the Courts may require documents to be submitted in a certain word processing format that the Court's computers can open. It is not unusual for the Courts to have older technology and word processing programs, and you do not want to submit a filing that the Court cannot open. If the Local Rules do not specify a program for electronic filing, check with the Clerk of Court or the judge's bailiff to determine what program you need to use.

Respectful

No matter how bad opposing counsel is, or how irrational you think the judge on the case is, resist the temptation to express your feelings in a document. Outrage never impresses the reader, and some attorneys have been sanctioned for spitefully attacking a judge in writing. If you must refer to the other attorney's or the judge's behavior, simply describe the situation without embellishment. Avoid using pejorative adjectives, no matter how tempting.

EXAMPLE

In a personal injury case, plaintiff's counsel had tried repeatedly to obtain plaintiff's medical records for plaintiff's treatments for a pre-existing injury affecting the same body part that also had been injured again in the motor vehicle accident that was the subject of the lawsuit. Defendant's counsel claimed that that physician's records had been destroyed in a fire and could not be provided. At trial, however, the defendant's attorney sought leave to admit these same records, and the judge allowed them into evidence. The following paragraph would be very satisfying to write, but it actually would hurt the plaintiff's case.

BAD EXAMPLE

Plaintiff's counsel repeatedly subpoenaed his medical records, and his former physician repeatedly, and obviously falsely, claimed that the records had been destroyed in a fire. The dishonest physician swore that the records no longer existed. Despite counsel's zealous but futile attempts to obtain the records, somehow, opposing counsel managed to produce them, apparently out of thin air, on the first day of trial. Rather than comply with the rules and provide them to Plaintiff's counsel, however, opposing counsel instead chose to ambush the Plaintiff and withhold the evidence until the beginning of trial. Worse, the Judge exhibited outrageous bias by allowing these surprise documents into evidence. Clearly, a gross injustice had been inflicted on the Plaintiff.

The following version of the events seems bland, but anyone with a knowledge of the law can see the two significant legal errors described in it:

GOOD EXAMPLE

Despite plaintiff's numerous discovery requests for the Plaintiff's previous medical records, his former physician informed counsel that the records had been destroyed in a fire and he could not produce them. On the day of trial, however, opposing counsel moved to introduce these same records into evidence. Despite the prejudice this late evidence presented to the Plaintiff, the Judge allowed them into the record.

An attorney submitting a brief like the first example not only hurts his current client, but the attorney also damages his or her reputation in the legal community and with the courts. Judges may not get along among themselves, but they work together closely. They talk among themselves, and an inflammatory court filing like the first example will make its way through the court.

Additionally, a party should never threaten another party, either with further litigation or with anything else. This behavior, in addition to being unprofessional, is unethical.

BAD EXAMPLE

Attorney Dowling, who represented the Plaintiff James Kovach in the lawsuit against Thomas Williams, Sr., initially wrote the following Statement of Facts in his Motion for Summary Judgment.

BLINDED!

Through gross recklessness, stupidity, and animalistic indifference, a hard-working husband and father may have been reduced to begging with at tin cup on Parkhurst Square. He certainly clearly cannot return to his previous employment, employment that supported his family, employment he had studied and worked for. NO. This once productive, law-abiding citizen is now dependent on his children to find his clothing, bring him his food, and guide him to his bed.

IN STARK CONTRAST, defendant Williams has not worked a day in his life. Instead, he spends his time – when he is not in an alcohol-induced stupor – drinking and bragging at the Dew Drop Inn.

BRAGGING! BRAGGING ABOUT HAVING BLINDED MR. KOVACH AND GETTING AWAY WITH IT!!!

The facts of this case are disgustingly, pathetically simple. Mr. Kovach was returning home after spending a Saturday morning working at his office. He was eagerly anticipating watching his oldest son (who is working toward qualifications to be an Eagle Scout) play soccer with his championship team. Mr. Kovach, through no fault of his own, never arrived at his son's game. Instead, he spent the time he should have been watching the game being extracted from his mangled, crushed auto and being raced by ambulance to Parkhurst emergency room. By the time his son's team had won the soccer game, Mr. Kovach was having an emergency, but alas futile, surgery to try to save his vision.

What disastrous turn of events possibly could have changed Mr. Kovach's afternoon, indeed the rest of his life? The idiocy, irresponsibility, and moronic behavior of the Defendant, and his callous, heartless, cruelty.

Not only did Defendant transport a 1,000 pound refrigerator in the bed of his truck unrestrained, HE DID NOT EVEN PUT THE TAILGATE UP!! Driving recklessly over pot holes and bumps, a beer in his hand and five more already in his belly, Defendant's incredible recklessness resulted in the refrigerator flying off the back of his truck. Now perhaps we should forgive stupidity. The stupid are already sentenced to live with themselves. **BUT WE CAN NEVER FORGIVE CALLOUS INDIFFERENCE!**

When Defendant realized that the refrigerator had fallen off the truck, did he stop to give aid to the person his stupidity had injured? **_NO!!! HE PICKED UP THE REFRIGERATOR, PUT IT BACK INTO THE TRUCKBED, AND DROVE AWAY!!!!!_**

HE LEFT A MAN, BLEEDING AND TRAPPED, AND **HE DROVE AWAY.**

GOOD EXAMPLE

Compare the following Statement of Facts to the one above, and note how much more effective this one is.

This case demonstrates how bad decisions, compounded by even worse decisions, can ruin several lives. The first bad decision involved Defendant's poorly planned attempt to transport a refrigerator in the bed of his pickup truck. The refrigerator was not secured in the truck bed properly, and it bounced out of the truck while Defendant was driving.

Although transporting the refrigerator in this manner was a bad decision, it was Defendant's response to the damage his refrigerator caused that was a worse decision. The refrigerator in question crashed through the windshield of the car behind Defendant's truck. The driver of that car was the Plaintiff in this case, James Kovach.

Instead of seeking to assist Mr. Kovach, or at least calling for assistance, Defendant retuned the refrigerator to the bed of his truck and drove away.

Mr. Kovach was trapped in his car. The refrigerator had shattered his windshield, and the glass became lodged in his eyes. Initially, he did not realize that he was blinded. When he reached to touch his face, he felt the warm stickiness of blood and assumed that the blood was obstructing his vision.

Mr. Kovach soon lost consciousness, and when he awakened, he learned that his sight could not be restored. Since that time, Mr. Kovach has been unable to work, and his house has gone into foreclosure. His electricity has been turned off because he cannot pay the bill. Having been a commercial artist, he now is without a career.

EXERCISE

In the following paragraphs, circle the sections, words, or elements that are likely to elicit a negative response from the Court.

ANTOINE TAYLOR AND HIS ATTORNEY ARE LIARS!! Taylor falsely claims he did not think that the property disclosure form was wrong. *THAT IS BOGUS!!* **He has lived in Parkhurst all of his life!** How can he claim that he did not know the Rod and Gun Club were adjacent to the property he sold to the innocent buyers, Karen and Floyd Green.

Don't think that they do not realize, now, that the reason Taylor sold the house in the winter was to hide the presence of the shooting range. THE SHOOTING RANGE THAT WAS NEVER MENTIONED ON THE PROPERTY DISCLO-SURE FORM!

The Greens also wonder how Taylor's counsel can represent him; attorney Smith has lived in Parkhurst all of his life too as well, and he knew that the Rod and Gun Club was there since 1980. HOW BIG A SHYSTER IS THIS SMITH DUDE ANYWAY? Attorney Smith's interrogatories were unethical and offensive, and the Greens have no intention of answering such lame, inappropriate questions.

If Taylor does not make the Greens whole by refunding the amount they paid for the house, they will prosecute him for fraud. The Greens are not joking. They will expose him as the crook that he is. And the Greens also suspect that the Supreme Court of Ohio would be interested in the defamatory nature of the interrogatories attorney Smith submitted to them.

EXERCISE

In the following paragraphs, circle the sections, words, or elements that are likely to elicit a negative response from the Court, then revise the draft and write a final copy to hand to your attorney.

This Honorable Court should find in favor of Gisele Harrington, the true victim in this case. A newcomer to town, Ms. Harrington was hounded, demeaned, and besmirched by the vicious, callous, and, dare we say, jealous actions of the Defendant in this case, the owner of Chez Cherelle.

Ms. Harrington did Chez Cherelle the honor of patronizing the déclassé, proletarian shop. Despite immediately recognizing the shop for what it was, a small town pretension, a would-be high fashion salon, Ms. Harrington graciously deigned to select the least offensive gown in the shop and purchase it. She reasoned that she could deduct the cost from her taxes when she donated it to a thrift shop in a real city.

Rather than appreciate a visit by a person accustomed to (MUCH) better quality stores, Chez Cherelle's owner, no doubt in response to feelings of severe inferiority, proceeded to attack Ms. Harrington and to destroy her reputation in her new community.

Perhaps the biggest loser in this case, however, is the quaint little town of Parkhurst. If she had had to opportunity to make her own reputation in town, Ms. Harrington could have shown Parkhurst how it could have improved itself from being a backwater and turned it into a DESTINATION.

Now Ms. Harrington is forced to defend a specious, frivolous lawsuit and try to recover her disturbing losses. Ms. Harrington only hopes that, with this being a small, inbred town, Chez Cherelle's inept attorney is not friends with the marginally competent judge.

EXERCISE

In addition to identifying the errors in the following paragraph, write a paper explaining why each constitutes an error. This document is Winnie Whiner's brief in response to Brad Smith's Motion to Dismiss, which you will find in chapter 17.

Defendant, Dr. Nasty, is ABSOLUTELY, TOTALLY WRONG when his attorney says that there is no actionable claim in Ms. Whiner's lawsuit. Until discovery can proceed, Ms. Whiner cannot prove her well-founded allegations of an unhygienic waiting room. A physician has a duty to keep his patients healthy, not expose them to illnesses. MS. WHINER WAS NOT SICK UNTIL SHE WASTED HALF A DAY IN DR. NASTY'S WAITING ROOM. We need to obtain evidence of when Dr. Nasty last had his waiting room cleaned, how often he has it cleaned, and how many other patients waiting in that waiting room got sick that day.

Ms. Whiner has clearly established that Dr. Nasty had duty to prevent injury and/or illness to his patients. Ms. Whiner has further established that Dr. Nasty breached that duty, and that his breach was the cause of her illness. She has also clearly stated her damages, and the dollar amount of those damages can only be established with a trial on the merits.

Defendant's attorney also said it was acceptable for a doctor to be indifferent to his patients and for his staff to be rude to them. I don't know what type of quack doctor attorney Smith goes to, but if he had any brains, he would realize that the doctor's staff has a duty to the patients, just like the doctor does.

TIME IS MONEY, PEOPLE! The staff should have known by the middle of the afternoon at the latest that the doctor is not coming in. What makes doctors think that they are above the law? If Dr. Nasty shows up late for the trial, will the Judge sit still for it? I don't think so!

Ms. Whiner's time is as valuable as Dr. Nasty's is, and his staff has an obligation to respect that without patients, Dr. Nasty would be very hungry indeed (and the staff would be out of a job- wouldn't that serve them right! Ha ha.)

Lucky for Ms. Whiner that Dr. Nasty got an incompetent lawyer- all the easier for her to win the case!

■ ETHICS

You have been exposed to ethical dilemmas throughout this book, but because you will confront situations that require you to make ethical decisions throughout your career, we wanted to present a separate section addressing potential ethical issues that paralegals can face.

Ethics are the moral principles upon which you base your actions, both professionally and personally. Although the difference between right and wrong may seem obvious, when an attorney is zealously representing a client, the line between ethical and unethical can blur. While an attorney cannot tell an outright lie, the attorney has a duty to present the client's case in the most favorable light possible.

Ethics are easy to define, but the definition is abstract. The words "moral" and "principle" are abstract concepts, and it is not until you apply them in flesh and blood situations that they become clear and very real.

In the law, we refer to the "slippery slope." The line between ethical and unethical is at the top of the slippery slope, but that slope begins very gradually, sometimes almost imperceptibly. Many a well-meaning and dedicated attorney has found him or herself on the wrong side of that line, despite the best of intentions.

In a previous chapter, we cited to a case in which an attorney notarized a signature that she had not personally witnessed. The attorney probably did not intend to violate legal ethics. Instead, she was taking a shortcut. Amazingly, staff members in some law offices routinely notarize signatures the notary did not witness.

It is possible that the staff in those offices is not aware that notarizing those signatures is an ethical violation.

You can picture a situation in which this might not seem like such a bad idea; it is a blustery winter day, and you do not want to make your elderly client drive to the office to sign a medical authorization. You have the client's signature on another document. It is very tempting to trace that signature on the medical authorization after you have asked the client's permission to obtain the medical records.

If you do so, however, you have crossed the ethical line. This is where you start down the slippery slope: notarizing traced (legally, they are forged) signatures becomes routine for you. Eventually, you might forget that this is not an ethical practice.

It is impossible to anticipate every ethical dilemma you will encounter in your paralegal career. Nonetheless, we will present you with several situations and explain the ethical and unethical choices available, as well as why the unethical choices cross that line between ethical and unethical.

Remember that online, you can find your state's Rules of Professional Conduct or the equivalent. With these you will find some form of Professional Ideals for Lawyers and Judges. These provide excellent guidelines for avoiding the slippery slope.

BAD EXAMPLE

The attorney you work for represents the plaintiff in a medical malpractice suit. He had held a deposition of the defendant doctor in the conference room in the office. You are clearing up the conference room after the deposition and notice that opposing counsel has left a large folder behind.

Although you know that this folder contains attorney-client privileged work product, you photocopy its contents before you return it to opposing counsel. After reading it, you find a fatal flaw in the opposing side's case. You know you can find the evidence you need for your client to win, now that you have read this privileged attorney-client work product.

Copying and using opposing counsel's work product violates ethical conduct. Just because you happened upon it due to opposing counsel's inadvertent neglect does not make your intrusion into that work product ethical. Opposing counsel has also violated an ethical rule, because he or she had a duty to protect the client's confidences. The attorney's error does not make your viewing that work product right, though.

GOOD EXAMPLE

You are assisting your attorney in a trial. On the lunch break, one of the jurors sees you eating lunch in the Courthouse cafeteria. She approaches you, and before you can stop her, she tells you that your client's case is very strong and that all the jurors dislike opposing counsel.

You realize that your client has a very good chance of winning the lawsuit. You also realize, however, that you are employed by the attorney, and he is bound by the Ohio Rules of Professional Conduct, and that Rule 3.5 states in pertinent part:

(a) A lawyer shall not do any of the following: . . .

(3) communicate *ex parte* with either of the following: . . .

(ii) a juror or prospective juror during the proceeding unless otherwise authorized to do so by law or court order.

You therefore inform your attorney of this *ex parte* communication with a juror, so the attorney can inform the Judge.

EXERCISE

Read the following situation and identify the unethical behavior. Write a paper explaining what an ethical response would be.

Pat Paralegal works for a divorce attorney. The attorney has warned Pat repeatedly not to divulge the identity of any of the firm's clients. "Like I care who is getting divorced," Pat thought when told this.

One day, however, a famous actress, Lisa Luscious, who was one of Pat's favorites, came to consult with the attorney. Shortly after Pat left the office for lunch, a man approached Pat and said he had seen Lisa Luscious entering the building. He asked Pat whether she had come to see Pat's employer. Pat tried to walk around the man, but then the man held out $1,000 in $100 bills and told Pat that it would all be public record soon anyway, and if Pat gave him the scoop, the $1,000 might find its way into Pat's pocket.

Still, Pat remembered the attorney's warning, so Pat just responded, "She might have." The man slipped the money into Pat's coat pocket and jumped into a waiting car.

EXERCISE

Select the most ethical choice for each of the following ethical situations.

1. You realize that the statute of limitations for a complaint in a case your attorney just took will expire at the end of the day. You quickly draft a complaint, but your attorney is out of the office, in fact, out of the county. You:
   a. Write your attorney's name on the complaint followed by your initials.
   b. File the complaint without any signature and hope the judge will let your attorney file an amended complaint.
   c. Locate your attorney and fax the complaint to him for him to sign and fax back to you.
   d. Find an attorney who is friendly with your attorney to sign the complaint in his place.

2. You are having lunch with another paralegal from your firm, and this paralegal begins loudly discussing one of the firm's clients. You:
   a. Tell the paralegal to use a lower tone of voice.
   b. Point out to the paralegal that opposing counsel is sitting nearby.
   c. Remind the paralegal that it is unethical to discuss clients outside the office.
   d. Report the paralegal to the attorney when you get back from lunch.

3. One of your friends is on jury duty, and she has told you all about the testimony in the case. You:
   a. Remind her that she is not allowed to discuss the case.
   b. Tell all your friends what she said – it is a really juicy case!
   c. Tell your attorney, even though she is not on the case.
   d. Telephone the judge and inform her of what you heard.

4. Opposing counsel sent discovery requests to your attorney two months ago, and now opposing counsel has called your attorney to ask about when the attorney will respond. Your attorney tells you to inform opposing counsel that he is in court and you will give

(continued)

the attorney opposing counsel's message when the attorney returns. You:

a. Tell opposing counsel what your attorney tells you to say.

b. Tell opposing counsel that your attorney told you to lie to him.

c. Tell opposing counsel that your attorney is not available to take the call.

d. Put the call through to your attorney; he has a lot of nerve asking you to lie.

5. You have become concerned about your attorney, a sole practitioner. She has come to the office with the smell of alcohol on her breath most mornings, when she comes in at all. She has had to ask an attorney from another office to cover for her at several pretrials and even a trial. You:

a. Ignore her erratic behavior; you need your job.

b. Make sure another attorney is willing to cover for her.

c. Report her to the police. She has been driving to work while drunk.

d. Report her to the local bar association for intervention.

6. You have just become a notary public. Your attorney is thrilled, because he is tired of notarizing all the signatures he needs. He has asked you to notarize the signature of a new client, who is standing with him. The client has already signed the document, but the attorney tells you that the client signed it.

You:

a. Take your attorney's word for it – the client is standing right there.

b. Ask the client to re-sign the document and swear to its contents.

c. Tell your attorney to notarize it because the attorney saw it being signed.

d. Tell the attorney you forgot your notary stamp at home.

7. Your attorney calls you from his car and tells you that he is stuck in traffic. He is due at a pretrial in ten minutes, but he is still half an hour away from the Courthouse and traffic is not moving. He tells you to go to the pretrial for him and pretend you are an attorney. You:

a. Tell the attorney that the connection is bad, and you cannot understand him.

b. Go to the pretrial and say nothing during the pretrial.

c. Call the judge's bailiff and tell him your attorney is stuck in traffic.

d. Go to the courthouse and tell the judge what your attorney told you to do.

8. Your attorney has three trials in the next three weeks and is overwhelmed by trial preparation. The Brief in Opposition to a Motion for Summary Judgment is due in three days, and the attorney does not think she will have time to write it. She asks you to write it for her, and when you give her what you have written, she signs it without reading it and tells you to file it with the Court. You:

a. File it with the Court; it is her license on the line.

b. File it with the Court; you are better writer than she is anyway.

c. Tell her you are not comfortable with filing it until she has read it.

d. Tell her that you are not about to engage in the unauthorized practice of law.

9. Your attorney tells you to call opposing counsel and talk to the attorney. He tells you not to tell opposing counsel that you are recording the call, but to record it. He assures you that in your jurisdiction, it is legal to record a conversation if one of the parties knows the conversation is being recorded. He tells you he cannot do it, because it would be a violation of the Rules of Professional Conduct, which is why he is asking you to do it. You:

a. Record the phone call; it is legal because you are not an attorney.

b. Tell him you will, but pretend the recorder broke and did not record the call.

c. Tell opposing counsel that you are recording the call, and then turn on the recorder.

d. Tell your attorney that as his agent, you cannot ethically do something that he could not do.

(continued)

10. Your attorney hands you an unsigned Medical Authorization and a photocopy of a client's signature. He tells you to photocopy the signature onto the Medical Authorization. He tells you he will notarize it himself, because he knows that you will refuse to do so. You:

    a. Photocopy the signature onto the Medical Authorization and give it to the attorney.

    b. Pretend to be unable to photocopy the signature in a way that looks authentic.

    c. Tell the attorney that photocopying the signature onto the Medical Authorization constitutes forgery, even if you are not notarizing it.

    d. Report the attorney to the bar association or the Supreme Court.

EXERCISE

The paragraphs below present an ethical dilemma. Identify what the dilemma is and name it. Write a paper describing how you would have responded in this situation and defend your decision.

The attorney you work for has filed a complaint for wrongful death on behalf of a mother whose newborn died within hours of birth. The mother, Ms. Carson, has five other children at home. She does not own a car, so she has to use public transportation to come to the office. She has to change buses to get to your office from her home, which requires her to wait in the cold for twenty minutes while waiting for the second bus. She does not have access to a fax machine, and she does not have the money to use one at a copy store.

The attorney needs to have Ms. Clark's signature on a form that needs to be filed in Probate Court within the next three days. You know that Ms. Clark has not been in the office since her initial consultation two months ago. Your attorney asks you to file the form with the Court. You notice that Ms. Clark's name written in the space where her signature belongs, and that it is written in your attorney's handwriting.

EXERCISE (IN-CLASS)

Your instructor will present you with ten situations that present ethical challenges. Divide into pairs and discuss what the best ethical response would be. You will then present your responses to the class.

SUMMARY

- Effective legal writing requires attention to many details.

- Passive voice weakens writing and dilutes the writer's argument.

- If a document is not grammatically correct and well organized, the readers are distracted and the document loses its persuasive power.

- A concise document is always more effective than a wordy one.

- It is imperative that legal writers are honest, yet persuasive, in everything they write.

- Good writing is clear and avoids jargon, excessive legal terminology, and obscure acronyms.

(continued)

- Good legal writers know that they must avoid tactics that are counterproductive and annoying, like underlining, bolding, and capitalizing.

- Good legal writers also know that they must avoid florid prose and hyperbole.

- Good legal writers carefully proofread their documents and edit as needed.

- Good legal writers are compliant with the Civil Rules and Local Rules.

- Good legal writers know that a respectful tone is more effective than a sarcastic or angry one.

- Good paralegals always comply with ethical behavior while still assisting their attorneys in zealously representing the client.

ASSIGNMENTS

I. The following fact pattern contains examples of both ethical and unethical behavior. Identify the ethical dilemmas, and determine which responses were ethical and which were not. Write a one-page paper explaining why one of the options was unethical.

You work in a medium-sized law office, and there are five paralegals in the office. The other four paralegals are named Abby, Brenda, Carl, and Jim. Abby and Carl have been dating for six months, and they have started taking turns coming in late. All employees are supposed to be at their desks at 8:30 am. Whichever one of them arrives at 8:30 am, however, will turn on the other paralegal's computer, open a document on it, and send an email from it, so that it appears as though the paralegal were present in the office but had stepped away from the desk. The tardy paralegal then arrives at the office around 10:00 am.

This has caused the workload that falls to the other three paralegals in the office, Brenda, Jim, and you, to increase. The attorneys assign the work to the paralegals as a pool, so they are not aware of how much work any one paralegal is doing. Needless to say, the three of you are getting resentful.

Brenda, Jim, and you have decided to go to lunch together to discuss the situation. Jim is a quiet, shy man, and although he produces more work than any of the other paralegals, he suggests that the three of you should ignore Abby and Carl's behavior and not "rock the boat." Brenda is not shy, but

she prefers to achieve her goals indirectly. She suggests that they find a reason for at least one of the attorneys to unexpectedly need to talk to the missing paralegal just around the time the tardy paralegal would be arriving at the office. Since it is winter, the tardy paralegal would be wearing a winter coat. Neither Abby nor Carl smokes, so there would be no reason for either of them to be outdoors at 10:00 am.

Alternatively, she suggests sending an office-wide group email requiring an immediate response while the paralegal who came in on time was conferring with one of the attorneys. Then she would ask another of the attorneys to come to the paralegal pool and ask the tardy paralegal for his or her opinion.

You suggest the three of them approach the managing partner as a group and report Abby and Carl's behavior.

II. Read the following fact pattern and write a two-page essay explaining what ethical dilemma or dilemmas it presents and how you would respond ethically to the situation.

You work for a sole practitioner. You have noticed that at times the pupils of her eyes are dilated and her speech is slurred. You have mentioned to her that you are concerned about her health and suggested that she get a medical examination. You are fairly certain that she is not drinking, because you have never smelled alcohol on her breath.

The attorney is scheduled to start a big trial this morning, and because she is a procrastinator, you both were up all night preparing for the trial. She has gone into her office, which has a bathroom, to freshen up. When she comes out, you notice that she suddenly has far more energy than she did prior to going into the bathroom, and you suspect that the pupils of her eyes do not look right. She will not look directly at you, so you cannot be sure what her eyes look like. She suddenly is speaking very quickly and is drumming her fingers nervously.

You go into her office to use the restroom before you both go to the courthouse for the trial, and you see a syringe with the cap off the needle and a tissue with spots of blood on it.

You are scheduled to meet your client at the courthouse in fifteen minutes. You know that the judge assigned to this case has always refused to reschedule trials, even when the attorneys are ill.

III. Read the following fact pattern and write an essay at least two pages long explaining how you would choose to respond in an ethical manner that avoids engaging in the unauthorized practice of law. Then explain how you personally plan to integrate ethical behavior into your paralegal career and avoid unethical practices.

You are at a family picnic, and one of your cousins, Chuck, informs you that he has gotten a ticket for driving under the influence of alcohol (DUI). Your Uncle Harold overhears your conversation and begins to give Chuck advice.

"I know what you have to do, Chuck," Uncle Harold says. "You have to tell the judge that you were taking medicine for a cough and you did not know it had alcohol in it. Isn't that right, Paralegal Eagle?"

Uncle Harold looks directly at you and insists that you respond and affirm his statement. Uncle Harold continues to give Chuck legal advice and continues to turn to you and say that you are a legal expert because you are a paralegal. Uncle Harold tells Chuck to save his money and that he does not need a lawyer because you are the legal expert in the family.

INDEX